JAMES J. HILL
AND THE OPENING
OF THE
NORTHWEST

James J. Hill in 1910. Photograph by Pach Brothers, New York.

JAMES J. HILL AND THE OPENING OF THE NORTHWEST

Albro Martin

WITH A NEW INTRODUCTION BY
W. Thomas White

Minnesota Historical Society Press
St. Paul

Minnesota Historical Society Press, St. Paul 55101
Copyright 1976 by Oxford University Press, New York
New material copyright 1991 by the Minnesota Historical Society

International Standard Book Number 0-87351-261-8
Manufactured in the United States of America
10 9 8 7 6 5 4 3 2 1

Library of Congress Cataloging-in-Publication Data

Martin, Albro.
    James J. Hill and the opening of the Northwest / Albro Martin ; with
a new introduction by W. Thomas White.
        .p. cm. – (Borealis books)
    Reprint. Originally published: New York : Oxford University Press, 1976.
    Includes bibliographical references and index.
    ISBN 0-87351-261-8
    1. Hill, James Jerome, 1838-1916. 2. Great Northern Railway (U.S.)
3. Businessmen – United States – Biography. I. Title.
HE2754.H5M37 1991
385'092 – dc20
[B]

                                                         90-26749
                                                             CIP

For My Mother

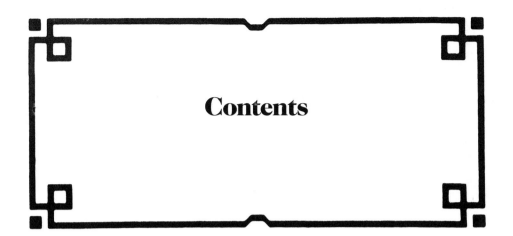

Contents

Introduction to
The Reprint Edition   xiii

PART ONE—SEEDTIME, 1838–1879.   1

1. The Making of a Pioneer   7
2. "I Took a Notion To Go and See Saint Paul"   26
3. Northward the Course of Empire   58
4. Energy Revolution in the Northwest   88
5. 1877: Year of Decision   114
6. 1878: Year of Miracles   146
7. 1879: Year of Triumph   174

PART TWO—GROWTH, 1879–1895.   199

8. New Railroad Star in the Northwest   207
9. Canadian Interlude   237
10. The Best of Times, the Worst of Times   272
11. New Friends, New Horizons   301
12. On to Montana   332
13. Purple Mountains, Shining Sea   366

PART THREE — HARVEST, 1895–1916.   **399**

14. The Worst of Times   403

15. Star Ascendant   430

16. Empire Builder   460

17. "Great Cases . . . Make Bad Law"   494

18. A Public Man   524

19. "The Way for Me To Quit Is To Quit"   561

20.   "The Lilacs Are Slow this Year"   582

Notes   617

A Note on the Sources   659

Index   665

Acknowledgments

This biography owes its existence, first of all, to the foresight of those who brought the James J. Hill Papers into being at the Hill Reference Library in St. Paul. Gertrude Hill Gavin and Rachel Hill Boeckmann, late daughters of Mr. Hill, lent their consent to the establishment of the collection and contributed the special room in which it is located; and a generous grant from the Louis W. and Maud Hill Family Foundation made possible the cleaning, arranging, and cataloging of the Papers, which was superbly carried out by Dr. Grace Lee Nute and her assistants. I have been but the first of many scholars who will benefit from their labors.

Many people and institutions lend a hand to a biography project along the way, and I can mention here only a few while extending my thanks to all. Sheila Ffolliott was a prime mover in the earliest stages of this project, and has since given me advice and encouragement which I can repay only with admiration and appreciation. The Hill Reference Library, at which Dr. Virgil F. Massman presides over an admirable staff, provided an ideal setting in which to carry on my research, and I heartily thank all those who, over a period of two years, submitted cheerfully to my increasingly numerous demands. Duane Swanson and his colleagues at the Minnesota Historical Society provided vital advice and help, and I was graciously received on several occasions at the Library of the University of Minnesota and the Public Library of St. Paul.

Four major collections of manuscripts outside of St. Paul were vital to this biography, and I thank their staffs for their assistance: the Newberry Library in Chicago, the Library of Congress, the National

Archives, and especially the Public Archives of Canada, which made a special search for hard-to-find items. At one time or another I have used the New York Public Library, the Butler Library of Columbia University, the Library of The American University, the Library of Western Connecticut State College, and the Public Libraries of Bethel and Danbury, Connecticut. I thank them all, and all those whom I have inevitably overlooked.

Chairman David J. Brandenburg of the Department of History, The American University, enthusiastically supported my request for two years' leave from teaching, without which this book would have been much longer in the making. Indispensable financial assistance, which carried with it no literary or scholarly restrictions of any kind, was provided by a group of sponsors, all of whom have made other contributions to the project as well: Louis W. Hill, Jr.; Cortlandt T. Hill; Maud Hill Schroll; Mary Boeckmann; Gertrude Boeckmann Ffolliott; Mrs. G. S. Reny; Anson Beard; the late G. Norman Slade; the Avon Foundation of the late James Jerome Hill II; and John M. Budd. Several of these sponsors read all or part of the manuscript, providing valuable suggestions which I have accepted or rejected according to my own final judgment. To my inquiries about the papers of Jacob H. Schiff and Edward H. Harriman, John M. Schiff and W. Averell and E. Roland Harriman responded graciously.

Others who have read some or all of the manuscript are Richard C. Overton; Ralph W. and Muriel Hidy; Lewis L. Gould; Charles W. ("Dinty") Moore of the Great Northern Railway, now retired; James H. McKendrick; and Howard L. Dickman, who allowed me to read a draft of his monograph on Hill's agricultural interests. All made helpful suggestions. None, of course, is responsible for what I have done with them. Among the many members of the Burlington Northern who have helped me are Robert W. Downing, Albert M. Rung, and P. W. Stafford. Anthony C. Morella, general counsel of The American University, and Irving Clark of the firm of Doherty, Rumble & Butler handled the legal details of the project as efficiently as Thomas Proulx and Carole Hodson of The American University administered it. At the St. Paul Athletic Club, which provided me with a cheerful home for two years, the "knights of the round table"—the resident members—unfolded each morning at breakfast an authoritative oral history of the Twin Cities and the Northwest that has enriched these pages. Sheldon Meyer, Vice President, Caroline Taylor, and many other members of Oxford University Press performed the perennial miracle of turning a manuscript into a book.

I thank Mrs. Heather Gilbert, author of the first volume of a biography of Lord Mount Stephen, for allowing me to read portions of the manuscript of her second volume, and Warren L. Hanna, for showing me a chapter from his forthcoming history of Glacier National Park. I appreciate permission granted by Glenn Porter, Editor of *The Business History Review,* to reprint that part of my Chapter Four which first appeared in the Summer 1976 issue of the *Review;* by *The Sunday New York Times Book Review,* to quote a review by C. P. Snow that appeared in the August 12, 1973, issue; and by Farrar, Straus & Giroux, to quote several lines of poetry from *A Book of Americans,* by Rosemary and Stephen Vincent Benét, published in 1933 by Farrar & Rhinehart.

My greatest debt is to Mrs. G. S. Reny, whose knowledge of the early history of St. Paul and the Northwest qualifies her to become a historian in her own right whenever she chooses to do so. In addition to providing me with a wealth of information about the domestic life of James J. and Mary T. Hill, Mrs. Reny also extended to me a sympathetic understanding of the distance by which a biographer's reach to recreate a life must exceed his grasp. *Aujourd'hui, nous voyons comme dans un miroir, d'une manière confusé; alors, nous verrons face à face.*

A. M.

"Great Maple"
Bethel, Conn.
August 1975

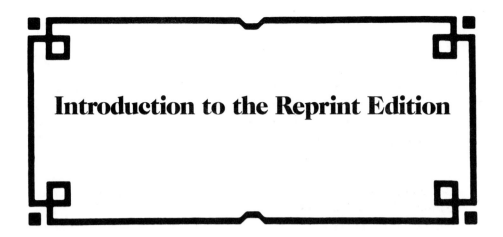

Introduction to the Reprint Edition

The Ontario-born James Jerome Hill rose to preeminence as an American railroad leader of the first order, exercising control of the transportation system of the entire Northwest and playing a fundamentally important role in national economic and political affairs. The folk belief in the Horatio Alger rags-to-riches myth of opportunity in America may have had little basis in most Americans' experience. The experience of James J. Hill, or the Empire Builder as he came to be called, was an important exception, however, and one that easily supported rather than denied the popular myth.

Despite his stature, Hill has received comparatively little serious attention by scholars. He is commonly mentioned as president of the Great Northern Railway (GN). In connection with his part in the mammoth Northern Securities Company he along with Edward H. Harriman became the objects of President Theodore Roosevelt's Progressive wrath. Mention of Hill and his significant role in a wide variety of national and regional developments commonly is limited to these cursory treatments or ignored altogether.

Joseph Gilpin Pyle's two-volume biography, completed shortly after Hill's death in 1916, has been the standard work and the source of any treatment of Hill. That study was written in a stiff, formal style with little attempt at detached analysis. The uncritical, sympathetic viewpoint undoubtedly was a consequence of the work being commissioned by Hill, who was Pyle's employer. Pyle had been the editor of the *St. Paul Globe*, which Hill controlled, and had drafted most of the railroad leader's speeches after the turn of the century. Following Hill's death, Pyle was the first librarian, or head, of the James Jerome Hill Reference Library, which the Hill family constructed in St. Paul. As such, Pyle traveled throughout the United States and Europe purchasing books and other materials to stock the new cultural institution that opened in 1921.[1]

Subsequently, Stewart Holbrook published a short biography of Hill in 1955.[2] Yet Holbrook's treatment necessarily was based on secondary material. At that time Hill's papers were housed with the Great Northern corporate records at its headquarters in St. Paul. Consequently those rich collections were not available to scholars.

Albro Martin was the first author since Pyle to obtain access to Hill's documentary legacy, consisting of more than 450 linear feet of material, spanning the years from 1856 to 1916. In the early 1970s Martin obtained special permission to use the papers, then housed in a specially constructed vault in the Hill Library. The result was this biography, originally published by Oxford University Press in 1976. Yet the Hill Papers remained closed and unavailable to other scholars until 1982.

Since the early 1970s historiographical concerns have changed, and individual perceptions and interpretations of Hill and his activities remain varied and subject to debate. Increased attention to the issues raised (or in many cases, renewed) by the "new social history" within the history-writing community over the last two decades has considerable bearing on treatments of Hill and the railroads and their impact on the United States' northwest quadrant.

Writing generally about the Trans-Mississippi West – the location of most of Hill's domain – Patricia Limerick, Rodman Paul, Michael Malone and Richard Etulain, Robert Athearn, and other scholars have summarized many of these concerns in their recent works. Limerick in particular focused upon the "conquest" of the western territories. That view has particular merit for consideration of Hill's and the railroad's entry into the region stretching from St. Paul to Seattle. For the plains and mountains of the Northwest were not unpopulated. Native Americans already held the land. They had lived and contended for its uses for centuries until the arrival and comparatively quick conquest by technologically knowledgeable white populations, which after the initial frontier period, arrived largely on the new trains that carved "metropolitan corridors" for full development of the region's mines, forests, and farms.[3]

While much work remains to be done on this subject, Native Americans' experiences in the wake of the white onslaught spearheaded by the railroads (aside from the more spectacular armed conflicts) already have received initial attention. As Dennis Smith noted, the arrival in 1887 of Hill's St. Paul, Minneapolis & Manitoba Railway (the Manitoba, which became the Great Northern in 1890) was followed within a year by a catastrophic reduction in Blackfeet and Sioux lands in northern Montana and western North

Dakota. While Hill's construction crews laid rail at a frenetic pace across the northern Great Plains to Butte, Montana Territory, the Northwest Commission led by Senator Henry L. Dawes of Massachusetts negotiated with the native populations for land cessions. (Dawes was chair of the Senate Indian Affairs Committee and author of the 1887 Dawes Severalty Act.) The result, ratified by Congress in May 1888, was an agreement by which the affected tribes ceded to the federal government more than nineteen million acres abutting the Manitoba's line, a reduction of the Blackfeet Reservation in Montana by 80 percent and the Fort Berthold Reservation in North Dakota by 60 percent.[4]

The circumstances surrounding that dramatic cession, often neglected by scholars, remain mysterious. At one level, the negotiations are simple and uncomplicated. An overwhelming majority of whites in the late nineteenth century favored continued acquisition of land for settlement. Moreover, Hill maintained a close political relationship, including making substantial campaign contributions, with President Grover Cleveland. Given that the whites wanted land and Cleveland owed Hill a favor, the outcome of federal and private efforts to garner new tracts of land from western tribes seemed predictable and unremarkable.[5]

What is remarkable and remains something of a mystery is Cleveland's veto of the initial right-of-way legislation, vitally necessary for construction of the Manitoba across the northern Great Plains. Worse, the president ignored Hill's last minute pleas and publicly insulted his ally and friend in his veto message, charging that the legislation would open "Indian lands to a class of corporations carrying with them many individuals not known for any scrupulous regard for the interest or welfare of the Indians." Further, the railroads (and presumably Hill's Manitoba) would be "strongly tempted to infringe at will upon the reserved rights and property of Indians and thus are apt to become so arbitrary in their dealings and domineering in their conduct toward them that the Indians would become disquieted."[6] Hill was furious, as were his allies. Minnesota's Republican Congressman Knute Nelson concluded that "on the whole we are in the hands of the Philistines," while former St. Anthony Falls entrepreneur Paris Gibson wrote from Montana Territory, where he was boosting Hill's Great Falls townsite company, that "Cleveland may be qualified for sheriff or Mayor of Buffalo, but beyond that, he is not safe."[7]

What makes this episode even more odd is that Cleveland signed what was essentially the same legislation several months later. An enormous land cession that, indirectly, proved a great boon to the new railroad followed. Presumably, the anti-Manitoba lobby that included the Northern Pacific and Union Pacific roads remained active, as it was before the veto.

Those railroads, already established in the new territories, desperately wanted to prevent any new transcontinental lines traversing the Northwest to Puget Sound. More immediately, the NP and UP sought to protect their absolute control over access to the rich copper mines of the Butte/Anaconda region that they enjoyed through a joint pooling arrangement to keep rates artificially high. That year the Montana mines surpassed the Michigan mines as the nation's principal copper-producing region. Hill, aware of his rivals' maneuvers, groused to his ally, Canadian financier George (later Lord Mount) Stephen, that the NP received "$500,000 per annum for keeping out of Butte."[8] Despite the continued pressure exerted by the NP–UP forces, however, Cleveland abruptly changed his mind within a few months of delivering his scathing veto message. Perhaps another of Hill's allies – Pennsylvania rail and coal industrialist and Democratic Congressman William L. Scott – had the best explanation for Cleveland's peripatetic behavior. Convinced the president was a bumbler, he contended that "the only wonder . . . is he does not make more mistakes than he does."[9]

Another of the "new social history's" themes is labor, important in and of itself but of even more concern in view of the GN's pioneering role that intrinsically placed a significant part of its employees on what Carlos Schwantes has characterized as the "wageworkers' frontier."[10] Martin touched on this subject at various points but did not give it extended attention. Typically Hill's attitudes toward organized labor were divided. He made his peace with the national leadership of the so-called Big Four, the operating brotherhoods that represented roughly 20 percent of the railroad work force and consisting of engineers, firemen, brakemen, and conductors. In the turbulent 1890s his relationship with the rank and file of those craft unions and with the remaining 80 percent of the work force was a much different matter.

For Hill and those who worked for him, the Great Northern strike of 1894 proved to be a pivotal event. Erupting in the midst of the great economic depression following the Panic of 1893, the conflict pitted the industrially organized American Railway Union (ARU), founded the previous summer and led by Eugene V. Debs, against Hill and the GN management. Hill's transcontinental line had reached Puget Sound in 1893 – arguably the worst year of the nineteenth century to begin operating such a line. The depression caused widespread distress and forced all transcontinentals, aside from the Great Northern, into bankruptcy.

Shortly after completion of the railroad, Hill commenced a series of layoffs and wage reductions. In April 1894, a wildcat strike erupted in western Montana when employees learned that the railroad planned to clean house, discharging all real and suspected dissidents working in the freight yards. The GN's main line was immediately cut in two, and despite Debs's pleas for restraint, the work stoppage spread both east and west to cover the entire system. In a common Gilded Age pattern – one foreign to our own time – the general populace of the communities, caught up in the anti-railroad Populist revolt, disregarded class and occupational lines to support the militant insurgents enthusiastically. In doing so the strikers challenged the established, conservative national leadership of the brotherhoods as well as their newly chosen leaders in the ARU.[11]

On the other side, Hill tried desperately to end the conflict quickly. He successfully allied himself with the Big Four national leadership, but the brotherhoods' chieftains had little influence over their members, who dared to rip up their local charters rather than desert the ARU cause. At the same time, Hill begged Cleveland, who had returned to the White House (again, with substantial support from the Empire Builder), to call out federal troops to "restore order" and curb what he characterized as the "turbulent mobs" that "defied and ridiculed . . . the authority of law and its officers."[12] Cleveland refused to provide any substantive help, keeping the army on a nervous watch of the bands of Coxeyites who were attempting to move on Washington, often by commandeering trains.[13]

Anxious to keep his newly completed, financially fragile line solvent and under great pressure from shippers, Hill had only one option if the GN was to resume operations in the near future. Reluctantly, he agreed to arbitration. At the GN president's and Debs's request, a panel chaired by Charles Pillsbury and composed of prominent Twin Cities businessmen convened immediately. Surprisingly, they found in favor of the strikers. The ARU claimed a great victory. That widely proclaimed boast helped to swell their membership rolls throughout the country and particularly in the Far West. Yet, closer examination of the matter suggests that the infant union's gains were more modest. Essentially the Great Northern's ARU members had won only a rough wage parity with their counterparts on the Northern Pacific, which was in receivership and had sharply reduced wages and instituted its own widespread layoffs. For his part, Hill instructed his subordinates not to contradict the ARU claims.[14]

Two months later the ARU fought its principal battle in the Pullman boycott, the largest strike of the century, which paralyzed most of the nation's rail network, including all transcontinental railroads aside from the Great Northern. The coalition of the Chicago-based General Managers Association with its allies and the Cleveland administration, which called out the entire western garrison to enforce injunctions issued by a friendly judiciary, proved to be too much for the ARU. Hill may have found some satisfaction in Debs's loss and the dissolution of the American Railway Union. Yet at the same time, those feelings probably were bittersweet. His supposed friends in the administration, having ignored his own pleas for support, had provided overwhelming, decisive aid to his rivals.[15]

The Pullman boycott, to which the GN strike was an important prelude, was a watershed in railroad labor relations in a variety of ways. The ARU's defeat and demise ended the last serious attempt at pure industrial unionism in the railroad industry. What is less well recognized was the impact of the union's defeat on the demographic composition of the railroad work force in the Northwest. The fact that workers on the GN and the region's other principal lines were relatively ethnically homogeneous, as were the new towns where many resided, was an important factor in forging their militant solidarity and popular support. That fact was not lost on railroad managers. After the 1894 turbulence they immediately altered their recruitment methods, hiring instead a much more diverse group of employees to perform the unskilled, often seasonal work on their lines.[16]

On the Great Northern, the Northern Pacific, and other northwestern lines, Japanese immigrants increasingly occupied an important position. Following the anti-Chinese movement of the 1880s, the established transcontinentals, joined by the GN after its completion, employed native-born whites and northwestern European immigrants to do unskilled work, while they experimented with using Japanese and southern and eastern European immigrants. After the Pullman boycott, the influx of large numbers of Japanese workers signaled a new era in labor relations.[17]

Desperate for a large, seasonal, docile work force, managers on the Great Northern and other lines felt they had found the ideal solution in the Japanese workers supplied in abundance by West Coast agencies and dispersed largely over the western half of their lines. "Jap section laborers . . . are certainly more reliable than either Greeks, Italians, or white labor generally," Hill's subordinate, H. A. Kennedy, wired from the important rail hub at Spokane. Equally enthusiastic, F. E. Ward, Kennedy's supervisor, was overjoyed that "the Japs are turning out so well," and he urged the Great Northern to place its "main reliance on them and hav[e] nothing to do with Italians or other outside labor."[18]

As the Japanese presence grew dramatically — by 1906 they numbered thirteen thousand on the western roads, including an estimated five thousand on the Great Northern — their arrival sparked an intense opposition by whites reminiscent of the earlier anti-Chinese agitation. "The Northwest is on the verge of [another] gigantic struggle with Oriental labor," Gordon A. Rice, editor of the *Seattle Union Record* (a prominent labor paper), thundered in 1900 in a protest that was carried in nearly every issue of his and other newspapers throughout the region for nearly a decade. In a more explicit but equally common vein, the *Butte Reveille* charged, "J. J. Hill is very fond of the Japs; they work cheaper than the Irishman, or Englishman, or Dutchman, and then besides they will stand all kinds of abuse from their employers."[19] In addition to the obvious racism in such statements, there was an element of truth, since Japanese workers for most of this period received substantially less pay than what the GN and others gave to workers they dubbed "foreign" (southern and eastern European) and "white" (native born and northwest European). The myth of contentment and docility proved decidedly false after the Gentleman's Agreement of 1907–08 curtailed immigration, and Japanese workers signaled their disaffection by returning to their homeland or to the coastal ports.

Suddenly, the "foreign" workers, including Italian, Greek, Bulgarian, and other immigrants on the second rung of the railroads' unskilled labor pyramid, took on a new importance, adding still greater ethnic diversity to the work force and the region. While they were paid more — roughly twenty-five cents per day — than Japanese laborers were, they received less than "white" unskilled labor. Consequently cultural prejudice again meshed with economic fears to spark intense opposition to the newcomers, whom Hill and his counterparts were importing. Former Portland ARU leader Ed Teasdale warned of "the evils impending from a flood of unskilled labor from Southern Europe," while Washington State labor commissioner William Blackman, also an important former ARU spokesman, declared "the immigration of labor from the South and East of Europe is a menace to the American standard of living." Not to be outdone, newspaper editors and the American Federation of Labor (AFL) pounded home the constant refrain that this was a "white man's country." Simultaneously the weak AFL-affiliated Brotherhood of Maintenance of Way Workers limited its own growth by adamantly retaining its color bar and constantly declaring its opposition to "Italian and Greek labor that takes from honest American laborers the money and work that are rightfully theirs."[20] For all that, the new immigrants continued to arrive, and although many did not remain long on any of the railroads, they added to the diversity of the developing Northwest.

Outside the parameters of the "new social history," researchers have suggested other ways in which James J. Hill influenced developments in "his" domain. That arena, obviously, included his hometown and GN headquarters in St. Paul. Robert Frame outlined the Empire Builder's material legacy in *James J. Hill's Saint Paul*. As the city's most prominent citizen, Hill had a pervasive presence as reflected in the library that bears his name,

railroad shops and headquarters building, St. Paul Seminary, and many
other structures related to his business and philanthropic activities. The
latter included the College of St. Thomas, Macalester College, Society for
the Relief of the Poor, Little Sisters of the Poor, Visitation Convent, and
the Home of the Friendless. Hill also was a benefactor of churches in St.
Paul and along his railroad. Hill, a Methodist, hotly denied the 1912 *Encyclopaedia Britannica* statement that he and his wife Mary (a Roman Catholic)
generously donated $1.5 million toward the construction of the Cathedral
of St. Paul.[21]

What is undeniable is the presence of his Summit Avenue mansion,
located diagonally from the Cathedral and the largest house on the city's
preeminent street that included the homes of his son and successor at the
Great Northern, Louis W. Hill, lumber tycoon Frederick Weyerhaeuser,
Northern Pacific president Edwin W. Winter, and other St. Paul notables
such as W. S. Dalrymple, Pierce Butler, Amherst Wilder, Frederick Driscoll,
Alpheus B. Stickney, Henry M. Rice, and Chauncy W. Griggs. Hill's home,
now administered as a historic site by the Minnesota Historical Society,
was completed in 1891 as he was emerging as a national figure. The Richard-
sonian Romanesque-style stone mansion measured thirty-six thousand
square feet and was completed at a cost of nearly $1 million after three
years of labor by more than four hundred workmen. It included a
remarkable art gallery, where Hill assembled a fine collection of Barbizon
School paintings.[22] Hill's mansion served as a symbol of the self-made industrial leader's wealth and stature. Because it has been preserved, it is
an important material reminder of America's Victorian age and a center
for the city's cultural life.

Outside St. Paul, Hill's and the Great Northern's activities have received
considerable attention. In their recent history of the railroad, Ralph Hidy,
Muriel Hidy, Roy Scott, and Don Hofsommer surveyed the part both played
in the recruitment of settlers and the development of agriculture, irrigation, and Glacier National Park with its related tourist industry. Donald
Pisani assessed the role of the federal government and the railroads in the
irrigation movement, while Howard Dickman made extensive use of the
Hill Papers in his study of agricultural developments on the northern Great
Plains. After geographer John C. Hudson explored Hill's and the railroads'
impact on the founding and development of towns in North Dakota,
John R. Borchert integrated that experience within his wider survey of the
Upper Midwest's economic and historical geography. Similarly, in impor-
tant new regional syntheses, Carlos Schwantes, John Fahey, and Gordon
Dodds examined the railroads' general role in the development of the Pacific
Northwest. To the north, John Eagle, W. A. Waiser, Gerald Friesen,

A. A. den Otter, and others treated Hill's involvement with the Canadian Pacific and development of western Canada.[23]

Folk wisdom has it that Hill forbade his employees from investing in ventures near the Great Northern lines, presumably to limit speculation. Hill did not apply the same strictures to his own activities or those of his northeastern or Chicago allies who often followed his advice for speculative investments in the developing lands. Hill's papers document a variety of Minnesota investments, including the St. Anthony Falls Water Power Company, the Red River Roller Mills at Fergus Falls, and the Mille Lacs Lumber Company at Milaca. At the latter location Hill and Jacob Schiff initially hoped to found an agricultural colony for Russian Jews fleeing the pogroms, but Milaca instead became a lumber town and, later, a real-estate venture. Finally and perhaps most notably, Hill and his sons played a major role in the development of Minnesota's iron ranges.[24]

Outside Minnesota, the Empire Builder was active in mining and railroading activities in Iowa. H. Roger Grant outlined the documentary sources for Hill's undertakings soon after the Hill Papers were opened to researchers. He noted particularly the Mason City & Fort Dodge Railroad and over a half-dozen soft coal mining operations (Hill had made a good part of his first fortune in the fuel business), which dealt with transportation, mining, labor relations, blacks, agriculture, town development, and other topics. Elsewhere Grant concerned himself with Hill's relationships with railroad leaders A. B. Stickney and Marvin Hughitt.[25]

In the Northwest, the Great Northern leader involved himself in similar activities, such as passenger travel and freight shipping[26] and an ill-conceived mining enterprise in Washington's Cascade Mountains. In Montana, Hill joined with local notables Charles A. Broadwater and former Minneapolis pioneer Paris Gibson to found the Great Falls Water Power and Townsite Company. Retaining over 90 percent of the company's stock, Hill periodically sold blocks to his principal supporters elsewhere, including John S. Kennedy, D. Willis James, Marshall Field, Leonard Lewisohn, Charles E. Perkins, Philip D. Armour, and John Murray Forbes. Yet, personal investments did not sway important decisions affecting the welfare of the Great Northern, whose main line ran north of and not through Great Falls to the consternation of Gibson and other locals but to the delight of Hill's Chicago, New York, and Boston investors.[27]

Apparently concern for the GN always was uppermost on Hill's scale of priorities, an important element in his campaign to promote consolidation of the region's transportation network, itself part of the general consolidation, or "incorporation of America," then sweeping the nation.[28] In the case of Hill, that development led directly into the formation of the

Northern Securities Company in 1901. The 1896 "London Memorandum" proved to be an important prelude to that event. Signed by Hill, J. P. Morgan, George (Lord Mount) Stephen, and Arthur Gwinner of Berlin's Deutsche Bank (representing the bankrupt Northern Pacific), the agreement ratified their determination to "form a permanent alliance, defensive, and in case of need offensive, with a view of avoiding competition and aggressive policy and of protecting the common interests of both Companies." Further, the signatories vowed that "all competitive business, such as . . . [that] of the Anaconda Copper Company," Montana's principal single shipper, would "be divided upon equitable terms between both Companies. Tariff Wars and rate cutting . . . [were to] be absolutely avoided," while neither the Great Northern nor the Northern Pacific would in the future "ingress into the other's territory by new construction or purchase or acquiring of control of existing lines."[29]

By this agreement the Minnesota-based opponents ended their long, bitter rivalry and consequently ended any serious competition in much of the northern-tier states. The Chicago, Milwaukee & St. Paul, which extended its line to Puget Sound after the turn of the century, was too late and too weak to mount any serious threat to what had become known as the Hill Lines. The stage was set for the larger, national rivalry between Hill and his allies, who controlled the GN, NP, and the Chicago, Burlington & Quincy, and Edward H. Harriman and his supporters, who dominated the Union Pacific, Southern Pacific, and other railroads. Following a sharp fight on Wall Street at the turn of the century, Hill and Harriman agreed to an armistice, forming the Northern Securities holding company in 1901. The largest railroad company of its day (and the direct predecessor of Burlington Northern Inc., formed in 1970), Northern Securities represented a major consolidation of the two rail empires, which included most of the rail traffic between the Mississippi River and the Pacific Coast.

Consequently, it drew the wrath of Progressives, worried about monopolistic power and the effective end of any meaningful competition in that vast region. Theodore Roosevelt, anxious to distance himself from William McKinley, responded to the Progressives' hue and cry and ordered his conservative attorney general, Philander C. Knox, to invoke the Sherman Anti-Trust Act and break up the Northern Securities Company. Predictably, Hill, who had played an active role in the Grand Old Party since 1896, was furious and felt betrayed by the president. "Possibly, the dazzling influence of the 'newly established court' at Washington, with all its tinsel and red-stockinged and gilded flunkies, has got the better of the other side of the 'Judicial Household,' " he fumed to CB&Q leader Charles E. Perkins when the U.S. Supreme Court in 1904 found for the Roosevelt administration and ordered the dissolution of Northern Securities. Other principals in the holding company were more detached. Harriman, for example, worked hard raising campaign funds for Roosevelt's reelection that year, while Hill's long-time London ally, Gaspard Farrer, opined that "in principle my sympathies are against allowing corporations to obtain unlimited powers, and I have a feeling in my bones that however unpleasant the judgment may be at the moment, we shall none of us have cause to regret it in the long run."[30]

The celebrated Northern Securities Case suggests another important area for investigation. Hill was extremely active in political matters in both his native Canada and his adopted United States. Martin touched on this at various important junctures, and I have noted the Empire Builder's growing and significant relationships with a succession of presidents from Grover Cleveland (first administration) to Woodrow Wilson.[31] Hill's extensive papers document a much wider network of political activity, involving senators, congressmen, governors, and their advisers of both parties in the states traversed by his railroad and elsewhere. Most published research on the railroad industry's political activities has had to do with analyses of lobbying efforts, commonly over rate issues. Representative of the two interpretive poles are Martin, who argued that the roads were adamantly opposed to government regulation, and Gabriel Kolko, who insisted from a New Left perspective that the railroad leaders sought a federal regulatory system that they could control.[32] Nonetheless, we still know very little about individual railroad entrepreneurs' ongoing political efforts, including influence, strategic advice, and financial support on both national and state levels. Hill's papers provide an unusual and rich field for further, much-needed inquiries into the nature of a powerful Victorian entrepreneur's activities in this arena.

This essay has highlighted some of the serious historical writing about Hill and the Great Northern published in the last fifteen years. Since Martin obtained access to the Hill Papers and wrote his biography of James J. Hill, the focus of much of the profession has shifted dramatically, opening and reopening topics for research. Because Hill and his railroad played such a decisive role in the history of the Northwest and, indeed, of the nation, and because their documentary legacies are so rich and extensive, they have provided abundant material for scores of scholars with both new and traditional topical concerns. Martin's suggestive biography has proven to be a central element in that ongoing scholarly process of constant inquiry and reevaluation. Martin's massive treatment easily continues to stand on its own interpretive merits as an arresting analysis of a major, although often neglected, figure, one who emerged as a pivotal voice, important ally, and, to many, a dangerous rival, taking his place in the first rank of American economic leaders during the nation's industrializing era. Martin's study of Hill remains central and contentious and consequently well worth his readers' serious attention.

W. Thomas White

NOTES

1. Joseph Gilpin Pyle, *The Life of James J. Hill*, 2 vols. (Garden City, N.Y.: Doubleday, Page & Co., 1916–17).
2. Stewart H. Holbrook, *James J. Hill: A Great Life in Brief* (New York: Alfred A. Knopf, 1955).
3. Patricia Nelson Limerick, *The Legacy of Conquest: The Unbroken Past of the American West* (New York: W. W. Norton, 1987); Rodman W. Paul, *The Far West and the Great Plains in Transition, 1859–1900* (New York: Harper and Row, 1988); Robert G. Athern, *The Mythic West in Twentieth-Century America* (Lawrence: University Press of Kansas, 1986); Michael P. Malone and Richard W. Etulain, *The American West: A Twentieth-Century History* (Lincoln: University of Nebraska Press, 1989). Malone has also commenced work on a new interpretive biography of Hill. For more on the general cultural implications of the arrival of the railroad, see John R. Stilgoe, *The Metropolitan Corridor: Railroads and the American Scene, 1880 to 1935* (New Haven: Yale University Press, 1983).
4. Dennis J. Smith, "Procuring a Right-of-Way: James J. Hill and Indian Reservations, 1886–1888" (Professional paper, University of Montana, Missoula, 1983) (copy in James Jerome Hill Reference Library, St. Paul, Minn.).
5. For more on Hill's political relationships, see W. Thomas White, "A Gilded Age Businessman in Politics: James J. Hill, the Northwest, and the American Presidency, 1884–1912," *Pacific Historical Review* 57 (November 1988): 439–56.
6. *Senate Executive Document 204*, 49th Cong., 1st. sess. (1886), 3.
7. Knute Nelson to Hill, July 15, 1886, Paris Gibson to Hill, July 13, 1886, James J. Hill Papers, Hill Library.
8. Hill to George Stephen, January 18, 1885 (quotation), Hill Papers; White, "The War of the Railroad Kings: Great Northern–Northern Pacific Rivalry in Montana, 1881–1896," in *Montana and the West: Essays in Honor of K. Ross Toole*, ed. Rex C. Myers and Harry W. Fritz (Boulder, Colo.: Pruett, 1984), 37–54; Malone, *The Battle for Butte: Mining and Politics on the Northern Frontier, 1864–1906* (Seattle: University of Washington Press, 1981), 40–41; Malone and Richard B. Roeder, *Montana: A History of Two Centuries* (Seattle: University of Washington Press, 1976), 134. For more on the Union Pacific's role, see Maury Klein, *Union Pacific: Birth of a Railroad, 1867–1897* (Garden City, N.Y.: Doubleday, 1987), and *The Life and Legend of Jay Gould* (Baltimore: Johns Hopkins University Press, 1986).
9. William L. Scott to Hill, July 22, 1886, Hill Papers.
10. Carlos A. Schwantes, "The Concept of the Wageworkers' Frontier: A Framework for Future Research," *Western Historical Quarterly* 17 (January 1987): 39–55.
11. For more on the Great Northern strike, see Tamara C. Truer, "Eugene Debs, James J. Hill and the Great Northern Railway's Strike of 1894," *Ramsey County History* 25 (Spring 1990): 12–13, 23; Nick Salvatore, *Eugene V. Debs: Citizen and Socialist* (Urbana: University of Illinois Press, 1982), 114–25; White, "A History of Railroad Workers in the Pacific Northwest, 1883–1934" (Ph.D. diss., University of Washington, 1981), 47–81; Great Northern Eastern Railway President's Subject files 107 and 2572, and Great Northern President's Subject file 2114, Great Northern Railway Company Records, Minnesota Historical Society, St. Paul.

12. Hill to Grover Cleveland, April 28, 1894, President's Office files, vol. 29, p. 591, Great Northern Records.

13. On the Coxeyite movement by unemployed, usually skilled workers, see Schwantes, *Coxey's Army: An American Odyssey* (Lincoln: University of Nebraska Press, 1985).

14. Pyle, *Life of James J. Hill*, 2:81.

15. White, "Railroad Labor Protests, 1894-1917: From Community to Class in the Pacific Northwest," *Pacific Northwest Quarterly* 75 (January 1984): 13-21.

16. For recent treatments of the Pullman boycott, see White, "Protest Movements on the Northern Tier: A Comparative Look at Railway Workers in the Pullman Boycott of 1894 and the 1922 Shopmen's Strike," in *Centennial West*, ed. William L. Lang (Seattle: University of Washington Press, forthcoming); Shelton Stromquist, *A Generation of Boomers: The Pattern of Railroad Labor Conflict in Nineteenth-Century America* (Urbana: University of Illinois Press, 1987); James H. Ducker, *Men of the Steel Rails: Workers on the Atchison, Topeka & Santa Fe Railroad, 1869-1900* (Lincoln: University of Nebraska Press, 1983); Salvatore, *Eugene V. Debs*; Jerry M. Cooper, *The Army and Civil Disorder: Federal Intervention in Labor Disputes, 1877-1900* (Westport, Conn.: Greenwood Press, 1980).

17. For more on the changing demographic composition of the railroad work force, see Yuji Ichioka, *The Issei: The World of the First Generation Japanese Immigrants, 1885-1924* (New York: Free Press, 1988), 57-145, and "Japanese Immigrant Labor Contractors and the Northern Pacific and Great Northern Railroad Companies, 1898-1907," *Labor History* 21 (Summer 1980): 325-50; White, "Race, Ethnicity, and Gender in the Railroad Work Force: The Case of the Far Northwest, 1883-1918," *Western Historical Quarterly* 16 (July 1985): 265-83; Yuzo Murayama, "The Economic History of Japanese Immigration to the Pacific Northwest, 1890-1920" (Ph.D. diss., University of Washington, 1982).

18. H. A. Kennedy to G. T. Slade, June 24, 1903, General Superintendent to P. T. Downs, June 7, 1900, Great Northern Vice President–Operating Subject file 34-01, Great Northern Records.

19. *Union Record* (Seattle), May 4, October 27, 1900; *Butte Reveille*, quoted in *Union Record*, August 10, 1901.

20. *Portland Labor Press*, May 16, 1912 (first quotation); Washington, Bureau of Labor, *Third Biennial Report*, 1903, p. 21-22 (second quotation); *Union Record*, February 9, 1907 (third quotation).

21. Robert M. Frame III, *James J. Hill's Saint Paul: A Guide to Historic Sites* (St. Paul: James Jerome Hill Reference Library, 1988); Marvin R. O'Connell, *John Ireland and the American Catholic Church* (St. Paul: Minnesota Historical Society Press, 1988); Joseph B. Connors, *Journey Toward Fulfillment: A History of the College of St. Thomas* (St. Paul: College of St. Thomas, 1986). For more on Hill's personal life, see Thomas C. Buckley, "Railroader as Yachtsman: James J. Hill and the Yacht *Wacouta*," *Ramsey County History* 25 (Spring 1990): 4-11, 16-19, 21; William B. McCash and June H. McCash, *The Jekyll Island Club: Southern Haven for America's Millionaires* (Athens: University of Georgia Press, 1989); Carol Ann Colburn, "The Dress of the James J. Hill Family, 1863-1916" (Ph.D. diss., University of Minnesota, 1989).

22. Jane H. Hancock, Sheila ffolliott, and Thomas O'Sullivan, *Homecoming: The Art Collection of James J. Hill* (St. Paul: Minnesota Historical Society Press, forthcoming). See also Sharon Lee Irish, "Cass Gilbert's Career in New York, 1859-1934" (Ph.D. diss., Northwestern University, 1985).

23. Ralph W. Hidy, Muriel E. Hidy, and Roy V. Scott, with Don L. Hofsommer, *The Great Northern Railway: A History* (Boston: Harvard Business School Press, 1988); Donald J. Pisani, *Building an Arid Empire: Water and Development of the American West* (Albuquerque: University of New Mexico Press, 1990); Howard L. Dickman, "James Jerome Hill and the Agricultural Development of the Northwest" (Ph.D. diss., University of Michigan, 1977); John C. Hudson, *Plains Country Towns* (Minneapolis: University of Minnesota Press, 1985); John R. Borchert, *America's Northern Heartland* (Minneapolis: University of Minnesota Press, 1987);

Thomas W. Harvey, "The Making of Railroad Towns in Minnesota's Red River Valley" (Master's thesis, Pennsylvania State University, 1982); Carlos A. Schwantes, *The Pacific Northwest: An Interpretive History* (Lincoln: University of Nebraska Press, 1989); John Fahey, *The Inland Empire: Unfolding Years, 1879–1929* (Seattle: University of Washington Press, 1986); Gordon B. Dodds, *The American Northwest: A History of Washington and Oregon* (Arlington Heights, Ill.: Forum Press, 1986). Mary Beth LaDow is completing a doctoral study of United States and Canadian plains towns and has published some of her preliminary findings in "Chinook and the Myth of Progressive Adaptation," *Montana, the Magazine of Western History* 39 (Autumn 1989): 10–23. For more on Hill's activities in Canada, see John A. Eagle, *The Canadian Pacific Railway and the Development of Western Canada, 1896–1914* (Kingston, Ont.: McGill-Queen's University Press, 1989); W. A. Waiser, *The Field Naturalist: John Macoun, the Geological Survey and Natural Science* (Toronto: University of Toronto Press, 1989); Gerald Friesen, *The Canadian Prairies: A History* (Toronto and Lincoln: University of Toronto Press–University of Nebraska Press, 1984); A. A. den Otter, *Civilizing the West: The Galts and the Development of Western Canada* (Edmonton: University of Alberta Press, 1982).

24. Norma Hervey is completing a dissertation in history at the University of Minnesota on Milaca. David A. Walker, *Iron Frontier: The Discovery and Early Development of Minnesota's Three Ranges* (St. Paul: Minnesota Historical Society Press, 1979). The recently opened (1986) Louis Warren Hill Papers, James Jerome Hill Reference Library, provide additional documentation on the Hills' activities on Minnesota's iron ranges.

25. H. Roger Grant, *The Corn Belt Route: A History of the Chicago Great Western Railroad Company* (DeKalb: Northern Illinois University Press, 1984); "The James J. Hill Papers: An Untapped Source for the Study of Iowa History," *Annals of Iowa* 46 (Summer 1982): 373–76; "The Mason City Road: From Iowa Shortline to Chicago Great Western Affiliate," *Annals of Iowa* 46 (Summer 1982): 323–36; "A. B. Stickney and James J. Hill: The Railroad Relationship," *Railroad History* 146 (Spring 1982): 9–21; "Midwestern Railroad Leader: Marvin Hughitt of the Chicago & North Western," *Hayes Historical Journal* 8 (Fall 1989): 5–17.

26. Howard B. Schonberger, *Transportation to the Seaboard: The Communication Revolution and American Foreign Policy, 1860–1900* (Westport, Conn.: Greenwood, 1971), 212–34. A number of scholars, including Carlos A. Schwantes, C. Vann West, William L. Lang, William G. Robbins, and Saul Engelbourg, are completing article and book-length studies that will deal with Hill's activities in the Northwest.

27. White, "Paris Gibson, James J. Hill, and the 'New Minneapolis': The Great Falls Water Power and Townsite Company, 1882–1908," *Montana, the Magazine of Western History* 33 (Summer 1983): 60–69; White, "Commonwealth or Colony? Montana and the Railroads in the First Decade of Statehood," *Montana, the Magazine of Western History* 38 (Autumn 1988): 12–23.

28. Alan Trachtenberg, *The Incorporation of America: Culture & Society in the Gilded Age* (New York: Hill and Wang, 1982); James Oliver Robertson, *America's Business* (New York: Hill and Wang, 1985).

29. London Conference Memorandum, April 2, 1896, Hill Papers.

30. Hill to Perkins, March 21, 1904, Gaspard Farrer to Hill, March 15, 1904, Hill Papers. For more on the Northern Securities Case, see Vincent P. Carosso, *The Morgans: Private International Bankers, 1854–1913* (Cambridge, Mass.: Harvard University Press, 1987); Hidy, Hidy, Scott, and Hofsommer, *Great Northern Railway*; Alfred D. Chandler, *The Visible Hand: The Managerial Revolution in American Business* (Cambridge, Mass.: Belknap Press, 1977); Balthusar Henry Meyer, *A History of the Northern Securities Case* (Madison: University of Wisconsin, 1906).

31. White, "Gilded Age Businessman."

32. Albro Martin, *Enterprise Denied: Origins of the Decline of American Railroads, 1897–1917* (New York: Columbia University Press, 1971); Gabriel Kolko, *Railroads and Regulation, 1877–1916* (Princeton: Princeton University Press, 1965).

Americans have a special gift, possibly unique, for demonstrating the silliest and ugliest faces of their society. It always puzzles outsiders that there is surprisingly little reflection, in the high literary art of the United States, of people doing serious and disciplined work, particularly work of human concern. This lack has made for major misunderstanding in other countries. —C. P. Snow.

PART ONE
SEEDTIME, 1838-1879

Summer deserts the land early on the northern Great Plains. By late September the thick tall grass, so recently lush and green, waves brown and expectant in a wind already edged with the arctic cold. The hot dry winds of summer have gone, the soft renewing breezes of spring are a distant memory.

Each year more millions of earth's people watch this sequence anxiously, for these plains are vital to the world food supply. They were not always so important. Long after the Roman peasant could no longer afford to own the land he worked, these plains lay deserted, unknown except to small bands of Indians who scorned to till the soil. For centuries Europe's masses toiled in feudal serfdom while not even their wisest men suspected the existence of these vast lands. Two hundred and fifty years after the founding of the first European settlement in the New World, and long after the younger sons of Quebec and Vermont, of Ontario and Pennsylvania, had begun to despair of finding farms for themselves, the northern Great Plains lay silent and unused behind the formidable barriers of Canada's granite shield, the Great Lakes, and distances which made men's heads swim.

Thus it was in September 1838. No outward sign, not the isolated campfire of an Indian band belatedly pursuing the buffalo before the threat of winter; not the lone trapper hurrying back to the haven of the primitive settlements near the mouth of the Red River of the North; none of these hinted at three widely separated events which in but one more generation would open these lands to the millions who would be denied them no longer. In a tiny village far up one of the countless fjords of Norway, Jacob Ryggen was born to a young couple who a year before had defied common sense by marrying. The young father could not afford a wife, much less a child. What member of the bønder, the Norwegian peasantry, could? Endless hours of hard work would never secure for him, his helpmeet, and the numerous children who were sure to follow more than a bare existence, with no assurance even of that. But not to have married would have contradicted all of the forces welling up in the young couple. Perhaps, somehow, if not they, their eldest son, or at least *his son, might someday find a little piece of land on which he could lavish the pride of ownership. . . .*

Halfway around the world, in a miserable hut in a miasmal settlement on Beaver Creek in Illinois, another Norwegian, not much older than Jacob Ryggen's father, lay dying. Ole Rynning, preacher's son, victim of an unrequited love affair back in the Old Country, and self-appointed champion of the bønder, had led one of the first parties of Norwegian settlers into Illinois just a year before. In "Providens," where their ship had touched briefly, he had seen his first railroad train, so backward was Norway. But the lowlands of Illinois proved even less hospitable to these Norwegians than their fjords had been, for they were unprepared for the heat and humidity of the American Midwest. By September 1838 half of the group of eighty-four were dead, and Ole Rynning was soon to breathe his last. News of his death, carried to Norway by his closest friend, was a sharp discouragement to emigration, but Rynning's friend also carried with him something of the dead leader's which quickly rekindled in his countrymen a mighty urge to cross the sullen ocean to the new land. It was the manuscript of Rynning's manual for prospective emigrants to America, which he had written during his last winter on earth. Published as A True Account of America for the Information and Help of Peasant and Commoner, *it answered dozens of questions for the barely literate Norwegian peasant. For the vanguard of what would swell to one of the greatest of the* Volkswanderungs, *it removed that outer web of ignorance which so often immobilizes even the most daring. "In America," Rynning told them, "one gets nothing without work, but by work one can expect some day to achieve better circumstances." How prosaic. How powerful.*

At almost the same moment James Jerome Hill was born on a stingy farm in the backwoods of Ontario. With many others, but chief among them, Hill would lay the highway which would lead the millions whom men like Jacob Ryggen would father, and whom prophets like Ole Rynning would inspire, to the land which would blossom under their expert hands. The coincidence of these three lives symbolizes the diversity of the forces behind the rise of the Northwest. They represent the inseparable end and beginning which make the common thread of all history. Ole Rynning was the first of his line to die in the New World, but, on the other hand, Jacob Ryggen was the last of his line to die in the Old, for his sons came to America. And James J. Hill was the first of his line to be born in the New World. His biography is, inevitably, about all three of them, and of the few who preceded them, and the multitude who came after.

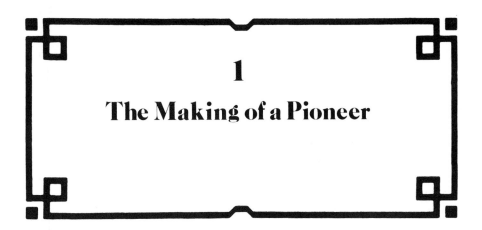

1

The Making of a Pioneer

What little success has attended my own labours as a teacher must be attributed to the felt necessity of knowing *each scholar as an individual, of sympathizing with them in their sorrows, of encouraging their feeble efforts and aspirations.*

—Rev. William Wetherald

I

Smart tourists in the Province of Ontario, heading west from Toronto, will avoid the monotonous superhighway and take Highway Seven. Fifty miles of driving through the prosperous, rolling countryside will bring them to the old Quaker village of Rockwood in the township of Eramosa. If they are looking for tourist sights and not motels, they will see on their left, just before they enter the village, a handsome stone building which might be a school. In fact, it *was* a school, one of Canada's earliest private academies, as they were called in Canada and the United States before the public high school destroyed them. A plaque, set in place in 1962 by the Ontario tourism officials, informs the visitor that Rockwood Academy was founded by the Rev. William Wetherald, one of the Quakers who were the earliest settlers of Eramosa, in 1850; moved into the present building in 1853; and ceased operations in 1882. Among its students were three who were thought to merit mention on the plaque: Adam Beck, founder of Ontario's hydroelectric power system; A. S. Hardy, fourth premier of Ontario; and James J. Hill, "pioneer railway magnate."

It is no traditional biographical cliché to emphasize the influence of

William Wetherald on young James Hill. There was little else to start a boy thinking, in Rockwood in the 1850s, that he might be destined to grow up and do great things. In the midst of his first great triumph as a railroad leader Hill would recall "my dear old master" with more than passing sentiment. The miracle is that William Wetherald ever became a teacher at all, and his power to stimulate a critical young mind like Hill's is an exceptional testament to the art of self-teaching. For Wetherald never set foot in a classroom as a student beyond the age of fifteen.

His education had begun auspiciously enough, although the prospect of entering an English public school—in this case, the Friends School of Ackworth, Yorkshire—appalled the lad, judging by the bit of doggerel with which he commemorated the event:

> I have entered thee for Ackworth,
>   Was all my father said;
> And turning quickly from the door,
>   He though he'd killed me dead.[1]

But while most students survive their years in bleak educational institutions by scheming to escape at the earliest opportunity, Wetherald survived by dreaming of how much better a school he might found someday. What he vowed to replace was the spiritual coldness of the typical school:

> The want of life and vivacity in the routine . . . , the cold rigid inflexible system of punishment, the generous want of sympathy between the teachers and the taught, the suspicion generated by a system of espionage (for the monitorial system is in its *essence* a spy system), these and other remembrances . . . affect me with painful sensations. . . . The punishment was lenient and judicious, but administered without *tenderness* with . . . no hope held out that by future efforts my lost position might be regained.[2]

Many a teacher might have taught James J. Hill the subjects which he studied under Wetherald, but few could have matched his constructive approach to what is for so many a painful process. And there was something else. Young Hill would suffer bitter disappointments in his few years in Rockwood, but in Wetherald he had a dramatic example of what one can accomplish if bitterness and self-pity are conquered. Wetherald had plenty to be bitter about, if he had been so inclined. When he was fifteen and beginning to soak up the culture of Ackworth, he suddenly found himself and his family set down in the bleakest intellectual atmosphere imaginable: a frontier farm in Upper

Canada, where there was nothing in prospect but unremitting toil, and not even a newspaper or a Bible to read, nor a pen or sheet of paper on which to scrawl one's thoughts. If we doubt that even in the wilds of Upper Canada a young Quaker had to start with such total intellectual deprivation, we can yet marvel at the intensity of the seven-year program of self-education which Wetherald set for himself. By the time he was twenty-two he had the equivalent of a college education, had learned to make do with four hours of sleep a night, and was ready to prove to any young charge who might benefit from it how little one could start with and how much he could make of it.[3]

The Township of Eramosa, in which the village of Rockwood is located, dates from 1784, when the land was surrendered by the Indians. As in the case of the American interior, it remained hard to get to, hard to stay alive in, and even harder to transport its small agricultural surplus to the outside world until well into the nineteenth century. When the Quakers founded the settlement of Brotherstown—later, Rockwood—in the early 1830s, Eramosa and neighboring Puslinch were so thinly settled they barely qualified as townships. By 1836, however, the Society of Friends had been persuaded to grant the little community the churchly status of Rockwood Meeting. To the community's slender income from farming was added the modest wealth created by a few grist mills which used the waterpower of the Eramosa River.

If education is the child of affluence, Rockwood and Eramosa had ample excuse for the slender schooling opportunities which James J. Hill encountered there in the 1840s. There was little educational capital, indeed, beyond that which Wetherald had stored up in his head, and the youngster would not encounter that for several years. While Wetherald had succeeded in getting a teaching post in 1843, when he was twenty-three, it appears not to have been in Rockwood, for the first teacher there, beginning in 1842, was one John Robertson. For the sum of £50 or less a year, collected from the parents of his pupils notwithstanding the fact that it was a "public" school, Robertson drilled his charges in the "three R's" and little more. This country schoolmaster, holding forth in his one-room school, was James J. Hill's only brush with culture for five years. Then, in 1849, came William Wetherald.[4]

One year of pinafores and blue-backed spellers appears to have been all that Wetherald could take. Realizing that Canada, though still closely tied to Great Britain's apron strings, would need its own leaders, and that the parents of Rockwood's more promising boys would gladly pay for advanced instruction, he bravely decided to open his own school. In the summer of 1850, through the columns of the Guelph *Advertiser,* he "intimates that he can accommodate a few additional pupils, to whose domestic comfort and literary progress the closest attention will be given." The subjects offered were English grammar, writing, arithmetic, bookkeeping, history, geography, Latin (Greek was offered later), geometry, theory of land surveying, and algebra—all eminently practical subjects except for English grammar and Latin, which seem to have been looked down upon by that utilitarian society. Young Hill saved a part of the £13 fee which boys his age were charged for board and tuition for the semester by walking four miles to the academy, but one winter the master offered him a chance to earn his keep by doing the chores around the place. In that era, before vegetable peelers, garbage disposers and indoor plumbing, the walk might have seemed the lesser evil, but to Hill the opportunity to become a resident boarding student must have been worth a good deal of menial labor.[5]

By his fourteenth birthday Hill probably knew more algebra and geometry, and certainly more bookkeeping and land surveying, than a typical high school graduate of today does. Wetherald knew the value of these subjects, but he seems to have impressed the boy even more with the beauty and power of the English language and its enormous literature. The articulateness of Hill's voluminous correspondence, so much of which was dashed off in his own handwriting with hardly a chance for revision, bespeaks an especially fine training in grammar, rhetoric, and literature. For Wetherald, if he saw that a bright lad was going ahead "too fast," knew how to fill in the chinks of time. "Glad as he was to assist an eager pupil," recalled one of the master's last students, "he would not let me rush the pace, but insisted on sandwiching in *Le Juif Errant, Don Quixote,* and *Gil Blas* between Anthony, Caesar, *de Bello Gallico,* and Horace. He also taught me to play chess, and in cricket and other outdoor sports, always joined us in them as one of ourselves. . . ." The boys and their master enjoyed themselves enormously. The mill dam behind the school supplied that winter pastime which makes northern boys and girls the envy of southern youngsters, ice skating; and the rugged glacial landscape provided limitless opportunities for exploring, with a lesson in geology thrown in.[6] And the best was yet to come.

So successful was the academy that in 1852 Wetherald began construction of a new building to replace the old log school. Jim Hill, at fourteen, had had four years of stimulating instruction under the master. He looked forward to four more and after that, somehow, college, for this farm lad was going to become a doctor. But Hill never became a doctor, and he never went to college, nor did he ever set foot in the new Rockwood Academy building as a student. On Christmas Day 1852 his father died, and there was no more money for tuition. If bitterness welled up in his heart as he walked past the fine new building on his way to his job at Passmore's grocery store, we have no record of it. Wetherald's story of whittling axe handles to exchange for a pen, a bottle of ink, a quire of paper and a Bible had not been lost on him. He had had one year less of formal schooling than his master, but, then, his master had not had the opportunity to study under William Wetherald. Jim Hill would make the most of what he had.

The business leader carried his memories of Rockwood Academy with him throughout the rest of his life. Not long after his successful acquisition of the St. Paul & Pacific Railroad and the organization of the St. Paul, Minneapolis & Manitoba under conditions which made him several times a millionaire, he wrote to Wetherald, who had retired from schoolteaching to become a Congregational minister in St. Catherine's, Ontario:

> Your letter with photo gave me more real pleasure than anything I have received for a long time. Herewith I enclose you passes from St. Catherine's to St. Paul and return, together with draft on N.Y. for $50.00 which I hope you will accept and take the time to run up and spend a month with me, during which time if you desire you can run down to Manitoba and see the Canadian northwest. I have a nice little family of children and my good wife will be more than happy to have you our guest. I have looked forward for some years to a time when I could have you pay us a visit and renew some of the days that were spent so pleasantly under your care.[7]

Wetherald did come, and, care-worn, stoop-shouldered, old teacher-preacher Quaker that he was, he enjoyed himself enormously on the trip down the Red River Valley as guest of the railroad in Hill's private car. On the train back to Ontario he thrust his hand into his coat pocket and pulled out an envelope. It contained a gift of $500. Two years later, in response to his timid request for help in building a new church, came a pledge for $1500. But he firmly resisted what Hill most wanted of him: to become the tutor of his sons. Perhaps he realized that a Congregational minister and lifelong Quaker was not the proper

William Wetherald, about 1880.

tutor to two lads who were preparing for confirmation in the Roman Catholic church. His diplomatic reply displays the rhetorical art which he had imparted to James J. Hill in a more robust strain:

> I have thought much of James and Lewis [Louis]. There are many teachers with scholarship enough to fill the bill, but none whom I would dare to recommend as likely to win the hearts and retain the confidence of the boys. Knowledge, after all, is to the teacher only what colors are to the artist. Tact, insight, patience, and sympathy are needed in order to give a fitting relation to light and shade and develop a perfect picture. . . .[8]

II

Who was this young Canadian who was to become such a famous American? What was the background of this would-be country doctor who became instead the leading figure in the development of the American Northwest? He was the oldest surviving son of James and Ann Dunbar Hill, who were part of that thin stream of Anglo-Celtic immigration which contributed to the slow growth of English-speaking Canada in the decades following the Napoleonic wars. The genealogy is a wild tale of Anglican missionaries, Scottish covenanters, and English civil servants persecuted by the religious orthodoxy; of families separated by emigration and reunited by the strong pull of family ties. Through the mists of three centuries we can dimly make out James and Mary Rogers, sent to Ireland as missionaries of the Church of England in 1640. The sons of St. Patrick, we are told, welcomed the pair by burning James at the stake and were preparing to do the same to Mary when she escaped with her baby girl, Jane, to the mountains.

Jane Rogers lived, married one Graem (Graham), and presented him with two sons who became ancestors of James J. Hill on both his paternal grandparents' sides. Each Graem had a daughter. Margaret married James Hill, a young man of their village of Armagh in northern Ireland, the religious center of all Ireland, where St. Patrick established his archbishopric in 445 A.D. Her cousin Agnes married one Alexander Riggs. A son of Margaret and James, James Hill (1780–1845), and a daughter of Agnes and Alexander, Mary Riggs (1780–1857), married and became the paternal grandparents of James J. Hill.

Hill's father, inevitably named James, was born at "Mars Hill," near Armagh, in 1811 and, as we have seen, died in Rockwood in 1852. His wife, whom he married in Canada in 1833, was Ann Dunbar Hill (1805–76), daughter of Alexander Samuel Dunbar, a government clerk, and Elizabeth Dulmage, who were married in County Limerick, Ireland, in 1797. The Dunbars, it is believed, had fled from persecution as "covenanters" (Presbyterians) in Scotland in the late seventeenth century, landing shipwrecked on the west coast of Ireland. Dulmage is the Anglicized form of the German, Dolmetsch. There were Dolmetsches in a shipload of Palatine emigrants headed for England which was wrecked off the Irish coast in 1709. Alexander and Elizabeth Dunbar left Limerick about 1800 on the advice of a loyal Catholic friend that they had best move on. They went to Templemore, in Tipperary, where other Dulmages were well established, and there Ann was born in 1805.

The Hills might have been content to remain in northern Ireland forever, producing one James in each generation until the end of time, but for an adventurous strain in the Riggs family. Mary Riggs, James J.'s grandmother, had a brother, John R., who had fought with Wellington at Waterloo, although not, despite family tradition, as a colonel. His reward upon retirement was a grant of land in Upper Canada. If nobody quite knew where it was, at least it was close enough to Lake Ontario to be warmer, and therefore somewhat more bearable to an Irishman, than the less favored interior areas of what eventually became the Province of Ontario. Thither sailed the hardy ex-soldier in 1819, taking with him his younger brother, Alexander, and James and Mary's eldest son, Graham (1804–49), who was barely fifteen years old. No letters or other word of the emigrants came to those who were left behind in Ireland. Mary Riggs Hill, despairing of ever hearing from son or brother again, determined to reunite the entire family in Canada. In 1829 she got her way, for by that time her son James was eighteen and her husband had secured a grant of two hundred acres in the township of Eramosa, not far from where John Riggs and young Graham Hill had settled. Four years after their arrival the elder James split off a fifty-acre parcel from his original two hundred, and on this small farm the future father of James J. Hill set up housekeeping with Ann Dunbar in 1833. Ann had arrived with her family the year before, and the two young people were soon promised to each other. Their first child, named James according to family custom, was born a year later and, like many an infant in those times, shortly died. Mary Elizabeth, named for grandmothers on both sides of her family, arrived on Christmas Day 1835, and on September 16, 1838, a second son, named James without deference to his dead predecessor, was born. A younger brother, Alexander Samuel Dunbar Hill, was born on September 6, 1839. The family was complete and, Ann noted with relief, her husband had finally cut down the last tree near their log cabin which, if it fell, could have landed on their house.[9]

James Hill provided his family with a better living from his fifty acres than that which is implied by the modern term, "subsistence farm," for the agriculture of Ontario, like that of western New York and northern Ohio, which it resembles so closely, was productive and well diversified. Young James had all that was necessary to produce a physically healthy lad, and he managed, moreover, to taste just enough of what the wider world had to offer to plant in him the dissatisfaction which would lead to greater things. He lived at a time when the tradition of picking up and moving on, over great distances and to the complete desertion of all that one left behind, was strong. Indeed, the society into which James J. Hill was born was so restless as to make our supposedly mobile modern society look nailed down by comparison. His part of Ontario was filling up rapidly, and the capacity of the land to produce wheat, the staple food crop of these northern people, had begun an alarming decline for reasons which would remain a mystery for many years. One would have had to love farming deeply to look forward to a lifetime in Eramosa. Younger brother Alec had such a love, and would find a way to stay. But James would forsake the land at his earliest opportunity, and would find a higher way in which to serve it and those who struggled on it. To these generalizations about why some stay and some press on to meet their fate, Joseph G. Pyle, Hill's first biographer, writing before the tyranny of the behavioral sciences, could confidently add "the blood of the Celt, which flows naturally toward greatness." [10]

Another who would find farming an incubus was James's and Alec's father. For fifteen years he labored on his acres. He raised the log house in which they lived, "in the bush," as Alec said, felling the trees from which it was built and later splitting the shingles with which it was rudely covered. Life was drab. There was little room for non-essentials. Newspapers provided the slenderest thread of contact with the outside world, and they were often weeks old by the time they had been passed along to those in the backwoods. Sleigh rides in season and an infrequent Saturday night dance, always over by midnight, provided what little social life there was. A volume of the works of Shakespeare, the boys would recall, stood on a shelf in the warm kitchen, which served as "family room," along with the Bible, the poems of Burns, and a dictionary—a well-stocked library compared with what had faced the fifteen-year-old William Wetherald ten years earlier.

James Hill was a Baptist and Ann a Methodist, while their children "were practically raised with Quakers," as Alec recalled. Immigrants and frontier people centered their religious beliefs on a certain surprise that they had been spared thus far, and the conviction that they had best be prepared to depart on short notice. It was a view of the spirit for which James J. Hill would find little use in later life. Perhaps he eventually read the smug, lugubrious letter which his fearfully religious Uncle Graham wrote to Uncle Alexander, who lived on another fifty acres which the elder James had sliced off the original two hundred, after the sudden death of their twenty-year-old sister:

> But I would say to father and mother, weep not for Mary Jane, but weep for yourselves and the rest of your children, that is still in this world of grief and sin, exposed to the tempter's powers. . . . How easy the soul that has left this wearisome body behind. . . . But I must tell you about our camp meeting that was held on the Sydenham about five miles from my place. The Lord was presant. . . .[11]

A few minutes spent dutifully reciting their assigned verses from the Bible on Sunday morning, followed by attendance at church, sufficed to release Jim and Alec for the real pleasures of country life in a land still close to the virgin forest. Jim became an excellent shot with the rifle, which was still a valuable tool for adding variety to the family's diet, and an expert at various methods of fishing. The two boys were close companions: less than a year separated them in age, although Alec always insisted that Jim had been born two years before him, thus disputing that most final of authorities, the family Bible. Jim had experimented with fashioning bows and arrows from the simple materials available to them, and one day when he was nine he was persuaded to make one for his younger brother. What happened then, although many youngsters have had the same mishap without injury, produced what was to be James J. Hill's most unusual physical feature. The bow snapped; the end of the arrow, held so earnestly to the right eye, was propelled backward; and the eye was badly injured.

In a miracle of frontier surgery, the local doctor managed to return the eyeball to its socket and restore muscular control over it, but the function of the optic nerve was permanently destroyed.

It is possible that James could perceive shades of light and dark with the eye. Both eyes twinkled with humor or flashed with anger equally well, and it is unlikely that those who did not know ever suspected that the Empire Builder was blind in one eye. Long years of intense work, involving the writing of hundreds of thousands of words by lamplight in his massive correspondence, seem never to have distressed the good eye.[12]

A one-eyed doctor would have been just as welcome on the Canadian or American frontier as a doctor with two eyes, and thus it is unlikely that it was young Hill's accident which deflected him from his early ambition. He was far from committed to a medical career at the age of nine, but for a rather bookish lad either the pulpit, the schoolroom, or the scalpel seemed a proper destiny. It was Hill's deep love of reading, in fact, and the obvious inability of the country schoolmaster to cultivate it, which led Hill's father to place him in Wetherald's academy, where his brother followed him the next year.

One day someone lent him a copy of Sir Walter Scott's *Ivanhoe*. He rushed through his chores that evening, then settled down with the book. Sent to bed just as the mantle of the Middle Ages was falling about him, next day the school-bound lad turned off the road at the thickest part of the forest and was soon again deep in the age of chivalry. His mind took a leap forward that day, but the prosaic fact was that he had played hooky. We should congratulate ourselves that this kind of indomitable spirit has not died: many of the weekday visitors to the branches of the New York Public Library, in fact, are bright, bored truants from the city's public school system.

Until he was thirteen this boy was simply James Hill, like numerous generations of first-born males in his family before him. Then, impressed by a biography of Napoleon, he took for himself the middle name of Jerome, after the emperor's brother, and so infectious was his enthusiasm for the man who remade the map of Europe that James Jerome's sister gave five of her daughters names from Napoleon's family. A year later a traveling lecturer came to town with his illustrated spiel on Napoleon's military genius. Eager to see the show, which consisted of a narration in front of a large, moving painted scroll, not once but over and over, young Hill offered to turn the scroll without fee. By the middle of the week-long engagement, however, he was ready to break the bargain, but the showman held him to his rash promise. Young Hill relieved the monotony and brought his servitude to an abrupt end by having Napoleon's famous cavalry gallop on the scene tail first.[13]

Hill's father said goodbye to farming forever in 1848, when he moved his family to the village of Rockwood and opened an inn and tavern "for the refreshment of man and beast." After certain difficulties in getting a license to serve ardent spirits were surmounted, the tavern became a place of fascination and education for the boys. The excesses of the rough men and, now and then, their women, repelled him, as they generally repel those entering the puritanical stage of early adolescence. Hill's lifelong moderation in food and drink probably owed more to his chemistry and the fact that he had many more interesting things to do than eat and drink, but passing one's formative years in a mid-nineteenth century inn on the Canadian frontier must either hurt or help in character development. It was hardly a neutral experience. But it certainly was better than the old farm, for there was more leisure and the family grew closer to one another. He soon came to love the ancient Scottish airs which his father played on his flute, the more so since now young James was reading the moving verses which Robert Burns set to them. Years later, around campfires in Montana or before the towering fireplaces of exclusive salmon-fishing lodges, James J. Hill would lead his distinguished friends in singing those old songs until long past midnight.

On Christmas Day 1852, after a short illness during which he barely had time to write out a confused will, James Hill died. His son, James Jerome, was just fourteen. His childhood was over.[14] Already a strong,

well set-up adolescent, with a nervous drive to keep busy, he was
soon employed at any odd farm or town job he could find.

III

The two years which James J. Hill spent clerking in stores in Rockwood and Guelph following the death of his father may have been one
of the most important phases of his education. His first job, at a dollar
a week, was in the general store of a hard-bitten Scotsman named
Passmore on the single street of Rockwood. Here young Hill had a
year's liberal education in what business was all about in that agrarian
age, for business then still meant mercantile activity. There were few
highly manufactured products, for the age of steel and chemistry and
electricity and the internal combustion engine were still decades in the
future. Such manufactured goods as found their way into the channels
of rural trade were produced in thousands of enterprises of which
even the largest were family-owned establishments. Most high quality
goods, notably textiles, were imported. Distribution was carried on almost exclusively by mercantile firms—jobbers, wholesalers, retailers—
as manufacturers had no distribution facilities and, indeed, little first-
hand knowledge of the thin-spread, far-flung market for their goods in
the countless little villages which served the farming communities that
surrounded them. A job in a general store in the 1850s could teach a
bright, industrious, ambitious lad a great deal about what farmers
wanted and needed, how much they could pay for it, and where supplies could be procured most easily and cheaply. Jim Hill acquired that
clear, legible handwriting which was the first thing an employer
looked for, a knowledge of double-entry bookkeeping, and at least a
good start toward the ability to tell which of his customers were going
ahead and which would inevitably fall behind—then, as now, the
basis on which credit could intelligently be extended.

After a year of trying to run the inn without her husband, Ann Hill
gave up, and she moved her family to Guelph early in 1854. There
James soon turned up a new position as clerk in McElroy and Mitchell's grocery store, but eight months later found himself, for the first
and last time in his life, without a job. What he did with himself in
the year between the fall of 1854 and the spring of 1856 we do not
know, but as scarce as work was, it is clear that young Hill did whatever he could to earn money, and that he saved a good portion of it.

By then he was seventeen, no younger than many another lad with no expectations who had set out to make something of himself in the world. His brother Alec was sixteen, old enough to take care of their mother and apparently quite willing to remain in Guelph and Rockwood for the rest of his life. His sister Mary, who had married John Brooks, a farmer, in 1853, seemed well provided for, although she was already burdened with several children. The path of adventure seemed to be open to the boy, almost whether he welcomed it or not. The urge to go was no more powerful, however, than the question of which direction to take was confusing.[15]

Marcus L. Hansen, the most promising historian of the immigration of peoples to and within the continent of North America, had time to complete a valuable study of what he called "the mingling of the Canadian and American peoples" before his premature death in 1940.[16] For at least a hundred years before the birth of James J. Hill, Hansen noted, the two young nations had traded populations in about equal streams, while a steady influx of immigrants from Europe made up for any losses at the border. "With the passing of the year 1837," however, "the wavering balance of population movements as between the United States and Canada began sharply to favor the southern country."[17] By that time Canada's two classic problems, population and geography, had begun to work strongly against her, a situation which would not be reversed until her harsh geography was finally conquered by the Canadian Pacific Railway in the 1880s. Yet, even today, Canada is a small country when measured by population, for despite her magnificent expanses of land she consists, in effect, of a "shoestring" nation some 3000 miles long and no wider than the roughly 150-mile-deep southern strip in which most of her people are concentrated.

In 1856 "Canada" consisted of the Province of Canada, an uneasy 1841 merger of Lower and Upper Canada, the present-day Provinces of Quebec and Ontario; the Maritimes, embracing Nova Scotia, New Brunswick, and Prince Edward Island; a vast, unexplored, and virtually uninhabited area known as Prince Rupert's Land, which was the domain of the Hudson's Bay Company; and the rugged but promising Pacific coast area bravely named British Columbia, which, Canadian statesmen uncomfortably admitted, had more in common with the American Pacific Northwest south of the 49th parallel than it did with eastern Canada. While the direct authority of the British sovereign had waned considerably by the 1830s, no real effort had been made to introduce the kind of representative government toward which England, in its Reform Act of 1832, was tentatively heading, and which America had enthusiastically adopted in the shape of Jacksonian Democracy. Rebellions in 1837–38 against powerfully entrenched old-line cliques in both Quebec and Ontario had failed, and severe punishment of the participants further encouraged emigration to America. Lord Durham, appointed Governor General in 1838, introduced substantial reforms, but the political future of Canada remained, in the 1850s, a great question mark composed of numerous imponderables, not the least of which was a growing agitation in the United States for annexation.[18]

It was the geography of Canada, however, which provided the most serious obstacle to any meaningful westward movement that might be contained within her own boundaries. It was not merely the appalling distances that separated her eastern cities from the Great Plains and British Columbia. The United States was also seeking to overcome heroic distances, but Canada had to contend with the fact that it is virtually bisected by the Great Lakes, which straddle the most important line of latitude in eastern Canada. As if this were not hardship enough for nation-building, the country north of the Lakes, through which any all-Canadian line of communication would have to run, is among the most forbidding in the world. Dubbed by geologists the "pre-Cambrian shield," it is a gigantic sheet of granite which extends right down to the water's edge at Georgian Bay and Lake Superior and is overlaid by a thin crust of soil grudgingly left behind by the glacier. The inability of such terrain to absorb moisture in an area of heavy annual precipitation has produced innumerable lakes and, where there is enough soil, the most treacherous of marshes and swamps. The climate is even more discouraging. Winter temperatures of 50 degrees below zero are common, while the short summer is made miserable by dense swarms of black flies and mosquitoes. And only a few hundred miles south of this complex, frustrating, physical obstacle, America's fertile Midwest spreads invitingly. Hansen's eloquent summary of the situation cannot be improved upon: "Canada had no Middle West of her own; . . . the one great Canadian frontier of settlement was in the United States."[19]

Rather than see her young people emigrate to the squalid, new, industrial cities of the eastern United States, where they would quickly lose all sense of religion and community, the government of Quebec actually encouraged movement of her excess population into the

American Midwest. Father Charles Chiniquy led several hundred families into the region around Kankakee, Illinois. By 1856 there were over 6000 persons of French Canadian origin there and, carrying the process of assimilation altogether too far and too fast to suit the Quebec authorities, many, including this pioneer priest, had switched to the Presbyterian church. By 1860 there were 8000 former Canadians in Iowa and 900 in Kansas. Then, just when it seemed that Canada would lose all of its "westering" people to the American Midwest, there began a train of events, one in which James Jerome Hill would play a major role, which deflected the westward movement northward as it rounded the southern tip of Lake Michigan.

One vital asset which the Americans who were spreading out on the treeless Midwestern prairies lacked was a suitable building material. The vast virgin forests of Michigan, Wisconsin, and Minnesota provided the lumber from which the Victorian houses of the midwestern American cities and towns were built. Young Canadians, having traveled as far as Detroit or Chicago in a vague drift toward Kankakee and Presbyterianism, got wind that their lumbering skills could be put to immediate, profitable use to the north. Canadian capital and business know-how, in fact, had preceded them. The ports on the east, and, later, the west shores of Lake Michigan and on Green Bay mushroomed. As lumbering expanded westward across Wisconsin, logs began to move down the Chippewa and St. Croix rivers into the Mississippi, which was then entering the final, golden era of the steamboat.[20] Then, suddenly, all eyes were on Chicago, as that booming terminal of rapidly growing east-west trade was connected with the Mississippi at Rock Island by man's first fully practical means of inland transportation, the railroad. The vector of western movement now added a strong northern component. On the northern reaches of the great river, at the point beyond which steamboats could not proceed, sprang up the lusty town of St. Paul. Farther north was the Red River of the North, and halfway down its tortuous course lay—Canada again!

There was much in the mid-1850s that America, east or west, could offer a young Canadian. But James J. Hill was no farmer, and he was sure that he had business talents which would be wasted in factory labor. "To seek one's fortune" was less of a cliché then than it later became. Among the richest men in America in 1855 were many who had sought and found their fortune in the Orient. Some, like the Astors, mined the riches of the North American wilderness in the form of exquisite furs and traded them to the Chinese for much more valuable goods. Others had provided a superior form of transportation to speed goods to and from the Orient, in the manner of the clipper ship operators of Boston and New York, whose exploits made the young nation a wonder to the Old World. Still others, like the seventeen-year-old John Murray Forbes, had actually gone out to live in the Far East in order to develop a lucrative trade at its source. A willingness to exile oneself to mysterious, dangerous corners of the earth was commonly conceived to be the best and quickest way to achieve one's fortune.

Perhaps Hill had lived long enough, and had seen enough of that mindless enthusiasm which led astray so many pioneers, to suspect that by the time a trend is universally accepted, it may actually no longer be valid. (If he suspected in 1855 that furs, clipper ships, and Oriental trade had just about had their day, as far as America was concerned, he was right.) That he was emotionally drawn to the Far East, however, is clear. He talked regretfully of unrealized ambitions in that direction, for himself and the nation, as long as he lived. But Hill believed in surveying all the possibilities. He already knew that what he had learned about the world and its opportunities was slight in comparison with what a little investigation could add to it. There were, after all, unknown opportunities in that vast empire which the United States had bought from Napoleon, a domain which Thomas Jefferson, urging the Louisiana Purchase, had said would require a thousand years to develop. And beyond Louisiana, the Republic had recently wrested from Mexico and Great Britain all of the North American continent between the 49th and 32nd parallels, westward to the sea. Even Rockwood must have felt some of the praise which writers, in crassly chauvinistic rhetoric, were heaping upon this new empire:

> The Land of Promise, and the Canaan of our time, is the region which, commencing on the slope of the Alleghenies, broadens grandly over the vast prairies and mighty rivers, over queenly lakes and lofty mountains, until the ebb and flow of the Pacific tide kisses the golden shores of the El Dorado . . .
>
> O, the soul kindles at the thought of what a magnificent empire of which the West is but the germ, which, blessed with liberty and guaranteeing equal rights to all, shall go on conquering and to conquer, until the whole earth shall resound with its fame and glory! [21]

But the importance of the West in mid-nineteenth-century North America has been vastly overdone. History, i.e. written history, has traditionally been concerned mainly with politics, and the bitter poli-

tics of Manifest Destiny in the decades just before and immediately
following the Civil War have obtruded on the story. As history has
become more specialized, we have come to realize the vital importance
of this period, and especially the decade of the 1850s, in the
emergence of a strong American economic society. And it is almost
entirely an Eastern story. The quickened economic pulse of the nation
from the early 1840s on produced a frontier which was less obvious
but more real than that represented by vast areas of land. This economic frontier lay to the east. At the very moment that Daniel Webster
was pleading for the Compromise of 1850 in his Seventh of March
speech, the most important single factor in the occupation of the
North American continent by western man was emerging. During that
fateful decade the cities of the Eastern seaboard—Boston, New York,
Philadelphia, and Baltimore—were linked to the Ohio River, the Great
Lakes, and the Mississippi by a revolutionary form of transportation
which was able to go anywhere, in any season, faster and far more
cheaply than any which had been known before. In a few short years
everything which Americans had learned about their internal commerce would have to be relearned. Politician and journalist Thurlow
Weed, traveling in the West in 1854, witnessed the revolution which
was taking place, and in his enthusiasm gave Americans one of their
most enduring hyperboles:

> Time is working a phenomenon upon the Mississippi River. In a business
> point of view this river is beginning to run up stream! A large share of the
> products of the Valley of the Mississippi are soon to find a market up in-
> stead of down the river. There is a West growing with a rapidity that has
> no parallel . . . while the railroads that are being constructed from Cin-
> cinnati, Toledo, Chicago, &c, to the Mississippi, are to take the corn,
> pork, beef, &c, &c, to a northern instead of southern markets.[22]

In the new railroad industry, although it required unusual foresight
to realize it in 1855, lay greater opportunities for more young men of
no family or fortune than any other calling in the nineteenth century.
And in its wake would come the steel industry, soon to be transformed by the railroad, which made possible the conversion from
charcoal fuel to bituminous coal, and by the introduction of the Bessemer steel-making process. Centering more and more in New York
was a rapidly evolving complex of business service institutions: banking, insurance, shipping, investment, and many others. The chief axis
of the rapidly expanding world economy was soon to be a line from
Liverpool to New York to Pittsburgh to Chicago. And thence—who

Anne Dunbar Hill, mother of James J. Hill, about 1856.

could say? Along that line there would be plenty of opportunities for a bright, hardworking lad who had the good sense to perceive them and the drive to make the most of them. They could not go uninvestigated.

And so it was that when James J. Hill left home he went, not westward, but to the East. Perhaps he hoped that nothing he would see there would deflect him from his great scheme to go out to the Orient. But he was no obscurantist, then or later. If there was a factor which bore on what he was about, it had to be checked out. Not long after his seventeenth birthday he began to make his plans. He would not require much in the way of baggage. The old-fashioned, brassbound leather trunk which his father had brought from Ireland would not do. Bestowing this heirloom on his brother, he decided to take a simple valise. What he did need, he thought, was something to add years to

James J. Hill, about 17, shortly before he left Rockwood.

his all-too-youthful appearance. He found the answer in a fashionable "Horace Greeley hat," a tall felt in a sporty, light shade. It was a bit loose on his head, but it was the best Guelph had to offer. Thus equipped, one cold, gray morning in February 1856 he said goodbye—not quite forever—to his birthplace and climbed aboard Guelph's shiniest symbol of the new age, the Grand Trunk Railway express to Toronto. As he turned his face toward his destination a sudden gust of wind whipped the new hat from his head. In consternation he watched it quickly disappear in the dusty wake of the train. Ah well, not to worry. He would not need a top hat where he was going.[23]

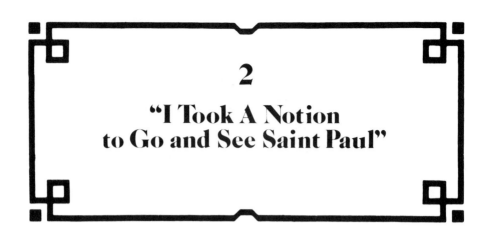

2

"I Took A Notion to Go and See Saint Paul"

Knocking about agrees with me. I will come out all right side up with care marked glass.

—James J. Hill, 1860

I

Father Lucien Galtier, anxious for the spiritual welfare of the motley band of misfits which the United States government had just expelled from the military reservation of Fort Snelling, built a rude log chapel on the bluff just above a great bend in the Mississippi River and named it for his patron saint. That was in 1841. Fifteen years later St. Paul, thus fortuitously perched on the most advantageous site at the head of navigation on the great river, was a bustling city of nearly 10,000, and Minnesota, which had reached territorial status only in 1849,was already agitating for statehood.[1] It was here that James Jerome Hill came on July 21, 1856. That spring he had seen more of the world than most of the citizens of Rockwood would see in a lifetime. We owe this earliest example of the lad's talent at letter-writing to his adventurous grandmother Hill's desire to share in some small way in a journey which she would never be able to take:

St. Paul Minnesota Territory Aug 1st/56

My Dear Grandmother

It is with a feeling of the greatest pleasure that I undertake to keep my word with you by writing as soon as I was settled. After I left Canada I went direct to New York and there I had a slight mishap which caused no injury except a pecuniary one. After leaving New York I went to Philadelphia, Baltimore, Charleston, Savannah and Pittsburgh, spending a good deal of both time and money and afterwards I came back to New York. I took a notion to go and see St. Paul so on the 11th of July I left and on the morning of the old 12th I was coming into Toronto on board the steamer Europa. After I landed in Toronto the cars were just going to Guelph and I could hardly refrain from going up but I thought if I went I should stay being a little homesick at the time.

So on I went and at Bronte the train stopped and Thos. McClenaghan got on. I was so tired and travel worn that he scarcely knew me. At Woodstock I saw Thomas Perry and his lodge waiting at the station for another lodge to come up and he was the last man I saw since I left Canada that I knew but three, one of which is Mr. Bookless from Guelph, he being on his way to Saint Paul. I overtook him in the city of Chicago quite accidentally but he was good companion for me up the river, we both being perfect strangers. I like this country very well and I think I shall like it still better the longer I live here. I am in the commission and shipping business. My salary is twice as much as I could get in Canada and work is easy, all done in an office. I have from 6 o'clock every evening to walk around and enjoy myself.

I intend to go and see you this winter or next fall and I hope to find you all in good health, the greatest of God's blessings. I should like to hear from you very often and let me know what course my mother is pursuing and what my brother is about. Also, what Robert Dunbar is doing, if he is still keep Alexander at his place at work. Give my love to Uncle Alex'r and his family and to Uncle John and Aunt Agnes and accept a large portion for yourself. In the meantime believe me to be

Your aff't grandson

James Hill * [2]

The odyssey which the lad described for his grandmother was both longer and less harrowing than that which his brother recalled sixty years later. Hill did not set out for New York State at the onset of the winter of 1855–56, as Alec believed, nor did he head for St. Paul as soon as spring came. What is now clear is that he left Canada in the

---

* In the "mishap" he had his pocket picked. July 12, Orangemen's Day, marks the victory of William III over James II at Aughrim, County Galway, in 1691, and the joining of Northern Ireland to England. Thomas McClenaghan (Jr.), a printer, was a son of Mary Riggs Hill's sister, Eliza. Thomas Perry was probably a relative of James Perry, the husband of "Aunt Agnes" Hill, who was James J. Hill's father's sister. Mr. Bookless was a business acquaintance. Robert Dunbar, for whom Hill's brother, Alexander, was working that summer, was their mother's brother. Uncles Alexander and John were his father's brothers. Mary Riggs Hill died the following year.

late winter of 1856 and went straight to New York. Nor did he go
without money, for he had been making his plans for a long time. He
undertook the trip with the same deliberateness and advance study
that he would give to much greater undertakings in the future. In his
pockets was $600, carefully saved during four years of hard work. For-
tunately, he was too shrewd to carry all of his money in one purse
while in New York, the capital city of pickpockets. When he got to his
ultimate destination, he had several hundred dollars left.

Philadelphia offered the young man his first taste of high culture.
Years later he recalled the beauty of the singing and the virtuosity of
the orchestra at an operatic performance, his first real lesson in what
great talent and uncompromising discipline could accomplish. The
music in Philadelphia was far more impressive than the few opportunities to go to the Far East which he could perceive in New York,
where a few days' sightseeing on the docks had quickly convinced
him that if the only way he could get to the Far East was to ship out as
a common sailor before the mast, then his destiny clearly must lie elsewhere. The eastern United States, indeed, turned out to be no land of
opportunity in 1856, for at that moment the great, protracted economic
build-up of the 1840s and 1850s was nearing its end. The panic of 1857
was to lay business low until the Civil War prosperity began in 1862.
There were two things he could do, once he had completed the tour of
the Eastern seaboard: he could go home in defeat, or he could "take a
notion to go and see St. Paul," a notion which had been growing in
his mind for a long time.[3]

St. Paul, the jumping-off point for the Northwest, had a special appeal to young men like Hill in the mid-1850s. The Compromise of
1850, the last work of Henry Clay and Daniel Webster, had been brutally disrupted in 1854 by Stephen A. Douglas's great political mis-
calculation, the Kansas-Nebraska Act, which reopened the wounds of
sectionalism and thus deflected the course of immigration to the mysterious but reputedly fertile lands beyond the Mississippi which were
bound to remain forever free. The Dred Scott decision further po-
larized Americans, reinforcing the attractiveness of the upper Midwest. Not political considerations alone, however, bent the course of
empire northwestward. Traveling journalists and lady sightseers alike
raved about this new land. C. W. Dana had written, in the same year
James J. Hill left Ontario, that

> this new town [St. Paul] will "go ahead" and must eventually become a
> depot of a vast interior commerce. It will receive and distribute the mer-

chant ware of the Upper Mississippi and the whole valley of the Minnesota, which is now being opened to settlement. Already the annual arrival of steamers from below averages 200. . . .[4]

Three years before, in a widely circulated book of travel, Mary Ellen Ellet had said some very attractive things about this boom town on the upper Mississippi:

The city of St. Paul must be the central point of business for the northwest. . . . Its growth has been one of unexampled rapidity, and fortunately for its prosperity and the well-being of its citizens, the Maine Liquor law is now in force throughout the Territory. The expenses of living are much more moderate than could be supposed possible. . . . Board at the best hotel costs but a dollar and a half a day, and from three to five dollars a week. Rent is high [but] labor commands excellent wages. . . . Mechanics can earn two dollars or more a day.

And the year after Hill arrived in St. Paul, Harriet Bishop saw the future of the new city clearly:

St. Paul is comparatively an infant city, with a population of probably 10,000 souls, but here "every man counts." Here, men are picked not from the fossilized haunts of old fogyism, but from the swiftest blood of the nation. Every man here, to use a western expression, "is a steamboat," and is determined to make his mark on the history of Minnesota. . . . It is a strange medley indeed, that which you meet aboard a Mississippi steamer. An Australian gold-hunter, a professor in an eastern University, going out to invest in Minnesota, a South Carolina boy, with one thousand dollars and a knowledge of double-entry. . . .[5]

To young Hill, whose faith in his own travel instincts was at that moment at a low ebb, there were more practical reasons for thinking about St. Paul. A former neighbor in Rockwood had emigrated there in the early 1850s and, when he went back home for a visit, had assured the teenager that he could get him a job on the levee, like the one he had, any time Hill wanted to come west. The boy also had some former schoolmates who had gone out a year or two before to look over the Red River country; one of them, William Farrish, was a close friend.[6] A shrewd young man like Hill would realize that much of their enthusiasm about Minnesota sprang from a desire to appear successful to those they left behind. Still, it was a gravitational force to a youngster who had no better plan and, he rationalized, it was on the overland route to the Pacific Coast and the Orient. And along the way, lay home.

The truth was, as he admitted to his grandmother, that he was more

than a little homesick. He traveled from New York to Toronto by the fastest possible means, taking the New York Central to Buffalo, a connecting train to Niagara, and, early on the morning of "the old twelfth," the steamer *Europa* across Lake Ontario to Toronto. Guelph was only about fifty miles farther, and the "cars" were about to leave the station when he arrived. But he found that he could not face his family as he was: tired, travel-stained, and empty-handed. "So on I went," he says, and to make sure that he did not weaken again he spurned the Grand Trunk's line to Detroit and Chicago, which would have taken him right through Rockwood and Guelph, for the Great Western's line via Hamilton and London.

Detroit and Chicago were new experiences for Hill, and he must have done some sightseeing there, since he took nine days to go from Toronto to St. Paul. From Chicago he took a train on the Chicago & North Western and Illinois Central lines to Dunleith, Illinois, just across the Mississippi from Dubuque. Only two years before the first railroad had connected Chicago with the river, but already navigation on its upper reaches had been greatly stimulated, and waiting for Hill's train was a northbound steamboat for which J. W. Bass & Company were agents. Within hours young Hill had become part of the convivial world of the Mississippi River steamboat. Two days later he stepped onto the levee at St. Paul. Above him he could see the wooded ridge of what became Summit Avenue where, sixty years later, his remarkable life would find its end.

II

St. Paul had been more than a little oversold in 1856. "One settler who arrived at St. Paul on the *Senator* in October was dumbfounded to find a rough frontier village, whereas newspaper accounts had led him to picture a city surpassed only by New York." Photographs from this period reveal a bleak collection of wooden buildings, many of them obviously dating from before the arrival of the first sawmill. The dreary, treeless prospect is no accident: all of the trees for miles around had long since been cut down to supply wood to keep the population from freezing in the winters. The citizens had already grown touchy about their climate, which made their convenient rivers and

St. Paul in 1857. The large building under construction is the county jail.

beautiful lakes useless for so much of the year. One Colonel Hewitt, "in order to quiet the eastern impression that Minnesota winters began in September," organized a steamboat excursion in December 1856. It was quite a success, to the pleasant surprise of the Catholic and Protestant charities which shared the proceeds. Caught up in the spirit of the affair, some of the passengers walked up the gangplank wearing linen dusters and waving palmleaf fans. None was so gauche as to point out that, although the narrow, swift-running stream did not freeze up at St. Paul until January in some years, broad, sluggish Lake Pepin, a wide place in the river a few miles below the city, always cut off access to and from St. Paul by the end of November, and each spring kept the city in a state of frustration while boats both above and below the lake waited well into April for the ice to break up.[7]

The "Maine Liquor law" may have diluted the frontier flavor of St. Paul life in the 1850s, as Mrs. Ellet noted, but the arm of the law was typically short and feeble. Crimes of passion and of greed were common, and seem usually to have gone unsolved. Twelve days before James J. Hill arrived, George B. McKenzie, proprietor of the popular Mansion House, who made a habit of carrying large sums of money, was robbed and his body thrown into the river from the bluff on which his hotel stood. A newcomer, one Robert Johnson, was also murdered and robbed; the perpetrators merely flung the body off the cliff, not bothering to conceal their crime. St. Paul was policed by a vigilance committee that summer, after which, we are told, things got better. Besides being a violence-ridden city, it was not a good place to get sick. A young doctor, recently arrived from the effete East, was shocked at being told, during a visit to the local hospital, that all pulmonary ailments, regardless of origin, were being diagnosed as "chest disease."[8]

Nevertheless, the progress of St. Paul, was distinctly upward, and there were many opportunities for those who wished to participate. In the main part of town, near the public levee in the vicinity of Third and Washington streets, things had begun to take on a look of permanence. Several brick buildings had gone up, or were planned, to accommodate the rising volume of business transacted and to provide for the growing stream of immigrant families and commercial travelers who thronged the area during the season of navigation. Among these were the Merchants' Hotel, a boarding house which Hill would patronize frequently, and the Mansion House. On the site of the burned-down Rice House, where one session of the territorial legislature had convened, the elegant Metropolitan Hotel was rising. Spiritual needs were beginning to be met more adequately. The Rev. John Mattock arrived in 1856 to be pastor of the Presbyterian Church, which overlooked the river at Third and St. Peter Streets. The Catholic population, greatly increased as a result of the Irish immigration after 1848, justified the creation of the diocese of St. Paul a year after creation of the Territory, and the consecration of Father Joseph Cretin to occupy the new see. In 1852 the first Catholic school had opened, numbering among its students fourteen-year-old John Ireland, who would personify the growth of the faith in the Northwest. Casper H. Schurmeier, native of Germany and a master wagonmaker, moved up from St. Louis. He and Conrad Gotzian, a flourishing shoe manufacturer who was also a German immigrant, built houses near Ninth and Canada streets, where, in a few years, James J. Hill would be their neighbor. In 1857 the new gasworks began operation under the aegis of Norman W. Kittson and the management of General Henry H. Sibley, the leading citizens of St. Paul, and three years later the new city achieved instantaneous communication with the rest of the nation by means of the magnetic telegraph.[9]

III

The steamboat was still the king of inland transportation in America in the 1850s. The railroad train, little more than a teakettle on wheels pulling a few oblong wooden boxes on spindly iron rails, was valued mainly as a means of connecting one navigable body of water with another. When James J. Hill arrived in St. Paul, the city was still eleven years away from a rail connection with Chicago. The first railroad wheel of any kind, in fact, would not turn in Minnesota until 1862. The 1850s, therefore, marked the zenith of the riverboat era, and it was almost inevitable that Hill's long career in transportation should begin on the levee.

Robert Fulton had demonstrated the practical application of steam power to navigation on the Hudson River in 1807, and only four years later the first steamboat on the Mississippi, the *New Orleans,* was launched. By 1817 upstream navigation by steamboat had been proved feasible by the *Zebulon M. Pike,* which ascended as far north as St. Louis. The tiny *Western Engineer* ventured as far as Keokuk, Iowa, in

1820, and, finally, on May 10, 1823, a date dear to the hearts of steam-boat enthusiasts everywhere, the *Virginia*, carrying supplies for the United States government, tied up at the mouth of the St. Peter River (now the Minnesota), near Fort Snelling. Only a few miles farther up the Mississippi were the falls of St. Anthony, beyond which no steam-boat could go, although some smaller boats were lugged around the falls and operated as far north as St. Cloud.[10] In the next two decades, while Minnesota awaited the tread of immigrants' feet, steamboating to St. Paul remained the province of the government and the American Fur Company, but by 1842 a former Hungarian count, Augustin Har-vaszthy, recognizing what the locals could not, decided that an in-dependently operated boat could make money that far north on the Mississippi. His little *Rock River* proved that he was right, and by 1848 "packet" boats, offering service on a more or less regular schedule, were in operation.[11]

The number of boats plying the upper Mississippi as far as St. Paul expanded from 85 in 1849 to 837 in 1856. In the year Hill arrived, navi-gation had begun on April 18, the earliest date since records had been kept. The river was a public highway, upon which anyone who had the capital could operate a steamboat. Not being common carriers, the boats could take what freight they wanted and carry passengers ac-cording to whatever schedule suited the operators. Sometimes freight was left on the docks, and passengers found on more than one oc-casion that the run had been terminated far short of their ticketed des-tination. The boatmen set whatever rates they chose, and assumed no responsibility for the safety of either passengers or cargo. Inevitably, therefore, the steamboat business, during its brief ascendancy, was even more chaotic than the railroad industry would prove to be during its formative decades. Had the steamboat proved to be as vital and as revolutionary as the railroad in the economic development of the na-tion, its chaotic structure would never have been tolerated. As it was, it all seemed rather picturesque, and certainly was a lot of fun. Rates came down rapidly: the charge between St. Louis and Galena fell from 50 cents per 100 pounds in 1841 to 22 cents per 100 in 1843. The size of the vessels and their comforts, if not their safety, were repeatedly enhanced as a constantly quickening national economic pulse drove the stakes ever higher. By the time young Hill reached the Mississippi at Dubuque, steamboating was big business.

A few face appeared on the steamboat scene in 1857, one who would transform the river boat business, combine and recombine the dozens of boats into ever larger organizations, and finally preside over the twilight years of this interim innovation in transportation. Beginning in 1857 with the *Franklin Steele*, his first steamboat designed for the Mississippi River trade, "Commodore" William F. Davidson saw the distinctive white collar of his companies painted on more tall, lean smokestacks than any other insignia. So long as James J. Hill remained a part of this romantic, if temporary, form of transportation, his fortunes would be closely tied to those of the Commodore.[12] During his early years in St. Paul, Hill watched the economic life of the city ebb and flow with the level of steamboat activity. At its height it was a wonderful thing for a lad from the back country of Ontario to behold:

> When the *Northern Light* arrived early in May the *Frank Steele*, the *Messenger*, the *Orb*, the *Golden State*, the *Equator*, the *Key Stone*, the *Saracen*, the *Sam Young*, the *Mansfield*, the *Ocean Wave*, the *Red Wing*, the *Golden Era*, the *Minnesota*, the *Conewago*, the *Kate French*, the *Time and Tide*, the *Hamburg*, the *Wave*, the *Excelsior*, and the *W. L. Ewing* lay diagonally with the levee. Instead of presenting the appearance of a city of houses, the levee looked like a city of steamboats.[13]

The lad made a strong impression on the older men with whom he traveled. By the time his boat reached St. Paul he had landed his first job with Brunson, Lewis & White, agents for the Dubuque Packet Co. It may seem strange that James J. Hill should have stood out among all of the immigrant men and boys who were flocking into the Northwest in the late 1850s. The fact is that then, just as now, the right combination of talents is always rare. And Hill was a steamboat agent's dream. He had the strong back and willing hands which were indispensable in that masculine calling, which might require the agent to drop his quill pen at a moment's notice, jump down from his high stool, and rush out onto the levee to help stop a fist fight, or quell a drunken passenger, or rescue a drowning one, or merely help load or unload cargo or baggage when extra hands were needed or a sudden rainstorm should come up. Much rarer were the bookish talents which constituted Hill's main "capital": his ability to write a fair hand, so important in the days before the typewriter, to add a column of figures accurately, and, rarest of all, to compose a clear and concise business letter. Young Hill soon demonstrated that he could get his work done, and with very little supervision, which counted for a great deal in the informal atmosphere of the St. Paul levee. Most men are good at something; what Hill did poorly, relatively speaking, he did very well. His work was not "all done in an office," as he bragged to his grandmother, but his aptitude for it was great, and it made him a prize catch for his new employers. Perhaps they knew they would not keep him long, but he was a valuable employee as long as they had him.

And what did he do on the levee, this new recruit to America's rapidly growing transportation corps? When he arrived in St. Paul, Minnesota still had a "deficit trade balance," in the jargon of economics. It was importing, so to speak, more than it was exporting, for the region had only begun its period of intensive development. In terms of value, the inbound cargoes of goods were much more important than those which the port of St. Paul was sending outward in the late 1850s. Practically everything necessary to support life above the simplest frontier subsistence level had to be brought in. So soon to become the greatest flour milling center in the United States, the area still was importing flour when Hill arrived. Nearly every form of manufactured goods— cook stoves for the new immigrant households; wagons, harness, and supplies for the horse-drawn economy; salt, nails, groceries, furniture; yardgoods for the home seamstresses; early versions of the machinery which would replace much of the manpower in plowing, tilling, and harvesting on the growing number of farms—all of these flowed off the steamboats and onto the waiting wagons and, later, onto the cars of the puny St. Paul & Pacific Railroad. None of this happened automatically. The transportation process had to be fussed and worried over every step of the way. Through waybills were unknown in that day, and a farmer's cookstove, for example, might pass through a dozen pairs of hands and several modes of transportation before reaching its destination. At each transfer point agents supervised the flow of freight. Inevitably, goods as well as baggage got lost, and somebody had to trace them. All of this greatly increased the already high costs of transport. Not the least of the railroad's cost-cutting virtues would be the development of through waybilling procedures, but meanwhile the steamboat agent played a vital role in the settlement of the new regions.

Slowly this "external investment" in the future of Minnesota and the new Northwest began to yield its fruits. When James J. Hill first saw St. Paul, the fur trade was still the Minnesota country's main reason for being. The Hudson's Bay Company's territory lay north of the international boundary, and during his first years at the great bend of the Mississippi, much of the inflow of goods would reflect that region's growing dependence upon the southern route, through the United States, for its supplies and for the goods which it traded for furs. And, inevitably, as the 1850s and 1860s unfolded, the southern route would come to be preferred for shipping the still enormous and valuable yield of pelts to the outside world. But the products of the fields were soon to replace those of the forests, and within a few years a thriving wheat and flour trade would spring up.

The first commercial grist mill in Minnesota had been erected at the falls of St. Anthony, a few miles above St. Paul, where unlimited water power was available. By 1854 millers were equipped to grind more wheat then could be supplied by the area, a deficiency which would be quickly rectified as the fertile lands northwest and southwest of St. Paul were settled. But the area's domination of the flour milling industry did not take place overnight. By 1861 it was producing some 250,000 barrels of flour a year, no more than a single large mill at Oswego, New York, turned out in what was then the breadbasket of the nation.

In 1870, however, man's ingenuity, as it so often does, entirely inverted the economic relationships which seemed to have been dictated by nature. The much colder climate of Minnesota had called for the cultivation of spring-planted wheat, rather than the winter-germinating variety which had been the staple food of western man since long before he left Europe. But the spring variety had a hard, brittle husk, or "bran," which, being pulverized during the milling process rather than winnowed out, was impossible to remove, or "purify," from the finished product, and yielded a dark flour which brought a lower price from the consumer than that made from soft winter wheat. Edmund N. LaCroix introduced the "middlings purifier" at one of the Washburn Company's mills in Minneapolis in 1870, and it, combined with grinding techniques more suitable to the hard wheat, solved these problems. From then on the nutritionally superior, hard spring wheat brought a better price than Eastern soft winter wheat, and the economic future of the Northwest was assured. It happened none too soon, for in truth the future of the Eastern wheat-growing regions had been foreclosed by factors which entomologists would not understand for another generation.[14] Thus, a few years after his arrival in St. Paul, James J. Hill found himself stenciling the consignees' names on some of the earliest commercial shipments of flour from the region.

Because the mills ground right on through the winter, when outward shipment of flour was prevented by ice on the river, warehousing of the temporary surplus became necessary, and as the St. Paul & Pacific Railroad began to haul flour and other goods in from St. Anthony in 1862, the efficient transfer of freight from the railroad station to the boats, and vice versa, introduced yet another business opportu-

nity. In 1859 Hill landed a better job with Temple and Beaupré, wholesale merchants, and in 1860 he began a four-year association with the
firm of Borup & Champlin, wholesale grocers and forwarding and
commission merchants, who sought to provide these services. During
the winter, when business on the river was at a standstill, he was free
to develop his initiative in a number of directions. He bought oats on
his own account, and frequently he was the low bidder in providing
feed for several hundred horses at Fort Snelling. Fuel—a constant
problem in that cold climate at a time when nothing more sophisticated than wood was used—had to be provided for every use, from
parlor space heaters to the boilers of the steamboats and the railroad's
new locomotives. Hill turned the problem into an opportunity, and in
his frequent trips farther and farther into the hinterland, in fair
weather and an occasional blizzard, he laid the foundations for his future success in the coal business.

Almost all of the goods and services which the region needed, Hill
realized, cost more than they should. Indeed they did, for transportation in the Northwest was still in a rudimentary state as the nation
entered the Civil War. Hardly a day passed in which he did not have
an opportunity to reflect on how much it cost to move things in his
part of the country. Freight charges frequently came to more than the
value of the goods. As he checked in a large shipment of salt (so vital
for preserving meats in the days before mechanical refrigeration) at
the very close of navigation in November 1864, he could see clearly
how much room there was for improvement on that score. The 560
barrels, which had come by rail from Milwaukee to Prairie du Chien
and thence by "the good steamboat *Milwaukee* whereof Holcombe is
master," to St. Paul, had cost over $1200 in shipping charges, of which
only one-third was for the rail portion of the trip.[15] Steamboat operators, it seems, had to recoup their losses from rate wars at the height
of the season by squeezing shippers who were desperate to get their
supplies in before the river froze. The young man could not suspect in
1864 how useful he would be in freeing the Northwest of such tyranny.

IV

James J. Hill would have been amused at the suggestion that a very
young man, so recently from his farm home, could have been either

homesick or bored in St. Paul in those year. For its size, "Pig's Eye," as some still insisted on calling the city, had more excitement than most places Hill had so recently visited. He moved into the household of V. K. Routt, a steamboat agent with whom he had become acquainted, as a boarder, but it was just a place to sleep and eat. He put in long hours at his job and, as he told his grandmother, after six o'clock in the evening he was free to walk around and enjoy himself. He would walk out along the graded but trackless right-of-way of the ill-fated Minnesota & Pacific Railroad, one of several which had been optimistically chartered by the state in the 1850s, and soon to be reorganized under the equally grandiose name of St. Paul & Pacific. It was a good way to learn railroading from the ground up. Sometimes he would stroll with his girl friend to the high points around the city, but not for the scenery alone, for in that day no one ever knew when the next boat would arrive, and up there on the bluff he had plenty of warning. When a boat rounded the great bend he would walk his girl home, hustle down to the levee, and get to work. It was a technique upon which he relied heavily in 1861 and 1862, when he carried the added responsibility of wharf master. More than anything else, he liked to put his ideas into words and try them out on his friends, who frequently had more than enough of it. Many years later a long-forgotten acquaintance reminded him of those days:

> I first knew you when I was selling steamboat tickets for Orrin Curtis and you were shipping clerk for Borup & Champlin down on the St. Paul levee. Later, when you used to drive Pat Kelly * nearly wild with your optomistic talk about the Northwest I always thought your head was levil. Pat likewise owned up to me in after years that he was to slow in comprehending our future. . . .

Life was anything but dull. One summer morning as Hill was working in his office he heard the cry, "Boy drowning!" and rushed outside to find his employer, Theodore Borup, floundering in the water in a losing effort to rescue an eleven-year-old immigrant boy who had decided to take a swim. Pausing only to peel off his coat, Hill was quickly in the water, followed by Captain Davidson himself. Soon all four were back on dry land, with no further crisis impending than that of preventing the boy's enraged father from taking a bull whip to his son. In the previous spring, "Jeems," as the newspaper editor liked to call him, had distinguished himself by racing up the street which led

---

* P. H. Kelly, a successful wholesale grocer, who was long a close friend of Hill's.

from the levee in a successful effort to catch a runaway dray horse, a
dangerous menace to other traffic. That winter "Jeems" and Theodore
Borup organized a bear hunt on the Eau Palla [Eau Galle] River in
neighboring Wisconsin, but that time Hill had only scratches to show
for his efforts.[16] Life's most exciting moment was narrated by Hill in a
letter of February 11, 1858, to his old friend William Farrish in Rockwood:

> Your epistle bearing date of the seventeenth ult came to hand in good
> time and your fertile imagination can scarcely conceive what an amount of
> pleasure I derived from it, as it was the first epistle of William to James at
> St. Paul for a "long back." My surprise on receiving your letter was only
> surpassed by my surprise at not receiving one from your after you left St.
> Paul or sometime during the ensuing season. Still, a good thing is never
> too late or *done too often.*
>
> It gave me much pleasure to hear that you were all well and enjoying
> yourselves in the good and pious (as I learn) little town of Rockwood. I
> did intend to go to Canada this winter but it is such a long winter trip I
> thought I should defer it until summer when I hope to be able to get away
> as I intend to go on the river this summer if all goes as well as I expect.
> Capt. W. F. Davidson wrote to me from Cincinnati about going with him
> as first clerk on the sidewheel packet Frank Steele, a new boat about the
> size of the War Eagle. The Capt is Letter A No. 1 and I think I shall go
> with him. If not, I have two or three good offers for the coming season on
> the levee besides my present berth, which is nevertheless very comfort-
> able.
>
> I think it mighty strange that some [of my letters] have not reached
> home as I wrote several times to my Bro. Alex and I never was more
> surprised than when old Bass handed me a letter of enquiry as to my
> *whereabouts.* But after the boats stop running our mails are carried so ir-
> regularly that whole bags of mail matter are often mislaid at way stations
> for weeks and some finally lost or otherwise destroyed.*
>
> On the tenth of November last I was returning from the Winslow House
> with Charley Coffin, clk of the War Eagle, about eleven o'clock and when
> we were coming down Fourth Street passing one of those low rum holes
> two Irishmen red mouths came out and following us asked if [we] would
> not go back and take a drink. Charley said no and we were passing on
> when two more met us who along with the other two insisted that they
> meant no harm and that we should go in and drink. I told them I did not
> drink and generally speaking I knew what I was about. We attempted to
> go on but they tried to have us go back so I hauled off and planted one
> two in Paddy's grub grinder and knocked him off the sidewalk about 8
> feet. The remainder pitched [in] and Charley got his arm cut open and I

---

* Wagon transportation was notoriously incompetent. On occasion bags of mail would
leave St. Paul by wagon and three weeks later would be returned, confused with the incoming mail.

got a buttonhole cut through my left side right below the ribs. The city police came to the noise and arrest[ed] three of them on the spot and the others next day and they turned out to be Chicago Star Cleaners, a name given to midnight ruffians.

I was not compelled to keep my bed but it was some 2 months before I was quite recovered from the effects of the cut. One day on the levee I was going aboard one of the boats and slipped on the gangplank and sprained my knee which laid me up for about 2 weeks. About a week since my pugnacious friend who gave me his mark escaped from the penitentiary at Stillwater along [with] all the rest of the prisoners confined at the time.

I am sincerely grateful to you for your generous offer in your letter and fully appreciate your *kindness*. But notwithstanding my bad luck I have still "a shot in the locker"—about $200—which will put me out of any trouble until spring. Our winter here has been very mild and open. We have scarcely had any snow but what was altogether unprecedented, rainstorms lasting three or four days in succession.Times have been mighty dull here this winter and money scarce. Write to me as soon as you receive this and give me a birdseye view of Rockwood and its inhabitants. Tell me also what you have done all summer for *horizontals*. Remember me to R. C. and Christy, and believe me,

Yours sincerely,

J. J. Hill

[P.S.] Send me some papers.

The best regimen for young, unmarried men in a largely masculine frontier society was long hours of hard work combined with hearty, physical recreation of the socially useful variety. Twenty-year-old James J. Hill, in company with other spirited young men in rough-hewn, fast-growing St. Paul, found that the volunteer fire department and the militia provided both great fun and a sense of civic service, the two not always being clearly separated. In an era much given to ritual and the strict hierarchical organization of virtually every phase of public life, the intrepid men who manned the pump-bars, the hoses, and the hook-and-ladders of America's volunteer fire companies developed a complex ritual which the modern city quickly outgrew in the years following the Civil War. Minnehaha Engine Company No. 2 was among St. Paul's proudest institutions in the 1850's, and Hill devoted himself to its activities. Proposed for membership in April 1858, he found himself a member just in time to contribute to a fund for painting the old engine. His $10 contribution was one of the largest, perhaps in recognition of which he was signally honored by election to one of the four positions of hoseman. By the end of the year he was parading up the bumpy streets of St. Paul behind the grunting enginemen who hauled No. 2, a fine new engine which had recently arrived from Philadelphia. Impressively uniformed in a red shirt faced with blue, his face stern under an enormous helmet, and carrying his fire nozzle at the ready, he marched smartly and democratically alongside his employer, Theodore Borup.

A man with administrative talent and an appetite for work seldom finds it difficult to rise to a position of responsibility in unpaid callings. By June 1859 Hill, elevated to the post of secretary, was writing up the minutes of the company's monthly meetings. He had to report both success and failure in the record of the Minnehaha Engine Company. He repeatedly put his finger on the chief problem faced by the firefighters: water—or, rather, the lack of it. On one lamentable occasion the men were unable to coax more than a puny stream from their engine, although they had extended the intake hose 250 feet to the nearest cellar and then to a mudhole in a vain search for water. The secretary was even more embarrassed to have to record during the dry July of 1859 that the company had been unable to stop "the progress of the 'devouring elements' until the cupola and a part of the roof was destroyed." That fire was in the engine house itself.

Late in the summer the firemen passed in review before City Hall, where they were gravely inspected by Mayor Kittson and his board of engineers. His honor addressed then at length, praising their devotion to duty and concluding "by telling the *boys* that they should have what they most needed, water, and that before the expiration of his term of office with, he added, the assistance of his colleagues, the aldermen." Minnehaha No. 2 and the engine Minnesota, from neighboring St. Anthony, then squared off to see which could throw the higher stream over the Catholic church. After a lengthy, sweaty competition it was decided that the two engines threw their streams to about equal heights, but Hill noted in the record "that Minnesota got tired first and ceased playing while No. 2 was doing her best throwing." The proceedings were brought to a fitting end when some thoughtful citizen rang in a false alarm, "after which several of the members adjourned to the Winslow House to partake of a supper . . . where all ate, drank, and made merry until about 9 o'clock." At the November meeting Secretary Hill's service was appropriately memoralized:

> At this juncture there was a neatly made up package with letter accompanying laid upon the table. The secretary opened the letter and found at-

tached to it the names of several members of the company and one or two well known citizens of Saint Paul presenting our worthy Secretary, J. J. Hill (alias the Old Lady) with an original and correct *likeness* of her Lady-ship. Here a motion was made that the picture and communication be laid under the table. After many discussions and witticisms on the part of the company, the subject was allowed to depart in peace.[17]

Alongside Hill's firefighting gear in his closet hung the uniform of a member of the Pioneer Guard of St. Paul. As clear and present as the danger of fire was in the wooden city, in that summer of 1859 the mili-tia must have seemed more likely than the Minnehaha Engine Com-pany to see real action. Gathering to have their pictures taken for the traditional photograph, Hill, Norman W. Kittson, Jr., and other members of the Guard had much to discuss. Down in Wright County a murder trial threatened to grow into a civil insurrection. The Sioux Indians of the Minnesota River Valley were being rapidly dispos-sessed of their lands, while Washington was stubbornly withholding the agreed-upon payment for them. The Sioux were in an ugly mood, which could spell danger for the defenseless settlers at any time. And on the national scene the specter of civil war grew ever larger.

Physical standards of the militia were low, as long as its operations remained a local matter. With his one eye James J. Hill was a better shot than most of the other militiamen (he took first prize for marks-manship one year), and he marched with them when the bloodless "Wright County war" actually flared up. The defense of St. Paul and the Union were the topics of conversation one evening when Hill in-vited a traveling businessman to spend the night on the folding sofa in his furnished room, for the visitor had been a captain in the regular army and had served in the Mexican war. Under the gaze of an old engraving of Mary, Queen of Scots, James J. Hill and Ulysses S. Grant discussed the situation at length. And when the call came for volun-teers in the spring of 1861 Hill responded as promptly as did the state itself, for the First Military Volunteers were to include the Pioneer Guard. He was genuinely disappointed at being rejected altogether, although he must have expected that the examining surgeon would refuse to approve a one-eyed man for active military duty. As his old company assembled for the march to the steamboat, however, Hill and Theodore Borup cheerfully prepared a sendoff for them. "Naturally presuming the boys stood in need of some change of diet, [Hill and Borup] took up a fine fat calf which was presented by Hill, accom-panied with an amusing and characteristic speech. The scene created a great deal of merriment and his calfship was sent off to the butcher's." [18] And when the company came back to St. Paul three years later to be mustered out at the end of their enlistment, they were not forgotten, for Hill wrote to its commanding officer on February 9, 1864:

> It is the wish of the citizens of this little burg to give the 1st a welcome in the shape of a public dinner, &c, and there is a committee at work to make all necessary arrangements. It will assist them very much if they can ascertain the number of men likely to come thro' to St. Paul, also when they would probably arrive so that if they could come nearly so or all together and it was generally understood so beforehand the whole town would go out to meet the boys.
>
> Now, Harry, will [you] telegraph me from Lacrosse how many men will come thro' and if they will all come together, and if they do not all come together, telegraph what difference there is in the time of starting from Winona.
>
> So now, hurry up for we want to give you a good sound threshing, and we'll do it too.

Hill's ties with Rockwood loosened rapidly after 1860. His obliging friend Farrish had gone back to spend the rest of his life in the fine old stone house on the maple-lined road which both boys had trod in their childhood. On January 30, 1860, Hill wrote him to ask a favor:

> I am glad to hear you are all well and also glad to say that my health never was better in my life—weigh 166 lbs, *gross huge ain't it*. I am not married *yet* and am not prepared to say when I will be. However, when that important step is about to be taken I will assuredly let you all know before hand unless when I take a wife I may make a mistake and take somebody else's and in that case mum's the word.
>
>   As regards the farm I would simply say that I would prefer selling it but if I cannot sell it I am in no mind to give it away. I want you to write me particulars what its worth and what it would rent for 1 or 10 years. Also if it is not too much trouble if James Black or some of the neighbors would not rent it.
>
> As regards the rent for the past year, pay my mother some considerable part of it and afterwards in amts as in your judgment she wants it.
>
> Write me particulars about everything and everybody. I have been up country most of the time since fall buying grain and have to make another 160 mile trip tomorrow. But knocking around agrees with me. Have not had first rate luck in business this season, however, will come out all *right side up with care marked "glass."*

The garbled deathbed will which William Wetherald had written out for James Hill in 1852 required James J. and Alexander to keep the farm until the younger son was twenty-one. In the winter of 1860–61, therefore, Hill made his first trip back to Rockwood and arranged to sell the farm to neighbor Black, whose descendant, William Black, was still farming the enlarged acreage more than a century later. James turned his $800 share over to his mother. Ann Dunbar Hill, who is remembered in Rockwood chiefly for her absent-minded tendency to go to milk the family cow while wearing her best silk dress, would soon need more.[19]

V

Hill's seven years with the firm of Borup & Champlin and its successors were his most significant apprenticeship in business. The long, busy days melted rapidly into years during the hectic period of the Civil War. Neither that great conflict, nor the tragic Sioux war which finally broke out, beginning with the massacre of New Ulm, only a few miles from St. Paul, could permanently stem the tide of immigration and commerce that caused the city to grow before the young man's very eyes. In the daily routine which swirled around them, some men saw the subtle signs of change—men like Horace Thompson, who founded the First National Bank of St. Paul and thus became one of the chief forces in the economic development of the Northwest; his young teller, H. P. Upham, who would become its president in the twentieth century; Norman W. Kittson, by then a leading citizen of St. Paul, whose years as a fur trader at Pembina, on the international boundary between Minnesota and what would become the Province of Manitoba, and later as agent of the Hudson's Bay Company, had impressed upon him the need for better transportation on the north-south axis between St. Paul and the future Winnipeg; and Edmund Rice, William Crooks, F. R. Delano, George L. Becker, and the Litchfield brothers, Edward and E. Darwin, who labored to bring Minnesota's first railroad into being. Every move James J. Hill made in his little office on the levee, every casual conversation with these and other men struggling to handle the booming trade of St. Paul, impressed upon him the urgent need for new and better ways of doing things.

The times were indeed changing. September 9, 1861, was a day to remember on the river. See Jim Hill, in the vanguard of the crowd gathered on the levee in a drizzling rain to greet the steamer *Alhambra*, which pushes ahead of her a barge bearing the iron and brass symbol of St. Paul's future: the locomotive *William Crooks*. Named for the first construction engineer on the Minnesota & Pacific Railroad, this first locomotive in the state had traveled under its own steam all the way from Paterson, New Jersey, to Prairie du Chien, on the Mississippi. From there it had been pushed upstream to St. Paul by the obliging steamboat whose breed it would soon replace. Whistles blew, bells rang, and the crowd roared its approval as the younger men threw off their coats, grasped the ropes, and pulled the engine up the temporary track which had been laid for it. Admiration for the high-wheeled, diamond-stacked, wood-burning machine was unanimous, but she was a long way from providing St. Paul with the improved transportation all longed for. Amid recriminations between the citizens of St. Paul and St. Anthony over the route which the new road should follow for the ten miles which separated them, the Minnesota & Pacific succumbed to financial starvation that winter. The *William Crooks* went into storage, while the man for whom it was named marched off to war at the head of the Third Regiment of Minnesota volunteers.

Next spring the newly organized St. Paul & Pacific Railroad rose from the ashes of the Minnesota & Pacific, with all of the latter's charter privileges intact, and construction on the ten-mile link to St. Anthony was rushed to completion. "A passenger train started from St. Paul in the direction of Puget Sound today," exulted a newspaperman after the first trial run between the two young cities on June 28, 1862. Three days later, James J. Hill helped load the three wooden freight cars with goods consigned for St. Anthony and beyond. Returning the waves of the crowd on the platform, the engineer opened the throttle and the first railroad in Minnesota was in operation.[20]

Fascinating as the railroad was in the 1860s, it was the steady procession of steamboats which called at St. Paul between April and November that paid Hill's salary. Into the business which the boats created directly, and into the broader opportunities which this transportation link made possible, the young man threw himself with enthusiasm, energy, and shrewdness. By the time the Civil War finally turned in the Union's favor, Hill had made himself an expert on the economics of the upper Northwest, mastering a wide range of trade secrets—from river transportation; to wholesale merchandising; to buying and selling of commodities; to the logistics of basic commodities like wood, coal, salt, and grains; and, most recently, to the new art of railroading. The steamboat industry had begun to reap the natural fruits of competitive anarchy by 1864 when Commodore Davidson was able to combine the weakened, once-numerous steamboat lines into his Northwest Packet Company, which virtually monopolized this waning form of transportation in the 1860s.[21] Like monopolists everywhere, Davidson needed lieutenants who could match his own aggressive, hard-working approach to business, and he had had his eye on James J. Hill for some time. But the Borups had been good to the young man, and he was inclined to be loyal to them. At least he would not leave them in the lurch, as he wrote Davidson on January 27, 1864:

> Your favor of the 22nd inst. is at hand. I spoke to Mr. Borup in regard to it, and he thought it would not be using him right and refused to let me go. I am very grateful to you for the interest you have taken [in] me and would like to work for you but you understand how things are in the warehouse, and I have been with him so long that it would hardly be right for me to break my engagement with Theodor. Again, I could not work for you for less than $1500 a year and a year's work guaranteed, you paying travelling expenses and I, of course, paying my own board, &c, for I would prefer not to work at all than in order to make anything for myself to be compelled to put items in my voucher that did not belong there.

By the end of 1864, as far as Davidson and his newly merged associates in the Northwest Packet Company were concerned, James J. Hill *was* Borup and Champlin. Since he was mainly responsible for the excellent freight forwarding service which the steamboatmen were getting at St. Paul, it seemed reasonable that the young man might do it just as well, or even better—and perhaps for less—on his own account. By the beginning of 1865 Hill had begun to benefit significantly from his close friendship with the genial William E. Wellington, who had recently been drawn into Davidson's empire. Wellington, who a few years before had endeared himself to the people of the river towns below St. Paul by rescuing a rhinoceros which had fallen overboard during a collision between Dan Rice's circus boat and the *Key City*, was one of the best-known steamboat operators on the upper Mississippi. After winding up the season accounts for Borup and Champlin and reporting to the local newspapers that freight on incoming shipments had reached the record total of $365,000, Hill took leave from his duties and went to Chicago on an extended visit.[22] Wellington had encouraged him to try for the full agency assignment at St. Paul, and had told him how to go about getting it:

> While you are at Chicago go to the Sherman House occasionally. Mr. Blanchard is liable to be at Chicago any day and you may meet him there. Should you meet him there, telegraph me immediately and I will come

over on first train and we will have a definite understanding about St. Paul agency. Telegraph me as soon as you arrive at Chicago as I may want to see you. . . .* [23]

The early months of 1865 were critical for the fledgling independent businessman. Wellington supported him at every point, feeding him confidential information in rambling, friendly letters marked "personal" with instructions that they be burned. (They were not, much to our benefit.) He wanted to hear the younger man's plans for improving the handling of freight at St. Paul, especially now that the railroad was beginning to alter conditions so fundamentally. He let Hill know that the Northwest Packet Company was going to make a strict, formal contractual arrangement for the coming year, but assured him that it would go to Hill. "Let us hear from you [as to] what you may want for the coming season, [so] that we may have a little time to think it over. . . . This had better be burned soon as read. . . ." [24] Two weeks later, having secured a bid from a supplier of ice for the company's boats at St. Paul, Wellington revealed the price to Hill and offered him the chance to better it, at the same time informing him that Borup and Champlin were out of favor:

> If you can make any arrangement by which you can do better, do so.
> . . . You had better get the control of the ice at that point. By so doing
> you may make a good thing out of it. You now know all arrangements I
> have made and can govern yourself accordingly. . . . Borup knows noth-
> ing [about the arrangements]. Neither does Davidson. . . . All I've said to
> Davidson was . . . that I did not like the way in which Borup and
> Champlin treated us . . . I thought them very expensive men and would
> not agree to appoint them as our agents. . . . You can rest easy on this
> point as they know nothing. [25]

Hill could be useful to Wellington, too. Business on the Minnesota River, which flows into the Mississippi just above St. Paul, far exceeded available facilities now that the pacification of the Sioux had greatly stimulated immigration to the beautiful, fertile valley. He notified Hill that he was going to put the steamer *Julia* on the Minnesota that spring, and he wanted the young man to find two pilots for her, taking them away from Davidson, if necessary, and to watch over things in general:

> B. & W. have plenty of funds and can back up anything they undertake.
> So when you see anything there is money in, we can let the St. Paul line

---

* Wellington was in charge at Dubuque. Blanchard was secretary-treasurer of the Northwest Packet Co.

have funds at a fair rate of interest. . . . In the meantime, look out for all chances and keep us posted. *Let no one know we are together. Much will depend on that.* They may *suspect* and *hint* as much as they please, but if they *know nothing,* all will be well.* [26]

The St. Paul newspapers reported in the first week of March 1865 that James J. Hill had been appointed freight and passenger agent for both the Northwest Packet Co. and its important ally, the Milwaukee and Mississippi Railroad. The *Daily Pioneer* congratulated the companies on their choice: "Mr. Hill is well known in this city and throughout the State, as an active thorough-going businessman, and enjoys the confidence of the business community to an eminent degree." The bumptious *Daily Press,* noting that the change would mean the merging of two formerly separate offices operated by Borup and Champlin for freight and Orrin Curtis for passenger services, adopted a sardonic tone: "Go it, James! We always knew you could do a heavy business, but we confess to a little surprise in seeing you commence by monopolizing to such an extent." [27]

The people of St. Paul had little idea of what Hill was up to. Ever since the St. Paul & Pacific Railroad had replaced the ragged lines of teams and wagons which pulled up at the levee to deliver the produce of the country and to load on the goods which the steamboats had delivered, Hill and his colleagues had wrestled with the problem of transferring goods between the boats and the trains. To be sure, the local draymen were willing to do the job, but it seemed wasteful to load the wagons for a trip of only a few hundred feet, and it was certainly expensive, adding one dollar to the cost of every ton of freight shipped through St. Paul. Hill's plan was to build an all-weather warehouse at the end of the public levee just below the grain elevator. The floor of the warehouse would be on the same level as the steamboat dock, and would have one or more railroad sidings. Freight and baggage could then be transferred with a minimum of lifting, dragging, and hauling, and would be protected from the elements during the process. Storage space would be available for a few days or, as in the case of flour, throughout the winter in anticipation of the opening of the river in the spring. The facilities would be unique—and the right to make the transfers through the warehouse would be Hill's alone. The charge for the service would be attractive when compared

---

* B. & W. (Blanchard & Wellington) was Wellington's side-venture in the operation of the *Julia* and other enterprises. He was anxious to keep Davidson in the dark about such activities.

with its alternative, but, as James J. Hill said about his farm, he would not be inclined to give it away. On February 6, 1866, he signed an agreement with the St. Paul & Pacific to lease what eventually became one of the choicest pieces of commercial real estate in St. Paul. On it he would build his warehouse. The railroad reserved the right to buy back the lease and the warehouse at cost, but by the time that happened Hill would have gone on to bigger things.[28]

A month later the *Daily Pioneer* carried an advertisement, signed by "J. J. Hill, General Transportation Agent, St. Paul, Minn." and "F. R. Delano, Sup't. First Division St. Paul & Pacific R. R., March 15," announcing that

> The merchants and shippers of freight in Minneapolis, St. Anthony, Anoka, Dayton, Elk River, Monticello, Clearwater, St. Cloud and other points upon or connecting with the First Division of the St. Paul & Pacific Railroad are hereby notified that all freights intended for transportation over said Railroad arriving at this port by steamboat and marked, Care of J. J. Hill, St. Paul, will be transferred from the boats to the Railroad Company, if landed at the Transfer Depot, or from the Railroad to the boats free of the usual transfer charges at this point. . . .[29]

This was what he had been saving his money for. To the $2500 which Hill invested in the new business, his partners, Blanchard and Wellington, added $5000. In April the parties signed an agreement providing that Hill, who would give all of his time to the business, could draw up to $1500 a year in lieu of salary. (Good clerk-solicitors were getting $1000 to $1200 a year then.) All of the annual profits (his drawing account included) from this "general transportation, storage and commission business" up to $3000 were to go to Hill. All of the profits between $3000 and $5000, and all but $1000 of the profits between $5000 and $12,000, would go to Blanchard and Wellington. Of the profits above $12,000, the agreement optimistically apportioned one-third to Hill and two-thirds to his silent partners. Hill's backers, it seems, expected to derive their main benefit from the existence of a first-class freight transfer facility at St. Paul for their steamboats, which had come to dominate the business.[30]

The proud proprietor of the newly formed James J. Hill Co. went out to the stationery store and bought, not a 300-page or a 500-page letter-book, but a 1000-page volume in which to copy the outgoing correspondence of his firm. Hill thought big, even then. But within a little more than two years the book was almost filled with copies of the flood of letters which he loosed upon the businessmen of mid-century mid-America, all in his own handwriting. He improved upon much otherwise idle time by writing letters promoting trade in one form or another. The first letter in this letterbook, dated April 2, 1866, was to a railroad freight agent in Chicago, introducing a St. Paul man who was going east to lay in a stock of groceries for his new wholesale business. "His shipments will be large," Hill promised, "and he may want to make some special arrangements about a portion of his stocks— some fine liquors which he wants to ship through from New York without change of cars." This policy of helpfulness was to convince a growing number of substantial people that it was good to have Jim Hill on their side.

He could soon report to Wellington that the new warehouse was almost ready for use, but he was waiting until the snowed-in lumber mills could bring out new materials, which would save him $1000. Meanwhile, he had been up the St. Croix River (which forms the boundary between Minnesota and Wisconsin north of the St. Paul area) to solicit the business of the merchants and the big new flour mill at Hudson, Wisconsin, for the boat which his partners were about to put on that river.[31] The new warehouse was an immediate success:

> The Levee was a busy scene yesterday. Several boats from above and below were unloading, and the levee was crowded with grain and merchandise. The splendid freight transfer house of J. J. Hill greatly facilitates business. It gives in effect just so much more levee room. A boat can be unloaded and a tremendous quantity of freight stored away there, without any confusion or crowding. Both the steamboatmen and the mercantile public vote it a big thing.[32]

But the young entrepreneur quickly learned one of the hardest lessons of being in business for oneself: splendid facilities, hard work, and the best relations with other businessmen still do not add up to immediate success. Until a new enterprise builds up volume, and until would-be competitors fall by the wayside, it is lucky to break even. Hill's report to Wellington on January 12, 1867, after the results of the season had been totaled up, was discouraging. "My whole income account is but about $2000 for the season, and if it were not for the way I looked after [the business] I would have run a way behind." It was a bitter struggle competitively, too, as his negotiations with the Milwaukee & St. Paul Railroad, which was about to enter St. Paul from the south, taught him:

I have had a terrible long siege of it figuring and figuring and when I thought I had it all right before I went to Chicago as far as it could go until the proper officers of the road arrived from N.Y. to sign the agreement, I received a despatch that other parties were ready to give a bonus of $3000 to take it off my hands.

Still, he had more than one string to his bow, and it was good for his morale to list his bargaining points to the sympathetic Wellington:

However, I have got the contract for the term of my warehouse lease to do the business of the St. Paul station for 40¢ per ton mdse and 20¢ per ton flour, 30¢ per ton wheat, 25¢ per M ft lumber &c, on all freight going or coming by the road [the St. Paul & Pacific] and the road put in a new dock extending from the lower end of the warehouse 250 ft below the [grain] elevator with a side track the whole length . . . on a level with the lower floor of the warehouse. . . . With the splendid facilities I have for doing a packet business—a warehouse 100 by 330 [feet] and an additional dock of 300 feet immediately adjoining it, with a track the full length and also the business of eighty miles of railroad, it certainly seems to me that my chances for the whole agency are much ahead of anyone else. . . .

The important thing was to maintain an air of confidence, especially since he was about to sign an agreement with the St. Paul & Pacific which would give him control of that railroad's entire terminal facilities at riverside in St. Paul.[33] He explained all this to H. B. Wilkins, general superintendent of the Milwaukee and St. Paul Railroad, in a letter of January 15, 1867:

I am going to be situated to accommodate the millers at the Falls to any extent they may require and I find already they are anxious to take advantage of it. They have engaged all my storage capacity and I expect to have 30,000 bbls flour to start in on when the river opens, all or nearly all of which will be sold in Chicago for the reason that Chicago houses have advanced on it and will hold the receipts. I suppose of course that you want it by Milwaukee. . . . The Packet Co. have not made definite arrangements as to . . . another season, but I feel that I can give them ten dollars [worth of business] to anyone else's one, and as dollars and cents generally govern business transactions I feel pretty easy on that score. . . . Whichever way they decide I feel I am all right as long as I have control of

The levee on the Mississippi River at St. Paul, about 1867. The warehouse of James J. Hill & Co. is the low building with the large door at the edge of the water. On the same level as its upper floor are the tracks of the St. Paul & Pacific Railroad, whose depot and grain elevator are just behind the warehouse, and across the tracks from the warehouse is the depot of the La Crosse & Milwaukee Railroad (later part of the Chicago, Milwaukee, St. Paul & Pacific Railroad), which had just established through rail service to Chicago.

the amount of business which my new arrangement will give me. Somebody will want to carry it. . . .*

Hill was merely "running scared," as would always be his policy. No sensible businessman could miss the fact that he had the business sewed up, creative monopolist that he was. He had taken the broad view of things, and, by moving to solve problems which another man in his position would have considered none of his affair, if he were aware of them at all, had ended up with the high cards. Take the matter of the "millers at the Falls." All winter long they would be grinding wheat into flour to be sold in the South and the East. Hill provided them with a place to store it, a place where it would be assured of space on the first boats to go south in the spring. While he was in Chicago he had convinced the grain merchants that they could make a good thing out of advancing funds to the hard-pressed millers against the huge inventory which was piling up in his warehouse.[34] Right from the start the Milwaukee & St. Paul Railroad, which was about to join St. Paul (via a rather circuitous line) with the eastern trunklines at Chicago, would take an enormous volume of southbound traffic away from the steamboats, if their rates were attractive and if they dealt with Hill. Besides, the Milwaukee railroad people, he knew, were going to end up using the St. Paul & Pacific's terminal facilities—which meant the James J. Hill Co.—anyway. Indeed, nine railroads eventually came together on the spot after the St. Paul Union Station was built.

And so business boomed in that prosperous, optimistic post-war year of 1867. By the middle of April Hill had already put on the steamboats more than 7000 barrels of flour, and it was only the beginning. At the end of the summer, by now overwhelmed with the volume of the business he had created, he admitted an active partner to handle the transportation business while he moved on to greater things. The Litchfield brothers, who had become the chief protagonists of the St. Paul & Pacific Railroad project, had a young half-brother, Egbert S., who needed a situation. On September 16, 1867, Hill and Litchfield signed articles of co-partnership in the firm of James J. Hill & Co. Under the agreement, which was to run until 1872, each put up $5000, and Litchfield, in return for his full-time attention to the business,

* Hill was in a position to dispatch the flour by the conventional river-and-rail route, which would have given the Milwaukee & St. Paul Railroad only the business between Prairie du Chien and Milwaukee; or by all-rail, thus giving the new railroad all of the business via the city of Milwaukee and thence to Chicago over a line which the Milwaukee road was in process of taking over.

would receive two-thirds of the profits. By December the warehouse, emptied of the thousands of barrels of flour, echoed to the thump of a hay-baling machine. Said the *Daily Press*, "J. J. Hill has, with a spirit of enterprise which is commendable, converted his immense warehouse into a mammoth 'hay pressing' establishment. There is a spirit that is not daunted by difficulty. If he can't handle freight he can press hay." [35]

Hill guarded nothing that was stored in his warehouse more closely than he guarded his business reputation. Much of his time was spent in tracing lost shipments, and he could not bear to be branded as the weak link in the transportation chain. "I am well aware there are parties who have an interest in having freight shipped over a different line . . . ," he wrote one shipper; "to them I would say if they will confine themselves to *facts* I shall be satisfied. Whenever your freight *is* delayed at this point over night I shall be satisfied to lose your business." He had tried unsuccessfully to get the agency for the Red Line or the Blue Line, express companies which operated through fast-freight cars over the trunklines between Chicago and the east in the days before the railroads rose to the challenge of directly providing such premium quality service. Thus, when the Red Line's Boston agent dropped remarks about Hill's losing freight at St. Paul, Hill instructed the Easterner, "The next time you have occasion to air your spleen, if you are called upon to use my name be kind enough to confine yourself to the facts." [36]

Hill rode the crest of the rapid shift from river to rail transportation in the late 1860s. He pressed tirelessly for rates that were at least as low as other agents' customers were getting, demanding rebates, as was the custom of the time, as aggressively as anybody. "The present rate on flour from Mendota to Chicago or Milwaukee is 70¢ per bbl," he wrote a shipper in Faribault, Minnesota. "But the regular rate can hardly be said to be established," he went on. "I will take your 1000 bbls at 67¢ and if the rate is any lower until May 10th you shall have the benefit. Say nothing to brokers about this." To the New York Central's agent in Chicago, he laid it on the line: "I would like very much to do business with the N.Y.C. line but your rates are, as they were last season, about 10¢ higher than on other lines. . . . Will do what I can with you when rates are within reach." He saw clearly that the railroads could not remain a high-rate, low-volume kind of business, specializing in high-value merchandise and allowing the burden of putting together a through service to fall on the shipper or his agent. And so he pressed for lower rates, encouraging the railroads to bid sharply for the large volume of freight which he could guarantee them. For higher class merchandise, he encouraged shippers to use the through, fast-freight lines whenever they proved to be cheaper—even if he did not get a commission from them. A wool-buyer in Faribault, Minnesota, who had always shipped his goods to the market in Boston by the familiar boat-and-rail combination, was delighted when Hill showed him how he could ship by rail all the way from St. Paul, via the Red or the Blue Line, in only six days from Chicago, and at no more than the slow, traditional routing would cost. The secret, as Hill saw clearly, was that the shipper would save 20¢ per hundred pounds for insurance, which was required on the steamboats but not on the common-carrier railroads. It was the club which would lay the steamboats low in another decade, and James J. Hill wielded it without mercy. As 1868 began, he advertised, "Through contracts given on freight to New York, Boston, Philadelphia, and all principal points East. TIME GUARANTEED IF DESIRED." [37]

Through Hill's office there passed a constant stream of people who were down on their luck. Some were going home, defeated by life on the frontier. Others had little deals they could not quite carry off without financial help. Many were drawn to this bustling, self-confident young man who seemed to run things in St. Paul, who could answer their questions about where to go and what to do, and who was able to help them out financially if he chose to do so. And so the bad debts piled up. In June 1865, when he was putting aside every cent he could spare for the new business he was planning, he paid for a forlorn young man's ticket to New York. A year later he was still trying to collect the $44.85 it had cost. To a man in Shakopee, Minnesota, he wrote asking for a repayment of a $20 loan, asserting, "Now, John, I have no such amount to loose and hope you will not take as a jest any longer. . . ." A man in New York whom Hill had lent $10 apparently believed that out of sight was out of mind. When his first dunning letter went unanswered, Hill let off steam with the sarcastic demand that "If I am to contribute to your support, I want due credit for same acknowledged through the 'public press.' " [38]

VI

There were other things to think about besides business as the summer of 1867 wore on. Certain plans were maturing which Hill had been turning over in his mind almost as long as those which made him the transportation leader in St. Paul. To H. W. Carr, agent for the Red Line in Chicago, for whom he had done countless favors, he sounded a distinctly domestic note in a letter of July 9, 1867. He wanted to bring a piano from the East, and, he declared, "I think the Red Line can carry my music box 'Phree' without any loss." W. G. Swan, a close friend and general superintendent of the West Wisconsin Railroad, which eventually became the Chicago & North Western, received an unusual request: "Will, I want you to get me 200 cards, 'Mr. and Mrs. James J. Hill,' 'Mary Theresa Mehegan,' also a plate and 100 cards for Mrs. James J. Hill, and send by express C.O.D. Have them leave Chicago by the 10th or 12th at latest and oblige." And to J. J. Merrill, general manager of the Milwaukee & St. Paul Railroad, "If not against your rules I would ask you to send me a pass from La-crosse to Milwaukee and return good until Sept. 10. I am about to take unto myself a wife and have to take the customary 'trip.' " William E. Wellington heard the news and wrote in delight:

> Am pleased to learn there is every prospect of soon having a 'Mrs. Hill.'
> Go it, Jim. It's a good institution and the only way for a man to live. May
> the 'little Hills' spring up thick and fast around you, and all bear the
> marks of being 'chips off the old block.' [39]

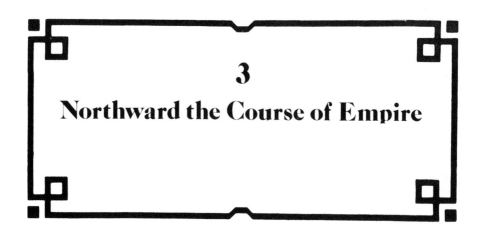

3

Northward the Course of Empire

The mace of the Provincial Parliament of Manitoba was fashioned out of the hub of a Red River cart wheel.

—Heather Gilbert

I

Saint Joseph's, the oldest Roman Catholic Church in New York City, has stood on Sixth Avenue between Waverly Place and Washington Place, a block from Washington Square, since 1833. The epic northward sweep of the great city flowed right by its doors until the name of Greenwich Village seemed incongruous for what was no longer a semi-rural neighborhood by the time of the Civil War. The dignified Greek revival structure was more than half a century old when the shadows of the elevated railroad crept about it in the 1880s. For another fifty-five years the aging structure endured the roar of rapid transit until the "el" was dismantled and sold as scrap to the Japanese. The city's fashionable shopping center, which has constantly moved farther uptown, paused just to the north of Saint Joseph's at the turn of the century, when stores like Siegel-Cooper's lured the ladies of New York's growing middle class. For a brief time Saint Joseph's watched the golden era of the Village's true Bohemians on the eve of the first World War, and then endured two decades of fake Bohemianism in the 1920s and 1930s. Now, in the last quarter of the twentieth century, it lies in gentle equipoise between the Jefferson Market Courthouse (itself elegantly restored as a branch of the public library), the high-rise apartments which house the affluent of the city's population, and the sordid drug culture to which the Village's Bohemian tradition has sunk.

None could have dreamed of such a future for this Manhattan landmark in the winter of 1844, when Timothy Mehegan brought sixteen-year-old Mary McGowan there to make her his wife.. The young couple set up housekeeping on Greenwich Street, on New York's bustling Lower West Side. There, two years later, on July 1, 1846, their first daughter, Mary Theresa, was born. A few days later the future Mrs. James J. Hill was baptized in near-by Saint Peter's Roman Catholic Church on Barclay Street, which, like Saint Joseph's, is still standing, more than a century later.

Timothy Mehegan and Mary McGowan were in the vanguard of that historic multitude of Irishmen who crossed the ocean to America in the nineteenth century, from the 1830s on, making the hard choice between the very real possibility of starvation in the Old World and an uncertain fate in the New. Clara Hill Lindley, second daughter of James J. and Mary, liked to point out that both of her parents owed their births in the New World to the adventuresome spirit of the women of their families. Just as Mary Riggs Hill had pressed her husband to follow her brother and son to Canada, Timothy Mehegan's two spirited younger sisters, Margaret and Catherine, had conspired with their younger brother, Edward, to engineer the two girls' departure for New York. There, according to everything they had heard, their very slight expectations could be vastly improved upon. As soon as their ship had sailed from Queenstown, Edward revealed the scheme to their mother, who entreated Timothy to pursue them on the next ship. Once in America, he stayed, for his prospects of success in his father's tailoring trade were slender indeed in the Ireland of the 1840s. He married Mary McGowan, and opened a shop near Chatham Square. But the shop soon proved incapable of supporting his family, which had grown to include two daughters by 1850. The standard remedy then was to keep going west. The harried young husband, who had been hearing the same glowing reports about the new Northwest which James J. Hill was beginning to hear in Ontario, bought land, sight unseen, near the falls of St. Anthony. There he brought his wife and two little girls on May 21, 1850.

Timothy Mehegan's land turned out to be good for nothing at that early stage of St. Anthony's development, so he backtracked to St. Paul. There he tried to support his family again setting up in his trade and by dealing in town lots. But the disappointed young Irishman, who by then must have wondered bitterly where the vaunted opportunities in America were hiding, was up against the hard fact that he whose needs are great and whose capital is slight has no place in an undeveloped frontier settlement. Evidently a man of refinement, if not formal education, with a taste for the good things of life, Timothy Mehegan never adjusted to the rudeness of the frontier. His family soon found their staunchest support, if not their only friends, among the priests, nuns, and students of St. Paul's Roman Catholic institutions. In the modest little school which the Sisters of Saint Joseph founded in 1851, Timothy's daughters would find a refuge from their bleak home life. Soon they would count the friendship of Father Ravoux, Bishop Cretin, Father Caillet (who had just arrived from France), and young John Ireland and his sisters among the few certainties in an alien environment. Mary Mehegan Hill would not forget them.

She was eight when Christmas Eve, 1854, was changed in a few hours from a time of excitement and expectation to one of bitter bereavement. Timothy Mehegan fell sick about dinner time, and by midnight, before the frontier doctor could make even a clumsy attempt at diagnosis, the defeated young man from Cork gave up the struggle. The little girl remembered with a shudder something she saw through the window of the room where her father was laid out. It was the exultant look on the face of "Old Betz," a tough, ancient Indian woman against whom Timothy had once committed the unpardonable offense of catching in the act of stealing his best trousers. As bad as things had been for the Mehegans, they soon got much worse. The twenty-seven-year-old mother, desperate to provide for her little girls, quickly made a marriage which turned out badly.

Mary's prospects were bleak, but life and the new land both lay before her, and she was ready to make the most of what they had to offer. A cat may look at a king, and when Ole Bull, virtuoso violinist, fresh from his efforts to start a colony of fellow Norwegians in Pennsylvania, played a concert at the Capitol, Mary Mehegan was in the audience. And forty years later the wife of the railroad millionaire, sitting in a box at the Metropolitan Opera, could tell her rich and powerful companions about the sixteen-year-old girl who sang one evening in rough, backwoods St. Paul, and who later became famous—Adelina Patti.

Little is recorded of Mary Mehegan's life in the years before her engagement to James J. Hill in 1863. It was humble enough, to be sure. If, as tradition insists, she worked as a waitress in the Merchants' Hotel, where Hill and his friends took many of their meals, her independence and resourcefulness thereby qualified her for full-fledged membership in that very democratic society. She had a grave, dignified bearing that impressed young Hill, and her fresh, colleen beauty and fierce devotion to the strict precepts of the Roman Catholic upbringing, which were her most valuable inheritance, made her one of the most attractive young women in St. Paul. James J. Hill's intentions regarding Mary Mehegan were soon a settled matter among his friends.

Father Caillet, who would be a close friend of the Hills throughout the rest of his life, was the fatherless girl's strongest support in those years. Caillet sized the situation up shrewdly and intelligently. It would be a mixed marriage, to be sure, but that was nothing unusual on the frontier. More to the point was the fact that this ambitious young man, who clearly would be one of the most important citizens of St. Paul in a few years, was about to found a family which would be an ornament of the Catholic Church in St. Paul, in the Northwest, and perhaps in the United States as well. Caillet impressed upon Mary the importance of preparing herself to be the wife of a man with such expectations. It would not do for her to be a source of embarrassment to him in later years. She would be expected to preside at his table with grace and self-assurance and as a social equal of whomever he might bring there. Taste flowed from the top down in those days. It was an era in which men and women were determined to smooth the rough edges of human existence. Nearly everyone believed in progress, and gentility was its surest sign.

With help from her fiancé and some of his young friends at the Merchants' Hotel, Mary Mehegan rose to the challenge. "Your life may not be an easy one," Father Caillet told her, "but you must continue to educate yourself to be his companion." So off she went to the convent of St. Mary's Institute, which the School Sisters of Notre Dame had recently founded in Milwaukee as a finishing school of the best upper-middle-class Roman Catholic tradition. Mary mastered French, the language of culture, and won a prize in it. She learned something of music, practiced calisthenics with Sister Hilaria, and excelled in the arts of needlework, tapestry, crochet, and knitting. "In youth," said Clara, "she worked for her home and children; in old age she was

James J. Hill in 1865, aged 27, two years before his marriage and shortly before he went into business for himself.

knitting for the poor." Mary Mehegan Hill's destiny was to create an atmosphere of simple dignity at a major seat of wealth and power. She recognized its importance, and she prepared herself well for it.

The young couple became engaged in June 1864, and saw each other often during the winter and spring of 1864–65, when Hill made his extended business trip to Chicago. Nearly every Sunday he was in Milwaukee, where, chaperoned by one of the lay sisters, they strolled along the bluffs overlooking Lake Michigan. He described his visible prospects, as well as certain dreams that had not yet died. He warned her that he might yet go to India to run steamboats on the Ganges. Meanwhile, he was just about to start in business on his own, which would take every spare dollar he could scrape up for at least two years. Fortunately, long engagements fit Mary Mehegan's ideas of propriety

Mary Theresa Mehegan Hill in 1867, aged 21, shortly after her marriage to James J. Hill.

perfectly, and besides, two years later he would still be only twenty-nine and she a genteel twenty-one.

Two years later they were married. It was a very simple ceremony. Hill was not joining the Church, at least not yet, so a service in the sanctuary was out of the question. On August 17, 1867, he took out the marriage license, engaged the parlor of the Bishop's house, and sent word to Father Caillet by Father Ireland that they were expecting him to marry them. Two days later the wedding took place but, to Mary's disappointment, Father Caillet did not officiate. Young Father Ireland had forgotten to deliver the message. Declining the embarrassed young priest's offer to read the service himself, Mary asked for Father Oster. Sanford Newel, James J. Hill's closest friend, was best man, and Mary's only attendants were the members of her family. It had all been done with dispatch, before ten o'clock in the morning, for the young couple had a train to catch for their honeymoon trip to Milwaukee. Soon they were settled in a modest house on Pearl (later Grove) Street in St. Paul. "I am the head of the house now and live at home," Hill wrote to his friend Swan; "all's well." [1]

II

James J. Hill's reputation as the Empire Builder who pushed the Great Northern Railway west to Puget Sound in the last decade of the nineteenth century has obscured the significance of the first two decades of his career as an independent businessman. From the close of the Civil War to the time of emergence of Canada as an integrated nation with its own transcontinental railroad, the fortunes of Hill and the people of the new Northwest were closely bound up with the development of the lands which lay on the north-south axis between St. Paul and Fort Garry (now Winnipeg), Manitoba. "Melody," a musician has said, "is something which flows over the bar line." He meant that the theme, or basic meaning of music, cannot be made to conform rigidly to the meter. In the same sense, the promising territory just west of the Great Lakes and north of St. Paul could not be effectively divided into two isolated spheres by the artificial political bars which men had placed along the 49th parallel to mark the boundary between the United States and Canada. In our day the considerable interdependence of the Canadian and American economies is a highly sensitive matter, but in the 1860s and 1870s the people of the new country between St. Paul and Fort Garry could hardly afford such touchiness. It would be developed as an economic unit.

The unity of this area flowed over natural boundaries, too. St. Paul was the northern limit of navigation on the Mississippi River, but almost from the day the first white men arrived in the area, traders stubbornly insisted on going farther north with the goods of civilization and returning with the furs and other produce which the wilderness offered. Chief among the reasons for this northward course of empire was the existence of one of nature's great curiosities, the valley of the Red River of the North. This twisting stream rises 200 miles south of the boundary and flows into Lake Winnipeg 75 miles north of it. The Nile excepted, it is the most celebrated northward-flowing river in the world. The receding glacier which pointed the Red River northward likewise deposited upon the land for a hundred miles on either side some of the richest soil in the world. Until the middle of the nineteenth century it was the fur trade which drew men there, but ultimately the exploitation of this awesome fertility would mold the careers of men like James J. Hill.

"*Le commerce est libre—vive la liberté!*" is what the independent traders around Fort Garry are supposed to have shouted one day in 1849, upon learning that the local courts would no longer support the trading monopoly of the Hudson's Bay Company. Like all pinpoints in history, the episode was the culmination of a long series of events which finally destroyed the mercantilist privileges of this great enterprise, thereby removing the last barrier to the free colonization of the new Canadian-American Northwest. But the fact that the Hudson's Bay Company, in its original seventeenth-century form, was an anachronism by the middle of the nineteenth should not be allowed to obscure the vital role which it played in the early development, political as well as economic, of the vast area which had been named Prince Rupert's Land. After its amalgamation with the rival Northwest Company in 1821, this company of "gentlemen adventurers trading into Hudson's Bay" became the virtual government of all of Canada west of what was to be the Province of Ontario.

It was the Hudson's Bay Company itself, during the years that it was controlled by Thomas Douglas, Fifth Earl of Selkirk, that laid the foundations for the eventual extinction of its quasi-sovereign powers. By the beginning of the nineteenth century the dramatic rise in the population of western Europe, which explains so much of the history of the colonization of the New World, had produced intense hardship in the Highlands of Scotland. That rugged country could support no more than a few people per square mile, but by 1800 the cottage of nearly every crofter, or tenant farmer, sheltered one or more boys or girls for whom no place would ever be found on the land. Determined to resettled these surplus people in British North America, Lord Douglas gained control of the Hudson's Bay Company and bought from it 116,000 square miles of land in the Red River Valley.

The mixed group of colonists who came to the forks of the Assiniboine and Red rivers in 1811 under the auspices of the Earl of Selkirk suffered hardships and disappointments that presaged what later generations of settlers would face. Early snowfalls and interminable winters in which the rivers froze to a depth of five feet were followed in the spring by thaws and rains which flooded out those who had not already been frozen out. "Grasshoppers," as the locusts were called, and even a massive infestation of mice devoured the settlers' pathetic crops, leaving them without seed for the next year. The colony did not prosper in these years, for the age of commercial agriculture on the Northern plains was not to dawn for another half-century. But two steps taken by these premature pioneers to alleviate their hard lot set the stage for the real colonization of the Northwest. Many of the Selkirkers moved southward into the United States, where they founded the first outposts of civilization along the Red River. And those who remained in Canada began to engage in direct trade with the half-breed fur trappers, in defiance of the Hudson's Bay Company monopoly. For this they required "trading goods," those simple but necessary products of civilization—tobacco, liquor, ammunition, tea, and textiles, to name the most obvious—which had to be brought in from England, over great distances and difficult terrain.

The Hudson's Bay Company itself required huge quantitites of trading goods. As long as it had no competition it was content to bring these goods down from a settlement called York Factory, which lay on the southern edge of Hudson's Bay. All of the goods for the ensuing year were brought from England and unloaded there during the short season in which ocean-going ships could enter the Bay. Then they had to be carried over several hundred miles of lakes, dense forests, and swampy marshes to Fort Garry. It was an economic vacuum into which other forces were bound to flow. By 1843 Norman W. Kittson had opened a trading post at Pembina, which the Hudson's Bay Company men suspected lay in American territory. They were right, but discovery of that fact had little effect on Kittson's dealings with trappers and settlers. The duties which he had to pay on goods imported from England into the United States were more than offset by the natural advantages of the American transportation route, which ran south of the Great Lakes, through St. Paul, and up the Red River valley. The Hudson's Bay Company's old mercantilist structure quickly gave way under the onslaughts of the new reality. By the time James J. Hill arrived in St. Paul in the mid-1850s the future Province of Manitoba and the emerging State of Minnesota were an economic unit.

Hill had had nothing to do with these complex events. The key significance of St. Paul as the transportation hub of this exciting new land was determined years before he stepped onto the levee and began to stir things up with his search for better ways of doing things. But trade grew rapidly on this north-south axis during his first decade in

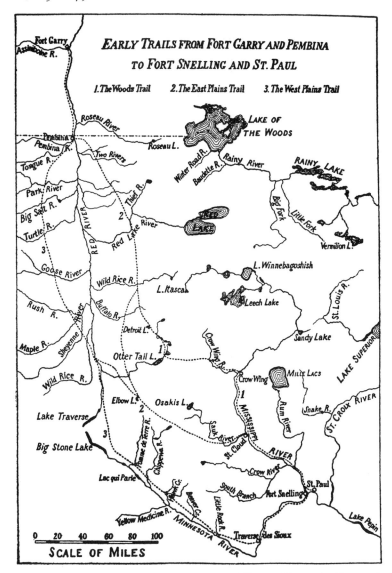

EARLY TRAILS FROM FORT GARRY AND PEMBINA
TO FORT SNELLING AND ST. PAUL

1. The Woods Trail   2. The East Plains Trail   3. The West Plains Trail

From Grace L. Nute, "Red River Trails," *Minnesota History*, VI, 279–82. By permission.

St. Paul. The goods were carried on the Red River carts, which left their unique mark on the history of Manitoba and Minnesota. These primitive all-wood conveyances, each with two huge, ungreased wheels, creaked down from Fort Garry in early June as soon as the grass was high enough to provide food for the oxen which pulled them. After discharging their cargoes of furs, buffalo robes, and little else, they returned to the north country piled high with the goods which would make another winter in that bleak land bearable. When Hill first saw them the carts covered the entire distance between Fort Garry and St. Paul. By the late 1860s they came only as near as St. Cloud, about seventy miles north of St. Paul, to which point the St. Paul & Pacific Railroad had been extended. Every mile of their route which was replaced by more modern forms of transportation would bring dramatic reductions in the cost of developing the frontier. James J. Hill would play a major role in supplanting these gallant cara- vans which served the Northern plains so well during their short chapter of history.[2]

The growth of the Red River trade was breathtaking to the people of St. Paul, who had once thought of their city as the northern limit of commerce. "The other day we saw passing through our streets a number of Red River carts, laden with some of Atkins' Automaton Reapers," marveled a local editor in 1856. "Who would have thought five years ago that in so short a space of time, St. Paul would be supplying the settlers of that region with these labor-saving imple- ments of husbandry." A rival editor, not to be outdone in enthusiasm, proclaimed that "the people in [the Red River country] now look to St. Paul for the supply of almost every utensil in the household econ- omy." Two years later the Hudson's Bay Company experimented at bringing its goods from England via New York and St. Paul under bonding arrangements which exempted from American tariff duties goods not destined for the American market. Nor did the violent events of the 1860s reverse the trend, at least not permanently. "The bonds between St. Paul and Fort Garry were tighter in 1865 than they had been in 1861," writes a modern historian. "The bonds were com- mercial, and the hand that had drawn them tighter was British. . . . The Sioux and Civil Wars built up the commercial frontiers more than they tore down the already unsteady agricultural frontier."[3] That is all true as far as it goes, but the Americans, notably James J. Hill, were to see to it that nothing happened to loosen those bonds.

III

In 1867 James J. Hill was a transportation agent, concerned primarily with promoting someone else's business, for which he received com-

missions. He was very good at it. As long as the independent agency
system prevailed in the nation's rapidly growing railroad network, as
it had always prevailed in the steamboat business, no railroad executive could hope for a better agent than Hill. But the young man could
see plainly enough that the system would be doomed, sooner or later.
In the first place, there were not enough people of exceptional ability
to carry on independently the very important but routine, thankless,
and not very well paid work of soliciting and handling freight. As the
railroad era unfolded, it gradually became clear that the agents, who
were primarily interested in volume of business at whatever rate they
could get, and the railroads, who wished to maximize their profits and
therefore had a strong interest in maintaining published rate schedules, were frequently working at cross purposes. Even Hill, who understood the railroads' problems at least as well as they did, had to cut
rates and demand rebates for good customers when everyone around
him was doing the same. The railroads were just beginning to turn to
the question of rational management structures, and Hill put himself
in their place: would he want his business to be handled by independent agents if he owned a railroad?

About the time of his marriage and the founding of the partnership
with Egbert S. Litchfield, he began to develop new business opportunities. The fast-moving events in the Red River Valley provided the
basis for his new ventures. One of these was his brief but profitable
participation in .the fur trade, which he entered when Norman W.
Kittson turned over to him his trade with Winnipeg.

Kittson, who had dominated the fur trade through St. Paul in the
decade before his young friend arrived, had reported in 1856 that
93,000 pelts, worth $97,000, had passed through the city. Most were on
their way to Europe, but he noted that more and more were for the
American market. By 1870, when the trade had already begun to decline, more than $500,000 worth of furs passed through the city. Hill
handled at least $100,000 worth of those sales. The business drama-
tically revealed the rapid rate at which the buffalo was being made to
disappear from the plains. When the Red River carts arrived in mid-
July 1870, they carried 225 bales of buffalo "robes" consisting of 2225
skins, worth $30,000. The year before, Hill had noted in his diary the
extent of his fur trading for the year: besides the 25,000 muskrat skins
which were the backbone of the business, there were 1200 beaver
(worth almost as much as all of the muskrat); 780 mink; 11 precious
silver fox; and 55 black bear, 12 brown bear, and 6 grizzly bear, tes-

tifying to the fact that there still was a lot of excitement in frontier trapping.[4]

The services which the James J. Hill Company provided the isolated fur traders were comprehensive. A good example is the large transaction, made during the season of 1868, which he handled for William Inkster, a leading trader on the Canadian side of the boundary, for whom Hill realized over $19,000 in the sale of mink skins. For the first time, apparently, the mink were set aside for shipment to New York, where the domestic fur-garment business was thriving. The lot was bought by J. Ullman & Company, whose finances were limited. Inkster had to wait an uncomfortably long time for his money, for reasons which Hill explained to his London correspondent:

> Mr. Inkster felt very sore about the delay of [payment of the] draft and was rather inclined to blame us, but we wrote him the facts—that the [dealers] to whom he sold had not a dollar of sterling in the bank and were unwilling to do anything else than give their own draft on London. As we had no assurance that they had any money in London and we would not take their check here unless it was certified we did not feel at liberty to accept any such paper.[5]

Besides handling the receipt and sale of Inkster's furs at St. Paul, collecting for them, and safely remitting the money to the trader, Hill arranged for all the trading goods required to support such a remarkable dollar volume of fur business. It was this kind of business which Hill, the transportation specialist, wanted to develop, for it was obvious that the volume of freight then moving from the East through St. Paul and up to "Assiniboia" and points between was a fraction of what it would soon become. To his London agent, through whom he procured so many of the English goods that made up a trader's stock, Hill wrote in 1868, a month before the Red River carts were due:

> It being our first year in this Red River business, we feel anxious to do our work well as a guarantee for the future, therefore we feel it our duty to try and have these excessive charges reduced and have no doubt but we will succeed in so doing. . . . There has been a strong competition between the leading [railroad] lines from N. Y. to the west the benefit of which the Red River goods have not received.[6]

He was as good as his word, pouncing upon an overcharge which the Michigan Central Railroad was making on goods coming through New York; no one else had noted it. The indifferent railroad agent, he discovered, was passing along an exorbitant charge which the New

York cartage men were collecting for transferring the goods from the docks to the railroad cars. He notified the general superintendent of the railroad that other lines were eager to get the business at New York, without transfer charges. A month later goods were being billed on a through rate of $3 all the way from Liverpool to Chicago, where before the rate had been $2.80 for the New York-to-Chicago segment alone. Hill blandly informed the embarrassed Michigan Central officials that the new charge was "entirely satisfactory." [7] Meanwhile, he patiently explained to many a Red River trader the mysteries of shipping goods in bond through the United States, which made such rates possible.

Hill went to considerable lengths to be sure that his clients in the Red River country got goods which would please them and their customers, a job which was considerably complicated by the fact that they seldom knew what was available, and often did not even know what they wanted. They drank great quantities of tea up-country, presenting a business opportunity which Hill explained to a Boston tea merchant: "We are anxious to do as well as possible on this lot of tea . . . and if we can compete as to price and quality with the London agent we will get orders for 1200 or 1500 chests annually." [8] Where a staple like pork was concerned, quality was all-important, as Hill pointed out to Philip D. Armour:

> Please ship 200 barrels clear mess pork *without any bones,* care of N. W. Kittson, St. Paul. The pork is for the Hudson Bay Co. and has to go in carts from St. Cloud to Red River, therefore we ask you to be very particular. Mr. K. had an offer $1 per bbl less than yours but we told him that he could depend upon the meat packed by your house being as good as you represented. [9]

The future of the Red River settlements hung in the balance in these closing years of the pre-railroad era, and the solicitousness of St. Paul businessmen like James J. Hill was often a critical factor. In the late summer of 1868 the "grasshoppers" returned, and the news from the prairie farms, which were still a long way from self-sufficiency, was heartbreaking. Writing to another London agent, Hill summed up the situation. "Owing to the grasshopper plague there will be a great amount of suffering and possibly starvation among the Red River people the coming winter. We are raising 500 bbls flour to send to them among the citizens of St. P." Not ten years later the call would come again. Meanwhile, the spiritual as well as the physical side of life had to be provided for, as anyone who had ever spent a winter on the prairie well knew. To the Reverend H. George, pastor of St. Mary's Church at Red River, Hill's letter of May 23, 1868, was reassuring:

> We have purchased for you everything ordered except the tuning forks. We can only get "C" and "A" as these are the only ones used by teachers in this country. We think we have got some O.T. [old time?] Gin that will suit you. We could have purchased a domestic gin (quack stuff) for $10 per dozen but thought it would not pay to haul it so far. The article we send is bought and put up for medicinal use and if it is not good we have no good in this market.

> Enclosed we send you 6/ worth 12 ¢ stamps. The editions of Tennyson and Longfellow are bound in green cloth, very handsome—but our American print is not as good as the English and I fear that unless you have bought American books before you will be disappointed. Mr. Tennyson has just published a new poem * in London but not in this country. If you order many books we can often get English editions in half calf in private library catalogues for sale at less than London cost, but in such cases we would have to have a little time to look them up . . .

It paid to do business with Hill.

IV

The Dominion of Canada passed through its worst birth pains in 1869 and 1870, the time of the Riel Rebellion. The Rebellion grew out of the efforts of the new nation to establish territorial status for Manitoba. After many years of negotiation during which it often seemed that the differences between the groups making up the settled provinces of Canada could never be resolved, the British North America Act of 1867 had established a self-governing Dominion. The first objective of Prime Minister John Macdonald was to confirm the sovereignty of the new government over all of British North America as rapidly as that awesome feat could be accomplished. To begin with, he had somehow to carry out an arrangement to bring the prairies of modern-day Manitoba, Alberta, and Saskatchewan into the new confederation, an arrangement under which the rights of the Hudson's Bay Company to this vast area were to be extinguished by payment of $1,500,000.

Thus began a tumultuous series of events during which it often seemed that a unified Canada might never come into being. It was one

---

* The first expanded edition of *Idylls of the King*.

thing to buy up the claims of the Hudson's Bay Company; it was quite another to bring under the political domination of eastern Canadian politicians the *métis*, or French-Indian half-breed, who made up most of the population of "Assiniboia" at that time. No one had thought to assure these hardy, independent people that their claims to the land on which they had lived for many years would be respected, nor that their language, Roman Catholic religion, and unique culture would be protected. A leader of these people, Louis Riel, emerged; he swore either to secure these guarantees, or to set up an independent nation, or, if necessary, to seek annexation by the United States. The new governor, Lord William McDougall, was more the victim of the almost total lack of communications than the potential dictator which he seemed to Riel, but when he sought to take office before any of these matters had been settled, Riel and his followers met him and his party twenty-five miles south of Fort Garry and sent them packing.

James J. Hill plunged into the thick of these events. He had watched with keen interest the emergence of the Dominion, for he had been born a Canadian and as far as anyone knew he still was a citizen of that country. He was anxious, moreover, to see the Red River country, for the rapid growth of trade on the north-south axis since the Civil War had convinced him that even greater opportunities lay ahead. In March of 1870 winter's hand still lay heavy on the land north of St. Paul, but by then Fort Garry had been in Riel's control for five months, and matters were obviously approaching some kind of climax. The government in Ottawa was grateful for any information or counsel which would help them remove this potentially fatal obstacle to union. Donald Smith, the highest executive of the Hudson's Bay Company in North America, had been sent to try to deal with the rebels. Archbishop Taché, brother of the late Quebec statesman who had worked long and hard for Canadian unification, and a staunch friend of the *métis*, hurried home from Rome, where he had been attending the Vatican Council. But no one knew what was going on. There was no telegraphic link between Ottawa and Fort Garry, and travel north of Lake Superior and across the morasses between the Lake and Fort Garry was well-nigh impossible.

Hill offered to make the trip north from St. Paul to find out what was happening, and Joseph Howe, Secretary of State for the Provinces, quickly accepted. It meant leaving Mary, who was suffering from a disturbing chronic cough, with a two-year-old daughter and a month-old son, but her sister, who was in a convent in Milwaukee, consented to come to St. Paul to keep her company. The St. Paul & Pacific Railroad took Hill, then thirty-two years old, as far as St. Cloud, from which he traveled another hundred miles by stage, pausing frequently, for he and his fellow passengers had to shovel it out of the snowdrifts. At the end of the stage line he hired a dog team and two sleds which Oscar Malmros, the American consul at Fort Garry whom he met en route, assured him were as good as money could procure. His half-breed guide, however, turned out to be a less fortunate choice. Tiring of the man's dark threats to abandon him, and fearing even worse, Hill sent him back to the village and continued alone. He was now in half-breed country, and suddenly realized that as participants in the rebellion, these people might not take his appearance on the scene as a friendly gesture. He decided to cross to the west side of the river, where he was less likely to encounter strangers on the trail. He made a little raft of tree branches for his outer clothes and then, stripped to his underwear, splashed through the frigid, ice-choked stream to the other side. That night he and his dogs slept in one touseled heap, their body heat and his blankets and robes providing the only warmth. Next day he traveled for some distance on the west side of the river, then crossed to the east side again and resumed his journey. Arriving at Pembina at nightfall of the third day, he was glad to accept the hospitality of C. T. Cavileer, the customs collector he was to visit many times in the next several years as his interests in the valley developed.

On he pressed, for north of Pembina lay even snowier wastes than those he had just come through. Six years later, bound for Montreal on a train which crept through a snowstorm, he would note in his diary, "Storm very much like the same time of winter of 1870 when I went to Ft. Garry with dog train." Out of the swirling snow emerged a southbound party, among whom was Donald A. Smith, head of the Hudson's Bay Company in North America, who was then quitting Fort Garry to make his report to Ottawa. This peppery little man, whom Hill had met once before in St. Paul, bore a remarkable resemblance to Santa Claus in the wintry landscape. Soon the two men were deep in conversation, exchanging observations on the frightful travel conditions, the rebellion at Fort Garry, and the bright future of the Red River country—once problems of politics and transportation were solved.

Smith told Hill that he was going to recommend that Macdonald send troops to put down the rebellion. Riel's execution of Thomas

Scott, one of his bitterest opponents, had convinced Smith that only a
show of force by the Dominion government would resolve the situation. But, as Hill would soon learn from Riel himself, it would take
more than a simple show of strength to work things out. One key to
the situation was the avoidance of clashes between the numerous
tribes of Indians, who would go to war with each other if the white
men did not settle their own differences very soon. The day Hill got
back to St. Paul, on April 22, 1870, he telegraphed Howe in Ottawa the
essentials of the situation, and then wrote him a long letter which
emphasized the Indian problem:

> Almost the entire English speaking population and fully one-third of the
> French are looking and hoping anxiously for the early assumption by
> Canada of the government of the country. Many of the better class of the
> French and a large number of the English around and north of Fort Garry
> contemplate moving to Saint Joseph and other points in the States unless
> the Canadian government speedily acquires control of the country. . . .
>
> There is a great deal of anxiety and fear on account of the Indians and in
> the event of trouble with the Indians the people want Canadian or British
> troops to protect them or else they will leave in large numbers for the
> United States. . . .
>
> If the Dominion government desire [sic] to send supplies thro' by way of
> Pembina in bond from Canada, we will see that they go through safely.
> We are now sending supplies to H[udson's] B[ay] Co., and the missions
> and . . . it need not even be known but that [the government's supplies]
> were trading goods. . . . If you think it would be of any advantage I
> could go to Ottawa and assist in bringing thro' any amount of goods the
> government might desire . . .*

Hill's trip back to St. Paul was as grueling as the trip up, and put his
resourcefulness to an even greater test. He told the story hundreds of
times as his life unfolded, and in 1910 included it in a speech at the
University of North Dakota:

> Soon after daylight we started. I was on horseback and had a half-breed,
> or a breed and a half, for a guide, and he had a cart and an extra pony.
> . . . That afternoon it turned cold. It got very cold. . . . [We went] into a
> grove and camp[ed]. . . . In going out of it and across the stream, my

* Hill's offer to carry supplies ("even gunpowder," he wrote later), might have precipi-
tated an international incident, for it was strictly illegal. The Canadians, however, never
allowed themselves to be humiliated to the extent of asking permission to transport military forces or supplies across American soil, preferring a heroic trek across the appalling wasteland between Lake Superior and Fort Garry.

breed and a half had to lift on a cart wheel . . . and he put his shoulder under the spoke of the wheel . . . and the wheel came around and struck his arm and dislocated it. . . .

The next day I had to set the man's arm and I did it. Down below there were some box elder trees growing . . . I cut a box elder stick about five or six feet in length with a crotch or fork at one end. I made a bundle of my underclothes and put the roll under his arm. Then I got him under the cart with a spoke between his legs. I put the fork against the bundle, cut a notch in the end and let the rope twist in through that notch and back to the wheel. Then, I took a twist on it so that the same power that hauled his arm ahead pressed through this forked stick and pushed the end of it down tight. I took care to sit across him. . . . When I got a good strain on him he began to yell but I kept it going until I felt the joint pressed into its place. . . .

As soon as I got the horse hitched up and our things in the cart and was ready to start he wanted to say his prayers. He was a very devout fellow and had a little bit of a French prayer-book. Some of the missionaries had given it to him or, maybe, to his mother. He got it out and wanted to say his prayers and I . . . suggested that if he would repeat after me I could probably do the work quicker. I commenced at the beginning and went through the various services—marriage service, christening children, baptism, burial of the dead. I took a line at the top and one in the middle and sometimes one at the bottom. I got through the entire prayer-book in less than twenty minutes. He felt he had done the biggest day's work in his life. . . .

On April 22, after more than a month of wondering whether she had become a widow, Mary was vastly relieved to see a shaggy, dirty apparition burst through the door. She was still suffering from her cough, and her thinness must have given him a twinge of conscience, but life was soon serene again in the little house. Lunching with his friends at the new club they had organized, Hill was more enthusiastic than ever in telling them about the future of the Red River country. That summer he began to build flatboats at the head of navigation on the Red.[10]

V

Steamboats made their final contribution to the opening of the Northwest on the Red River of the North in the 1870s. Until the completion of the railroad link between St. Paul and Winnipeg, at the end

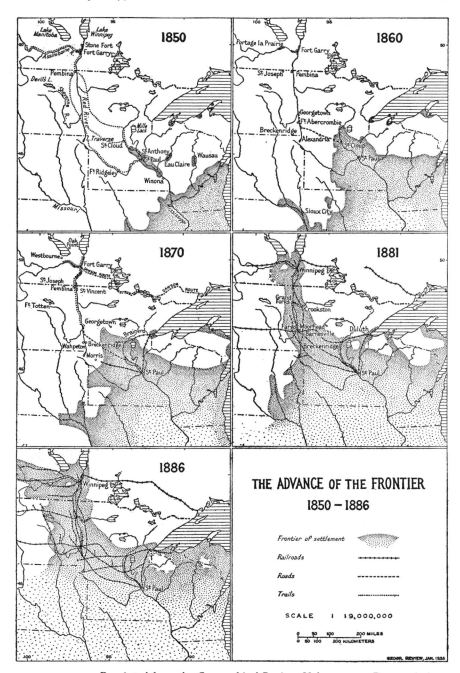

Reprinted from the *Geographical Review*, Vol. 25, 1935. By permission.

of 1878, the boats carried the stream of immigrants, their belongings, and their supplies, which grew rapidly after the establishment of the Province of Manitoba in 1870. The main figures in the establishment of regular steamboat service on the Red during these years were Norman W. Kittson, pioneer trader between St. Paul and the Hudson's Bay Company's territory; Colonel Chauncey W. Griggs, who was Hill's business partner in the early 1870s; Alexander Griggs (no relation to the Colonel) and E. V. Holcombe, veteran steamboat captains; and Hill.

The value of the Red River as a cheaper, faster and easier transportation route between the United States and Canadian Red River settlements had been urged as early as 1849 by Father Georges A. Belcourt. In the 1850s there arose a flourishing overland trade which the half-breeds carried on with their carts. When the Hudson's Bay Company arranged to ship goods in bond from American Atlantic ports via St. Paul and the Red River Valley in 1858, the merchants of St. Paul began to encourage basic improvements in transportation. They sent Captain Russell Blakeley to study the prospects for navigation of the Red as far south as Breckenridge, where it began, and Blakeley obliged them with a highly optimistic report. Lured by a prize of $1000, which the St. Paul people offered to the first person who would put a steamboat on the Red, Captain Anson Northup removed the machinery from his *North Star,* with which he had gained experience in navigating shallow waters on the Mississippi above St. Anthony's Falls, and lugged it 150 miles to a point on the Red where the Sheyenne flowed into it. There he installed it in a hull which had been built on the spot, and the little *Anson Northup,* as he named the boat, became the first steamboat to reach Fort Garry.

But Captain Northup did not find Red River steamboating to his taste. He sold the little boat to J. C. Burbank, who had begun to operate a line of stagecoaches to the Red River settlements from St. Cloud, the farthest point on the Mississippi to which above-the-falls steamboats could go and the announced goal of the branch line of the St. Paul & Pacific Railroad. Burbank found that he still had a great deal to learn about the technological aspects of steamboating, yet that was not his chief problem. The greatest weakness in his transportation system was the fact that the stagecoach and steamboat segments were hopelessly out of phase with each other. Early in the season, when the river was full of water and the *Anson Northup* could sail blithely over such trouble spots as Goose Rapids, the roads northwest from St. Cloud were frequently impassable, even though Burbank and his partners built 150 miles of corduroy road at their own expense. By the time the roads were fine and dry, the water level in the Red would have fallen very low, so that navigation above (i.e. south of) Georgetown was out of the question. It proved impossible to maintain any kind of regular service. Placing a second boat, the *International,* on the river improved matters only slightly.

It was human factors, however, which blighted Red River navigation in the 1860s. The Sioux uprisings of 1862, which included a massacre at Breckenridge, and the difficulty of protecting settlers at such advanced outposts during the Civil War, disrupted operations. Alarmed at the fratricidal conflict, the officials of the Hudson's Bay Company reversed their policy of trading by the southern route and announced that in the future they would operate their own ship across the Atlantic and into Hudson's Bay. The interests of the Burbanks and the Company, in fact, had not turned out to be identical, as Captain Blakeley recalled many years later in a talk before the Minnesota Historical Society. "We wanted immigration and trade; they did not want immigration, nor mails, nor any one to trade in the Hudson's Bay Company territory but themselves. The expectation that [Manitoba] would be opened proved a delusion." By this time Norman W. Kittson, so long the champion of free trade in the face of the Company's monopoly, had become its agent at Georgetown, and when the Company bought the *International* from the Burbanks, Kittson was put in charge. Her trips were "few and far between" for the rest of the decade.[11]

Paradoxically, the golden age of steamboating on the Red from 1871 to 1879 was made possible by the railroad, with which it then had a symbiotic relationship. The main line of the St. Paul & Pacific was making for Breckenridge in a more northwesterly direction than the branch line, which was advancing via St. Cloud. When it reached the town of Morris in 1870, less than a hundred miles of relatively easy stagecoach travel separated end-of-track from Breckenridge, and that nominal head of navigation on the Red was reached the following year. After thirteen years of struggle, Minnesota's pioneer railroad had finally achieved the traditional objective of the early railroads, which was to link navigable bodies of water. Transportation in the Northwest had then reached that stage which Hill had learned to recognize as the point of opportunity: prior conditions which had produced only frustration had been removed, and the time was at hand for someone to capitalize on the opportunities which had unfolded.

Hill had bought back Egbert S. Litchfield's interest in the James J.

Hill Co. on August 19, 1869, for $11,000, which represented Litch-field's original investment plus $6000 in accumulated profits. The next day Hill formed a partnership with Chauncey W. Griggs, a former New Englander who had earned the rank of Colonel in the war and who had been a good friend of Hill since his days with Bass and Company. Griggs's main strength was in the fuel business, and it was in that line that their partnership was most productive, but out of that association had grown their collaboration in a steamboat line on the Red River. Alexander, the other Griggs, was a Mississippi River steamboat captain with an ambition to run a line of his own. On August 2, 1870, Hill and the two Griggs's signed a contract to carry on "a merchandising and transportation business on the Red River of the North."

Recognizing that flatboats, which could only go down the river, would not serve their purposes, the partners signed a second agreement, on February 20, 1871, to build and operate a steamboat. Alexander had a one-sixth interest, while Hill and the colonel split the other five-sixths equally. Christened the *Selkirk*, after Manitoba's early noble patron, the new boat was a trim stern-wheeler, 110 feet long, with a 26-foot beam and a shallow draft that came as close as possible to meeting the jocular requirement that a Red River steamboat be able to navigate on a heavy dew. Late in April 1871 she left Fort Abercrombie, "loaded to the guards" with 105 tons of freight and 100 passengers, and "with the gallant and delighted Jim Hill himself on the hurricane roof." Rumor had it that the new operators expected to clear $7000 profit on the first trip.[12]

Hill had his hands full from the moment he became involved in the Red River trade on such a scale. In September 1871 he left St. Paul on a long, arduous trip to inspect the operation of the *Selkirk*, to see how their competitor, the *International*, was doing, and to straighten out a host of problems involving agents' salaries, lost freight, unpaid bills, and drunken employees. Morris, the end of track on the railroad, was his first stop, where he noted in his diary, "Spencer [the agent] I find considerable the worse for a touch of colar [cholera] morbus and a 'little by the hind.' Spencer says Kittson is very tired of Red River freight business and thinks there is no money in it."

After having dinner (he noted that while he had paid 75 cents for dinner, "Mr. Royall and party travel very economically by having cold ham and Rye bread made into sandwiches"), Hill pressed northward. Bouncing along on the top seat of the stagecoach, he smiled at the driver's complaint that he repeatedly had to "double up"—drive two segments of the run with the same horses—because "the stage company have made more and done more business this year than in two years before over the same route." Hill was aware, even if the driver was not, that Jay Cooke's Northern Pacific Railroad, building west from Duluth on Lake Superior, was about to reach the site of present-day Fargo, North Dakota, on the Red River, and would greatly increase the inflow of passengers and freight looking for transportation on down the river. Everywhere he frowned at the evidence of low water, a problem for which no solution lay in sight, and at reports from southbound travelers that they had passed the *Selkirk* and the *International,* both going very slowly. He was pleased to find that the Hudson's Bay Company agent at Grand Forks "seems very well disposed towards crew of *Selkirk* and thinks the *International* crew rather slow." But when he finally caught up with the *Selkirk* he was disgusted at what he saw:

I find the Cabin outfit in shocking condition all broken up, misused, lost and destroyed and all thro' bad management. The Cabin crew consists of Steward, Cook & two cabin boys when all the work should be done by Cook and one Cabin boy as the boat is not carrying passengers.

The Furnace is entirely used up and is unsafe for an hour. Every night the whole brick work has to be pulled down and built over unless it has already fallen down. The boilers have fallen thro' onto the bottom of boat and the whole thing is in worse shape than I ever saw a steamboat. . . .[13]

Meanwhile, another dramatic episode of Canadian-American history was about to unfold before his eyes. In the late 1860s the idea of annexing western Canada had thrilled such earnest men as James W. Taylor, pioneer publicist of the upper Midwest; Oscar Malmros, American consul at Fort Garry; and even Senator Charles Sumner of Massachusetts—as well as Midwestern demagogues like Alexander Ramsey and Ignatius Donnelly. By 1871 such sentiment had all but died out, and only the Irish-American Fenians, who were more interested in twisting the British lion's tail than securing the blessings of United States citizenship for Manitobans, still sought to stir up trouble. Hill wrote about the unedifying events which he saw unfold at Pembina, on the international boundary, beginning on October 5:

This A.M. at 7 o'clock a band of thirty Fenians under Gen'ls Jas. O'Neill, Curly Donnally & O'Donahue composed of about twenty of the hardest looking roughs and ten Pembina loafers made an attack on the H[udson's]

B[ay] Post at North Pembina which was occupied by one of the H. G. Co. officers and his clerk and captured it without resistance being offered. They at once set about clothing their half naked squad of roughs and loading up a wagon with provisions. Either the plunder had too much attraction for them or they thought they could rest on their freshly gained laurels for they remained in the Post until 11 o'clock A.M. when they were surprised by Col. Wheaton with 23 men from Fort Pembina coming down the road in an army ambulance and a few Mule Wagons. . . . In about twenty minutes he [Wheaton] returned with Gen'ls O'Neill, Donnally and Curley in the ambulance and about ten men on foot. . . . O'Donahue made good his escape. . . .

I was a close eye witness of the whole affair and I never saw a more ridiculous scattering or silly farce. It certainly looked as if the leaders would have been very much disappointed if they had not been kindly taken charge of by the U. S. Troops and in that way kept out of harms way . . . O'Donahue got hungry or dry and went into a half-breed's house and was then taken prisoner by the breeds, but not until he had made them pledge that they would not deliver him to any but the United States authorities [would he lay down his pistol].

Fenian trial continued all day [Oct. 10] and was a contemptible farce and a burlesque as . . . Stutsman & Potter [defense counsel] simply bullied both the court and Col. Wheaton. Prisoners were acquitted on ground of want of jurisdiction by court as the arrests were made on what has heretofore been known as British soil. . . .* [14]

The brief heyday of steamboating on the Red River began in 1872, when the Hudson's Bay Company was removed from the scene, and Kittson merged his interests with those of Hill, Griggs & Company. After launching the *Selkirk,* Hill had waged a campaign to eliminate the Canadians. He persuaded the United States Treasury Department that goods could be carried in bond in the United States only by a firm which was itself bonded, and that a Canadian firm could not legally operate a vessel in American waters. He was on firm ground on the latter point, for the United States Congress had specifically reserved shipping within the territorial limits of the United States to American vessels. The Hudson's Bay Company responded by transferring the *International* to Kittson, who was a naturalized American citizen (which was more than Hill could say at that time) and had no difficulty in get-

---

* The Fenians knew that they would be dealt with lightly by United States authorities because of the large number of Irish-Americans in the area, but that if they had been captured by the Canadians, who labored under no such handicap and against whose newly unified country they had led an armed raid, they might well have been executed.

ting a bond. There followed a period of rate cutting which satisfied nobody. The result was an agreement, made on January 19, 1872, establishing "Kittson's Red River Transportation Company." Explicit arrangements were made to split the business between the *Selkirk* and the *International,* and minimum rates of $1.50 per hundredweight (except for the rate of $1.00, which Kittson was obligated to give the Hudson's Bay Company) for freight and $8.00 per passenger, from Moorhead (where the Northern Pacific Railroad was to cross the Red) were established.

Except for a brief period in the spring of 1875, when a short-lived competing line put the *Manitoba* and the *Minnesota* on the river, the Hill-Griggs-Kittson combine had an absolute monopoly of the business. One afternoon in early March of 1873 Hill noted in his diary that his entire family were sick with colds, while he not only had a cold, but was threatened with an attack of pleurisy. Propped up in bed, he observed that the thermometer outside his window registered $-27°F.$, and that there was a foot of new snow. Having nothing better to do, he was going over the books of the Kittson end of the business, preparatory to merging all of the partners' interests in a new corporation. Kittson's amounted to $75,000, while Hill had only $18,000 worth, and the Griggses had reduced their interest to $7,000. But Hill would be running the business. Kittson, whom a friend had described in the 1850s as "a sprightly, fine-looking man, cleanly and really elegantly dressed, hair just turning gray, eyes bright, with a quiet, pleasant voice, genial in nature," was unmistakably growing old. When his French-Indian wife had died (March 1868) he had taken her body by dogsled to St. Boniface, opposite Fort Garry, to be buried. Remarried, he indulged a love for race horses and, when winter came, went off to Florida or New Orleans to warm his bones. He was destined for one more great adventure, however, one into which this dynamic young man who had made him a transportation monopolist of the Red River Valley would draw him.

The people of the United States, like the Canadians, have a profound distrust of concentrations of power today. It was no different in the 1870s. The monopoly which Hill had established was deeply resented, the more so by the Canadians because they lacked the resources to put up any competition, and because the United States shut them out of the trade south of the boundary. Meanwhile the people of the Red River country enjoyed a transportation system which had not been dreamed of a few years before. Five boats plied the river where

only two had recently been, and rates had come down as fast as prudent operation and the demand of the owners for a handsome return
on their labors and substantial risk would permit. Freight, which had
been carried for $6.00 per hundredweight in 1860, cost only $2.25 by
1875, while passengers, who rode all the way from St. Paul by train
and boat, paid $19 instead of the $35 which the uncomfortable stagecoach and boat trip had cost in 1860. [15]

VI

On New Year's Day, 1869, James J. Hill noted in his diary that there
was new snow on the ground that morning. Snowy holiday or not, the
business had to be looked after. "I went to the office during the forenoon," he noted; but toward midday he apparently caught the spirit
of the occasion, and "gave the hands at the warehouse a half-holiday
in the afternoon." There were few days when Hill was not in his office, for the business was the kind which demanded daily attention.
Attendance at mass was the high point of Mary's Sundays, and as the
children grew older, Hill went to church with his family occasionally.
If Mary was sick he might take Mamie, as their oldest child was called.
He himself would have been welcomed enthusiastically into the
Church if he had shown more interest, and he was the object of a little
understated proselytizing. "Father Caillet spent the evening at the
house and presented me with a missal," he noted in his diary early in
1869. [16]

Even on Sundays he was usually back at the office by noon. It was a
day for catching up on his large correspondence, which he carried on
in his own handwriting, that reflected the three roles he was playing—
in railroad transportation, in steamboating, and in solving the serious
fuel problems of that land. New interests crowded alongside the old
ones. In April 1869 he consented to sit on the board of directors of the
newly formed City Bank of St. Paul, which was headed by the very affluent William B. Litchfield, with Hill's close friend and neighbor,
Henry P. Upham, in the cashier's cage. General H. H. Sibley, St. Paul
pioneer and head of the gas works; George L. Becker of the St. Paul &
Pacific Railroad; and Norman W. Kittson were also on the board. The
depression of the 1870s was not kind to small banks; while the City
Bank managed to avoid both death and dishonor, it was eventually
absorbed by Horace Thompson's powerful First National Bank of St.

Paul.[17] James J. Hill's important role in St. Paul banking would come many years later.

Land speculation in the new territory to the north was a fascinating, sometimes rewarding sideline. Hill invested substantial sums, and unwonted hours of his time, in dealing in Sioux half-breed scrip, which entitled the bearer to lands, and in foreclosed and abandoned town lots and farms in Dakota Territory. John J. Jackman, the United States Commissioner at Bismarck, wrote frequent, lengthy letters promoting various money-making schemes which he thought he saw around him. "Come up here by fast train and look the ground over," he urged Hill. "I think there is $500 or more worth of furs and skins here which could be purchased by anyone who is a judge of such things at a good figure."

If Hill could have foreseen the morass of litigation into which Jackman was leading him, he would have thought better of these dealings. Nearly all of the lands on which the Dakotan, acting for Hill, took options turned out to be of questionable ownership. Jackman claimed to represent the settlers who had the best claims to these lands, and that they would share the profits with Hill if he would finance the presentation of their claims before the Secretary of the Interior at Washington. The Secretary threw most of them out, and shortly thereafter Hill learned that Jackman had deliberately misrepresented many. Totaling up all that he had spent to keep Jackman's house of cards standing, Hill arrived at a figure of $6100. Oscar Taylor, his lawyer at St. Cloud, advised a lawsuit to collect damages from Jackman, but Hill had clearly wasted far too much of his time on such empty pursuits. The experience was easily worth $6100.[18]

William E. Wellington, who had hoped that the "little Hills" would "spring up thick and fast," would have been pleased with the Hill family. James J. and Mary's first child, Mary Frances ("Mamie"), was born in 1868, the year after their marriage. Most of Hill's friends were still bachelors then, and Stanford Newel, Henry Upham, and Greenleaf Clark showered gifts and affection on the new baby. Two years later Hill's first son was born and, following family tradition, was named James, though his father, who had had to acquire his own middle name, saw to it that James Norman Hill suffered from no such deficiency. A second son, Louis W., joined the family two years later.

In 1871 Hill had paid $5000 for a cottage on a choice lot at the corner of Ninth and Canada streets, where Henry Upham was already building a house. He gave a one-year note for $2000, on which he paid interest at the rate of 12 percent. Then the depression of the 1870s closed in, and the "spacious and handsome residence" which, gossip had it, was to rise on the new lot was delayed three years. The Hills settled for an expansion of their old house.[19]

Despite her strong constitution, Mary Hill was showing the strain of regular childbearing by this time, although her loss of weight and chronic cough were eventually to be traced to other causes. The household had its full share of ailments, since the building up of antibodies was a business which Nature took just as seriously then as now. "Little Jimmy" had a severe case of what Doctor Hand "thought" was the measles. Then one cold Saturday morning in January 1873, when their mother was sick abed, Hill sent the children for a ride. Mamie returned with her face frozen, "but not badly." A few days later the doctor was treating her for worms, but he soon concluded that what she had was typhoid fever. The family physician in those days was Daniel W. Hand, a native of New Jersey who had arrived in St. Paul in 1857. A graduate of the Medical College of the University of Pennsylvania, he was as well prepared to treat the Hills as anyone else they could get. But St. Paul was still not a good place to be sick.[20]

Hill made what was to be his next-to-last trip back to Rockwood in the early spring of 1869. His mother was not managing her affairs very well, and Alexander seems to have been able to contribute very little in the way of money or management. The two brothers paid a visit to the family burying ground, but were disappointed that they were unable to find the grave of their grandfather Hill, whose body was supposed to have been moved there years before. Hill took the opportunity to go on to New York, where personal calls on railroad agents and importers could be of great value to the development of the Red River trade. Leaving New York City at 11:30 the morning of April 1, he got no farther than Hudson, where the breakup of ice in the river had flooded the tracks. The passengers had to make themselves as comfortable as they could, for the train stayed there all night.

He was glad to get back home and into the easy-going pattern of St. Paul life. An occasional game of cards with the P. H. Kellys or other friends, a lecture or concert, with an infrequent gala affair, such as the governor's inaugural ball, was their social life. It left Hill many evenings to do what he still enjoyed best, which was to read widely. His companions before the fire on such evenings may have included the newest addition to the family: the lead sled dog from his Fort Garry trip, which he had brought back to St. Paul with him. "That is the dog that saved my life," he told his brother. He eagerly pressed upon his friends books which he had found worthwhile. One evening he could not find *The Decameron* of Boccaccio, which he had just finished reading. Mary, with a frown of disapproval, dug it out of her sewing basket for him. She had sewed a new cambric cover for it, and for good measure had decided to sew it entirely shut.

Life was simple and informal in the bustling little capital city. After the rigors of December and early January, there was usually a brief, deceptively balmy thawing period. Strolling down the street one bright January afternoon in 1869, Hill noted that the weather had warmed up and that the sleighing "was going very fast." Spying Henry A. Swift, who had served briefly as governor of Minnesota when it was still a territory, he grasped him by the arm and insisted that he came home with him to dinner. "The Governor thought I ought to congratulate myself on my wife, child, and prospects of domestic happiness," the young husband noted proudly in his diary.[21]

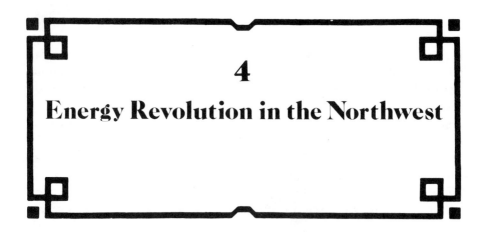

4

Energy Revolution in the Northwest

My idea is to get as many people using coal as possible. In a country as thinly wooded as this and settling up so fast a large coal business must build itself up in a very short time.

—James J. Hill, 1867

I

By the middle of the nineteenth century Americans knew that their young nation was blessed with the largest reserves of the best quality coal in the world. The anthracite, or "hard" coal, of eastern Pennsylvania, where fabulous quantities lay buried under the agriculturally worthless hills, gave a unique solution to man's age-old effort to warm himself in the cold climates where western civilization flourished. For those favorably situated to use it, it yielded more units of heat per unit of cost than any other fuel ever known. Further west lay great beds of bituminous, or "soft" coal—just how much people could still only guess—which would provide one of the keys to America's supremacy in the industrial world when the time came. In 1859, three years after James J. Hill arrived in St. Paul, the United States was mining nearly ten times as much anthracite as it had produced just twenty years before, and by the time Hill was established as an independent businessman it was evident that the age of coal was rapidly approaching, even in the isolated Northwest.

It had been a long time in coming. Although a tenfold increase in anthracite output from 1839 to 1859 is impressive, the fact is that only a small part of the existing United States was meeting its energy requirements with coal of any type, even as late as the Civil War. Indeed, before the War of 1812, although Americans were aware of their coal, it was virtually unknown as a fuel to most people. When President and Mrs. Washington treated themselves to the warmth and cheerfulness of a coal fire in the grate of the first executive mansion, on New York's Cherry Hill, the fuel was likely to have been brought from the near-by East River docks, where it had arrived not from a few miles away, in the inaccessible hills of Pennsylvania, but from England. Incredible as it may seem, the English coal mining industry had progressed so far by the end of the eighteenth century, and the fuel was so prized by the affluent for space heating, that considerable quantities of coal were imported for use in East Coast cities in the years just before and just after the Napoleonic Wars. Throughout the young Republic, moreover, in hundreds of small furnaces back in the hills, iron was smelted from its ore with charcoal fuel supplied by the virgin forests. Although the English had begun to smelt iron with coal fuel a hundred years before and had perfected the process fully by the 1780s, Americans continued to make most of their iron by a backward, expensive, and futureless technique until the Civil War.

The factor which explains these differences was cheap, dependable inland transportation: its availability in England and its absence in the United States and most of the rest of the civilized world. In the early nineteenth century, except in England, where no place is more than about sixty miles from the sea and the relatively flat lands are crisscrossed by navigable rivers, no nation possessed a practical means of dragging such a bulky, heavy product as coal out of the often rugged areas where it was found and hauling it over the considerable distances which separated the mines and their markets. Heating coal had to be taken to where the people were, which in America meant within a few miles of the seaboard. And iron-smelting coal, even if one had mastered the technique and had the right kind of coal, had to be combined with the iron ore, which was seldom found in the same place as the coal. The first break in the fuel stalemate in the United States came with the canal-building era of the 1820s, when several canals were built to carry the anthracite coal of Pennsylvania to tidewater, where it could be placed on coastal vessels for transportation to the cities. But the nation moved westward and the population moved into the interior, so canals proved to be no final answer to the American fuel problem. It was, in short, the railroad, once it had been extended throughout the nation to virtually every trading center, which, at first gradually, and then with amazing speed, brought coal as an energy source to preeminence—a preeminence which was not seriously challenged by other fuels until the second quarter of the twentieth century.

It would take much more than the building of railroads, however, to establish coal's superiority as a fuel, especially in places which were far from the mines and relatively well supplied with wood. Three elements, elements which James J. Hill and his associates would provide in the 1870s to bring this about in the Northwest, were essential. The first was know-how; coal was a relatively new product, it came in a bewildering variety of qualities, sizes, and sources, which met various kinds of needs, and the economics of getting the fuel from one place to another involved much knowledge of a rapidly changing business. Considerable capital, moreover, was required to get a coal business going on a scale which could prove the virtues of the new fuel. This was "risk capital," money which its owners were willing to sink into a new business with no past record of success and which they were prepared to lose if the whole idea turned out to be a bad one. Naturally, such capitalists would expect that the rewards, if any, would be substantial. And, finally, the men who brought this new business into being in a market like St. Paul and the Northwest had to have absolute control of the situation, at least until the greater efficiencies of their way of doing business had had a chance to be fully demonstrated. Coal had first to be established as a preferred fuel among a majority of consumers, and efficient mass handling facilities had to be installed and paid for. Then the new ways of doing business had to work themselves out. Until these steps in the innovative process were complete, the men who had big ideas for the future of coal had to see to it that cutthroat pricing, dishonest grading and weighing, poor service, and all of the other symptoms of business anarchy were avoided. To do this they had to monopolize the business during its formative years. This is what Hill and his associates did in the coal business in the 1870s. It was, in fact, much the same kind of constructive monopoly which Hill and Kittson were simultaneously bringing to the steamboat business on the Red River. Hill's success in the coal business provided much of the seed money for what later proved to be his most important work.

II

In a land as thinly populated as the antebellum United States, with the great majority of its people living on isolated farms in densely forested areas, it is not surprising that wood remained the most important fuel before the Civil War, even though the advent of cheap transportation had begun to bring coal to the fore after 1840. The widespread availability of wood in the years before the population spread out onto the prairies and plains gave that fuel a large, if temporary, advantage, particularly since it was also well adapted to the simple uses of an unsophisticated society. Moreover, until the Civil War, and for some time later in backward areas, wood was the fuel used in nearly all of the rapidly multiplying locomotives in the country. Designing a locomotive boiler which could use coal satisfactorily, especially one which could use the anthracite, which was so plentiful in the East, had turned out to be very difficult, so the temptation to keep on using wood was strong. The St. Paul & Pacific Railroad was still using wood exclusively when James J. Hill and his associates acquired control in 1879.[1]

As long as there was money to be made in the wood-fuel business in St. Paul, Hill had a hand in it. Even before he had gone into business for himself he had dealt in the commodity, buying quantities where it lay in the woods from some farmer who wanted cash, arranging to have it brought to the city, and negotiating its sale. With the warehouse facilities which he built in 1867, he was able to accumulate substantial inventories in the summer and hold them for sale until the heating season began. The large, guaranteed market for wood, however, was the railroad, which entered into contracts with various parties, including James J. Hill & Company and, after 1869, Hill, Griggs & Company. Hill and Griggs brought John A. Armstrong, a Minneapolis fuel dealer of considerable experience and excellent connections, into the partnership, largely because he held permits to cut hardwood logs on certain public lands to the north.

The price of wood was always a hot issue. To the woodcutter, who saw the commodity as a cash "crop" which he could produce during the winter, and to the dealer, who had to provide the cash for its purchase and haulage, sometimes months in advance of its resale, the price was never high enough. To the consumer, especially during the long winter's siege, it was galling to pay several dollars a cord more than the price of the previous spring and summer. Suppliers were regularly accused of monopolizing the business and keeping prices at artificially high levels. By the time wood was delivered to the user's bin it had a large "input" of labor embodied in the price, and labor was always relatively scarce in the West in those years. In February 1870, Hill, Griggs & Company advertised reductions in wood, but a cord of dry maple (the best grade) still cost $7.25. Allowing for changes in the purchasing power of the dollar, this was as much as a householder had to pay for fireplace wood in the Danbury, Connecticut area, for example, a hundred years later.[2]

The wood business demanded the services of a young, active man. Hill's diary reveals that it was a strenuous life, requiring him to travel out into the "sticks" to check the progress of cutting and hauling out of wood and to see to it that other dealers were not buying up supplies which he himself was counting on. He carried large sums of cash to pay off the woodcutters, and constantly plunged deeper into the forest in search of likely stands of timber. One such trip found Hill on the road for over a week in January 1876, staying overnight with farmers, general-store owners, and wherever else he could find a bed for the night. By then he had made a stunning success of the coal business in spite of the general depression which had settled on the nation in 1873. There was no substantial market left for wood except for the locomotives of the St. Paul & Pacific Railroad, and Hill had plans which would make the wood-burning iron horse a relic of the past.[3]

III

Whoever could claim the distinction of having introduced coal into the Northwest at St. Paul, it was not James J. Hill. As early as 1856 one David O. Oakes advertised that he was establishing a "stove coal yard," from which he would be able to supply "blacksmiths, furnaces, hotels and private families with coal at reasonable rates," and would also stock coal stoves and grates. Such coal, sold in sacks or casks, was brought in by steamboat, and was correspondingly expensive. For the premium market at which Oakes aimed even expensive coal was widely favored, but before a true mass market for the commodity could be developed for less demanding applications, ways would have to be found to make it much cheaper. This would mean stocking other sizes and varieties of coal, which were best adapted for specific applications; drastically cutting the cost of transportation from the distant coal fields; lowering the cost of handling the coal locally; and, perhaps most difficult, promoting the natural advantages of coal to users who had always considered wood perfectly satisfactory. The man who was to do these things most successfully was James J. Hill.

Americans took coal much less for granted in the middle of the nineteenth century than they do today, when there is little interest in what is considered a prosaic subject. Hill sought out and read everything he could find about coal, which combined so many knotty problems of geology, chemistry, and economics. He was thoroughly familiar with, and often quoted, the leading authority on the subject, James Macfarlane, whose *Coal-Regions of America* was published by D. Appleton in 1873. He was probably familiar with the statistics on coal reserves published in 1856 by Richard C. Taylor, whom Macfarlane called "the most distinguished geologist of his time," and with the work of J. P. Lesley, who published an early formal treatise on the geology of coal in 1856.[4] Hill's main sources of information, however, were his own remarkable powers of observation and his indefatigable correspondence. He bombarded railroad superintendents and coal sales agents in Chicago with numerous questions about coal:

[To "Friend Swan," Chicago, April 11, 1867:] I wish you would give me the best figures you can make *in Chicago* on Pittsburgh, Lehigh and Bloseburg coal per ton in bulk and also in sacks. . . . I am going to try and sell . . . 2000 tons and I think I can sell 200 or 300 tons of other coal. . . ."

[To Swan, June 4, 1867:] The gas Co. want another 100 tons of Pittsburgh but are not quite ready to receive it and pay for it, but will be in a week or two. . . . I have not more than a week's supply of Bloseburg left and it will not do to be out of it even if we have to pay . . . $12 for one car load to keep running. . . . Please send me quotations on Lackawanna (lump and egg) also cheap coal for furnaces, grates, etc., delivered on cars.

[To Swan, June 6, 1867:] Robert Law is sending Lackawanna coal here in casks . . . at $18 per ton. How does he do it? I can sell 100 tons if I can get it at figures to compete. What is Brice Hill coal and what is it used for? . . . I will get up a big trade for coal here if I can get it to compete with Law. . . . When Blosburg is plenty and cheap let me know as that will be the time to order.

[To Swan, June 6, 1867:] Would it not be well to see Robert Law about coal as Mr. Law might be willing to sell coal in Chicago instead of sending it up here to sell on commission. If we can get Law's coal out of the market any way we can have a margin of $2 or $3 per ton. . . .

[To Robert Law, June 17, 1867:] I think with your advantages and some that I have we could make an arrangement that would drive any outside competition out of the market.

[To Swan, June 24, 1867:] My idea about this thing is to have this coal in *one* man's hands and instead of his trying to see how low he can sell to try and see how much he can get for it.*

Hill was moving to develop the coal business in St. Paul in a way which would make it profitable for him to assume certain risks which would be unavoidable if the market were to be expanded to the extent he believed possible. Working through sales agents in Chicago, the leading producers in the various Pennsylvania fields had been selling coal at prices delivered in St. Paul on consignment to small-time fuel dealers. These retailers played a largely passive selling role, letting the producers carry the inventories, bear the burden of sudden declines in market price, and perform other functions normally assumed by entrepreneurs located near the consumer. Hill wanted coal priced at Chicago, for he knew perfectly well that although he might be 400 miles farther along in the marketing process, he was capable of driving just as hard a bargain with the steamboat and railroad lines as the industry executives in Chicago were. In fact, he probably expected to do even better on that score. Especially in dealing with the one big volume user in St. Paul, the gas company, he was willing to buy and pay for gas-making coal purely in anticipation that the company was going to need it and that they would be willing to buy it from him.

Hill also pressed for better prices on cheap coals, realizing that the broader the consumption base he could develop for mineral fuel, the quicker people would become accustomed to use it for all purposes. But he had his eye on the main chance in the coal business, which was to get and control the St. Paul market for the fine anthracite coals produced by companies allied with the Lackawanna and Lehigh Valley railroads, coals which commanded a premium price and were strongly preferred for domestic heating. These mining companies were banded together in a sales agency in Chicago which attempted, generally with only modest success, to control production and prices. Hill realized

---

* W. G. Swan was general superintendent of the Chicago and North Western Railroad and Hill's close friend. "Pittsburgh" was a steam-making coal; "Lehigh" and "Lacka-wanna," the best anthracites. It took Hill some time to get the spelling of Blossburg coal, which blacksmiths preferred, just right. Robert Law was the general sales agent in Chicago for a group of leading anthracite producers.

that, however energetic he was, he could not make a go of selling
these coals on his own account if he had to pay the same price that
passive fuel dealers in his city paid. What he wanted Robert Law, the
Chicago sales agent, to do was to step out beyond Chicago, sell
anthracite to Hill, Griggs & Company at a special price which would
be justified by the large quantities involved, and let them make the
best thing they could out of it. Law and his principals back East were
quite willing to do this if they could be sure that the increase in the
amount sold would more than offset the reduction in their net realized
price per ton. It was a classic case of an industry poised between a
low-volume, high-unit-price business and a truly mass consumption
industry. Before the summer of 1867 was over, Law received a letter
which convinced him that Hill was in earnest. He was asking for a
price on coal loaded into cars which he himself would arrange to have
switched into Law's coalyard in Chicago:

> The coal market is very quick here. . . . My idea is to get as many people
> using coal as possible. In a country as thinly wooded as this and settling
> up so very fast a very large coal business must build itself up in a very
> short time. . . .[5]

A few weeks later Hill told Law that he was pressing the St. Paul &
Pacific Railroad to use coal in their shops and forges. "I am working
with some of our leading men," he confided, "to have them try coal
for fuel." The following year, as the time to lay in stocks arrived, the
Milwaukee Railroad began to feel the pressure. Hill wrote the general
superintendent about rates:

> Now, we shall bring another year [i.e. next year] to this market 3000 tons
> of coal for ourselves and the Gas Co., and unless we can do as well from
> Milwaukee as from Chicago on the present shipment we shall find no
> fault but another time we shall give the preference to those who do the
> best for us. We do not think it right that we should be obliged to pay the
> same rate on 500 or 1000 tons as any blacksmith has to pay on 3 tons.[6]

It was a classic statement of the philosophy which would lead to the
rebating controversies of the 1870s and 1880s. Hill had put the same
case to "Will" Wellington of the Northwest Packet Company:

> Law, I think, is willing to give us a good thing on coal as he is afraid that
> we will take the trade away from him. I am now selling about all the coal
> that is sold here and the field is enlarging all the time. . . . Goodrich of
> the Gas Co. is now East and he may call on you for a special rate on coal
> which you must look out for. I want to sell that Gas Co. all their coal and I
> want to take the order down with me when I go the last of this month.

Every day convinces me more and more of the wisdom of a fair policy
with [Captain Davidson, president of Northwest Packet]. . . . I think it is
best to keep far enough away from him to make him think he has no sure
thing unless he deserves it and I will constantly keep the "fire of the Lord
before his eyes" at the same time showing that His Mercy Endureth Forever to those that believe.[7]

That summer he had begun to advertise aggressively in the St. Paul
papers, offering coal "at Chicago quotations, with freight added," and
offering to deal with large users "at prices to suit them." [8]

IV

Leadership in the St. Paul-Minneapolis coal business was not to be
resolved without a struggle. By the latter part of 1873 it was obvious
that the nation was sliding into a business recession at least as serious
as the one which had terrified men in 1857–61. The panic of 1873 did,
indeed, inaugurate the first great depression of the industrial era,
which ripened in turn into a financial shakeout that left the structure
of American business greatly altered. Most of the nation's attention
would center on the railroad industry, where innovative use of the
common law's equity receivership would greatly strengthen the transportation network, and upon the fast-rising young petroleum industry, in which one group of men, the Standard Oil "crowd," were
emerging as leaders. The coal business, however, and especially the
Eastern anthracite branch, was shaken to its foundations. And in the
Northwest began the contest between the two leaders of the fuel business, Colonel Chauncey W. Griggs and James J. Hill, which was to
lead first to violent price competition, then to vindication of Hill's
anti-price-cutting policies, and finally to the tying up of all of the
warring elements in a single enterprise.

The firm of Hill, Griggs & Company had prospered in the years
before the depression. From total sales of 3500 tons of all kinds of coal
in 1870, the firm expanded to at least five times that much in 1874,
when they sold 5000 tons of anthracite alone. The partnership was
founded in August 1869, and shortly thereafter Hill and Griggs admitted William B. Newcomb, along with John A. Armstrong, into the firm
in order to concentrate on the business in the Minneapolis area.
Profits were to be split five ways: one-fifth each to Hill, Griggs,
Armstrong, and Newcomb, and the fifth share "to the said Griggs and

Armstrong to be expended by them for the benefit of the whole concern," thereby anticipating a financial formula which would be used
in Hill's first railroad undertaking. By the end of 1871 the business had
grown to the point where a new partner was needed, particularly since
Armstrong had drifted away by then. Young George S. Acker, who
was to handle much of the firm's correspondence and other internal
matters, was brought in on January 1, 1872. He was to be a strong
pillar of Hill's coal empire throughout these trying years.[9]

Price instability had already begun to appear by the middle of 1872.
In May the firms of Hill, Griggs & Company, Garrett and Johnson,
both of St. Paul, and B. S. Russell, of Duluth, through which port most
of the coal then reaching St. Paul was brought, signed an agreement to
support prices, pool their buying power, and present a united front to
the railroads in bargaining for railroad rates. The arrangement did not
work, and a year later this "Minnesota Coal Association" met at the
Metropolitan Hotel to terminate itself and divide the coal on hand. By
then signs of the depression were everywhere. Hill, Griggs & Company got behind in paying their trade bills. A. B. Hinman, a distribu-
tor of lubricating oils, in which the firm had been doing a growing
business, had to dun them repeatedly. He received payment for his
invoices nearly six months late. By 1875 Morehouse Oil & Wax Company, a Cleveland firm, was pressing them for overdue amounts and
asking them to sign a note for the balance. Others were in bad shape,
too. One of their smaller customers, Mrs. William J. Smith, who struggled against overwhelming odds to run "Norwood Hall," a genteel
academy for young ladies, asked Hill, Griggs & Company for repeated
extensions on what she owed for coal. Eight of her best pupils, she
confided, had failed to return from the Christmas holidays owing to
the hard times. Even George L. Becker, President of the St. Paul & Pacific Railroad, was in trouble. "I have a note for $1000 due at First Na-
tional next Monday, which I must provide for," he wrote Colonel
Griggs. "I do not feel like asking you for money, but if you can give
me [a loan] on note it will oblige me greatly." [10]

Relations between Hill and Griggs deteriorated under these strains,
and both men began to feel they could do better on their own. Griggs
was not eager to subordinate himself to the younger man in making
important decisions, while Hill had formed a poor opinion of his partner's business judgment. "Griggs took Dutchus's order for wood until
Jan. 1st, 1874 @ $7.00 per cord," Hill noted in his diary on May 3,
1873, "and BH [Brice Hill] coal as called for 500 tons @ $11. Had regu-

lar collision in p.m. with Griggs about above." Hill was aghast at his
partner's recklessness in making long-term price quotations for such
products as wood and coal. "Spent forenoon talking over matters with
C. W. Griggs," he noted the following Monday. He expressed much
sorrow for his conduct on Saturday and desires to try and do better."
Less than two years later, on May 1, 1875, despite the firm's continued
profitability, Griggs agreed to sell out to Hill for $35,000. The parting
was friendly, but there was no implied promise on either side to yield
an inch in the fight that was coming. On the same date Hill formed a
new partnership with Acker; Armstrong, whose support he would
need in Minneapolis; and Edward N. Saunders, a prominent Minneapolis dealer whose descendants would continue in the Northwest
fuel business.[11]

The new partnership was capitalized at $50,000, which was to be
shared equally at the beginning, although Hill apparently invested
more in the next year or two. The partners were to share equally in the
profits, and Saunders, in addition, was to have a drawing account of
$2400 a year in lieu of salary. Hill was anxious to have Saunders in the
firm. Ten years later Saunders would recall their first discussion of the
partnership. "I was at that time in the coal and wood business. . . .
We were competitors; and this meeting was with a view of seeing if
we could arrange to go into business together. He mentioned this fact
of his proposing to engage in a railroad enterprise . . . and that it
would be a great benefit to me to take hold of the fuel business with
him . . . [as] he didn't expect to devote a great deal of his time to the
fuel business after . . . this railroad scheme of his was running." It
was indeed a golden opportunity, and Saunders used it well.[12]

Hill laid down the law on proper business deportment, now that he
was the unquestioned senior member of the firm. Making one of his
usual Sunday afternoon visits to the office, he was furious to find
Acker playing draw poker with two of the employees. "Told Acker I
hoped he would never again let himself indulge in any such game."
And they were all to stick strictly to their legitimate business. When
Hinman, the oil jobber from Detroit, came by to offer them 10 per cent
in stock if they would help him dispose of $100,000 worth of stock in
something called "Detroit Utah Silver Mines," Hill threw him out.
"Informed him that I . . . was opposed to *stock jobs* on principle." [13]
And he redoubled his efforts to make the new firm the leader of the
coal business in the Northwest. He was no longer dealing through
Law in Chicago. On May 3, 1875, he wrote to C. M. Underhill, who

was in charge at Buffalo of all Anthracite Association sales, to tell him
about the new partnership:

> This we think will more than double our Minneapolis tonnage and our St.
> Paul tonnage I will hope to increase largely over last year. . . . I will meet
> you in Chicago and hope to make an arrangement that will be to our mu-
> tual advantage. We want the sale of all your coal in this market, and while
> that may look to you somewhat arbitrary I am satisfied that I can show
> you that you will get a larger tonnage than by selling to different dealers.

He came down hard on price-cutters. To R. C. Elmore & Company
of Milwaukee he wrote on June 9, 1875, that D. W. Jones, a local coal
dealer, had reported that Elmore was cutting prices in order to sell in
the Minneapolis market. "If Mr. Jones' statement is correct we will
most certainly retaliate and you will hear from us right in Milwaukee.
. . . We had hoped the season would run along without anything
more than good, ordinary business competition. . . ." He increased
the firm's standing order from Underhill, "so as to have the market already nearly filled and so cut their [local competitors'] amount down."
He wrote to Mark Hanna, whose Lake steamers were now bringing
Hill and Company's coal to Duluth by the boatload, pressing him to
crowd as much on board each sailing as possible so that there would
be no danger of their running short when Lake navigation closed in
November. He passed along to Underhill the information that Griggs
was going into the coal business on his own, and his own theories
about where Griggs might expect to get coal. Underhill, he warned,
should be on the lookout, and keep him informed about Griggs's
movements. At the end of June Hill brought off a major coup, for Underhill finally agreed to allow Hill, Saunders, and Acker to sell large
coal accounts in the Twin Cities area directly at the same price which
the Anthracite Association charged Hill for coal, with a small commission for each such sale. Hill and his partners thus had become, by
mid-1875, the *de facto* representative of the Association northwest of
Chicago.[14]

V

Coal did not sell itself, no matter how much of a staple it had become
by the mid-1870s. Hill did not rest on his oars as the leader of the
business in the Northwest, for he knew that the situation was far from
being stabilized, and that the entire coal industry, from the eastern

Pennsylvania fields all the way to the general store in Yankton, Dakota Territory, which had recently begun to buy small lots of coal from him, would be under severe pressure as the depression deepened. He was frequently on the road, meeting with customers, large and small, hearing their complaints about service, quality, and prices, and taking orders wherever they could be found. Travel was not easy. Although the St. Paul area had railroad service in several directions by then, schedules had not yet been integrated and equipment was primitive. To the northwest, as far as the head of navigation on the Red River, ran the insolvent St. Paul & Pacific Railroad. The Lake Superior & Mississippi, one of the most important early railroads of the region, ran north to Duluth, and it provided Hill with his cheapest source of coal during the six or seven months that shipping could move on the Great Lakes. To the southwest ran a railroad which was really two companies: one, the St. Paul & Sioux City, had been built toward that important Iowa city, while the other, built northwestward to meet it, had been named the Sioux City & St. Paul. From St. Paul southeastward to many important river cities and to Milwaukee and Chicago ran the Milwaukee & St. Paul, the most important railroad in the Northwest at that early date. And eastward to the St. Croix River country at Stillwater, Minnesota, and Hudson, Wisconsin, where it turned southeast toward Chicago, was the West Wisconsin Railroad, which, like the Sioux City roads, was soon to become a part of the Chicago & North Western system. It was on this railroad that Hill set out via freight train one cold night in March 1874 on a coal-selling trip to Chippewa Falls and Eau Claire. "Arrived at Eau Claire at 5 a.m. Spent all of night in freight car & feel quite tired," he noted in his diary the next day.

His efforts paid off. Of about 40,000 tons of coal which passed through Duluth on its way to St. Paul in 1873, some 15,000 tons were sold through Hill's firm. Two years later the company was selling more of the premium-priced Lackawanna coals than he had sold of all types in 1873. Their sales of such coal amounted to nearly $85,000, and the firm was doing close to a $200,000 business in 1875, at the depth of the depression.[15] Such a volume could never have been handled with the receiving and distribution facilities which had existed in St. Paul just two years earlier. Hill and his partners built alongside the tracks of the Duluth railroad an all-weather coal receiving shed, 60 feet wide and 160 feet long. By protecting their stock from repeated drenching, freezing, and thawing, which tends to degrade coal, they realized a higher net price for it and significantly cut down on the most common consumer complaint—that the customers were paying for "screenings," or pulverized coal which they could not use.

To serve this new facility Hill arranged with the railroad to run a private siding through the street to the structure, and when politicians tried to make capital of this diversion of public property to private use, Hill fought back in the best nineteenth-century style. "Alderman Fisher threatens an injunction to restrain Ry. Co. from putting tracks in front of warehouse. I told Sewell [superintendent of the railroad] to get all ready tonight & lay the track Sunday," he wrote in his diary. At the same time the partners built a receiving dock at Duluth for coal arriving by Lake vessels, with facilities for storing and cleaning it and loading it onto railroad cars. This early bulk-handling Lake-and-rail facility was one of Hill's most important contributions to the energy revolution in the Northwest. Every year as the trees turned scarlet and gold around Duluth, the dock would become the scene of feverish activity as A. C. Jones, Hill's man in charge, tried to squeeze through as much coal as possible before winter set in.[16]

It was a constant struggle to maintain a dependable local delivery service. Whatever doubts we may have in the last quarter of the twentieth century about the motor vehicle's contribution to progress, there can be no doubt that Hill, Saunders, and Acker, working a century ago, would gladly have traded their teams and wagons for motor trucks. Teams would get lame or catch cold and have to remain in the stable all day. Good drivers were hard to get, and the way they treated their teams on the public streets could affect the firm's public relations in an age when Dobbin was man's best friend. "You have a man in your employ who abuses one of your tames very badley [sic]," wrote an irate animal lover. "I think he does not feed or water them. . . . It is a sin and a shame to allow poor dumb animals to suffer. . . . The team I have spoken of one is a gray and the other a dark one. Have him take better care of them and oblige a Friend of dumb animals." Hill gave such teamsters short shrift, for the heavy coal season coincided with the release of men and teams from farm and construction work. "We are offered a good team and driver for the winter for $25 per month and board the man and feed the team," he wrote to Armstrong in Minneapolis. "Now if our teams are costing more, let one of them drop out without delay and we will send this team up. . . ."[17]

The shortage of railroad cars was as much of a problem then as it is today. Coal was usually carried in boxcars, since gondolas were difficult to unload and hopper-bottom cars were as yet unknown. The cars had one-tenth the carrying capacity of today's, with a rated payload of 10 tons, but they were often loaded with 12 tons, especially when a flat rate per carload had been exacted from the railroad. Any evidence that his firm was not getting at least as good treatment as his competitors in the allocation of cars brought instant, indignant reaction from Hill.

Meanwhile, there was constant controversy over weights, for at that time weighing procedures had not been standardized. Hill's firm used the St. Paul public scales for its deliveries, and steadfastly refused to accept claims that short weights were being given, but in their inbound shipments they had constant trouble. Hill picked the brains of a friend at the Northern Pacific Railroad, who told him what the difficulty was. A typical railroad car, he learned, might have as many as four tare weights (the empty weight of the car) painted on them; scales were old, rusty, and generally unreliable; and to save time the railroads tried to weigh loaded cars without uncoupling them as they passed over the scales, which gave spurious results. Ordinary coal dealers might complain about such sloppy practices without result, but Hill, who sometimes found that actual weights ran as much as 3 per cent below the billed weights, demanded and got improvements, to the benefit of all.[18]

The most important development during Hill's last years in the coal business was the trend toward lower railroad rates and the shift away from dependence upon Lake transportation. As each summer waned, Hill devoted a considerable part of his time to a running correspondence with Mark Hanna, pleading for boats to ship as much coal as possible to him from Buffalo, Cleveland, and other Eastern Lake ports. With the arrival of fall, Lake rates shot up because everybody wanted coal to fill out their winter stocks. By the middle of October Hill and Hanna were all but on their knees, begging ship captains to make just one more trip before laying up. But there were more fundamental drawbacks to water transportation. On one occasion an entire vessel was lost, and it was many months before the insurance claim was paid. Hill often had to take more coal in a given shipment than he wanted, because of the comparatively large capacity of a boat, and when it arrived, especially at the end of the season, it was often frozen into one gigantic lump, which A. C. Jones had to find some way to break up. By mid-October Jones and his gangs were working around the clock, Sundays included, unloading coal. One year Jones managed to keep this gelid commerce moving until the incredibly late date of November 29. Then, taking refuge in his little shack at the end of the dock as the weak winter sun sank below the horizon, Jones wrote Hill that the switching engine had frozen up and that pouring boiling water on it did no good. The temperature was −29°F. The season was over.[19]

The railroads were hungry for freight by the mid-1870s. The depression had taught them a bitter lesson: most of a railroad's expenses are fixed, and go right on regardless of the volume of traffic carried. The roads had also made another important discovery: their ability to carry the nation's burden was far greater than had been realized up to that time. The era of high rates and low volume was over. With a relatively modest investment in heavier rail, especially the much tougher steel rails which Andrew Carnegie was turning out at such attractive prices, and with larger rolling stock, more powerful locomotives, and stronger bridges and roadbeds, the tonnage which they could carry was capable of being not merely doubled, but quadrupled and more, and the future promised further vast increases, not only in railroad mileage, but in the carrying capacity of each mile laid down. No one understood these basic economic facts better than James J. Hill, and he took advantage of the situation to beat down rates and shift as much of his inbound coal shipments to rail as possible. Having extracted a flat carload rate from the railroad at Duluth, for example, he encouraged Jones to load 12 tons into each nominally 10-ton car. Sometimes the railroad objected; more and more frequently it pretended not to notice. It was only one of countless ways shippers found to whittle down rates.

Hill preferred to make a frontal attack. By mid-1877 the tonnage he controlled could have made the difference between profit and loss for a railroad like the Chicago & North Western. Hill pointed out to its general freight agent that he could have a good share of 18,000 tons a year when his rates became competitive with Lake-and-rail via Duluth. In any event, the agent had better not give rebates to anybody else if he did not see fit to give them to James J. Hill & Company. "We have only to say that we are protected against such a course and that we all live here and expect to for some time to come," he warned. But a substantial shift toward all-rail transportation was already taking place, even for such a cheap item as gas-making coal. "We have as a general thing bought our coal at Lake Erie ports and taken it by vessel to Duluth but the low rate we have from Chicago would enable us to bring [it] that way provided we can buy at a low figure on cars in Chicago," he told a New York sales agent who was eager to break into the Northwest market. Much coal was coming west on the New York Central, which had so recently priced coal out of the market, and when that line's crack passenger train fell through the bridge at Ashtabula one cold night in December 1876, in one of the most spectacular railroad accidents of the era, the result was a substantial delay in receipts of coal at St. Paul. Demand that winter had far exceeded expectations, and coal was being brought by all-rail routes from as far east as Ohio. Much of this traffic was not to find its way back to the Great Lakes when spring came.

To the disgust of William H. Vanderbilt of the New York Central, the Baltimore & Ohio Railroad had forged ahead with its trunk line to Chicago, completing it in 1874. This development, along with the revitalization of the Erie Railroad during its receivership, caused a major break in through railroad rates between East Coast cities and Chicago, and changed the trunk-line situation into one of active rate competition. "As the B. & O. have their own line into Chicago of course they can give you a rate," Hill wrote a Baltimore dealer in gas-making coal. "If we can get this coal at Chicago at the price named for it at Detroit, we think we can use quite a large amount of it." All of this added up to two decades of sheer hell for the trunk-line railroads, which were not to succeed in stabilizing their rate structures for twenty years, and as a result they suffered bitter condemnation from all sides of Victorian society. One hundred years later the railroads still bear the stigma, but historians have finally come to realize what businessmen of the nineteenth century knew at the time: that this shift from a high- to a low-rate policy, however unseemly and inequitable the process by which it was achieved, transformed the American economy as no other single factor did. James J. Hill had played a vital role in this transformation, and he would continue to do so.[20]

VI

After Chauncey W. Griggs and Hill had decided to go their separate ways, Griggs found himself of secondary importance in the coal business of St. Paul and Minneapolis. This was because Saunders and Armstrong had chosen to make common cause with Hill, who kept the railroads from giving special rates to Griggs. As long as the Easterners were able to maintain the price of anthracite, therefore, the Colonel had no foothold from which to increase his share of the coal market in the Northwest. But by late 1875 Eastern prices had begun to slip, and the railroads were desperate for business. Griggs began a campaign to weaken Saunders's reputation, and word of it quickly reached Mark Hanna. "We are sorry to hear that a war is necessary in the St. Paul coal trade," the Clevelander wrote. "We saw Griggs' letters in Buffalo, in which we see that he has also gone into the *mud* business, throwing it fast at Saunders." Armstrong confirmed that there were similar doings in Minneapolis. "They [Harrison and Knight, local coal dealers] say that Griggs told them that he was after Saunders in this fight, and he has done all he could to poison Harrison against Saunders." Hill sent assurances to the Anthracite Association in Buffalo that his firm would hold fast:

> We have in this market some 7 coal dealers, large and small, and the en-
> tire consumption of hard coal is only about 10,000 or 11,000 tons. While a
> run on coal will cost us some money, still we incline to the belief that we
> will have the market *very* much to ourselves and later in the season we
> can get good sound prices.[21]

And two weeks later he outlined his strategy to the Easterners:

> Griggs has never had any occasion to find fault with the manner in which
> we have treated him. . . . Now his last opportunity with his last cargo
> occurs and he shows his hand fully by trying to break the Mpls market.
> . . . We have concluded to allow him to sell at his figures provided he
> takes no orders for anything more than 300 tons. . . . If he desires to keep
> on at the above prices [as quoted in the advertisement] we will sell at
> same figures. . . . Our idea is to keep the fight in as small a compass as
> possible. We think Griggs is now so sick of the coal business that he will
> let it alone hereafter. . . .[22]

But at that same moment Underhill was sitting at his desk, writing his strong man in St. Paul that events were rapidly moving toward a separation of the men from the boys:

> The war has actually begun! I shall trust the whole campaign to your
> generalship. There can be no back-down on your part. You must adapt
> your methods to theirs somewhat, and not be scared by any price how-
> ever low, but go down to them with good grace. You must wear a smiling
> face, keep up your nerve, and treat your families with tenderest consider-
> ation. . . . I shall feel grieved and ashamed of you if you do not toss up
> the scalps of these offenders into mid-air at the end of the fight.[23]

Hill managed to get a special rate from the Duluth railroad to ease his firm's losses in the price war which ensued, and the Anthracite Association reluctantly made up a part of the losses, but the firm of

Hill, Acker & Saunders took the brunt of the warfare, which lasted into 1876. As the largest and most popular fuel dealer in the area, with the largest stocks of coal on hand, they had to sell much more coal at a loss than their competitors did. Even so, the warring St. Paul businessmen were eager to make peace by early spring of 1876. In March they had all met to discuss pooling arrangements whereby they would split up the Twin Cities market and keep prices up. Hill refused to accept a 35 per cent share for his firm, but a month later agreed to 39 per cent. On April 13 he wrote to Underhill, explaining the new arrangements: Hill and Acker, 39 per cent; Saunders, another 24 per cent; St. Paul Coal Company and Griggs & Johnson, 18.5 per cent each. The Anthracite Association was guaranteed two-thirds of all the hard coal tonnage. On May 30 Hill mailed a letter to "Dear Colonel" assuring him that all was now well. "We feel that everything is going to run smooth and harmonious [sic] and that our sales will aggregate over 40,000 tons this year and the profit will be full." [24]

As a result of the treaty thus concluded, the recently warring Northwestern coal dealers proceeded to cash in on the chaotic state of the economy elsewhere. While they maintained prices of coal at attractive levels, if somewhat down from earlier years, they bought from the Anthracite Association and others at prices reflecting a depression that was beginning to have revolutionary overtones in the industrial areas of the East. The president of the Duluth railroad, in the East for a conference with the executives of the Northern Pacific, with which his railroad was closely allied, wrote Hill, assuring him that their "exclusive contract" would be adhered to and pleading with him not to talk about it in St. Paul, where "considerable 'talk' upon the streets has rather embarrassed us." Hill had promised him 35,000 tons at Duluth if the price was right; otherwise it would come up by rail from the East. Now acting for virtually all of the coal dealers in the Northwest, he applied pressure on the powerful Milwaukee & St. Paul Railroad. There was reason to believe, he said, that dealers in Milwaukee and perhaps Chicago were getting rates which enabled them to sell at certain points just below St. Paul which the Twin Cities men considered their preserve. O. E. Britt, the road's general superintendent, piously protested that no one was getting any such rates as Hill had heard about, and then (in the florid style of the period) proceeded to offer just such rates to the St. Paul combine: "We don't propose to put our hands to the plow and look back. We are passing forward, hunting for nett [sic] earnings. If you want to sell any coal at Red Wing or Hastings you can do so on a $3.50 [per ton] rate, which is as well as anybody does." [25]

By October of 1876 prosperity was returning to the coal business across the country. "The demand for anthracite is far ahead of the supply and it now looks favorable for dealers who have stock," wrote one Eastern shipper to Hill. The Northwestern dealers not only had the stock, thanks to deliveries by rail which made up for deficiencies in Lake transportation, but they also had a strong organization which assured a certain amount of business to everyone, high quality coal and service with a smile for consumers, and absolutely no "bargains." Everyone was delighted with the season's business, and the next spring they came together to form something that was still rare on the business scene in the Twin Cities: a corporation. The Northwestern Fuel Company, incorporated for twenty years with a capitalization of $100,000, began operations on May 1, 1877. Hill was elected president; Griggs was vice president; William Rhodes, Griggs' erstwhile ally, secretary; Acker, treasurer; and Saunders, superintendent of operations.

The Northwestern Fuel Company provided a stable, well-financed, and expertly run instrument by which the people of one of the fastest growing areas of the country could take full advantage of the energy revolution of the nineteenth century. From 1877 until coal was abandoned as a consumer product in the 1940s, the Twin Cities were among the most important fuel distribution centers in the United States. The company's formation was an impressive beginning for the Cities' appearance on the national fuel stage, and the company itself was an equally impressive valedictory to the coal business for James J. Hill. In a little more than a year, true to his prediction to Saunders, he would forsake it for greater things. In barely a decade, at the head of a group of energetic men, he had helped to propel the Northwest into the industrial era. In doing so he had made a good profit, averaging about $8000 a year. Consistently reinvested in the business in good years and bad, these profits in coal eventually provided much of the seed money with which he would enter the railroad business. [26]

VII

"I have much to be thankful for this year. I have had a fairly prosperous business and my wife and five children are all in good health and happy. Spent the evening at the P. H. Kelly's." James J. Hill thus greeted the New Year in 1876. At that moment a similar stock-taking was occurring across the land, for it was America's centennial year. Few had come through the cruel depression of the previous three years as prosperously as Hill, especially in the East, where the rising industrial working class was suffering from unemployment and shrinking wages. Farmers everywhere had seen the high prices of the post-Civil-War era replaced by much lower returns for their labor, and it was not much of a consolation that the prices of nearly everything else were also in a steep decline. None could know it then, but the Western world was entering one of the most complex and confusing periods in modern history, a period in which a high and growing level of economic activity on the one hand would be contrasted with a stubborn, twenty-five-year decline in average prices and a corresponding appreciation in the value of the dollar which would transfer enormous power to those who controlled large amounts of liquid assets. It was to be a period in which the clever, the enterprising, the hardworking, and—not infrequently—the unscrupulous would prosper mightily, while those who sought certainty, security, and stability would look in vain. It was a terrifying, exhilarating time to be alive.

Hill, just turned thirty-seven, was in the prime of life. Although he claimed to have been a 135-pounder, with a 29-inch waist, on his wedding day, he was well on his way back to the "gross huge" 166 pounds to which he had confessed a decade before. Although never overweight by the well-fed standards of his time, he had the long torso and rather short legs which give the impression of burly strength. His hair was going fast, while his beard had not yet reached the patriarchal whiteness which would make him a rather forbidding figure to all but his close friends. The over-all effect was one of great physical power, a valuable asset in the active outdoor work ahead, where he would often find himself shoulder to shoulder with some of the roughest men in a still-rough land. Apart from a tendency for colds (when he got them) to develop into pleurisy, he was seldom sick. One can hardly believe that an insurance company doctor set him down for a high premium rate on his life policy because of an irregular heart beat. No one, it seems, ever suffered from this defect except coffee merchants, whose product Hill thereafter forsook. Through long hours of reading and thousands of words of writing, the one good eye served so well that its owner did not even require eyeglasses in these years.[27]

He had decided at the time of his marriage that a fortune of $100,000, enough to enable him to live the leisurely life of a gentleman, was his ultimate goal. Like Andrew Carnegie, who had also made youthful plans to retire from money-making, Hill passed his established goal without even slowing down to reflect upon the fact. While he had not yet begun to keep the elaborate accounts from which his net worth in the years after 1885 can be easily calculated, it is clear that on the eve of his participation in the acquisition of the St. Paul & Pacific Railroad he had net assets of about $150,000. His interest in Hill, Saunders & Acker, which continued in business until 1878, amounted to $36,000, while his stock in the Northwestern Fuel Company had a par value of $25,000. His most important asset at this time was his share of the Red River Transportation Company, which had a conservative value of $75,000. Personal property and real estate easily brought the total to $150,000.[28]

He was always occupied with a wide variety of business deals in those years. He, Saunders, and Acker continued to deal in a range of staple commodities, as had his earlier companies. On his own account, he frequently purchased the assets of bankrupt businesses and resold them at good profits. When the hapless firm of Corning Depew & Company, iron founders, succumbed to bad times in 1874 he bought the assets at the sheriff's sale for $3600 cash. His sharp eye had detected scrap and pig iron in the storeyard, and it was worth, it turned out, $6600. A little patience and investigation turned up a party who was anxious to go into the iron founding business and who was delighted to buy the valuable set of mold patterns for $2000. The building was disposed of later for $4400 and the boiler and miscellaneous items for $1760. The entire process took about two years, and well repaid his tireless search for buyers and his faith that good times would return. No business was too small or of too dubious social value if its salvage was worthwhile: in 1876 he performed a similar operation on the remains of Brown & Donnelly's saloon. And not even something as prosaic as apple cider, in season, deserved to be ignored for its profit possibilities. At the end of 1875 a general-store proprietor in Maple Plain wrote him to ship another barrel. "The one you sent last is only about half gone. But there is to be a shooting match here near the store on Christmas day [and I] will probably need the cider on that day."[29]

Hill was sickly during the winter and spring of 1873. He had been pushing himself quite hard on his rigorous trips to the Red River country in the dead of winter. Pleurisy was threatening in February, and not even a "Turkish bath" seemed to help. "My good neighbor C. H. Schurmeir died this evening," he noted sadly in his diary as he lay on his own sickbed. A week later he was up, but complained to Doctor Hand about "catarrh in my head." He improved rapidly once his dentist discovered and removed the roots of two teeth which had been pulled some time before. As soon as spring came the family was ready for a change of scenery. He took Mary and five-year-old Mamie to Milwaukee, where they visited friends at the convent where Mary had gone to school. Then they went on to Chicago. They stayed at the New Sherman House, and while Hill talked business, Mary and Mrs. W. G. Swan thoroughly investigated the latest spring fashions.

St. Paul's short, hot summer was in full season by the middle of July, and Mary was expecting again. For the first time, the Hills felt affluent enough to go to a resort for the season. All five Hills and a "nurse girl" boarded the steamer *Clinton* and sailed fifty miles down the Mississippi to Lake Pepin, where they put up at one of the Hotel Frontenac's cottages. Hill, always the careful spender, noted in his diary that "They rate my family, exclusive of myself, as three persons." For the rest of the summer he went down on Fridays by boat or by the new railroad line which the Milwaukee Railroad was building along the river, returning Sunday evenings by boat, which he often found uncomfortably hot. Breaking away from the office posed the same problems encountered by later generations of "summer bachelors." One Saturday he had to remain in St. Paul for the meeting of the State Agricultural Association. Missing both the boat and the passenger train, he hitched a ride on the freight train which got to Frontenac at 10:30 that evening. The bill for the season, which ended September 5, came to $319.40. The Hills would see more elegant resorts in later years, but they loved Lake Pepin, with its legend of the Indian maid who jumped to her death from the high rock above the lake rather than be separated from her lover who, inevitably, belonged to another tribe. That summer Hill commissioned a local artist to paint "a moonlight view of Maiden Rock with sunset effect as seen from the Hotel at Frontenac Aug. 7th. Cost framed and packed $100." It hung in their bedroom for years, and, long after, "Lake Pepin by Moonlight" would grace the walls of their eldest son's New York apartment.[30]

Sitting before the fire on the evening of December 3, 1873, he read, while Mary, feeling better than she had for some time, made a flannel skirt for little Louis, who was still in dresses. Both enjoyed such moments, which seemed to become rarer as his interests grew, and their bedtime, 11:30, was late for those early-rising years. At one o'clock Mary called her husband, who sent for Mrs. Gooden, the nurse, and Dr. Hand. "A little girl was safely born at 3:30 a.m. this Thursday, December 4th," the sleepy father wrote in his diary. It was more than two months before Mary felt well enough to attend mass, but she was present, along with her sister Anna and brother-in-law, James Phelps, and neighbor Henry Upham, when Clara Anna Hill was baptized by Father Caillet on January 11. As times got better they talked about the new house they were planning to replace the cottage at Ninth and Canada, where the block was filling up fast with close friends like the Uphams and the Gotzians. They were already living on a comfortable, upper-middle-class scale, as Mary's household accounts, which totaled over $400 in April 1874, attest. She managed the house in the conviction that the less notice her husband took of domestic affairs the better, but he did not always think much of her choice of domestic help. "The cook left this a.m., for which I am thankful," he growled in his diary one Sunday.[31]

The thermometer registered −27°F. on the evening of January 27, 1873, but that did not keep the Hills from going to hear Ignatius Donnelly deliver his famous lecture on "The Authorship of the Plays of Shakespeare," and a few weeks later when they went to the Opera House to hear Mrs. Scott Siddons read selections from the same plays, they were "highly pleased both with her reading and appearance." The following year, curious to see a feminist close up, Hill went by himself to hear a lecture on "Political Matters Unmasked," by Victoria Claflin Woodhull. "Aside from her good and fluent delivery," he noted grudgingly, "the entire lecture was disgusting and unclean." Like the Women's Liberation leaders a hundred years later, Mrs. Woodhull inspired strong *ad hominem* criticism. When Hill shared a railroad coach with her a few days later he wrote in his diary, "Victoria C. Woodhull, the female champion of Free Love & Free Lust on the train from Hudson [Wisconsin] to St. Paul. She apparently is an unchaste Charlatan whose aim is notoriety with an eye single as to what she can make out of it." There were more uplifting things to do, however, and he took Mary, Annie Phelps, and Mrs. George Acker to a concert of sacred music at St. Mary's Church and to other musicales that winter.[32]

Defeat in the race for alderman of St. Paul in 1870 ended Hill's brief career in politics. His mother, who was visiting them at the time, wit-

tily condemned the obtuseness of the electorate, but her son realized
that a person with his blunt, matter-of-fact personality, could make
his best contribution to politics from behind the scenes. A life-long
Democrat of the conservative, pre-Bryan variety, Hill did some of the
paper work in the congressional elections of 1876 and 1878, helped
raise campaign contributions, and ended up lending $2000 to W. M.
McNair of Minneapolis, the unsuccessful congressional candidate, in
1876. Hill showed a spectacular lack of political acumen when he
threw his influence behind McNair for the nomination over Knute
Nelson, whom he considered to have only ethnic appeal, for the Norwegian immigrant was on the threshold of a brilliant career that would
carry him to the United States Senate.[33]

Horses were much more fun than politics. William Henry Vanderbilt, the richest man in the world, had his Gentlemen's Driving Park
in New York's Bronx; these Westerners had theirs, too, which Hill had
helped to organize and run. He bred his sorrel mare to a local Hamble-
tonian trotter, officiated at races (which drew 2000 spectators on the
Fourth of July, 1873), and, as steward of the club, checked conscientiously into the pedigree of both horse and owner when an outsider
sought to enter the contests. When the bank went looking for someone
to make good on the Driving Park's note, they knew just where to
go.[34]

The ties with Rockwood slipped away. Anne Dunbar Hill, so bright,
witty, and determinedly optimistic, seemed to age rapidly as she approached her seventy-first birthday in 1876. As thoughtless as ever
where money was concerned, she was a burden to Alec, whose farming and schoolteaching brought in little enough for his own family.
Their sister Mary's large brood were beginning to grow up, and the
question of what James Brooks, the eldest boy, should make of himself
was worrisome. Hill sent his periodic contribution to the two women
in care of Alec. "Mother is well but I don't think she ought to get all
the money at once as she does not take good care of it," Alec reported,
adding that she resented having it doled out to her. "I gave Mary
some and am applying $50 to paying for her son's instructions in tele-
graphing. I got him in at the station in Rockwood by paying $50 to the
agent to learn [*sic*] him." One summer James J. invited Alec and his
wife to visit them in St. Paul, and he got them a pass from the Lake
shipping company so that they could make the leisurely trip from Sarnia, Ontario, through Lakes Huron and Superior to Duluth. A week
before Christmas 1876, not quite a quarter of a century after her hus-

band, Anne Dunbar Hill died. Their two sons, lingering in the little graveyard next to the Everton Christian Church where the funeral service had been held, were pleased to note that Anne and James Hill were resting side by side. Next to them lay Alec's first wife, and the younger man was content to know that he would one day rest there too. That evening the two brothers sat talking and smoking in the parlor of the old home. From his coat pocket James took some sheets of paper on which were many figures pertaining to bonds of the St. Paul & Pacific Railroad. He asked Alec, who had always been proud of his own head for figures, how much money he thought would be required to take over the railroad. About five million dollars, calculated the thoroughly impressed younger brother. James J. left next day. He never came back to Rockwood again.[35]

Throughout these years Hill was becoming deeply involved in the acquisition of coal lands in Webster County, near the town of Fort Dodge, in north-central Iowa. By 1877 he had invested several thousand dollars in the drilling operations which were being carried on there by Hamilton Browne, the enthusiastic son of the federal land commissioner in the area. There was coal there, as Hill had long known from his reading of Macfarlane's geological treatise. As far as anyone knew then it was the most northerly point to which deposits of useful coal extended, and by building less than a hundred miles of railroad northeastward, connections could be made with railroads serving the Twin Cities, thus reducing their dependence on Eastern sources. It was a soft coal which Iowa produced, good only for burning under boilers. Why should Hill be interested in such a coal? His letter of February 4, 1873, to Browne, reporting on the results of tests of a sample, contains the answer:

> I have put the car of coal to good use. Had several of the stationary engines try it and also had Supt. Lincoln of the Sioux City RR try it under a stationary boiler and on two locomotives. In every single case it gave entire satisfaction and proved itself superior to the ordinary western coal.

If Hill had his way, the demand for locomotive coal in the Northwest was going to boom in the next few years. As usual, he chose to control events rather than let them control him.[36]

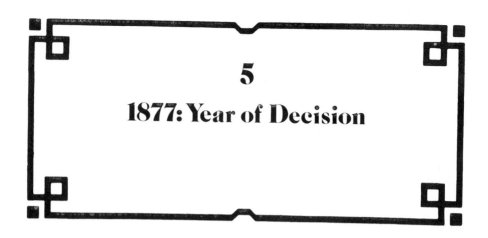

5

1877: Year of Decision

The early development of the Red River Valley, the Black Hills and the Upper Missouri will make this railway one of the very best paying roads in this country. I have the greatest confidence in the enterprise and am willing to assume personal liability for the amount.

—Norman W. Kittson, 1877

I

Captain E. V. Holcombe, who was in charge of the five steamboats which the Red River Transportation Company operated between Fisher's Landing and Winnipeg, found himself with an entire day to kill in late August of 1877. It gave him plenty of time to brood over his problems. The water level in the river was low, and falling. If he did not keep a sharp eye on the men who were loading his boat at the landing with goods bound for points north of the end of the railroad, they would overload it. He would then have to go through the tiresome, undignified process of hauling the boat over the shallow places with a line looped around a tree on the bank and wound on his own capstan. It had been a poor season, for the grasshoppers had reappeared. They had eaten everything but the beet tops, for which they had no taste, and the promising wheat crop had been much reduced. All of this, however, was not enough to explain the long, gloomy, and slightly reproachful letter which Holcombe wrote his employer, James J. Hill, that evening. Sitting at a desk in Fargo's Headquarters Hotel, he filled page after page of his writing tablet with thoughts of the future. "The business of the River is gradually undergoing change," he noted, "which I can see better here than my employers can being located in St. Paul. Not to be caught with a lot of unavailable property on hand when the *great change* comes is the problem."

The captain had just come from St. Paul, where he had hoped to get instructions from his employers on how elaborately they wished to prepare for next year's season. "I had hoped to have seen more of you when in St. Paul," he complained. The great increase in immigration during the summer of 1877 was all the more remarkable in view of the grasshopper plague, but he doubted that his recommendation for an extra passenger boat would meet with much enthusiasm. Still a relatively young man, Holcombe had had many years experience as a riverboat captain, and had moved from the Mississippi to the Red when Hill and Kittson had made navigation on that stream a practical reality. It was all too clear, however, that his talents would soon be extraneous to the transportation picture in the Northwest.[1]

Holcombe's depression was hardly irrational. It was common gossip in St. Paul that Hill, Kittson, and what the newspapers referred to as "some of the heaviest capitalists in Canada" were working on a scheme to buy up the bankrupt St. Paul & Pacific Railroad and complete it to St. Vincent, on the Canadian border, where it would connect with the branch of the new Canadian Pacific Railway, then being built south from Winnipeg. Hill wrote the captain an immediate reply, assuring him that there were at least two more seasons (1878 and 1879) of navigation remaining on the river, but he did not bother to deny the rumors.[2] People who did not know Hill personally professed to be surprised when he burst so suddenly into the affairs of the much-abused railroad, but his close friends were not. "I heard him constantly speak of it," Henry P. Upham recalled, "from early in 1874 . . . daily and weekly. . . . It was a matter that he incessantly talked about. . . . The nearest I can come to fixing a date when these conversations commenced is prior to May 2, 1874 . . . at the old [Minnesota] Club house on 8th St. . . ." More than one person, in fact, could recall seeing Hill, index finger stabbing the air in the general region of his listener's midsection, lecturing Kittson or whomever he could find on his favorite topic.[3]

Hill had really been in the railroad business almost from the moment he helped drag the *William Crooks* off the river barge at St. Paul. No one knew better than he the savings to be realized from the replacement of earlier forms of transportation with continuous rail service from St. Paul to Winnipeg, especially after the capital of Minnesota itself had achieved all-rail service to Chicago in 1867. He well knew that the Red River Transportation Company, from which he and Kittson had made so much money at the depth of a great national depression, was a mere transitional development. After 1873, as the need to establish coal as the standard fuel in both cities and towns of the Northwest became apparent, the demand for through railroad transportation to the north had also become critical in his eyes.

More than anything else, however, it was the growing stream of immigrants to the Red River country, which seemed almost ready to back up all the way to the East Coast for want of adequate transportation to the valley, that caught Hill's imagination. He had perceived something which few others were aware of and none articulated: a railroad into the valley could save settlers not just a few months, but virtually an entire year. Because the boats had to wait until mid-April for the river to be free of ice, settlers arrived on the ground too late to put in a cash crop of grain. This meant that the capital cost of settling in the valley was increased by the amount needed to sustain a family for a whole year. It was Hill's ability to perceive not merely the minor, obvious advantages of a railroad, but the truly revolutionary nature of basic transportation improvements, which set him apart from most of his contemporaries.

During his twenty years in St. Paul Hill had made himself the best expert on railroad economics in the Northwest. Constant poking around the properties of the St. Paul & Pacific and other railroads, and a decade of critical observation of the more highly developed lines between Chicago and New York, had given him a practical knowledge of the physical side of railroading which was seldom found in one with neither formal engineering training nor long years of experience in railroad construction and operation. He had long since come to understand the most important fact about railroading: the combination of the self-propelled vehicle and the iron rail roadway was a unique and virtually universal solution to the problem of inland transportation, because a locomotive pulling a train of loaded cars on a low-friction track was far cheaper than any other form of land transportation, and the rails could go almost anywhere.

Hill had followed the progress of the St. Paul & Pacific closely since its inception, and his papers contain many documents which he acquired, in one way or another, to enable him to master the intricacies of its legal and financial history. The critical year was 1872, when one of the two companies making up the railroad was placed in receivership after defaulting on the interest on its bonds. Before that date there had been no place for Hill in the picture, no matter how great his railroading talents. Until 1870 the road had been in the apparently competent hands of George L. Becker, the local man who was its president, and E. B. Litchfield, a highly successful Eastern railroad contractor who, with his brothers, had undertaken to complete the St. Paul & Pacific to the head of navigation on the Red River and, eventually, to the international boundary at St. Vincent. When these gentlemen failed in their mission, the day had been saved, or so it seemed, by William Moorhead of the Northern Pacific, who had finally convinced Jay Cooke that the St. Paul & Pacific was vital to the interests of the road which they themselves were building from Duluth to the Pacific Ocean. Few railroad enterprises have so consistently failed to comprehend their true interests as the Northern Pacific, which only looked upon the St. Paul & Pacific as a road which would feed traffic to its main east-west line at Brainerd, in central Minnesota, and Glyndon, near the Red River. But in 1870 the Northern Pacific was (apparently) a powerful organization, well-financed by the celebrated Jay Cooke, who had helped finance the Civil War for the federal government, and after it gained control of the St. Paul & Pacific in 1870 the little railroad's future seemed to have been settled. The combination of Becker, Litchfield, and the Northern Pacific people, of whom Moorhead was the most sensible, succeeded in completing the "main line" of the St. Paul & Pacific to Breckenridge, at the head of navigation on the Red River, and the "branch line" to Melrose, about thirty-five miles west of St. Cloud, at the point where the road crossed the upper Mississippi River.

The most important development during the Northern Pacific's stewardship was the so-called St. Vincent Extension, for which special legislative provision, including a further land grant, had been made some years before. Logically a continuation of the St. Paul & Pacific's main line from Breckenridge to the boundary, the Extension was to be exploited by the Northern Pacific as merely a north-south "feeder" for its main line to Duluth, so it was built north from Barnesville, a few miles south of Glyndon, where it intersected the Northern Pacific. The southern end of the Extension was deliberately left unconnected with the main line of the St. Paul & Pacific at Breckenridge. The Northern Pacific's idea was that traffic for the Red River country ought, in season at least, to come by the Great Lakes to Duluth, by the Northern

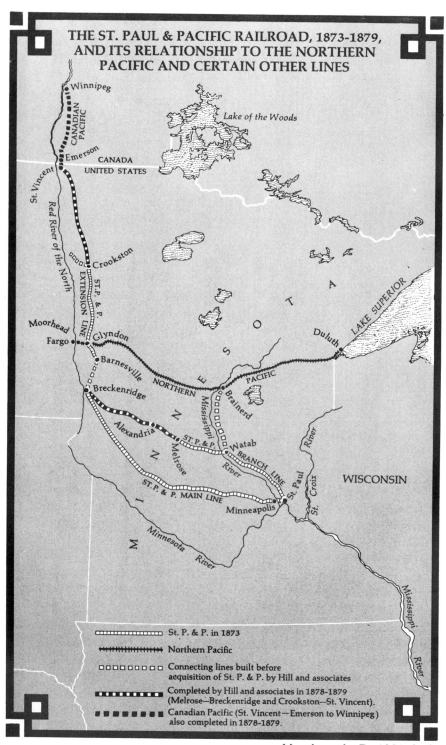

THE ST. PAUL & PACIFIC RAILROAD, 1873-1879, AND ITS RELATIONSHIP TO THE NORTHERN PACIFIC AND CERTAIN OTHER LINES

Winnipeg

CANADIAN PACIFIC

Emerson

St. Vincent

CANADA
UNITED STATES

Lake of the Woods

Red River of the North

Crookston

ST. P. & P. EXTENSION LINE

Moorhead
Fargo
Glyndon

Barnesville

Breckenridge

NORTHERN PACIFIC

MINNESOTA

Mississippi River

Brainerd

Duluth

LAKE SUPERIOR

Alexandria

ST. P. & P.

Watab

Melrose

BRANCH LINE

River

St. Paul

St. Croix River

WISCONSIN

ST. P. & P. MAIN LINE

Minneapolis

MINNESOTA

Minnesota River

Mississippi River

	St. P. & P. in 1873
	Northern Pacific
	Connecting lines built before acquisition of St. P. & P. by Hill and associates
	Completed by Hill and associates in 1878-1879 (Melrose—Breckenridge and Crookston—St. Vincent).
	Canadian Pacific (St. Vincent — Emerson to Winnipeg) also completed in 1878-1879.

Map drawn by David Lindroth.

Pacific to Glyndon, and then north on the Extension; and traffic which stubbornly insisted on coming via St. Paul, as more and more did, could proceed northeasterly via the Lake Superior & Mississippi Railroad (soon to be renamed the St. Paul & Duluth) to a junction with the Northern Pacific a few miles outside Duluth, and then westward and northward on the Northern Pacific and the Extension line. Such a patently impractical arrangement would be replaced before long, or so it was believed, by an extension of the St. Paul & Pacific's branch line north from St. Cloud to Brainerd. The entire strategy was one of subordinating the St. Paul & Pacific and the Twin Cities to the interests of the Northern Pacific, which continued to think of itself as a grand transcontinental railroad between the Great Lakes and the Pacific Ocean.

So little did Cooke and the president of the line, J. Gregory Smith, both absentee managers, think of St. Paul as the major terminal of the Northern Pacific that they never quite got around to building the Brainerd connection. Had they done so they would have had a continuous short line from St. Paul to Crookston, only sixty-two miles from the international boundary. The St. Paul & Pacific would have become merely the eastern terminus of a much stronger Northern Pacific than the one which Cooke and his successors eventually built, and the Great Northern would never have come into being. But the Northern Pacific's early promoters could never rid themselves of the notion that the way to make money in railroads was not in operating them, but in securing and selling off the lands which had been granted in support of construction. That is why they pushed construction of the Extension, which had extremely valuable grants in the promising Red River Valley, while neglecting the Brainerd connection, which would have made the Northern Pacific a rational railroad.[4]

The Northern Pacific failed as the instrument for completing the St. Paul & Pacific because the Northern Pacific was itself a house of cards. If Smith's management had matched Cooke's financing skills, the railroad might have succeeded in its original objective: reaching the Missouri River at Bismarck, Dakota Territory, and cashing in on its enormous land grant before the Panic of 1873. But expenditures got out of control during the early years, Cooke himself was brought to ruin by making enormous short-term loans to the mismanaged company, and by 1873 the Northern Pacific, unable to avoid its own bankruptcy, was out of the picture. The St. Paul & Pacific was left lying, a shattered but sill valuable piece of railroad crockery, waiting for someone to pick up the pieces. When it had defaulted on the interest on some of its bonds in 1872 the court had appointed a receiver to manage the property, conserve its assets, and complete the construction of the Extension line if he could find a way to work such a miracle in the depression which had begun. But during the 1860s, in a legal maneuver to give the railroad more flexibility in borrowing money, all of the then existing railroad line was conveyed to a second company, the First Division of the St. Paul & Pacific Railroad. When E. B. Litchfield had taken on the job of completing the main and branch lines, he had acquired all of the common stock of the First Division in part payment for his services and subsequently transferred it conditionally to the Northern Pacific. If someone else did not salvage the St. Paul & Pacific, Litchfield might.[5]

The First Division had floated about $11 million of a huge bond issue of $15 million, which, in the madcap finance of the era, netted the railroad barely $5 million. Most of the buyers of these bonds were Dutchmen, who were eager for a high-interest security that also held out the possibility of long-term appreciation because of future profits from the land grants. Prudently, or so they thought, they had held back enough of the proceeds of the loan from the railroad company to guarantee that they would get their interest for the first three years. When relations with the Northern Pacific first caused acrimony over the divergent interests of the two railroads, and then collapsed altogether, the Dutchmen were anxious to get their property, as they thought of it, under the protection of a receiver as soon as possible. But it was not their property, at least not yet. It belonged to E. Darwin Litchfield, the London financier, who had reclaimed the family's common stock from the Northern Pacific, which had been unable to carry through their conditional purchase contract. Since the First Division would not be in arrears on the bonds for two more years, the court, not unaware of the strong anti-Dutch sentiment which was building up in Minnesota, refused the foreigners' application for the appointment of a receiver. The horrified Hollanders sought to compromise with Litchfield under an agreement which, had the requisite 90 per cent of the bondholders ratified it, might well have given him permanent control of the company. Litchfield wanted a compromise very badly, realizing perhaps that the foreclosure suits which had been instituted under the mortgage provisions of the bonds would hold his equity at naught if they were ever settled by the courts. He therefore agreed to allow the bondholders majority representation on the board of directors. As soon as the First Division was six months in arrears on its interest, however, John S. Kennedy, a New York banker with great skill in such matters, invoked the provisions of the mortgage which put the trustees, of whom he was one, in charge. Shadow-boxing though this all may seem, the "Litchfield agreement," which acknowledged his nominal ownership of the First Division, made Litchfield a factor to be reckoned with.

The railroad, meanwhile, was in poor physical condition, but it was making a little money and promised to make more. The receiver, J. P. Farley, a plodding, semi-literate man in his sixties, took charge of the First Division as general manager under the trustees. Farley was a tactless man, and may have been suffering from the beginnings of senility, but his conservatism and deliberate methods seemed to work well when applied to sickly railroads. He proceeded to improve the property as his limited funds would allow. Since it made little sense to have the Extension stop in the middle of the prairie north of Crookston, he went along with a bright idea which Hill gave him. The Extension had been built about ten miles east of the Red River, which regularly flooded the adjoining land each spring, and it had been necessary to transfer freight by wagon between the railroad and the steamboats. Hill and Kittson formed the Red River Valley Railroad, taking care to avoid being further branded as "monopolists" in the Valley by remaining off the board of directors, and reimbursed Farley for taking up ten miles of rails north of Crookston and laying them westward to a place called Fisher's Landing, a short distance up the Red Lake River from the point where it flowed into the Red. Now, if a thirty-three-mile link could be built between the end of the main line at Breckenridge and the southern end of the Extension line at Barnesville, there would be a continuous railroad all the way from St. Paul to Fisher's Landing on the Red River. Hill and Kittson had expected that their little Red River Valley Railroad would also undertake this link, but the Dutchmen, who had been smarting under massive criticism from Minnesota politicians, submitted to an assessment, and Farley completed the link in 1877.[5]

By the end of 1877 the St. Paul & Pacific held out great promise to anyone who could get hold of it and guide it through the obstacle course which lay before it. It had to complete the Extension and branch lines soon, or forfeit the land grants which, in a country so ripe for settlement, were clearly going to be worth a great deal more per acre than the uninhabited plains which the Northern Pacific had touted so loudly to investors. It had to find as much as $500,000 to satisfy unpaid contractors who had built the Extension line or see the Minnesota legislature give these men some of the railroad's lands instead. The Litchfield claims, which were legally dubious but capable of tying the company up in lengthy, costly litigation, had to be settled. And the Northern Pacific, which was coming back strong after its bankruptcy and had no intention of being frozen out of a St. Paul gateway that now began to look absolutely indispensable to their plans, would have to be dealt with. Who could do all these things? Not Farley. He could barely get along with the Dutchmen, taking it as a personal affront that they sent their own representative to oversee his work, and he could not get along at all with contractors like William Crooks and William Moorhead, whom the railroad owed more than just money. Not the Dutchmen. Their standing in the eyes of Minnesota politicians was about as low as it could go, and they had no agent through whom the railroad could be completed and skillfully managed. Certainly not Litchfield, who merely wished to cash in his stock at the right moment for the greatest amount it would bring. It had to be done by local people, men who had the full support of the community, who knew just what needed to be done and who had the skill to do it, and who had or could raise the money to buy the Dutchmen out of this miserable situation into which their greedy investments had got them. It turned out to be not one man, but five who would resolve the situation and, just as prosperity returned to the nation, would give Minnesota and Manitoba the transportation facilities for which their people had so long yearned.

II

The Litchfields might see the St. Paul & Pacific as an easy way to increase their already substantial wealth. The Northern Pacific might see it as an expedient for achieving its grandiose designs west of the Red River. Even James J. Hill might emphasize the tremendous savings in the cost of development of northwestern Minnesota and the handsome profits to flow therefrom. But to two men who had been intimately connected with the flow of commerce on the north-south axis between St. Paul and Manitoba, and between eastern and western Canada, the railroad would eliminate transportation hardships which they had wrestled with for most of their lives. Norman Wolfred Kittson, one of Hill's oldest and closest friends, was St. Paul's leading citi-

James J. Hill in 1878, aged 40, about the time the associates assumed control of the St. Paul & Pacific Railroad. Photograph by Zimmerman, St. Paul.

zen and the very embodiment of the fast-growing city's northward thrust. Born in Canada, he had been a citizen of the United States for many years. For most of his career he had been an antagonist of the Hudson's Bay Company, working first for the American Fur Company and later for himself. As a fur trader at Pembina, just south of the international boundary, he had represented the spirit of free trade between the future state of Minnesota and the province of Manitoba, and since 1854 had lived in St. Paul, which he had served as mayor in 1858–59. Dignified and courtly, remarkably easy in his relations with others, he had made a good deal of money in St. Paul real estate and his tentative entry into the Red River steamboat business on behalf of the Hudson's Bay Company had blossomed into a substantial addition to his fortune after he formed the partnership with Hill. In 1877 he was sixty-three, in poor health, and not eager to spend another winter in St. Paul. But he had one more role to play in the history of the Northwest, and it would be his most important. No more serious obstacle stood in the way of anyone who would take over the St. Paul & Pacific than the anti-Dutch attitude of politicians who threatened legal and legislative actions which would vastly complicate any orderly transfer of control such as Hill had in mind. If an antidote to this xenophobic sentiment was needed, there would be found no more powerful one than Norman W. Kittson.

Donald Alexander Smith was the Canadian counterpart of Kittson in the activities of the "associates," as the men who joined to take over the St. Paul & Pacific came to be called. Born in Scotland in 1820, he had come to Canada at the age of eighteen as an employee of the Hudson's Bay Company. He had spent much time in the future province of Manitoba, knew the Red River country well, and was thoroughly acquainted with the realities of Canada's transportation problems. In 1870 he had become Chief Commissioner of the Hudson's Bay Company, and, as a member of both the Manitoba and the Dominion parliaments, he was one of the most authoritative voices in the debates over the various schemes to bind eastern and western Canada together. John A. Macdonald, leader of the Conservative party, detested Smith, who had denounced him on the floor of the Canadian parliament for his role in the "Pacific scandal," which had torpedoed the Dominion's first effort to build a transcontinental railroad. But the episode had vastly increased Smith's prestige in Canada and had placed him, a Conservative, beyond the stigma of partisan politics.

Hill knew that once the associates had control of the St. Paul & Pacific, they would have virtually a free hand in developing it in the most rational manner. But the railroad he had in mind would be an international organization, in fact if not by law, and it was just as important to control the situation north of the boundary as south of it. To the north they would be dealing with a government bureaucracy, with all that that meant in red tape, delays, interposition of political expedients, and the rest. Smith's position in Canadian politics, despite Macdonald's bad feeling, might make the difference between success and failure in Hill's plans. For Hill wanted much more from the Canadians than a railroad from the boundary at St. Vincent (or Emerson, as the settlement on the Canadian side of the line was called) to Winnipeg. He had hopes that the Dominion would ignore the insistence of impractical politicians that Canada must have her own all-Canada railroad north of Lake Superior, and concentrate her all-too-slender resources, instead, on a railroad built westward across the vast, fertile plains between Winnipeg and Puget Sound. What Hill foresaw for the St. Paul & Pacific, in short, was a double role: as carrier of traffic between the Twin Cities and Winnipeg through the Red River Valley, and as the key link in a "trans-Canadian" railroad route which would lie within the territorial limits of the United States, between Sault Sainte Marie on the east and St. Vincent on the west.[6]

James J. Hill had met Donald Smith for the first time on Christmas Day 1869, in St. Paul, where Smith had paused on his way to Fort Garry to treat with Riel and his rebels. They had talked about the need for better transportation on the north-south axis, and when Hill, northbound late that same winter, ran into Smith again on the prairie they talked further about what needed to be done. There were meetings again in 1873 and 1874, when Smith, making his annual spring trip to the parliamentary sessions at Ottawa, was the guest of the Hills in St. Paul. By then, he told Hill, the Dutch had broached the possibility that the Hudson's Bay Company would take over their beleaguered railroad. "I considered the idea of acquiring the road originated with myself," Smith later recalled, "and that it was at my instance in 1873 and early in 1874 that Mr. Kittson acted in getting all the information he possibly could. . . . It was in no sense the proposition of Mr. Kittson and Mr. Hill in the first instance. . . ."[7]

There was enough glory for both Smith and Hill, eventually. Smith had yearned for possession of the road since the moment there had been a Dominion of Canada to weld together and, not incidentally, since the Hudson's Bay Company had received nine million acres of land upon surrender of its rights to Prince Rupert's Land. But Hill had coveted it at least since it became clear that the Litchfield/Northern Pacific/Dutch stewardship was a failure. Smith dealt with Kittson at first, but the information Kittson gave him came from Hill. The 1873

TWO OF THE ASSOCIATES: THE PIONEERS.

and 1874 dealings which Smith recalled involved the question of acquiring the branch line which ran from St. Anthony to St. Cloud, and
building to a junction with the Northern Pacific at Brainerd. Hill, Kittson, and several others actually secured a charter for such a railroad
link in 1874. In return for trackage rights over this Western Railroad of
Minnesota, as it was to be called, the Northern Pacific offered the incorporators all of the capital stock in the First Division—not a very
grand offer, since the Northern Pacific had not secured clear title to the
stock. These arrangements, toward which Hill was never more than
lukewarm, would have subordinated the St. Paul & Pacific to the
Northern Pacific, so it was fortunate that Smith was unable to interest
any of his "heavy capitalists" in Canada in the undertaking. Four
years later they would be able to take over the entire railroad and give
Minnesota and Manitoba the kind of railroad service their people
wanted with a minimum of interference from the muddled Northern
Pacific promoters.[8]

LEFT Norman W. Kittson, about 1878.

ABOVE Donald A. Smith (later First Baron Strathcona and Mount Royal) in 1871, two years after Hill met him. Notman Photographic Archives, McCord Museum, McGill University, Montreal.

Hill continued to gather information on the legal, financial and legislative tangle in which the St. Paul & Pacific was involved, and by 1876 could see that the time was fast approaching when the lengthy impasse would be resolved. Also, the truth was dawning on the Dutchmen that they would be lucky to salvage only part of their investment in the bonds of the railroad. Francis R. Delano, former superintendent of the St. Paul & Pacific, rose to his feet in the Minnesota House of Representatives on February 23, 1875, to fan the flames of prejudice against the foreigners, and the lawmakers passed an Act transferring part of the land grant to DeGraff & Company, one of the unpaid contractors on the Extension line, if their claims were not otherwise settled.[9] John S. Kennedy, trustee in the mortgages which the bondholders were trying to foreclose against the St. Paul & Pacific, and representative in the United States of a committee which the Dutchmen had formed to protect their dwindling interests, was aghast at the thought of where this kind of anti-Dutch feeling could lead. He wrote to the chairman of the Minnesota House's Committee on Railroads early in 1875:

> Relying upon the representations made regarding the value of the property by its managers, . . . the Dutch public bought these bonds to the amount of about $11,000,000. . . . The purchasers of these bonds comprise over six hundred individuals, nearly all of whom are persons of moderate circumstances—small farmers and trades people, who believed they were investing their savings in a reliable American enterprise. . . .

> To all intents and purposes the enterprise was abandoned, and its affairs in utter confusion. There was no one in the country who had any pecuniary interest in the property, or who would acknowledge any responsibility for or on account of it. . . .[10]

The implications were clear. If a responsible and competent party should enter the picture prepared to pay the Dutchmen a fair price for their bonds, they would do well to entertain any offer he might make. Hill was already on this trail. Clearly, the Dutchmen possessed the only equity that existed in the railroad, and, since they had deposited a majority of all classes of bonds with a committee and authorized it to negotiate for them, the time had come to take a look at the price tag on this most interesting merchandise. Hill's source of information at the St. Paul & Pacific offices warned him that E. D. Litchfield intended to make trouble, but the future railroad magnate might have responded that when it came to placing obstacles in the way of what he hoped to bring off, there were plenty who would make trouble, so Litchfield would just have to get in line with the others.[11] Hill was fortunate to have a neighbor, C. Klein, who not only had come from Holland, but was related by marriage to one of the partners in Chemet & Wetjen, one of the banking firms which represented the Dutch bondholders. Klein translated letters and Dutch financial periodicals for Hill and delivered messages for him when he was in London.[12] Matters rested for the most part, Hill learned, with one Johan Carp, a prosperous manufacturer from Utrecht, who headed the bondholders' committee. He would be coming to the United States sometime in 1876. Meanwhile, Hill might get an idea of the possible sale price from Kennedy or his partner, John S. Barnes, but he realized that before any definite steps could be taken he had to make formal common cause with Donald Smith.

Smith was in Ottawa in March 1878, attending a session of the Dominion Parliament, when Hill decided the time had come to take action. At Smith's home, "Bank Cottage," over a leisurely breakfast which lasted until the member had to leave for the day's session, they discussed the situation. Smith agreed to proceed on the best lines Hill could work out, and indicated that he felt sure he could raise whatever funds were needed by buy the Dutchmen's bonds. Hill had reason to believe that Smith could do it. Sir John Rose, governor of the Hudson's Bay Company, would need little assurance of the importance of the acquisition to both Canada and the company, Smith believed, and Sir John was a partner in Morton, Rose & Company, one of the largest banking houses in London.

Elated, Hill returned to St. Paul. On the train out of Chicago he ran into his old friend, Stanford Newel, and proceeded to tell him all over again, and at length, of the possibilities in the St. Paul & Pacific. Then he got to talking with a genial, portly gentleman who turned out to be "Captain" John S. Barnes, partner of John S. Kennedy and absentee president of the First Division, who was going out to St. Paul to look the situation over. "Mr. Barnes was anxious to learn all he could," Hill recalled. "He asked a great many questions. I remember Mr. Newel remarking to me that he thought Mr. Barnes was industriously using his pump and that he hadn't got any information I didn't want him to have." Barnes remained in St. Paul for several weeks, during which time Hill tried to get him to suggest a price at which the Dutch bondholders might be willing to sell. Barnes was not talking at that stage, but he was clearly interested in this possible escape hatch for his Dutch clients, and he promised to keep Hill informed of developments.[13]

III

Throughout the year 1876, while the nation celebrated its centennial and nervously faced the future, James J. Hill fretted under the frustrations of poor communications and the law's delay. He was greatly pleased when the Legislature passed a law making it possible for the bondholders of a railroad chartered in the state to take over and reorganize a bankrupt railroad and inherit, unimpaired in any way, the land grants made to the original corporation. This served only to whet his appetite for the St. Paul & Pacific even more, but, shrewd trader that he was, he knew it was pointless to consider making an offer to the Dutch committee for the bonds until he had some idea of how low a price they might entertain. And so he busied himself with other things. The coal business in the Twin Cities was at a critical stage; perhaps it was a good thing that Hill was free to cultivate the sentiments which led to the combination of the leading companies in the Northwestern Fuel Corporation.

That summer death drove other thoughts from his mind. It was little Katie, his youngest child, not quite a year old. She had been a frail, delicate baby at birth, and worry about her had taxed Mary's own uncertain health. As soon as the hot, humid weather of the Eastern seaboard gave way to a golden October he took Mary on the first visit she had made to New York since she had left there as a little girl a quarter of a century before, and to the Centennial Exposition in Philadelphia. As the train crossed the state of Ohio they got a good look at the Republican candidate for President, Governor Rutherford B. Hayes, who was on their train, and between Cleveland and Pittsburgh they saw the disappointed runner-up for the nomination, James G. Blaine.[14]

Late in the year word came that Johan Carp, the Dutchman, was in the United States. Farley told Hill when Carp was expected in St. Paul, and together they went to the railroad station to meet him and Captain Barnes. Losing no time, Hill took Carp to Kittson's office for discussions, which they continued in the suite at the Metropolitan Hotel where Carp and Barnes were staying. Carp took no pains to hide his disbelief in the ability of two provincial businessmen, at the depth of a worldwide depression (when not even the leading American financier, Jay Cooke, could avoid bankruptcy), to raise the several million dollars required to buy the St. Paul & Pacific. But the earnestness of the two men from St. Paul, and especially Hill's thorough grasp of the situation, impressed him, as did the realization that if he helped negotiations along, and they did succeed, these men would obviously be very much in his debt. Hill, imitating Carp's thick accent, recalled that the Dutchman had a "sheme" for the associates to buy the property and let the bondholders keep the land grant. Hill knew that Smith would never agree to such a proposition, but at least it was a starting point. Next month Hill and Kittson wrote to Carp in New York, pressing him for a price for a complete sell-out, and when the Dutchman returned to St. Paul for further talks in February 1877 he gave them some figures.[15]

Now Hill had something to work on, and his pencil flew fast as winter passed into spring. He had assembled everything he needed to work out a tight estimate of what the railroad would be worth to the associates once it was completed to St. Vincent, and how much money they would have to put up to carry out the entire deal. He estimated that a majority of each class of bonds outstanding could be acquired at prices ranging from 80¢ on the dollar of face value for the most senior security down to 11¢ for the infamous $15 million loan. Total cash required for this purpose would be $4.3 million. To this had to be added $300,000 to buy up bonds not held by the Dutch committee and to foreclose the various mortgages, and $910,000 to complete the road to St. Vincent. Grand total required: $5,540,180. And what would this sum buy the associates? Railroad track worth $11.4 million, Hill calculated; equipment worth another $800,000; $400,000 worth of surplus property which they could sell off; $200,000 worth of townsites on the main line; and a land grant of 2,643,482 acres "lying for the most part in well-settled counties and of a quality much above the average of western land, worth at least the U.S. government minimum price for lands within the limit of the grant, $2.50 per acre," or a total of $6.7 million in land. The grand total value of the property as Hill saw it, once safely in their hands, completed, and judiciously operated: $19,402,923.[16] The figures were breathtaking. Yet the actual value turned out to be even greater.

It was not the land grant, however, but the prospect of sharply increased earnings which caught Hill's eye, for the land could be sold only once, while earnings were a continuing source of income and would certainly increase as the country grew:

> It is difficult to estimate the increase of earnings, however, we believe that $600,000 per year would be a low estimate and with fair average crops the net earnings would undoubtedly reach $700,000 or $800,000, which amount will increase from year to year as the country is settled up.[17]

How could he be so sure? Quite simply, Hill's intimate contact with the prosaic, day-to-day problems of the rising tide of immigration into the Northwest gave him the basis for his confidence in the future.[18]

At last the time had come to put the enterprise on a firm footing. Hill and Kittson had warned Smith from the beginning that they would be able to contribute very little to the undertaking financially, and would therefore defer to the money men when it came time to determine how the various parties would share in the profits. Of course the project could not move forward one inch without the St. Paul men, but it was not going very far until there was a "heavy capitalist" in the picture. By the spring of 1877 it was clear to Hill and Kittson that the person whom Smith had in mind to play that role and entice outside capital into the venture was his cousin, George Stephen, president of the Bank of Montreal.

Tall, slender, impressive of countenance, sartorially elegant, Stephen was also a shrewd judge of money-making opportunities and a skilled negotiator whose self-confidence, bordering on arrogance, was a telling asset. An immigrant like Smith, he was one of the most successful businessmen in Canada and a leader of the Scottish business community of Montreal. By the time Hill met him in 1877 he had multiplied the small fortune that he had made in the dry goods business into a much larger one in worsted mills, a rolling mill which made iron rails for Canada's expanding railroad system, and a company which turned out railroad cars and locomotives to run on them. In 1871 he had become a director of the Bank of Montreal and since 1876 had been its president. At the moment that the St. Paul venture came to his attention he was fending off criticism from stockholders at the reduced size of the dividend, a situation which, he explained, was due to the bank's excess liquidity in the absence of investment opportunities in the depression-ridden United States. James J. Hill would show him how to correct that.[19]

In May 1877 Smith wrote Hill and Kittson, telling them to meet him and Stephen in Montreal as soon as they could. The older man, having business in Chicago, took the morning train, while Hill followed on the overnight. Calling at the Mattison House, Hill found his friend sick abed and under the care of a doctor. He wrote a letter for Kittson to sign, took his leave, and pressed on to Montreal alone. There Smith took him to Stephen's office for the first meeting of the two men. Convinced of the feasibility of the St. Paul venture, Stephen confidently predicted that when he went to England that fall he would have no difficulty in raising the $5 million in short-term funds necessary to close the deal. He explained that this would be achieved by offering to give an equal share in the profits to a banking concern he had in mind. English capital was still the most impressive in the world, and to Hill, George Stephen's optimism settled the matter. Off he went to the telegraph office, where he cabled Carp, "Finances arranged letter on Friday." [20]

Back in St. Paul, Hill set to work drafting a formal offer to be mailed to Carp in Utrecht, so as to get his committee moving on the tedious job of soliciting the ratification of the bondholders as early as possible. A most careful choice of words was required. A firm offer to buy the bonds could leave the associates open to a ruinous lawsuit if Stephen subsequently failed to find financing in London, but Carp, on the other hand, would probably not submit a tentative offer to the bondholders and in fact might conclude that the associates were just talking. Hill, Kittson, and R. B. Galusha, their lawyer, "puzzled over it" until late into the night. The next morning Hill, walking down Third Street to his office, saw George B. Young, whose office was one floor above Hill's, leaning out of his window and enjoying the fine spring day. Young was one of the ablest lawyers in St. Paul, and within a few minutes Hill had him working on the problem of producing a document which asked for an option to buy while appearing to be a firm offer. Young's handiwork, mailed to the Dutchmen May 26, 1877, served the purpose:

> I now beg to inform you that I have made arrangements with George Stephen, Esq., President of the Bank of Montreal and the Honorable Donald S. Smith, Commissioner of the Hudson's Bay Co. representing Canadian and English capital who have agreed to furnish the money in case we shall conclude a contract with you for the purchase of the bonds of the Main & Branch lines of the First Div. of the St. Paul & Pacific Railroad Comp. and the Extension lines of the St. Paul & Pacific Comp. held by your Committee as per your letter bearing date N. York Feb. 28th, 1877.
>
> After a careful examination of the property we have determined upon a valuation of the whole on the basis of which we are prepared to purchase the several issues of bonds (with all unpaid coupons attached) held by your Committee as above specified at the following prices. . . .
>
> While we consider the above prices an equitable valuation for the respective classes of bonds your Committee may make such changes in prices as they think best, provided such change in prices does not increase the aggregate amount to be paid by us.
>
> If the purchase is made the bonds are to be delivered in London, England at such banking house as we may select and to be paid for on such delivery.
>
> As the amount required for the above purchase is very large and is to be furnished by our friends, we desire that as short a time as possible should elapse between closing the contract and the time fixed for the delivery of and payment for the bonds, in order to avoid contingencies which might happen during that period.
>
> In case therefore your Committee is prepared to sell us the bonds on the terms above mentioned we shall require 60 or 90 days (the latter if pos-

sible) after receipt of advices from you to that effect in which to take the
necessary steps for completing the transaction by closing the bargain and
obtaining the necessary funds to pay for the bonds. Upon receipt of this
we ask that your Committee shall advise us by cable as soon as possible if
they are willing to dispose of their bonds on above terms, also naming the
time for closing the transaction.

We hereby beg to withdraw our former offer for the First Div. Lines. We
have the honor to be,

Very respectfully,

N. W. Kittson
James J. Hill * 21

While this letter was making its slow progress halfway across North
America and across the Atlantic, there was plenty for Hill to keep an
eye on. He went to New York in June, where he met John S. Kennedy
for the first time. Captain Barnes gave him a coded cablegram, dated
May 22, 1877, from Carp. It read, when decoded: "Serious measures
B & B [Breckenridge and Barnesville] line are taken here. We will advise you as soon as possible next week. Think very well of proposal of
Kittson. Our acceptance probable. Otherwise procure funds ourselves.
Therefore suppose Farley could commence work now." This meant
that the missing link of railroad in the Red River Valley would soon be
undertaken, and that the Dutchmen would either approve a contract
with the Red River Valley Railroad (Hill and Kittson) to do the work,
or would furnish the money themselves, as they in fact did.[22]

The Supreme Court of Minnesota meanwhile had invalidated the
law which had given DeGraff & Company, the unpaid contractors on
the Extension line, the railroad's land grant, but these creditors were
back in court on another tack. The Northern Pacific, barely recovered
from its brush with financial death, was making trouble again. It agitated against the construction of the Breckenridge-Barnesville link,
and when that move failed it demanded a perpetual lease on both the
Extension line and the Brainerd connection, when built. It was the
Northern Pacific's last-ditch effort to gain an entrance into St. Paul and
keep the St. Paul & Pacific a purely local affair. The new management
of the Northern Pacific was eager to face the truth from which their
predecessors had shrunk: they had built the wrong railroad! It

---

* Carp's letter of February 28, 1877, has not been found. The "former offer" was Hill and
Kittson's tentative offer for the railroad without the land grant.

required no prophet to see that this influential group might indefinitely delay foreclosure of the mortgages and takeover of the St. Paul & Pacific by the bondholders who, Hill hoped, would soon be the associates.

Dealing with the Minnesota politicians finally produced results. An omnibus Act, passed on March 1, 1877, effectively transferred the unbuilt Brainerd branch to the Northern Pacific by giving the St. Paul & Pacific only until May 1, 1877, to build it or forfeit the right—a date which the embattled railroad could not possibly meet. Such a compromise was all right with Hill. To ensure settlement of the DeGraff claims, the Act reserved the proceeds of the eventual sale of 300,000 acres of the land grant. Most important to the associates, who expected to pay off DeGraff and keep the land, were the provisions liberalizing the timetable for completion of the St. Paul & Pacific. They would now have until January 1, 1879, to complete the Extension line to St. Vincent; until December 1, 1879, to complete the branch line to Alexandria; and until January 1, 1881, to finish it to Glyndon. It was an easy schedule; Hill expected to beat it.

The United States came close to revolution, in the eyes of many observers, that summer of 1877. Large-scale pay cuts by the Baltimore & Ohio and Pennsylvania railroads resulted in strikes which deteriorated into the most widespread civil violence and property damage the country had ever witnessed. At one point two-thirds of the nation's total railroad mileage was out of service. Coming only a few months after the presidential succession had been resolved at the very last moment, and to cries of fraud from the supporters of Samuel J. Tilden, the unrest might have destroyed any plans for major capital ventures but for President Hayes's use of federal troops to restore order. Through it all, Hill kept relations with his Canadian associates at the boil. To Smith he sent a detailed map of the railroads in Minnesota, actual and projected, with details on the stage of completion of each. "I also enclose you a view of the manner of opening up 'Big Farms' in the Red River Valley," he wrote; "this view is from the Dalrymple Farm between Elm and Grove rivers." The reference was to the so-called bonanza farms, the vast commercial farming operations which would rivet the world's attention on the money-making possibilities of commercial exploitation of the Northwest's wheat fields.[23]

Hill wrote Kittson at the end of July that "Mr. Smith says that both himself [sic] and Mr. Stephen are very much pleased with the look of the St. P. & Pac. matters as shown in our statements, maps, etc., and

TWO OF THE ASSOCIATES: THE FINANCIERS.

George Stephen (later First Baron Mount Stephen) in 1871, six years before Hill met him. Notman Photographic Archives, McCord Museum, McGill University, Montreal.

that he thinks the money matters will be very easy in England, in fact I think he said it was about arranged." Lord Dufferin, Governor General of Canada, and his party visited Winnipeg that August, and returned via St. Paul. Hill busied himself with making their visit as interesting as possible. At Hill's request the general superintendent of the Milwaukee & St. Paul Railroad personally conducted the party over the company's new route to Chicago. "I need not tell you who have been over the road how enjoyable a daylight ride along the banks of the Mississippi will be," Hill wrote Smith.[24] By the end of August, with Stephen's trip to England in the offing, he put on more pressure:

> I learn that the prospects are very favorable for a heavy immigration this fall and next spring. Every indication leads us to think that the present is the favorable time to purchase this property. In fact I do not think we

John S. Kennedy, about 60, in the mid-1880s. Burlington Northern.

could get it for less than a million dollars increase after the present indications are realized.[25]

Learning that Stephen would be in Chicago at the end of August, Hill grasped the chance to get him to come to St. Paul and see the railroad, for he knew that the first thing an English banker would ask Stephen was what the proposition looked like at first hand. "I hope you can spare the time to make a trip over the St. Paul & Pacific RR," he wrote, "and for that purpose we can take the business car which has good sleeping accommodations. You can both transact business and see the property at the same time." On the first Sunday in September Farley conducted a party from St. Paul to inspect the railroad. Besides Hill, Smith, and Stephen, it included Richard B. Angus, general manager of the Bank of Montreal, whose Scottish skepticism Stephen had thought it wise to have in reserve, and John Knuppe, who had just married Carp's sister and for whom the Dutchman hoped to find a place in the St. Paul & Pacific organization. To Stephen the prairie at its best would have looked bleak in comparison with his beloved Quebec. On that hot bright Sunday morning the ravages of the grasshoppers cast a further pall on a scene which he had begun to find depressing, but then the train chugged around a curve to disclose a country church with several dozen wagons drawn up in front. "Our Catholic friends," Farley noted. Hill explained that the Reverend John Ireland, by then one of the most progressive new bishops of the Roman Catholic Church, was successfully planting colony after colony of the faithful in the Red River Valley. Perhaps a mental picture of dozens of neat European farms ran through Stephen's mind; in any event, the valley seemed desolate no longer.[26]

Later that month Kittson made his delayed trip to Montreal for a conference with Stephen, who was about to sail for England. While there Kittson gave a letter to Stephen, prepared by Hill and intended for the eyes of the English bankers. It set forth Kittson's faith in the project, and attached to it was Hill's prospectus, which set the cost of the takeover at $5.5 million and the total value of the property at $19.4 million:

> While the amount required to purchase the bonds held by Dutch Committee ($4,330,180) is very large and the security unusual, still I am fully satisfied that if the bonds were all of the same class, and there were not such jealousies among the Dutch Bondholders themselves, as to prevent their agreeing upon a plan to adjust their respective interests, we could never get the bonds at the prices named . . . [S]o far they have been unable to agree upon any definite plan of organization. . . .

> The settlement of the Red River Valley, both in Minnesota and Manitoba, has been very rapid during the past two years, and the early development of that section, together with the increase of traffic from the Black Hills and the upper Missouri, will make this railway one of the very best paying roads in this country.

> I have the greatest confidence in the enterprise, and am willing, with those associated with me, to assume personal liability for the amount, and depend upon the revenues of the property to repay myself and friends, after paying all interest charges. . . .[27]

Meanwhile, the enemies of the associates were making their final efforts to upset the negotiations. While contending with various rumors planted in Holland by the Northern Pacific and certain others, among whom Hill suspected were their lukewarm friends at the Chicago & North Western Railroad, he had to contend with the Dutchmen's Old World zeal for haggling. Steadfastly opposing any effort to raise the purchase price, or to slice off the land grant, or give Carp's brother-in-law a job on the railroad, or even to cut Carp in with a large block of the stock, presumably to be issued by the reorganized railroad, he was greatly comforted by the letters which Farley periodically received from J. S. Kennedy & Company in New York. Concerning the Northern Pacific people, "While regretting that we cannot have the satisfaction of defeating these scamps . . . we hope that in the change of ownership we shall see all of them placed where they deserve to be." Concerning brother-in-law Knuppe, his "intervention is nothing but a little game of our young friend Carp . . . ; Kittson and Hill should ignore him [Knuppe] altogether." Concerning the long time which the Dutchmen seemed to be taking to make up their minds, "We are having long cables from the Committee full of absurd propositions, which show that there is a great deal of selfish 'hugger snugger' going on, and that the Dutchmen don't trust one another very much, and are scrambling for 'front seats.' " [28]

The position of J. S. Kennedy & Company in the negotiations was extremely delicate. As trustees of the mortgages which secured the bonds and as representatives in the United States of the Dutch committee, they had a double responsibility, moral and legal, to advise the Dutchmen solely in accord with the Dutchmen's own best interests. But Kennedy and Barnes were also in the railroad finance and supply business, and it was already clear that if the St. Paul & Pacific could be got into the hands of a live-wire group like the associates, they would stand to get some very profitable business. What they wrote to Farley, they told the receiver, was also to be conveyed to Hill. Astute Scotsman that he was, Kennedy walked the tightrope gracefully from start to finish, but it is clear that his firm, fatherly advice to the Dutchmen, also delivered via Farley, was a deciding factor:

We are inclined to advise our friends to take the matter into consideration, and have mentioned prices which would in our opinion be more in accordance with our ideas of the value of the property, although it cannot be expected that parties will buy these bonds except with a pretty sure prospect of a large profit; and except these Canadians, there would not be found persons ready to give any such sum in these times as is now offered. [29]

By September 1877 the Dutchmen had decided they had a deal, and when George Stephen sailed for England late that month Hill was laying his optimistic plans to put into practice what he had so long preached as the solution to the Northwest's transportation problems.

IV

One of the shepherdesses, Rachel Hill remembered, had six toes. Thus did August Jacacci assure immortality for the pastoral scenes which he was painting for the Hill family's new dining room. It was a good thing that the family would soon get settled in a spacious, modern house which Mary and three or four servants could run smoothly, for her husband was entering the most hectic year of his life. The "cottage," as Mary described it, in which they had been living since 1871, had been torn down in 1876 to make way for the new house. In the interim, the Hills lived on a small farm on Dayton's Bluff, overlooking the great bend in the river just south of the main part of the city. There they produced most of their fruits and vegetables, milk, and eggs. The stone house was hardly old by Eastern standards but in its lack of running water, indoor plumbing, or gaslight it was just the kind of farmhouse in which a prosperous yeoman of New York or Pennsylvania might have lived a hundred years earlier, except for the kerosene lamps, which had replaced the candles of an earlier day.

To the house on Dayton's Bluff Hill had brought Mary and their five children—Mary Frances ("Mamie"); James Norman, who owed his middle name to his father's friendship with Norman Kittson; Louis Warren, named in honor of Father Louis Caillet and in memory of the legendary Admiral Warren Riggs; Clara Anne, whose names were also those of Clara Jestin, her second cousin on her father's side, and Aunt Annie Phelps, her mother's sister; and frail little Katie who would not live through the summer. Another daughter, Charlotte, would join the family before they left the Bluff. In the meantime the children were beginning to enjoy the rewards of membership in a large, close-knit, middle-class Victorian family. There were books to read, or just to look at, pictures, good horses and comfortable wagons to go to town in, and even a beautiful watch and a diamond ring which they might admire (their father had presented them to their mother). But most impressive of all, Clara thought, was the grand piano which her parents had bought in New York, before which her father loved to stand and lustily sing the Scottish ballads and Methodist and Baptist hymns which were his Canadian heritage.[30]

Somehow Hill found time to act as his own contractor on the new house. He was determined that it should be as comfortable and convenient as possible: in a day when many houses, even in town, still had outside toilets, he wanted not one, but two bathrooms for his rapidly increasing tribe. Pushing aside the stack of papers which cluttered his massive mahogany rolltop desk, he wrote to his builder, explaining how it could be accomplished: "I though by' moving the partition back one joice [joist] where we closed the door along side the chimney we could do better in placing the water closets and disposing of the pipes." And he added a plea for greater economy in those hard times: "Please see that the bricklayers do not break up too many bricks—they are a little careless." The "hot water back" on the kitchen range, which delivered hot water right to the bathtub and lavatory and which greatly impressed Clara, was her father's idea. He had seen such a device in an advertisement for a Philadelphia firm and had pressed the innovation upon his plumber. Not every innovation passed the test, however: "The patent gutta percha bath[tub] is not as durable as I thought it would prove," he wrote the plumber, who must have been greatly relieved to learn that the gadget had been rejected; "a friend of mine has used one for a year and says that although it does not leak, 'it is hourly expected to.' " [31]

At the end of January 1878 the family moved into the handsome new mansion. A solid, mansard-roofed structure in the style which symbolized mid-Victorian American bourgeois strength, the house still managed an air of gracefulness, for Hill had specified white brick (especially imported from Milwaukee) and had avoided the gingerbread excesses of the period. The neighborhood was one of the best in St. Paul, boasting a number of such fine new residences. The Conrad Gotzians were around the corner, at Tenth and Canada streets, and the Uphams were right next door. Across the street was a spacious yard fronting a row of stables which served all of the houses in the block and included quarters above for the men who, in the bright mornings of summer or the cold gray dawn of winter, regularly produced the miracle of a horse and carriage before the front door on short notice.[32]

The house was to be furnished in the solid black walnut furniture which Mary, knowing that her husband liked things that worked and gave no trouble, had picked out at Messrs. Herts Bros. on lower Broadway during their New York trip. Besides the painted shepherdesses, the dining room would also boast striking stained glass windows made by a rising young American artist, John LaFarge, who had just been highly praised for the windows which he had created for Trinity Church, Boston. Sunday dinner in those surroundings was the high point of the week to Clara, who remembered "the leisure of the day, the luxury at table and everyone in his best clothes." [33]

John Brooks, who had married James J. and Alexander's sister, Mary Elizabeth, could not support her and their brood of children, which would soon number eleven. That fact had to be faced, and by early 1877 James J. was shouldering the responsibility of settling them on a small farm where his brother-in-law's labors might at least keep them fed, and of finding a job with hope of a future for their eldest son, James. With a frankness that he hoped would forestall future misunderstandings, he wrote on February 23, 1877, to "my dear sister":

> In reply to your letter of the 24th ult I have to say that I hope to be able to get a station for James early this spring and will let him know promptly. I note what you say about trying to keep a little store. . . . I think the money so invested would be as good as wasted for . . . your best customers would be your own family. If you can find a nice comfortable place with five or ten acres of good land near the factory so that the girls can get there on time you would be able to do better and John might raise enough to feed the entire family except flour, provisions, etc. I hope to be in Canada in a short time again and will I hope be able to help you to something permanent. . . .*

The day before, Hill had written his brother that he was counting upon Alex's judgment of what was best. "I hardly like the idea of paying 8% interest [in] these times on farm purchases . . . but if you think best to buy I can let you have the $2500 on the 1st of July and will make any arrangements to do so if you buy the place. . . ." A year later the problem had been compounded. He sent Alex $50 to spend on Mary's family in whatever way would do the most good, but he would not send anything more directly to her because he knew it would not be applied wisely. [34] He told his brother of his most recent disappointment with the Brooks clan, and then explained to his sister:

> I am sorry to tell you that [James] has quite disappointed me, but I think after he has been obliged to earn his own living in his own way for a few

---

* James Brooks had learned telegraphy, and his uncle hoped to use his influence to get him a job at a way station. Although Hill made several trips to Montreal in the next several years, there is no evidence that he ever visited Rockwood after his mother's funeral in 1876.

years he will understand his duty to the world better than he does now. He is not a bad boy, but he is downright lazy and does not want to depend upon himself for anything. He would like to wear good clothes, etc., if someone else would find them for him. Now I like to see a boy of his age have some pride and ambition and try to be somebody. I think you should hereafter let him take care of himself and while it may look hard, it is very much better for his future. Depend upon it, if he ever amounts to anything at all it will be in the next four years and I am afraid you have already indulged him too far.

Alexander has a message for you and I hope you will be soon able to get a more comfortable home for yourself and children. I will be glad to aid you to that end but must feel some certainty that it will be used to do more than give you temporary help only.[35]

In the few hours a week which he needed or wanted to take from his work, Hill found relaxation in the not-so-simple pleasures which his twenty years of hard work had made possible. There was less time after 1876 for the gentlemen's driving park, but the countryside provided him with the bird-shooting that he had loved in the fields of Ontario. Soon James Norman and Louis would be able to keep up with him as he tramped through the underbrush, his gun held (left-handedly) at the ready, his dogs scampering ahead of him. As with most things, he found that not even the hunting dogs of the North-west were yet up to his standards. On February 23, 1877, he wrote to a man in Quincy, Illinois, offering to buy his orange and white pointer bitch, which he wanted to breed to his own "large orange and white pointer dog, [which] weighs 72 lbs and [is] the cleanest male pointer dog you ever saw. He was imported from England in 1871. . . . Now, I want to save the blood and if I can get a good bitch I feel quite sure that the puppies would be the finest in the country."

V

As the Hill family made preparations for their second Christmas on Dayton's Bluff, the associates still hoped that a line of credit with which they hoped to pay for the Dutch bonds would be arranged before 1877 was over. George Stephen reported from England that, in addition to having a number of conferences with Johan Carp and the Rosenthals, who had been members of the "$15 million loan" syndicate, he had engaged the strong interest of Sir John Rose, governor of the Hudson's Bay Company and a partner in the London banking house of Morton, Rose & Company. "What I proposed was this," Stephen later recalled. "Here is an enterprise to carry through which requires an advance—I think I named the sum of eight hundred thousand pounds. If you will advance this money to . . . us four gentlemen, . . . [we] to pay interest on the advance . . . at the rate of five per cent, . . . we will give you an equal interest with us in the final outcome." In the hands of a man of Stephen's reputation, and with Hill's detailed prospectus to back it up, the proposition was tempting. If an independent investigation on the spot supported Stephen's enthusiasm, the money would be forthcoming. The Londoners cabled Morton, Bliss & Co., their correspondent house in New York, to have such an investigation made as quickly as possible.[36]

The New Yorkers chose General Edward Winslow, one of that breed of Civil War heroes who had successfully transferred their leadership on the battlefield to the Victorian business world, to do the investigating. Ten years' experience in the construction and financing of railroads had made Winslow one of the leading authorities on such new ventures, and he was shortly to become a founding partner of the investment banking firm of Winslow, Lanier & Company. But the General believed in fishing where the fish were, not where they might be later, and he was partial to very big fish. He was already planning the most spectacular venture of his career, a new double-track railroad running up the west shore of the Hudson River, which was expected to cut itself a slice of the richly profitable territory already developed by the Vanderbilts and their New York Central. If the new railroad did not turn out to be especially profitable, it was widely hinted, Winslow would proabably force the Central into a rate war and eventually sell the New York, West Shore & Buffalo Railroad, as it was to be called, to the Commodore's timid son, William H. A mind preoccupied with such high-flying financial schemes could not see much opportunity in a rundown, bankrupt railroad out on the edge of nowhere which could look only to the future growth of the country for its earnings.[37] Stephen returned to Montreal on Christmas Eve with the news that Morton, Rose & Company had decided not to advance the funds.

Eighteen seventy-seven was the year of decision for George Stephen, Donald Smith, Norman Kittson, and James J. Hill. They had to decide whether they themselves were prepared to assume the enormous risks in the complex project which they had so blandly laid before the astute London bankers. They were discovering something which none of them could articulate, but which they must already have known deep in their hearts: that there is a vast difference between investment capital and risk capital, and that it is rare that the twain ever meet. Investment capital, which is what Morton, Rose & Company had to offer, looks for established or at least pre-tested business ventures in which the rate of return is commensurate with the prior removal of all but the most conventional, calculable risks. Risk capital, by contrast, is what is required for undertakings in which the risk is beyond calculating, or is of a peculiar, unprecedented sort, while the returns are, at least theoretically, unlimited. Investment capital looks for interest and dividends, which are at least approximately foreseeable on the basis of past history of similar enterprises whose securities are traded on the exchanges. Risk capital aims for "profit," which is quite another thing.

As Hill remembered years later, "it was difficult to get capital to invest in so big a law-suit." [38] There were psychological and political imponderables which neither Winslow nor the Londoners could intelligently assess, as Hill had. The associates could not offer their proposition as an investment, but as a gamble, and floundering Northwestern railroads were not Winslow's or Rose's game. Was it the associates'? That was what they now had to decide. If they had ever had any real faith in the project—especially Hill, who had preached it to every businessman in St. Paul within reach of his index finger— now was the time for them to show it. There were other ways in which the money could be raised. If the railroad was going to produce the kind of profits Hill had outlined on his sheet of foolscap, the associates had the chance to reap them, but Hill and Kittson, at least, would have to be willing to risk everything they had. It was a hard decision to make in the cold, gray days of a Minnesota winter, in the fourth year of a great depression, especially for a sixty-three-year-old man in poor health and a proud, forty-year-old man with a wife, five young children, and a new house. Failure might not merely wipe out their modest fortunes; it might also saddle them with debts which they could not repay in their lifetimes. But if they did enter the fight under their own colors, theirs would be the victory and theirs alone the fruits thereof.

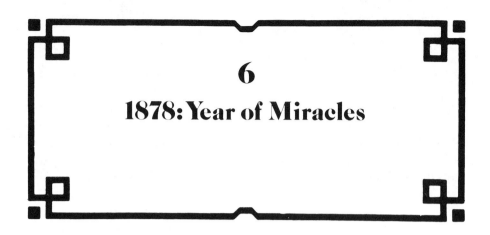

6
1878: Year of Miracles

I have been up at the front on both lines, and I find it pays to be where the money is being spent.

—James J. Hill, 1878

I

If in the fall of 1877 James J. Hill thought that the success of the associates' plan to take over the St. Paul & Pacific Railroad rested solely on George Stephen's efforts in England, he was wrong. A delicate balance had to be maintained at home in the interim, and that was not easy. The St. Paul *Pioneer Press* plastered the front page of its October 26 issue with an embarrassingly complete account of the negotiations, and, to make matters even worse, it reported that the deal was all sewed up. Donald Smith, handed a copy of the paper on October 31 at his desk in Hudson's Bay House, Montreal, wrote a troubled letter to Kittson:

> As nothing has been settled . . . the article . . . may probably be fatal to the project, and . . . the sole chance of success may now be in your coming East immediately, after undoing as far as may be possible the effect of the communication . . . by a personal denial. . . . The statement should be scrupulous by avoiding to mention in any way either Mr. Stephen's name or the Bank of Montreal in connection with the affair.

Hill had already seen the danger and taken steps to get the story retracted. He had a good idea where the leak was, but since he had been the beneficiary of many a leak himself he was in no position to complain. It was fatuous to suppose that negotiations which promised such momentous changes in the transportation situation in the Northwest could be kept secret. Nervous congratulations, in fact, were already coming from various men whose affairs were bound up with those of James J. Hill. Hamilton Browne, still prospecting for coal in Iowa, wrote to say that he was "glad to learn the good news." Captain Holcombe complimented Hill heartily, "knowing as I do that to you belongs the credit as originator of the whole scheme," and then grasped the opportunity to remind him of "the old and still important—for one year—subject of steamboating." [1]

George Stephen, still empty-handed, lost little time in calling the associates into conference in Montreal and pushing ahead aggressively with alternate plans to finance the takeover. A refinancing operation, in which the old securities of the bankrupt company would be exchanged for new bonds in a reorganized and revitalized one, seemed possible. Stephen's failure to raise the cash in London, in fact, could be put to good psychological use in further convincing the Dutch that they had better seize whatever offer the associates ultimately produced. While the associates were disappointed to learn that they would now have to work out a deal which the Dutchmen would consider less desirable and would therefore be more costly, and that they themselves would have to shoulder the burden of the risk directly, the route which they did follow to success was just the kind of alternative these clever men were prepared to take.

The Hill and Galusha children saw nothing of their fathers that holiday season, for Hill and his lawyer were on the overnight train to Chicago when it pulled out of the St. Paul depot on that frosty Christmas Eve of 1877. Kittson, who was in Chicago, took a dim view of such unseemly haste, but two days later all three pushed on to Montreal, where they arrived on December 29. Hill's first act was to lay out $4.30 for a dozen collars, a scarf, and two neckties for Kittson, who was out of clean linen. After two days of discussion, during which they were joined by Donald Smith, all five took the train to New York. That was New Year's Day. Arriving on the morning of January 2, they went directly to Kennedy's office at 41 Cedar Street. Kennedy and Barnes, they learned, were anxious to keep the deal alive, for they were in danger of embarrassment with the Dutchmen, who believed that they had a firm contract. Throughout the day they worked on the complex problem of buying and completing a railroad without money, and by late afternoon had agreed upon the main features of a new plan. After a quick dinner Hill and Galusha divided up the subject matter and retired to their rooms at the Hotel St. Denis to draw up an agreement.[2]

The Dutchmen, it was decided, would be paid for their bonds in cash if they insisted, but the associates planned to make it very attractive for them to take not cash, for they would only have to find some way to reinvest it, but bonds of a new railroad company, which would acquire all of the assets of the St. Paul & Pacific upon foreclosure of the mortgages. Upon signing a contract to buy the bonds, the associates would deposit with Kennedy, the Dutch committee's New York agent, $125,000 in gold which the associates agreed to forfeit if the deal broke down. Pending successful completion of the foreclosure suits and organization of a successor company, they would pay the Dutchmen interest on the full net amount of the purchase (about $4 million) at the rate of seven per cent per year, payable semi-annually.

In addition to the deposit and interest money, about a million dollars cash was required to complete the railroad from Crookston to the international boundary and from Melrose to Alexandria. The latter amount was raised by means of "receiver's debentures." Kennedy was sure that the United States District Court in charge of the receivership would authorize Farley to issue such securities upon seeing evidence that substantial parties had entered the picture and were ready to assume responsibility for the entire outcome. But debentures were not cash; they were the I.O.U's of a bankrupt railroad. Who would take them in return for iron rails, or rolling stock, or, for that matter, for the cash that would be required to meet payrolls and pay local suppliers? That was where J. S. Kennedy & Company came in, for Kennedy's word was better than gold; the associates could have marketed Confederate bonds with his guarantee. In retrospect it is difficult to say at just what point Kennedy had become a *de facto* member of the associates—he never admitted to playing any such full-fledged role—but he had obviously been of the utmost value to the four ever since they had first tried to get Carp to say what his people might take for their bonds. Once it was clear that Stephen could not carry out the financing by himself, John S. Kennedy had held the key to success.

So much, Kittson may have thought, for the big money. But how about the seed money, which, he could plainly see, the associates themselves were going to have to provide? It would take at least a year, probably more, to finish the railroad, tie up all the loose legal and political ends, take possession of the property, and issue new bonds to the Dutchmen. The amount of seed money involved was not less than a quarter of a million dollars, and after further negotiations with the Dutchmen, inevitable delays, and unknown contingencies, it could easily become half a million. Where could he and Jim Hill get such a sum as $125,000 apiece in ready money? They would have to liquidate most of their business holdings: Kittson, his stock in the Red River Transportation Company and some of his most desirable real estate; Hill, his steamboat stock, his interest in the Northwestern Fuel Company, and perhaps more. Suppose there were no ready buyers except at a bargain price, which was entirely likely, since the depression still raged? Clearly, there was no way in the world they could put their signatures to a piece of paper which required them to raise *any* specific sum of money from the sale of their assets.

Hill knew what was going through Kittson's mind. He had reassured the older man as persuasively as he could, but still he was not looking forward to the time when the associates would have to face the problem. Late on Saturday afternoon, January 5, the nettle still had not been grasped. Smith and Stephen had tickets on the evening train to Montreal, while Hill and Kittson were about to leave via the New York Central for Chicago. What happened then is not clear, but Kennedy apparently reminded them as they were putting on their hats and coats that each would have to be prepared to forward a substantial sum of cash on short notice. The men from St. Paul, Stephen replied, were good for such an amount. Hill's jaw dropped. Whatever his choice of words in setting Stephen right on this point, it was highly effective, for both Stephen and Smith lapsed into embarrassed silence. Kennedy tactfully ignored the entire contretemps. A family fight, he may have reflected, must be worked out in the family, and he had not yet married into this one. The New York discussions were thus concluded on a distinctly ragged note. Back in Montreal, Donald Smith wrote his old friend Kittson in anguish:

> The little episode just as Mr. Stephen and I were leaving Mr. Kennedy's office for the train on Saturday last greatly surprised and I must add not a little pained me, as I felt there must be some grave misunderstanding. . . . I regretted extremely that it should be made to appear to our friends Messrs. J. S. Kennedy and Barnes that there existed between ourselves any thing other than the utmost cordiality where we have one and the same intent to serve. I . . . hope to have from you an explanation. . . .[3]

Kittson came to Hill's office with Smith's letter in hand, wondering what to do or say. To Hill it could only have appeared that George

Stephen had been tempted, at nearly the last minute, to back out of the oft-implied arrangement to have the Bank of Montreal lend the associates whatever short-term money they needed on the excellent security they could furnish. Indeed, Hill had repeatedly disavowed any specific percentage share in the profits of the undertaking for himself or Kittson, since they could not furnish their share of the seed money on their own. He let the Canadians stew for over a week, and then wrote Stephen a frank but courteous explanation:

> I am very sorry indeed that our time was so short on Saturday [Jan. 5] P.M. in New York, which prevented our more fully explaining the matter to Mr. Galusha and having the whole thing closed up at the time, and I am especially sorry that yourself and Mr. Smith or either of you should have got the impression that I differed with you in any way, or that I thought for one moment there was any want of mutual confidence, personal cordiality, or good faith, for I beg to assure you that I had no such feeling, and I trust that nothing that has occurred will be allowed to disturb the absolute confidence and mutual trust necessary in an affair of the kind we are endeavoring to carry out. . . .

> My hesitation was solely due to my desire that neither Mr. Kittson or myself should undertake to do what was totally beyond our power—while at the same time we are ready and entirely willing at all times to risk everything we have got in the world upon our faith in the property, and will gladly join in securing to the fullest extent of our means whatever loans may be necessary to carry out our offer to the Dutch Committee, *but we cannot alone furnish our share of the money.* . . .

> I feel quite sure [Kennedy] took no notice of it, for as we were leaving he gave us assurance of his entire satisfaction with what has been done. . . .[4]

If George Stephen had had any doubt about the key role he was expected to play in the takeover of the St. Paul & Pacific Railroad, James J. Hill removed it.

II

Kennedy had lost no time in sending the associates' new offer along to the Dutch committee, mailing it the same day the associates had walked out of his office. The associates had agreed, upon his suggestion, to allow the $125,000 deposit to be retained by the committee in lieu of reimbursement for its expenses, and to pay the Dutchmen for the Breckenridge-Barnesville link exactly what they had advanced for it. The bonds of the new company would bear 6 per cent interest, and, to make sure that very few Dutchmen would ask for cash, a bonus of $250 in a new preferred stock, paying 6 per cent, would accompany each $1000 of new bonds accepted. Kennedy urged the foreigners to accept, but of course Carp and the Dutch bankers felt that counterproposals had to be made. Hill had warned repeatedly that the price of the property would soon begin to rise steeply, and he had been right. The Dutch raised their price for the $11 million worth of bonds of the "$15 million loan" from 11¢ to 13¾¢. They then demanded, and got, a 7 per cent coupon for the new bonds which they would get in exchange for the old; and for those timid souls who would choose to eschew the bonus of preferred stock, they got a 10 per cent discount on the new bonds in translating old bonds into new. Interest on the purchase contract would begin not as of the date of signing, but as of December 22, 1877, the day when the original purchase agreement had foundered. Of more immediate importance to the associates, who were already going through their strong boxes to see what collateral they could put up on a loan of seed money, the deposit was increased from $125,000 to $280,000, all of which was to go to the committee for expenses. Carp would have his pound of flesh, one way or another.[5]

During these transatlantic negotiations, which were filtered through the offices of J. S. Kennedy & Company, Smith and Stephen journeyed to St. Paul for conferences on one occasion and met Hill and Kittson in Chicago on another. Despite the distances separating the various parties and the slowness of telegraph and cable communication, the associates reached agreement on a financial plan by early February. A red-cheeked messenger boy, hands clapped to his frostbitten ears, burst into the welcome warmth of the Northwestern Fuel Company offices on Third Street one morning with a telegram for James J. Hill:

SEND ME IMMEDIATELY NOTE PAYABLE DEMAND TWO HUNDRED AND EIGHT *
THOUSAND DOLLARS ORDER BANK OF MONTREAL SIGNED YOURSELF KITTSON
BY ATTORNEY WILL COMPLETE WITH OUR NAMES ON RECEIPT.

It was from George Stephen. Hill's letter, enclosing the promissory note, went out next day with the news that Kittson, who had gone south, reported his health much improved. "We hope nothing will

* It should have read two hundred and eighty.

occur to prevent the Dutchmen carrying out their part of it," he added anxiously.

Stephen reassured him. "I think you may take it for granted that the Dutchmen will take our offer of bonds at par with preferred stock, and you may safely gird yourself accordingly." [6]

Hill and Kittson had to gird and regird themselves financially throughout 1878. As their share of the collateral for the four-party note which Hill had sent to Stephen, they put up all of the stock they owned in the Red River Transportation Company except what they required to qualify as directors. The four associates were binding themselves, jointly and severally, to repayment of the loan, which the Bank of Montreal could demand at any time it chose. If one or more failed to pay up and his collateral proved worthless, the others would be liable for his share. The degree of trust which the associates placed in each other was remarkable. Neither Hill nor Kittson had any first-hand knowledge of Stephen's or Smith's financial condition, nor did the Canadians know anything about the affairs of the men from St. Paul except what they had been told. Smith and Stephen, furthermore, were cousins, and both were directors of the Bank, the latter enjoying all of the privileges of an insider, since he was also president. What assurance had Hill and Kittson that they were indeed sharing alike in the risk? Smith did not wait to be asked, but provided it in a letter he wrote to Hill on April 4, 1878:

> You should retain a sufficiency of the stock [in the Red River Transportation Co.] to qualify you as a director of the Company and Mr. Kittson should do the same, making transfer of the remainder to me "in trust" as in your own case. As Directors of the Bank of Montreal you will at once see how Mr. Stephen and I desire that any responsibility of [*sic*] yourself, Mr. Kittson, and we jointly undertake should be amply covered by our joint securities and I need hardly say that there we deposit equally as yourselves, not at all as a condition required by the Bank but to avoid the possibility of cavil or misrepresentation as to our being borrowers while Directors of the Bank.

"I am anxious to have this property take care of itself," Hill wrote on April 8 to Hamilton Browne, concerning the Iowa coal lands, "as I am now engaging in enterprises connected with the St. Paul and Pacific." He assured Browne that he was confident that a railroad would soon be built into their coal fields, but by May 10 he had had to pledge his deeds against the Bank of Montreal's loan of money for the first semi-annual interest payment, which was due the Dutchmen on June 22, 1878. As of June 1 Hill stepped out of the Northwestern Fuel Company altogether, selling his 300 shares of stock to Edward N. Saunders for $21,500. On June 4 Smith wrote urgently from Montreal, asking for Hill and Kittson's signature on a second note, this one for $140,000, for the first interest payment. From then on they would have to scrape up cash, and for that purpose their steamboat company performed admirably. It was making money almost faster than they could count it, carrying record numbers of immigrants down the river, as well as unprecedented tons of rails, ties, and rolling stock (including the first locomotive ever owned by the Canadian Pacific Railway) for use on both the St. Paul & Pacific extension to the boundary and the Canadians' project southward from Winnipeg. By the first of November Hill had extracted at least $75,000 from the enterprise and had sent it to Stephen.[7] No possible way of raising cash was overlooked. At the height of his labors to complete the railroad that summer, Hill was writing sharp letters to delinquent customers of the fuel company, demanding that they pay accounts as small as $27.50.

The lamp atop his big rolltop desk was lit long before closing time on the gloomy February afternoons as Hill waited for word from the Dutchmen. To Kittson, who was warming his bones in New Orleans, he wrote reassuringly on February 13: "Mr. Merrill [superintendent of the Milwaukee & St. Paul Railroad] is here and says his road would like to have a small interest at any time if we would allow it. If we should want to sell our contract the Milwaukee road would pay $1,000,000 *cash* for it and let us step out." Definite word was expected soon. Meanwhile, he advised his friend to take long drives, eat plenty of fruit, and enjoy the Mardi Gras. On February 23 he was penning a letter to Stephen when the news came. "We have virtually crossed the Rubicon," he noted; "this is a great relief." To Smith he wrote jubilantly that same day, "I have a telegram from Kennedy and Co. saying that a majority of all classes [of bonds] has accepted our proposal, which no doubt settles it. I cannot omit expressing my gratitude to yourself and Mr. Stephen for the confidence you displayed in this matter, and I am now sure you will not regret it." Carp and others were sailing for New York immediately, and the signing of the formal contract would take place there in two or three weeks. On March 8 Kennedy telegraphed Hill and Kittson to come East.

But where was Kittson? Hill learned that he was somewhere between Chicago and St. Paul, and decided that he would just have to turn around and head for New York with him as soon as he stepped off the train. But one look at the older man told Hill that Kittson should go home and go to bed. He was in no shape to attend the signing in person and, in fact, was so agitated at the thought of what he was getting into that he did not dare tell his old friend, General Henry H. Sibley, for fear that his fellow pioneer would think he had taken leave of his senses. When the impressively engrossed and be-ribboned document was spread before the principals in Kennedy's office on March 13,[8] Galusha signed for him.

Not until March 27 did the associates get around to formalizing their own arrangements, although a preliminary draft of what came to be known as the "associates' agreement," drawn up in Hill's own handwriting, had been signed by Hill, Smith, Stephen, and Galusha (as Kittson's attorney) on January 21. Each of the four was to share equally in the expenses and the net profits to be realized from completing and reorganizing the railroad. That is, each would get one-fifth of the residual value (to be evidenced by bonds and stocks of the new company) after all claims had been satisfied. The "fifth fifth" would go, in trust, to George Stephen, "for the purpose of securing the cooperation of an associate or associates in said enterprise through whom the financial aid necessary to enable us to complete such purchases [of Dutch bonds] may be obtained as understood between us in New York at the time of making our said offer of purchase." J. S. Kennedy & Company would play such a role, and the cooperation of R. B. Angus, general manager of the Bank of Montreal, would not be forgotten. Even Farley, who was expected to be helpful but could be dangerous, was to receive some kind of "bonification," as Stephen called it. The associates would forget Farley, however, and they would be sorry.[9]

Hill, his style more than a little influenced by that of Thomas Jefferson, grandly penned a final paragraph to the associates' agreement:

> Having full confidence in each other and in the success of said enterprise we hereby mutually agree to become responsible for the repayment of all moneys required to be advanced to us in carrying out said purchase (if said offer be accepted) and to join in the execution of any papers or securities which may be required in obtaining such advances.[10]

III

"St. Paul To Join Hands with Winnipeg and Also To Clasp Alexandria and Intermediate Points in Fond Embrace," exulted the St. Paul *Daily Globe* on April 1, 1878, "All-rail Connection with Winnipeg in October!" The reporter had just come from an interview with James J. Hill, who knew that an atmosphere of optimism and confidence was just what the associates needed as they prepared for the hard work that lay ahead. But he had no illusions about the obstacles that lay in their path and the heavy burdens, in every department of railroad finance, engineering, and politics, which they would have to carry. Thirty years later he may have smiled wryly at the laissez-faire picture which the Progressive historians were beginning to draw of the era in which he and his friends had taken over the St. Paul & Pacific Railroad, for in fact they had had to contend at every step with the indifference, ambivalence, inefficiency, and venality of government—permanent features of civilization which their enemies sought to use to thwart the associates' program. By early 1878, in fact, prosperity was rapidly returning to the United States, and various parties had begun to take an interest in the neglected St. Paul & Pacific Railroad. But the people of Minnesota and Manitoba now felt acutely the lack of modern transportation on the north-south axis, and their leaders had come to realize that the associates, a group of local and Canadian men who seemed to know how to give them what they wanted, held the region's future in their hands. The associates occupied a strong moral position which, Hill suspected, would give them the margin they needed to succeed where others had failed.

He first applied the full weight of popular support in the state legislature, where men had threatened to pass laws that would have destroyed the St. Paul & Pacific as an independent railroad. The legislators changed their tune when faced with proof that the associates had indeed bought the bonds. On March 8, just as the message arrived from Kennedy to come east for the signing, Hill was writing the New Yorker of their great victory in the legislature:

> It was very late before we felt able to say that we represented ourselves and not the Dutchmen and consequently we had to make our fight a bitter one. The whole pack, "Tray, Blanche and Sweetheart" *—DeGraff, Crooks, Becker and all excepting old Delano fought hard and had letters and cables from Holland fresh every day or so saying that we had bought no bonds, that our negotiations had entirely fallen through and some one from Holland cabled Governor Pillsbury to say that we had not closed any bargain for the bonds. I speak of this to show you that great reliance was placed . . . upon the old feelings against the Dutchmen. . . .

* "The little dogs and all, Tray, Blanch, and Sweet-heart, see, they bark at me." *King Lear,* III, 6.

Don't worry about the $125,000 worth of land which the legislature had awarded DeGraff in settlement of his claims, Hill counseled Kennedy, for the price of land had begun to go up rapidly, and the acreage involved would be considerably less than had originally been estimated.

At the same time Hill confronted the Chicago & North Western Railroad with evidence of the associates' independence from support by other railroads. The North Western executives had believed that the associates were in league with the Milwaukee & St. Paul Railroad to form a through line from Chicago to Winnipeg, thus excluding the North Western from a share of the traffic. "We have assured our friends we would have no opposition from North Western," he wired Marvin Hughitt, general manager of that road at Chicago; "we depend upon your immediate action withdrawing all opposition to us as the best interest of all." Hughitt was in New York, but back came a quick telegram from Albert Keep, president of the North Western, assuring Hill that they were not opposing the associates in any way. It had not been easy for the highly placed executives of well-established railroads to believe that provincial businessmen, with no formal experience in railroading, could be anything but a front for one of their competitors. Once they grasped the facts, however, they were delighted with what was happening.[11]

Political pressure and the law's delay were heavy burdens throughout the year. By June it was clear that it would be December at the earliest before the courts would rule on the foreclosure suits. Knute Nelson, on his way to becoming the most important political figure in Minnesota, wanted a job for a constituent. A state senator "who stood by us last winter" asked that spring for a round-trip pass to Crookston, Minnesota, in the Red River Valley, for his brother. From Winnipeg the United States consul, James W. Taylor, who was extremely popular among the Manitobans, wrote to remind Hill of the valuable work he had done as a publicist for the St. Paul & Pacific in the past. He noted that he had written F. W. Seward, Assistant Secretary of State in Washington, advising him to oppose efforts of the Northern Pacific to have the St. Paul & Pacific land grant abolished, and wondered if a small monthly retainer "which would enable me to live in St. Paul with my family" might not be in order. It was all worth it, however, for by the time Farley, with Hill peering over his shoulder, was beginning construction work that spring the associates' enemies had been deprived of their political leverage.[12]

In pressing the foreclosure suits Hill was confused and troubled by the problem of the "non-assenting" bonds, those held by people whom the Dutch bondholders' committee had not been able to persuade to accept the associates' offer. In the eyes of the court, the signing of the purchase agreement had made the associates the owners of a majority of each of the several issues of bonds, but this did not mean clear sailing in the foreclosure suits, for the court might place onerous conditions on the associates by way of protecting the interests of the minority bondholders. The best thing, the associates had agreed, was to buy up as many of these bonds as possible.[13] There was reason to believe that the Dutch bankers, particularly Lipman, Rosenthal & Company, were encouraging the non-assenters to stand fast, so Kennedy sent Barnes off to Amsterdam to straighten things out. Stephen was delighted to learn that the portly, genial Barnes had known how to use a little friendly blackmail:

> Mr. Barnes' account of his visit to Amsterdam is very amusing but too long a story to bother you with. He . . . succeeded in making our Dutch friends see very clearly that they had as much interest almost as we in carrying the operation . . . to a successful conclusion. . . . Mr. Barnes thinks they will aid us in every possible way they can . . . to get the outstanding bonds on the best possible terms. . . . I fancy Mr. Barnes gave George Rosenthal a hint that he might be under deep obligations to us before he had got out of the difficulty about his firm's title to the 4 million odd bonds and perhaps that made him see things a little more clearly.[14]

"We have wary foes in front of us, and many men connected with it here, whose salaries will be sorely missed were the foreclosures made," Hill reminded Stephen on June 23, thinking of the men who were hanging onto their positions with the St. Paul & Pacific, their trusteeships, and their jobs in Receiver Farley's office. The greatest enigma was Litchfield, who still owned the common stock and, by pretending that the "Litchfield agreement" between himself and the Dutchmen was still in effect, could delay matters indefinitely if he was not dealt with somehow. Hill considered him little more than a thief. Hard at work on June 23, he wistfully wrote Stephen and Kennedy, who were fishing at Causapscal, Stephen's summer home on the St. Lawrence River: "I have a good man ready to shadow [Litchfield] to N.Y. and get service on him . . . [We] have concluded that [we] cannot lock him up in New York, but can sue him for the $1,500,000 diverted. . . . Hope both yourself and Mr. Kennedy have a good time with the salmon."

George Stephen's emotional detachment from local St. Paul matters and his remarkable blandness in negotiation would be the key to the Litchfield problem, and would also open the door to a reasonable compromise with the Northern Pacific. Hill had infinite patience when he was dealing with the forces of nature or with people whose standards matched his, but in the poker game between the associates, Litchfield, and the Northern Pacific he was rather ineffectual, for he allowed his contempt for the manner in which the other players had acquired their cards to blind him to their strength. When it came to relations with the businessmen of the Twin Cities, however, Hill was very effective. Learning that certain interests in Minneapolis planned to isolate their sister city by encouraging the Northern Pacific to duplicate the St. Paul & Pacific's facilities north of St. Anthony, Hill helped the city fathers see reason. "There has been a convention going on at Mpls of all the roads running into that city, [and I spoke to them] in terms all parties present could not fail to understand," he reported. The convention passed only one resolution, "a declaration on the part of the Millers' Association that they would not do anything in connection with any railroad that was unsatisfactory to the St. P. & Pacific." [15]

IV

As spring crept northward in 1878 it was clear to the associates that the St. Paul & Pacific Railroad had to be completed to the Canadian boundary that year. But that was all that was clear, for the questions of who would do it and precisely how the money was to be supplied were still unanswered. The court considered that the person in charge would be Joseph P. Farley. As receiver he was the court's choice to conserve the assets of the railroad until permanent arrangements could be made for it, and that meant that Farley would have to operate it, and apply its profits, if any, as well as such funds as could be raised from any other legitimate source, to whatever end would strengthen the property, including carrying out the construction program on his own account. To accomplish this the court was willing to authorize the receiver to issue as much as $5 million worth of debentures if he could get anyone to take them in exchange for goods, services, or cash.

The associates, however, had the credit which could turn a sheaf of receiver's debentures into all of the things necessary to build a railroad—if they could just get their hands on them. Hill helped Farley draft a petition to Judge John F. Dillon of the United States Circuit Court, which was then sitting in Des Moines. Hill recited the facts about the imminent change of ownership of the bonds, and urged that authority be granted to issue up to a million dollars' worth of debentures to complete the Extension line to St. Vincent and the branch line from Melrose to Alexandria. Dillon had no doubt that this was the best possible thing that could happen to this railroad, which had sought shelter under his common-law wing. But he was super-sensitive to criticism that he had shown favoritism toward the St. Paul & Pacific and its various despoilers in the past, so he refused to do anything until he had an independent report on every aspect of the situation, including the financial standing of the associates and the existing status of the railroad's land grant. To make the report he appointed two special commissioners: John B. Henderson, former United States Senator from Missouri and special United States prosecutor in the whiskey ring trials of the Grant administration, and Thomas C. Reynolds, former governor of Missouri. Hill devoted days of precious time to explaining the situation to the commissioners, preparing the way for them to visit Kennedy in New York and the Department of the Interior in Washington, and dancing attendance on Judge Dillon at Jefferson City, Des Moines, Davenport, or wherever he happened to be. Hill wrote Stephen on June 1 that Dillon had authorized the debentures, but he added, regretfully, the judge would not permit a single one of the certificates to be signed by the receiver until the work had been done, and they were to be, furthermore, not a first lien on the assets of the entire system, but only on the mileage of railroad for which the proceeds had been used, and would therefore be somewhat less negotiable than the associates had hoped.[16] Under the circumstances, the backing of John S. Kennedy would be not merely desirable, but vital.

Because he withdrew from his private banking and railroad supply businesses in 1883, on the eve of the vast growth and wholesale reorganization of this gigantic American industry, John Stewart Kennedy has been all but forgotten in the annals of American finance. Only fifty-three at "retirement," he continued to work hard at overseeing his large investments and the vast private charities of New York City, whose fund-raising activities he consolidated. Upon his death in 1909 these charities received about one-half of his entire estate, which was reported to be at least half again as large as that of J.

P. Morgan. Born near Glasgow, Scotland, in 1830, he came to the United States in 1850 and was associated with the private banking firm of M. K. Jesup & Company. He recognized very early that Chicago was to become the railroad hub of the nation, and established the firm of Jesup, Kennedy & Company to sell railroad supplies in that city. A rich man by 1868, he founded the banking firm of J. S. Kennedy & Company in New York and, in partnership with "Captain" John S. Barnes, helped numerous fledgling railroad concerns through the fifteen hectic years of prosperity and depression which followed. It was an era when it was difficult to tell whether a given financial scheme was a valuable innovation in the rapidly changing world of finance or a new technique for robbing the people. But this dour man, whose dignified demeanor hid a nervous, hypochondriac nature, remained above criticism, and he became a United States government member of the board of the Union Pacific Railroad in the aftermath of the Crédit Mobilier scandal. At a time when little thought was given to limiting even the possibility of conflicts of interest, Kennedy demonstrated that it was possible to be simultaneously a banker, a guardian of aggrieved investors' interests, and an innovative reorganizer of vital railroads. In no instance did he employ his talents more dramatically than in the rebirth of the St. Paul & Pacific Railroad, but the price he ultimately paid was nervous exhaustion and chronic insomnia. John S. Kennedy was an utter failure in one way: he simply did not fit the Robber Baron stereotype. It is a sad commentary on American historical writing that he has, accordingly, been forgotten.[17]

Kennedy, Stephen, and Hill worked perfectly together. Remarkably similar in background, they shared some of the few interests which they were able or willing to engage in apart from their work. Not the least of these was fishing for the Atlantic salmon. For more than a decade after the success of the associates' first undertaking, Kennedy continued to take an active part in Hill's subsequent ventures. No golf club ever provided so exclusive a setting in which to discuss new projects as the Restigouche Salmon Club in New Brunswick, of which Kennedy was president, or Stephen's summer place at Causapscal, or, in later years, James J. Hill's own salmon-fishing lodge on Quebec's St. John River.

Once Kennedy had given his nod to the associates' venture in St. Paul, the cash which was required to complete the railroad, buy up the outstanding bonds, pay off Litchfield, and meet a hundred miscellaneous expenses which added up to substantial sums was amply provided. This is not to say that Kennedy took over all the risks, for the associates themselves were very far out on a financial limb before the frantic year of 1878 was over, but by lending his name at critical points the enterprise had available to it credits which might not otherwise have been found. Most notably, Kennedy used his influence to get the Cambria Iron Works, which supplied most of the rails and fastenings for construction in 1878, and in which he had a financial interest, to accept the receivers' debentures as temporary payment for several hundred thousand dollars worth of their products—or, more accurately, to accept the *promise* of such debentures, which were not available until the work had been completed. All of this had to be kept quite confidential, for ordinary men would conclude that the potential conflict of interest mean that someone was being robbed. In later years Kennedy always maintained that his participation in the associates' enterprise had been largely passive, that he had not been promised any specific share in the profits, and that what he ultimately got out of the venture remained his own business. Perhaps it was only the happy circumstance that virtually everybody, and most notably the people of the Northwest, came out of the process better off than they went in, that made such an Olympian attitude possible.[18]

V

Hill was determined to meet the legislative deadlines for construction of the branch line to Alexandria by December 1 and the Extension line to St. Vincent by the end of the year. Both achievements were vital if the associates were to reorganize the railroad on a permanent new financial footing early the following year, issue new bonds to the Dutchmen, and relieve themselves of further interest payments to the foreigners. Hill wanted Farley to let the construction contract to him and the associates and to lease the Extension line to the Red River & Manitoba Railroad, the formal name of the Breckenridge-Barnesville link, which the associates were buying as part of the deal with the Dutchmen. These arrangements would have given Hill complete control of the situation, relieved him of any necessity of deferring to Farley in both construction and operational matters, and enabled him to get service north of the international boundary going as quickly as possible. But it was not going to be so easy. Judge Dillon, conferring with Hill and Farley in his chambers, brought up the subject, and what happened then left Hill flabbergasted:

> The judge suggested that [the associates] might take the contract from the receiver, but much to our surprise Mr. Farley said he could build the road himself better and cheaper if we simply furnished him the money. In order to get the matter [settled], Kennedy is to advance the money and Stephen and Smith are to write Farley expecting it to be done in that way.[19]

Hill tried to put the best possible face on what to him was a patently undesirable arrangement, but his early avowals of faith in Farley were replaced by increasingly frequent, and indignant, expressions of dissatisfaction as they got deeper into the work. Farley seemed to feel that nothing had really changed when the associates entered the picture, and he continued to see himself as the key man. He wrote Kennedy early in June to assure the banker that he had everything under control:

> You will pardon me for the suggestion, but you are aware that Mr. Kittson is an old gentleman and does not intend to trouble his head much about this railroad matter. J. J. Hill is all right but a very sanguine man. Messrs. Stephens and Smith are a good ways off, and I do not feel at liberty to annoy them on the subject, and will have to rely wholly upon you to financier this matter.[20]

In fact, the receiver himself was past sixty and subject to periods of exhaustion at which time he customarily returned to his Iowa home for several days' rest. Kennedy could only counsel him to be guided "by your own views of your duties and responsibilities," but at the same time he wrote Stephen that he was worried about the arrangement. Relaying Kennedy's concern to Hill, Stephen noted that the weather was too hot and Farley was too busy to "run down to New York" so that Kennedy could explain a number of things to him, but it was nevertheless urgent that the receiver understand the situation. "Tell Mr. Farley," pleaded Stephen, "that he [must] not overlook the fact that whatever be the amount of *debentures* issued, *we* have to pay the amount in cash before we get possession of the road. . . ." Hill took nothing for granted. "I have been up at the front on both lines," he assured Stephen, "and I find it pays to be where the money is being spent."[21]

By midsummer there was grave doubt that the first deadline, which called for the branch line to be completed to Sauk Center by August 1, could be met because of Farley's agonizing slowness. Hill went up to end of track on July 21 and on his return reported to Kennedy, "I got Mr. Farley to go up with me and when on the ground showed him the trouble, and today steps have been taken to remedy it. . . . I am going up to end of track again tomorrow to see there is no hitch. . . ." By the time the first train chugged into the town, just twenty-four hours ahead of the deadline, Hill was deeply worried. "As you know, I think everything of Mr. F[arley]," he wrote Stephen, "but I do not think he fully appreciates the situation and thinks by going slower he will do the work cheaper. This would hold good if there was no winter." [22] But, of course, there was.

Things got worse. The associates had been after Farley to sign a contract with them for the work he was doing, inasmuch as they were paying for it, but he put them off, week after week. Hill was red-faced at having blasted the Cambria Iron Works for failing to deliver iron on schedule, only to be told that Farley had informed them he was in no hurry for it. But when he found out why the Extension was progressing so slowly toward the Canadian boundary, it was the last straw:

> Mr. Robbins had to discharge one of Mr. Farley's favorites who had full charge north of Crookston and who spent half his time at Crookston with a strumpet, and took her on the road with him on the engine, or at times would take the engine off the work in the middle of the afternoon to run down to Crookston in order that he could keep some of the other employees out of his preserve. . . .[23]

After the close call at Sauk Center, Hill had insisted that Farley subcontract the remaining work on the branch and Extension lines to David M. Robbins, the man he had wanted to do the work in the first place. Farley scorned Robbins as "a Livery Stable man with no knowledge of railroad work," but Hill came to depend upon him almost completely. "Now, old friend," he wrote at the end of a long letter in which he meticulously described to Robbins how he wanted the work done, "I have given you our side of it, and I know you will do it the best and fastest way you can. Do not allow any trifle to stand in the way of doing the work. Have every man do his full duty or clean him out. Call loudly whenever you want anything." [24]

VI

The big rolltop desk, where he toiled away at a massive correspondence, remained Hill's base of operations throughout 1878. As the associates' enterprise moved toward its climax, he was their man on the spot. At first his main responsibility had been to oversee Farley's construction work, but he had virtually taken it out of the receiver's hands by early fall, and meanwhile kept a sharp eye on the quickening day-to-day operations of the railroad. He nursed along the matter of the debentures, keeping Judge Dillon and the two commissioners posted on construction progress, and at the same time worked hard to get at least a temporary settlement of the simmering dispute between the St. Paul & Pacific and the Northern Pacific over sharing of business between Duluth, St. Paul, and the Northwest. Donald Smith was in Ottawa much of the time, trying to get Liberal Prime Minister Alexander Mackenzie to negotiate a lease of the Winnipeg-Emerson line of the Canadian Pacific Railway to the associates so that they could inaugurate efficient through service early in 1879. In Montreal George Stephen kept a wary eye on international financial conditions and prayed from day to day that he would get the debentures from Farley in time to prevent a financial crisis at the Cambria Iron Works. Hill had to keep all of these men fully informed of what was going on, and his letterbook rapidly filled up with seven- and fourteen-page letters—sometimes more than one a day—to Stephen and Kennedy. Mary Hill, despairing of seeing anything of her husband during the lovely summer days, walked down to the office to keep him company in the evening. He never forgot the scene:

> I often worked in my office until one in the morning. One night my wife said she would go to the office with me and bring me home at half past ten. It was a summer night and I gave her a book and a chair by the window, where she presently fell asleep. At two I waked her and took her home.[25]

Before the first hint of spring, Hill had turned his attention to the problems of supply that he knew would develop later. It was not grading of the roadbed, or the laying of iron (if they could get deliveries), which worried him, but the prosaic matter of crossties. There were the woods, full of trees waiting to be cut and adzed into ties for his railroad, but as a wood dealer of long experience Hill knew that getting them out was the problem. "There is no snow to haul on [it had been an "open" winter]," he explained to Stephen, "and wagons cannot be used as well now as later. I think the best and cheapest way will be to take a small portable saw mill into the woods on the river . . . and saw them and ship them on the road." Farley, of course, would simply have waited until the farmers had nothing better to do than cut ties and sell them to him cheaply, but Hill had no intention of letting the work bog down. When Hill and Farley had taken up the rails at the north end of the Extension line to build a line to Fisher's Landing, thousands of old ties had been left there. Hill told Robbins to use them as far as they would go—"the farther the better." As summer waned it was clear that they were not going to have enough, so he took the train to Stillwater, on the St. Croix River, where he paid whatever the farmers were demanding until he had 20,000 ties on their way to the Red River country. But ties continued to be a problem. "Our construction has been going slow on the [northern] end owing to our being out of ties a great deal too often," he reported to Stephen. "In fact, if I could afford to I would feel discouraged, but we must do the best we can with what we have." [26]

"The trouble with Farley is, he is slow," Hill told Stephen. One way to speed him up was to make him see that, with labor hard to get in a country that was opening up rapidly to farming, new labor-saving equipment would be called for. Hill could not bear the sight of men laboriously shoveling gravel out of rigid-sided gondolas to ballast the newly laid track. He took the initiative: he procured the kind of equipment which he had seen doing the job quickly and effortlessly on Eastern railroads. "We have finally got the center dumps [cars] at work and the gravel will be put out at the rate of from 80 to 120 cars a day," he proudly told Stephen. He also found a better way to provide water for the locomotives. In this Diesel age we do not bother to think of such problems, but the steam locomotive used then was more likely to run out of water for its boiler than fuel for its firebox. The old management, anxious to save money on both machinery and labor, had erected along the railroad windmills which pumped away, unattended, as long as there was a good wind, and kept the trackside tanks filled. But with several locomotives chuffing back and forth on construction errands, in addition to regular traffic, the capacity of the windmill pumps was quickly overtaxed. Hill nagged Farley to procure larger, steam-driven pumps and install them wherever a man was available to stoke them. [27]

Sooner or later, Hill knew, iron would be the critical factor. Apart from labor, rails were, by a large margin, the costliest item required in building a railroad, and they were about the only thing which otherwise resourceful frontier railroad builders could not improvise on the spot from local materials. The St. Paul & Pacific was being completed at the very moment that iron rails were beginning to be replaced by steel. After Sir Henry Bessemer demonstrated his method of producing steel cheaply in 1858, it had slowly caught on, first in England and later in the United States. Andrew Carnegie, who had sole rights to the process in America, built the first large-scale Bessemer steel works at Pittsburgh in 1874; within two years his entire capital investment had been returned and the future of steel was assured. Actually, Bessemer steel in certain respects was inferior to wrought iron. It was more brittle, and it had a strange tendency to break for no apparent reason. But it was some twelve times as hard as iron, and that is what would make the difference, for the cost of taking up iron rails every year or two in heavily traveled stretches of track, sending them to a local rolling mill to be heated and re-rolled, and then replacing them, was growing prohibitive. Hill convinced Farley that the rails on the oldest and most heavily used part of the railroad should be replaced with steel, and the old iron, re-rolled, sent farther out on the line for new construction. But, in general, the associates could not afford steel in 1878.[28]

About one-half of the cost of construction in 1878, $500,000, went for rails. Kennedy had made a deal with Cambria: that company would furnish some 8650 tons and take most of the payment in receiver's debentures when they became available, on the understanding that, come what may, the entire indebtedness would be liquidated within two years. Kennedy did more than arrange for financing, however, for he kept close watch over Cambria's work schedules, production problems, and labor difficulties, and saw to it that the associates' orders received high priority at a time when the tempo of railroad building was quickening throughout the nation. By the end of June Farley was laying rails on both the branch and the Extension lines, and Hill was reporting to Commissioner Henderson that they expected the line to be competed by October 10.

But then things started to go wrong. The Cambria Works began sending through shipments of rails without the fishplates required to fasten them together, and about the middle of August there was a massive breakdown at the Works. Hill had managed to get the track-laying rate up from less than a mile to over two miles a day, which he had known from the start was possible, but he was beginning to run out of rails. The panicky Stephen hurriedly bought 1000 tons at a premium price from the Springfield Iron Works while they were still committed to a like amount from Cambria. By the end of October the crews were only three miles from Alexandria, their goal on the branch, and eight from the international boundary on the Extension, which only added to Hill's sense of frustration as materials ran short and winter closed in.[29]

Passengers who crowded aboard the cars in the little station at the foot of Sibley Street in St. Paul stared at the strings of flatcars loaded with iron rails that filled the adjoining tracks. As their heavily laden train puffed through Minneapolis, out over the main line through Willmar and Breckenridge, and on up the Red River Valley, they were seldom out of sight of a freight train panting on a siding or, more than once, impatiently passing them as they deferred to it. The surge of traffic which Hill had been predicting for several years had begun.

All the rolling stock, engines, and coaches now on the road are in use and there is not enough to do the business. Last night the Fisher's Landing train ran with five coaches and two baggage cars, all crowded. As soon as Farley returns I think we will want more rolling stock.[30]

The road is doing a very heavy business and today [we] had to hire two engines from the Duluth road. The Fisher's Landing train is the largest and fullest train leaving St. Paul and it certainly looks as if we would have more of it. The Extension lands north of Crookston to the end of track are all applied for and in fact I believe all the extension lands outside of the limits disputed with the N.P. have been applied for. . . . We can have a wheat crop on that line next year of 500,000 bushels. You can have no idea of the rush of immigrants to Minnesota this year. . . .[31]

The farming folk wanted the railroad immediately. One man in Grand Forks, Dakota Territory, wrote to say that they badly needed a siding there, but, knowing how busy Hill was with the main line, they were willing to put it in themselves. Hill thanked him warmly, and took the opportunity to ask how much wheat would be brought to the railroad there when the harvest began.[32] Meanwhile he had noted that the railroads between Chicago and St. Paul were fattening on the huge volume of freight coming through for both the St. Paul & Pacific and the Canadian Pacific projects, and he quickly got the rate on rails reduced by fifty cents a ton. There were other ways to save scarce cash. Learning that there were fifteen new flatcars on a siding in Chicago waiting for his orders, he wired the railroad to hold them there until the lake steamer arrived with their consignment of rails, for the flats might as well come up loaded as unloaded. Hill hated deadheads.[33]

VII

As eloquently as he could, knowing that his words would be passed along to the highest persons in the Canadian government, James J. Hill explained to George Stephen why it was so important to Canada that the line from St. Paul to Winnipeg be completed by the end of the year:

> It is most important for us to have the Pembina [St. Vincent] branch [of the Canadian Pacific Railway] finished this fall so that we can make season contracts and begin our Manitoba trade in March before the Lakes open, and it is of great importance to Canada and Manitoba to have the connection this fall to move the crop during winter, and emigrants from [eastern] Canada can put their effects into a car in Canada and take them out in Manitoba, and arrive early enough to prepare a little crop for the first year, while passengers who wait until the Red River opens are too late for anything of the kind.[34]

He was willing to make almost any deal with the Canadian government, just so long as he could get control of the situation. He yearned for a contract which would make it possible to operate the St. Paul–Winnipeg railroad as a single company, not, as he would repeatedly explain, to extort monopoly profits from the Canadians, but rather to save them from paying an over-all rate which, being the sum of the rate from St. Paul to St. Vincent plus the local rate from St. Vincent to Winnipeg, would be excessive. What he had in mind was to make the rate from points east of St. Paul all the way to Winnipeg equal to the rate from such points to the international boundary, for he had long since learned that nothing promoted Western settlement more rapidly than such long-and-short-haul discrimination.[35] Early that year an article in the Montreal *Gazette* had charged Hill and Kittson (foreigners, as the paper considered them both) with conspiring to prevent any railroad from being built in order to save the profits of their steamboat line. In a cold fury, Hill wrote an influential Winnipeg editor:

> Let me say right here that *if we get the property (and of this we have no doubt)* we will have the cars running to Pembina by the first day of November next [1878] and the only thing to prevent this is the opposition of interests which inspire the very article in the Montreal *Gazette* and for which I most firmly believe that paper was paid. The idea that a steamboat company with a capital of $150,000 could or would invest seven or eight million dollars simply to prevent the completion of 65 miles of railroad is entirely too absurd. . . .

The fact that after so many years waiting, we should be concerned in the only effort made by anyone to render it possible to complete the line to St. Vincent should, we think, meet with more praise than has been accorded us; at least we should have fair play.[36]

If the Canadian people's interests had coincided as closely with their leaders' as they did with Hill's, he would have gotten all he wanted in the matter of the line to Winnipeg. But at just about the same time two of his locomotives were colliding head-on, Ottawa was witnessing an equally violent collison between Donald Smith and homely, bibulous John Alexander Macdonald, "the Old Chieftain," the leader of the Conservative party whose ejection from the prime ministership Smith had had so much to do with in 1873. If a politician could be all but destroyed for permitting favoritism toward a railway enterprise, reasoned Macdonald, perhaps he could be rehabilitated by detecting the same in others. Macdonald had no intention of allowing the timid Mackenzie, who (he accurately predicted) would be roundly defeated in the coming elections, to lease the road to Smith and the other associates. At the height of a filibuster on the last day of the session Macdonald condemned the proposed lease in terms which Smith found objectionable. At once the little Scotsman from Manitoba was on his feet exchanging insults with Macdonald and his overbearing lieutenant, Charles Tupper. Pandemonium reigned in the aisles. The stenographer caught more blows from flying arms than words in the "debate." "Black Rod," the official usher, was ignored as he rapped on the door to summon the members to the Senate chamber for the closing ceremonies. The session broke up in confusion. "That fellow Smith is the biggest liar I ever met," bellowed Macdonald. The bottom was out of the tub, the train was off the track. The Old Chieftain was swept back into office in the elections, while Smith managed to be returned for his district of Selkirk, though only by a hair. Once again the associates would have to find a different route to their goal. There would be no lease.[37]

The Canadian government, meanwhile, was making no effort whatever to get the contractors to finish the railroad to Emerson (across the boundary from St. Vincent) that fall, though it had previously agreed to a deadline of December 31, 1879. Upper and Murphy, the contractors, were losing money, or claimed they were, and saw no reason to lose more by pushing construction in bad weather. Their contract gave them permission to operate the line for the first year after its completion, and they looked forward to making a killing. But Hill was determined to have the line finished according to his deadline, not the Canadian government's. There ensued a round of haggling via telegraph. And, as a result, H. B. Willis, a contractor in whom Hill had more faith, bought out Murphy's interest for $15,000, which Hill guaranteed.

"Blood will tell," Hill wired Upper on September 14, "we will meet you half way." And he did. A month before he had bought fifteen flat cars on his own account and sent them up the line to give the Canadian contractors the equipment for lack of which they were laying so little track. He wired Smith to get the revenue collector at the border to allow an American locomotive to enter Canada in bond to help in the track-laying. To help the road across a small stream, Hill called in a firm of builders in St. Paul, sketched a bridge for them, stood over them while they knocked it together, and dispatched it north on a flatcar. And when the pilots on the Red River steamboats, reasoning that they were the key figures in the drama since they were carrying all of this material down the river to the Canadians' railhead, struck for a wage of $200 a month, Hill, who had already arranged for their replacements, fired them without ceremony.[38]

VIII

Not the least of the risks that the associates were running in 1878 was the danger that Stephen or Hill might be laid low by sickness or death. It is unlikely that Hill could have shouldered Stephen's load in the financial East, since he was already doing the work of three or four ordinary men, and none of the other associates could have carried out Hill's role. Both thrived on the exhilarating work in which they were engaged, but the physical burdens and the extraordinary tensions were bound to take their toll. At first, however, Hill had worried about Kittson, whose weak heart was further strained by the succession of anxieties which the enterprise encountered. In October he wrote to the older man in Chicago to offer reassurances and a word of advice:

> Now my dear Mr. Kittson, I trust nothing whatever will prevent your letting me hear from you and especially so if your health does not improve materially. I am afraid you allow matters of business to annoy you when really everything is going well. It has occurred to me that you must be very lonesome and that if you had Norman [Kittson's son] or one of the [other] boys with you for company it would be much more pleasant for

you. Should you think so I will get passes, etc., for him. . . . About
Wednesday I could take a run down to Chicago to see you. . . . Let me
ask you to write me a short note, if only two or three lines every day or
so, as I assure you I am always uneasy if I do not hear from you, and bear
in mind that I can come to you at a moment's warning.[39]

Donald Smith might find distraction in Canadian politics and the
cliff-hanging canvass in his home province of Selkirk, but George
Stephen was as deeply immersed in the associates' enterprise as Hill,
and, as the chief worrrier over money matters, he was subject to even
greater frustrations. By early summer he was showing his concern: "I
am decidedly of opinion that you ought to get rid of [those] in whose
loyalty to us you have not the fullest confidence; in short, we are in a
battle for life, and must not neglect even the smallest source of
help." [40] He had not been prepared for Judge Dillon's stipulation that
the debentures would not be issued until the work had been performed, which meant that by late fall the associates would be in debt
to the extent of nearly a million dollars above what they had originally
anticipated. By October Stephen was almost frantic, seeing in every
bearish report that the Atlantic cable brought him the toppling of the
first domino in their shaky enterprise:

> You know that we have calculated on getting [the debentures] on 1st
> November at latest, and I much fear delay beyond that date will cause us
> great loss and serious embarrassment. . . .

> You will see by yesterday's European cables that serious financial difficul-
> ties have appeared at Glasgow and elsewhere with strong indications of
> increasing and spreading all over the country. If this occurs, it may not be
> possible for the Bank of Montreal, in justice to itself, to do all for us that it
> might otherwise have done. . . .

> This [the debenture problem] is a matter of supreme importance. . . .
> Things are so squally that I am quite uneasy about our Bank liabilities.
> . . . I have written about the distribution of the steamboat earnings. . . .
> We *must* get that money to pay our December interest. . . .[41]

Hill, at least, could choose from a variety of headaches. By early fall
he had fairly well solved his problems in human relations, although
the associates would pay dearly for his having ridden roughshod over
Farley's ego. But Nature was fickle, and what she gave with one hand
she took back with the other. By midsummer, when navigation on the
Red River should have been at its height and all of the boats crammed
to the gunwales with railroad construction materials, the water level
on the river was the lowest on record. By mid-July, Hill wrote Kittson,

the level at Goose Rapids, one of the most troublesome spots on the stream, was only two feet and falling fast. No technique known to these resourceful river men could carry the steamer *Grandin* over the barrier, and she was laid up for the season. Captain Holcombe must have thought Hill had taken leave of his senses that fall when he bought a second-hand locomotive from the Northern Pacific, had the name "Countess of Dufferin" painted gaudily on her cab, and dispatched her north toward Winnipeg on a barge:

> Now, we have two or three boats that must be hauled out before there is *any ice.* . . . What may happen to the balance of the line in the next month is more than I can tell. Our two best boats, the *Minnesota* and the *Manitoba,* leak like two old baskets, and the wear and tear at this stage of water is perfectly fearful. . . . While I don't have the least particle of faith in the completion of the RR to Pembina [St. Vincent] before the close of navigation . . . I am still hoping that it will be done in order to be able to run our boats from there for a week or two. . . . The car barges were started from Fisher's [Landing] * Tuesday evening . . . It was an awful [*sic*] job to get them out of the Red Lake River; the one carrying the locomotive draws more water than there is in the river. . . .[42]

When the rains finally came, they came in torrents. The Extension line, where several hundred men were at work, was under water for weeks that fall, although it had been laid down several miles from the river to avoid just such a possibility. Soon the workmen were breaking thin sheets of ice on the water barrels each morning, and the "two old baskets" were crunching through ice which was a little thicker each day as they came up to the landings. Traffic on the unseasoned new line was far greater than it could handle safely. Two locomotives crashed into each other near Crookston one day, and derailments were common:

> We have had four trains off the track—one passenger and three freights. One of the freights damaged 14 cars more or less with their contents and the other damaged 4 cars; the third, only the engine. The passenger train [accident] was caused by a broken rail and the air brakes saved the train. . . .[43]

Remarkably, Hill noted, no one had been killed in these mishaps.

By October Stephen, in a dark mood, was writing Hill on the subject of the extraordinary sacrifices the two of them were making. In addition to substantial sums which Stephen had laid out for expenses, no-

---

* Fisher's Landing, where the contents of railroad cars were loaded onto steamboats or barges, was on the Red Lake River, which flowed into the Red River a short distance to the west.

tably on the trip to Europe, he had given up business activities which, he said, had been netting him $35,000 to $45,000 a year in order to work full time on the takeover. Reminding Hill that he, too, had made similar sacrifices, Stephen suggested that when the profits of the enterprise were calculated, the two of them should receive an additional $25,000 apiece in recognition of these financial hardships.[44] The letter found Hill, who was worried about his wife's health, in a similar state of mind. Mary was expecting again, and seemed little prepared for the winter that was approaching. He was still determined to complete the St. Paul & Pacific to the boundary before December 1, and even to get some kind of train service to Winnipeg shortly thereafter, but when he replied to Stephen's letter on October 19, it was in the same minor key:

> I have always supposed that at the proper time such a settlement as you mention would be made, as of course the burdens whatever they may be should be divided as fairly as possible.
>
> We all know how you have devoted your time, money and credit to bring about the results arrived at. I am sure no one connected with the enterprise either would or could object to the sum named by you for yourself, but in my own case you are too liberal.
>
> The business which I gave up yielded me an income of about $15,000 per annum and I do not look to be reimbursed to an extent beyond my income at least. My travelling expenses, cables, telegraph bills, &c, which included travelling expenses for Mr. Kittson, attorneys, &c, except about $400.00 paid by Mr. K. amount in all to about $4200. It seems to me that if you would reduce the amount named for me to $15,000 and increase your own that amount the proportion would be more equitable, in any event that amt named for me is too high, and [I] should feel that I was being preferred above others, in fact that I am not entitled to it.
>
> I know both yourself and Mr. Smith will wonder why our track is not nearer the boundary, and I can only say that we have not had the material to lay as fast as we otherwise could, and we have had fearful weather. The wet country passed over by Mr. Smith has from further rains become entirely covered with water on the East side over a foot deep and it has been impossible to crowd the work. We have lost several days on account of ice and snow.
>
> The work seems to drive and control everybody in place of being controlled and driven.

Ten days later the railhead was still eight miles from the Canadian boundary.[45]

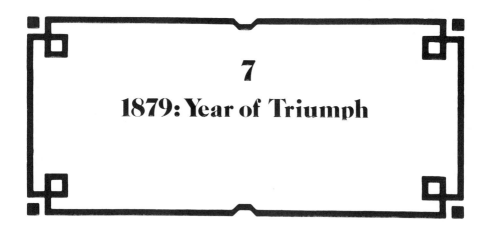

7

1879: Year of Triumph

Stephen writes that he has settled with Litchfield. This is the happiest news I have received for many a day. Mr. Kittson will have to go to the Psalmist to express his joy.

—James J. Hill, 1879

I

Like many another diarist, James J. Hill began the new year with the best of intentions, but quickly found that it was an onerous task to live a full, energetic, exciting life and note it all down in a book as well. With notable exceptions, as when he had just witnessed the Fenian raid across the Canadian border at Pembina, or when he was indignant at the successful posing of a feminist lecturer, his diaries often petered out as the year progressed. The hectic year of 1878 found him far too busy for such chronicles. Fortunately, his duty to keep his partners informed of his progress on the spot in Minnesota while they stuck to their posts in Ottawa, Montreal, and New York resulted in a rich legacy of information on the takeover of the St. Paul & Pacific Railroad. The outlines of his family life in this critical year are less clear, the more so since his daughter Clara's reminiscences end with dark hints of a personal crisis in late 1878. But from the little evidence we have it is clear that at the height of his titanic labors to complete the railroad into St. Vincent, and to get the Canadians to do likewise, Mary Hill almost died.

By November 1878 Mrs. Hill was seven months pregnant. The previous February she had supervised the exhausting job of moving her large family from Dayton's Bluff to the new house at Ninth and Canada streets, but that was just the beginning of her tasks. From New York arrived two thousand dollars' worth of new furniture—which began to come apart almost immediately in the cold, dry climate. Yards and yards of heavy raw silk draperies, also from the East, had to be hung in the lavish folds, so dear to the mid-Victorians, in room after room of the new house. What seemed like acres of carpet had to be cut and laid, wall to wall, in what was then not so much a symbol of bourgeois success as a practical concession to the Minnesota winters. The children were demanding more thought and attention every day. Mamie, only a year or two from adolescence, was in the best of hands with the sisters at Visitation Academy, but James Norman and Louis, who were eight and six years old, needed a strict disciplinarian. Hill found the answer in August N. Chemidlin, a Frenchman who had been educated by the Jesuits in Nancy and was a close friend of Father Caillet, who recommended him as a tutor. It was the beginning of a long friendship between two generations of Hills and this gentle, stoop-shouldered man, so typical of that now-forgotten class who, with dignity and loyalty, served the rich and powerful upon whom they were totally dependent to make their way in the world. Mary was glad to get Jimmie and Louie settled with M. Chemidlin in the schoolroom on the third floor, and delighted to find that little Clara liked to wander in and out of the boys' lessons when she tired of the work Miss Adams, her kindergarten teacher, had set for her.[1]

In the critical third and fourth months of Mary's pregnancy, her worried husband insisted that she and the children spend the short, hot summer at a resort, even though he knew it meant that he would see very little of them. He packed them off to Elmo Lodge at Lake Elmo, Minnesota, about fifteen miles east of St. Paul, near the beautiful valley of the St. Croix River. Hill managed to get out there for one day in the first month of their stay, and he brought with him his brother Alexander and Alec's wife, who were on a visit from Rockwood. At the end of July he came out again, this time with R. B. Angus, general manager of the Bank of Montreal, and his family. Back in St. Paul by the first of September, Mary quickly found herself caught up again in the routine of a large, busy, and somewhat noisy ménage. But she was feeling fit, and worried about nothing more than maintaining the tranquillity of her household for the sake of her hard-working husband. Tired but generally happy, except on particularly frustrating days, Hill seemed replenished by the hour or so dinner took from his preoccupation with business. Almost every night, however, he went into his study to write the massive letters which were Stephen's and Kennedy's only means of keeping abreast of their affairs. Long after the clock had struck midnight, Mary, seeing the lamplight shining under his door, and hearing nothing but the scratch of a pen and the rustle of letters being folded, was tempted more than once to urge her hard-driving husband to bed.

In the cold, wet days of November a bad cold brought her chills and a high fever, and Mary took to her bed. Doctor Hand confirmed what her husband dreaded to hear: pneumonia. At that moment Hill's epic labors were being crowned with success as the last rail was laid into St. Vincent, but it was no time for celebration. For one thing, it brought more problems than it solved, for now men and equipment had to be shifted north to help Willis in the last desperate drive to finish the line from Winnipeg. "Will try to go up Monday," he wired Willis on November 14. "Wife very ill. Iron and spikes will be there. Robbins [the associates' contractor] will turn in seven horse teams and iron horse." The feeble attempt at a joke must have cost him great effort, for Mary and their unborn child were near death. In this age of penicillin, we have forgotten the anguish of those who watched helplessly while the pneumonia victim's lungs gradually filled with the fluid which, if her natural bodily defenses proved insufficient, would inevitably drown her. Faithful Doctor Hand, assisted by Dr. F. R. Smith and his son, were in almost constant attendance. Worried servant girls moved noiselessly into and out of the sick room, carrying out the orders of the physicians. The odor of the aromatic substances which the doctors used to help the patient's breathing hung depressingly in the air of the overheated room. The children, aware that something terrible was happening to their mother, anxiously plied their nursemaid with questions as she urged them into bed.

But Mary Hill was not going to die. The life within her, the new world that was opening up for her husband in which she was vitally needed, and, not least, her hardy Celtic constitution triumphed over the disease and the clumsy efforts of her doctors. Once the crisis was past, she found the long convalescence that her bout with pneumonia demanded to be a boon in her last weeks of pregnancy. Soon she was commiserating with her husband, who plaintively announced the arrival of his first case of rheumatism. By late January she was up and around, dropping by his office on the twenty-ninth to remind him to wire her favorite nurse to come over from Minneapolis. Two days later she called her husband early in the morning, "and at 8 a.m. we had a splendid little girl born," the vastly relieved husband noted in the diary which he had again resolved to keep in the new year. Little Clara, deeply impressed by these events, would tell the story of her mother's illness and her sister Ruth's birth many times.[2]

II

Smiling nervously as the section hands showed them how to grasp the rail carriers, twenty well-bustled Manitoba ladies lifted the last rail of the Canadian Pacific branch line into place at Emerson on December 3, 1878. The continuous rail line from St. Paul to Winnipeg was now complete, and the dream of two decades had been realized—but just barely. For the rest of the winter the line from the international boundary to Winnipeg would be "very little better than no railway," as Hill put it. The contractors, claiming a $26,000 loss, were insisting on their right to operate the line to the end of 1879 in hope of recouping their stake and making a good profit. The Canadian government inspector had a long list of items which the contractors had not yet furnished, and it required all the persuasiveness Hill and Donald Smith could muster to get him to approve the line at all. Most disturbing was the fact that Hill had forgotten to get Willis specifically approved by the government when he had bought out Upper's partner's contract, and now the new government—Macdonald's—refused to recognize the arrangement.

The last weeks of construction had seen a virtual takeover of the project by Hill. As soon as the St. Paul & Pacific had been completed to St. Vincent, on November 10, he had sent every man and piece of equipment north to help the Canadians. "Fix Flannagan [the Canadian foreman] up with outfit to lay Canadian iron," he wired Robbins on November 14. "Can send you all the men you want." Two days later he laid down the law to Willis. "What is to prevent track-laying?" he wired. "Answer fully. It must be laid." Now that there was a semblance of a railroad it was possible to run a train almost every day in each direction, but because of the shortage of watering points the runs had to be held down to a couple of passenger cars and one freight car.

The northern terminus, which would be at St. Boniface until a bridge was built across the Red River, had no turntable or "wye" track, so the little train had to make the return trip to St. Vincent in reverse.[3]

Without fanfare, the branch line of the St. Paul & Pacific had reached Alexandria on November 5 with nearly a month to spare. At almost the same time the last mile was being hammered through on the Extension line to St. Vincent. On November 9 Farley and Hill, accompanied by a number of friends, had come up to end of track in the first two Pullman Palace sleeping cars which the line had ever owned, the "St. Paul" and the "Minneapolis," and on the tenth they made a triumphal run all the way from the international boundary into the Twin Cities. Drawn by Locomotive No. 1, the "William Crooks," patriarch of a rapidly increasing tribe, the train had clipped off the miles at the rate of forty-two per hour. This was good news to the jittery George Stephen in Montreal, but the best news of all would be that the receiver's debentures had been issued and were on their way to Kennedy. The associates' indebtedness, on their own signatures and Kennedy's, was approaching a million dollars by this time, over and above what they owed the Bank of Montreal for funds advanced to pay the Dutchmen, and another $140,000 interest payment was due shortly. The debentures had been one long series of disappointments. By October Stephen had begun to fear the worst, warning that any delay beyond November 1 "will cause us great loss and serious embarrassment." [4]

Hill was pressing Judge Dillon to issue at least part of the debentures before construction was finished. He reminded Kennedy that the Judge had agreed to do so with the express approval of the Dutchmen, and he encouraged the banker to get their assent, but without success. At the end of October he hustled Farley and George B. Young, his most able lawyer, off to Des Moines to plead with Dillon. "I have it arranged with the Governor to send a friendly engineer to inspect the road and have it accepted by the state the day it is completed," he wrote Stephen soothingly. But two days later he had to telegraph the bad news to Montreal: "Receiver and Young here. Debentures will not be issued before December 10th." Then he wrote an explanation:

> The judge expressed great satisfaction that the work had been done and said it was the most successful operation his court had, and generally pleased at the result. However, it would be necessary for him to guard the interests of the minority bondholders inasmuch as we were asking for a lien ahead of all others on all the property. . . . He said his liberality

towards railways had been made a subject of very severe and hostile criticism in the "Iowa Central" case and he desired to put himself in as strong a position as possible in this case. . . .

Hill may have reflected that if Dillon was not able to make a distinction between their straightforward operation and Russell Sage's Iowa manipulations, then justice was indeed blind.[5]

Dillon's deliberateness was agonizing. He put the case on the docket for the December term of the Circuit Court in St. Paul, and then blandly announced that he would not be on the bench himself, but on circuit in Arkansas where, he may have noted, the weather would be considerably milder. Hill was horrified; what a strange judge might do could not even be imagined. Upon his earnest application, Dillon reluctantly agreed to come and hear the case himself. Stephen had repeatedly urged Hill to have the certificates all printed up and ready for Farley's signature as soon as the Judge ruled, but that proved impossible, for the Judge reserved the very wording of the debentures until the last. When he finally handed down his ruling, on December 21, the securities, as Hill had feared, were made a first lien only on those portions of the railroad which they had built that year. It was far better than nothing, however, and J. S. Kennedy & Company would simply have to work one more financial miracle in getting them accepted by their creditors.

Off he rushed to the printing office, where he waited while 800 $1000 certificates were run off. He had warned Farley to stand by in his office, pen poised, ready to scratch his name painfully at the bottom of each one if he had to sit up all night doing it. Next afternoon a brown-wrapped package, carefully sealed with wax in several places, was handed over to the express agent at the railroad station in St. Paul, and two days later the delighted Kennedy received it in his office on New York's Cedar Street. It was almost exactly a year since Hill and Galusha had turned their backs on their Christmas firesides and headed for Montreal to help revive the associates' project. Now the season and a great feeling of relief were making Hill feel benevolent even toward Farley, with whom he still had numerous bones to pick. Discovering that the older man had left for Dubuque to spend the holidays, Hill sent him a jovial Christmas Eve note: "I hope you will have the merriest kind of Christmas and let me ask you not to spoil it by being uneasy about things here. If the boys will keep the trains moving, everything else will keep until you return."[6]

Stephen must have known, as Hill did, that despite the obstacles which had been thrown in their way and the frustrations which had ensued, their project was developing an almost irresistible momentum. Hill had peered over the bookkeeper's shoulder every month when the operating results were totaled up, and by the first of November it was clear that the railroad was going to end its first eleven months since the associates began their takeover with a net profit of more than $600,000. Hill's original estimate had been $400,000. Throughout the year he had pried ever larger sums out of Farley to be remitted to the railroad's creditors in the East, so that the difference between the $800,000 of receiver's debentures and the $980,000 which Hill estimated the year's work had cost was taken care of. Kennedy, whom both Hill and Stephen would later remember as nervous and erratic, in fact displayed a welcome imperturbability. On November 25, with Mary well past the crisis in her fight with pneumonia and with Kittson feeling better than ever, the two men and Galusha went to New York for a conference with Smith, Stephen, and Kennedy. Meeting at the Windsor Hotel, which was near Kennedy's 57 Street brownstone residence, they concluded that only two difficult problems remained: the working out of a *modus vivendi* with the Northern Pacific, and a settlement with Litchfield. And the closer the associates came to bringing off the foreclosure suits the better their bargaining power would be. "Interview very satisfactory," Hill wrote elatedly in his expense notebook. "Messrs. Kennedy & Co. gave assurance of their robust cooperation. Pair of canes, N.Y., $6.00." If the canes were for Kittson and his friend to use in a triumphant stroll down Fifth Avenue, they had earned it.

III

"It brings an empire to our very doors," exulted the St. Paul *Daily Globe* at the end of 1878, referring to the 343 miles of railroad which had been built in Minnesota during the year. Railroads "now gridiron the empire state of the northwest, and Dakota clasps hands with the commercial emporium," bragged the editor. Nearly one-third, or 96 miles, of this new railroad had been laid by the new owners of the St. Paul & Pacific, and the editor headlined their accomplishment in linking St. Paul with Winnipeg. But he also found it exciting that the Northern Pacific had finally built the "Brainerd branch" which connected the main line of that road with the St. Paul & Pacific branch line from Sauk Rapids into St. Paul. "Supplemented by permanent running arrangements over the branch line of the St. P. & P.," the editor explained, the new Northern Pacific line made St. Paul "the eastern terminus of this great transcontinental railway." [7]

The editor made it all sound so easy. Seven years had passed since William G. Moorhead and James W. Taylor had finally convinced Jay Cooke that he had built the wrong railroad, and that the natural eastern terminus of the Northern Pacific was not Duluth, but St. Paul. Time was running out when the Northern Pacific gained control of the St. Paul & Pacific at the end of 1870, and barely two years later the Northern Pacific men had not only failed to integrate the St. Paul road into their scheme, but had lost their grip on the transcontinental line as well. By 1878 a new team was in charge, chief among whom were President Charles B. Wright, a hard-working, shrewd, but rather sickly Pennsylvania banker who had built the Philadelphia & Erie Railroad; General George Stark, who was in charge of operations; and Frederick C. Billings, the most able of the group, who had been author of the plan under which the bankrupt Northern Pacific had been reorganized.

The Northern Pacific faced a policy decision of the most fundamental kind. Ideally, they would have liked to grasp the lucrative Red River Valley business, which was about to enrich the smart operators who had just taken over the St. Paul & Pacific, but that opportunity was gone forever. At the same time, their main goal, which was to build westward into Dakota Territory and on to Puget Sound, beckoned as enticingly as ever. But at the very least they had to have access to St. Paul (or to Minneapolis, which, they intimated to leaders of that ambitious city, would be just as good) as an eastern terminus. The importance of Duluth in their traffic with the East was obviously going to diminish. The directors of the Northern Pacific quickly divided into two camps: those who, like Wright, wanted to meet the St. Paul & Pacific head-on in competition for the business between the Twin Cities and the Red River country by building their own "west-side line" down the west bank of the Mississippi from Sauk Rapids into St. Paul, and another "west-side line" north from Fargo to the international boundary; and another group, followers of Billings, who wanted to husband the Northern Pacific's scarce resources to press toward Bismarck, Dakota Territory, and beyond, as rapidly as possible. The latter group were willing to compromise with the St. Paul & Pacific, recognizing it as a predominantly north-south line in return for the associates' recognition of the Northern Pacific's claim to east-west business and for running rights over the St. Paul & Pacific into St. Paul.[8]

Hill got set for a brawl right from the start. He had nothing but contempt for the Easterners who, ignorant of the real transportation needs of the Northwest, had bungled the Northern Pacific project so badly for a decade, and he knew full well that George L. Becker, a trustee of the St. Paul & Pacific, was still trying to deliver the road into the Northern Pacific's hands. Hill's espionage system worked well. In the fall of 1877 Captain Holcombe had notified him that the Northern Pacific was trying to get control of the Canadians' Winnipeg branch. Fortunately for the associates, the confusions of Canadian politics were working in their favor in this instance, for if the Northern Pacific had got hold of the line and had built its own line on the west bank of the Red from Fargo north to meet it, the future of the St. Paul & Pacific would have been dim indeed. Even so, Hill was repeatedly angered by the hostility of the Northern Pacific, whose general superintendent, Homer E. Sargent, used various tactics to keep business on his line and away from its rival. Agreements on rates and on division of receipts for business carried jointly were made and almost immediately broken, until Hill realized that only sheer necessity would force them to keep their word:

> We do not expect they are going to act fairly in anything until they are compelled to, and we hope to be in the position to compel them in a very few days. We have received nothing from them but broken faith and insufferable arrogance.[9]

In the heady days of June, with the associates' plans proceeding smoothly, Hill had exuded confidence. "We do not think the Nor Pac people intend to build any road in Minnesota, either in the Minnesota Red River Valley or from Sauk Rapids to Mpls. If they build any road, they would be more apt to build west of Bismarck and earn their land grant," he assured Stephen. As for the efforts of the Northern Pacific to make common cause with the railroads to Chicago, both of which also had ambitions west of the Twin Cities, Wright's statement that the Milwaukee road was going to join them "is a ———— lie." The Chicago & North Western, he noted, was already using the St. Paul & Pacific's yards in St. Paul, and the Milwaukee road was begging him to enlarge them so that they could use them too. He wrote S. S. Merrill, general superintendent of the Milwaukee, an expansive letter emphasizing the value to that line of "the friendly cooperation of the St. Paul & Pacific," and reminding him that of the 9000 tons of rails which they were bringing in that summer, one-half would be carried by Merrill's railroad to St. Paul. Two weeks later he was not so sure of himself, for his sources had notified him that the top Northern Pacific executives were arriving in St. Paul on their way to the Red River to make arrangements for building a west-side line, and that Alexander Mitchell, president of the Milwaukee, was with them. By the end of October Hill was threatening Mitchell with a boycott of the Milwaukee road by St. Paul shippers unless the Chicagoans demonstrated their unmistakable loyalty to St. Paul.[10]

It was time to bring up the big Eastern guns. When Hill went to New York early in July he asked Kennedy to invite Jay Cooke to a meeting to discuss their problems. Cooke struck a haughty pose at first, but as Hill and Kennedy laid out the situation for him, he soon "talked as if he desired to have all matters fairly adjusted between the companies." But Jay Cooke was not running the Northern Pacific any longer. Although Merrill assured Hill at the Minneapolis railroad convention a few days later that the Northern Pacific, on the advice of the Milwaukee, would abandon its plans to build from Sauk Rapids into St. Paul or Minneapolis, and despite the Northern Pacific's willingness to sign an agreement to submit their rate disputes to arbitration, Sargent was as hostile as ever. Informed that the Northern Pacific man was putting off naming his arbitrator from week to week, Stephen voiced complete support for Hill's tough policy. "Deal with them fairly," he wrote, "as a line running to *Lake Superior,* and have nothing to do with any pretension they may set up as a line to St. Paul, to which they have no claim. If they will not settle with you on some such basis we shall be obliged to pitch with them all we can, hot and heavy." Even the cautious Kennedy was ready to fight.[11]

Hill took his friends at their word. When Wright was in St. Paul in early September, Hill had several meetings with him and tried to beat the stubborn Easterner into immediate submission. But Stephen was appalled at the belligerent stance which Hill adopted. Hill had written Stephen:

> I have seen Wright several times and have just left him about to start for Philadelphia to prepare his report for their annual meeting on the 26th. I have given Mr. Wright to understand that we wanted it settled . . . whether we were to [be] friends or enemies. . . .

I told him that . . . if he persistently attacked us we would make a struggle for life and would not come off second best—that we would at once
survey a line from Grand Forks to Fort Buford at the mouth of the Yellow-
stone which was on a good and easy line all the way, through a country as
good for agriculture as the very best portions of his road, and we would
ask Congress for half of his grant to the *Rocky Mountains, &c,* and that he
knew there were strong interests opposed to him who would be only too
glad to help us. . . .[12]

This was no way to talk to the man who welcomed evidence that
Billings's policy of compromise with the associates was impractical.
Although arbitration, which had finally taken place a few days after
Hill's warlike letter, had resulted in a highly satisfactory arrangement
for the St. Paul & Pacific which gave the Northern Pacific only re-
stricted use of the branch line, there was no guarantee that even this
limited settlement would endure. Hill returned from the Northern Pacific's annual meeting more belligerent than ever, convinced as he was
that Wright's board would not let him build his own line into St. Paul.
From this point on George Stephen took over negotiations with both
the Northern Pacific and the Litchfields, for it was evident that Hill
was too close to the problem, too emotionally involved, and too well
identified with a particular point of view. As Captain Barnes would
put it in another context, "Hill is inclined to make messes of negotiations in which he has no special experience." Stephen wrote to Stark
in a conciliatory tone, encouraging the Northern Pacific men to
suggest an annual rental for sharing the branch line into St. Paul. In
mid-October he spent several days in New York conferring with
Wright and Stark, but he refused to accept or reject any specific offer
until Hill had studied it.[13]

Why were the associates so worried about the Northern Pacific? The
answer is that an accommodation which would give that railroad
access to St. Paul and its freight and passenger handling facilities was
a life and death matter to the Northern Pacific. They were willing to
play every card in their hand to get it, and it was a good hand. Their
best card turned out to be the rivalry between Minneapolis and St.
Paul. Men like W. D. Washburn, the leading miller in the "Mill City"
and himself a power in Minnesota's evolving railroad system, tried
every blandishment they could think of to get the Northern Pacific to
build down the west side of the Mississippi from St. Cloud, by-pass-
ing St. Paul altogether. The city fathers had a charter for such a road

and public opinion was clearly in support of a bond issue to help finance it.

A second card was the fact that the St. Paul & Pacific was no longer the only rail link between the Twin Cities. The Milwaukee Railroad was building its "short line," which would take it along the Mississippi directly into Minneapolis after pausing at the St. Paul & Pacific station in St. Paul, and the Northern Pacific was flirting with the Milwaukee. President Mitchell of the Milwaukee was in an uncomfortable position. General Stark, writing to inform him that Stephen had asked the Northern Pacific to make the associates an offer to settle their difficulties, reminded him that he, Mitchell, had promised Billings the use of the Milwaukee's short line if their negotiations with Hill and Stephen failed. To the citizens of Minneapolis this was all beside the point, because their civic ambition ran so far as to encourage the Northern Pacific to make their city its terminal and main headquarters, thus ignoring St. Paul altogether. At the end of October, although things looked favorable for a settlement with Stephen, Stark dropped in on Mitchell in Milwaukee, later reporting to Wright that "they do not want to put anything on paper, but he assures me that if we get down to Minneapolis, they will provide without delay a short route to St. Paul." [14]

The Northern Pacific never let up until the last card was about to be played, because by fall it was clear that the associates had an Achilles heel in the uncertainty they faced at the international boundary. The overthrow of the Mackenzie government, in view of Donald Smith's poor relations with Macdonald, seemed to give the Northern Pacific's Manitoba ambitions new life. While accepting Hill's blood, treasure, fifteen flat cars, and the "Countess of Dufferin," Joe Upper, the Canadian contractor, was simultaneously dealing with Stark. Wright sent Stark off to Ottawa to disrupt the delicate negotiations between Stephen and Macdonald, explaining to Sir John that "[Stark's] mission is to call your attention to the desirability of securing and strengthening mutually advantageous and permanent relations and connections between our railroad and the international and through carrying business of Canada, more especially with reference to that of Manitoba." [15] It was a very good hand.

Horace Thompson, president of the First National Bank and one of St. Paul's leading citizens, broke the deadlock. By late October Stephen realized that the associates would have to make the branch line available to the Northern Pacific for joint use, and probably would have to yield to their demand for a free gift of ten acres of the St. Paul & Pacific's increasingly valuable land on the river front for their own yards. The trouble was that, assuming the two railroads were to operate entirely separate facilities, the Northern Pacific needed much more land there to accommodate a roundhouse for its engines and allow for future growth. This was what made Minneapolis' siren song so attractive—beyond its value as a club to wield over the associates. Thompson had besought J. S. Kennedy to stop such thinking, and Kennedy had replied that he had warned Jay Cooke not to proceed with that kind of blackmail: "If [the Northern Pacific] can stand it, I think the St. P. & P. can also . . . but after the many follies committed by the NP Co., I should hardly think they would want to add to them by building a line from Sauk Rapids to Mpls . . ." But Thompson and other civic-minded citizens, unwilling to risk a development which could lead to St. Paul's withering on the transportation vine, produced a plan to convey to the Northern Pacific as much as seventy-five acres of land, at a bargain price.[16]

Early in November Stephen notified Stark that he was coming to New York to seek a solution. "I find the practical difficulties in the way of an arrangement . . . are greater than I had anticipated," he warned, "but I will do all that lies in my power to overcome them." Two days later, on November 8, Stephen and his adversaries settled in principle the main elements of their controversy, and later that day the Northern Pacific's board adopted a resolution empowering Billings, Stark, and Mitchell to go to St. Paul to work out a formal "protocol," as they called it. The associates had bought a few years' time, during which the pretense that the St. Paul & Pacific was strictly a north-south line and the Northern Pacific an east-west line would be observed. It was all Hill really wanted. The secret was well kept for more than two weeks. On November 16 Billings was handed a plaintive telegram from Washburn, in Minneapolis: "Hope you will not commit yourself on railroad question until friends here can see you. . . ."[17]

IV

Pity the harried businessman who finds it necessary to deal with an elderly, stubborn, garrulous opponent who has plenty of time to devote to the struggle! Such was George Stephen's lot at the end of 1878, when the associates faced the necessity of settling with Litchfield. As winter approached, Hill had come to realize that "the stock [of the First Division of the St. Paul & Pacific, which Litchfield owned] is the 'bridge' that will carry us over." The associates' takeover strategy was based on using the bonds, nearly all of which they owned by then, to buy in the railroad at a sheriff's foreclosure sale. This would have the effect of extinguishing Litchfield's equity, but with the railroad's earnings increasing to the point where it might well be able to pay the interest on some, if not all, of its bonds, a court might be reluctant to order foreclosure sales. Litchfield's chances of dragging out the lawsuits were excellent, and the prospect of "the old fox" sitting down with George L. Becker and his ilk at a First Division board meeting, while the associates were reduced to no other function than to clip their coupons, was more than Hill could bear.

Hill had approached Litchfield about a settlement as early as May 1877, when he was in New York to confer with Kennedy. At that time Litchfield maintained, as he always had, that his agreement with the Dutch bondholders for operation of the First Division by trustees was still in effect, and that nothing short of a full participation in the associates' enterprise would satisfy him. Hill informed him that that was out of the question, and left with the impression that Litchfield could be bought off. A year later Litchfield named his price: a round million dollars, a figure at which Hill hooted. By late fall Hill and Stephen had agreed on a payoff of $200,000, and Hill was not reluctant to turn the negotiations over to his friend. "It is a good thing for you to see him and endure him," Hill wrote, "and I am sure his long-winded accusations will be sooner ended with you than with anyone else." [18]

In the dark days of November Hill and Stephen had concluded that a settlement with Litchfield was bound up with reaching a *modus vivendi* with the Northern Pacific. From the moment Stephen and the Northern Pacific reached agreement, Billings had begun to use his good offices to conclude a deal with Litchfield by means of a united-front strategy. "Litchfield has sent me 16 closely written pages arguing his case," he moaned to Stephen, enclosing a copy of his reply, which concluded with a warning and a threat:

> Suppose Mr. Stephen should take it into his head to join the NP in building [the line from Sauk Rapids into St. Paul]. . . . What becomes of all your figures as to value [of your stock]? I believe Mr. Stephen and his associates will win in the end. Mr. Stephens [*sic*] is fair and frank. What he offers you I suppose is to hurry up his foreclosure and get rid of litigation.

. . . Now, what I want to know, in confidence, [is] if I can get him up to $500,000, will you come down to that sum? . . . You can readily see that if litigation is to go on I must do all in my power to aid Mr. Stephens." [19]

But Litchfield *was* an "old fox." He had already got wind of the settlement between the associates and the Northern Pacific, and with great gusto wrote a cocky letter to Stephen, rejoicing in this victory for "our property." [20] Meanwhile, Stephen was trying some tactics of his own. To Billings he sent a strangely indifferent letter:

> My friends in St. P. and N.Y. do not hesitate to say that my offer [which had been increased to $400,000] was absurdly too high. Notwithstanding all that I wrote to Mr. L. from Chicago giving him to 2nd Dec. to say yes or no. If he says yes I shall be pleased. If he says no all my friends will be pleased.

But there was another letter to Billings in the same envelope, which he was supposed to read first:

> If he [Litchfield] were like men generally and as wise as he is able he would at once accept your suggestion and offer to mediate. . . . I have written the enclosed for *his eye* if you should think proper to send to him. The point to impress upon him is . . . *time*. . . . I must close with him one way or another before leaving New York next Thursday. [21]

But he did not settle, and the matter dragged on through December and into January. Billings wired Stephen for permission to offer $400,000 plus $25,000 for "expenses," and Stephen gave his assent through Captain Barnes. What sent Stephen scurrying back to New York, however, was the news from St. Paul about the rate at which money was rolling into the coffers of the St. Paul & Pacific "These figures," Hill warned him, "under all the circumstances are to me the strongest argument in favor of settling with William Street [Litchfield's office was on William Street] before he learns the situation. . . ." Lawyers Young and Galusha had rendered a written opinion of the value of Litchfield's securities to the associates which further convinced Hill that a settlement was vital. He was crushed, therefore, to get Stephen's telegram on January 15: "Leaving for Montreal. Negotiations postponed." [22]

But Stephen, it seems, did not trust the telegraph operators at St. Paul. Two days later, just before leaving for Ottawa and discussions with Tupper, Macdonald's lieutenant, he scrawled a letter to Hill:

> My wire from N.Y., announcing the postponement of negotiations must have been a great disappointment to you and to Mr. Kittson. The fact is I have settled with the "old rat" on the basis of $500,000. . . .

Now, not a word about a settlement must be said, and no one in St. Paul must know about it, except of course Mr. Kittson. . . . The old rascal's idea is to bring Bigelow & Becker to N.Y. to *make* an *agreement;* they must not know that we have made one already, or all the fat would be in the fire. Old L. wants to cheat both of them, & it is not our policy to interfere. . . . I had a terribly wearisome 4 or 5 days in N.Y. with the old fellow.[23]

Hill was elated, for the New Year could not have opened more auspiciously. Mary was well again, his family circle had been increased once more, and now the stone of Litchfield had been lifted from his heart. "Since the acceptance of our offer by the Dutchmen," he told Stephen, "nothing has happened which gives me so much joy. Mr. Kittson will have to go to the Psalmist to express his joy." Out came the diary. "This is the happiest news I have received for many a day," he wrote.[24]

V

It is a fact of little historical significance that James J. Hill was for a time a director of the First Division of the St. Paul and Pacific Railroad, and George Stephen its president. Early in February Hill and Galusha checked into the Westminster Hotel, on 16 Street, east of New York's Union Square, which they had decided to try because it operated on the American plan (meals included). After hours of "negotiation" with Litchfield and his associates, all returned to the "old rat's" office that evening for the resignation of the Litchfield board and the election of Barnes, Stephen, Hill, and Galusha to replace them. Now the associates owned the railroad in every sense of the word except one. They held virtually all of the bonds, the stock of the First Division was theirs, and the stock of the St. Paul & Pacific Company would be theirs as soon as the "protocol" with the Northern Pacific had matured into a formal agreement. But the properties represented by these securities were the subject of foreclosure suits under the various delinquent mortgages, and until Judge Dillon finally saw fit to issue decrees of sale under which the sheriff of Ramsey County could knock the properties down to the highest bidder, they could not formally take possession.[25]

Foreclosure was the goal toward which Hill now aimed. "If Dillon delays foreclosure it will forfeit six hundred thousand acres of land for want of necessary construction this year," he wired George Young, who had gone to St. Louis to try to hurry the all-too-deliberate Dillon.

"He must know we cannot build any more road under a receiver." Hill thought Dillon was stalling until he could get another federal judge to sit with him in reaching a final decision. "I think with you," he wrote Kennedy, "that Dillon's conduct has been pusillanimous. He has apparently been trying to renovate a damaged reputation because he thinks he has the power and opportunity to do it at our expense." Just when the court seemed to be moving ponderously toward the issuance of the longed-for decrees, lawyer Young dropped out of sight. Hill was frantic. After several days without any news or answers to his telegrams, he wired Stephen, "No word from Young. Starting Newell to find him." Newell, Young's law partner, feared that he had been taken sick. Apparently Young had been in St. Louis all this time, but we shall probably never know any more about what he was up to than what is contained in Stephen's telegram to Hill: "I hope Young has woke up at last and that our interests will not suffer in consequence of his breakdown." The decrees, five of them, finally came through between March 15 and April 11.[26]

Kennedy and Stephen had been looking forward eagerly to the month of June, when the salmon-fishing in Quebec and New Brunswick would be at its best. It had begun to appear, however, that the reorganization of their railroad properties into a new corporation might claim their attention well into the month. Hill had written to Marvin Hughitt, general manager of the Chicago & North Western Railroad, for a copy of his company's by-laws to use as a model for the new corporation, and H. R. Bigelow had been hard at work for weeks on the legal documents. His office, at 25 East Third Street, thus became the scene of one of the historic events in the Northwest, for there, on May 23, 1879, Barnes, Stephen, Smith, Kittson, and Hill held the last meeting of the associates and the first meeting of the new company. Barnes called the meeting to order, and on his motion, seconded by Hill, Stephen was elected chairman. Hill acted as secretary as Stephen formally received the notice of foreclosure of the branch line, which had taken place on May 7. Captain Barnes, seconded by Kittson, moved that "we now proceed to organize a corporation pursuant to the statute in such cases," and proposed that it be named the St. Paul, Minneapolis, & Manitoba Railway Company. They then elected themselves, with Bigelow and Galusha, its board of directors.[27]

The first meeting of the board of the new company was called to order on the spot. Barnes presided temporarily as George Stephen was elected president; Kittson, vice president; and Edward Sawyer, who was running the land department, secretary-treasurer. Donald Smith then proposed that the company's equity capital consist of $15 million in $100-par-value shares, and that $2 million worth be issued to the four associates immediately, as these hard-pressed men could make good use of this fresh collateral for their outstanding loans. It was all over by 2 p.m. Early in June, as the new owners began to take over the operations of the railroad, they selected Kittson, Hill, and Galusha to constitute an executive committee, and later that month they officially appointed Hill general manager at an annual salary of $15,000. The most significant financial step was the authorization of $8 million in first-mortgage, 7 per cent gold bonds. Of the $6,780,000 actually issued in 1879, more than two-thirds were turned over to the associates, who in turn passed them along to the Dutchmen as final payment for their old bonds, which Kennedy and two special messengers lugged on the train all the way from New York. Most of the remaining first-mortgage bonds were sold through J. S. Kennedy & Company, to liquidate receivers' debentures and other outstanding obligations. And 125,500 shares of the common stock were issued to Captain Barnes to hold in trust until the associates decided how this evidence of the equity value of the company was to be divided. [28]

At the end of September it was much more clear what the associates had left to divide among themselves. The board decided on September 30 that the company would execute a second mortgage on the property and issue under it up to $8,000,000 in 6 per cent bonds. This second issue was required for two purposes. Some $77,000 worth were issued to the Dutchmen who were holding out for their right to take first-mortgage bonds at par and a 25 per cent bonus in preferred stock. (The associates decided not to make a preferred issue, and the bondholders were delighted to take bonds instead.) Barnes had not been able to talk all the Dutchmen out of the bonus option, although he claimed that without his eloquence fully 75 per cent would have chosen it, and it was Kennedy who suggested that they be given bonds. The second-mortgage bonds also provided the associates with their first taste of profit, since these securities, supported by the excess of earnings over the interest required for the senior issue, went, with the exception noted, to them. The problem of how to raise the substantial amount of cash required for that season's new construction was solved when the associates promptly lent the company back $2.8 million worth of those bonds. [29]

Hill was wary about plunging further into this golden stream at a

time when various malcontents were bringing suit against the associates for lining their pockets at the expense of the old bondholders.
Stephen wanted to sell the stock and turn the proceeds over to the associates, but to Hill this made no sense at all. "If after the stock is
divided," he wrote to Montreal, "any one of the holders desires to realize, of course he can do so, but Mr. Kittson is entirely unwilling to
sell any of his stock and I fully agree with him until we can show some
surplus earnings which will give the stock some value." On November
22 certificates for this "valueless" stock, which was to become the
foundation of so many fortunes, were issued to the associates. Each
received 29,993 shares except Stephen, who received two-fifths, or two
certificates for 29,993 shares each. It was then decided that the bonus,
which everyone had assumed R. B. Angus would receive for holding
the suspicious stockholders of the Bank of Montreal at bay, would
come directly out of their shares. Each anted up 1100 shares (Stephen
put in 2200) to make a handsome purse of 5500 shares for Angus.[30]

Eighteen months before, the associates had stood alone, their
scheme spurned by a shrewd English banking firm and by the knowledgeable railroad specialist who had investigated it. When they decided to go ahead it had been fully understood on all sides that they
were risking all they possessed, and that theirs alone would be the
fruits of victory. But neither they nor the increasingly envious on-
lookers had been prepared for the richness of that harvest. The ultimate reward which the associates realized depended upon how long
they retained the securities which constituted the bulk of their profits,
and the price at which they eventually disposed of them. For Norman
Kittson the rewards were considerably smaller than for the others,
because, old, sick, and nervous as he was for the future, he sold out
not long after the Manitoba road was organized. To Kennedy the
profits meant merely that an already very rich man would be just that
much richer. To George Stephen and Donald Smith, who would retain
their investments in the Manitoba road and its successor companies
well into the twentieth century, the gains made possible *their* great adventure—the building of the Canadian Pacific Railway—and then a
life of dignity and power as peers of Great Britain. For James J. Hill,
who remained the largest investor in the railroad and dedicated to it
the rest of his life, the profits of "George Stephen & Associates" was
the foundation of a great fortune and the basis for his rise to preeminence among the nation's railroad leaders.

In May of 1880 John S. Kennedy & Company, which had kept detailed records of the cash inflows and outflows for the associates, reckoned that there remained in the account, after satisfaction of all claims, a balance of $278,044.18, which, divided four ways, came to slightly less than $70,000 for each man.[31] The second-mortgage bonds and common stock of the company, which, as will be seen, presently were divided five ways, had no market value on the day they were distributed to the associates, but the market soon bid them up to and then above par when the earning power of the Manitoba road had been proved. By November 1885 a one-fifth share in these securities was worth $4,970,000.[32]

As for the "missing fifth," it went, for the most part, to John S. Kennedy, who had bridged the gap between the Dutch bondholders and the associates, and filled the breach between the associates and the sources of short-term capital which made the miracles of 1878 possible. His vital services would not now be available to any such enterprise, for today fears of conflicts of interest run deep. Even in the 1870s, Kennedy had had to steer a very risky course between potentially conflicting groups—the Dutch bondholders, whom his firm represented in America; the bondholders of the First Division Company, for whose mortgages he was a trustee; and the associates, in whose behalf he encouraged the Dutchmen to accept the purchase offer—and he had found a taker for the receiver's debentures. Hill, Kittson, and Smith always insisted that they had no knowledge of what Stephen did with the fifth fifth, and Kennedy even disclaimed any knowledge of its existence. Under oath during the Sahlgaard and Farley litigation in the 1880s, Kennedy came through unscathed and apparently unperjured. He declared in 1881 that he owned only 2000 shares of Manitoba stock, bought at market value, which undoubtedly was true, but his correspondence with Hill throughout the 1880s reveals that he controlled some 25,000 shares, most of it held by "fiduciaries"—i.e. his clerks, lawyers, and bankers. Many years later Stephen arrogantly tossed off the entire matter in a letter to the Prince of Wales's secretary:

When I first knew Kennedy in 1878 he considered himself a *very rich* man, having by 20 years hard work accumulated $500,000. He was agent for the Dutch Bondholders from whom I bought the Bankrupt St. Paul & Pacific Railway, which became the St. Paul Minn. & Manitoba Railway in 1879 & years afterwards the Gt. Northern; Kennedy was very useful to me. To reward him *I gave* him 1/5 interest, making him equal to Hill, Kitson [sic], Smith & myself & that is how he became the Scotch millionaire.[33]

VI

Hill's cares showed no signs of slackening as he entered upon the duties of general manager. The challenges of 1878 were but a preview of the labors which he faced in getting the dilapidated and badly run railroad into shape. At the same time he had to work out a final agreement with the Northern Pacific under the "protocol," get his plans for further construction under way, and find some way to make the "lunatics," as he called the Canadians, John A. Macdonald and Charles Tupper, see reason in the matter of operating the branch from Winnipeg. Not the least of his problems was to recruit competent railroad men to take over from Farley's "favorites," as well as to find some way to get rid of the "old gentleman" himself.

Farley turned out to be more of a problem than anyone had ever thought possible. As his empire began to fall away from him, Farley's opinion of his importance in the associates' enterprise grew. Stephen, who had assumed that Farley would be sent on his way with thanks and a "bonification," made a grave tactical error: he had promised Farley a seat on the board of directors of the new company. Kennedy threw cold water on any such hopes by pointing out that for much the same reason that he, Kennedy, would have to remain off the board, Farley was also ineligible. Kittson had expected "to do a little something" for the receiver when things had been successfully concluded. It developed, in fact, that in the dark days of early 1878 when the associates were scrambling to raise money, Hill and Kittson had offered Farley a share of their interest, but the receiver had declined because he had no money to invest.

Hill, who had suffered a year of frustration in trying to get things done while supporting the charade that Farley was the real mover, ran out of patience early in 1879. "I am getting on nicely with Mr. Farley," he wrote Stephen, "and will continue to do so, but I am daily made aware of the fact that I am looked upon as a censor. When I see you I will give you some points that may make it worth our while to look for others." But he could not wait, and launched into an indignant description of Farley's bookkeeping methods:

> I find that the construction account has been made a slop bucket of from the very beginning. The cost of repairs for the collision at St. Vincent, $2500, which happened long after the road was finished, and in fact so many things that would fill a page have been charged to construction account, amounting in all to certainly over $30,000 and possibly over

$50,000. The only way I can explain it is that Mr. Farley did not think it made any difference what account he charged the bills to, or else he tried to pay out as little of the Receiver's money as possible. . . .[34]

He had stopped trying very hard to get along with Farley by the spring of 1879. His indignation, released by a natural preference for bluntness of expression, churned to the surface. Things came to a head a few days before the meeting at which the Manitoba road was organized, when Farley summoned Hill to his office late one day, after everyone else had gone home. The receiver launched into a tirade over the fact that he was not to become a director of the company, demanding to know what he was going to get for his past cooperation. Hill suggested that he put his demands in writing and submit them to the company, but Farley growled that that would not do much good as long as Hill was against his getting anything. He *was* against it, wasn't he?

Hill retorted that Farley's combined salary as receiver and manager, which totaled about $20,000 a year, was generous compensation for what had averaged about twenty days' work a month, and, therefore, if the board asked him for his opinion, he would recommend that Farley had already got all that was coming to him.

Livid with rage, the receiver wildly threatened to block the final foreclosure sale. Hill coldly remarked that he had better not forget that as receiver he was bound by law to see to it that the bondholders got the best possible price at foreclosure, and that the associates were the bondholders. Bidding Farley a curt good night, Hill turned on his heel to leave and at that moment heard a chair creak in the adjoining office, the door of which was half open. The receiver, he realized, had gotten him there in the hope of extracting a promise from him, and had planted his own witness behind the door. Farley immediately wrote Kennedy a bitter (and badly spelled) letter:

Since the election of Bigelow & Galusha as Directors in the New Company, Men of no money, railroad experience or Influences, And myself left out in the *cold* I am forced to the conclusion that My time and claims on the St. Paul & Pacific is Short, I did expect better things of Hill & Kittson. I had a talk with Jim Hill last knight. He Disclaims any intention on his part to ignore my claims. But he is such a Lyer cant believe him. It is a matter of astonishment to every Person in St. Paul to see the way Jim handles Mr. Stephens. He is notoriously known to be the biggest lier in the State. Mr. Kitson has told me time and again that Jim Hill was the worst man he ever saw. Upham, P. H. Kelly, Thompson, and in fact every citizen in St. Paul if they would Speak their sentiments would all tell the

same story. You must not blame me if I should try to get even with Jim Hill before I leave here.[35]

Barnes realized that Hill had stirred up a hornets' nest. "Hill is such a loose talker and so inclined to make messes of negotiations in which he has no special experience," he wrote Kennedy on June 9, "that I shall not be surprised if he at one time gave Old Farley ground to indulge in hopes of some sort." Farley's bitterness meanwhile grew apace. "I have had some sharp talk with Mr. Hill," he told Kennedy some days later. "If he persists in his Present course to ignore all my claims to share in the *honours* or *profit* to some small degree, He may have cause to Regret it." Eventually he professed to feel sorry for anyone who had "to breathe the foul air connected with everything Jim Hill has anything to do with." By then he had filed a lawsuit claiming that he had a contract with the associates to help place the St. Paul & Pacific Railroad in their hands and that they had failed to honor it. It was a suit to compel men to perform on a contract which, if it had ever existed, was illegal to begin with. But Hill and his friends were to be surprised to learn how much vitality such a flimsy cause would have.[36]

Meanwhile, the press of day-to-day business continued. Early in May Hill had severed his last tie with the fuel business. His former partner and fellow incorporator of the Northwestern Fuel Corporation, John A. Armstrong, had died in the latter part of 1878, and Armstrong's widow leaned heavily on Hill's business advice, but her plea that he continue to look after things was impractical, since he had no intention of serving as president for another year. He knew that Mrs. Armstrong would be destitute if anything should happen to the value of her Northwestern Fuel stock, but he had full confidence in E. N. Saunders's abilities. On May 1, in fact, he had arranged to sell her stock and his own remaining shares to Saunders and to an Erie, Pennsylvania, concern at their full market value.[37]

The general manager of Minnesota's newest railroad relaxes with his neighbors in 1879. James J. Hill looks on in mock disgust from behind the stuffed buffalo (restrained by Emerson Lewis) as Henry P. Upham presents a "new" shotgun to shoe manufacturer Conrad Gotzian. William R. Merriam, soon to be governor of Minnesota, with the help of a neighbor's pet dog demonstrates an alternate method of killing grouse—seize one and club it to death. This is the yard in front of the row of carriage houses across from the Upham and Hill houses (center rear and right rear, respectively) on Canada Street, St. Paul. The Gotzians lived around the corner on Ninth Street.

Hill planned to devote all his time to the railroad business, realizing that during the company's infant years his best efforts would be barely sufficient. He was to spend almost every waking hour of the next decade assuring the survival of the new company. In the job of land commissioner he placed Edward Sawyer, making him responsible for locating, mapping, and selling the company's lands, and he appointed a new general superintendent to take care of the day-to-day operation of the trains. Late in the year the St. Paul, Minneapolis & Manitoba Railway Company published its Timetable No. 1, which included the operating rules of the railroad. At the very end, in bold-faced type, appeared this stern warning:

> Study well the regulations for the running of trains and directions concerning signals. Important changes have been made, which must be understood alike by all. In cases of doubt, take the safe course.

Jas. J. Hill, General Manager.[38]

PART TWO
GROWTH, 1879-1895

The first-class passengers on almost any steamer sailing out of Oslo or Stavanger, Kristiansand or Bergen, in the 1880s might look down at a miniature drama unfolding in steerage. A young widow, her last farewells made to the Old Country, would be timidly asking her way to her quarters. Clutching at her skirts would be several young children, while a thirteen-year-old boy struggled under the heavy, old-fashioned trunk which was balanced on his strong young shoulders.

Lucky to have found even one husband in a land which so many young men were leaving, a widow like Mrs. Jacob Ryggen could not hope for a second. It was the same in Sweden, they said. So to America she and her five children must go, in hopes that the vast lands of that far-off place would provide all that was lacking for a hard-working Norwegian family determined to survive in a hard world. By the time the smaller children were asleep in their narrow bunks that night, Engebord Ryggen and her son Knute would be talking of the new life they would make in Minnesota. Many days later, after arriving in St. Paul, they would pause only long enough to transfer to the new railroad, which would make their journey to the valley of the Red River of the North so much easier than it had been a generation before.

Northward the course of empire. . . .

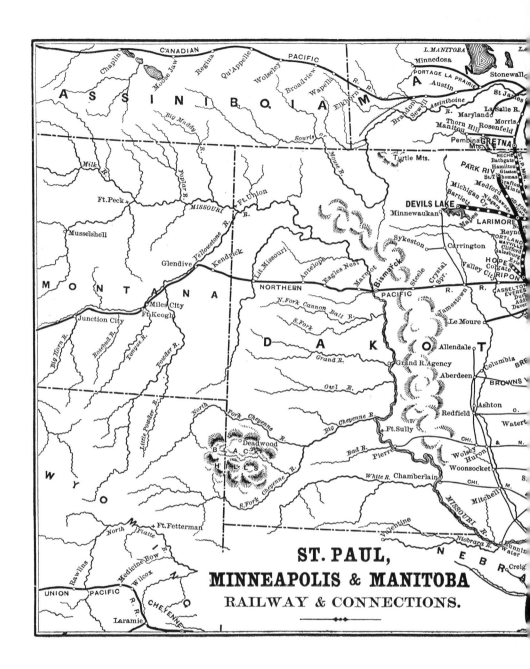

ST. PAUL,
MINNEAPOLIS & MANITOBA
RAILWAY & CONNECTIONS.

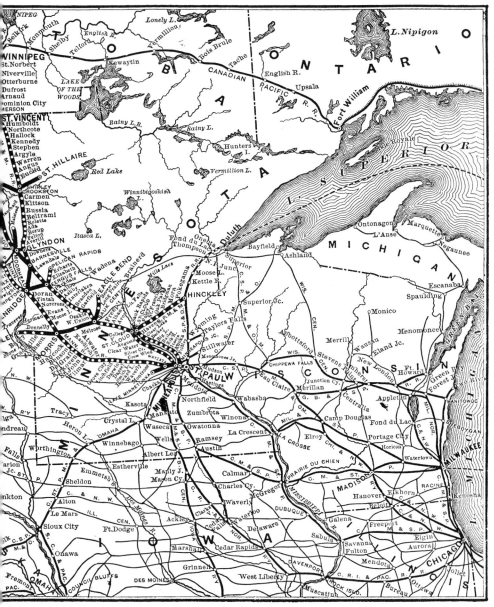

1885 *(Commercial and Financial Chronicle.)*

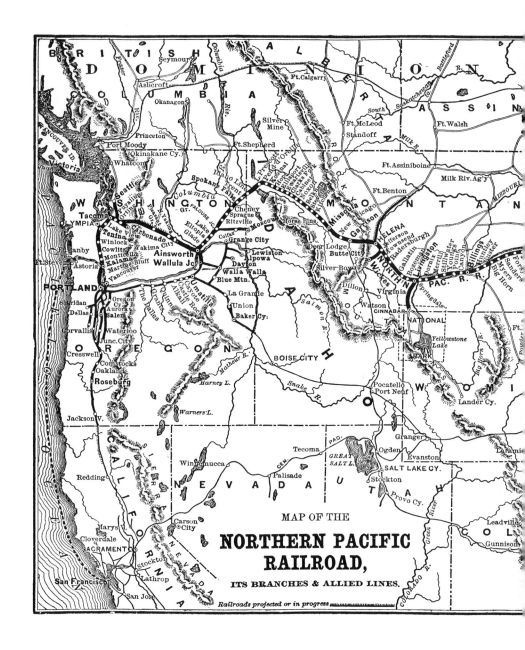

MAP OF THE

NORTHERN PACIFIC RAILROAD,

ITS BRANCHES & ALLIED LINES.

Railroads projected or in progress

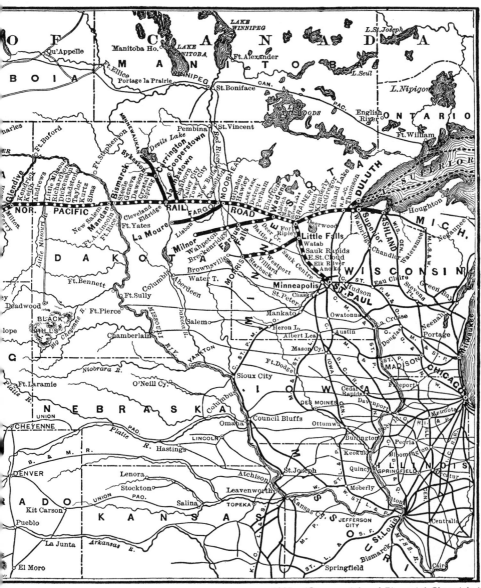

1885   (*Commercial and Financial Chronicle.*)

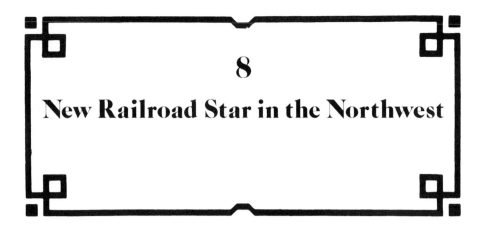

8

New Railroad Star in the Northwest

When we are all dead and gone the sun will still shine, the rain will fall, and this railroad will run as usual.

—James J. Hill, 1880

I

One bright morning in October 1880, following the earliest blizzard in Minnesota history, James J. Hill, general manager of the St. Paul, Minneapolis & Manitoba Railway, lowered the top of his mahogany desk, clamped his big-brimmed, Western-style homburg on his head, and briskly walked the short distance to the Federal courthouse. There, before James O'Brien, deputy clerk of the court, he raised his right hand and, forsaking all previous allegiances, became a citizen of the United States of America. Since he had arrived in St. Paul almost a quarter of a century before, he had played as full a role in politics as a busy man of affairs could manage, marching proudly in the torchlight parades of the St. Paul Democratic party organization, raising funds for its candidates, and faithfully voting in every election. The event in the courthouse marked the end of an era for Hill, an era in which he had moved swiftly from one enterprise to another at a speed which mere red tape could not match. Now he was a rich man, managing one of the newest and most promising railroads in the nation. Tidying up his citizenship status was only one example of the deference which in the future he would be obliged to pay to the formalities of the law and to the increasingly bureaucratic world in which he found himself.[1]

Even before the Manitoba road had been formally organized in the spring of 1879 it had been obvious that Hill was going to bear the heavy burden of its day-to-day operation. "I hope you will be able to be about a good deal when we are at work on the new road," Stephen had told him; "your eye is the best foreman we can have." Filing away Governor John S. Pillsbury's proclamation of acceptance of the completed railroad, which formally conferred the grant of lands in Minnesota, Hill contemplated the housecleaning that faced him. Farley and his trouble-making nephew, Fisher, who was still serving as the "old gentleman's" assistant, had to go. E. B. Wakeman, whom Hill had insisted upon hiring as general superintendent over Farley's bitter objections, made a hasty inspection of the property and reported that, with a few obvious changes in operating procedures, they would be able to get by for a while without all of the new equipment that Farley had wanted to buy. Before summer came Hill was running the railroad, with Wakeman's indispensable assistance, and Farley was conferring with his lawyers about the lawsuit he was bringing against the associates for refusing to cut him in on the deal.[2]

Hill was the only member of the associates who was on the scene and prepared to take a direct hand in running the railroad. Kittson, who considered himself well out of it, notwithstanding his nominal rank of vice president, joyfully devoted himself to breeding thoroughbred race horses, the one activity he expected would fill the few years left to him. By 1882 he had invested $100,000 in his stables. Donald Smith stayed in Montreal, taking care of the affairs of the Hudson's Bay Company, when he was not in Ottawa attending to his parliamentary duties; or else he was on one of his increasingly frequent trips back to the land of his birth, where he virtually occupied the status of Scottish laird. George Stephen, like Hill, had discovered that great success brought even more money-making opportunities to his door. Busy with a variety of interests, he was about to embark on the greatest adventure of his life, the building of the Canadian Pacific Railway. John S. Kennedy would be Hill's strong right arm in financial matters, despite his frayed nerves and increasing susceptibility to respiratory ailments; he would head the New York office, which every Western railroad, no matter how self-sufficient, had to have. But operating a railroad was a ceaseless, day-in, day-out grind, involving an incredible volume of details, doing frequent battle with the rugged climate of the Northwest, and constantly grappling with a burden of freight and passengers, which grew rapidly, without respect for the limited resources of the region's railroads. Soon Hill would realize what any railroad manager in the country could have told him: in the growing and changing world of the late nineteenth century, the railroad impinged upon every aspect of human life, making some men and, intentionally or otherwise, breaking others. Inevitably, the railroads were becoming the lightning rod for the countless discontents of an ambitious, bumptious society whose political structure would sway alarmingly with one social gale after another. "I have been quite busy getting well settled in the harness and find all my time occupied from morning until night," Hill wrote Stephen during his first summer as general manager. Not for more than thirty years would he put that harness by.[3]

What Hill was responsible for, he tended to dominate. The organizational structure of the Manitoba road was simple in the extreme. Under the continuous, close supervision of Hill, Wakeman ran the trains and W. S. Alexander, who would have a long and distinguished career with the railroad, handled the increasingly complex relations with shippers and passengers. Hill poked his nose into every aspect of the road's operations whenever the opportunity arose, and he warned his associates in the East to keep hands off. Concluding an eight-page letter to Stephen, whom he kept well informed on the railroad's affairs, he noted that it was midnight and he had to be up in time to start for Alexandria at seven o'clock—not a pleasant prospect for a man who for years had hated to get up almost as much as he hated to go to bed. But he had one more thing to say:

> Before closing I have to ask that you will not send any more men out here for employment. . . . We have during the past two months laid off several good, faithful men who have been in the Company's employ for a long time . . . and I cannot discharge old and faithful employees to make room for strangers.

No defect in the railroad escaped being jotted down in his diary, which is full of comments on bad places in the track, poor housekeeping around depots, insufficient sidetrack facilities, and the absence of the station agent from his desk as Hill's private car swept by.[4] But not even Hill could wring more than twenty-four hours out of a day. Never a deep sleeper, and constantly loath to put his cares down at bedtime, he developed a cumulative fatigue which complicated, or was complicated by, the neuralgia that bothered him more and more frequently. Stephen realized that it was unfair to expect Hill to continue making vitally important decisions without the moral support of at least one of the associates on the spot. But none of them could come, and it was soon agreed that the next best thing would be to send R. B. Angus, who faced no more challenges to his superb business talents at the Bank of Montreal, to St. Paul in the post of vice president. Affable, diplomatic, and a shrewd and efficient businessman, Angus had hit it off well with Hill when the associates were leaning so heavily on the Bank of Montreal to help them over the rough spots in their takeover of the St. Paul & Pacific.

Hill was delighted to learn that Angus had consented to come to St. Paul. In view of the deep financial commitment which both men had to the enterprise, titles meant little, and no one ever thought of Hill as Vice President Angus's subordinate. "I am anxiously looking for you as I assure you that I cannot get over all the ground as it should be done," Hill wrote him, "and there are so many questions coming up daily which require an immediate decision that I feel the need of someone with whom I can at least advise." But the period in which Angus was to help Hill with his burden was woefully short. In less than a year Angus was spending weeks at a time in Montreal, where he was helping Stephen convince Prime Minister John Macdonald that the associates were the best group he could select to revive the project of a Canadian railroad to the Pacific. By the winter of 1880–81 Angus was doing most of his work in the East, while Hill had the added task of dropping in on Edith Angus and checking on the progress of their sickly daughter, Peggy, who had what the doctor airily described as "a low form of malaria with typhoid symptoms, usually simple." By March of 1881 Angus was in England seeking support for the Canadian Pacific project, and General Manager Hill was back where he had started.[5]

"At last along came 'the man for the occasion,' James J. Hill—'Jim' Hill, everybody here calls him," gushed the St. Paul *Daily Globe* in its 1880 annual summary of the railroad situation in Minnesota; "a young gentleman that some of these days will contest the kingship in railway chess playing with little Mr. Gould of New York." The hard truth was that sooner or later Hill would have to give up trying to run the Manitoba single-handed. Meanwhile, he rebuffed the general manager of the Chicago, Milwaukee & St. Paul Railroad, who offered to take over Hill's operating duties if Hill would move up and let him have the title. "We have not felt that any stranger could do either himself or the road justice in the matter of the commercial and territorial interests of the company until he had an opportunity to become actually acquainted with both." He did not believe that his associates would ever approve of his "handing over the entire control of the property" to someone else. Meanwhile, as long as Hill insisted on receiving only the rather modest salary of $15,000 as general manager, he could not hope to get someone like C. C. Wheeler, already holding that position on the Chicago & North Western, to come to St. Paul, where he could expect only $10,000. Wakeman, however, was clearly not going to grow to the stature of a general railroad officer, and in December 1880 Hill opened negotiations with Allen Manvel, general superintendent of the Chicago & Rock Island, to take over similar duties on the Manitoba road.[6]

Sitting in his modest private office, his door slightly ajar to welcome the steady stream of visitors who wanted something from the general manager, Hill handled the multitude of details which demanded the attention of him and his two clerks, H. C. Ives and William Secombe (for his personal business). Hill clung to his policy of overseeing everything that went on. If farmers who wanted to make a little extra money cutting logs trespassed on railroad land whose timber the Manitoba road badly needed for its own use, he pounced upon them. If minor accidents occurred in the railroad yards, he demanded the details and decided for himself whether gross negligence made the unfortunate employee ineligible for help from the railroad's till. Each morning's mail brought pleas for free passes over the road from employees, shippers, friends, officials of other railroads, and a motley band with nothing but their own gall to recommend them. If the representative of the American Bible Society asked that brackets be installed in the Manitoba road's coaches to hold the Bibles which they wanted to supply free, the general manager had to decide whether the good books would stay in place long enough to make the expense worthwhile. A farmer who insisted on a permanent pass because, he claimed, the railroad was helping itself to all of the water in his well, had to be checked up on. Not until a painstaking investigation disclosed that only the thirsty passengers, and not the panting locomotives, were drinking at his well, could the general manager conscientiously rebuff the demand. No coffee breaks interrupted the long, hard work day. To Kennedy, who had a friend who wanted to send his twenty-one-year-old son to St. Paul to learn the railroad business, Hill warned that "the cold winter and long office hours (8 to 12 and 1 to 6 and sometimes later) would be harder on him than the shorter hours of New York." [7]

A heavy blue pencil was Hill's device for indicating the disposition of most of the problems that came in the mail. If a letter could not be dismissed with "F/P" (for "file, personal"), a few sentences scrawled directly across the face of the letter was generally enough to instruct the quiet, meticulous, accommodating Secombe what to reply. "Don't want to buy any land," Hill wrote over and over on hopeful letters from real estate dealers. For matters of a more technical nature Hill relied on H. C. Ives, whose title of clerk masked his training as a civil engineer. Both men personified a vanished breed of office worker, the male clerk-secretary whose propensity to go into business for themselves required their employers to continue to write their more confidential letters in their own hand. Only the most routine of Hill's correspondence was in Secombe's hand, for Hill rarely wrote Stephen or Kennedy anything but the most personal and confidential letters. Stephen, who had painfully bad handwriting, was sometimes forced to the more modern usage, but Kennedy, frequently propped up in bed in his West 57 Street brownstone, would continue to pen Hill long letters in his spidery handwriting. In 1881 a typewriter appeared in the office, but several more years passed before Hill would consent to sign a typewritten letter.[8]

"Matters on our road have assumed a position which render it imperative for me to have some one to whom I can turn over the active affairs of this company," Hill wrote Manvel in December 1880, "and the present outlook makes it almost a certainty that our line will soon be a leading feature in the railway geography of the west." From Philip D. Armour of Chicago, to whom Hill addressed inquiries about Manvel, came assurances that "there is not a railway man in all of Chicago who has the confidence of the leading business men more than Manvel." A few days later Hill wrote Manvel a long letter, summarizing the spectacular financial performance of the Manitoba road and emphasizing the degree of responsibility which he wished to bestow on a new general superintendent, especially in the acquisition of large numbers of locomotives and rolling stock, which were desperately needed. Next month Manvel, who was a year older than Hill and had completed twenty-five years of responsible railroad work, turned him down.[9]

Nothing could have done more to convince Hill that he had to have Manvel in St. Paul. In the next spring there was a vast increase in traffic volume, and Hill knew he needed help. He made Manvel the usual $10,000 offer, considerably sweetened with an immediate bonus of

$25,000 ($10,000 in Manitoba bonds and $15,000 in stock), the title ("if you wish") of assistant general manager, the promise of a larger salary in the future, and a five-year contract. Not until late that year could Manvel tear himself away from the Rock Island, which could ill afford to lose that outstanding railroad manager. But by December he had taken over a desk in St. Paul, where he continued the fourteen-hour workdays that would put him in an early grave. Angus resigned, and Hill took the title of vice president. The other associates were delighted and greatly relieved. "I hope and trust you will put a big share of the work on to Mr. Manvel and take some leisure yourself," wrote Stephen; "it is simply impossible you can go on working as you have been these last three years. Were you made of *steel* you could not stand it for long." [10]

II

"Wakeman tells me he never saw so many miles of road being so badly operated in his life," Hill reported to Stephen a few weeks before the Manitoba road took over from the St. Paul & Pacific.[11] As far as anyone could see into the future, the new owners would be simultaneously struggling to carry a heavy and rapidly growing burden of freight and passengers, to up-grade the physical condition and operating efficiency of the existing railroad, and to expand it into new territory. To these one might have added a fourth objective: James J. Hill had to be educated in the arts of railroading. In the end Hill would be the best possible leader the Manitoba road could have, but in 1879 he barely qualified for the job, at least on the basis of direct experience. He made up for lack of expertise by meticulous attention to detail and a thorough knowledge of the economy of the region; and he was a fast learner, which was a good thing, for railroading in the Northwest in the early 1880s was a hard school.

The rapid growth of the Manitoba road's freight and passenger traffic in these years was a dramatic vindication of the forecasts Hill had made almost a decade before. Total road mileage only doubled from 1879 to 1883, but passenger miles tripled and freight ton-miles (a measure of gross freight services provided) quadrupled. Thus, while passenger rates were cut slightly and freight rates were slashed by a remarkable one-third, revenues climbed steeply, and net profits, bolstered by a rapid improvement in the condition of the road and, consequently, its operating efficiency, grew even faster than the associates were willing to admit. Somehow the road managed to keep up with the dizzying growth of the Northwest. As spring arrived in 1882, Hill was goading the Canadians, who were now running the trains from the boundary to Winnipeg, to keep things moving. "I have told them that we would be unwilling to acknowledge to the world our inability to handle the traffic now being forced upon us," he thundered to Angus. Not for fourteen years would the incredible pressure let up.[12]

The opportunities were taken at the flood, whatever the burdens they placed on Hill and his hard-working men. As the tentacles of a rapidly growing railroad network crept into what had once been exclusive Manitoba road territory, a competitive strategy had to be devised. Farmers had once pleaded with the St. Paul & Pacific to take their wheat to market, but now many lucky grangers had a choice of railroads to whose grain elevators they could deliver their crops. Hill was ready for the new order of things, and his intimate knowledge of life on the treeless prairie paid off. Farmers needed wood for fuel, and it made sense for them to take their wheat to a depot which had cords of wood for sale at reasonable prices. It made a return load for their otherwise empty wagons, and it did the same for the Manitoba road, whose general manager was to abominate one-way hauls all his life. "The large wheat receipts on the main line go to prove this," he explained to Angus; "we have all we can do to keep the elevators open at the leading points." Nearly a hundred years before the energy crisis of the 1970s Hill knew the critical importance of fuel supplies for those whose labors support the population, and the popularity of the subject in the newspapers bore him out. He sent the farmers wood, and he soon would be introducing them to a far superior fuel: coal.[13]

The Manitoba road made good profits from its passenger business in an era when virtually all travel was by rail. The average American passenger train, even on the more highly developed Eastern railroads, consisted of a single, light, eight-wheeled locomotive, pulling at most four or five wooden coaches. Citizens of the Twin Cities watched in amazement, therefore, at some of the trains which the Manitoba road dispatched northward at the height of the immigration season. One train left the Minneapolis depot on June 3, 1880 with twelve cars bound for points on the main line. "Ten of the coaches," the Minneapolis *Tribune* remarked, "were filled with emigrants." Railroad men dared not forget that they were carrying a precious cargo. "I have stopped running night passenger trains on the north end," Hill explained to Kennedy on Christmas Day of 1879; "we now lay over night at Breckenridge or Crookston. . . . With the thermometer from 30 to 50 below zero neither trainmen, passengers or machinery is safe if they strike enough snow to stop them at night." [14]

The public was a demanding, thoughtless beast. H. C. Ives, reporting to Hill on a slight accident during the great blizzard of 1881, revealed his contempt for the local sawbones who tried to make a good thing of it. "Dr. Mitchell magnified a scratch on one finger into a badly mashed hand. . . . The doctors [we] sent up could tell little about [the victims] as he had them so covered with bandages and plaster. . . . Dr. Mitchell could not stand so much prosperity in so short a time and feeling obliged to brace himself against the 'bloody work,' as he termed it, succeeded in getting drunk by the time he reached St. Paul." It was the sort of thing a general manager quickly became used to, but a letter from W. D. Washburn, leading citizen of Minneapolis and a Representative in Congress, complaining bitterly about train service to near-by points on the branch line, was upsetting. Anxious to show the citizens of the Mill City that the Manitoba road was not a parochial St. Paul institution, he had insisted that Minneapolis be included in its corporate name, and he winced at Washburn's words. [15]

When the Minnesota winter descended upon the railroad its operations became sheer hell. Writing to C. C. Andrews, former chief engineer of the Northern Pacific, who was surveying railroads in Brazil, Hill grumbled one winter that "the upper part of the thermometer has been of no use at all in this part of the country . . . and there is more snow on the ground now than I ever remember seeing before." Climatologists may be right in their insistence that winters in the 1880s were generally more severe than those of the twentieth century, for nearly every season brought at least one major blizzard. Bitterly cold winds of gale force, slamming down from Canada, caught up great masses of moist air and dumped foot after foot of dry, drifting snow on the hapless railroad. Locomotives lost half of their steaming capacity in the sub-zero cold, and Hill had them equipped with two boiler feedwater pumps so that if one failed the other would keep the locomotive, the train crew, and the passengers from an icy death. Hill was glad that they could keep things moving at all, but he admitted that in spite of their efforts "there will be much suffering on the plains in southern Dakota and northwestern Iowa." [16]

After a blizzard there might be no mail service in any direction for days at a time, and even the telegraph failed, especially to the north. The puny Minneapolis & St. Louis Railroad, over which the Manitoba road received coal from its Iowa mines, was stopped dead for nearly a month one winter, and the huge fuel stocks which Hill had insisted upon were amply justified. As he had always said they would, once the railroad was available, immigrants wanted to proceed north before winter was over, which put the railroad in the hotel business for a while each year. "During Friday and Saturday we accumulated about 1500 people in St. Paul," Hill reported to Angus after what he was sure was the last snow storm of the season, "all of whom were sent out yesterday. . . . They were all well cared for and satisfied except about 15 who wanted to hold indignation meetings and pass resolutions." Two weeks later King Boreas, before taking his delayed departure, presented the Twin Cities with another three feet of snow. "The 'oldest inhabitant,' " Hill sighed, "says that no such storm has occurred for thirty years." The Northern Pacific, true to form, did not know when to come in out of the weather. Eager to have the only train moving between St. Paul and Fargo after the big blizzard of 1881, they dispatched a train in spite of Wakeman's warnings. A few hours later the Manitoba road had to send three engines to dig them out.[17]

The severe winters made careful maintenance of the roadbed all the more important, and each fall Hill had hundreds of men out on the line getting it in shape for cold weather. As the first frosts appeared he was rolling over every foot of the railroad in his business car, "Manitoba," looking for weak points. "We will go into winter with the best track we ever had this time of year," he reported proudly to Stephen in 1882; "we do not find one low joint between St. Paul and Kennedy and but very few north of there." But spring brought its problems, too, for severe flooding was inevitable when all that snow began to melt, and with the line in the valley under water, freight piled up to the south. By the time the road was dried out in the spring of 1882 there were 1000 loaded cars held up in the yards at St. Paul and another 1500 bound for the valley which were embargoed between Chicago and the Twin Cities. The road was using twenty locomotives borrowed from the Chicago lines, which had a direct interest in seeing the Manitoba road unclog itself, and Hill had learned another valuable lesson about railroading in the Northwest. The building of north-south railroads, he reflected, with their embankments a foot or two above the general level of the prairie, tended to hold the wayward river within abnormally narrow limits when spring freshets came, thus creating even worse flooding. Perhaps, he told Angus, this had its bright side, if the discovery could be used to discourage competitors from building parallel lines.[18]

III

A railroad took enormous resources to build, and required constant care and improvement thereafter, but once built, it could at least be counted on to *be* there. Much more complicated was the problem of motive power and rolling stock. There would never, it seemed, be enough boxcars, gondolas, and flats to carry the freight; they seldom seemed to be in the right place; and division superintendents never seemed to think they had locomotives enough to move them about. In the spring of 1882 the Manitoba road had 100 new box cars, 15 coaches, 5 sleeping cars, and 35 locomotives arriving or on order, and Hill thought it would be barely enough to handle the expected increase in business. One of the tasks which kept Manvel chained to his desk, or off on exhausting trips, was the design and procurement of all of these costly pieces of equipment. Hill was glad to have Manvel to do this work, for it was the subject on which he was furthest from being an expert, even if he had gratified his ego by taking out a patent on an idea he had for converting flat cars into dump cars for spreading gravel. (Almost a year before he took over the railroad he had discussed with Horace Thompson the possibility of starting a shop to manufacture rolling stock in St. Paul, and he was constantly on the lookout for better dump cars than the one he had devised.) [19]

It was in the soot-blackened stables which held the iron horses, however, that the major investment in rolling stock was concentrated. Railroad men would laugh today at the price of $6000 or so which the Manitoba road paid for a locomotive in the early 1880s, but it was no laughing matter to a railroad which had half a dozen demands for every dollar in its capital budget. The small locomotives of the era were a direct reflection of the light-duty character of American railroads at that stage of their development, and of the relative cheapness of labor, two factors which made it feasible to put two, three, and sometimes more locomotives to work tugging and shoving a single train. Hill wanted all the motive power he could get for his money, and he bid an unsentimental goodbye to the gingerbread era of locomotive design when he told Kennedy, who negotiated with engine builders before Manvel arrived, "Please have all trimmings good and *plain* [underscored twice] such as will not be hard to keep up." [20]

The up and coming Baldwin Locomotive Works, which was rapidly taking over leadership in a traditionally chaotic, individualistic industry, received Hill's hearty approval for its designs, attractive prices, and ability to deliver. He turned his back on the older Rogers Company because they charged too much and their locomotives did not stand up in the Minnesota climate. He wanted the finest steel tires on the five-foot drivers, and he reminded Kennedy that their locomotives had to have two sets of feedwater pumps. Toward the end of 1879 he made one of his most important decisions: due to the high cost of wood and the need to save dwindling supplies for the farmers, in the future all Manitoba road locomotives would be coal burners. Meanwhile he pitched into the big job of replacing iron rails with steel, a task which admitted of no delay in view of the enormous operating economies which would result. He watched the scrap-iron market like a hawk, and when the price was right sent off dozens of flat cars loaded with old iron to Chicago. Little things like that, which cut the net cost of new steel rails by more than one-half, gave the profit-and-loss statement its own welcome, metallic ring. [21]

Expensive hardware notwithstanding, railroading was first of all a business that dealt with human beings who could be counted on to concentrate just so much on their duties and who would submit to just so much regimentation. In an era when automatic block signals and safety interlocking devices were unknown, when preoccupied conductors might pocket unread the orders thrust upon them by way station telegraphers, and when potbellied stoves sometimes made funeral pyres out of wooden coaches, the Manitoba road was lucky. No major accidents marred its passenger service, although each year brought fatalities to a few passengers, crew, and bystanders, most of whom had themselves primarily to blame. Especially unfortunate was a gang of fifty Swedes riding in the empty cars of a work train which was making for the gravel pits on the main line near Willmar, Minnesota. Their engineer, a "hot pilot," in modern slang, backed down the grade to the loading point at nearly forty miles an hour, dumping the entire train on the curve and crushing thirteen men fatally. The coroner's jury, showing no bias toward either labor or management, cited the engineer for going too fast and the railroad for not having a published speed limit for gravel trains. This first major disaster cast a pall on the associates. "This is one of the uncomfortable things about railroading," Stephen wrote Hill; "the liability to accident to life and limb is great." [22]

The time was growing late for a paternalistic attitude of management toward labor, but in the 1880s Hill still hoped, as did virtually every other employer in the western world, that wages and conditions of employment would remain a matter between individuals: the employer on one side of the table, the individual worker on the other. Collective bargaining was a new idea, labor unions were considered little better than conspiracies, and strikes were condemned as destructive blows against property. Employee relations were carried out in a fatherly atmosphere, which meant that father knew best. When H. M. Jordan, a hostler in the roundhouse at St. Cloud, wanted to get his wife, "who has bin sick," down south for the winter, he had only to ask for a pass and one was granted. Did Peder Rasmusson, who was injured on the ill-fated gravel train, need further treatment? Twenty-five dollars was forthcoming. When passenger rates were lowered 20 per cent in January 1880, wages were cut the same amount. Later in the summer it was decided that the wage cuts could be partially restored, and it was done "without either demand or request on the part of the employes," the *Globe* noted, admiringly. [23]

It could not last. Hill had his first taste of the trend toward concerted action by working men in August of 1880. Only two weeks before then he had filled one of the most important jobs on the railroad, that of master mechanic, whose duty was to keep the hissing, clanking machinery of the age of steam in good working order. His domain was the company's shops in St. Paul, which, Hill knew, had not been well run. The new man, A. A. Ackerly, confirmed that there were more men on the payroll than could be profitably employed and that some were actually engaged in "busy work." Without much regard to seniority he suspended more than a dozen. They reacted bitterly. Moving from work bench to work bench the aggrieved men whipped up latent anti-Ackerly feelings among the men, who much preferred the easygoing policies of his predecessor. Soon 200 men had walked off their jobs, and they laid siege to the office of J. B. Rice, assistant superintendent, demanding Ackerly's immediate removal.

It could not have happened at a more awkward time, for Angus, Hill, and Wakeman were all out of town. Rice promised to have Hill back within twenty-four hours, and the men dispersed. By late afternoon on the following day at least 500 people, not all of them workmen, had gathered in the Manitoba railroad yards. At 6:30 Hill strode through the crowd and climbed up on a box from which to address the milling throng. All of the air of confidence which had brought him to such a position of authority was marshalled in this, his first effort at mass persuasion. His voice was deep and resonant, and no pince nez was perched on his nose; otherwise this stocky, powerfully built man, his indignation under full control, might have been giving the men a foretaste of Theodore Roosevelt's earnest, explosive style. His oratory got better as he went along:

> It is my desire to have every man make known his grievances. If the charges are true, the man making them is entitled to the respect, confidence and protection of the company, but if untrue and made through malice, that man cannot work for the company an hour. Work has been stopped in the shops and to that extent you have assailed the company. The time will never come when you can dictate who shall be hired and who discharged. I work for a living, as you do, and always expect to. I am going to the bottom in this matter, let the blame fall where it may and to whom it belongs. When we are all dead and gone the sun will still shine, the rain will fall, and this railroad will run as usual.[24]

The men returned to work next day and the suspended men were soon back at work, thanks to the general prosperity, but the old way of labor relations was gone forever.

IV

Hard at work in their lush, green fields, farmers who paused to wipe the sweat from their foreheads watched as a stocky, bearded man drove his buckboard off the road and straight across their acres. James J. Hill was out prospecting again, looking for that intangible yet very real optimum combination of short length, gentle grade, and freedom from curvature which would make the ideal route for a line between two points he wished to connect with rails. Hill knew very well what it was never possible to explain adequately to investors: that a railroad was never really finished, that it had constantly to be ready to extend the main line here, put out a branch there, and alternately make war and peace with neighboring railroads as the highly fluid situation demanded. One could not stand still. To do so would be not only to lose out on new opportunities as they emerged, but also to jeopardize the advantages with which one had begun.[25]

The Manitoba road in its early years had many advantages, thanks largely to Hill's foresight, but it had to fight continually to keep and build upon them. The Manitoba road's prosperity, at least in its early years, lay primarily in protecting and exploiting its territory on the north-south axis between the Twin Cities and Winnipeg. At the same time it had to see to it that the produce of the rich country to the southwest of the main line, in the general direction of northwestern Iowa and southeastern Dakota, was not drained off by the "Chicago lines," which eyed it hungrily. The objective was to get as much traffic as possible, as far out on your own line as possible, and to keep it on your line for as long a haul as possible. Those were the conditions and the general principles which explained Hill's strategy of expansion in the early years.

In the beginning the Manitoba road could not even count on its connection north of the international boundary. For over a year Hill and Stephen, each from his own location, struggled to reach a definitive agreement with slippery politicians for operation of the "Pembina branch," as the link with Winnipeg was called. They bombarded Ottawa with letters, telegrams, and, in Stephen's case, personal visits, and they sympathized with each other in letters in which they condemned the hollow men, the "lunatics," as Hill called them at one point, who agonized over the political implications of every move they contemplated. Finally, at the end of May 1880, Collingwood Schreiber, chief engineer of the Canadian government's railroads, came to St. Paul to conclude a contract with Hill. By the end of the year the entire picture had changed, for Stephen had accepted, on behalf of the associates, a contract to build "the national dream," an all-Canadian railroad from coast to coast, and the Pembina branch would soon become part of the new Canadian Pacific Railway.[26]

Before rushing to do battle in the field, however, Hill knew that the first order of business was to lay the firmest possible foundation for the railroad in Minneapolis and St. Paul. He had observed that more than one old, established road was already beginning to regret the inadequate terminal facilities it had acquired in its early days, when urban real estate was cheap and the land unoccupied by substantial buildings. The Manitoba road, thanks to the old St. Paul & Pacific's early appearance on the scene, was in good shape in St. Paul. The sole remaining need there was for a union terminal, one that all of the railroads entering St. Paul would own and jointly use. The idea, which had been gestating for some time, came to maturity just as the associates were organizing the Manitoba road. Hill had finally decided to sell to the terminal company the necessary land at the foot of Sibley Street, from which the *William Crooks* had departed at the head of the first railroad train in Minnesota not twenty years before. He agonized over the decision. He told Stephen,

> I assure you that it was the hardest thing I have had to do in the whole enterprise . . . to forever part with terminal property, knowing that my views might not prove to be as advantageous as I now believe them to be. The price is a very large one and the money will be of great use to us, and I believe we have everything left which our line can possibly want even if it were 2000 miles long. [27]

Hill would live to see the Manitoba road's successor considerably longer than 2000 miles and the St. Paul Union Station one of the busiest and most efficient railroad terminals in the world.

Between St. Paul and Minneapolis a great deal of work faced Hill and his helpers. The Manitoba road had an excellent line from St. Paul to St. Anthony (the original main line of the St. Paul & Pacific), and it would make a good thing out of the rentals from other railroads, which would use these tracks to get into Minneapolis from the east and south, or into St. Paul from the west. But a better access to the center of Minneapolis, which was growing rapidly on the west side of the Mississippi, depot facilities at the center of the city, and freight transfer facilities between the two metropolises, were pressing needs. Hill advanced one of his most dearly held projects: a jointly owned central freight yard between the two cities to which all of the railroads could bring cars of freight to exchange with connecting railroads. Like a clearing house for banks, the Minnesota Transfer, as it was named, has been a boon to the efficient exchange of railroad traffic ever since. Another valuable facility was a Manitoba road subsidiary, the Minneapolis Union Railway, which gave all of the railroads equal access to the flourishing industries of the Twin Cities and a better route into the center of the Mill City. [28]

Between the east bank of the Mississippi and downtown Minneapolis, Hill left an indelible mark. A passenger depot rose on ground which had been prudently acquired earlier. Three other railroads immediately applied to rent space in the new station, and, at a rental of 6.5 per cent of the cost of construction, the new facility became a profitable investment for the Manitoba road. The terminal bonds were for two generations one of the bluest blue-chip investments which the Twin Cities ever produced. But it was in crossing the river that Hill created his monument in stone and mortar. For, although it has never been called anything but the Stone Arch Bridge, the massive yet graceful series of curving arches by which the Manitoba road spanned the Mississippi was unmistakably James J. Hill's. Here was something which would go on serving "when we are all dead and gone." Paris has her Eiffel Tower; London, the Houses of Parliament along the Thames; and New York, the Statue of Liberty. For years the bridge, emblazoned on countless business letterheads, was Minneapolis' trademark. In the 1920s the limestone stele of the Foshay Tower upstaged the aging bridge, and in the 1970s all eyes turned to the soaring, glass-walled IDS building. But in the years when Minneapolis shouldered its way to front rank among American cities, its symbol was Jim Hill's great Stone Arch Bridge.[29]

V

By the end of 1883 the Manitoba road had built 937 miles of new line, counting the 96 miles which the associates had built in 1878 and 43 miles taken over from the Northern Pacific in one of the recurring adjustments between the two companies. During 1879 Hill had pressed to completion all of the mileage required under the Manitoba road's charter, and in the years that followed he consolidated its position in the Red River Valley, put it in a position to take advantage of certain changes in the transportation pattern in southwestern Minnesota which he knew were on the way, and pushed the line westward to Devil's Lake in Dakota Territory. Hill's strategy, translated into action, had preserved the Manitoba's domination of the north-south axis, had prepared it for the emergence of Duluth as a major eastern terminus for the burgeoning produce of the Northwest, and had provided it with a convenient springboard for westward expansion when the last great explosion of railroad building arrived toward the end of the decade.[30]

He did not have everything his own way. At the outset he had had to build fifty-one miles of railroad which he did not want, on the west bank of the Mississippi from Minneapolis to St. Cloud. This was the "west-side line" which the Northern Pacific had threatened to build as its independent entrance into St. Paul, and, protocol or no protocol between the two railroads, Minneapolis was determined to have it. To keep it out of hostile hands, the Manitoba road built it. Eventually, it would be a valuable additional channel in a heavily traveled region. Meanwhile, initial relations with the Northern Pacific went smoothly. Before snow fell in 1879 Hill could report to Kennedy that "the branch line [jointly used by both roads] is now entirely laid with steel and has had almost as much work done on the grade as was originally done in building it." With the Northern Pacific so well served by the Manitoba road under their agreement, the future looked promising.[31]

When the agreement with the Northern Pacific was finally signed in August 1879, lawyer Bigelow warned Hill that the explicit description of the Manitoba road as a north-south line might eventually prevent it from having its own line from the Red River Valley to Duluth. But in the end President Billings had demanded deletion of the clause which explicitly designated the Northern Pacific an east-west line, so the way was left open for disagreement on that point in the future. Again, Hill wanted only time to mold the Manitoba road into a strong property, and he agreed with Kennedy that parchment bonds would not restrain the Northern Pacific from moving into Manitoba territory when it thought the time was ripe. Kennedy was even more emphatic to Stephen:

> I consider it of the utmost importance that you break ground, and make a vigorous demonstration from Breckenridge north, on the west side of the Red River. . . . Your surest method of protecting your property and keeping others off is by beginning, and that immediately.[32]

It was the situation in Canada which lured the Northern Pacific into building north into the valley on the west side of the Red River. Stephen had told Prime Minister Macdonald that no sane party would undertake to build hundreds of miles of railroad across the wastelands of the pre-Cambrian shield unless they absolutely controlled all lines that were built southward to the boundary in the western provinces. Otherwise these lines would drain off all of the Canadian Pacific's through traffic, rust would devour the tracks, which, against every experienced railroad man's better judgment, were to be built north of Lake Superior, and the national dream would turn into a nightmare. "Monopoly!" screamed the Grits, Canada's equivalent of America's Populists, and one Dr. John C. Schultz, among the grittiest of them all, secured from the provincial parliament of Manitoba a charter for a railroad to run southward from Winnipeg on the west side of the river, a line with the jawbreaker name of Manitoba & Southwestern Colonization Railroad. The bumbling Northern Pacific, apparently not pausing to reflect on the fact that the Dominion Parliament was honor-bound to disallow the charter, began to build north from Casselton, Dakota Territory, to meet it. Before the dust settled the Manitoba road had taken over the Casselton branch from the Northern Pacific, which had little use for a line that could not make connections at the boundary. The Manitoba also bought the Manitoba & Southwestern to hold for the Canadian Pacific (even though it had no power to acquire a foreign corporation), and then spent many anxious months waiting for the hard-up Canadian Pacific to find the money to pay for it.[33]

Hill did little to hide his contempt for the Northern Pacific's chronic inability to stick to its knitting and stop trying to cut itself in on the rich territory it had let slip through its fingers ten years before. During a meeting on the arbitration of freight rates, the Northern Pacific's representative had pointedly referred to the road's recent successful refinancing. "He thought," Hill sarcastically remarked to Angus, "that [the Northern Pacific] would use some of their recently borrowed $40,000,000 if he couldn't have all he wanted out of the rate north of Glyndon." The Northern Pacific did try to make trouble, but a handful of Easterners sitting in stuffy offices at the tip of Manhattan island were a poor match for James J. Hill on his home turf. When the Northern Pacific threatened to make the Manitoba road go through the injunction process to win permission to cross its line at Moorhead, Hill belligerently wrote Kennedy, "I had a letter from a leading Moorhead merchant today offering 500 good citizen tracklayers to help us at the crossing." [34]

When Henry Villard entered the Northern Pacific picture, Stephen feared the worst. "As matters stand," he warned Hill, "and while a man of the egotistic stamp of Villard is in control, it will not be easy to arrive at any reasonable and permanent agreement. Villard's vanity will be apt to lead him to reject any treaty of peace that does not seem to gratify his vain desire to obtain a triumph." Hill, in fact, had already put a spy into the field to check up on suspicious moves the Northern Pacific was making in the highly desirable Pelican Rapids region. But with Villard's appearance the center of interest on that road rapidly moved westward, and in two more years it would finally be linked to the West Coast. Mr. Manvel journeyed to New York, from which he soon returned with a highly satisfactory arrangement to pool freight with the Northern Pacific in their competitive areas. Two months later Villard called on Hill at the Manitoba road's office, "and in a few moments [we] settled all points which he raised satisfactorily." Hill's jaw jutted more confidently than ever. "You are right in supposing that we are not gobbled up by Mr. Villard, or anyone else," he wrote a friend; "that can only be done when we are ready to be gobbled." [35]

So much for the flabby Northern Pacific. The rich, powerful, aggressive Milwaukee road would be a different matter. Having connected St. Paul with Chicago and the rest of the young nation when the St. Paul & Pacific was still two streaks of rust between St. Paul and St. Anthony, the Chicago, Milwaukee & St. Paul claimed the right to be a major factor in the development of the Northwest. The trouble was that it could not seem to make up its mind as to just how to go about it, and fifteen years after reaching St. Paul it was still probing a bewildering number of possibilities. If it had taken over the St. Paul & Pacific when it had had the chance, the railroad history of the Northwest would have been vastly different. As it was, the Milwaukee still longed for a piece of the Red River Valley business, and was determined to advance westward to ensure that the wheat of southwestern Minnesota and Dakota would continue to move eastward via Chicago. This was the "blow to the midriff" which Hill feared. Evading that blow would tax all his skill at bluster and bargaining, and he would not be entirely successful.

Westward from the Mississippi, the Milwaukee road, through Russell Sage, controlled the Hastings & Dakota line, which became the Milwaukee's instrument for westward expansion. Hill warned them not to wander an inch north of Big Stone Lake, which, in his opinion, was the boundary of Manitoba territory. He spied out all of the local railroad projects, for he knew that if they were not inspired from the beginning by bigger roads, which liked the anonymity a local corporate name gave them (or so they believed), they soon became the protégés of railroads like the Milwaukee. Talking as if the Manitoba road already controlled the Northern Pacific, Hill warned S. S. Merrill, the Milwaukee's general manager, that the two sister railroads had already split up the northwestern country to their complete satisfaction, and that the area was not open for further colonization by other railroads. Merrill planted a rumor that the two sisters were about to become alienated by an attractive offer by the Milwaukee to allow the Northern Pacific to use the former's new "short line" between St. Paul and Minneapolis, at which Hill sternly warned Merrill that the Northern Pacific had signed an ironclad contract with the Manitoba for the use of the latter's trackage between the Twin Cities.[36]

By 1883 it was obvious that in the near future Duluth and the newer Lake Superior port of Superior, Wisconsin, were going to take a much larger share of the Northwest's wheat crop to market. While the Lake was open, farmers realized several cents more per bushel for their wheat there than at Chicago, because the cost of completing its journey to Liverpool was less from Duluth than from Chicago. The Milwaukee desperately drove a line of its own, fatuously disguised as the Fargo & Southwestern, into the Red River Valley. It was a classic act of frustration, for Hill and Stephen froze the interloper out without mercy:

> I did not hesitate to say in strong terms [wrote Stephen] in the presence of people whom I knew would repeat it that any road going down the Valley to the boundary line expecting to get a connection with the C.P.R. would be hugely disappointed; that the connection between the two Companies no matter what might be said by some to the contrary was a *family* one and could be strengthened, as is always the case in domestic matters, by any outside attempt to interfere.

The associates were still an effective team.[37]

How did Hill accomplish all of this railroad building, while running the mileage that was already in operation? The answer, to a great extent, lies with one of Hill's closest friends and longest associates, David C. Shepard, first chief engineer of the old Minnesota & Pacific, railroad builder *par excellence,* and a shrewd businessman who never ceased to inspire Hill's admiration and confidence. "I will telegraph you from either Montreal or New York," Hill wrote Shepard early in 1882, after the builder had been absent in the East for some months; "it is so long since I have seen you that I am really lonesome and when I meet you again I will try and get you under where I can sit on you and squeeze you thoroughly." No longer did Hill have to get up before dawn and head up the line "where the money is being spent." Now the Manitoba road could afford the best, and Shepard was only one of several first-class contractors upon whom Hill, while looking over their shoulders to be sure they followed *the* best route, depended to advance the road's rapidly growing empire.[38]

VI

James Bryce, Scottish don and perceptive student of the American commonwealth in the 1880s, was deeply impressed by the striking dif-

ferences between American and British methods of financing large-
scale enterprises such as railroads. English investors expected their
managing directors to pay out all of the earnings of a railroad as dividends, looking to debt issues (bonds and debentures) as their sole
source of fresh capital for improvements or expansion. But in America
the officials of a railroad operated with a degree of independence from
stockholders which amazed Bryce. The revolution that railroads were
working in American life, in fact, was being reflected in a volume of
profits for well-planned and well-run companies which was far greater
than a "normal" rate of return on the stock. As long as interest was
paid on the bonds and an attractive dividend rate (say, 6 per cent) on the
par value of the stock, American railroad managers were free to reinvest the surplus to make even bigger profits. The Manitoba road was
an outstanding example of what Bryce was talking about.[39]

Hill had predicted that large profits would be made from the operation of a reorganized, rebuilt, and efficiently operated St. Paul & Pacific Railroad. By the time the associates took over in 1879 he thought
that operating expenses would come to no more than 45 per cent of
gross revenues, leaving the rest for interest, dividends, and surplus.
Although the road reported an "operating ratio," as it was called, of as
much as 50 per cent in its first five years of operation, the truth is that
Hill's prediction was not only realized, but considerably bettered. It
was common practice for highly profitable railroads to treat as current
operating expenses many outlays which had been made for basic,
long-term improvements in the system. Not only were the better
railroad managers, like Hill, fundamentally conservative in their bookkeeping philosophy, and loath to capitalize many items which the
profit-oriented executive of today would eagerly capitalize, but they
were admittedly embarrassed by the spectacular profitability of their
properties, and they took every legitimate opportunity, and, perhaps,
some that were not legitimate, to minimize reported profits. It was not
that these moneys were going into the pockets of the owners, for they
were being recommitted to a railroad which was as greedy for fresh
capital as a baby robin is for worms. Concealing "excess" profits in
this way did not bother Hill, since most of the criticism of railroads
was that they were *overcapitalized*—i.e. that they carried their property
on the books at a larger amount than had actually been invested in the
property—and Hill, like many of his breed, abominated the "watering" of a railroad's securities which such practices implied.[40]

During its first five years the Manitoba road plowed back some $4 million in *reported* net profits. As Hill would later maintain, the actual amount of money reinvested from earnings, including that which was "expensed," was much greater. But it was never enough, for in a rapidly growing enterprise, profits are seldom reflected in cash. Both the times and the nature of the Manitoba road's needs ensured that Hill would constantly be short of cash and would have to watch closely the balances which the company kept with J. S. Kennedy & Company. It was Kennedy's firm, and primarily the superb financial acumen of its principal partner, which lent the modest Northwestern railroad a degree of financial strength and stability which was the envy of many a bigger railroad. Personal differences had led to Captain Barnes's departure from the Kennedy firm in 1880. He had been replaced by J. Kennedy Tod, who had been so conscientiously trained in banking by his uncle, John S. Kennedy, that his signature for the firm was a virtual copy of the older man's. Three years later Kennedy liquidated his firm (it was reorganized as J. Kennedy Tod & Company), but he continued to oversee the financial affairs of the Manitoba road in which, like Hill, he owned nearly 30,000 shares of stock, worth, at one point in the early 1880s, some $4.5 million. When Hill could not scrape up the cash required to make regular interest or dividend payments, Kennedy quietly arranged for short-term loans to tide the company over. Such loans were always paid off just in time to permit the Manitoba road to publish a balance sheet that was free of such debt. And, as the short-lived but deadly panic of 1884 approached, Kennedy was working hard to get the company in a cash position which many considered unduly conservative—until the blow fell.

Hill fully supported major changes in the company's financial structure, which became necessary as it developed. The capital stock outstanding was soon increased to 200,000 shares (par value $100), all that the Manitoba road's charter allowed. Construction of the line westward into Dakota Territory was financed by "Dakota Extension" bonds which were issued only as sections were completed, a hand-to-mouth arrangement which Kennedy found inconvenient. "Another year we must manage this thing differently," he grumbled to Hill. When Kittson decided to sell his stock in 1881, the other four associates formed a syndicate to take it at a price of $60 per share. Anticipating that the stock would soon go much higher, Hill took his full allotment. "I firmly believe none of us have yet gauged accurately the position the road will occupy as a property in five years hence," Stephen declared, but he warned that everything depended upon the ability of the road to continue to produce heavy profits. "We should have been in a rather tight place without these big increases," he noted; "we must get our house more 'snug and weatherproof.' " Hill could not have agreed more, so in 1883 the company authorized a $50 million issue of consolidated bonds. These securities were to be used to redeem earlier bond issues and to provide up to $20 million for new construction. They were also part of a scheme which turned out to be the worst public relations mistake that James J. Hill ever made.[41]

Hill and his accountants calculated that at least $13 million of profits had been spent on permanent improvements to the railroad which directly increased its earning power. This was, in effect, a forced loan, and the associates, who were the majority owners of the property, wanted to receive in return for it a dividend-paying stock. But additional stock could not be issued without applying to the Minnesota Legislature for an amendment to the charter—a Pandora's box which no one wanted to open. So the distribution was made in bonds. The plan was to give each stockholder an opportunity to buy $500 worth of consolidated bonds for every $1000 worth of stock which he held, at a price of 10 cents on the dollar. A limit of $10 million was set on the total amount of this "bond grab," as it came to be called. Since the value of securities distributed "free" to the stockholders under this plan was, therefore, only $9 million, while the physical assets represented had cost $13 million, Hill could not see how anyone could find anything dishonest or even the least bit immoral in the affair. But they did, then and later. From 1893 onward, as the age of reform blossomed, cartoonists, financial editors, and muckrakers joyfully seized upon the episode to justify placing Hill alongside the other robber barons. Forget it, a Morgan or a Rockefeller might have told him; if they don't impale you for one thing, they will for another. But he never could forget it, and for the rest of his life he would reflect that even the conservative John S. Kennedy had had similar ideas.[42]

When it came to financing branch feeder lines, Hill's philosophy was both unique and refreshing. He believed that the initiation and financing of such projects should come from the top down. Many communities which had not yet been reached by a railroad were voting local bond issues to finance independent lines that might then be sold to established companies. But Hill felt that if the only way a branch could be financed was to place a tax burden upon the local citizens, something was wrong. Branches ought to be built, he maintained, as part of an over-all plan, and be surveyed and located by the standards of the railroad that sponsored them. In the first year or two of the Manitoba's existence he had been willing to accept local bond subsidies; in fact, politician-promoters like Ignatius Donnelly, whose star would rise once more, briefly, during the Populist revolt of the 1890s, frequently gave him no choice as they sought to play one railroad off against another. But he fought the idea when he had the means. In the fall of 1879, hearing that the Northern Pacific was dickering with the citizens of Sauk Center for a branch, he got in his buckboard and scouted a much better route than the town's surveyors had located. When the Manitoba road announced that it would build the branch with its own funds, both the bonding agents, who were already counting their heavy commissions, and the Northern Pacific stole silently away. Two years later, as Fergus Falls was about to heed the siren call, Hill discovered that a leading supporter of the bond issue was the holder of an annual pass on the Manitoba road, and he had the conductor lift it, "in the usual manner of seizing stolen passes," the irate citizen said.

The Manitoba road had the country so well supplied with railroad lines, Hill explained to August Belmont, Jr., who was interested in becoming an important investor, that even the Fargo & Southwestern, which the Milwaukee road was building into the Red River Valley, was doomed to lose money. The figures spoke for themselves, and he could not imagine how the Milwaukee people could be so obtuse as to spend their funds in that manner. By 1884 the railroad boom was six years old, and showing signs of weariness. Despite "the many railway schemes in the air," Hill told Kennedy that he would build no more than twenty-five miles that year, except where rival railroads forced them to. Some local communities still sought to have a railroad link, and Hill talked good sense to them:

> It has not been our policy at any time to burden the communities along our lines with additional taxes for railroad facilities. . . . If the people [in your] county will give us their moral support in procuring what right-of-way we require at fair and reasonable prices, we will build the road and have it completed this year on condition that the bonds voted for the $65,000 [bonus] be returned to the officers of the county and by them burned or destroyed.

> The people of your county will largely have to support the road when it is built and the additional burden of the bonus would be a hardship to them. . . .[43]

VII

Preoccupied as he was with the affairs of the Manitoba road, Hill still found himself involved in numerous other enterprises. He was determined, however, to get out of the steamboat business, even if it meant practically giving the Red River boats—the "two old baskets"—to Captain Holcombe. He had a large interest in vital and profitable grain elevators, notably the huge installation at Minneapolis. Also, along with the stock in the St. Paul & Pacific, the associates had acquired the majority interest in the still-important water-power facilities at the falls of St. Anthony, and Hill later took over sole ownership. The Minneapolis *Tribune* then said that Hill had "bought out Minneapolis for $425,000," but the age of water power had not long to run. He was on the verge of going into the flour milling business, though he shied away from that risky industry.

In 1882 Hill took under his wing Andrew Tod, younger brother of J. Kennedy Tod, who had come west to seek his fortune in lumbering and in flour mills in the Red River Valley. The young man proved to have no business ability, and Hill, to his dismay, found himself running both the Mille Lacs Lumber Company and the Red River Roller Mills. Lord Elphinstone, an important English investor in the Manitoba road, also put Hill to work. Lord Elphinstone was interested in electric lighting (as was his son, who was later knighted for his pioneer work in establishing central station electric light plants), and he sent Hill some equipment for a trial. Hill's men set it up, got the steam engine going, and turned on the incandescent lamps. They marveled at this glowing evidence of scientific progress for a few hours, then shut the equipment down and relit their kerosene lamps and gas jets. Alas, it was a bit early for electric lighting in St. Paul. Hill had the further task of saving face for Lord Elphinstone; his "toy" was never started up again.[44]

Hill hoped to develop his Iowa coal properties into a major, dependable source of locomotive fuel. The acquisition of the lands had been accomplished by Hamilton Browne, Hill's man on the scene. Browne had been perfect for that job, for he was an enthusiast. But he was also a chronic optimist, and now they had come to the hard, sometimes discouraging work: sinking shafts, bringing up the coal, and getting it to market. Hill began to have doubts about Browne's value to the enterprise, but he still backed the man. The cost of coal depended upon how far it had to be carried, and it was that which eventually led Hill to get into the railroad business in Iowa. The Iowa mines were served by the Rock Island Railroad, and the coal completed its journey to St. Paul over the Rock Island's weak sister, the Minneapolis & St. Louis. By 1880 the Manitoba road was getting five to seven cars of coal a day from its Climax mine, and as much more from the What Cheer mine. The Northern Pacific, which got its coal from Indiana, was paying at least two dollars a ton more than the Manitoba road was, while the North Western was so desperate, Hill said, that it had even "tried corn in the ear as fuel." He invited just about everyone to join in opening more mines, including George Stephen, and he lent money to Browne and to E. N. Saunders, his former partner in the fuel business, so that they could pay for their shares of the stock. By 1884 he valued his own holding in Iowa coal properties at $400,000.[45]

Now and then the mail brought letters which reminded him of events that were slipping from his memory. A scrawled note from Georgetown, Minnesota, brought the past back in a rush:

> Are you the same man that came through here from Fort Garry about 12 or 14 years ago in the spring and had to break the ice and wade through the water up to your waist until you got to the bank, and when I came to take you across the river you made the remark that "If I ever like to see a man in my life that's you." [46]

as did a more proper one from Canada:

> It is now some ten years ago since I first made your acquaintance at North Pembina . . . at the time of the O'Donahue raid. I often think of the ideas you advanced which have since been adopted by the government in their agreement with the Canadian Pacific Railway. I have always considered it *your* scheme *in toto.*[47]

Meanwhile, opportunity to do good was never lacking. Captain Holcombe asked for a job for his twenty-two-year-old son, whose hanging around the house was getting on his mother's nerves. The following year Holcombe needed Hill's signature on his note for $10,000, and he got it. John Proctor, who had done some work for Hill in the old days of land speculation in Dakota Territory, had got in a scrape with the law and was in "limbo" in the Detroit House of Correction. Hill foiled Proctor's voracious wife, who was busily putting the unfortunate man's property in her own name and filing for divorce, and arranged to have her spouse freed. Through his office trooped one westward-bound young man after another, each bearing letters of introduction from Eastern friends. When they told Hill of their plans to become "settlers and cowboys," he listened patiently and gave them valuable advice.[48]

It all left him little time for relaxation. "I have not had a good shoot all year," he complained sadly to a New York friend who was on his way to Dakota to hunt prairie chickens. Except for brief trips to take Mrs. Hill south, which were usually made in his official business car, he traveled in modest style. There were frequent, grueling trips to New York. A Pullman section was good enough, he thought, and he was content to splash away next morning in the washroom alongside the drummers who peddled the myriad goods that railroads like his had been built to carry. He promoted Ives and Secombe to better jobs, and Charles H. Benedict and W. A. Stephens were working in the office when a fire in the building next door would have consumed all of his records but for their stout assistance in getting everything out into the street. His attention to detail, by now legendary, never flagged. Thus he instructed J. S. Kennedy & Company to remove a charge of $2.19 for telegrams from his personal account, noting that the message had been sent on company business. He spotted errors in the accounts of the Climax Coal Company, informing the manager that "it rather interferes with the conclusions you have drawn." He reminded one of his lieutenants in Montana Territory that corporate charters had to be filed with the Secretary of the Interior at Washington as well as in the Territory.[49]

He still had not brought himself to turn operating details over to Manvel. It was hard to believe that someone else, no matter how dedicated, could run the Manitoba road properly. Manvel adapted as well as he could to the situation. He contrived to let Hill know beforehand when he was about to make an important, though purely routine, decision, for experience had taught him that Hill frequently expressed his anger at officials without taking into account the niceties of the organization chart. Hill's reluctance to let go of details almost lost him the services of this man, who was giving his life's blood to the Manitoba. E. B. Wakeman went over Manvel's head and asked Hill for the title of assistant general superintendent, and Hill thoughtlessly assented, but it was Manvel who should have made the decision. When Hill raged at him for showing sympathy for a subcontractor who had exceeded his cost estimates, Manvel decided the time had come to have it out:

> I have thought it best to place my resignation in your hands. . . . . I seem
> to be unable to get at what your wishes are or to carry them out to your

The new president of the St. Paul, Minneapolis & Manitoba Railway. James J. Hill in 1883. Photograph by Ludovici, New York.

satisfaction. . . . For this I must to a degree hold you responsible. . . . Work was stopped by you upon the depot at Ada after orders had been given regarding it. Some weeks ago you ordered rails unloaded at Minneapolis Junction after I had given orders as to their disposition. The effect is to induce a hesitating and uncertain policy in me for fear a positive order on my part will be met with an equally positive counter order from you. The effect of this is to destroy my standing and influence with those under me. . . . Work on the line is now reaching such proportions that no one can give it that detailed attention heretofore possible and it will be necessary to leave it to heads of departments. . . .[50]

Manvel was right, and Hill knew it. The simple days of the past were gone. He had to take a broader view of things, as he told Stephen, but he would not relax his vigilance:

> I would certainly rejoice if I could have more time to rest and be with our children, who are getting to an age when I might be of use to them, but our railroad is unlike old roads, whose staff has been doing the same things at the same place for years. . . . Every day's observations convince me that in a new country a railroad is successful in the proportion that its affairs are vigilantly looked after.

> There is no substitute for hard work, and the value of a railway is its capacity to earn money.[51]

The time had come for Hill to exercise that vigilance from a higher level, and he consented to move up to the presidency when Stephen, preoccupied with the Canadian Pacific, resigned in 1882. From Angus came hearty congratualtions: "It is an honor that you should wear, and I wish you long life to enjoy it." [52]

9

Canadian Interlude

The only reason for going into the Canadian Pacific scheme was for the purpose of benefitting the Manitoba road, but now it assumes the position of a deadly enemy. I fear the result much more than I can tell you.

—James J. Hill to R. B. Angus, 1880

I

George Stephen's first trip back to the British Isles after the associates' spectacular triumph in the St. Paul & Pacific enterprise was deeply gratifying. He had come to Canada, an all but penniless teenager three decades before, and it pleased him to reflect on the fact that if he so desired he could now settle down in England as a rich, respected member of the community. His wealth would buy him a great landed estate, still the chief criterion of a commoner's social standing, and would assure the onetime draper's apprentice an important voice in the commercial and industrial affairs of the nation.

Before the end of the century Stephen would return permanently to England, and not as an ordinary citizen, but as a peer of the realm, a distinguished vassal of Queen Victoria, for whom he had performed a spectacular service in tightening Britain's hold on her slippery North American empire. For just as James J. Hill was about to become the leader in the emergence of the American Northwest, George Stephen, more than any other man save one, would help weld eastern Canada, the vast prairies of the West, and the forests of British Columbia into a true Dominion of Canada. The Canadian Pacific Railway was the product of thousands of hands, but it was George Stephen who was chiefly responsible for setting them to work and keeping them supplied with materials until the job was done.

If Stephen was the chief agent by which the Canadian Pacific project was resurrected and continued to completion, however, the essential political support and protection from a host of demagogues who had learned in the 1870s how to climb to political office over the ruins of the first Canadian Pacific Railroad was provided by John A. Macdonald, Conservative prime minister and the most important figure in the rise of modern Canada. In one of the most amazing phoenix-like comebacks in parliamentary history, Macdonald had rehabilitated not only his party and himself, but also the idea of a privately organized national railway, in the years following the devastating Pacific scandal of 1873. By 1878 Alexander Mackenzie's Liberal party, which housed the agrarian Grits for want of more suitable shelter just as the United States' Democratic party would provide an uneasy abode for the American Populists, had been swept out of power, and Macdonald was back in the prime minister's chair at Ottawa. One of his first moves was to cast about for someone to build his railroad.

The Canadian Pacific is usually described as having been more political than economic in its conception, a generalization which is supposed to explain why it emerged just when it did, and why its builders, in the face of abundant advice to the contrary, agreed to build an all-Canadian line from the beginning. It is an explanation which explains less and less the more one thinks about it. For most great railroad enterprises in North America have been as much "political" as they have been economic in origin. The government-aided Union Pacific, for example, was as much an instrument for binding the West to the East at a time of Civil War as it was a money-making investment, and the Union Pacific was a much longer time becoming a profitable enterprise than the Canadian Pacific was. But the influence of political ends is obvious from the earliest stages of the railroad age in America. The Erie Railroad was pushed primarily to give the residents of the southern tier of New York counties a transportation facility balancing the remarkably successful Erie Canal. Even the Pennsylvania Railroad, by 1880 one of the most successful enterprises in the world, began as a heavily state-aided project to keep the state of Pennsylvania in the westward expansion stakes. All, except the financially victimized Erie, turned initial obstacles aside and became healthy business organizations.

George Stephen knew this, and from the beginning he accepted, however reluctantly, the obligation to build the segment north of Lake Superior as a condition for the contract which he proposed that the Canadian government give to George Stephen & Associates. One who accepted the obligation with strong mental reservations, and with the determination to dissuade the government from it, if possible, was James J. Hill, whose chief concentration was on the practical realities of Canada's transportation needs. To Hill there was a deep and obvious community of interests between the Canadian nation, the Manitoba road, and the Northwest. Transcontinental movement of freight and passengers between the eastern cities of Canada and the vast empire for which Winnipeg was the jumping-off point could most expediently utilize an American link from either Detroit or Sault Ste. Marie, via St. Paul and the Manitoba road to Winnipeg, and thence westward on a Canadian railroad that would not come any nearer the boundary than 100 miles. The first Canadian Pacific Railroad syndicate, which had gone down amid cries of political corruption and Yankee influence in 1873, had never really accepted the idea that the Lake Superior segment would be built during their lifetimes, if ever, and Hill had not accepted it in 1880.

It was the impending completion of the Northern Pacific to the Pacific Coast which impelled Hill to go into the Canadian Pacific syndicate despite all his mental reservations. He knew that once the Northern Pacific was completed, the volume of traffic which would move through St. Paul bound for the West Coast would be very large, and if the Manitoba road were to share in this business it would have to have a line to the coast too. The Canadian Pacific would give it such a line, and, in addition, would provide the Manitoba road with an entrée into the vast lands which promised to be far more bountiful wheat-producing areas than the bleak plains of Montana, through which the Northern Pacific wound its way. John S. Kennedy shared Hill's common sense and his mental reservations, but went along with his decision to accept Stephen's invitation to join the syndicate. The confidence of both men was bolstered by the knowledge that Sir John Rose, who had rejected the associates' offer to finance their efforts to buy the St. Paul & Pacific in 1877, was bringing his firm into the group, and that the Continent would be represented by a group of French and German capitalists.[1]

"Consult the annals of Canada for the past fifty years at random, and whatever party may be in power, what do you find? The government is building a railway, buying a railway, selling a railway, or blocking a railway." [2] Thus did Paul-Émile Lamarche, Quebec Nationalist, express his contempt for the Dominion in 1917. It is true that no other nation of so small a population and such slender resources has ever been so preoccupied with the subject of railroads, but then no people ever rattled around in vast spaces more than the Canadians. The very magnitude of the gap between the job to be done and the resources available, however, seemed to convince nearly everybody, from the grittiest Grit to the most capitalistic Conservative, that the enterprise had to be scrupulously free from alien influence or control. Stephen had his work cut out for him, therefore, when it came to getting Sir John's approval of those who were to be the controlling members of the Canadian Pacific syndicate, and he was not above dissembling to minimize the danger of Yankee taint:

> Here is what the St. Paul papers say of the syndicate: it is rather curious that all my Minnesota associates are Canadians. Mr. Kittson is a native of Sorel, brother of the collector of customs at Hamilton, and Hill is from Guelph. Not a Yankee in the concern. Kennedy, whose position and reputation in New York stands hardly second to any, is a Scotchman, President of the N.Y. St. Andrews Society, and by the way he has not one dollar of interest in the St. P., M. & M. Railway. I mention these things in case you may be exposed to attacks of selling the country to a lot of Yankees. [3]

Stephen faced an impossible problem in getting Macdonald to accept Donald Smith as a member of the syndicate, for the Conservative leader had been his sworn enemy ever since Smith had sided with the Liberals in the Pacific scandal. Smith remained a silent partner at first. "I had to omit his name as a member of the syndicate," Stephen recalled thirty-four years later, "which he did not like at all." Even so, the syndicate, with the addition of Angus, was remarkably similar to the group of associates who had taken over and reorganized the St. Paul & Pacific, and, until their withdrawal in 1883, Hill and Kennedy would perform very much the same services in this even more daring enterprise. On October 21, 1880, the contract was signed with the Canadian government, calling for what then seemed generous cash and land grant subsidies, and after a long and bitter debate in Parliament it was confirmed on February 1, 1881. Sixteen days later Hill sent Stephen his check for $150,000, a one-third installment on his subscription to 5000 shares. [4]

II

"I am hardly an active member of the C.P. Co.," Hill wrote to Walter Moberly, who had been one of the early railroad surveyors in the mountains of British Columbia and hoped to be taken on by the new syndicate to help find the best route through the Canadian Rockies.[5] Hill, more than fully occupied with the affairs of the Manitoba road, never managed to apply to the Canadian Pacific his policy of "being where the money is being spent." The work in 1881 west of Winnipeg was managed primarily by the contractors, and while they performed great feats of railroad construction, they could not give the business the continuous, official supervision it required. Hill depended upon agents to reassure him that the rails were headed into inhabitable country as they proceeded westward, which was all the more important since he had persuaded Stephen and Angus to make sweeping changes from the route originally surveyed. "The man sent over the work . . . went as far west as the Moose Jaw," Hill wrote Angus, "and reports that the country after getting 30 miles west of Brandon is equal to the best portions of southern Dakota as regards the soil, with the advantage of more timber and an abundance of good water." [6]

It was no way to build a railroad, and by the end of 1881 Hill was trying hard to get a first-class railroad man to take over the responsibility for building the Canadian Pacific and putting it into operation as its sections were completed. Angus was trying to run the road's office in Montreal, but the amiable, incompetent Duncan McIntyre, who had been taken into the company largely because he controlled an Eastern railroad which the syndicate intended to amalgamate into the new transcontinental road, was a grievous handicap. To Angus's great relief, Hill finally persuaded William C. Van Horne, general superintendent of the Chicago, Milwaukee & St. Paul Railroad, that his greatest challenge and brightest future lay north of the border as general manager of the promising Canadian Pacific.[7]

Meanwhile, corruption had threatened the very existence of the enterprise. The temptation to make big profits out of speculation in town lots as the road crept westward from Winnipeg proved too much for Thomas Lafayette Rosser, former Confederate general and in 1881 the chief engineer of the Canadian Pacific. Rosser peddled information about the route to real estate promoters, and that crass breed moved in, encouraged by railroad sidings which had been laid solely to facilitate construction, not to serve new towns. Winnipeg had to endure a land boom, with all its attendant demoralizations and inevitable, resounding crash. Van Horne, whose imperious manner, stern bearded countenance, and awesome proportions led to his being mistaken for King Edward VII in later years, ousted Rosser. And Hill backed Van Horne up all the way:

> It looks as if everyone holding any position of responsibility on the C Pac at Winnipeg from Genl Rosser down has been engaged in townsite operations. It is openly advertized that Genl Rosser is a promoter of the town of Raeburn. Yesterday Mr. Van Horne issued a circular notifying the public that the locations of towns and stations . . . would be made officially from his office and that present side tracks &c were only temporary.[8]

Not even a tearful letter from Mrs. Rosser could make Hill deal leniently with this man who had almost discredited the fledgling enterprise. Hill was willing, however, to take the word of A. B. Stickney, one of the contractors, that Stickney was not involved with Rosser, and Stephen was relieved to hear it, for this man was already a substantial figure in railroad construction and operation in the Twin Cities area. Hill would not be sorry, in the years to come, that he kept Stickney's friendship.

Meanwhile, Rosser, unchastened by his disgrace, intercepted a courier from one of the surveying parties at the railroad station. Pretending that he was still chief engineer, Rosser accepted a packet of maps showing the probable route of the railroad in what became the Province of Saskatchewan, and within hours departed for the west and one more try at townsite speculation.[9]

James J. Hill's permanent mark upon the Canadian Pacific lies in the route which it follows from Winnipeg to the Pacific. Sandford Fleming, the Canadian government's chief engineer of the railroad in the 1870s, had planned it to run through the valley of the North Saskatchewan River, far north of the route that was eventually selected. When John Palliser, the adventurous Irishman who was largely responsible for the myth of the "Great American Desert," explored what later became northern Montana and southwestern Canada, he was convinced that the region was too arid to support any kind of farming. But he found what he dubbed a "fertile belt" much farther north, and conceded that a railroad at that latitude would be practical. Less than ten years later three factors combined to change the path of railroad development in Canada from what Palliser's findings dictated: the onset of the humid phase of the rainfall cycle; James J. Hill's overriding desire for a Canadian Pacific Railway which would be, if nothing else, a direct extension of the Manitoba road to the Pacific that could compete with the Northern Pacific; and the persuasiveness of John Macoun. Where Palliser, exploring at the very depth of the drought of the 1870s, had seen a desert, Macoun, a stubborn, wiry Scotsman, insisted on seeing a land that could become the breadbasket of the world. During summer vacations from his post as professor of botany at a small college in Ontario, he persuaded the government to send him as far as the foothills of the Rockies on an extended field trip during his summer vacations in 1879 and 1880. Neither Macoun nor Canada was ever the same again. All of the arts of persuasion, oral and written, he could marshal were devoted to singing the prasises of southwestern Canada. He had little difficulty in persuading Hill, and Stephen, who could already see that the cash subsidy was never going to stretch as far as his railroad had to go, eagerly agreed. A year after the decision to build due west from Winnipeg was made, Hill was more convinced than ever that it was a good one, as his own man began to send back reports of the territory:

> He reports the country as a whole as being the best large section of farming land he has ever seen in the west. . . . His report of the country is very satisfactory, coming as it does to confirm our recent information, and the result will I am sure justify the change we have steadily advised from the Northern route. It would be a fatal error to leave the southern route open for some rival to occupy and in doing so get the shortest and best line.[10]

III

The shortest and best line: that was always Hill's formula for the location of a railroad. But no southern route through the Canadian Rockies and the Selkirk Range was known to exist, for Fleming's survey had sought out northern passes. It was an act of bravado on Hill's part, and in fact an almost irresponsible risking of the "national dream," to write Stephen that "I have little or no doubt but we will get a good pass through both ranges on the line we have taken." All of his hopes were pinned on a scrawny, dundreary-whiskered, tobacco-stained, and foul-mouthed little man, an Army engineer—"poor old Major Rogers," as Hill called him. But Hill saw that A. B. Rogers had a consuming ambition to become the discoverer of *the* passes through the Rockies and the "mysterious" Selkirks, and a singleness of purpose

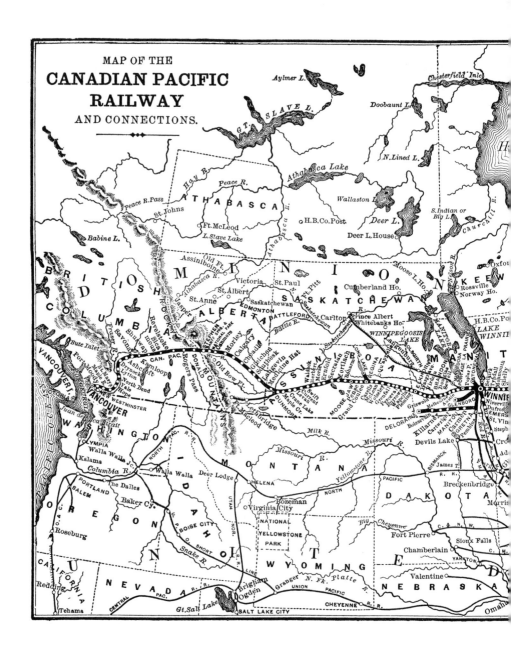

MAP OF THE
CANADIAN PACIFIC RAILWAY
AND CONNECTIONS.

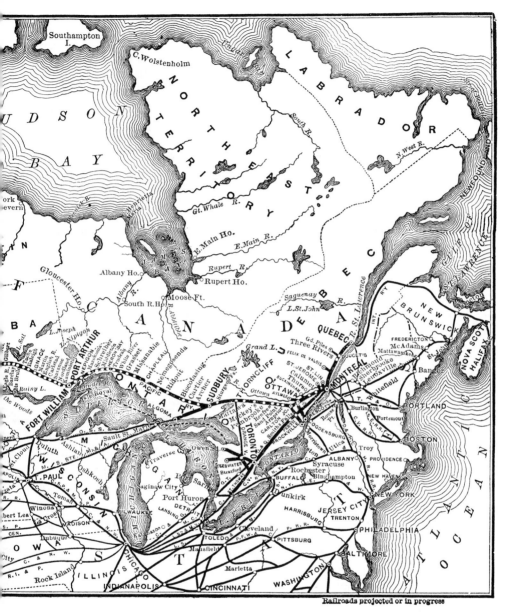

1885   (*Commercial and Financial Chronicle.*)

which would keep the little man driving his surveying party up and down the rugged, trackless slopes, with little more than a few pieces of hardtack in their knapsacks, to the very verge of winter. Hill knew his man, and he was not to be disappointed.[11]

"I feel certain that a good practical man like Rogers can with a comparatively small outlay get a good line through the mountains and save nearly 150 miles of heavy work," Hill reassured Angus, adding seductively, "and [thereby] closing the way for other ambitious parties who may come after us." When the spring of 1881 was still no more than barely begun, Hill had Rogers on his way. As summer waned he posted frequent encouragements to the little band of men who were stumbling through the rugged defiles of the mountains. "Mr. Stephen, and Mr. Angus, as well as myself, have read your letters with great satisfaction and they desire me to express to you their confidence in your judgment and perseverance," he said.

Then, a few days before Christmas, an untidy little man stumped through the office door, demanding to see Hill. "Major Rogers has returned and is in good form," Hill joyously wrote Van Horne, who was about to leave Milwaukee to take up his new duties with the Canadian Pacific: "he reports that he has a good and very direct line through the Kicking Horse Pass [of the Rockies] and says that he has enough information to remove any serious doubt about our being able to find a pass through the Selkirk range." Another spring came, and another summer of exploration went by. As the maples began to turn on the hills of Montreal, Stephen, whose burdens as president of the road were becoming almost unbearable, was relieved to get a triumphant note from Hill. "Poor old Major Rogers has redeemed his promise and the pass through the Selkirks is better than the Nor Pacific's [through the American Rockies], and with the further advantage of saving the tunnell [sic]. It is hard to estimate the value of this pass to our enterprise." The major's claim to have found a line with a maximum grade of 2 percent (a 100-foot rise to the mile) turned out to be optimistic, but when he died it was in the knowledge that his life's ambition to be the pathfinder through the mountains had been realized.[12]

Hill had had his way about the southern route and the passes through the mountains, but he would not get his most ardent wish. The Canadian government put first what Hill put last—a transcontinental railroad route every foot of which would be on Canadian soil. Never again, Sir John was determined, would his or any other Canadian government face the humiliation of even considering the dispatch of peace-keeping troops westward through the United States. And so the "Nipissing line," as the segment north of Lake Superior came to be called, was made a mandatory condition of the contract with the syndicate: no matter how fast or how well they built the line eastward from Winnipeg to Thunder Bay, on Lake Superior (a region so cluttered with lakes and swamps that no one yet knew how it was to be done), if the syndicate reneged on the Nipissing line, or even sought to delay it, the deal was off. Unable to believe that the government would be so unreasonable, Hill wrote a long letter to Angus, pleading with him to see if something could not yet be done:

> After the line is completed I cannot see that it would have any local business whatever for some time and the through traffic would not afford it enough money to meet the payrolls and fuel, saying nothing of repairs and renewals. . . . I write thus at length because I believe a great deal could be done to settle up the prairie within a comparatively short time and every effort should be turned to that end [while] the line from Thunder Bay to Nipissing will not be of any service whatever for many years to come. Would it not be a much better arrangement for the government to have the all-rail line run via the Sault Ste. Marie, where it would have a local timber and mineral business both sides of the line?

> After there is a settled belt along the line to the Rocky Mountains, the back country would begin to open up and when the people are in the country and there is some business created, a line east via the north shore might be considered. . . .[13]

It was not to be. Hill began to realize that eventually the Manitoba road would have to have its own line to the Pacific, for the Canadian Pacific surely would not give him eastbound freight at Winnipeg once it had its own traffic-famished line to look out for. Still, from a practical point of view he was right, as the Canadian Pacific eventually acknowledged when it acquired the "Soo" Line to give it precisely the American middle link which Hill had hoped would be the Manitoba road's role. Before 1880 was quite past, and when the Canadian Pacific project was just getting under way, he could see the beginning of the end of his participation:

> As it presents itself to me I can see nothing but absolute loss of everything invested before five years unless the plan is to borrow money that can never be repaid to an amount that will tide over. . . . The only reason for going into the scheme was for the purpose of benefitting the St. P. M. & M. Ry., but now it assumes the position of a deadly enemy. I sincerely hope I am all wrong but I fear the result much more than I can tell you.[14]

IV

Hill continued to take an active role in the formation and execution of important policies of the Canadian Pacific until well into 1883. Many questions remained after the basic decisions on routes, mountain passes, and the Lake Superior section had been made, and the road's understaffed executive office, isolated in Montreal, would have been even less effective than it was without Hill's help in resolving crises. He threw himself into the fight to prevent parallel railroads such as Dr. Schultz's Manitoba & Southwestern from being built southward from Winnipeg, and he went to the provincial capital with Angus to argue against the $200,000 subsidy that the Grit-fearing legislators were on the point of voting. While he shared the Canadian Pacific men's eagerness to promote immigration from eastern to western Canada as vigorously as possible, he stood fast for the Manitoba road's long-run welfare when Angus pressed him for ultra-low through passenger rates.[15]

The Canadian Pacific syndicate's members found themselves forced on more than one occasion to lend their personal credit to the enterprise, which was constantly short of cash. Early in 1882 Hill authorized Kennedy to use $500,000 worth of his Manitoba road stock as collateral for short-term loans so that the Canadian Pacific could buy rails before the price went up. "I do not want to sell any of my Manitoba stock," he said, "but you will consider yourselves at liberty to use it if required for the [Canadian Pacific] advances." Closer to the work than any of the other senior Canadian Pacific men, and more familiar with the problems of railroad building, he flashed warnings to Angus and Stephen when things threatened to go wrong. He repeatedly urged Stephen to come west, "as many things can be put into better shape than at present." There was little margin for error in the affairs of the enterprise, he realized, and McIntyre could not be trusted to exercise sound judgment. "We have an enormous task to perform and every effort . . . will be required to make it a success," he warned; "McIntyre . . . is too sanguine of results to lead in so large an affair as ours." Hill had not stopped believing in the value of constructive anxiety.[16]

Much has been made of the lifelong feud which their early relations on the project engendered between Hill and Van Horne. But if history offered more examples of the creative relationship which existed between these two men then and for the rest of their lives, man's story would be a happier one. It is true that sparks flew on more than one occasion as these two proud, gifted, and supremely motivated men set about solving the numerous problems which the imperial objectives of the Manitoba road, the Canadian Pacific, and, later, the Great Northern Railway presented. Both men had more than the usual amount of intellectual and artistic temperament. Van Horne was a talented painter and accomplished geologist, while Hill's aesthetic makeup could be seen in nearly everything he set his hand to, from the rhetoric of his letters to the strikingly severe decorations of the Manitoba road office building in St. Paul, to the elegance of his art collection. But to historians and biographers who yearn for snappy items for their books, Hill and Van Horne's relations look like those of two prima donnas.

Hill, to be sure, could never think of Van Horne other than as a young man who owed his first grasp on a ladder that led to spectacular success and a knighthood to James J. Hill. And Van Horne, determined to bask fully in the spotlight which he had earned, seldom missed an opportunity to suggest that luck had played a large part in Hill's career. In 1914 he seduced Donald Smith's biographer into believing the legend that Stephen's trip to St. Paul in 1877 to inspect the St. Paul & Pacific had been decided by the toss of a coin:

> How wonderful the result of that toss! If it had fallen for St. Louis there would have been no Lord Mount Stephen or Lord Strathcona, and Jim Hill might have become mayor of St. Paul or something of that kind.

but he came stoutly to Hill's defense against woolly-headed socialist critics:

> I have not seen that book of Gustavus Myers', but if he says that Lord Strathcona or Lord Mount Stephen or Jim Hill ever made a dollar in any but an honorable, legitimate and unquestionable way, he is a damned liar.* [17]

Hill never had any reason to change the opinion he had expressed when he was urging Stephen to hire Van Horne as general manager: "I have never met anyone who is better informed in the various departments, machinery, cars, operation, train services, construction and

---

* Stephen, or Lord Mount Stephen, as he was entitled to be called, was past eighty by that time. Donald Smith became Lord Strathcona and Mount Royal. Gustavus Myers's *History of the Great American Fortunes,* first published in 1907, is full of historical errors, but it sowed many seeds whose harvest later exploiters of the robber baron legend reaped.

general policy which with untiring energy and a good vigorous body should give us good results." Nor did he, when the going got rough, ever go back on the pledge he had made Van Horne in welcoming him to his new position: "It will always give me great pleasure to assist you in all ways in my power and . . . I fully pledge you the support of the company." Years later, when William Graham Sumner, Yale sociologist and ardent champion of free enterprise, coined the term "antagonistic cooperation," he might well have had William C. Van Horne and James J. Hill in mind.[18]

By the following spring the Canadians were more grateful to Hill for pressing Van Horne's appointment than Stephen could adequately express. "It was indeed a happy hit getting him," he wrote. Van Horne's charismatic presence had been inserted into the situation west of Winnipeg just in time. The Rosser scandal, the land boom, and a scarcity of labor were threatening to demoralize the contractors. Hill gave Van Horne vital assistance at that juncture by secretly sending an engineer from the Manitoba road to select the best point at which to cross the South Saskatchewan River, and the new general manager was grateful for the advice. Hill continued to view Van Horne as an able, trusted lieutenant. Soon he was lecturing him on personnel policy, impressing on him that, as difficult as it was for the Canadian Pacific to attract and hold good engineers, he should not quibble about salary. Less than two months later he was singing a different tune, for Van Horne, taking advantage of the painfully short summer to push the rails westward at a dizzying clip, had increased wages to what Hill considered unjustified levels. High wages, Hill argued, with peculiar logic, would make the men think they were indispensable, and increase the danger of a strike.[19]

Hill repeatedly interposed himself between Van Horne and the contractors, pleading that no time should be lost in standing on ceremony, and tended to take the contractors' part in disputes. Van Horne, eager to become master in his own house, resented the intrusions, and Hill finally realized that he could not wield the power of president, the only official to whom Van Horne was responsible. He urged Stephen to come west, survey the problem, and assure himself that the contractors understood who was boss. "It would not do to have Langdon & Co. coming to me for decisions that properly belong to Mr. Van Horne," he told Stephen, piously; "Mr. Van Horne is our man and the company should support him where he is right and where he is wrong he should be set right. . . ." The Canadian Pacific

William C. Van Horne in 1886, two years before he succeeded George Stephen as president of the Canadian Pacific Railway. Notman Photographic Archives, McCord Museum, McGill University, Montreal.

never did achieve a strong executive organization during this period. Angus, in fact, was so frustrated with the jerry-built arrangement that he threatened to resign. But once Van Horne was in command, he would turn such frustrations into the kind of challenge that even the most gifted get only once in a lifetime. By the time Donald Smith drove the last spike at Craigellachie, Van Horne was the unquestioned master of the Canadian Pacific.[20]

Van Horne's ascendancy in the road and Hill's alienation from it proceeded apace throughout 1882. After backbreaking work, and a ter-rifying period when it seemed that the marshy terrain between Winnipeg and Thunder Bay would never be mastered, Van Horne had completed the link to the western end of Lake Superior. He was anxious to demonstrate to the Canadian people before the close of navigation on the Lakes that they now had an all-Canadian (if not yet all-rail) transportation system from the Atlantic all the way to the railhead out on the plains of Saskatchewan. As Hill had expected, he adopted a rate policy designed to keep as much of the eastbound freight as possible on the Canadian Pacific at Winnipeg, rather than see it continue via St. Paul. "While we make no complaint as to what the Canadian Pacific Co. may deem its best interest," Hill sulked, "it would only be common courtesy to a connecting line to have at least given us sound notice, and not leave us to get our information from the newspapers." Besides, he wrote Kennedy, the Thunder Bay Branch was not supposed to have gone into operation until the following spring. He confided that there was "a feeling in the Can Pac board of ill concealed hostility towards this company." There was bitterness over the Manitoba Southwestern matter. The Manitoba road had scraped up $1.1 million to buy the interloper, which was a much greater threat to the Canadian Pacific than to the Manitoba road, and now the Canadians were acting as though it "was not so much an affair of the Can Pac as it was of the Manitoba Co." Well, Hill blustered, perhaps it was, and he threatened to keep the line and use it to draw traffic from the Canadian Pacific at Winnipeg whether they liked it or not.[21]

By the middle of 1883 the Canadian Pacific had solved most of its problems, except the financial one, which would all but destroy it, while Hill was completing the Manitoba road's original expansion plans in Dakota Territory and casting serious glances toward Montana. He was ready to pull out of the Canadian Pacific syndicate, and Kennedy, who was going through a crisis of nerves that was all but disabling, shared his views. Hill had acquired a total of 25,000 shares of the company's stock since its inception, and, although he knew that it would make Stephen's financial tightrope walking just that much more difficult, he was tempted to throw on the market all 15,000 of the shares he had left by 1883. He complained that "our Canadian friends" had reduced their holdings of Manitoba road stock considerably, although he well knew that only dire financial need would have led Stephen and Smith to sell their stock. It did reduce the associates' margin of control over the Manitoba road, however, which worried Hill. They might soon be in the minority, he told Angus, "and I have too large a holding to be in a minority. . . ."[22]

Angus opposed Hill's threats to resign only feebly, whereupon Hill became more conciliatory:

I have made up my mind to hold $1,000,000 of my Can Pac stock, if it is only one of the bonds that bind the old party together. . . . I think you know I am not anxious about the money part of it. I have all and more than I will ever want and all that will be good for those who come after me. . . .

But he began to work out an arrangement with Kennedy whereby both could pull out with as little embarrassment to the Canadians as possible. Before spring was over Hill's resignation from the Canadian Pacific board was in the mail:

I have felt for some time past that [because of] the great distance between St. Paul and Montreal, and the fact that my time is so fully occupied with the business of the St. Paul Minn. & Man. Ry. Co., it will be impossible for me to . . . serve as a member of the board during the coming year.

In taking this step I feel that . . . however reluctantly I close the official connection, I will always feel the same interest in the success of the enterprise, and of the friends with whom I have been so long associated.

But he was not optimistic about the future relations of the two companies. "I have repeatedly pointed out the necessity of putting the joint business on a fair and equitable basis," he told Kennedy, "but Mr. Van Horne is inclined to take the view that the St. P. M. & M. are powerless to help themselves and must simply accept any situation that may be assigned to it by the Can Pac. I think Mr. Stephen would prefer a good fair arrangement, but he has to rely on some one else to tell him what that should be." [23]

V

George Eastman introduced his "Kodak" camera in 1888. It was loaded at the factory with a roll of flexible film on which as many as a hundred snapshots could be made by the most inexperienced operator, after which the film, still in the camera, was returned to Rochester for processing. One of the first families to record their domestic life on the round, red-tinted pictures that Eastman's gadget produced were the Hills of St. Paul. During the 1880s men like James J. Hill extended the railroad to nearly every village and town of any consequence, and in doing so they changed the character of American life forever. Now,

as the decade drew to a close, Hill could steal a few minutes from his important work to watch the new American ritual of picture-taking. A fresh snowfall has always been the signal to get out the family Kodak, and St. Paul seldom lacked this stimulus once winter held sway. Striding briskly down the walk on a whitened morning in 1888, amply protected against the sub-freezing temperature by a substantial Victorian breakfast and a heavy coat which further exaggerated his air of solid power, James J. Hill could look with pleasure across Ninth Street to the broad yard where the toboggan slide stood. His daughters were taking pictures.

"Like stairsteps," that was the cliché Hill heard a thousand times about his daughters. It was not quite accurate. Mamie, almost twenty years old and engaged to be married by the time the Kodak made its appearance, was not a member of the group posturing in front of the camera. The younger girls, however, industriously posed for their pictures, singly, in groups of two or three, sometimes atop the big wood-frame toboggan slide and sometimes self-consciously at its foot, or at other times on the front steps of the mansion, vainly trying to get their pet Newfoundland to hold still for his portrait too. There was shy, petite Clara, not looking her fifteen years, yet the eldest; there were Charlotte, a gregarious twelve-year-old who usually directed the photographic activities, and Ruth, old enough at nine to challenge her leadership; little Rachel, born only five years before; and Gertrude who, at four, might have been her twin; and finally a tiny toddler, barely three, whose long stockings and warm, heavy skirts made him a miniature replica of the others. The sixth little Hill in these scenes is not another girl, but Walter, with whose arrival in 1885 James and Mary Hill's family of nine living children was complete.

Affluent twentieth-century American families have discovered that mere money is no substitute for a large staff of cheerful domestic servants in raising a large family. They would have envied the Hill ménage of the 1880s. Save for the traffic problems which eleven family members and a staff of resident servants must have caused in an era when private bathrooms were all but unknown, the Hill household ran like a well-oiled machine. But it did not run itself. Managing her

The house at Ninth and Canada streets (later numbered 259 East Ninth Street) before the art gallery was added to the right front. This was the Hill family home from 1878 to 1891. The Gotzian house is at the rear, fronting on Canada Street, and the Upham house is to the left. Winter 1884.

domain was a full-time business for Mary Hill, who though thrifty, disbursed a monthly sum which many a nineteenth-century working-class family could have lived on for a year. Except for Mamie, who attended day classes at the convent, the children were all at home, every day, all day, and their innumerable needs had to be met. To Mary, who had been brought up to believe that there was no substitute for seeing what you were getting, and for checking frequently on what the shop-keepers had to offer, every day required a lengthy shopping trip. Never quite approving of the shopkeepers' eagerness to charge her purchases and deliver them, she frequently dug down into the purse which swayed from her belt to pay for packages which the clerk carried out to add to the others in the carriage. Her husband expected, and Mary was determined to provide, a tranquil, dignified atmosphere in which his very domestic nature might be fully satisfied on the increasingly infrequent occasions when he was free to indulge it.

It was an unpretentious household in which plain food, conventional crises, stern discipline, and simple pleasures followed in predictable sequence. When the girls and little Walter went out into the fresh snow to dispose of a few more shots in their Kodak, they were well bundled in Astrakhan coats and Angora bonnets. Gertrude's coat had been Rachel's the year before, and Ruth's had been Charlotte's, and so on—but, as Rachel recalled almost eighty years later, one kept one's own bonnet as long as it would fit. When they got cold they could slip into the row of carriage houses across the street, visit with the coachmen, and pat the horses, of which the Hills alone had six. Sometimes the groom in the adjoining stable would allow them to sit in the Uphams' beautifully decorated old sleigh. It had known the Red River country long before their father had seen it, for Mrs. Upham, born a Burbank, had inherited the sleigh from forebears who had operated the first stagecoach line northwest of St. Paul.

Busy, important, rich though he unquestionably was, Hill was surrounded by as wide a range of domestic sounds, sights, and smells as any more modestly situated householder. For twenty years there was an infant in the family circle, and bills from the druggist came regularly for all of the appliances supplies that babies required, as well as large quantities of Pear's soap for everybody. M. Chemidlin held classes in the third-floor schoolroom, where he fully earned his seventy-dollar-a-month salary as he struggled to give the children a foundation on which other, more fashionable tutors, professors, and finishing-school mistresses would build. The Hills got the normal childhood ailments, multiplied by nine, which means that someone was nearly always on the sick list. In 1882 Hill was especially worried that "little Clara, although growing fast, is not strong."

Hill's interest in art was growing rapidly at that time, and in 1884 he resolved to have five-year-old Ruth's portrait painted by Bouguereau, the fashionable French painter. Both painter and subject were spared an Atlantic crossing, still a dangerous and uncomfortable adventure, for Hill asked Julius Oehmer of M. Knoedler & Company, New York, to see if the painter would not do the picture from a photograph. M. Bouguereau may have been insulted by the suggestion; if he was a $4000 fee mollified him. If Mr. Hill would send him a good photograph, the Frenchman replied, he would look for a little girl like Ruth to do the posing. And so the rosy-cheeked child of what had so recently been a raw town on the Northwest frontier had her portrait painted by a bohemian resident of Montmartre, and without either of them leaving home.[24]

All of the children were receiving a Catholic education in one way or another, and Hill gave Father Caillet little to criticize as an ideal *pater familias,* save for the fact that his appearances with his brood at church became more and more infrequent. One by one the children made their First Communion, a solemn event though modestly commemorated, as when Clara's photograph was put up in a small gilt frame that cost $1.15. It was Christmas that brought the family closest together and made for the greatest high spirits. A week before the great day in 1884 the Hill children entertained the Upham and Gotzian children, and many more, at a party which required three dozen papier mâché cornucopias for the place settings, the same number of party hats, two dozen candles and holders, and ten pounds of candy, all supplied by St. Paul's only fancy grocer. The night before Christmas the Kellys, Uphams, Gotzians, and Manvels dropped by to enjoy Rockaway oysters from the barrel which Eugene Mehl, manager of New York's famed Brevoort House, had sent his friend. They agreed with Mehl's description of a new cheese which he had also sent: " 'gorgonzola,' which you will find far superior to Roquefort or Stilton." Family dinner the next day was plain but ample, requiring 26½ pounds of roast chicken.[25]

The gifts were worthy of the Three Kings. That year Hill started the children in photography with $35 worth of equipment and supplies, including a copy of "How To Make Pictures." This was nothing, however, compared to the gleaming ebony grand piano which had miraculously appeared in the parlor during the night. It was Mamie's Christmas present, and she was instructed to thank Mrs. Samuel Thorne, wife of one of the New York directors of the Manitoba road, for having gone to Steinway's showrooms on 14th Street to select it. One year the girls were deeply impressed by a handsome sealskin "dolman," a large-sleeved coat which was to give their mother a little of the Turkish effect then so popular, but next year there was a present for their mother that really made their eyes light up: a big, beautiful, brilliant-cut diamond from a jewelers in Chicago. They should have been impressed, for the $11,000 it cost would have seemed a vast sum to their father barely ten years before.

As with all men and women of strong personality, Hill's own tastes were reflected in many of his gifts. Precious stones fascinated him, and, although he scorned personal jewelry for himself, he liked to carry a diamond or ruby or emerald as a pocketpiece. Mary Hill's superb diamond joined other pieces bought in Chicago and New York: a thirteen-carat sapphire worth $1000 in 1883; a string of pink pearls in 1884; pearl-and-diamond pendants and a yellow diamond ring worth $7200 in 1885; in the same year, a ruby and a diamond ring worth $4000, and, for Mamie, a diamond-studded comb for her long, flowing hair, a woman's crowning glory in that era.[26]

VI

Hill's sons, Jimmy and Louis, were reaching the age at which, their father reflected, "I might be of use to them," and he regretted that he did not have more time for them. They had never gone to a real school, a tutor being the diplomatic compromise between a public grammar school, with its Protestant influences, and the inadequate parochial schools of St. Paul. Soon Mr. Chemidlin would have to be replaced by a real "professor" who would be willing to move to St. Paul to prepare the boys for college, and Hill had his New York friends on the lookout for such a person. Meanwhile, he did what he could: he saw to it that the lads spent the usual dreary hours proving that they had little musical talent—in their case with the violin—and the Victorian ideal of thrift was held constantly before them. Plain, serviceable clothing was good enough for all the children, and even when the boys were ready for their first long trousers, the outfits came ready-made from the Boston One-Price Clothing Store in St. Paul.

For Hill the happiest times were the summers, when he spent as much time as he could at their new farm at North Oaks. There, one year, Jimmy helped raise two fawns, progeny of the tame deer that devastated the lawns. The problem of what to do with the pets, in view of a deer population explosion, was solved by allowing Jimmy to sell them to Mr. Secombe, who was moving north to take over the Mille Lacs Lumber Company for Hill. Jimmy's father showed him how to write out the receipt, and a copy was duly filed away in the family accounts. Business training cannot begin too early. Patriotism, too, was important, and it was combined with the excitement of a Victorian Fourth of July, for which $19 worth of fireworks were required one year. The summer when the boys were sixteen and fourteen, Hill packed them off, with a new professor, in the private car, "Manitoba," on a trip out West, via the Northern Pacific. The high point of the tour was Yellowstone Park.[27]

If the tribe of children did not drive the Hills, sooner or later, to a larger residence, Hill's growing art collection would have. In 1882 he ordered a large room to be added to the front of the structure as a gallery for his pictures. To match the house, three carloads of special white pressed brick were brought up from Milwaukee; and, to keep things reasonably clean during the short dry summer, Hill paid a man $8.00 a month to sprinkle the still-unpaved street in front. The establishment grew more substantial with each passing year, as Emerson Lewis, the trusted, well-paid Negro who had the responsibility for thousands of dollars worth of vehicles and horseflesh in the carriage house, could verify. As soon as the art gallery was finished the St. Paul tax collector came around for a look, and when the year's assessed valuations were announced, James J. Hill's increase, from $50,000 to $75,000 led all the rest.[28]

The unwillingness of skilled Eastern cooks to move to St. Paul was almost as much a problem to Hill as the same reluctance in professors, although the latter probably had less choice about it. Eugene Mehl, who should have been able to find a good cook if anybody could, reported that a woman who would remove to the Northwest could not be found, and Hill, against his wife's better judgment, agreed to take a French chef into his establishment. The result was disastrous. "He was not up to his work," Hill reported to Mehl. The problem was solved when the young man's relatives wrote, urging him to get back to France as soon as possible to fulfill his military obligation.

Each morning saw a steady stream of delivery boys coming up the back walk at Ninth and Canada. Bread, rolls, and cookies, to supplement the great quantity made under Mary Hill's supervision, came from the Portland Vienna Bakery, and numerous other establishments furnished the green groceries, fancy goods, Havana cigars, and Anheuser beer which disappeared in quantities. Park & Tilford, in New York, and Cavaroc & Company of New Orleans and Chicago, provided imported delicacies and wines and spirits. Ehrmantraut, the butcher, submitted a bill each month for as much as $200 (at least $800 in late-twentieth-century money) for beef, veal, lamb, and pork, and the many saddles of mutton for which Mary herself put up gallons of currant jelly each summer. Sixty years after Hill's death, old men remembered trotting up the walk day after day with packages of sweetbreads. They were not wrong. One month Hill had his favorite dish on eight different occasions.[29]

"I don't want a team for speed," Hill explained to Hamilton Browne, who was buying horses for him, "but more for size and weight to haul a heavy carriage about the city. If they are well matched and good lookers without faulty dispositions I can forgive them any want of speed." A large family needed a big carriage—a "road wagon," as the manufacturer called it—and strong horses to haul it. Hill took a lighter carriage to the office in bad weather or when he was in a hurry, or burdened with baggage. For a while he drove himself; then, growing bored with it, he turned the job back to the coachman. But when he could, he preferred to walk the few blocks. He frequently had lunch at the Minnesota Club, of which he was a charter member, and he was upset to learn, as the good old days receded, that politician friends such as Knute Nelson could no longer afford to be seen in such nests of privilege. A game of whist at the club, or in the evening at home with the Uphams, was a genuine pleasure, though it was growing rarer. (In later years he eased many a lonely hour at the huge mansion on Summit Avenue with a game of solitaire.) From the St. Paul Book & Stationary Company, one of downtown St. Paul's oldest institutions, came a steady stream of magazines, and he devoured the best of them: *Century, Harper's, Leslie's,* the *North American Review,* and the *London Graphic.* It was a time when New York businessmen chatted easily about a great range of subjects, and Hill never hesitated to join the Easterners.[30]

During his first four years as general manager and president of the Manitoba road Hill seldom took a vacation, and when he did it was usually to accompany Mary Hill to the southern resort where she spent several winters in the 1880s. "I feel that I should go south and get Mrs. H. settled for the balance of the winter," he explained to Angus in December 1880; "she is much better but cannot stand any cold or dampness and will not be permanently cured until she can go about in the open air." Mary Hill, the doctors would discover years later, had a spot on her lungs—tuberculosis in an early stage, or a "consumptive tendency," as it was more delicately put then. By the mid-1880s such trips were no longer necessary, or so they believed.

To ease the loneliness which, sooner or later, Mary felt in her southern retreat, Hill usually spent a few days with her, and he returned for her when the first sign of spring appeared in St. Paul. The first such excursion was a rather gala affair, duly noted in the local papers, as the Hills and their guests, the Uphams, and several of the older children headed for New Orleans in the "Manitoba." It was not as extravagant as it seemed, for the Associated Railways of Virginia hauled the car at a cost of only five cents a mile. At the time, it cost one person three cents a mile or more to ride in an ordinary coach. (Of course, the Manitoba road frequently had to return the favor to Eastern railroad magnates who wanted to look at the great American Northwest.) Hill grew fond of the southeastern Atlantic coast,and later in the decade, when Mrs. Hill was well, he liked to take her with him on business trips to New York, then on to Washington, where business of a different sort was transacted with politicians, and then to the South.[31]

As the busy years passed, Hill's personal interests and his ambitions for the railroad and the Northwest tended to merge. On the shores of Lake Minnetonka, west of Minneapolis, he built a mammoth residential hotel, the Lafayette. Assisted by young Samuel Wetherald, one of his "old master's" many progeny, who worked in Hill's St. Paul office for a time, Hill personally supervised the hotel's furnishings, the assembling of the staff, and even the selection of musical numbers for the grand opening in 1882. Eugene Mehl, who had retired after twenty-three years with the Brevoort, came west to manage the hotel, which was intended to provide profitable business for the branch line that Hill built along the lake and on its way to protect the midriff of the Manitoba road to the southwest. Until the automobile changed all that, the Lafayette provided a respite for prosperous Midwesterners from the subtropical climates of cities like St. Louis.

A beautiful, big new steamer, the *Belle of Minnetonka*, plied the lake during the summer, and over the bitter objections of her captain, a displaced Mississippi riverboat man, Hill insisted that incandescent

electric lighting be installed throughout. As Hill came to dominate the increasingly popular Lake Minnetonka area, the reactions of the many other influential residents were predictable. Hill had to return numerous cases of wine to the fancy grocery concern in Chicago which had stocked the Lafayette. "I am sorry but the town is a temperance town and will not grant license to sell," he wrote. To Hill, whose own hotel bills in New York, Washington, and other civilized places often listed a bottle of champagne or claret, it seemed a provincial attitude. When making plans for a streetcar line in the town, he ran into what looked to him like sheer perversity on the part of the citizens. His engineer agreed: "It appears to me that if they believe you favor electricity they will pray for steam." [32]

Hill also sought to combine business with pleasure by breeding improved beef and dairy cattle at a large new farm, North Oaks, located to the northwest of St. Paul and embracing beautiful Pleasant Lake. Here he began to find the ease which he would not take as long as he was within walking distance of the Manitoba road office. The summer days at North Oaks were almost lazy in their tempo, while the evenings, surprisingly warm for a climate with such bitter winters, were a time for contemplation of a future which seemed a host of question marks. He had time to read a few pages of "Notes of a Trip Around the World," which Andrew Carnegie had had printed up and sent to his good customers. In the summer of 1886 the Hills welcomed Jan Chelminski, a Polish painter who had lived for some years in France, whom Hill had imported to record on canvas the family's life at North Oaks. Chief among his pictures is one which portrays Mrs. Hill and the entire brood engaged in characteristic activities in front of the old-fashioned farmhouse, then still the main residence at the farm, while the master quietly reads his newspaper on the porch. Then the painter posed Mamie, self-conscious in her elegant Eastern riding clothes, on her favorite saddle horse. And that fall, armed with sketch pad instead of shotgun, he joined Hill, Jimmy, and Louis on a grouse shoot. [33]

The Hill family in front of the farmhouse at North Oaks. Summer 1886. Hill reads his newspaper on the screened porch while Mary trims a hat and Mary Frances ("Mamie"), 17, looks on. Rachel, 5, and Gertrude, 3, are on the steps near their mother, while Ruth, 7, leads the dogs (of which she was, in fact, terrified). Charlotte, 9, driving the pony cart, is accompanied by a nervous passenger, Clara, 12. In the distance a nursemaid props up Walter, barely 1, and James Norman, 15, leads Louis W., 13, in taking a spin on their velocipedes. From a painting by Jan v. Chelminski.

The more important the Manitoba road and James J. Hill became, however, the more frequent and insistent grew the calls to New York. By the middle 1880s he was making at least half a dozen trips east each year, and besides the intense tête-à-têtes with John S. Kennedy at 63 William Street, where the Manitoba road now maintained a New York office, there were increasing social obligations. For his evening engagements, of course, only New York clothes would do. Netzel & Frambach, on Union Square, outfitted him with an elegant full dress suit for $83 and a handsome brown beaver overcoat for $75, prices which make 1885 seem distant indeed. The tailors also furnished him with the proper "hunting suit," at $55, for his trips to the Currituck shooting lodge in North Carolina, while Daniel Youmans's shop in the Albemarle Hotel, where he usually stayed, fitted him with the mandatory black derby as well as a more comfortable cloth hat. During the business day, however, plain sack suits, or sometimes a cutaway, were good enough. They were made for him by George Palmes, whose tailor shop was just a few doors down Third Street from the Manitoba road's offices in St. Paul.

He made elaborate arrangements to keep in touch with Mary and the children, and required constant reassurances of their welfare. Mr. Secombe, and, after him, W. A. Stephens, were instructed to send a messenger to the house every day to see if all was well, and Mary was to summon the secretary if need arose. By the mid-1880s there were telephones in the house at Ninth and Canada, and also at North Oaks, but they did not always work. Away on a trip, Hill, like many another traveling man, dreaded opening telegrams, so frequently the bearer of sad tidings. Standing in the lobby of New York's Albemarle Hotel late one January afternoon, a black calfskin glove clamped between his front teeth, Hill frowned as he scanned the message which the clerk had just handed him. He might have sworn at Stephens's ineptness in phrasing a message with the bad news first:

CLARA, CHARLOTTE, RACHEL, RUTH AND SERVANT WHEN DRIVING TODAY WERE RUN AWAY WITH. DRIVER LOST CONTROL OF HORSES. ALL ESCAPED SAFELY. CHILDREN ALL RIGHT WITH VERY SLIGHT BRUISES. NO CAUSE FOR ANY UNEASINESS.[34]

VII

As the Canadian Pacific began to grow into an independent operating company under the leadership of Van Horne, Hill came to realize that eventually the Manitoba road would have to be prepared to go it alone. In 1882 and 1883 the alliance between the two railroads was subjected to continuous strain. Van Horne, for his part, acted as though he believed that the Canadian Pacific, living a hand-to-mouth financial life, could succeed only if it grasped every possible advantage for itself, and he was right. Hill knew this, and as much as it galled him, had to return good for ill on more than one occasion. Throughout these hectic years, as strong, ambitious men sought to ascertain what their genuine self-interest was, the deep feeling of a common bond between Stephen, Angus, Hill, and Kennedy was one factor that prevented a serious rupture in the pattern of their cooperation. But there was another. Although Hill adopted an increasingly independent pose as disappointment followed disappointment in their relations, he knew that the Manitoba road's interest in transcontinental railroad business could only be served by the Canadian Pacific, unless and until he was prepared to buy or build a road to the Coast.

The spring of 1882, when the Canadian Pacific, though still feeble, was coming to life in Manitoba, was a time of troubles. As the colossal snows of the record-breaking winter began to melt, St. Vincent, the boundary transfer point for the two railroads, found itself under four feet of water. Hill persuaded Alexander Griggs, who was still trying to make a living oprating the *Selkirk* in competition with the railroads, to transfer freight from the Manitoba road north to a dry point on the Canadian Pacific. Griggs and his men responded heroically, working around the clock until several of the men collapsed from exhaustion and exposure. Even more drastic measures had to be taken to prevent real hardship at Winnipeg and the back country. Inevitably, the break in the flow of supplies had led to profiteering, and the settlers could not afford the prices that the storekeepers were demanding. Hill bought up twenty carloads of hams, bacon, pork, and beef—all he could find on the open market—and rushed it north, ordering the first two boxcars to be coupled to the regular passenger train. The Canadian Pacific itself, which at that time owned little rolling stock, depended upon Hill to send construction supplies north in Manitoba road cars and to keep encouraging the railroads from Chicago to do the same.[35]

Working with Van Horne, however, meant a steady stream of surprised, hurt, indignant, and, finally, angry letters, with the stream flowing almost exclusively from south to north. Hill was convinced that Van Horne was badly abusing the privilege of using other railroads' cars, and wrote to him in increasing irritation about the evil consequences of such a policy.[36] By June, when both the Manitoba road and the Canadian Pacific had track-laying programs in high gear, the Canadians pleaded that they not only could not get the cars of rails and other supplies unloaded out on the increasingly distant railhead, but that they could not take delivery on them at all at the moment. Hill was furious at the sight of 254 badly needed flatcars, loaded with rails for the Canadian Pacific, sitting in the Manitoba road's yards in St. Paul waiting to go north:

> Your people do not get to work early enough. . . . We have so many cases reported of their neglect that your messages [of denial] can only be accounted for on the ground that you are not well informed. . . . Mr. Manvel left for St. Vincent last night prepared to take such action with you [as] he can, or without you if you are not ready. . . . If he finds it necessary your men will either work under our orders entirely while south of the boundary or he will deliver the freight [across the boundary].[37]

"It is hard for me to see things out of joint and keep my hands off," Hill confessed to Angus, who was desperately trying to prevent an open break. "But it has to be done," he reluctantly concluded. Almost immediately he was meddling again. "Mr. Van Horne is a little vexed at my persistent efforts," he rationalized to Stephen, "but that will be over when I see him and in the meantime the situation is improved." Van Horne was, in fact, working a minor miracle in finding a place to dump staggering quantities of railroad building materials and supplies at a railhead which probed deeper every day into the heart of the desolate Canadian plains. As for the delays at the border, that problem was finally solved, as Van Horne told Hill it would be, when the customs officials of both countries finally recognized that the great increase in traffic demanded a twenty-four-hour border service to pass the cars without delay.[38]

But it was over the question of the Manitoba Southwestern Railroad, the Grit-inspired line southward from the Canadian Pacific at Winnipeg which the Manitoba road had bought from the Northern Pacific, that relations most nearly came to grief. Hill was determined that the Canadian Pacific should take it off the Manitoba's hands, and while he knew that the Canadians simply did not have the money to pay for it as yet, he was furious at suggestions that the Manitoba should hang on to it indefinitely. In the summer of 1883, after a year of stalling by the Canadians, he wrote D. Willis James, an influential New York businessman and recent recruit to the Manitoba road's board of directors, the most scathing remarks he ever made about George Stephen:

> Judge Clark, our counsel, says [that] Mr. Stephen who [as president of the Manitoba Road] gave the instructions to buy the [Manitoba Southwestern] from Villard exceeded his power and was liable to the stockholders of the Manitoba Company for the sum paid for it. I think Mr. Stephen means well but has pursued a vacillating course. . . .[39]

James conveyed the substance, if not the raw threat, of Hill's anger to Stephen, who vacillated no longer, and the albatross was soon hung around the proper neck. However, the long-term problem, which would never be solved permanently until the Great Northern Railway was completed, involved the matter of how the Manitoba road and the Canadian Pacific were to divide east-west traffic and the revenues that flowed therefrom. Van Horne, stopping by the Manitoba road offices in St. Paul on his way to Chicago, left Hill livid. "He considers Winnipeg a local station on the Can Pac Ry, and that we had no more right to look for a rate to Winnipeg than to any other point," he wrote Angus. In his letters to Angus and Stephen, Hill adopted the psychology of making the strongest possible case against Van Horne's transgressions, then switching abruptly to a description of how tidy things were on the Manitoba road, continuing with protestations of his determination to cooperate fully, and closing with cheerful predictions for the future. To Kennedy, however, he was unrestrained in his pessimism about what was coming:

> When last I saw Mr. Van Horne he plainly stated that he did not consider we had any business north of the international boundary. . . . They have simply taken all the advantages they can for the benefit of their own company, which of itself is quite proper for them to do. If our company should go on and take advantage of whatever situations may favor us, we on the other hand would during the season of navigation be able to divide the business with them and in fact would make their Pembina Branch of very little use, and in the end their business for 150 miles west of Winnipeg would be practically reduced one-third, all of which would end in a freight war and a compromise that could and should have been made in the beginning. . . .[40]

Stephen, locked at that very moment in a financial death struggle which he was to win by only the narrowest of margins, tried desperately to keep the peace. "It would be the silliest thing that ever was seen to see our two roads at loggerheads, or even not on the best of terms, and I will do all I can to prevent anything of the kind happening," he pledged. Within a month, however, Hill was prepared to declare war on Van Horne. It had become an intensely emotional matter, and one in which personal honor was at issue. Hill found out that

Van Horne had told Stephen that the Manitoba road was changing freight rates without advance notice to the Canadian Pacific. "I can not admit the truth of his statement," Hill declared, and he sent Stephen copies of telegrams which, he claimed, constituted full advance consultation between the roads' respective freight agents. "If the General Manager of your company is acting on the basis of his statement," Hill threatened, "the natural result will soon be far from harmonious. . . ." Soon someone was whispering in Stephen's ear that Hill had condemned the entire Canadian Pacific project as an inefficient, costly enterprise that was bound to fail sooner or later.[41]

The Manitoba road, fortunately, had acquired in D. Willis James a director of great astuteness, and he succeeded in patching things up. A grave, highly religious Anglo-American in whom the regard for dignity and scrupulous honesty in business amounted to an obsession, James impressed upon Hill that he must "get Mr. Stephen feeling cordial again" at any cost. "They cannot quarrel with me even if they should try," growled Hill, but he took what was obviously very good advice.[42] Stephen was doing the same thing, also at James's prompting, and he wrote Hill earnestly:

> I most thoroughly concur in every word you say about the personal relations that ought to exist, not only between you and me, but between all the members of the original firm of "George Stephen and Associates," as well as between the two companies which owe their existence to that firm. It will be simply a *scandal* and reflection on the sense and wisdom of all concerned if foolish and hostile views gain the ascendancy. The interests of the two roads, properly understood, is to work together, each respecting the interests and the rights of the other, standing shoulder to shoulder against all intruders. . . .

> Though *very* sorry not to have your countenance and cooperation in carrying out our contract with the Can. govt., I have felt for some time back that with your views as to the future of our N.W. and of the C.P.R., it would be an advantage that you had no pecuniary interest in the Company and would, I thought, go a long way towards placing the relations between the two companies on an *easier* footing. It is very important to this end that on both sides we avoid all idle and unfriendly talk which only irritates and gives comfort to our enemies. The two roads are so linked in the public view that the very appearance of a disagreement between them does infinite harm to both. . . .

And he closed by asking Hill's opinion of his new move to get the Canadian government to guarantee the Canadian Pacific dividend for ten years.[43]

Hill was pleased to hear all this from Stephen, and flattered to be asked for his opinion about Stephen's desperate financial measures:

> You have been most successful in many ways in bettering the position of the Company's financial resources, but the [dividend guarantee] is of greater value . . . than the others combined, provided always the cost of completing the work . . . does not materially exceed your estimates; you have now made what may be considered your final and definite financial plan, and the garment must be made from the cloth provided.

Thereafter, relations between the two companies eased remarkably. Stephen's financial agonies continued, and Hill, who had been more than a little awed at his friend's valor from the beginning, was not disposed to make things any harder. The Canadian Pacific, at the very last moment, gave the people of Canada dramatic proof that the game had indeed been worth the candle: in the spring of 1885 it carried troops to quell the second Riel rebellion, and did so in a fraction of the time that had been required to get them there on foot fifteen years before. Hill sent his congratulations, and rejoiced at the news that the last spike would soon be driven. "It must be a great satisfaction to you to know that the 'great work' is so near completion. Your courage and faith [are] equal to harder tasks, if possible, but I think you have done your share. . . ." When Stephen wrote proudly to say that everybody was at last congratulating him on the associates' daring decision of five years before to reject the original survey in favor of the southern route, and to invite Hill to join the first inspection tour, Hill was deeply touched:

> Nothing would give me more pleasure, and I will shape my matters to that end. I am sure there will be many things of great interest to look at, inasmuch as neither you nor I have ever seen the country west of the mountains and through which the road was located against the advice of a great many who thought they knew the country.[44]

VIII

No one knew better than George Stephen what James J. Hill wanted from his participation in the Canadian Pacific enterprise. "I hope the time is coming," he wrote Hill on Christmas Day 1885, "when we shall be able to give the Manitoba road a through line from St. Paul to the Pacific Ocean and on to Japan and China. This is a forecast which I feel sure the near future will see realized." And no one knew better than Hill that any railroad that did not assure itself through connections to the Coast would sooner or later wither away. After 1900 the slow, steady decline of the Chicago, Milwaukee & St. Paul and the Chicago & North Western Railroads, both of which failed to get such connections while conditions were still favorable for railroad construction, proved him right. At mid-point in the 1880s he still hoped that the Canadian Pacific would provide the Manitoba road its route to the Pacific, and he wrote to Van Horne urging him to do all he could to develop a transcontinental business, noting that there would be precious little local traffic for some years to come. At the same time he told young J. Kennedy Tod, "I am anxious to get St. P. M. & M. matters so that they will stand on their own bottom. With the Nor Pacific on the south and the Canadian Pacific on the north, both of whom a financial squeeze would materially affect, we must be in a position to show our ability to maintain ourselves under all circumstances." [45]

Meanwhile, the Northern Pacific had finally reached the West Coast. Herman Haupt, who had solved the Union's transport problems during the Civil War, was closing a checkered career in railroad engineering as general manager of the Northern Pacific when that much-battered railroad was finally joined to Henry Villard's Oregon Railway & Navigation Company in 1883. By one expedient or another Haupt found enough sleeping cars and locomotives (some borrowed from the Manitoba road) to haul into St. Paul all of the financiers, newspapermen, and liberal Republican friends of Villard's who came to make the gala Northern Pacific celebration a success. But the people of the Twin Cities hardly needed such help in marking what the Minneapolis *Tribune* called "the great event of the nineteenth century," for they were ecstatic at having become the eastern terminus of a new transcontinental railroad. At the grand banquet which closed the week-long festivities, Mr. Villard was the star. The hour was growing late when the last speaker, the mayor of Minneapolis, finally sat down and the toast was offered to "the railroad system of Minnesota—the cause of the wonderful development of the State." Called upon to respond was James J. Hill, who was properly modest in the face of warm applause:

> I have listened to our honored citizen, Governor Ramsey, and I look around me, and I see Mr. Rice and our old pioneers who came here in that heydey of their manhood, when I was a boy, and I feel that you have called upon the wrong man. [Cries of No! No!]
>
> We [of the Manitoba road] have met Mr. Villard, and feel that in the future, as well as in the past, our work will go on, each one seeking to de-

velop new territory, taking ground to the front, step by step, to the usefulness of the public as well as ourselves. . . . I wish the president of the
Northern Pacific railroad all the success which he so well deserves.

Thereupon the toast was given to "The Press," and Carl Schurz, editor of the New York *Evening Post* and the greatest Mugwump of them
all, was called upon to respond. But Schurz, who had listened atten-
tively to Villard, was not there. He had not stayed to hear what this
unknown railroad man had to say.[46]

10
The Best of Times, the Worst of Times

The time is at hand when railway property will be tested, and we have some neighbors who will surely have difficulty in making both ends meet. . . . The Manitoba road is in good condition and the country thro' which we run is full of freight, and we have only to see that the work so well begun is intelligently taken care of. . . . Our policy is to cut down our grades and put the whole road in condition to give such low rates that opposition enterprises must be bankrupted.

—James J. Hill, 1882–86

I

During the decade of the 1880s James J. Hill emerged as the most promising figure in the tangled transportation affairs of the Northwest. New faces appeared on the world scene, too, as the United States and the new German Empire threatened to move ahead of Great Britain, which was beginning to show the strain of a hundred years of world leadership. It was a decade of vast and rapid change, and it revealed almost every modern symptom of feverish prosperity save one: far from rejoicing in the bountiful feast, American economic and political institutions creaked and groaned at every joint, as if loath to leave behind the idyllic world of hardy, self-reliant farmers and high-minded, small-bankrolled commercial men which Thomas Jefferson had told Americans was their true destiny.

For the businessman the 1880s were a terrifying era in which familiar rules had been suspended. No longer, it seemed, had he the option of playing it safe, or plunging recklessly into new ventures, as he chose. Suddenly the penalty for merely standing still, or trying to, had become as great as the penalty for miscalculating among the myriad expansion opportunities which sprang up as American industry recorded its first significant growth. There was to be no standing still in Hill's business, whether one ran an established Eastern railroad, on which, as he said, people had been doing the same thing for years, or found himself instead in a fast-growing region like the Northwest, where the ultimate outlines of the transportation system had yet to be revealed.

The railroad boom was everywhere in evidence in the 1880s, for the decade truly belonged to the iron horse. Dozens of new securities were added each year to the list of those traded on the New York Stock Exchange, and almost all of them represented the enormous values—actual, potential, and barely to be hoped for—which had been sunk in the railroads. By 1893 the frantic construction race had given America the largest, most efficient, and, in many respects, most uncoordinated transportation system in the world. Nearly 75,000 miles of new railroad were laid in the United States in the decade, far more than the total in existence in the United States in 1870. Much of this new mileage had been inspired by sterile competition between the hundreds of independent corporations which, by the end of the century, would be reduced to at most a few dozen. Hill and his associates laid only 2700 miles, which, although less than 4 per cent of the total, were some of the most important stretches of track in the nation, for they formed the basis of a consolidation of virtually all of the railroad facilities of the American Northwest under the control of a man who barely fifteen years before had been an unknown coal dealer.

Output of the nation's goods and services soared in the 1880s, while unemployment was rare among men who had a useful skill, good health, and the willingness to go where the jobs were. Contrary to the great weight of normal human experience, prices declined consistently throughout the 1880s, throwing everybody off balance. Businessmen as well as farmers constantly found themselves paying back their creditors with dollars that were more valuable than those they had borrowed. Employers also found, to their intense frustration, that their workers took a dim view of any concurrent reductions in the dollar rate of their wages. What slim statistical evidence we have for the period indicates that wages did go down more slowly than prices, thus giving workers an increase in "real" wages, but as the decade went by labor more and more militantly resisted decreases in dollar wages. Farmers had already been in trouble for five years when the great depression began in 1893, not only with falling crop prices and burdensome mortgages, but with the weather as well. By the end of the 1880s the nation saw a major reform movement, not inaptly termed the Populist revolt, which severely strained both of the major political parties and destroyed forever the individualistic atmosphere in which America's industrial foundations were laid.

But farmer and labor unrest was a long way from being the businessman's chief concern in the 1880s. It was the need to keep moving ahead, to tread the turning mill, without looking back and without making a misstep, which established the psychological climate of the decade. Men like John S. Kennedy, who helped Hill build the Manitoba road into one of the soundest railroad properties in the nation in these years, eventually would not be able to bear the strain, and by 1889 Hill would find it necessary to fill their places with quite a different breed. The unique feature of the decade that produced this dizzying, headlong movement of men and money was the steady reduction in the cost of production of virtually every good or service the nation turned out. The remarkable decline in prices from 1878 to 1893 was not chiefly a monetary phenomenon, a golden "crown of thorns," as articulate politicians and myopic economists have insisted, but rather the grand payoff of a broad array of investments which had been made in cost-cutting innovations, starting even before the Civil War and accelerating after prosperity returned in 1878. Progressive American businessmen put every spare dollar they could scrape up into improved ways to use nature's resources and human brawn, ways such as the Bessemer process for making steel; the refining of petroleum, to make abundant, cheap, illumination available; improvement of the steam engine, to give it vastly increased capacity and efficiency; and, perhaps most important of all, the development of a transportation system, which brought the blessings—and the problems—of regional specialization to the United States to a degree that no other nation would ever achieve.

Such innovations, and many others in less prominent industries, quickly lowered the production costs, and, eventually, the price, of nearly everything. Technology was still in the trial-and-error stage, but the errors were getting fewer. Thus, the businessman who tried to stand still by paying all his profits out in dividends, or who sank them in emotional or egotistical expansion projects, or who dissipated them in sterile price or rate wars, eventually lost out to the man who consistently sought ways to invest profits and new money in order to produce more cheaply than his competitor. The losers did not go down quietly. The bitter cries which they raised when the chastened survivors came together in the "trust" movement in industry and the consolidation movement in railroading would be heeded after 1900. But in the 1880s men either cut their costs of doing business or they stood aside for those who could. Few men saw the reduction of operating costs as the key to the economic puzzle as early in the decade as James J. Hill, and even fewer were as successful as he in using that key.

II

"Times have never been harder in Canada, between short crops and the tightness of money," wrote William Farrish, Hill's boyhood friend, from Rockwood in 1887; "I am anxiously trying to get rid of my property, for this line of business is completely overdone." Farrish was struggling to raise wheat on a farm much like that which Hill had turned his back on thirty years before, and to run a grist mill to which fewer and fewer farmers brought less and less wheat of poorer and poorer quality. Four years before Hill had advised his old friend to buy Manitoba wheat for his mill, and Farrish had been so delighted with the results that he visited St. Paul and Manitoba as Hill's guest, for the purpose, he said, of arranging to relocate himself and his family of stalwart young sons. "In that section," he said of Manitoba, "I saw the greatest wheat field I ever saw in my life; the settlers were principally [eastern] Canadians, and I found them all very proud of the President of the Manitoba Railway." Farrish returned to Rockwood, however, with a $5000 loan from Hill with which he tried to modernize his mill.[1]

Other Canadians were more self-reliant. A. V. McCleneghan, a bright, ambitious cousin of Hill's, wrote to say that, since moving to Winnipeg, with Hill's help he had passed the bar examinations with high honors, and he looked to a bright future as a lawyer. Sam and Charlie Wetherald, two of his "dear old master's" many offspring, came to St. Paul to work for Hill, Sam as an office clerk and Charlie as a farm laborer, in the early 1880s. After a time they, along with great numbers of their countrymen who were quitting the crowded older areas of eastern Canada, disappeared into the Northwest, which the

Manitoba road and the Canadian Pacific had made so accessible. The tide of immigration was swelled by their counterparts in the United States, who moved to the west and added to the confusion of the U. S. Post Office by naming town after town in Dakota and Montana Territory after the places they had left in Connecticut and Pennsylvania, in Illinois and Michigan. Most dramatic, however, was the European tide, which ran full in these years. The number of men, women, and children who came from Norway was equal to one-half the "natural growth" (births minus deaths) that would otherwise have over-populated that rugged, stingy little land. Sweden's outpouring of immigrants was smaller, relative to its national population, but the number of Swedes was greater in the absolute. Germans, who had been coming to the new Northwest since before the Civil War, continued to arrive, while other ethnic groups, notably Archbishop John Ireland's urban Irish from the East, and even some contingents of eastern European Jews, were less successful in adapting to the shocks of such a major transplantation.[2]

They came, in the last analysis, in order to survive as members of the human race. Territories were organized to provide a modicum of government for the new populations, and the Indians were shunted aside to make way for the great numbers of human beings whom this fertile land was now to support after countless centuries of being the domain of the nomad and the buffalo. The Manitoba road welcomed them as enthusiastically as other railroads did, and solicited them just as aggressively in their homelands. It maintained a land office to sell farms to bona fide farmers, and Hill rejected at least one offer to sell the Manitoba road's land grant *en bloc* in 1882. Once here, the immigrants yielded to the temptations of commercial agriculture, with its promise of cash profits and a surplus which, prudently saved, could buy more acres. In two short decades following the Civil War the area of North America west of the Mississippi and the Great Lakes and north of Texas became a gigantic wheat "factory," providing that traditional food for more and more Europeans as well as for the growing populations of the United States and Canada.

Hill fostered the colonization efforts of the Manitoba road through his extensive correspondence with English and Scottish gentlemen who were fascinated by the new Northwest. He sought better strains of wheat, particularly Russian varieties of spring wheat, which he pressed Knute Nelson, his friend and Congressman, to procure through the consular service. The wheat crop grew rapidly, year after year, requiring a remarkable expansion of elevator capacity in the Twin Cities and along the railroad. "I can truly say I have never seen such grain," he wrote George Stephen in the late summer of 1884, after a trip over the railroad. "Last year we carried over one-fifth of the entire spring wheat crop of the United States and this year I think we will carry one-fourth," he bragged to Kennedy the next year. At the end of the decade he reported to the manager of the Crédit Lyonnais, influential Parisian bankers, that elevator capacity had grown fifteen-fold in the ten years that the Manitoba road had been in existence. Falling prices were a worry, as was the inconstancy of the climate, but even as reports of distress began to come in from the lower plains states, he was reassuring Kennedy that "emigration is greater than for two years past into both Minnesota & Dakota." [3]

Beneath Hill's enthusiasm, however, lurked deep-seated doubts about the course of development of the Northwest, and of the railroads which served it. It bothered him to see farmers, poor businessmen that they were, involving themselves so deeply in the intricacies of commercial wheat farming. The trend was already leading to surpluses which only promised to grow more unmanageable as the vast plains of Montana and western Canada were settled by hundreds of thousands of farmers with the same motivations as those of Minnesota and Dakota. The wheat-eating population of the world could consume only just so much, he noted, and they could not afford to pay much for it, so the surplus grew while the price of wheat sank lower and lower during the decade. Deep down in his ethical origins, he perceived the real problem: how, he asked himself and anyone else who would listen, how could Northwestern wheat farmers expect to live for twelve months off the fruits of seven months' labor? The answer was that they could not. They had better find a way to busy themselves the other five months of the year. In the introduction of enlarged and improved herds of beef and dairy cattle, Hill was convinced he saw the outlet not only for the underemployed energies of the farmers on whom the Manitoba road was so dependent, but for their surplus grains as well.[4]

Perhaps because of the highly competitive nature of its chief industry, the economic weather was seldom clear in the Northwest. No one connected with the growing, buying, shipping, or milling of wheat in the late nineteenth century seems to have been any more content with the working of the complex mechanism than people are now, a hundred years later. Farmers compared the market price of their "number one hard red spring wheat" at Minneapolis, Chicago, or Duluth with the much lower price they netted at the country grain elevators to which they delivered their hard-won product, and they were discontent, especially as the entire structure of prices throughout the world drifted ever downward. Millers in Minneapolis, which by the 1880s had ousted Buffalo as the flour-producing capital of the nation, begrudged every carload of wheat which rattled past them to mills in the East. They felt they had the right to mill every bushel produced to the north and west of them, and, quite naturally, they wanted to pay the lowest possible price for it.

The pointless argument over whether the farmers expected too much or the millers were offering too little went on until it was finally resolved in a manner which railroad men like Hill had dreaded for a long time. Although railroad rates declined even faster than other prices in the decade, the commanding role played by the constantly evolving railroad system in the economics of the Northwestern wheat industry grew more and more obvious. Remembering the days of the Granger "revolt" in the 1870s, when threats of regulatory legislation had brought rates down with a rush (as they liked to believe), farmers, millers, and politicians decided that the railroads were the true villains, and joined forces against them. Hill and his fellow railroad leaders saw in their critics a set of millstones which might grind the carriers to death. He dreaded the outcome, and he vowed to redouble his efforts to reduce the dependence of the Manitoba road, if not that of his fellow Minnesotans and Dakotans, on this deeply troubled industry.[5]

As the decade drew to its close, the old enemies, insects and the weather, returned with a vengeance. In 1887 chinch bugs (not so deadly as the grasshoppers of the 1870s, but bad enough) had appeared in the areas to the southwest of the Twin Cities, and the lower Midwest suffered a crippling reduction in the harvest. Throughout the early summer of 1888 Hill wrote influential Boston financiers like John Murray Forbes that he was convinced the upper Midwest was to be spared. He was tempted to gloat over a letter in which Kennedy, who was soothing his nerves at Interlaken, Switzerland, reported that "the weather in Europe this season has been terrible . . . ; it has been cold and rainy, one of the worst seasons for agriculture that ever was known, and there will be a large shortage which will have to be made good out of the surplus in India, Russia and America. . . ."[6]

Six weeks later his tone had changed. An early frost, that worst nightmare of the upper Midwest, had hit the region, and thousands of acres of swelling ears of wheat stood blackened in the fields. Extra cash earnings which Hill had counted on to smooth his ambitious operations in Montana never materialized. By October he was begging the governor of Dakota Territory to lend farmers public funds with which to buy seed wheat, which the Manitoba road offered to carry free. Otherwise there would be no crop at all next year. In mid-November Hill had the agents at fifty Manitoba road stations canvassing the countryside for 15,000 bushels of oats to feed the blooded stock at his North Oaks farm, where the crops had also failed, that winter. By the spring of next year he was making no effort to hide his pessimism. He wrote to an old friend at Grand Forks, Dakota:

> As matters stand it will be impossible to obtain money to build more railroad lines in either Minnesota or Dakota. . . . I think that the conditions settling in now are worse in many respects than in 1873, because larger amounts are involved, and the entire country is suffering. . . . If you have any money it will be of more value to you *as money* than if invested in lands. I do not want to unnecessarily alarm you, but, as an old acquaintance I desire to tell you that this part of the country has to "go through the fire" before it will start on a new era of prosperity.[7]

Barely four years remained before the great depression of 1893 would settle upon the country. Despite all the storm signals that flashed around him in 1889, Hill sensed that the decade of the 1880s would be the last time he would have a chance to make the Manitoba road into a transcontinental route, one free of the vagaries of a regional, one-crop agricultural economy and free to establish through rates from Chicago to the Pacific Ocean and the Orient. It was the extraordinary financial and managerial strength of the Manitoba road, reorganized as the Great Northern Railway, which would make it possible for Hill to "play it big" at a time when railroads like the Northern Pacific were being driven to the wall. Hill and his associates attained this strength during the decade of the 1880s by hard work, shrewd and intelligent cooperation, and more than a little good luck.

III

John S. Kennedy, vice president of the St. Paul, Minneapolis & Manitoba Railway, recently retired private banker, leader of the organized private charities of New York City, and one of the most sagacious financiers in the world's most rapidly growing financial center, felt exceptionally good. Walking briskly to his office on William Street, he observed that the bright blue skies of that sparkling October day in 1884 had much to do with his good feelings, which had grown all too rare in recent years. But there was much else that he could be cheerful about. In the preceding year and a half the Manitoba road had encountered the stormiest financial weather to which any new and untried business enterprise could be subjected, and it had come through triumphantly. That triumph was, in no small measure, due to his own prodigious efforts. The traumatic recession which had begun in May 1884 had shaken some of New York's most prestigious institutions and individuals, but those interests which over the years had cast their lot with John S. Kennedy had come through stronger than ever. He had managed to get to his fishing lodge on New Brunswick's Restigouche River, where the Atlantic salmon, game fish *par excellence*, had felt his wrath. Returning to the workaday world holding the record for the largest number of salmon taken on a rod in a two-week period, he slept well. For the moment at least, he had calmed the nervous disposition which sometimes disabled him.

Arriving at his desk, Kennedy penned an aggressive letter to James J. Hill in St. Paul. "I feel like doing something to stop such people from making money out of their neighbors," he wrote, referring to the stock exchange speculators whom he and Hill both abominated. "I am disposed to make up a party to go in and give the bears a twist!" [8]

Much of Kennedy's efforts, and those of Hill and the other major stockholders of the Manitoba road, had been devoted to keeping the bears from giving *them* a twist in the five years since they had organized the railroad. Getting control of the predecessor railroad and reorganizing it had been one thing; holding control over it in the rugged financial world of the 1880s had been quite another. By 1883 only Hill and Kennedy, of the five associates who had originally owned virtually all of the 200,000 shares of common stock of the railroad, were still unequivocally committed to its welfare. Stephen and Smith, although they still owned most of their original holdings of Manitoba stock, were deeply involved in the finances of the Canadian Pacific. Stephen never missed an opportunity to praise "the blessed old road" for the handsome dividends it paid, but the Canadians might at any moment be tempted, or even be forced by circumstances, to sell a large portion of their holdings of a stock which in barely four years had gone from zero value to a quotation of nearly 170 on the New York Stock Exchange. As long as the old group stuck together, they represented almost one-half of all the stock, more than enough to control the company, but meanwhile, speculation in the small amount of "floating" stock was a constant problem.[9]

The 1880s were the decade of the bears in Wall Street. The Stock Exchange, subject to no government regulation, was largely a private club, run by a board of governors whose members were as susceptible as anybody else to the temptations of a largely amoral financial community. The volume of securities available for buying and selling in the open market was small, and large price rises and declines frequently took place on relatively small transactions. Totally groundless rumors could set off a buying or selling wave. And rumors were the life of the market. Brokers, many of whom had the assets of the city's fast-growing commercial banks behind them, traded on their own account. Since the days of Daniel Drew, the favorite game had been alternately to bull and then bear a stock: buy it cheap, talk it up to a much higher price, sell out, start rumors of some disaster about to befall the company, and buy the stock back at a much lower price. A company whose stock was a favorite of the bears developed a bad name, which made it difficult to raise fresh capital from the investing public. The Manitoba road's stock was a favorite of the bears in the early 1880s and one of Kennedy's and Hill's first objectives was to remove it from their clutches. They did so in two steps: first, they showed New York that they could and would fight any bear raid to a finish; and, next, they placed a large block of Manitoba stock with some of the most conservative investors in the United States.

In the summer of 1883 the two gave the bears a "twist" which they never forgot. Trouble had been brewing as early as March. Hill was embarrassed and angered to learn that P. H. Kelly, his old St. Paul friend, was being led on by the bears, who were trying to use his inside knowledge of Manitoba road affairs to raid the stock. Tongues wagged knowingly at the split between Hill and his Canadian associates which seemed inevitable once the Canadian Pacific was completed and became the Manitoba's full-fledged competitor. Hill himself was worried, and asked Kennedy whether he thought they should sell all their Manitoba road holdings over 30,000 shares each. Absolutely not, Kennedy wrote back. He was convinced that the stock was worth, conservatively, 120, no matter how far the bears might beat it down temporarily; besides, it was rumored that the Vanderbilts were trying to buy control, and this they would have to prevent at all costs.[10]

By July 17 Manitoba stock had broken to around 105. Thomas W. Pearsall, a broker who played both sides of the game, sometimes simultaneously, wired Hill that "parties are now offering to bet, in the open board room, that Manitoba will sell at 80 or below." Pearsall, who was associated with the banking firm of George S. Scott & Company, wanted to form a pool to support the stock. Meanwhile, Hill had wired Kennedy's partner that "J. J. Hill has sold nothing and will not. Buy at prices not exceeding 105. . . ." The following week the bears attacked. "Bold raid against Manitoba," wired George Stephen, who was determined that the "blessed old road" should not be used in such fashion. To prove to the widows and orphans that Manitoba was a respectable, investment-grade stock, he urged the immediate formation of a million-dollar pool to support it in the market. Hill's pledge of $250,000 came without delay, and even Kennedy, who was in agony whenever anybody but himself was manipulating his money, joined. The bears pulled out all the stops. An obscure Wall Street gossip sheet carried a planted article which told the story of the bond dividend affair in such a way as to make it look as though insiders were looting the Manitoba road of all it possessed. But when the dust settled the stock had been held at about 104, the bears had been routed, and each of the participants in the pool had a quick profit of $2600.[11]

At the same time a very worried James J. Hill, with Kennedy's help, went to work to straighten out his tangled personal finances. The time had come, both men agreed, for Hill to stop lending money to the railroad, which he occasionally did by allowing it to use some of his bonds as collateral for short-term loans, and, in turn, for him to stop borrowing from the company. Even so, Hill began the New Year of 1885 with the sad confession to Kennedy that he was in debt to various New York banks to the extent of $600,000. He was heavily involved in coal lands in Iowa and grain elevator projects in Minneapolis; he was setting himself up on a grand scale as a breeder of blooded livestock at North Oaks farm; and he had bought thousands of dollars' worth of fine paintings. With Kennedy's help he managed to refinance his loans periodically without having to sell any of his Manitoba bonds or stock, but when he finally succeeded in getting out of debt at the end of the decade, he was greatly relieved.[12]

If anyone has a right to an equal share with Hill in the emergence of the Manitoba road as the strongest railroad property in the Northwest, it is John S. Kennedy. While Hill was at odds, at one time or another, with nearly everyone else connected with the company, his relations with Kennedy remained polite, dignified, even courtly. The degree of mutual respect was impressive, reflecting an absence of that synthetic first-name familiarity affected by the professional corporate managers of modern times. "My dear Mr. Kennedy," began the frequent communications from St. Paul. "My dear Mr. Hill," began the replies in the spidery handwriting which Hill came to know so well. If Hill, in those days the only senior executive concerned with day-to-day operations of the company, gave Kennedy to understand that he felt the weight of the world on his shoulders, the banker sympathized, and then replied that it was pretty lonely in the financial jungle, too, especially when he found himself out on a limb for unsecured million-dollar advances to the Manitoba company.

Stephen jeered at Kennedy's tenseness in business matters. "I fear his nervous anxiety about *nothing* will be too much for his strength," he wrote to St. Paul. But Hill knew how much it meant to the Manitoba road to be represented in financial circles by the cautious, yet courageous Kennedy instead of an insouciant public relations expert like Henry Villard of the Northern Pacific. He was deeply gratified that Kennedy had supported his role in what by the mid-1880s was widely and casually referred to as Hill's "bond grab." * To Stephen, who was inclined to rub salt in this deep wound, Hill tartly wrote on one occasion, "I did not undertake to set my judgment against that of men who had much longer and greater financial experience, but I hope I have learned a lesson that will be of some benefit in the future. . . ." [13]

Kennedy retired from his banking firm in 1883, turning the business over to his nephew, J. Kennedy Tod. Thereafter he worked even harder in the Manitoba road's interests, for a salary of $10,000 as vice president instead of a banking fee of $50,000. The issues of securities which Hill required to keep expanding and improving the Manitoba road passed safely through Kennedy's hands in steady succession: the Dakota Extension Bonds, the Consolidated Mortgage Bonds, and, beginning in the middle of the decade, a torrent of securities which reflected the railroad's commitment to expansion into Montana Territory. He continued to exploit his valuable contacts in the rail and

---

* See Chapter 8.

equipment industries to get the best goods and lowest prices for the railroad. He worked hard to broaden investment interest in the company's bonds, and was pleased when shrewd, sensitive Jacob Schiff opened for the Manitoba road Kuhn, Loeb & Company's broad doors to the Continental market for American railroad securities. He voiced his uneasiness at Hill's tendency to lean toward Boston financiers, who looked down their haughty noses at the likes of Jacob Schiff, sensing that alienation of the powerful New York interests would rise up to haunt Hill one day.[14]

Kennedy's greatest coup, however, was the master stroke of conservative finance which he brought off in mid-1884. At the depth of the first real recession since the 1870s, and at a time when the Manitoba road was making more money than ever before and was preparing to offer its securities to some of the most conservative investors in the land, he sensed that the smartest move the company could make would be to cut the dividend. His explanation of the idea to Hill is a gem of Victorian business philosophy:

> I do not see why we should keep on paying 8% with the stock selling at a lower price than it ought to do if we were only paying 6%. I think we should go to work and get ourselves into a very strong shape, ready for any emergency that can possibly arise. There is nothing so well calculated to make us strong as a good cash reserve, and were it known in the Street that we had a few hundred thousands on hand which we were lending, I am sure it would help us immensely. . . . I am certainly in favor of having some working capital in hand; a railroad needs it just as much as a businessman. . . .[15]

By the middle of the decade there were few shrewd Eastern capitalists who were not aware that the strongest railroad team in the Northwest was that of John S. Kennedy and James J. Hill.

IV

Leo Tolstoy scorned the idea that war is a chess game, and Hill's strategies and tactics in his relations with other railroads in the Northwest in the 1880s show exactly that. Railroading was war, and there were no real rules in railroading. The outcome of confrontations could not be predicted from relative strengths. If there was any necessary ingredient of success it was, as Tolstoy remarked, the will to win. But Hill knew that simple will had to be backed up with a detailed knowledge of all the factors in a given situation, and, when the facts seemed clouded, as they did in the great majority of cases, he tended always to fall back on the principle that he who could do the business at the lowest cost would be the winner in the long run.

To the southeast, Hill faced two strong Chicago-based railroads which entertained ambitions to expand into the Northwest. The Milwaukee and the North Western were already on the scene at the Twin Cities, and the Milwaukee had even invaded the Red River Valley, which Hill considered his exclusive preserve. The North Western, much more eager than the Milwaukee to keep the peace, was a good neighbor to Hill, but it can hardly be said that he returned the favor, and by the end of the decade the Manitoba ran deep into the North Western's territory. By the middle of the decade the farmers to the southwest of the Twin Cities—the North Western's preserve—were complaining loudly about their lack of a northwestern outlet for their wheat. Navigation on the Great Lakes was growing rapidly, and the lower rates by water between Duluth, Buffalo, and the East Coast ports meant that shippers who could dispatch the grain over that route could offer farmers several cents a bushel more than those who expected to ship via Chicago.

Kennedy advised the utmost caution in dealing with the Chicago lines, pointing out that these older, financially stronger roads could count on the financial assistance of Eastern trunk-line railroad men, like Vanderbilt, if the situation in the Northwest became disharmonious. Meanwhile, men like Rockefeller were generating huge surplus profits in the oil business, which they were seeking outlets for in other directions. The Burlington railroad, solidly financed and well run by Boston interests, was expected to make a major move in the direction of the Northwest very soon. It was a situation in which one ought to look for allies, not adversaries. Still, when the Milwaukee road, in which packing magnate Philip D. Armour had taken a large interest, sought to lease or buy the Manitoba road, Hill traveled to New York, listened politely, and then named a price they could not accept.[16]

It was in the Red River Valley that Hill moved most aggressively to protect the fundamental interests of the Manitoba road. By the end of the decade the region was over-supplied with railroad lines, many of which were to be streaks of rust by the middle of the twentieth century. Hill used his informal intelligence network to learn about "local" projects and discover which established railroad was actually behind

them, and, where advisable, he rushed in ahead and either built a better line or so improved the existing Manitoba line that the interloper,
if actually built, would wither. He had to be careful not to be caught
up in the enthusiasm of local railroad promoters; it was fever such as
theirs which had led the Milwaukee into its disastrous Fargo & Southwestern venture. If public relations permitted, he gave a firm "no" to
impractical projects; otherwise, a bag of dilatory tactics served to keep
the limited capital of the people of the Northwest from being sunk in
redundant railroad lines. Inevitably, he made enemies.[17]

If the Chicago railroads seemed to Hill to be poised for some kind of
leap into the Northwest, the Manitoba road, which in the early 1880s
terminated at Devil's Lake, Dakota Territory, must have seemed to the
Northern Pacific like a dagger pointed directly at its heart. The 1879
"agreement" by which the Manitoba was to remain a north-south line
and the Northern Pacific an east-west transcontinental was in tatters
by the middle of the decade, and by that time the building of the Canadian Pacific had changed everything. The Manitoba was going to
become a transcontinental competitor of the Northern Pacific or it was
going to disappear into the structure of one of the existing Chicago
roads, which would then build to the Pacific Coast. The Northern Pacific's leaders had no doubt which alternative Hill would choose.

Hill could never understand the men who ran the Northern Pacific.
They were constantly biting off more than they could chew, as their
badly engineered, poorly managed line to the Coast demonstrated.
Chronically short of funds, when they did get their hands on a substantial sum of money they often spent it in ways that made no sense
to Hill. At the very moment when they were behind in their rentals to
the Manitoba road they were planning their own "short line" between
St. Paul and Minneapolis. Hill was dumbfounded. The Manitoba road
had virtually rebuilt its own "short line"—the first railroad in Minnesota—and its four all-steel tracks stood ready to carry all the trains
that would ever conceivably run between the Twin Cities. Real Estate,
almost free for the taking in the 1860s, had become expensive, but the
Northern Pacific seemed willing to spend its last cent to prove that it
was independent of Hill. Such unbusinesslike moves convinced Hill
that sooner or later the road would have to be subordinated to wiser
judgments. Meanwhile he sternly reminded his good friend, Thomas
F. Oakes, vice president of the Northern Pacific, that the Manitoba
would expect that road to go right on paying its contract rental between the Twin Cities.[18]

"Any action that will place Canadian railways built with government bonuses in a better position on American soil [than U.S. roads] is unpatriotic and unworthy of public or private approval," Hill thundered at his Congressman in 1888. The entire Canadian question, on which he had spent so much time and worry in the last ten years, was more annoying than ever. While he was dropping hints that the Manitoba road might build its own line to Winnipeg, he had had to sit by and watch Canadian money, with the full conniving assistance of erstwhile friends in Minneapolis, move into Minnesota in direct competition with the Manitoba road. Eight years earlier he had offered the Canadians the sensible solution to their transportation problem, which was to use the Manitoba road from Winnipeg to St. Paul, and a line from there to Sault Ste. Marie, which would be built in a great hurry if the Canadians proved reasonable on this point. Sir John A. Macdonald, who insisted upon an all-Canada line, had sworn to George Stephen that the Dominion government would never allow the Province of Manitoba to charter local railroads to drain traffic from the Canadian Pacific to American lines to the south. Now the Dominion's nationalistic policy was in ruins, shattered by the strident antimonopoly cries of the "Grits" in Manitoba. Hill had worked hard to adapt to Canadian nationalism; now Canadian provincialism saddled him with more worries.[19]

When the citizens of Minneapolis, who were determined to mill all the wheat the Northwest could produce, decided in the mid-1880s to build their own railroad to carry their flour eastward from Minneapolis to Sault Ste. Marie (the "Soo"), Hill grunted at such folly. He knew that the millers of Buffalo were not going to fold up their tents so supinely, not with the impressive growth of wheat traffic on the Great Lakes. Duluth, he saw clearly, was the future destination of more and more wheat, which, especially in the export trade, was more practical to ship than flour.[20] But he quickly discovered that there was much more to this Soo Railroad business than had met the eye. W. D. Washburn, leading citizen of Minneapolis and a powerful figure in the milling industry, was heading a movement to join the harmless Soo lines on the east with a new railroad, ominously named the Minneapolis & Pacific, which would run in a northwesterly direction from the Mill City to the wheat fields of Manitoba by a route which lay directly between the Main and Branch lines of the Manitoba road. But, he rationalized, people had been talking about paralleling his lines for years. Preparing for any possibility, he had cut down the grades and straightened the curves on the Branch line to the point where a single locomotive could haul an 800-ton train. "This all costs money, and plenty of it," he admitted, but no Soo line would ever be able to do the business at such low cost. The Manitoba road would continue to set the rates on wheat, the grain would continue to find its natural route to the hungry millions in the East, and Washburn and his cronies would learn once and for all that they could not win a fight in which both economics and James J. Hill were on the other side.[21]

Then he discovered that Washburn and his friends had much stronger strings to their bow than anyone had realized. Whether the millers could ever have financed the Soo line west of the Twin Cities is doubtful; they had repeatedly returned empty-handed from Boston and New York. But suddenly they seemed to have all the money they needed. In May of 1886 Hill made a startling discovery which resulted in a stern letter to Stephen, now "Dear Sir George" in recognition of the fact that Queen Victoria had recently knighted her faithful servant:

> Mr. Washburn's friends report that they have borrowed the money for their Sault Ste. Marie road from the Bank of Montreal. . . . I have to request that yourself and Mr. Smith, as directors of the Manitoba Company, will ascertain if possible and advise me, if it is true. . . .[22]

Indeed, it was true. Stephen urgently begged Hill to believe that he had had no idea that the Soo lines east of St. Paul were to be involved in any way with lines being built west of St. Paul in direct competition with the Manitoba. In fact, he claimed not to know that anybody was building in that area at all. The Bank of Montreal had advanced $750,000 to the Soo project east of the Twin Cities, but, he swore, no Canadian money was going into the project to the west. "The true policy of the Sault line people is to stop at St. Paul and Minneapolis and to make friends there with all the existing lines running westwards and northwards," he pledged.[23]

It was the involvement of Canadian money on any basis, however, which had made it possible for Washburn to raise all the money he needed. Canadian transportation policy, hopelessly muddled by the anomalous Canadian political situation, had brought this Frankenstein's monster into existence. The Grand Trunk Railway, bitterly regretting the day it had rejected a role in the Canadian transcontinental railroad scheme, was trying to get even by putting together just the kind of part-American, part Canadian system which sensible economics had called for in the first place. Having consolidated their hold on various Canadian lines leading to the Soo, they were ready to join forces with the people who were building the eastern Soo lines and, quite obviously, would bid heavily for any railroad that would complete the link northwestward from Minneapolis to the Manitoba border.

Recognizing this grave threat which the Soo line posed to the Canadian Pacific, George Stephen and Donald Smith, at almost the last moment, had acquired a controlling interest in the entire Soo enterprise. All right, Hill thought. Since the damned railroad was going to be built anyway, it was the best possible outcome, but he gave Stephen no grounds to hope that the Manitoba road would bail them out:

> I supposed . . . that you considered it would be a connection of some value to the Canadian Pacific, over which you would reach Minneapolis. If, however, it results in an attempt to build lines competing with ours, I think the value of the Soo . . . will be greatly reduced . . . and I would be sorry if any of the friends of this company were led, or rather, misled, into any undertaking that would have an unfortunate outcome.[24]

If Stephen somehow had gotten the idea that the Manitoba and the Soo were going to make common cause, track workers out on the line could have told him differently, for suddenly they felt more like soldiers than day laborers. Word had gone out from Hill to give no quarter in any confrontation which might ensue, and trouble was not long in coming. That fall, as both parties were rushing to make good use of the few days that remained before frost, twenty Manitoba road workers had attacked three Soo workmen near the village of Elbow Lake. "A very serious free fight" had ensued, and the lopsided odds had been quickly readjusted when a hundred men from the other side rushed to the scene, bottled the Manitoba road's men up in the courthouse, and threatened to set it on fire if they refused to come out. More such incidents followed. As soon as the Canadian Pacific had scraped up the money, Stephen sold the Soo to the transcontinental, in whose lap, through prosperity, depression, and several bankruptcies, it has reposed ever since.[25]

By the end of the decade Hill was demanding that the vague policy of the United States in regard to competition from Canadian railroads be clarified. Nothing short of reciprocity, he told John Murray Forbes, would do, and he threw down the gauntlet before the Senate Interstate Commerce Committee at an open hearing which it held in New York:

After allowing Great Britain to practically drive our ships out of the commercial carrying of the world's goods, leaving us without any considerable merchant marine on the high seas; . . . and after forcing us to remain walled up within our own territory, [should you not be] seeking information as to the best way to prevent the British Colonial roads in Canada from running away with our carrying business from state to state? [26]

Sensational as all of these matters were, however, it was the prosaic business of running the railroad which counted most. On the sagging shoulders of Allen Manvel, whom Hill had finally given the title of vice president and general manager, fell much of this crushing burden. In spite of his better nature, Hill developed a mild contempt for this plodding, unimaginative man, but whenever he was ready to show Manvel how he could run the railroad without him, worried letters from the New York directors of the company poured in and kept Manvel chained to his desk. By 1886 he was close to a breakdown and Hill, genuinely worried at the pale, wan face which smiled weakly at him as he passed Manvel's office, insisted that he take a long vacation in Europe. The tonic effects were remarkable. Hill laughed at the staid Manvel's increasingly witty descriptions of Continental European railroads:

I am emphatically against their style of passenger equipment. . . . No heat except a foot warmer, which is a fraud. No light more than a good candle would give. No water, no urinal, no arsenal. . . . All passengers on continental railways ought to be tested for pressure before starting out. [27]

These men took an intense pride in their railroad, which is not surprising in view of how closely they were identified with everything it achieved. The policy of plowing back surplus earnings into permanent improvements, rigorously followed, paid off handsomely in better and safer service as well as lower costs. They resented, even as they understood, the practical necessity of writing off such capital improvements as operating expense, rather than including the cost in net earnings, to which politicians would have pointed as a sure sign of monopoly power. Hill sought endlessly to match authority and responsibility, and he reported proudly to Frank Thomson, his close friend, and heir-apparent to the presidency of the Pennsylvania Railroad, that "I am getting up a working code of rules governing the relations of the different departments of the road to each other and the duties of the respective officers." Thomson, whose railroad led all the

TWO LIEUTENANTS:

Edward T. Nichols. Burlington North-   Allen Manvel. Courtesy of the late
ern.   G. Norman Slade.

rest in the introduction of scientific management, would do the Manitoba road a great favor, Hill wrote, if he would send him a copy of
their organizational manual.[28]

Meanwhile, economy continued to be the watchword. The Manitoba
road's New York business was placed in the competent hands of Edward T. Nichols, Jr., the son of a Navy admiral with no expectations, a
slight, mild-mannered, but spirited young man who had begun his
career as a clerk in Kennedy's banking office. His salary paid in part
by the Manitoba road and in part by Hill, he handled the enormous
volume of work which the railroad and Hill's personal business affairs
generated, and rose to be one of the most important figures in the
Eastern affairs of both Hill and the railroad. In 1889 the Manitoba
road's New York offices were moved into fine new quarters on the second floor of a seven-story elevator building at 40 Wall Street, under
the sober gaze of George Washington's statue in front of the Sub-
Treasury building. Almost immediately Nichols saw a chance to save
the railroad several thousand dollars a year. On the seventh floor, he
wrote, there was a suite, only one-half the size of their new quarters,

but really all the room they needed, for less than half of what they were paying. At the same time there was another railroad which was anxious to move part of its overgrown staff into the Manitoba road's space. Let the Northern Pacific have it, Nichols advised.[29]

V

Every stack of mail that was placed before Hill in his capacity as president of the Manitoba road contained requests for special favors of one kind or another. Few were as touching as one which came to hand in the early summer of 1885 from the most Reverend H. B. Whipple, Episcopal bishop of Minnesota and courageous friend of the unfortunate Indians of the upper Midwest. "Will you give Rev. I. I. Emmeqahbauh and wife and child a pass from Fargo to Devil's Lake and back," Bishop Whipple asked. "The poor Indians there walked all the way to Fargo to ask for a visit from a clergyman. I have asked my good Indian clergyman to go and see what can be done." Requests for free passes came in a flood, and each one posed special problems. It was a destructive system which made more enemies than friends for the railroads. Politicians, even those who had not yet been elected to any office, demanded passes as a matter of course. "I shall try to render you some service in return," one aspirant for public office told Hill during the campaign of 1884. Even the State of Minnesota took its pound of flesh: in 1880 the secretary of state sent Hill a list of twenty-one government officials, including the secretary of the historical society, blandly asking that they receive unlimited annual passes on the railroad.[30]

The free pass system has traditionally been held up as an example of the means by which venal railroad men corrupted honorable legislators and civil servants. It is more realistic to say that the hand was frequently outstretched to receive the favor before any was offered. "The tendency is to abuse the pass privilege," Hill grumbled in 1886, "[eventually] the firemen and porters will be looking for the same favors, and are, for all I know, as much entitled to them." By the Act to Regulate Interstate Commerce of 1887 Congress prohibited discriminatory rates, which effectively outlawed free passes to anyone not actually engaged in the railroad's business, but as late as 1889 Hill was complaining bitterly to Charles Francis Adams, Jr., president of the Union Pacific, that the Union Pacific and the Northern Pacific were still giving passes to important shippers. Hill himself defiantly renewed Bishop Whipple's annual pass in 1889, and when he was cautioned not to haul lumber free to the site of a little church out on the prairie, he sent a cash donation of $25 instead. Two years later the Bishop received Hill's personal donation of $1000 for the new gymnasium at the Indian school in Faribault, Minnesota.[31]

The railroads' customers often wielded a good deal of bargaining power, and those who exploited their power aggressively received special favors which made the difference between success and failure in business. Rebates, which permitted a hard-driving coal producer, for example, to quote lower delivered prices than his competitor, were widespread, and Hill as a user of railroad services was just as industrious at demanding rebates as Hill the railroad man was in discouraging them. In that deflationary age, the absolute level of rates had virtually ceased to bother people, but discriminatory treatment was a burning issue, and its elimination was the chief objective of the Act of 1887.[32]

By the middle of the decade it was clear to nearly everybody that strict government regulation at both state and federal levels was coming. Hill spent long hours studying the reports of the Railroad Commission of Massachusetts, the most prestigious of a number of such bodies which had recently come into existence. He saw that constructive regulation could benefit all parties, but he listened to the effusions of the Granger legislators at the biennial meetings of the state legislature with a heavy heart. The ignorance of these men, and their stubborn refusal to learn anything about the railroads' side of the case, depressed him.[33]

"I have always found in dealing with legislatures that you cannot reason with them," Kennedy wrote Hill early in 1885; "the majority are men who are ignorant, stupid, and full of prejudice who do not desire to know the truth and the more you try to enlighten them the more stubborn and unreasonable they become." Hill was inclined to agree, but still the effort had to be made, so he toiled over a carefully worded speech which he had been invited to make before the Railroad Committee of the Minnesota House of Representatives. He revealed a remarkable command of the subtleties and paradoxes of a problem which so many whose public duty it was to know about did not possess. First he took pains to point out that the railroads were not, as many seemed to think, primarily responsible for the farmers' troubles. (He could not resist this opportunity to condemn one-crop farming.) He presented statistics to show that rates were falling rapidly in Minnesota, and were lower there than in neighboring states. He demonstrated that enlightened railroads like the Manitoba would need no prodding to lower rates so long as they had reason to believe that the increase in traffic would be more than proportional, as so far it had. Growth in the general prosperity, not the taking from one group for the benefit of another, was the philosophy he preached.

> I urged upon our stockholders . . . that the interests of the railroad and the interest of the farmer were identical. . . . The prosperity of the farmer [is] necessary to our prosperity, and our work of peopling the new country served by our lines would be greatly retarded unless the farmers were able to make a fair living. We did not want those whom we had induced to come to Minnesota and settle on our lands to write back that they could not support themselves in Minnesota. . . .[34]

Well-informed though Hill was, his speech reveals how far he and other Americans had to go in comprehending the problems raised by the railroad revolution. He declared that rates were governed by the need of the railroad to earn a certain minimum income, which he believed was determined primarily by the capitalization of the road: the par value of the securities and the interest and dividends which it had to pay on them. Owners of railroad securities had a right to a fair return (he invoked the magic 6 per cent), and the rates paid by consumers, who pay for everything, ultimately, might be looked upon as a tax levied by a private enterprise upon the general public. It was deductive reasoning, very satisfying to the rationalist mind, but it had nothing to do with the way railroad rates were actually made, and the efforts of railroad men to demolish these inanities in later years was made all the more difficult by the fact that they had once believed in them as ardently as anyone else. Still, his speech was a *tour de force,* and when he had finished he must have felt, as Kennedy said, "thankful that we are only called on to submit meekly to the infliction once every two years." [35]

Almost from the moment the legislature's applause for Hill's speech had died away, the Minnesota commission began a ceaseless demand for lower rates. The result was a compromise. Hill noted that average rates had been cut by nearly one-half between 1881 and 1886 (from 2.84¢ to 1.49¢ to carry a ton of freight one mile), a trend which no reasonable man could expect to be continued, yet the commission was obviously just beginning to savor its new power.[36] "It takes about as much time to look after woodchuck bills and kill them off as it does meritorious legislation," a friendly state legislator told Hill, noting that Ignatius Donnelly, determined to rebuild his political power on a primitive concept of class conflict, was threatening to block even the appropriation for the state normal school unless his social-engineering ideas got full attention. "Our legislature is the worst I have ever seen," Hill commented to New York lawyer J. W. Sterling in 1889, "but I think we will get on without any serious trouble." [37]

While he fended off the worst excesses of emergent Populism, Hill followed closely the progress toward regulation in Washington. He corresponded with Joseph E. Nimmo, Jr., one of the most knowledgeable men in the country on the railroad problem, who was eager to follow the fast-moving developments in the Northwest. He studied the English experience at regulation with the help of thoughtful letters from Manvel, who was eager to get home and back to work. Like most of his fellow railroad managers, Hill was anxious to see Congress eliminate from the various bills pending in late 1886 a clause that would have rigidly prohibited the practice of charging more for a short haul than a long haul on the same line. As hideously unfair as this practice seemed on the surface, most railroad men, experts like Nimmo, and a few statesmen knew that the practice was fundamental to the American transportation system. "The interstate law, if enforced as it is written, would destroy the producers of the northwest," Hill told a friend. "[But] an intelligent commission [will] suspend its effect," he added, hopefully. And, "I am not so much afraid of the Inter-State Commerce Act as a great many," he asserted a few days after Cleveland had signed it into law. [38]

The long-and-short-haul agitation, in retrospect, was a slick effort by special interests and specific localities to beat down their rates, and if this "Section Four" of the Act had ever been rigorously enforced the nation's idealistic experiment with commission regulation might well have ended before it had fairly begun. As a compromise, to avoid a rigid long-short-haul clause, railroad men and their sympathizers accepted a clause which prohibited pooling (the great *bête noire* of the anti-monopoly forces) and thereby placed the industry firmly on the road to formal consolidation.

The arcane practice of pooling, a collusive practice which lacked any sanction under the Anglo-American law of contracts, had been the only mechanism for ameliorating the bruising rate wars of the 1870s and 1880s. Recent historians have persuaded themselves, perhaps because of the myth of J. P. Morgan's infallibility, that the great financier's rate associations, with which he proposed to replace the pools, worked even better, until they, in their turn, were outlawed, by the Sherman Anti-Trust Act of 1890. Hill could have told them otherwise. "If we cannot make arrangements with Union Pacific while keeping out of the association," he wired Manvel, "we had better join and try it, and if we find it works unfairly we can withdraw." The Manitoba road, because of its dominant position in the Red River Valley, had had to make only sparing use of pools, but Hill knew well the vital necessity of making some kind of agreement, especially on the intensely competitive Eastern trunk lines, which would guarantee weaker roads a piece of the business at established rates.[39]

Meanwhile, Hill, seeking to explain the fatuousness of a movement to push passenger fares down to the point where that phase of the business would have to be subsidized by freight earnings, succeeded in laying the foundation for his reputation of strongly opposing passenger service:

> The so-called "traveling public" [he wrote a legislative champion of lower fares] forms in reality but a small, and the more fortunate, class of the community; while the freight payers, direct and indirect, include all. Justice requires that railway systems . . . should not favor passenger traffic at the necessary expense of freight payers.[40]

Throughout 1887 railroad men anxiously compared notes on what the Act of 1887 was likely to do to their business. A. E. Touzalin, president of the Burlington railroad's new subsidiary line from Chicago to the Twin Cities, anxiously begged Hill not to jeopardize through business by raising long-haul rates if the Commission tried to put Section Four into effect. By the following year informed observers were aghast at the return of business practices which reminded them of the worst years of the 1870s depression. Hill wired the editor of *Bradstreet's Magazine* his thoughts:

> So far I do not see where [the Act] has materially benefitted the public, while through commissions [rebates] and other irregular methods, large shippers have evaded the law. An amendment allowing railways to agree upon equitable divisions of business would make rates equal to all . . . without increasing rates to the public.[41]

From New York, his close friend, H. W. Cannon, a shrewd, scholarly man who had recently attained the presidency of the Chase National Bank, wrote him just how bad things were in the country at large. "The 'straw that broke the camel's back,' " he declared, "was the action of the trunk lines lately which disclosed the fact of secret underhand rate cutting all over the country . . . ; all sorts of remedies are being suggested, among others the pooling of interests in different sections of the country by creation of great trusts or commissions." And he added, prophetically, "I believe that we shall have a considerable period of depression. . . ." [42] Henry L. Higginson, who had been following the progress of the Manitoba road for several years on behalf of its Boston stockholders, told Hill how he ought to lay his plans:

> The railroads *must* have peace, or the public will give them up in disgust. Every quarrel, every rivalry which is adjusted, by concessions or better still by consolidation, is wise. . . . Your Co., if joined with the N.P., would be a very stout concern. Of course you are far stronger than N.P. and can hurt it—but to what good end? The road is there to stay and more is the pity. . . . I believe this to be true: tie up always, when things can be tied up—all around. [43]

Hill was coming to the same conclusion. He did not agree with Albert Fink, guiding genius of the trunk-line pool association, that the time had come for a "corporation of corporations," taking in all of the railroads of the country, although the prototype of such a giant already existed in the Standard Oil Company and was being duplicated—with much greater chance of permanence—in the American Telephone & Telegraph Company. To a New York financier who had requested his views, he wrote:

> I do not think the time has come, or that it ever will come, when a general trust can be formed to include the chief lines throughout the country. The grouping of interests, the advantages of each being determined by the same controlling influences which will divide the country west of Chicago, between the Canadian border and the Gulf of Mexico, into three or four groups, might be brought about with excellent results. If something of this kind is not done the natural theory of the survival of the fittest must apply and some such harmonizing of interests will be the result through the bankruptcy of the weaker lines and their final absorption by the stronger ones. [44]

VI

H. B. Strait, who represented the southern portion of Minnesota in the United States House of Representatives, was enjoying the golden days of autumn in his home town of Shakopee in October 1888. One morning he received a letter from James J. Hill. He was pleased, and not a little surprised, to find that it contained a certificate for 100 shares of stock in the Great Falls Water Power & Townsite Company. "You will please accept my very hearty thanks for the same," he wrote Hill; "whenever I can be of service to you do not hesitate to command." [45] Hill's gift of stock in one of his less successful Montana projects was worth as much as $7000 to Strait if he sold it at the right time. It was small payment for the extensive lobbying services which Strait, following a common practice of the era, had carried on for Hill, the Manitoba road, and the people of Dakota and Montana territories for over two years, in the matter of the bill to allow the Manitoba road a right-of-way for its Montana extension through the Fort Berthold Indian Reservation. The bill had rattled around in the congressional compromise process all that time, during which Strait, staying on in steamy Washington summers after Congress had adjourned, kept it alive. Few people—not even the Indians—opposed the right-of-way, for the northern portions of Dakota and Montana were bound to have their railroad, come what may. Strait himself had never thought of voting against the bill. Only the vested interests represented by the Northern Pacific and Union Pacific wanted to block the Manitoba's westward march, and, true to form, they had cost Hill money, time, and much worry before the bill had finally passed.

Hill never had to make much use of such direct influence upon the governmental process. His wants were simple, and he had generally had the weight of public opinion and the onrush of events on his side ever since he and the associates had undertaken to revive the St. Paul & Pacific in 1878. Besides hiring a Congressman as a lobbyist, he had made modest loans to other politicians, notably D. M. Sabin, Minnesota's able Senator. He had accepted $1200 from Daniel S. Lamont, President Cleveland's secretary, to be very profitably invested in the city of Superior, Wisconsin, which Hill's Lake Superior branch created almost overnight. He paid an Indiana Senator more for his Montana Central Railroad stock than it was worth when the road was merged into the Manitoba road in 1888. "His cheek is immense, and there is no use in bothering with such people, and when you find one on your list it will be always the cheapest and best to get rid of him in the most direct manner," Hill wrote his lieutenant in Montana. A year later the Senator was inaugurated as President Benjamin Harrison. [46]

Hill reacted violently on the one occasion when he was openly accused of attempting to bribe a public official. It was in Manitoba, where the "Grits" were showing the way for demagogues like Donnelly, that the attack took place. Thomas Greenway, grittiest of the members of the provincial parliament, sent a telegram to the St. Paul *Pioneer Press* accusing Hill of offering him $20,000 to pass certain legislation for the Manitoba road. "Did you make such a statement?" Hill wired Greenway. "If you did I demand of you the time when, the place where and the person through whom such an offer was made." He had Greenway's retraction by wire later the same day.[47]

He was not especially effective in getting his way with the politicians. The man he wanted for territorial governor of Montana was rejected, and the worst man, in Hill's opinion, got the job. He could not understand why the first Democratic President in a quarter of a century would do such a thing, especially when Hill was one of those who had remained faithful to the party throughout the long, arid years. When Cleveland ignored his earnest, scholarly explanation of the Indian problem near the Canadian border and appointed a man from Tennessee—instead of Hill's man—to straighten out Indian affairs in the upper Midwest, Hill was genuinely hurt. But when the President vetoed the first version of the right-of-way bill, he was beside himself. Word reached Washington that Hill was reported to have condemned the President's intelligence or his honesty, or perhaps both. He hurriedly wrote a conciliatory letter to Postmaster General William F. Vilas, who replied that all was forgiven. With his friends, however, he continued to mince no words. "The only ones who will be benefitted are the G.O.P., as Dakota has not made any progress under Democratic rule," he told Strait. "I think we in the Northwest fared as well under Republican rule as we have so far under the [Democrats]," he confided to Knute Nelson; "if the G.O.P. were not so far gone on [tariff] protection I think they would sweep the country." [48]

VII

Hill had learned well the stern lessons of the 1880s. Never again would there be so much freedom for intelligent men of good will and broad vision to do what needed to be done, nor for corrupt, narrowminded financial opportunists to do harm. Never again, perhaps unfortunately, would the penalty for false moves be so quickly and unfailingly visited upon businessmen as in the rugged, final decade of the era of free enterprise. By 1889 Hill was ready for the bold moves which Cannon, Higginson, and his own vision told him would soon be necessary. At the same time he redoubled his efforts to apply the conservative, no-nonsense policies which had made the Manitoba road the strongest in the Northwest—indeed, in the entire West, except for Collis P. Huntington's Southern Pacific.

In 1884 he had received a letter requesting his comments on the Manitoba road as an investment. He got many such letters, frequently from very important people who had only recently heard of him for the first time, but this one he particularly enjoyed answering. It was from Sir John Rose, of the English banking firm of Morton, Rose & Company, who, in 1877, had declined the associates' request that Rose finance their takeover of the St. Paul & Pacific. In his reply Hill explained the policies by which he hoped to make the Manitoba impregnable:

> During the past two years we have spent a great deal of money for steel rails, ballasting track, transfer yards, terminal facilities, new equipment, new shops, and in fact we have put the road in better condition than any railway similarly situated that I know of in the west. . . . We have now over one thousand miles with a 26-foot maximum grade and only 220 miles with over a 30-foot maximum grade. The latter we expect to reduce to 26- and 30-foot maximum within the next two years. *When this is done no railway in the world of one thousand miles or more will have the same low gradients. . . .*
>
> I have today greater confidence in the present and future value of the property than ever before and am a larger holder of its securities. In fact, I am so largely interested in the property that I could not discontinue my connection with it if I would. Moreover, at my time of life there is no reason why I should not be good for some years yet of active service. . . .[49]

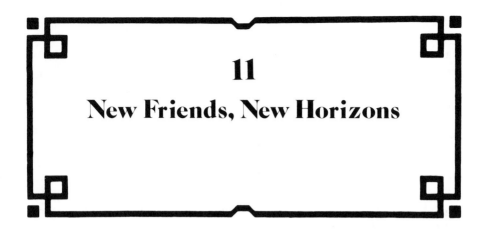

11

New Friends, New Horizons

I know that in the first instance my great interest in the agricultural growth of the Northwest was purely selfish. If the farmer was not prosperous, we were poor, and I know what it is to be poor. I always want to see the most made of our opportunities, because it will bring more grist to our mill. The man who takes another view of it falls far short of an intelligent grasp of it.

—James J. Hill, 1916

I

High on any list of nineteenth-century Americans who encouraged the importation, collection, and, eventually, public exhibition of the art masterpieces of Europe must be the name of Samuel P. Avery. Since the prosperous decade of the 1850s the business of this onetime engraver as art purveyor to New York's affluent middle class had grown steadily. As a founder of the Metropolitan Museum of Art, Avery had helped to raise the funds for what would eventually be one of the proudest cultural institutions in the world, and his remarkable skill in dealing with the rapidly increasing ranks of rich men who fancied themselves as art connoisseurs had gradually filled the walls of the Metropolitan and many a private gallery with some of the finest examples of European painting.

By 1880 the well-heeled private collector was just beginning to emerge as the critical factor in the art world of Europe and America. On their frequent trips to Europe, Avery and a few other pioneers in this esoteric new business sought out canvases and statuary which began to find their way into such soon-to-be-famous collections as those of Henry G. Marquand, William H. Vanderbilt, John Wanamaker, Benjamin Altman, the Morgans, the Wideners, and the Huntingtons.

But it was not to any of these Eastern potentates that Avery was writing in 1886 about some of his latest discoveries. A thousand miles from New York, in what had been little more than a frontier community two decades before, James J. Hill himself had fallen in love with collecting. Knowing how much Hill admired the work of Jules Breton, a leading star of the annual Paris Salon, Avery offered him Breton's latest, a picture of three peasant girls lunching in a field. Avery knew that a collector wanted, above all, a first-rate example of a painter's work, but any reassurance that it would appreciate in value and that there would not be, perhaps, too many more of them, was usually welcome, too. "*Enfin* a lovely and a saleable picture, '*pour vous*,' 80,000 francs," he purred; "I found Breton much changed since last summer, [he] has been sick for three months, is much thinner and his face has lost that sound, round healthy appearance of former days." [1] (Breton, then still in his fifties, lived to be nearly eighty.)

Hill did not rise to the bait in this instance, but he proved to be a good customer for Avery and a succession of other dealers, even though he never bought on such a grand, indiscriminate scale as those who assembled the great private collections. Soon George Durand-Ruel, whose Paris gallery had opened one of the most successful branches in New York, became his mentor. At the time, the Barbizon school of landscape painting was the height of fashion, but Durand-Ruel was already seeking to turn Hill's attention to the French Impressionists. In 1888 he sent his son to St. Paul with some pictures that would have raised eyebrows in New York. "Some of them are of the new French school," he wrote, "which though already admired and recognized in Paris, are yet comparatively unknown here. These painters are, in my opinion, of the same rank as the masters of 1830. . . ." [2]

In the 1880s, however, when Hill became an eager collector of "pictures"—*not* "paintings," he insisted to the secretary who drew up a catalogue of his acquisitions—it was the masters of the French school of painting that developed between 1830 and 1870 which he most admired. Durand-Ruel gave him instructions for collecting which Hill could immediately recognize as good advice in any line of business. "Anybody can tell," the dealer wrote, after one of France's greatest private collections had been sold, "that the very finest pictures are in great demand . . . and those only will keep their rank and their prices. . . . You can now easily get for one of the *chefs d'oeuvre* of our great masters several hundred thousand francs, while you can get cheap an ordinary picture of the same artists." Hill bought from Avery and from Durand-Ruel, but he also found satisfaction in M. Knoedler & Company of New York, successors to the French engraving firm of Goupil & Company, who sold him pictures to the end of his life.[3]

Hill had the usual motives of an art collector: a great love for the objects themselves and a profound respect for the talent and devotion of the artists. He felt pride in owning objects of great beauty and rarity which could be enjoyed not only by the owner and his family but by unlimited numbers of people who might come to view them. And, unmistakably, he liked the sweet smell of success, which was reflected in a steady appreciation in the market value of the pictures. Pictures had been mere decorative objects to Hill when he ordered a local artist to render "Lake Pepin by Moonlight," or had Jacacci paint the shepherdesses on the lunettes of the family's Victorian dining room. But the thrill of collecting grew and grew. Both Kennedy and Samuel Thorne sent him catalogues of the major auction sales in New York, and the library table in the house on Canada street was loaded with "editions de luxe" of albums of the William H. Vanderbilt mansion and its famous collection, the Durand-Ruel collection, and more. "Set your standard high," he advised the directors of the Minneapolis Institute of Arts near the end of his life. He did not hesitate to sell a picture when he found that it no longer moved him, however; he had discovered that "if you had to live with it, how soon you would grow to hate it." He smiled knowingly at a letter from Henry L. Higginson, who concluded his prediction of the great trust movement in business with the assertion, "It is the principle I am after—and then, pictures! They are a great refreshment after work, aren't they?"[4]

The walls of the gallery which Hill added to the front of the house at Ninth and Canada Streets filled up quickly, although pictures were hung, in the fashion of the times, side by side and from floor to ceiling. They were placed on the gilt bamboo easels in which the Victorians rejoiced, were propped against the plush banquettes, and overflowed into the other rooms of the house. In 1883 genre paintings by German art professors were still arriving, to be painstakingly unpacked and squeezed into the gallery. In that same year, however, pictures arrived by such artists as Dupré, Troyon, and Daubigny. Next year there was "Evening," by Corot—$1250, from Knoedler—and by the end of the decade much costlier Corots, as well as Rousseaus, Courbets, Delacroixs, and Millets delighted the eye of family, servants, and the gentlefolk who were freely offered tickets of admission by the proud owner. De Neuville's battle scene of heroic proportions, "The Storming of El Tel Kebir," for which Hill paid $20,000, dazzled the local citizenry, but in later years it proved that not everything he bought went up in value automatically.[5]

He began to share his paintings with the people of the Midwest almost immediately. Chicago's Calumet Club asked for the loan of two or three pictures for their annual art exhibit in 1881, and Hill consented. When the Chicago Art Institute asked for five pictures for its grand opening in 1887, it was delighted to receive thirteen. "I am proud to show some of my Boston friends such pictures," wrote the director. More than a dozen pictures made their way to Cincinnati for the Centennial Exposition of the Ohio Valley and Central States in 1888, and Kansas City, hearing of Hill's generosity, asked and received a similar loan. In 1889 six paintings were donated to the Minneapolis Public Library's Art Department; it was the first of a series of gifts of paintings and money to what became the Minneapolis Institute of Arts.[6]

Hill learned the hard way that a reputable dealer, whatever his wily ways of salesmanship, is indispensable to the serious collector who would avoid embarrassment and financial loss. In 1883 there had appeared in St. Paul, armed with impeccable credentials, including a letter of introduction to Hill's close friend, Judge Greenleaf Clark, a decayed English country gentleman named Major James Walter. The Major, like so many of his kind, had something to sell, in this case a handsome oil painting of Thomas Jefferson. It had been painted from life, and at Monticello, according to Walter, by James Sharples, a well-known English portraitist who, after the Revolution, had spent several years "taking the likenesses" of the Founding Fathers, and whose series of pastel portraits of George and Martha Washington were highly prized in England. Hill, a devout Jeffersonian Democrat, could not resist buying the portrait, and before long he had bought oils of James Madison and John Adams, too, both guaranteed by the Major to have been painted from life by a very busy James Sharples. Almost immediately, the Jefferson traveled to Chicago, where it was the hit of the Iroquois Club's Jefferson birthday banquet.

There were yet more treasures in Major Walter's bags. His most prized possessions, which he now reluctantly decided to part with, were three oil portraits of George Washington, painted, he said, by Sharples in 1796. Hill was impressed, but something held him back. Perhaps it was only the Major's price—$90,000. Even so, he paid Walter $750 for thirty sets of autotype reproductions which were distributed to the public schools of the Twin Cities amid considerable squabbling over who should get them. The Major did not give up. He wrote Hill from New York that he had been to the vaults of the Manhattan Storage Company to see the portraits. "They seemed to smile upon me," he oozed, "and I am not ashamed to confess [that] more than a tear fell from my eyes. 'Let us go home to our people in St. Paul, let it be our city [they cried out].' "

For the next four years the letters kept coming, and when the Major reported that the Washington portraits had been exhibited to great acclaim in New York and were to be acquired by the United States government, Hill wondered if he had made a mistake. At that point Francis Parkman, the celebrated historian, offered to head a commission of the Massachusetts Historical Society to study the portraits and the extensive documentation of letters which Walters offered as proof of their genuineness. The report, signed by Parkman himself, found the paintings to be spurious and, risking libel, noted that the documents contained "idiosyncrasies of Major Walter himself." Sharples, in fact, had never painted a single picture in oil while in America, preferring the faster and more spontaneous pastel technique. The following year Hill received a letter from Charles Francis Adams, Jr., asserting that the person portrayed in Hill's portrait of John Adams could not possibly be his great-grandfather. Adams thought he knew who it was, and offered to find out, but Hill tossed the letter aside, unanswered. After all, what difference did it make whether he owned a fake Sharples of Adams, or a fake Sharples of Albert Gallatin? [7]

II

Mary Hill, her own simple toilette finished, came to the rescue of her husband, who was struggling with the bow tie his elegant formal attire dictated. It was January 1889, and they were in the swaying drawing room of the Pennsylvania Limited, almost an hour late on the last leg of its run to Washington, D. C. The Hills were due at the White House at seven for what everyone assumed would be President Grover

Cleveland's last formal reception. Frank Thomson, vice president of the railroad, had wired them at Harrisburg to get into their evening clothes on the train. He would get the Limited to the capital as fast as he could without its jumping the track, and would have a carriage waiting at the depot to take them direct to the Executive Mansion. Tired as they were from their two-day trip from St. Paul, they enjoyed the dazzling event, at which Hill was more impressed by the popularity of Mrs. Cleveland than by the President's "deliberate movements [which] do not create much enthusiasm." [8]

Without great effort on his part, Hill had attained a brief importance in Democratic politics in the 1880s. The Hills had barely got settled at the Albemarle Hotel in New York, therefore, when Mary found herself thrown into a fresh flurry of activity. "Send Mr. Hill's best Prince Albert coat and vest by express today," she wired the housekeeper in St. Paul. A telegram had arrived from Washington, asking Hill to come back down in three days for an important meeting with the President and Calvin S. Brice and W. L. Scott, leaders in the Democratic party organization, to discuss the Minnesota legislature's election of a United States Senator. [9]

Ignatius Donnelly, radical member of the Minnesota legislature, seldom agreed with James J. Hill on anything, but both had opposed the election of W. D. Washburn, Minneapolis flour-milling magnate, to a Senate seat. Learning that Washburn's election was inevitable, Donnelly stomped out of the chamber, snorting that it was "the worst legislature that had ever been known." That same day he sat down to write his highly successful novel, *Caesar's Column.* Minnesota was a long way from the sadistic revolution which Donnelly's novel imagined, but its people were far from happy. Both major political parties seemed to grow less and less sensitive to the problems of the West. Donnelly was dissatisfied with the Democratic party's apparent inability to detach itself from the "Eastern monopolists," who were supposed to be as firmly in control of it as they were of the Republican party. Hill was, if anything, even unhappier. After thirty years as a faithful Democrat in a state still dominated by memories of the free soil agitation of the 1850s which had joined the West to the Republican party, Hill had suffered the frustrations of living under a Democratic administration that had given the West none of the economic relief which, in his opinion, it required so desperately. [10]

Historians who have preferred to see American political history in the late 1880s and 1890s as a confrontation of social classes rather than

of geographical sections have emphasized the efforts which Minnesota
political leaders like P. H. Kelly, Michael Doran, and their more or less
silent partner, James J. Hill, exerted to keep radicals like Donnelly
from sharing in the fruits of Democratic victory. But for Hill the victory had been a slender one indeed, as the irritatingly middle-of-the-
road Cleveland refused to push either the tariff relief or the monetary
reform which Hill and many of his Eastern friends such as Kennedy
and Thorne demanded. These men admired the fine steel rails which
the English and the Germans were exporting to America, and they
resented paying at least 50 per cent more for them than they would
have if American ironmasters had not been protected by a high tariff.
Kennedy was rabidly anti-protectionist, and Hill, congratulating Congressman Knute Nelson, the darling of the Republican Scandinavians
of Minnesota, for his vote against the tariff, warned that unless the
high protection were reduced or eliminated there would sooner or
later be overproduction in American steel mills, which would cause a
depression.[11]

Kennedy was also worried that the severe money stringency which
marked the 1880s would bring about remonetization of silver, and that
the destruction of the gold standard would follow. Hill agreed, but he
further condemned Cleveland's failure to do anything about the surplus in the federal budget, which was "locking up large amounts
every month in the Treasury." And Hill warned a senior New York
politician that the party had better adapt to a stronger future role of
the labor movement in politics. "Wise men of all parties [should] keep
it [the movement] out of American politics, [but] it may be like Ban-
quo's ghost and will not be laid." [12]

Hill and the other Democratic party regulars in Minnesota knew
what Donnelly was after: the leadership of the party, on his own
highly individualistic terms. The future Populist, more showman than
statesman, was constitutionally incapable of working as a member of a
political team. This trait accounted for much of his appeal to a substantial minority of the electorate and at the same time was the reason
why he would gain little power in Minnesota politics. By 1885 Hill was
willing to see Donnelly read out of the party:

He is a man of undoubted ability and industry [he wrote Kelly] and none
more likely to make a favorable impression where he is not known, but
looking back to his career in this state [and] his refusal to maintain Cleveland in the last campaign, I cannot but wonder that he is tolerated among
people who have proper self respect.[13]

Hill proceeded to throw his weight against men like Donnelly when it came to ladling out the patronage after Cleveland's inauguration, but he could have saved himself the trouble. The President seemed to develop a strange distaste at the mere thought that there was a patronage arrangement in Minnesota. Hill received numerous requests from office seekers for his nod of approval, but he got very little more than he himself wanted, and that took quite some doing. The last thing he wanted was any office for himself. Meanwhile, he found that just having a hand on the ladle made enemies, and he was not reluctant to hand over the details of running the Minnesota Democratic party to others.[14]

He cherished his newly powerful friends in the national Democratic party, however, and cultivated them in the little time he could spare. When a group of rich Eastern Democrats, including Samuel Thorne, John G. Moore, Edward Tuck, and Grant B. Schley, gave a testimonial dinner for party wheelhorse Brice at New York's Union League Club in 1886, he was there. In the last summer of Cleveland's first administration he joined a party on the Presidential yacht to go after bluefish, which were running strong off Fire Island. That September the Democratic Campaign Committee was pleased to receive his contribution of $10,000 to Cleveland's unsuccessful re-election bid. Hill and Cleveland remained good friends, both throughout the turbulent second administration and after the President was back in private life. Of all the industrial leaders Cleveland had known, he was most impressed by this Western railroad man. "I am perfectly sure that I have never known a man who was at once familiar with so many big things," he recalled, "and also had the gift of carrying about and comprehending what most persons so situated would deem too small for their attention."[15]

Politics brought Hill three close friends and valued advisers: John Jay Knox and Henry W. Cannon, both of whom were comptrollers of the currency and important financial advisers to Cleveland during his first administration, and Daniel S. Lamont, the President's private secretary. Knox and Cannon were both former Minnesota residents, having emigrated from the East as young men, and had been highly successful bankers. They possessed a knowledge of monetary theory which was unique in men of such considerable practical business ability. Knox was one of the authors of the so-called "Crime of '73," which had dropped the silver dollar from the coinage, and an expert on unsecured paper money. Hill had urged him to accept the presidency of the National Bank of the Republic in New York, on the eve of the great growth of commercial banking. Cannon, the grave, dignified investment genius who became Knox's vice president not long thereafter, was soon offered the presidency of the Chase National Bank, which he helped build into one of the great financial institutions of the world. Lamont, a short, baldheaded man who sported a bristly moustache, had been an Albany newspaper reporter. He was still in his thirties, and Hill was to make good use of his boundless energy, shrewdness, and efficiency over the next decade.[16]

III

St. Paul's civic leaders were proud of their city's role as the eastern gateway to the expanding agricultural economy of the Northwest. They spared no effort, therefore, to impress a group of Montana stockmen who visited their city in May 1886 to consider St. Paul as a site for fattening and slaughtering the herds of beef cattle that were beginning to dot the plains of Montana. They were tendered a banquet at the Minnesota Club, and the toastmaster, A. B. Stickney, made haste to introduce to them his good friend, Minnesota farmer James J. Hill. It was a merry crowd, and Hill had to wave goodnaturedly at numerous catcalls about wheat prices and railroad rates as he rose to speak.

"A few years ago," he recalled, "it was said that a man was pretty far from home when he was where they could not raise corn." But now, he noted, he was getting fifty-three bushels to the acre from his farm near St. Paul, and other Minnesota farmers could do as well. "Nowhere is the soil cultivated with as little intelligence as in Minnesota," he lectured. Farmers ought to do more stock raising, he insisted, as his own experiences at the Illinois Fat Stock Show in Chicago proved. His cattle entries there "made them [the exhibitors from the lower Midwest] look blue." He had taken the sweepstakes for the best two-year-old, he said, then slaughtered and dressed it and took the prize for the best carcass, and all of this in competition with 600 animals. It was done, furthermore, without using any corn for feed—only cabbages, turnips, and ground oats. Switch to cattle, he pleaded: "We shall have a market, feed our own fodder, and not go broke on wheat." [17]

Regulars at the Minnesota Club who had wondered what James J.

Hill would bore them with once he had exhausted the possibilities of development of railroads in the Red River Valley soon learned that his new cause was the pressing need for diversification of agriculture. By 1886 he had begun to make an impression. On the day after his speech, congratulations flowed in. "You can say more in a short space than any after dinner speaker I ever knew," the governor of Dakota Territory told him. "I believe the time will come when the farmers will appreciate what you are doing for their best interests," Cannon wrote him from New York. And Charles B. Lamborn, land commissioner for the Manitoba road's arch rival, the Northern Pacific, asked permission to quote the speech at length in their colonization literature.[18]

Feeding and selling fattened stock, Hill preached, was a more profitable way to use the fertility of the soil and the labor power of the farmer than growing and selling wheat was. The low world price for wheat, he noted, was due to the existence of a marketable surplus in the United States and elsewhere, and that surplus dragged the price down to a level not very far above the bare cost of handling and transportation. If American farmers would divert, say, 15 per cent of their acreage to some other crop, and, instead of marketing the produce of this portion, use it for feed, they would balance wheat output with domestic needs, or even create a comfortable deficit, which would raise prices considerably. He spread the gospel far and wide. When Joseph Nimmo, Jr., the knowledgeable former government statistician who was setting up in business as a lobbyist for the railroad industry, wrote to inquire about the prospects for stock farming in the Northwest, Hill delightedly sent him a pass over the Manitoba road, and offered to sit down and go over the economics of it with him. For several years he supported the unsuccessful efforts of a not-too-competent newspaperman to publish *The Farmer*, which publicized improved farming methods. (He even dutifully followed the suggestion of his peppery old friend, General William LeDuc, that they investigate the potentialities of the yak and, when the consul general at St. Petersburg finally reported to them, agreed with LeDuc that the best place to file the report was the wastebasket.) But his most notable contributions to the improvement of agriculture were the activities which he carried on at his farm at North Oaks, a few miles northwest of St. Paul.[19]

"I have lately looked at a place of about 3000 acres, 400 to 500 cleared and grubbed, three farm houses &c and a meadow capacity for 500 tons of hay," Hill wrote a friend in May 1883. Later that summer he closed the deal on the place, acquiring over 3000 acres of rather poor farmland from C. D. Gilfillan for $50,000. The property, which was near enough to St. Paul to be reached in a couple of hours by carriage, included lovely Pleasant Lake. It became the place where Hill liked most to be whenever he got the chance. The family would establish residence there every spring and stay on well into October or November. From 1883 until his death, Hill's real home would be North Oaks Farm. As adjoining land became available he bought it, until the property included over 5000 acres. For two years Mary labored to get the farmhouse ready for the family, and the boarding house, which Hill had built to house his hired men, properly furnished with everything from cast iron stoves for the drafty rooms to $143 worth of crockery for the long dining room table.[20]

Where Hill found the time to set up and run North Oaks Farm in the mid-1880s is not readily apparent. The paper work was enormous, due in large measure to his perfectionism. He wrote Sam Thorne for "the address of the party in Vermont who makes the 'vacuum creamer' " (he was the first person in Minnesota to use a cream separator), and carried his fancy ideas of farming to the point of advertising for a gardener "experienced in the growing of grapes under glass." His temper found plenty to vent itself upon as he sought to staff his farm with twenty-one people, more than half of them rough, unruly bachelors who made life miserable for the married couple who ran the boardinghouse. The payroll at North Oaks was almost $900 a month for farm labor alone, and he was constantly driving his manager to do a better job. "Possibly I am hard to please," he had told John Gibson, when he persuaded him to come from Ontario to run the place. Gibson had good reason to agree.[21]

Most of the time and much of the money that he devoted to North Oaks in the next several years went into his program to establish herds of cattle, swine, and sheep. The first occupants of the stalls were his Jerseys, which he found came through the Minnesota winters "all right," but he theorized that the breeds which would do best to the north of the Twin Cities were those which thrived in the highlands of Scotland. This inspiration was the beginning of the Northwest's great herds of polled (hornless) Black Angus beef cattle and shorthorn dairy cattle. He had worked out a plan to make the best Scottish bloodlines the basis for agricultural diversification in Minnesota and Dakota, which he explained to a friend:

To induce our farmers to take a more active interest in [livestock] I propose to offer a certain number of young bulls and rams annually as premiums for the best progress made in cattle raising counties, which I will select. I have imported from the best herds in Great Britain (mainly from the north of Scotland, on account of their strong constitutions and good feeding qualities) a number of cattle and sheep and from them I expect to be able to send out four young bulls fit for service next summer and after that about twelve yearly, and from twelve to twenty rams yearly.

I have not as yet fully decided as to the conditions upon which they will be distributed further than that they will be free of charge and must be kept in good condition for service, and the fee for service must be low enough to enable every farmer to avail himself of the benefit. . . .[22]

He had remitted to his New York agents over $6000 in the summer of 1883 for imported animals, but it was only the beginning. He retained David Hume, a Scottish expert, to buy the "best showyard bull you can find," and the result was the "roan Berkeley Duke of Oxford," price $5250. The cows were just as expensive, and Hill soon realized that such valuable property took a great deal of looking after. He sent his best man, W. A. Dolby, off to Scotland with a draft for £300 for his expenses. When Dolby arrived in Boston with the first shipment of bovine royalty, he found that Hill had had a special "house" and exercise yard set up for them, at a cost of $300, so that their weeks in quarantine would not result in injury or infection.

But Hill's worries had just begun. When a special stock car bearing the $5000 shorthorn cow, "Grand Duchess 43rd," on the Boston, Hoosac Tunnel & Western Railway caught fire, burning Her Grace to a crisp, he collected only $50 in damages, despite an energetic lawsuit. His tenacity and resourcefulness were severely tested when it came to getting valuable animals safely to St. Paul from the distant seaboard, as the odyssey of the "fine shorthorn cow, 'Sweet Pea,' " and her calf bear witness. When this elegant creature arrived at Glasgow to take passage, she was found to be too far advanced in pregnancy and had to wait until her calf was born. Arriving in Quebec in October, she faced a long, slow trip across the frigid Upper Midwest in January, when her quarantine would be up. Despite Hill's pleas, the Canadian Minister of Agriculture, John H. Pope, refused to waive the quarantine. When "Sweet Pea" and her daughter resumed their journey, they rode in a special heated boxcar of the Grand Trunk Railway, escorted by one of the railroad's own conductors.[23]

Soon Hill had blooded bull calves of his own from the Scottish

stock, and they were carefully entered in the official herd books. His
secretary, W. A. Stephens, filled in his time by carefully engrossing
the pedigrees and copying them in the letterbooks. By the spring of
1884 he proudly told Thorne, whose father had been one of the pioneer breeders of shorthorn cattle in Dutchess County, New York, "I
will have 30 imported bulls distributed along our lines this year, one
in each county at least, which will do for a beginning." The blooded
stock, he explained to a farmer in Dakota Territory, would put on
more weight per unit of feed than scrub cattle could, and the meat
would be worth more per pound. Farmers who agreed to service their
neighbors' cows for $1 each, and take good care of the bull for three
years, could thereafter call the bull their own. Two responsible
members of the community would agree to see that the recipient of the
bull carried out the agreement. Meanwhile, Hill would have his own
veterinary surgeon, traveling full time, calling from farm to farm to
check up on things. The following year, 1885, he expected to have
sixty-five bulls to distribute.[24]

By the time the spring of 1885 was over, he had actually sent out 100
bulls, and, he wrote Kennedy, 500 bulls would not supply the demand. His mail, in fact, had begun to bulge with requests for bulls,
ranging from the arrogant to the pleading. What had begun as a pleasant and useful hobby became more and more of a care. The veterinary
bills piled up, and more than once he had to send someone to hunt
down a bull which a farmer had "sold" to someone else. Some of the
animals were poorly cared for, and many farmers turned out to be
poor husbandmen. " 'Beaumont' is somewhat slow," Hill patiently
explained to one farmer, "but if you will turn him loose with the cow
in the field and let him take his own time, I think you will find that he
will have no trouble." If a bull did not turn out to be a good "calf get-
ter," however, he was turned into roasts of beef very soon.[25]

In 1888 Hill told Sandford Fleming, chief engineer of the Canadian
Pacific, that he had given away about 200 bulls. "The result has been
. . . that there are fully twenty times as many cattle in the districts
reached by me as there were when I began this distribution." Anxious
to advertise Black Angus beef, he sent Philip D. Armour three steers
with a request that he slaughter them and send generous roasts by
express to a list of Hill's friends. "I never ate a better piece of meat in
my life," Armour reported enthusiastically. Marshall Field sent
thanks, and a wisecrack: "I am more than ever satisfied that you will
yet make a good Granger." Frank Thomson told him that A. J. Cassatt,

a vice president of the Pennsylvania Railroad whose stock farm was the showplace of Philadelphia, wanted to know where he could get some good Angus heifers.[26]

Meanwhile, so many blooded pigs and Shropshire lambs went out over the Manitoba road—at the nominal price of $5, delivered—that Hill lost count. Of all the compliments he received, none was more eloquent than one in a letter from a Minnesota farmer, painfully scrawled on a page torn from a child's school tablet:

> The lamb came in a nice cage, all right, looking as fine as a new hat. I had hard work to put the same clothes on this morning that I have been wearing for the last few weeks, I felt so much pleased. . . . If there ever may be in the balance of my life any way that I can serve you, I shall be happy to render you any kindness. . . .[27]

IV

A close observer of the Wilder business block in St. Paul would have known when James J. Hill was in town and when he was off on one of his increasingly frequent trips. Most mornings his carriage arrived from North Oaks by eight o'clock, whether in bright sunshine or driving rain. When he was away, the farm staff had strict orders to report to his secretary that everything at home was all right, and on most such days the farm wagon was at the office building door by ten o'clock with a note from Mrs. Hill. One day it was a request for a dozen glass jars "with the best kind of tops for keeping preserves—I want them tonight," for when the currants were ripe they admitted of no delay. When she and Mamie planned a trip into St. Paul for a performance of "Faust" or "A Daughter of the Regiment," given by a traveling opera company, she needed her ruby earrings. On other days the driver merely handed in a plaintive request that someone prod the telephone company into finding out why their new-fangled instrument was out of order again.[28]

Hill planned many "good shoots" at North Oaks with his sons and friends. He was delighted to find that 200 pheasant eggs, which he had imported from England and which J. Kennedy Tod himself had escorted from the steamer to the train in New York, had hatched successfully. Bird hunting was Hill's favorite sport. He admired the sight of his fine English hunting dogs, which had been carefully "broken in" by a local expert, working in the field. He exchanged dogs with

Sam Thorne and other Eastern friends, joined them for a shoot at their places when he could, and repeatedly begged them to come to St. Paul for the next board of directors meeting and, incidentally, a little shooting. He was heartsick when his best dog was stolen in the field by trespassing hunters, and overjoyed when his trainer wired that "Jim" had been found, "just about starved to death," but alive, twenty miles from where he had disappeared.[29]

Hill continued to worry about his sister's large family back in Rockwood. The solution, he decided, was to buy them a farm that was big enough to keep them all busy, and he did. It seemed to work. "The little girls are busy hoeing the roots and all hands are trying to do all they can," his brother Alec reported, adding that their sister was "as happy as possible, and says you have now given her large family of 16 a chance to do well for themselves." The oldest boy, Alec wrote, wanted very much to go to college: "He is a good deal like what you were when a boy, always reading." A few years later Alec decided that farming was what he himself was best suited for, and, with $14,000 from his brother, he bought a farm in Rockwood.[30]

As Hill's fame and fortune grew, so did the size and scope of his charitable gifts, which his secretary recorded carefully in a special ledger. Catholic and Protestant causes were treated about equally; if Hill deliberately balanced his gifts to the two branches of the Christian faith, he had both civic and personal reasons to do so. As the Twin Cities' colleges and universities multiplied, he helped make successes of numerous fund drives. Professor William W. Payne of Carleton College in near-by Northfield was overjoyed at a gift of $5000 which made his dream of an astronomical observatory a reality, and thereafter he peppered Hill with invitations "to visit the observatory and do a little star-gazing." Letters from young men who needed money to finish college were carefully investigated. A student at Dickinson College, in Pennsylvania, who asked for a loan of $300, turned out to be the best orator and one of the best students in his class. The loan was paid off, on time and with interest, along with the gratifying remark that "in after years, perhaps I will be able to return your favor by assisting some young man, circumstanced as I was." Another supplicant, also investigated, turned out to be a lazy, whining hypochondriac; his professor offered to give Hill the names of several truly deserving students.[31]

Sometimes the calls for help were more dramatic. One afternoon in April 1886 Hill was handed an urgent telegram from Sauk Rapids: "We need ten doctors at once; we are totally destroyed." A tornado had touched down. It had hit the Masonic Cemetery, swept away a farmhouse with all thirty members of a wedding party inside, and left a swath of devastation. Sixty were dead and no one knew how many injured. Within hours all the doctors who could be spared in the Twin Cities were on a special train, heading for the disaster area. By the time the relief work was over, Hill had given $5000 and had secured other gifts from as far away as New York. J. S. Kennedy sent $1000.[32]

Sometimes small gifts were repaid many times over by the unconscious eloquence of the recipient. An industrious pioneer woman, who had dutifully converted from Methodism to Congregationalism to strengthen the little church they were organizing in Dakota Territory, wrote to ask Hill to help them buy a bell. Fearful that such an expenditure would strike a man of business as frivolous, she explained: "We know that, dwelling as you do in the midst of a great city, where bells are almost an annoyance, you can scarcely realize how a small church bell will be appreciated out here in this little prarie [sic] town." The bell, a seventy-five pounder, was soon on its way. It was, in fact, a very familiar kind of plea to Hill, for in those days new communities were springing up on the prairie every week. His procedure was always the same. The closest station agent for the Manitoba road was asked to investigate. If the new church was still in the talking stage, he made a pledge. When the roof was on, the contribution of $25, $50, or $100—rarely more—was forthcoming.[33]

And always the past came back with a rush when he least expected it. Eighteen years after his memorable trip by dogsled to the Red River Valley, he received an almost unreadable note. It was from the half-breed guide whose dislocated shoulder he had set and who had sold him his lead sled dog:

> You tuck the stage and when you was going to get in you asked me to buy my dog and I ask you what you want to do with it you toled me it was for your little boy and I gave it to you. You tank me for the dog and you said when the care track would be maid [i.e. when the railroad was built to that point] if I wanted to go and visit you said you would give a raid [ride] free. There I taught when you had said that I have surve you well. Now I would like you would do me that survice now to go and see my children and you all so before I die, me and my wife. . . .[34]

As the railroad claimed more and more of Hill's time, it was difficult to carry even the minimum burden of civic leadership which his position demanded of him, but he made his influence felt when it counted most. He vigorously encouraged William T. Booth of the New York Life Insurance Company to build a large regional office building in St. Paul, and the handsome structure, with its striking bronze eagles modeled by Augustus Saint-Gaudens, was a downtown landmark for seventy-five years. The ponderous building which for many years housed the St. Paul *Pioneer Press* likewise received his enthusiastic support. In the fall of 1885, Kennedy, who worried about Hill's refusal to take a vacation, urged him to remain at the farm at least until cold weather, but by October 1887 he was finding less and less time for North Oaks. "I am too busy day and evening to finish my work," Hill complained to Thorne; "I am not able to go out, and I will be glad when we are all at home in town." He had wanted to visit England for so long, he could not remember when he had first started making plans. But from 1884, when he regretfully declined the Earl of Latham's invitation to visit his famous breeding farms, to 1889, when he refused George Stephen's offer of a trip through the Highlands of Scotland, it was always "next year."

Meanwhile, he cheerfully arranged junkets for others, sometimes promising that he would go along, then, at the last minute, deciding to stay at work. In the summer of 1886 he bundled New York politico Smith M. Weed, the Thornes, Mamie, and even Mr. and Mrs. Kennedy into a private car for a trip out west, then strode out of St. Paul's Union Station, across Third Street, and back to his desk.[35]

V

Boards of directors took their duties seriously in the 1880s. Whether they had financial interests in the corporations they directed, as they frequently did, or donated their talents in recognition of the fact that others were doing the same for enterprises in which they were heavy investors, these men expected to participate in all important decisions. Of the seven directors of the Manitoba road in the mid-1880s, only Hill and Kennedy were executives of the company, but they as well as Stephen and Smith were major holders of its securities, and two more—Samuel Thorne and Marshall Field—were substantial stockholders. All of the day-to-day decisions of the company were made by Hill, and important policies generally originated with him by reason of his obviously superior knowledge of the company's situation. He could not well forget, however, that six highly successful and superbly talented businessmen were passing frank and independent judgment on his every move.

By 1888 the physical surroundings in which Hill would carry out most of the rest of his life's work had been established. For over two years he had watched from his office window as the new St. Paul, Minneapolis & Manitoba Railway office building slowly rose on Third Street, across from the St. Paul Union Station. "I notice that some of the piles being driven under the foundations are going in faster than others," he wrote the contractor, reminding him that in such soft places piles should be placed just that much closer together. He kept three assistants busy. William Secombe had left to manage the Mille Lacs Lumber Company (which Hill had found on his hands after disaster had overtaken the enterprises of Kennedy's nephew, Andrew Tod), to be replaced by W. A. Stephens as Hill's personal secretary and clerk. As his affairs became more complicated, he hired the efficient, personable Charles H. Benedict as general administrative assistant, while Hill's voluminous correspondence as president of the railroad was handled by F. L. Moffett.[36]

Past associations were receding rapidly. Near the end of 1883 he had received his copy of the document which formally dissolved "George Stephen & Associates." He saw little of Norman Kittson, who spent much time with his beloved race horses at "Erdenheim," his breeding farm near Philadelphia. When Kittson's wife died while on a trip to New York, Hill was saddened to see the profound effect on the old man. "He is quite feeble . . . and I am afraid he will not last long," he wrote their long-time mutual friend, Charles Cavileer, customs official at Pembina, and enclosed passes so that Cavileer and his wife could visit Kittson one more time. Since his Canadian friends were plunged deep into the affairs of the Canadian Pacific, it had become a rare event when Stephen or Smith attended a board meeting or even the annual meeting. Stephen, for his part, was glad that Hill had the counsel of a man like Kennedy, whom he hoped would overcome his nervous debility, for "he is too good a fellow to lose." Stephen and Smith offered to resign from the Manitoba board whenever Hill decided that an unmanageable conflict of interest existed, but made it clear that they wanted to keep their stock in the "blessed old road," and that they thought it would be bad public relations for them to resign at that particular time. Despite the grudge that Kennedy had developed against Stephen, he tended to agree. So Hill and Kennedy limped along from year to year with a board which could barely summon a quorum and which required one or the other repeatedly to make the wearying trip between St. Paul and New York.[37]

By 1886 Hill was ready to demand the resignations of Stephen and Smith, but the Canadians hung onto their positions with the Manitoba road. At the time, their reasons were far from clear, for it seemed that Stephen, then rounding out his career as the head of one of the greatest business enterprises in the British Empire, would find little interest in the Manitoba road. But the frustrations of Canadian politics, and the exciting future which opened for the Manitoba road after 1886, made Stephen reluctant to sever the old ties. Toward the end of 1886, Hill was angered to learn, almost by chance, that Stephen was leaving for a year's residence in England. He dashed off a grumpy letter to his friend: "I have to ask that you will, before you sail, send me your resignation. . . . [But if] you have the least reason for preferring to remain no one will be more ready to do his share and get along the best we can than myself." Then, cooling down a bit, he decided to send the letter, unsealed, to Kennedy in New York, with instructions to read it and, if he, Thorne, and D. Willis James approved, to deliver it to Stephen before he sailed. They did indeed approve, but Stephen, who had already boarded the Cunarder *Etruria,* played for time. "Will reply from the other side," he wired Hill, as the gangplank was being raised. The reply never came, Stephen remained a member of the board, and Hill was soon glad that he did.[38]

The first "outsider" to join the Manitoba board had been Marshall Field, the spectacularly successful Chicago merchant, and innovator of the modern department store. Field had been an early investor in the railroad, whose performance impressed him deeply. Hill realized that Field would not be a very active director, and confessed to Kennedy that he had reservations about appointing someone "merely on account of personal grounds or public standing," but he felt, nevertheless, that a strong Midwestern personality like Field's would be a "real acquisition to the board." It proved difficult to get Field to come to St. Paul for board meetings, however, and when Field thoughtlessly joined the board of the Rock Island Railroad, a potential antagonist of the Manitoba road, Hill eased him out.[39]

Thus, frequent shuttling back and forth between New York and St. Paul was necessary. There was much besides business to entice Hill to New York, not the least being the annual dinner at Delmonico's of the St. Andrew's Society, of which Kennedy was president; but there was little to bring Kennedy and the others to St. Paul. As a result, financial decisions tended to be delegated to the executive committee, which was composed of directors resident in New York, and the consequences were not always satisfactory or pleasant. Kennedy insisted in the spring of 1884 that new appointments be made. Noting that James Roosevelt, one of the trustees of the Manitoba's mortgages, had declined membership (perhaps because he wanted to spend more time at Hyde Park with his young wife and three-year-old son, Franklin D.), he proposed Samuel Thorne. A genial man with a shrewd head for business, Thorne had been an investor in the Manitoba road since he had bought a large block of receiver's debentures from Kennedy in the exciting days of 1878. He knew the Manitoba road's situation intimately; he had been a breeder of shorthorn cattle; he ran a small railroad in New Brunswick Province, which endeared him to a would-be salmon fisherman; and he delighted in bird hunting. Hill was greatly pleased when Thorne agreed to serve. D. Willis James, the dignified Anglo-American who had made a fortune in iron and steel, was no great social asset; his major avocation was the furthering of religious education, which was to culminate in a large bequest to the Union Theological Seminary. But he had a mind for railroad finance, which, along with his exalted view of business ethics, made him one of the most valuable directors the Manitoba road ever had. James would be a godsend to Kennedy, who felt the need for moral support as the Manitoba road's growing capital demands had to be satisfied in the increasingly uncertain financial climate. Hill and Kennedy, however, continued to bear the major part of the burden after 1884, and they continued to grumble to each other that it made little sense for them to work so hard when, as Hill said, "it would be far more profitable for me if I was at liberty to employ my knowledge and capital for my own benefit." [40]

By August 1884 Hill and his colleagues were congratulating themselves that the Manitoba road had come through the May panic so well. The reduction of the dividend, so unpopular at first, now seemed to have been everybody's idea, while Hill was not slow to take credit for the timely pause in the Manitoba road's ambitious expansion program. Even so, isolated as he was in St. Paul without another director to keep him company, and with financial decisions tending to center in New York, Hill's sense of insecurity grew. He felt a mounting need to assert his authority, and it was reflected in displays of temper. When a tipsy newspaperman blundered into his business car in the

TWO IMPORTANT NEW YORK
FRIENDS IN THE 1880s:

Samuel Thorne. Burlington Northern.   D. Willis James. Burlington Northern.

Minneapolis depot one night, Hill ejected him so violently that the
man admitted that he had been "partly sobered by the shock you gave
me." A few weeks later he arrived at North Oaks Farm about 7:30 p.m.
to discover that the hall floor was on fire. A hasty investigation disclosed that the builder, contrary to Hill's explicit instructions, had
notched the beams ten inches into the brickwork of the chimney, and
"the whole was a mass of charcoal." "Find the carpenter," he fumed to
the contractor, "and if he is still working for you, discharge him." [41]

That winter he lost his temper with the man who was least likely to
put up with it: D. Willis James. The executive committee, contrary to
what he thought the board had agreed upon, had listed some bonds
on the stock exchange even though they did not intend to sell them at
that time. James was the only director who had not quit New York for
warmer latitudes, and he felt Hill's wrath:

> I have always tried to shape my official business with the Board so as to
> accommodate them most fully, and I feel many times I have to administer
> the important affairs of the company without any board, and unless I can

feel that I have the full cooperation and confidence of the Board I will either let some one else do this work [or will change the by-laws to] compel all meetings of the board to be held within this state. . . .[42]

James gave him the same kind of shock treatment Hill had given the drunk:

I feel greatly surprised and much hurt at the tone of your remarks. . . . I reserve my decision as to what action I ought to take, in view of this remark, until Mr. Kennedy's return, but if it was not for the illness of his wife, I should call him back at once.

To delay listing would lead to the implication that the Directors were holding back . . . for stock jobbing purposes, or that the Manitoba Road was being run on the principles advocated by Jay Gould & confederates.

I may say, perhaps under present circumstances, that since I have been officially connected with the Company, that my *sole* effort has been to build up its credit and standing; there has been much, very much, to undo on account of the prejudice arising from the *very foolish* 80% Bond Dividend and also, from the Company's intimate relations to the speculative and stock jobbing Canadian Pacific.

I have labored steadily to bring up the credit of the Manitoba Co. while my connection with it has resulted in a very large pecuniary loss to myself while of course to you it has yielded a vast fortune. . . .[43]

No one had spoken so bluntly to Hill in a long time, and it is probable that no one ever did so again. He may have written James a personal letter of apology, especially since Thorne told him he was clearly in the wrong. In any event, he was soon in New York to make peace in person, and a year later James was protesting his full confidence in Hill: "I have no fears about our road so long as *you* are at the helm." [44]

Hill's relations with his business friends was almost as much social as otherwise. George Clark offered Hill two shares in the Currituck Shooting Club, an exclusive duck blind in North Carolina, which had belonged to sugar magnate Henry O. Havemeyer. It was a sure sign that he had entered the most exclusive of the Eastern financial circles. Three or four weeks of shooting at Currituck between Thanksgiving and Christmas was the custom, and Hill actually managed to get there for a couple of years. He showed up the first year with a set of expensive, handmade decoys and 200 of the finest Havana cigars, and barely managed to get back to St. Paul in time for Christmas. By 1888 he had accepted membership in the salmon-fishing club on New Brunswick's Restigouche River—it cost him $3750 plus an annual assessment of

$350—and William Rockefeller had sent him a certificate for one share in the ultra-exclusive Jekyl Island resort off the coast of Georgia. He quickly earned the reputation as the most indefatigable songster at Currituck. One of his favorites was something called "The Oratorio of the Deluge," which all agreed was appropriate for a rainy day. Dr. John T. Metcalfe, private physician to Thorne, and a witty septuagenarian, joined Hill and Thorne in shooting prairie chickens in Dakota, during which he and Hill practiced "Scotch songs." [45]

H. W. Cannon, meanwhile, finally induced him to accept a seat on the board of the Chase National Bank, alongside Calvin S. Brice, John G. Moore, and Edward Tuck. George Stephen's lawyer, John W. Sterling, became a valued counselor and a good friend. This lifelong bachelor, whose talent for making and saving money ultimately redounded to the spectacular benefit of Yale University, smoothed over more than one dispute between Hill and his Canadian friends. The beginning of an important London connection were made in 1888 when young Gaspard Farrer, of H. S. Lefevre Company, wrote to ask if Hill would allow him to try his hand at placing the bonds which Kuhn, Loeb & Company had declined. And always there were the junkets to arrange, a chore which Hill genuinely enjoyed. Late one summer Frank Thomson wired that he was coming west with a hunting party which would include General Philip Sheridan. Hill smiled at the Eastern tenderfoot's plaintive request: "One thing I wish to avoid is the 'local gunner,' who usually drives out with the gentlemen from the east merely to show them the country and ends by shooting all the birds off the end of his own gun." [46]

VI

Sitting at the visitor's desk in the New York offices of the Manitoba road, James J. Hill penned a frank letter to Kennedy on the subject of the railroad's need for strong alliances. "The personal burden is too heavy," he wrote, "and we will never find it lighter as long as [the ownership] is held as at present." On that hot day in July 1885 Kennedy was in Boston, seeking an infusion of Eastern equity capital that would permanently strengthen the Manitoba road. For more than two years the two men had been maneuvering closer and closer to the group of Bostonians, led by John Murray Forbes, who controlled the Chicago, Burlington & Quincy Railroad and who represented the most venerable fountain of capital from which the nation's Western railroads had been financed.[47]

Hill and Kennedy had known from the beginning that sooner or later the stock of the Manitoba road would need to be spread over a larger number of persons who would hold it for investment purposes and who would not be tempted to throw it on the market whenever it rose above par on the stock exchange. Furthermore, as an operating man, Hill realized that before long the confused, unstable, overbuilt railroad situation between St. Paul and Chicago would force the Manitoba road to make a dependable and lasting alliance with one or another of the powerful railroads between the two cities, while still maintaining its own independence. The Forbes group offered the best chance to achieve these two objectives, and Hill had missed no chance to cultivate the interest of the careful, slow-moving Bostonians. When Charles E. Perkins, hard-driving president of the Burlington, rode with a party of Boston people over the Manitoba road during a trip through the Northwest in 1883, Hill felt that they had been pleased with what they saw. "Every one of these people who go over the property come back delighted," he bragged to Kennedy, and in this case he was not misled. The Manitoba road, Perkins reported to Forbes, was "probably the snuggest and best of the properties lying beyond St. Paul, [with] every mile of it in the best kind of wheat country." Forbes himself spent a day with Hill in St. Paul the next year, and the year after that he was back for a second, longer look.[48]

In 1885 the Burlington interests committed themselves to a strong role in the Northwest: they finally decided to build their long-rumored line from Chicago to the Twin Cities. Projected as a well-built, double-track line which would hug the east bank of the Mississippi for most of the distance, it was to be built by a subsidary company, the Chicago, Burlington & Northern, which was led by an ambitious, aggressive president, A. E. Touzalin. By mid-1886 Touzalin had rushed to completion a railroad which would meet Hill's own high standards for low operating costs and which would eventually become one of the brightest gems in the Hill railroad diadem. Hill made the Burlington's entry into the Twin Cities easy, leasing to the new line valuable acreage for freight yards and granting it trackage rights over the Manitoba road's line between St. Paul and Minneapolis. Hill's faith in the project, reflected in his open-market investment of nearly half a million dollars in the new road's securities, eventually yielded him a handsome profit.[49]

Meanwhile, the Forbes group had made discreet inquiries, both in New York and in Montreal: would the major stockholders of the Manitoba road be willing to sell them a large interest, perhaps as much as 20,000 shares? Neither Hill nor Kennedy had any doubt that this was the break they had been looking for. Kennedy wrote in April:

> I will be glad to join you heartily in concluding a trade and I think it will be a relief to both you and me to have it done, for it will relieve us from care and responsibility which . . . has been burdensome and wearing, and both you and I can turn our time to better account . . .

And as negotiations approached the critical stage, Hill observed:

> I am quite sure our earnings will be greater the coming fall than ever before. Still, I am confident that the policy talked over by ourselves so many times and always with one conclusion is the only thing that will prove permanently satisfactory. . . . I think that with the following that will in a short time become interested in the property and the direct benefit of strong association there can be no question as to the wisest course. . . .[50]

Neither man had ever come up against such a group of perfectionists as the Bostonians. Although every mortgage of the old St. Paul & Pacific Railroad had been foreclosed in open court, and every requirement of the New York Stock Exchange had been met, the Yankees had their own ideas of legitimacy, and they insisted on having their own lawyers go over the voluminous records. Both men suspected that Forbes was stalling for time, that he wanted to get a look at one more semi-annual earnings statement by the Manitoba road. "We must just be patient and wait," Kennedy wrote wearily; "there is no use pressing them." There was also a question of representation of the Bostonians on the Manitoba board. One seat could be made available easily enough by asking Marshall Field for his (Field had not yet been eased out), but the Yankees wanted two. Perhaps, however, if a seat on the board and an executive post in St. Paul as well could be offered to Henry D. Minot, that might be satisfactory, at least for the present. Minot, brilliant scion of an old Boston family, at seventeen the published author of a book on ornithology, nephew of John Murray Forbes, and a lawyer, had investigated the Manitoba road in 1884. His report was only one of a number he had made on Western railroad properties which marked him as eminently qualified for the post. Kennedy had strong misgivings—Minot was, after all, only twenty-six, and Kennedy believed that there was much about business which

THE BOSTON ALLIES:

ABOVE LEFT John Murray Forbes, about 70, in the 1880s, when Hill first knew him. Burlington Northern.

ABOVE Charles E. Perkins at "The Apple Trees," his home in Burlington, Iowa. About 1890. Burlington Northern.

LEFT Henry D. Minot. Burlington Northern.

could be learned only with the passage of time—but he went along with the idea, and before the summer was over the big step had been taken. Still fiercely independent, the Manitoba road was now recognized by everyone as a staunch ally of the Burlington.[51]

The healthful effects of the stock sale began to be felt almost immediately. There were thirty-six new names on the list of stockholders, Nichols reported to Hill, and Minot had undertaken on his own to place an additional 2000 shares with conservative investors who were his personal friends. Minot's perspicacity, and his quick transference of loyalty to the Manitoba road (which he professed at length to Hill) made a good first impression on Kennedy. When Minot urgently advised them not to sell any more stock in the St. Paul & Duluth Railroad, the Manitoba's link with Duluth, until the intentions of other railroads who jointly owned it became apparent, Kennedy had to admit that they had been saved from a major blunder. "The more I see of him the better I like him," he wrote Hill, but the honeymoon did not last long.[52]

If he had not been so impatient to get ahead, and if fate had not had such a cruel end in store for him, Henry Minot might have become the leading figure in Northwestern railroading in the twentieth century. As it was, Hill made good use of him during his four years with the Manitoba road. He often sent him into the field, where he scouted out opportunities, aggressive as well as defensive, to build or acquire branch lines. The expansion into southwestern Minnesota and Iowa owed much to his work, as would the extension to Duluth. He helped to lay the groundwork for the Manitoba road's advance into Montana. Eager to tackle the administrative organization of the railroad, which had never been set down on paper, he drafted a "code" of operations for which Hill had great hopes, as the railroad became larger and harder to run. Minot repeatedly vowed his loyalty to Hill, but never missed an opportunity to advance his own cause. "Your principle is right, to put before a young man the largest incentives that you fairly can. . . . I foresee no difficulty in our working together, in good faith and fellowship to the same ends. I mean my allegiance to the Manitoba property . . . to be wholly undivided. Whenever the matter of the Second Vice Presidency is formally settled, please let me have notice." [53]

There was a great deal of genuine affection between the two men. Minot's brilliance and his extraordinary motivation pleased Hill, but it was Minot's vision which impressed him the most. It was what Hill had found lacking in Manvel, and what he knew he would have to find in a subordinate before he could seriously consider—some day— turning the railroad over to him. Minot thought not in terms of today or tomorrow, but next year and the years afterward. But he had faults that many found glaring. One was his cocksureness, stemming from the social, economic, and intellectual security which had been his birthright, and which was bound to irritate those who did not have it or were afraid to reveal that they did not. Another was his outspokenness. He wanted to get all of his thoughts out in the open, and he frequently made fatuous and insulting remarks. Kennedy must have frowned when the young man informed him that "there is already here an abundance of work for me to do, and . . . Mr. Hill and I will have our hands very full."

It was an age which laid great stress on personal loyalties, and Minot tended to belittle those around him. He tried to undermine Kennedy's faith in Charles H. Benedict, Hill's chief clerk, who was investigating the situation in Montana, when Kennedy knew perfectly well that H. W. Cannon, for whom Benedict had worked in New York, thought highly of him. He sneered at George Stephen, calling him "the honorable baronet," and pressed Hill to replace him on the board with a Boston man. Kennedy was furious when Minot tried, as Kennedy believed, to alienate the senior officers of the company by insinuating that Hill was withholding information from the New York directors. "There have been details that I had prepared to communicate," he wrote Kennedy, "but that Mr. Hill thought better to withhold. . . . Possibly Mr. Hill's habits of reticence and of independent thought and action prevent him from appreciating your demands." [54]

It probably would not have surprised Kennedy to know that it was his own job Minot was after. "I think with proper persuasion he would willingly retire at any time," Minot wrote Hill, "or . . . at the next annual meeting would give up his own place for me, should you approve and desire." Minot's handling of the Mason City & Fort Dodge matter was another opportunity for him to run afoul of Kennedy. Hill was determined to build this ninety-mile railroad, which had nothing to do with the Manitoba road, to connect his Iowa coal properties with a better route into the Twin Cities despite mounting evidence that Iowa coal had little future. He pressed Kennedy, Thorne, Knox, and Cannon to subscribe to the bonds. He turned the task of arranging the financial structure over to Minot, whose efforts to mask the true sponsorship of the project Kennedy found amateurish. Furthermore, Kennedy was convinced, Minot and his friends at Lee, Higginson & Company were aiming at an underwriting profit, which made no sense at all since the bonds were being bought by the principals in the company. Soon Hill received a twenty-three-page letter from Kennedy which condemned Minot in terms more intemperate than Hill had ever known Kennedy to use before. [55]

Hill remained loyal to Minot, however, and soon found a way to insulate him from Kennedy's wrath. He was enough of a psychologist to see that Kennedy was taking a highly emotional view of the situa-

tion. Vastly rich, yet childless, Kennedy resented the thought that
strangers would all too soon be taking over his life's work. He had
revealed the same resentment of his nephew when Tod took over the
banking business in 1883. Grateful as he was for the interposition of
Boston financial interests, he resented them, too, because John S. Kennedy was a leader of that breed of New York financial men who had
helped eclipse Boston in financial matters, and he had a low opinion
of Lee, Higginson & Company. "They are not the kind of people we
can negotiate with," he told Hill, "neither have they the connections
in Europe that are necessary to enable us to accomplish our purposes." [56] Most of all, Kennedy was contemptuous of Minot's compul-
sion to put things down on paper. In the past a good businessman had
always been one who divulged as little about his affairs as possible,
Kennedy believed, and he saw no reason to conclude that that would
not be true in the future:

> We [the executive committee] are all in doubt as to the propriety of bring-
> ing the matters [detailed expansion plans] before the board, but think
> they should be dealt with according to your own good judgment. You
> know we will ratify whatever you think it best to do . . . but you also
> know the trouble that may grow out of our spreading our intentions
> regarding our next two or three years work on our minutes now. In many
> cases "ignorance is bliss. . . ."

> For whose benefit have they [a digest of Manitoba road documents] been
> prepared? None of the present officers of the Co. or its directors want
> them or need them. . . . I am no means satisfied (judging by past occur-
> rences) that our young friend is entirely disinterested in getting up and
> publishing these documents. . . .

> He has been a fraud from the beginning, and an intolerable nui-
> sance. . . .[57]

It was good that it was someone else's season to be disgruntled. Hill
himself felt it had been a good year's work, and he was willing to take
the thin with the thick. Four years earlier he had been an unknown
operator of a regional railroad which, the know-it-alls had said, would
soon be gobbled up by one of the really important railroads of the
Northwest. He and a few loyal colleagues had gone to work to make it
"the snuggest and best" of them all. They had built a management
and a board of directors whose strength matched the physical condition of the railroad, and had cemented an alliance which overnight
had made the Manitoba road securities the bluest of blue chips in the

Northwest. He himself had graduated into the innermost circles of Eastern finance, and had attained the stature he needed to lead the Manitoba road's great advance to the Pacific. And he had gained the counsel of one of the nation's oldest and most respected financial minds, who, like Hill, smelled great trouble ahead. From Buzzards Bay, in the glories of a New England autumn, John Murray Forbes wrote him his fears:

> We are very scary here and some think the storm will be worse when the next big railroad gets sick, but if this is to come, is not then the time when strong people ought to be able to buy? If there is no hurry, please telegraph me and say, "No hurry," then leave me to my yacht sailing. . . ." [58]

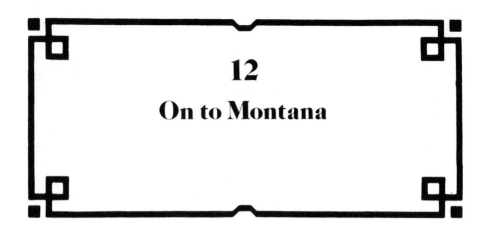

12

On to Montana

These lands, which may be classified as semi-arid, are better fitted for growing wheat than any lands I have ever seen. . . . There is more danger from too much moisture than from too little.

—Paris Gibson

This new country bids fair to surpass the Red River Valley in the quality of its wheat and the yield per acre, which is something I never expected to see in any section of the country.

—James J. Hill

It is always a good thing to have good soil and water under a railroad.

—John Murray Forbes

I

Relaxing at his big rolltop desk, James J. Hill wrote to his friend Frank Thomson of the good times he was planning for them. The year of 1888, then just three days old, offered a chance for some of the finest hunting either of them had ever seen. In Montana, to which the Manitoba road had been extended the previous year, "we have a country where the white breast has never been disturbed, plenty of ducks, geese, & brant. Elk, moose, and deer in the valleys and bighorn mountain goats & grizzly bear in the mountains, with first class trout fishing in the streams." And, he added proudly, "plenty of the best quality coal, iron, limestone, lead, copper, silver and gold—and all in as fine an agricultural country as there is on the continent." [1]

Hill had been interested in the Land of the Big Sky from the very beginning of his involvement in railroads. While still a young man on the St. Paul levee in the 1860s, he had watched the adventurers on their way to what was soon to become Montana Territory. They had expected to strike it rich digging for gold, but the placer mining boom lasted only a few years and by 1870 Montana probably had fewer residents than it had had five years earlier. A few miners remained behind to raise sheep and some cattle, but as long as Montana's major settlements were the Indian reservations and the army forts which watched over them, and as long as transportation over the formidable distances was by wagon train or by navigation of the tedious, treacherous Missouri River, Montana had little to recommend it. By 1880, however, the Union Pacific Railroad had pushed a narrow-gauge line northward into Montana from its main line in Utah, and the Northern Pacific was soon to pass through Helena, in the southern part of the Territory, on its way to the Pacific. Coal, copper, and silver had been discovered in abundance, and Montana began to stir with great expectations.

In 1883 the Manitoba road, ostensibly in deference to its "protocol" with the Northern Pacific, but more because of the rich opportunities it faced in the Red River Valley and eastern Dakota, had ended its westward march at Devil's Lake, Dakota Territory, eighty miles west of the Red. By then Hill was already personally involved in the future of Montana. Two long-time friends who combined their knowledge of the country with good business sense influenced him strongly. One was Martin Maginnis, Montana's Territorial delegate to Congress until the election of 1884, who had long been interested in the country farther west and who was to remain in Washington for several years more to serve Dakota and Montana as lobbyist. Such service was vital, for extensive Indian reservations had been established in this remote area years before, and the nation's promises to these people would somehow have to be redeemed before emigrants in great numbers could take up lands there. Meanwhile Maginnis saw to it that his friend in St. Paul did not forget the rich opportunities that were opening up in west central Montana between Great Falls, to the north, and Butte, to the south, as the region's mineral wealth began to attract the interest of Eastern financiers.[2]

The other was Paris Gibson, Montana's leading citizen. It was Gibson who did most to stimulate Hill's interest in the Territory in the early 1880s. This rather staid, colorless sheep raiser, a man whom ebullient men like Hill did not find very stimulating, was nevertheless almost a fanatic on the future of Montana. By the time depression hit in the 1870s, Hill had known Gibson for several years. Gibson, who had been a flourishing miller in Minneapolis, was ruined by the depression, and he emigrated to the virgin lands to the west but he and Hill kept up their correspondence. From the moment Hill and his associates took over the St. Paul & Pacific, Gibson had seen in these men and their new railroad power the means of unlocking the potential wealth of northern Montana. In 1881 Hill, his interest in Montana strengthened by constant letters, asked Gibson to find out all he could about the territorial laws as they related to railroad charters. "I may have to ask you to get up a local company in Montana," he wrote, "and will ask you to kindly treat this as entirely in confidence." [3]

Gibson replied that he was confident that "no road can ever be built into Montana as cheaply as by the Northern or Milk River route," and he even noted that in the northern section there was a certain mountain pass which would be "very valuable to you in case you should wish to push westward to Oregon and Washington." A few weeks later he wrote again, saying he believed that the territory south of Fort Benton (in northern Montana) could be more effectively reached from the north, rather than from the south, where the Northern Pacific and the Union Pacific already had lines. On these opinions, supplemented by shrewd observations of his own, Hill built his strategy.[4]

The water power at the falls of the Missouri River, Gibson and Hill agreed, was the key to future industrial development of the backbone of Montana. They joined forces to buy up large acreages of land around Great Falls, where, they were convinced, water power and townsite companies would sooner or later prove to be highly profitable enterprises. Gibson borrowed freely from Hill, as much as $15,000 at a time, and by 1886 Gibson had invested $72,000 and Hill $37,000. Gibson bought up land as it became available, but as rumors of what he and his powerful friend were up to leaked out it became harder to do so. One choice parcel remained out of reach until its owner shot a man in a barroom brawl—then he needed money for a lawyer. The land was soon part of the Gibson-Hill enterprise.[5]

But when it came to building a railroad to Montana, Hill repeatedly dampened Gibson's hopes. In September 1883, after a talk with Henry Villard, who was then completing the Northern Pacific's line to the Pacific, Gibson wrote a troubled letter to Hill, who replied coldly:

> Mr. Villard is quite right in saying that it is not our intention to build at present a line of railroad to Montana. . . . That country is now served by

the Northern Pacific Ry and there certainly is not business enough to warrant this Company in undertaking the construction of another line. I note what you state as to the effect our securing a charter from the Milk River Valley to the Great Falls would have on the town property, but you must bear in mind that my investment at Great Falls is an individual one with which this Company has nothing to do. . . .[6]

A year later, at the height of the panic of 1884, Hill was even more discouraging. He would have to have far more information about the country before he could entertain any ideas of building a railroad—which, he noted, would be unusually costly between Helena and Butte. "As far as the Grand [sic] Falls are concerned," he remarked, "they must 'stand on their own bottom' entirely except that I am willing to do anything I can fairly to give that location all the advantages of a railway if it can be done on a safe business basis." [7]

It was not Paris Gibson who was to be Hill's chief partner, but a big, genial, two-fisted man who spent as little time as possible behind his desk at the Montana National Bank of Helena. Charles A. Broadwater, president of the bank, was a shrewd businessman who was equally at ease out on the range, and he was an important factor in the outcome of the struggle between various interests to develop the region between Fort Benton and Butte. His reputation for settling unpleasant matters with his fists (as when the secretary of the Montana Central refused to accept the fact that he had been fired) did not cloud his reputation for financial solidity. At the time of his death (1889), Hill estimated his worth at $1,000,000. In 1884 Gibson and Broadwater finally persuaded Hill to come out to Montana. In particular need of a holiday at that moment, he was delighted with the country, and no less pleased with the hunting of prairie chickens. Long hours in the saddle and evenings around the campfire presented opportunities to talk about Montana which Broadwater did not miss. Hill resolved to return before winter with Sam Thorne and other influential Easterners; he felt sure that they would find the prairie chickens inducement enough.[8]

"Your recent trip has, as predicted, set the gossip going," Broadwater wrote Hill on his return to St. Paul, enclosing clippings from the Helena newspapers. The clippings, Hill replied, "show a lively imagination on the part of the editor, and a disposition to build largely on small hopes. . . . I cannot forget the many beautiful scenes of the few days spent with you in Montana, and I am more than ever impressed with the future of your territory." A month later he thanked Broad-

MONTANA ALLIES:

Paris Gibson. Montana Historical So-   Charles A. Broadwater. Montana His-
ciety.   torical Society.

water for suggesting the name, Montana Central, for the railroad they
were turning over in their minds at the time, but once again cautioned him to keep quiet about their plans. Meanwhile he had a local
Montana civil engineer make a quick barometric survey of the rugged
segment between Helena and Butte and learned, as he had suspected,
that several expensive cuts would be necessary to reduce the maximum grades to the low levels that he insisted upon and which, indeed, would be necessary for the heavy ore trains which would use
the line.[9]

II

"It will take two and a half days rail to Calgary; four days easy wagon
travel to Helena with relays, and two days rail to St. Paul," Hill explained to Sam Thorne that September. Thorne was eager to rid the
prairies of some chickens, and dallied just long enough to convince
himself that a friend of theirs, investment banker George Clark, was
not going to tear himself away from business to join them. By the end

of the trip Hill had done much to assure himself of the enthusiastic support of moneyed Easterners when the time came to proceed in Montana. One thing particularly impressed them: of the whole area northwest of the Twin Cities, it was Montana that was most likely to have coal of any real industrial value. Hill was having the best professional geologist investigate the deposits, and he and his Montana friends were convinced that, if the coal proved valuable for smelting the ores of the region, Great Falls' future was assured. "With a railway to the Falls and cheap coal, I see no reason why it is not the cheapest and best place in Montana to reduce the ores of that whole country," Hill told Broadwater.[10]

No less a person than Professor J. S. Newberry of the Columbia University School of Mines was retained to study the coal around Sand Coulee, near Great Falls, that summer. By October his thirteen-page report was in Hill's hands, and it was enthusiastic. The coal was definitely lignite (a "brown coal," somewhere between peat and bituminous coal), "but far better than the average of the coals to which it belongs; . . . the amount of sulphur is not greater than the average of sulphur in the Illinois and Iowa coals." But that was not all. The ores of the Red Mountain district at Great Falls, which Hill had also asked Newberry to take a look at, would produce "a very large and constant revenue" from gold and silver if sophisticated machinery and competent management were applied. The picture began to take definite shape in Hill's mind: coal, high-grade metallic ores, and a railroad to bring them together, the whole to be linked up with the Manitoba road, although not necessarily immediately. The professor agreed, and he asked that he be permitted to take his fee in the stock of such an enterprise. The studied pessimism which Hill had been expressing to Gibson and Broadwater about the coal deposits melted away. The negative opinion of Hamilton Browne, whom Hill had sent out with Newberry, and who was still stubbornly devoted to Iowa coal, was brushed aside. Meanwhile, Broadwater insisted that the Northern Pacific was their enemy, and urged that there was no time to lose:

> Jim, there is no doubt in my mind that he [Oakes of the Northern Pacific] has been double dealing all the time in this matter. . . . If you agree with me I think the sooner you have your atty draw up the papers the better. The Secy of the Interior is a friend of mine and I can leave them with him privately with the understanding that they are not to be placed on file unless other papers should be handed in. In that case ours would be filed first. . . .[11]

"Broad" rode back and forth through the hills around Red Mountain, picking up options wherever they could be had. The Christmas season slowed him down considerably. "I have the promise of the bond on the Chadwick and Gilmore property," he wrote Hill early in 1885, "but up to this time have been unable to get it drawn as they have both been drunk ever since Christmas." Hill tried to keep the damper on Broadwater's enthusiasm. "Remember always that bad news will not disappoint me half as much as it would yourself," he warned. But by spring he was making no effort to conceal his own enthusiasm from Kennedy. "It looks as if there was a chance to make not less than $3 million on an investment of $2 million," he reported after a visit from Broadwater. By the end of the year it was clear that either the Northern Pacific, building northward from Helena, or the Canadian Pacific, building southward to meet an independently chartered road at the boundary, would preempt their position unless they moved soon.[12]

What held Hill back? He was determined that his Montana operations, no matter how divorced from the affairs of the Manitoba road they might be in their inception, would fit into his long-range plans for the railroad, which would continue to be his chief interest. The Montana Central, envisioned as a heavy-duty road from Great Falls to Butte, and closely allied with water power, townsite, and coal and mineral holdings, would nevertheless wither on the vine or, less poetically, be gobbled by the Northern Pacific unless it could connect with an independent outlet to the east. Obviously, this outlet was to be the Manitoba road, which was to be extended some 800 miles from Devil's Lake to Great Falls in a gigantic burst of energy. Astride its path, however, lay the Indian reservations of Fort Berthold, in Dakota, and Forts Peck, Belknap, and Assiniboine in Montana.

Hill and nearly everybody else knew that, sooner or later, Congress was going to pass a law granting a railroad right-of-way through these areas. Nobody, certainly not the small Indian population that occupied these vast lands, opposed such a law—that is, nobody except the Northern Pacific, the Manitoba road's arch-rival. President Cleveland, however, seemed to get awfully nervous whenever this potentially controversial issue came up, and he made Hill and his lieutenants jump through many a hoop before he got a bill he was willing to sign. It was not just the right-of-way, furthermore, which had to be secured. Before the lands of Montana would become valuable the reservations would have to be opened to settlers, which meant that a new

set of treaties would have to be made with the Indians. The advice
from Washington, relayed by Kennedy, whose contacts in the capital
were at least as good as Hill's, was to go ahead, and so the ninety-
seven-mile Montana Central was built in the summer of 1886, all except for the laying of the rails. Next year it would have to be connected
with the Manitoba road, or the withering process would begin.[13] Hill
wrote the Assistant Secretary of the Treasury: Could not something be
done to speed up the slow-moving government commission which
was negotiating with the Indians? There were, he noted, other, more
humane reasons for haste than just the ambitions of railroad builders:

> The disturbance among the Indians will, no doubt, be greatly augmented
> if the Commission does not reach them before the severity of winter.
> There is absolutely no game in that country and nothing for the Indians to
> live upon except what they get from the government. The last two years
> many of them starved to death, and they will doubtless take advantage of
> the action of the Canadian Indians [who were drifting southward across
> the boundary] to kill the cattle of settlers and commit other depreda-
> tions. . . .[14]

"You will of course let me know when your Montana schemes are in
shape," Thorne wrote Hill anxiously on Christmas Eve of 1885. "I shall
be very glad to have all the interest in them you feel you can let me
have." Hill's associates seemed more anxious to move in Montana
than he was. In the gloomy days of the following February, Thorne
worried that the Northern Pacific would steal a march on them. "I
have looked upon it [the Montana Central] as a very important link in
your scheme . . . but you will have to move *very quickly*," he warned.
Martin Maginnis, on a trip to Montana, sounded the most urgent
alarm, writing that "the directors [of the Northern Pacific] were slow
and lethargic, but Hauser [Samuel T., president of the First National
Bank of Helena and Broadwater's main competitor for railroad supremacy in Montana] tackled them one day and stirred them up the
next, and . . . it was agreed that they would occupy the territory."
Hill must move now, Maginnis warned, for everybody's sake. "The
whole town is with you," he pleaded.[15]

Meanwhile Hill sent Manvel, who was in New York preparing to
sail for Europe on the extended vacation he needed so badly, to con-
front the Northern Pacific people. Manvel found T. F. Oakes, vice
president of the Northern Pacific, full of bluster. Oakes insisted, said
Manvel, that "they considered central Montana to be their province,
that they were now ready to serve it, and the Manitoba [road] had no

right to build beyond the Missouri River." The Montana Central disguise was fooling no one, Manvel wrote, and everyone expected the Manitoba road to proceed west of Devil's Lake, which, incidentally, he and his men were ready to do without delay. Thorne, Manvel added, was eager to begin. Even Kennedy, sitting before the fire in the library of his house on West 57 Street, snipped an item from the *Evening Post* which reported that the Northern Pacific was going to build a line parallel to the Montana Central.[16]

Hill, for his part, had already told Broadwater to proceed with grading as fast as the onset of spring would permit, and he was pleased to pass along George Stephen's assurance that the Dominion government, bravely facing up to outraged cries from the anti-monopoly demagogues, had disallowed the charter for the independent line which was supposed to run down from Canada to connect with the Northern Pacific at the boundary. If the Montana Central is built, Stephen promised, and wants a Canadian connection, the Canadian Pacific will build one without delay. Almost simultaneously word came from Washington that the Northern Pacific's credit had run out. Hauser, in the capital to seek permission to build his line under the aegis of the Northern Pacific (which was not supposed to build branch lines), discovered instead that legislation to punish the Northern Pacific for taking timber that did not belong to it was under consideration, and he returned to Montana. "Did you see Hauser when he passed through St. Paul?" Thorne wrote Hill from New York. "He left word with Geo [George Clark] to tell you and me that he . . . would be very glad to do what he could to facilitate the building of the M.C. north. He was evidently, as the boys say, all broken up . . ."[17] Most important to Hill, however, was the go-ahead he received from Kennedy:

> After the very satisfactory relations that have existed between us since I first had the pleasure of making your acquaintance, my confidence in your judgment and integrity is such that I am ready to go into anything which you ask me to, in which you are yourself interested and of which you have the controlling direction.[18]

Kennedy had always expected that Hill would get the information that would put the Montana enterprise "on a safe business basis." In fact, the Northern Pacific's agent at Helena had been Hill's spy for some time, and the intelligence he sent Hill was exciting:

> I have had some *careful* inquiry made as to the business of the Nor Pacific from Montana and find that . . . their earnings for March are $165,000

more than same month last year . . . all of which goes to show the value of an extension of our lines up the Milk River Valley to the mountains &c with a connection to Helena & Butte. . . .[19]

And his next letter removed what little doubt remained about the wisdom of a grand leap across Dakota and Montana:

Mr. Oakes said that with [few] river crossings and low grades the extension of the Manitoba road into Montana would ruin the Northern Pacific. . . . They find that we are in possession of all the advantages of location and there is no way left for them to oust us. . . .[20]

"From what you say, we cannot occupy the territory between Devil's Lake and the falls of the Missouri too soon," Kennedy responded. Next month Stephen came to the same conclusion. "It seems to me that the Manitoba road ought to extend as rapidly as may be expedient westward south of the boundary line," he wrote, and added, significantly, "no doubt some day reaching the Pacific Ocean." Everybody, in fact, wanted a share in the Montana enterprise, and Hill had to tread carefully to keep from disappointing important people. Even so, he omitted Stephen and Smith from the list of those who were invited to subscribe, at $1500 each, to "blocks" of shares in the three enterprises: the Great Falls Water Power and Light Company, the Red Mountain Coal Mining Company, and the Montana Central Railway. Hill took the largest share of each, and, with Kennedy, he wielded absolute control of the enterprise.[21]

Hill, many miles from the scene of operations, directed the difficult, expensive work of building the Montana Central through the Prickly Pear Canyon. The glory belongs, for the most part, to others, although Hill visited the scene frequently. He concentrated on the critical matter of the final location of the line, and his perfectionism paid off when the engineers so improved the difficult section between Helena and Butte that savings of $1 million were expected. Even adversity had its uses. The Northern Pacific tried to the bitter end to discourage Hill by steeply raising rates on rails between the end of the Manitoba road and Helena, and Hill decided to wait until the Manitoba itself was extended into Montana next year before "ironing" the Montana Central. Throughout the ensuing winter the citizens of the Land of the Big Sky gazed at their silent, railless roadbed, joking that stubborn Jim Hill was going to build the Manitoba road all the way to Great Falls just so he could haul his own rails. As for the butt of their jokes, he had not worked so hard since 1878, for the Montana Central was by no means all the railroad he built in 1886. "We have had a busy summer—774

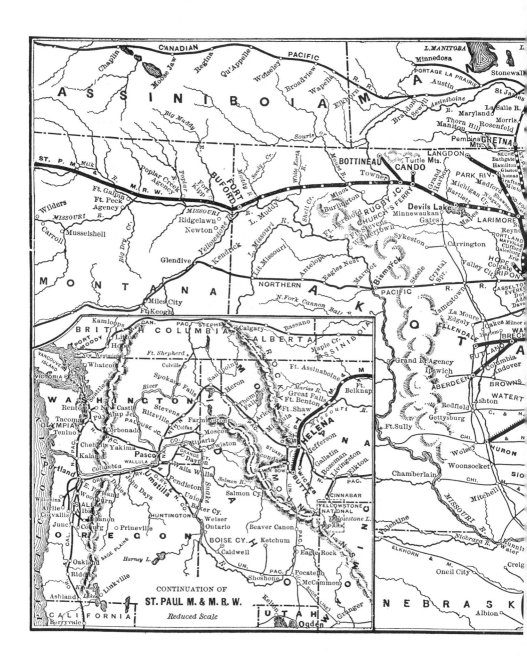

CONTINUATION OF
ST. PAUL M. & M. R. W.
Reduced Scale

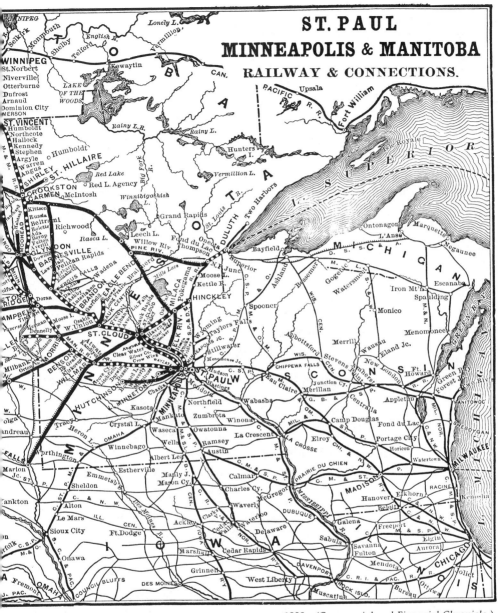

1888 *(Commercial and Financial Chronicle.)*

343

miles graded and 400 miles new track," he bragged to Frank Thomson, "but I do not feel at all tired." [22]

III

The postmark read Thomasville, Georgia, but the handwriting was familiar. Hill smiled as he read the blunt letter his old friend, David C. Shepard, prime contractor in the building of the new lines in Montana, had penned him from his vacation retreat. "Please cut short that call loan business in N. Y. and pay us up," he wrote. He was referring to the Manitoba road's policy of putting its cash reserves out at interest in the New York call money market. The railroad still owed his firm $150,000 for work done the previous year and, "D. C." noted, "we have plenty of ways to invest it in getting ready for the 'grand progress.' "[23]

Hill, too, had many things to do to get ready for the "grand progress," or the "long march forward," as he called it. His associates were uneasy about the magnitude of the undertaking, especially since the grading of the Montana Central the year before had cost much more than Hill had forecast. D. Willis James was concerned over the heavy capital demands which the extension would make, but he worried even more about the fact that the enterprise was almost entirely in the hands of one man, and a man who seemed to respond to every plea of his friends to slow down by working all the harder. The financial climate offered little but uncertainty, and there was hardly a business leader who did not expect a day of reckoning. The Montana extension would submit the directorate of the Manitoba road to such a strain that most of its members would not prove equal to the ultimate leap acrss the Rockies and the Cascades to the Pacific.[24] But in the fall of 1886 they had no choice except to press ahead, as Hill explained to Kennedy:

> We must build 783 miles of road next summer in eight months from the present end of track to Montana to insure our position of advantage. This has all to be done from one end and is more track than has ever been laid in ten months elsewhere, over twice this year's work, which has been carried on at four places, and will take a hundred million feet of timber and ties . . .
>
> With $5 million secured we can almost finish our line to Great Falls and in case financial trouble came next winter our main enterprise would be safe

. . . Our work for next year is subject to great peril from at least five distinct sources, any one of which might be fatal . . .[25]

Apparently he did not feel he had to spell out the five sources of peril. With James, he took the most reassuring stand he could, under the circumstances:

The future of this Company depends on our work during the coming year. . . . Our business will rest on solid foundations of agricultural, mineral, lumber, cattle, and mercantile products covering so wide a territory that any local failure of the one would not greatly affect any of the others, leaving us in a position to expect a good, steady average traffic at all times.[26]

Kennedy required no convincing that they should move forward, but he was adamant about financing. "I am not willing to go on contracting obligations . . . with provision made for but half the amount and trust to luck for the balance," he lectured. That fall he asked Hill to meet him in Chicago for a conference on the financial problems. It was getting very difficult to float new bond issues, for thousands of miles of new railroads were being built each year. The European capital market would have to be tapped more effectively than any Western road without a land grant had ever believed possible. This would mean attracting underwriters like Kuhn, Loeb & Company, with its unmatched contacts in Europe, and they would demand concessions. In November Kennedy reported that Jacob Schiff had dropped by his office with good news: the first offering of Montana extension bonds had been oversubscribed five or six times in Berlin. But Hill was unhappy about the concession Schiff had demanded: an option to take— or leave—large amounts of extension bonds in the future.

Henry Minot had sneered at Kennedy's ultraconservative financial policies, but the banker knew what he was doing. It was wise to make concessions to a strong firm with the best European connections, which could always get them money when it was needed. This was saying a great deal, Kennedy hinted, when Hill's estimates of construction costs kept falling so far short of reality. The following summer proved Kennedy right. His efforts to sell another batch of bonds had met a wall of indifference, but finally he could telegraph Hill that Kuhn, Loeb had agreed to take up their option on another $2 million worth. Future options were demanded, and the offer was good for one day only, but in Kennedy's opinion, considering the fear that was rampant in Wall Street as the aristocratic Baltimore & Ohio Railroad teetered on the brink of bankruptcy, it was an "excellent sale," and he delivered a rare ultimatum to Hill: "If this sale is not confirmed I must decline to undertake the conduct of the finances of Manitoba any longer. . . ." Hill knuckled under, but he grimly noted that his own young protégé, Nichols, believed that Schiff was at that moment engaging in some pretty devious tactics.[27]

If the financial jungle was terrifying, the political jungle was merely frustrating. The Manitoba road was poised on the edge of three Indian reservations, but the right-of-way bill was still hung up in Congress. Though Hill was busy with preparations for the coming season's work, he had to drop everything and go to Washington. He warned Minnesota's Senator McMillan that "all our contracts [are] in abeyance until [this] question can be settled." Finally the pieces began to fall into place. Cleveland signed the right-of-way bill in February, and the Manitoba road would now be free to cross the reservations, provided it paid the tribes a fair market value for the actual acreage taken.

Their foot in the door of the northwestern Great Plains, the new settlers who had been kept from sweeping across this former home of nomads could be denied no longer. While waiting for the reservations to be opened to settlement, Hill pressed the Commissioner of Indian Affairs to allow shippers to drive their cattle across the Indian lands on their way to the railroad that fall. In September of 1887 he took Senators Dawes, Morgan, and Davis of the Senate Committee on Indian Affairs on an inspection trip to Montana and got their assurances of "early ratification of the treaty which will throw nearly all that country open to immediate settlement." In retrospect it seems that Hill had never really had anything to worry about; still, in 1886 it had seemed risk enough for anyone's sense of adventure to build a railroad on the far side of a legal chasm which he might never have been able to bridge.[28]

There are probably enough "records" in railroad building to provide nearly every great tracklaying project with at least one. During the summer of 1887 the Manitoba road laid, between Minot, Dakota Territory, and Helena, Montana Territory, the longest stretch of track—643 miles—ever built by a single railroad in a single season entirely from one end of the track. Only about 140 miles of this track was laid on a roadbed which had been graded the season before, for in April 1887 some 500 miles remained to be built on virgin prairie. Day after day swarms of men urged their teams ahead, scraping two parallel scars, each about six feet wide, and separated by an untouched strip of the same width, across the prairie. Behind them more teams heaped the resulting topsoil on the median strip, thus producing above the plain a roadbed two or three feet high which, they hoped, would be blown free of snow when the blizzards came. Behind them came highly skilled Irishmen who laid the tracks. On August 8, 1887, they laid eight miles of steel, near enough to a record to satisfy anyone, D. C. Shepard thought.

Only the most careful, painstaking planning had made it possible. The year before, Hill had sent Minot back into the field to go over the proposed route once more, and the Manitoba road had been advanced 117 miles from its old railhead, Devil's Lake, to a raw new railroad town which had been named after Hill's none too modest assistant. And so Minot, North Dakota, remains to this day. As soon as the harvest of 1886 was over, every locomotive and every piece of rolling stock available was pressed into service to carry vast quantities of materials to the jumping-off point at Minot. Quietly and at the best prices, Kennedy bought rails, leaning heavily on English and German rail mills in spite of the detested tariff. Even before the hand of winter was lifted from the prairie next spring, Hill gave the signal to start. "The frost west of Minot is so deep that the earth has to be blown out with explosives," he reported to his associates.[29]

Hill was on the scene frequently, for only his insistence on making every day count could get the work done before winter closed in. In May he conducted a party of Bostonians, including Henry L. Higginson and the venerable Forbes, to the scene of operations. On his own inspection trips, Hill traveled over the route by wagon, an uncomfortable and exhausting experience for a fifty-year-old man. "The trip will be a hard one, and I would be glad to avoid it," he wrote Kennedy on one occasion "[but] there are two or three places which I must see before the final line is adopted." He goaded the contractors along, noting that it meant a million dollars in lost business to the railroad if they were not in Helena by winter. He was glad to find that the "great struggle" to haul all of the materials out as early in the season as possible had been a success, for by the first of September he was shooing many of the locomotives and box cars eastward to carry the new crop back to Minnesota. By the end of the month the track-laying crews were only a few miles from Great Falls, and Paris Gibson was eager to plan an arrival celebration. But Hill, who had observed the disabling effects of celebration hangovers many times before, insisted that they wait until they reached their real destination, Helena. "It would be

two or three days before we could get well under way again," he warned, and the morning after the rails arrived in Great Falls the men
were routed out before sunrise for the final push. On November 18
Hill set out from St. Paul in his business car for the ceremonies marking the arrival of the road in Helena.[30]

From mid-1887 on Hill was busy integrating the Montana Central
into the Manitoba road's corporate structure and aggressively seeking
industries to feed it traffic. He explained to Charles E. Perkins and
Higginson that, more or less by prior understanding, the purchasers
of blocks of his Montana enterprises a year earlier were acceding to his
request to turn in their Montana Central bonds for securities of equivalent value in the Manitoba road. The Bostonians, he hastened to add,
need not doubt "that the Manitoba interests were properly looked
after." Soon the Montana Central was an indistinguishable part of the
Manitoba road—as, indeed, no one had ever thought of it otherwise
from the beginning. By the middle of the next year the Manitoba road,
connecting with the Union Pacific at Butte, was carrying passengers
for the Pacific Coast and, Hill noted proudly, "our trains [are] arriving
[at Butte] from four to ten hours ahead of the Northern Pacific every
day." The ascendancy of Henry Villard in the Northwest was to be
brief indeed. But Hill's major victory was in securing the location of a
huge new copper-smelting plant on the railroad.[31]

At Butte, Hill had enjoyed cordial relations with Marcus Daly,
founder of the mammoth Anaconda Copper Company, who saw in
Hill a man who would bring in cheap, efficient transportation. "When
our lines are completed through to your place," Hill had promised,
"we hope to be able to furnish you all the transportation you want, at
rates as will enable you to largely increase your business. What we
want over our low grades is a heavy tonnage, and the heavier it is *the
lower we can make the rates.*" But he had his work cut out for him in
dealing with Leonard Lewisohn and his hard-boiled associates, who
were going to build a big copper refining plant at Helena or Great
Falls, depending on whether the Northern Pacific or the Manitoba
road offered the better deal. Charles O. Parsons, Lewisohn's partner in
charge of the negotiations, nearly drove Hill—and Nichols, on the
New York end—crazy with his nit-picking negotiations. "I will say,"
sighed Nichols, "I have never done anything less to my mind than trying to negotiate with these people. They are slippery, treacherous and
suspicious to the last degree—no confidence in each other or in anyone else." Forbes, with his usual disdain for New York capitalists,

warned Hill to tread carefully, but he devoutly hoped they would get the business in the end. Hill finally found the key to the negotiations when he quietly transferred 1500 shares of stock in the Great Falls Townsite Company to Lewisohn.[32]

The hard work and worry of the Montana extension during the summer of 1887 took a grievous toll of Kennedy's nerves. In May he had felt so well that he offered to come to St. Paul for a month or two to work alongside the hard-pressed Hill, but that fall he took a turn for the worse. He then announced his retirement as vice president. He would remain on the board yet awhile, he promised, but he was going to Florida and then to Europe in search of health. He regretted that one of the most important phases of his remarkable career was ending:

> After such close and confidential relations as we have held to each other for a period of nine years, and looking back at what we have been permitted to accomplish during that period—long in the prospect but short in the retrospect—it seems like tearing asunder old relationships, which, like you, I am most loath to do. . . .

Meanwhile, he had some sage advice for Hill:

> You are being admonished in more ways than one that you are overtaxing your strength; these neuralgic headaches and that weary feeling you complain of are both clear indications. . . . Your life and health are worth more than any addition you can make to your fortune or reputation. . . . The stockholders have no claim upon you, or me, to make such sacrifices for them and few, if any, of them would thank us for them or appreciate them if we did.

> We have strained our credit pretty severely during the last 12 or 18 months . . . but we cannot go on doing this indefinitely. Even parties friendly to us suggest that we are going too fast. . . . We have a great many bitter enemies. Time will cure them; but meantime, we must be wise as serpents and ever on the watch for them. . . .[33]

IV

In 1916 Louis W. Hill, Sr., and other leading citizens of St. Paul revived the Winter Carnival, which had been a neglected institution for nearly twenty years. In the mid-1880s, however, the Carnival served to brighten the short, frigid days and long nights of a Minnesota January, and to revive the animal spirits of the citizenry. People needed an alternative to hibernation. The Ice Palace, in those days actually built of blocks of ice sawed from the Mississippi River, was a popular tourist attraction; toboggans raced down the steep slope from Summit Avenue; torchlight parades up Fourth Street brought out crowds that are no longer seen in downtown St. Paul; and brigades of bizarrely costumed young men, claiming to be members of "ancient" orders that were more likely the product of a home-grown mythology, subjected young and old, male and female, to a boisterous hazing. "We are in the midst of the Winter Carnival," Hill wrote Frank Thomson in January 1887, "and the city is in the hands of the winter clubs." [34]

The Hills made the best of winter, which, as Minnesotans freely admitted, was all one could do. One year Hill had a handsome new sleigh delivered in front of his office. He drove it home to Canada Street to be greeted by squeals of delight. He insisted that, unless the children were sick, they be taken for outings in the carriage or the sleigh even on the coldest days, for the risk of a frostbitten ear or nose was a small price to pay for fresh air. A cruise on their own yacht to warmer climates would have been even better, Hill thought. It was an idea he had been entertaining for some time, since investigation had revealed that, for eleven Hills and several servants, it would be more economical for him to buy a boat than to charter one. In the fall of 1885, a comparatively quiet year for Hill, he negotiated for the ocean-going yacht, *Polynia*, built for James Gordon Bennett, publisher of the New York *Herald*, for a reputed $75,000, and for sale at $25,000. But if 1885 could be called a respite from Hill's labors on the Manitoba road, it was a short one, and although the agent reduced the price to $10,000, the ocean cruise went glimmering. [35]

Like many a busy man with a large family, Hill never solved the problems that separation on business trips presented. The heartaches engendered by the conflict of loyalties were a price of success which commercial travelers still pay reluctantly. Those left at home worried about "papa," hurtling along at forty, fifty, even a terrifying sixty miles an hour in a wooden Pullman car, on tracks which were crowded with the commerce of a prosperous, growing nation. The gory railroad wreck was a staple feature of the newspaper front page. Nor could the traveler return quickly at even the most tragic news from home—hence the dread of telegrams—and the larger the family left behind and the more dependent it was on the ministrations of servants, the more a man like Hill worried. Preparing to leave St. Paul for New York and then two weeks of duck hunting at Currituck in early December 1887, Hill was stunned to discover that five-year-old Rachel had been put to bed gasping for breath. "Diphtheria is of so sudden and terrible a nature that I could not leave Mrs. Hill with the children," he explained to Kennedy. Currituck was out for that year. And when he did go to New York a week later, after receiving the doctor's assurance that Rachel had passed the crisis, he still fretted. There were eight other children in the household, and the diphtheria germs could only have escaped from a leak in the soil pipes. He insisted that no opportunity to discover the leak be ignored. "Brodie and Holmes should test the plumbing with peppermint," he wired Mary, and the doubting but obedient plumbers were soon sniffing every soil pipe joint in the house.[36]

Hill had his own aches and pains. The neuralgia and the vague "weary feeling" he had complained about to Kennedy were with him much of the time, although, like the insomniac who finally gets a good night's sleep, he assumed that each respite was permanent. He found the trips to New York increasingly fatiguing, especially as art dealers began to besiege him with offers of paintings. A lover of good food and drink, he soon discovered that New York could offer more of it, and on a nightly basis, than he cared for. "My friend Cannon says you are dined to death," sympathized a man who was trying to sell him a painting. While in New York in the spring of 1888 he felt a bad cold coming on. He dropped everything, including an appointment with August Belmont, and took the next train to St. Paul, where his doctor put him to bed for a week. It was a summer of great strain, as Hill, with the "long march forward" barely achieved, tried to buck up his associates for the push to the Pacific. In August he came near to pneumonia and took to his bed, chastened by this proof that he was indeed not "made of steel," as Stephen had once warned him. Catching cold again at Christmas time, he (sensibly) received the holiday greetings of Mary and the children from his big bed. To his disgust, he spent the next Christmas in the same condition.[37]

"My hair is dark, with some grey hairs mixed throughout, possibly more gray in the beard on the chin than elsewhere," Hill told a writer in the East who was preparing an article on railroad leaders. The fact is that he was getting quite grizzled as he passed his fiftieth birthday in 1888, and his short, stocky build was more pronounced than ever as middle age brought added pounds. Even sixteen-year-old Louis would soon be taller than he was. Fortunately, the style in clothing which had favored tall, slender men like Prince Albert were being replaced by more sensible modes. Hill's tailor asked him whether he wanted some new suits he had ordered made up as cutaways, and Hill decided the time had come to switch to sack suits.[38]

When he went fishing with President Cleveland off Long Island in 1888, he proudly displayed in his cabin his "entire family," as Smith M. Weed, another member of the party, put it—a folding set of photographs of Mary and the nine children. By 1884 James Norman and Louis, aged fourteen and twelve, had outgrown the tutelage of Mr. Chemidlin, who was discharged with six months' salary. Chemidlin was replaced by Professor J. W. Fairbanks, who had been a principal in the school of Fitchburg, Massachusetts. Anxious to keep all of the children at home together, Hill had resisted suggestions that the boys go to boarding school in the East, but he would not entrust them to any of the local academies. John W. Sterling, the New York lawyer, had helped recruit Fairbanks. "I would make it a real good place for the right man," Hill promised, "if he could and would *take charge of their education.*" He was as good as his word: Fairbanks received a five-year contract and a salary of $4000 a year (the equivalent of $20,000 or more today) to "assume charge of the education of my sons until such time as they may be thoroughly prepared for college." He preferred to keep the girls at home, too. In the dog days of 1885 Mamie and Clara went east to spend a few weeks with the Manvels at a resort in Portsmouth, New Hampshire, but Hill was glad when they were all reunited at North Oaks. Soon the girls were helping their mother put up jar after jar of crabapple or grape jelly, while the boys, under the eye of the professor, sent up balloons and otherwise learned physics the easy way.[39]

It did not work. Like many another Ph.D., Fairbanks seems to have been a better administrator than teacher. By the spring of 1887 Hill could see that Jimmie and Louis were being allowed to get by with as little studying as possible. That fall he packed them off to Philips Exeter Academy, in New Hampshire. Meanwhile, Professor Fairbanks was left to vegetate in the house he and his wife occupied on Summit Avenue, but when Hill was told by the Exeter headmaster that both boys were a year behind where they were supposed to be, and would have to be put back, Hill angrily sent Fairbanks a check for $100 and told him he was breaking the contract, even though it had two years to run:

> I wanted the duties assumed by you to cover more than the simple recitation of their lessons; that they would be taught to do their work well and

thoroughly and must be taught good methods of doing their work. . . . I
told you if there was any want of application I would see that it was
remedied. . . . Both boys had to begin a good year behind where you left
off with them, and while their teachers say they are quick and apply
themselves, they did not know how to study and do good work. . . .[40]

Of course Hill could not get away with it, but it served to blow off
steam. When the professor called in his lawyer, Hill suggested that
Cyrus Northrup, president of the University of Minnesota, arbitrate
the matter. That Solomon, true to form, split the claim down the
middle, and Fairbanks returned to the educational jungles of Fitchburg while Hill's sons bent to the uncompromising discipline of Exeter.[41]

During the next several years Hill seldom went to New York without
making a side trip to see how the boys were faring. He generally used
business in Boston as an excuse. He set up his sons in a suite in a
private home where, the landlord assured him, they would be very
well taken care of. (Perhaps it was not so much indulgence as a compromise with the overly Protestant atmosphere of the residence and
dining halls.) Mary Hill, meanwhile, provided a good measure of discipline of her own. When the boys went two weeks without writing,
she sent stern telegrams to them. She saw to it that Jimmie, when he
went off to Yale in the fall of 1889, gave the chapel a wide berth in
favor of the nearest Catholic church. And when the boys took Alexander, Frank Thomson's ailing son, out on the prairie to shoot chickens,
she sternly wired them, "No shooting on Sunday." [42]

Hill was pleased that Jimmie had been elected manager of the football team that scored on Harvard in October 1888. Exeter lost, 39 to 6,
Jimmie explained, but he reported proudly that "this was the first time
Exeter or any other prep. school ever scored on Harvard," and he
wondered if he could have a stop watch. The boys had indeed been
poorly prepared to attend a first-class Eastern academy, but the Exeter
headmaster rose to the challenge by appointing several professors
(who were doubtless glad to get the extra stipend which Hill offered)
as their tutors. James Norman fared well under such intense discipline, and he gravely informed his father that Louis was "doing better this term but there is still room for improvement." When Jimmie's
graduation day arrived, however, his father was thousands of miles
away on an urgent trip to Butte, and only his mother and older sisters
were there to see him receive his diploma. From Yale, which he entered that fall, he wrote his father dejectedly that a childhood injury

would keep him from trying for the famous swimming team. But he consoled himself with his checking account and its balance of $300—*de rigeur* in his new world—and the thought that next year he would be a worldly Yale sophomore with a freshman brother. Meanwhile his father, grateful for the way things had turned out, treated the Exeter headmaster and his wife to a trip to the West that summer, and he found a job for their son "where he will have a chance to grow up with the country." [43]

V

Almost before he knew it, Hill had a grown daughter with children of her own. Mamie had been courted in the sedate, Victorian fashion by Samuel Hill, a young lawyer in Minneapolis, whose father, scion of an old Southern family and no relation to Hill, had bettered himself by moving north about the same time as Mamie's father migrated westward. Tall, good-looking, and gregarious, Sam was doing well in the firm of Jackson, Atwater & Hill, and when Mamie's father consented to the marriage in the spring of 1888, he thought he saw a future railroad man as well. Encouraged by nearly everybody to make it a short, Western-style engagement, Mamie and Sam were married in the house at Ninth and Canada (for Sam was a Protestant), Father Caillet officiating, on September 6, 1888. James J.'s tailor had worked at top speed to outfit the bride's father (a hard man to get onto a fitter's platform), and on the happy day Hill, in $108 worth of cutaway, embroidered vest, and striped pants, walked Mamie down the aisle. Mary Hill and her daughters, with considerable help from the Uphams and the Gotzians, had spent an exciting summer assembling the trousseau, most of which came from Mannheimer Brothers' dry goods store in St. Paul. It had a value of $1400 by the wedding day. With the help of $700 worth of glassware and the countless other niceties of a generation with an abundance of servants, the newest Hill family was soon established in a modest house of their own in Minneapolis.

The father's gift to the couple did not loom large among the forest of useful and frivolous, beautiful and ugly wedding gifts displayed in the parlor of the house on Canada Street, but it was the best one. It was 1000 shares of stock in the Manitoba road, par value $100,000. The $6000 a year in dividends would supplement Sam's earnings nicely, to say the least, and that winter the newlyweds set out to spend some of it on a grand tour of Europe. By the time they returned Mamie was expecting, and on July 3, 1889, Hill's first grandchild, a girl, was born. A week later he was in New York, where he had vowed he would buy the child a proper rattle, when Sam dutifully wrote to ask him to help name the baby. "Mary likes your mother's name," Sam hinted, but Hill suggested Mary instead of Ann, and Mary Mendenhall Hill, her middle name representing Sam's side of the family, was christened a few days later.[44]

The rising railroad baron of the Northwest acquired a proper chateau, if not quite a castle, in 1891 when he completed the ponderous, red sandstone mansion which frowns down on St. Paul from one of the finest sites on Summit Avenue. But it is the cheerful, dowdy, mansard-roofed house on Canada Street which more fully embodies the domestic history of James J. Hill. Four of his children had been born in that home, and even the youngest, Walter, spent his first six years there. Their parents were devoted to the place, and doubtless would have remained for at least another decade. But encroaching upon the quiet, tree-lined streets were the grim brick warehouses and noisy, smoky railroad yards that mushroomed during the rapid growth of St. Paul in the 1880s. Turning a deaf ear to the pleas of T. F. Oakes, who encouraged him to buy the place next to his because "Upham has had you long enough," Hill bought two of the last vacant lots on Summit Avenue, which was already becoming one of the country's most beautiful residential streets.

Filled though he was with plans for the new mansion, Hill decided to retain a proper architect, and the experience was not entirely a happy one. (Years later, while planning a new country house at North Oaks, he grew disgusted as a bevy of opinionated females wrangled over cupolas, wings, bay windows, and other protuberances. He turned the project over to the chief engineer of the railroad, and the result, a grandson recalls, bore more resemblance to a railroad depot than a residence.) This time he hired the firm of Peabody & Stearns, of Boston, who recommended that the grade of the lot be raised to that of the street despite the loss of several grand old oak trees which this entailed. By the spring of 1888 plans for the foundations were almost ready, and Hill decided that he would supervise the construction himself. The following winter he engaged a firm of New York interior decorators to design the rooms, concluding that a knowledge of English was not essential in a firm which assured him they could do the kind of job which "a residence of this caricature justly demands." [45]

Both the past and the future made demands on Hill. Early in 1889 he received a grateful note from Forbes, who, undertaking to raise a memorial fund for the late General Philip Sheridan, had found Eastern purses tightly closed. Acknowledging Hill's gift of $5000, Forbes asserted that Hill and Marshall Field had saved the day. "The fact is," the old gentleman gushed, "like the samples of grain & potatoes you once sent me, the west produces larger vegetables (and men) than our eastern fields do nowadays." That same year the men who were struggling to finance Chicago's World Columbian Exposition, already behind schedule, literally cheered when Hill's pledge of $25,000 was announced. By then he had begun to give some thought to a project which he had had in mind for a long time. What St. Paul, or any other respectable city, for that matter, needed was a "reference library," where young men and women bent on improving their minds and their vocational skills could find basic books in the sciences, engineering, business, history, and literature, instead of the sentimental female fiction which was all most public libraries seemed able to provide. His ideas were enthusiastically shared by the Reverend Dr. Edward D. Neill, who had provided Hill with much of the scholarly knowledge on the Indian tribes of Minnesota that he had passed along to Washington. Neill, who was also professor of history and librarian of Macalester College, a thriving local institution, welcomed Hill's offer to give $5000 for the purchase of books if the College would build a $20,000 building in which to house the new collection. "Franklin showed his common sense and perpetually blessed Philadelphia when he founded such a library," Neill told him. Hill committed himself to a monthly payment of $50 for books so that a beginning could be made, but neither man was to live long enough to see the reference library an actuality.

The past faded rapidly. In the summer of 1889 Captain Alexander Griggs, still navigating on the Red River, wrote to say that he had discovered some planking from the deck of the old steamer *Selkirk*. Send it to me, Hill replied, sentimentally.[46]

VI

In the spring of 1888 Hill spent nearly two weeks at some of the most exhausting and unproductive work of his life. The threats of J. P. Farley, receiver of the old St. Paul & Pacific Railroad, were finally bearing bitter fruit in a sensational trial which the citizens of St. Paul watched with special interest. True to his word, Farley had brought suit against Hill, Kittson, and the railroad not long after his services had been dispensed with, and by 1882 the case had come up before U.S. District Court Judge Samuel Treat. "I believe old Farley is quite capable of swearing to anything if he thought it would get him a few dollars," Hill warned Stephen, "and so far as making a showing for complaint is a dangerous man." Still, the suit seemed the height of arrogance, an effort to enforce a word-of-mouth contract which was alleged to exist between Kittson and Hill, on the one hand, and Farley, on the other, to deliver the bonds of the railroad to the associates without regard to the receiver's obligation, as an officer of the court, to get the highest price possible for the bondholders. Hill's and Kittson's lawyers, of whom George Young was the most important, entered a demurer, or counterplea, in which the defendants denied the facts as charged by Farley and further asserted that the suit was a nullity because the contract which the plaintiff sought to enforce, even if it had existed, called for the performance of an illegal act. It turned out to be some of the worst legal advice Hill ever received.[47]

Treat, to be sure, agreed heartily with the defendants' plea, and found in their favor. "This is a strange demand to present to a court of equity," he wrote indignantly in his opinion, "no court worthy of its trust would lend its aid to further a scheme so abhorrent to all recognized rules of right and justice. . . . Courts of equity will not . . . undertake to unravel a tangled web of fraud for the purpose of enabling one of the fraudulent parties . . . to consummate his fraudulent designs. The party complaining must come before the court with clean hands. In this case he has not. . . ." Treat, with more than thirty years' service on the federal bench, was one of the most honored jurists in the Midwest, and his colleagues had been saddened to learn that because of failing eyesight he would soon be forced to step down. He had disposed of hundreds—perhaps thousands—of cases involving such simple, well-settled principles of equity law, and he did not intend to allow Farley v. St. Paul, Minneapolis & Manitoba Railway, et al., to detain his court. He had a strong leaning toward just the kind of pragmatism which was the glory of the Anglo-American system of common law, and, as he would demonstrate two years later in the sensational Wabash receivership case, he had a talent for subordinating mere "law" to his sense of "justice," a view which would have struck judges a century later as modern in every respect.[48]

In the 1880s, however, the overwhelming philosophy of jurisprudence was that these were courts of law, not of justice. When the Supreme Court, in its leisurely fashion, decided five years later to review the Farley case, the associates were surprised and alarmed. Kennedy urged that they spare no effort in opposing the appeal, and engaged William N. Evarts to assist George Young in the oral arguments. Evarts, one of the ablest trial lawyers in the nation, had been counsel for the defense in the most sensational "trial" of the century, the impeachment of Andrew Johnson. He accepted Kennedy's check for $1000 with thanks, for in that innocent age the fact that he was also a United States Senator from New York was no obstacle to his continuing a lucrative law practice based on his unsurpassed contacts. He brought these contacts into play almost immediately when it was discovered that both he and Farley's counsel, George Edmunds, also a United States Senator, were scheduled to deliver speeches before the Senate on the very day that the court had set to hear their arguments. "The two Senators 'horse-shedded' * the chief justice and other judges in the robing room," the awestruck George Young reported to Hill, "and arranged that the case should go over until Monday. . . ." Evarts, in fact, had already given Young a chill, one which he attempted to shrug off. "I'm inclined to note a tendency . . . to make out his patient rather sicker than he is," he wrote Hill.[49]

The Supreme Court's decision, handed down February 7, 1887, was a bitter disappointment to Hill and his friends. Because of a mere technicality, or so it seemed to them, they would now have to endure a full-scale trial and answer the accusations of Farley with all of the evidence and wit they could command. The court had declared that a defendant who hoped to avoid a trial could not answer a plea in equity with another plea unless that defendant admitted the truth of the facts as the plaintiff had stated them. Obviously, the associates had never been willing to do that. They had based their plea on the point that the contract was illegal. This, said the court, could only be done by demurrer—i.e. a complaint against the entire proceeding—but they had denied the facts as stated by the plaintiff, and now they would have to answer him in open court. Kittson and Hill dreaded the trial, not only because they had so many more important things to do, but because of the fish-bowl atmosphere in which it would take place.

---

* Old-fashioned lawyers' slang. A lawyer would often approach a judge on behalf of his client while the judge was tying up his horse in the shed behind the courthouse before convening the session.

There was much feeling in the Twin Cities that Hill and his friends had made off with a far greater prize than they had earned, and many would enjoy seeing Farley, the aging underdog, give them their come-uppance. It was widely believed that Kittson had offered Farley some kind of reward for his "cooperation," and that only Hill's stubbornness had prevented Kittson from paying Farley off. The associates had no choice, however, so they paid Young $7936.30 for his firm's poor advice, and girded themselves for the ordeal.[50]

Hill bore almost the entire burden of the trial. The two weeks he spent in the witness chair, for three or four hours on some days, produced a remarkable oral history of his early career in steamboating, railroading, and the coal business, and of the evolution of transportation between the Twin Cities and the Red River Valley. Kennedy, who was in Europe, testified by means of interrogatories administered by the United States consul. George Stephen steadfastly supported the effort to defeat "the old rascal," while Donald Smith's five days of testimony, which included an impressive recounting of his early talks with Hill on the transportation needs of the Red River Valley, demolished Farley's claim that the entire venture had been his idea. Still, the old man was able to put into the record some intimations that Kittson, at least, had offered to reward him for services rendered, and St. Paul waited expectantly to see whether Kittson would testify or, as the know-it-alls insisted, would buy Farley off. They were never to find out.[51]

Farley was willing to be bought off, but Hill had Kittson's positive assurance that there would be no bribe. "Mr. Kittson returned yesterday looking better than I have seen him for some years," Hill noted in mid-April, as his own testimony neared its end. The two men went over the testimony given to that date and reviewed their strategy; then Kittson went back east, prepared to return to testify in mid-May. On a warm, muggy evening a month later, he wearily crawled into a lower berth on the Chicago & North Western's overnight train to St. Paul. He slept fitfully as the train puffed through one small Wisconsin town after another, headed for the cities in whose history he had played so significant a part. As the dark shapes of pine trees slipped past his window, his heart stopped beating. Next day Stephen and Smith entrained for St. Paul, where a saddened populace prepared to lay to rest one of their most beloved citizens. But Kittson's death had no effect on the outcome of the trial. On September 14 of the following year, Judge David Brewer, soon to be appointed by Benjamin Harrison to the

United States Supreme Court, handed down the decision of the Circuit Court.

Avoiding the question of the illegality of the alleged contract, Brewer noted that the plaintiff had two witnesses (himself and his nephew, Fisher) to the existence of a "parol" (oral) contract, and the defendants had only one witness, Hill, who claimed that there was none. Even so, the idea that such an important agreement would not have been put in writing, and that in the course of three years it would never once be referred to in the voluminous correspondence which had passed between the parties, was more than the Court was willing to swallow. No contract had ever existed, the Court decided. Congratulations rolled in. "I am extremely glad you have laid the gang out," wrote Senator Comstock. "The decision never will be reversed," Greenleaf Clark declared. He was right. Four years later, when Hill was deeply immersed in more important things and Farley lay beneath the sod of Iowa, the Supreme Court affirmed the decision. Minnesota's strangest lawsuit had finally ended.[52]

VII

If there had remained any doubt in 1886 that the Manitoba road had abandoned its early intention to remain a north-south railroad, the events of the following two years removed it once and for all. Not only on the western end, where the railroad had leaped across the vast prairie which separated it from the Montana Central, but on the eastern end as well, the Manitoba road expanded. By late 1888 it would be in the transportation business all the way from Buffalo, New York, to western Montana. At the same time that he was marshalling his strength for the westward push, Hill was bringing to fruition plans that he had been making for nearly as long as the Manitoba road had existed. These plans would give it an independent connection to Lake Superior; a fleet of boats to ply the Great Lakes between Superior, Wisconsin, and Buffalo, New York; and a set of tendrils to the southwest of the Twin Cities to carry the grain northeastward, away from congested, high-cost Chicago, to the higher prices that it could get at the lake ports.

He had to tread lightly, for the powerful millers of Minneapolis frowned at the slightest hint of a move in this direction. When, in 1881, Hill acquired the charter of a defunct railroad which would enable him to build northeast from St. Cloud to the lakes, W. D. Washburn, on vacation at Hot Springs, Arkansas, interrupted his course of baths to write that "such action . . . will cause a damage to our two cities that *cannot be measured. . . .*" But Hill knew better. The golden age of transportation on the Great Lakes, hastened by the development of the all-steel ship, was at hand. Grain, more and more of it, was going to the Lakes, and if the Manitoba road did not carry it, the Northern Pacific, and probably one or more newcomers, surely would. Hill knew that Minneapolis' position as chief flour miller for the nation was secure; in fact, he subscribed heavily to the merger of the Washburn & Crosby milling interests in 1889. As for the Chicago roads, Hill regretted that these developments strained his relations with his good friend, Marvin Hughitt, of the Chicago and North Western, but they were powerless to resist the changes that were taking place in transportation.

By 1886 Duluth, Minnesota, was one of the fastest-growing cities in the country, and, just to the east, Superior, Wisconsin, also was about to boom. Hill watched these developments closely, with a view to how they would fit into his long-range plans. When the Army Engineers began to take an interest in Duluth and Superior, Hill wrote his Senator, detailing just what kind of improvements would be useful. He bore down on the reluctant Northern Pacific to make sure that that company's new bridge between Duluth and Superior included a lift span so that ships could come and go freely. He enthusiastically supported efforts to enlarge the Sault Ste. Marie Canal between Lakes Superior and Huron to accommodate boats "even larger than are now in general use." [53] And in 1886 he took the fateful step which drew the Manitoba road lakewards:

> I have felt quite clear for some time [he wrote a local man] that the large and rapidly growing lake business of Duluth could not be done with any degree of expedition or for reasonable cost without largely increased terminal facilities and I have so far as the Manitoba Co. is concerned taken time by the forelock and our new elevator at West Superior can handle as many cars daily as all the elevators combined on the Duluth side. . . .[54]

The Great Northern Elevator Company, which Hill had given a name that he had begun to find fascinating, only served to make the shaky St. Paul & Duluth Railroad more inadequate than ever. For the next two years Hill peppered W. H. Rhawn, chairman of the board of the Duluth road, with warnings that the Manitoba road might have to build its own line from Hinckley, its most northeasterly point, to the

Lakes. His interest grew as Chicago men repeatedly invited him to join in plans to exploit the "huge" iron ore deposits of northeastern Minnesota. To learn more about these deposits, which had remained shrouded in mystery, for so long, he sent his own "iron explorer" to find out what he could, warning him not to set out until August if he wished to avoid the vicious black flies for which these desolate regions were notorious. Meanwhile, he turned his attention to the construction of lines to the southwest of the Twin Cities, lines which would cut in a northeasterly direction across the original Main and Branch lines of the Manitoba road like one leg of an "X," and give the farmers in those areas their long-sought short line to Lake Superior. In this, and in the extension of the Hinckley line to the Lakes, Hill would have the indispensable help of Henry D. Minot.[55]

"Harry" had grown as much in Hill's favor as he had fallen in Kennedy's. He was a strong lieutenant to a man like Hill, not in routine matters, which were well provided for, but in planning future moves. There was no one in the organization, besides Hill and Minot, who seemed able to grasp the broad spectrum of factors—surveying, engineering, cost estimation, competitive relations, and expected traffic growth—which Hill required as a firm basis upon which to commit the company's capital resources. Hill knew that Minot was ambitious, but the young man made no attempt to hide the fact that he looked forward to filling Hill's shoes, and Hill recognized that the company was better off for having someone coming along who combined confidence with mere ability. And Minot was a good lightning rod for Hill's temper. After angrily firing an engineer of many years' experience with the Manitoba road for being involved in a "tail-end" collision, Hill got Minot to rehire the man, who had a large family, on the Lake Superior branch. Minot, for his part, had been enthusiastic about expansion southwestward and northeastward almost from the time he had joined the company. "Delegations and appeals from the country southwest of us increase with alarming rapidity," he wrote Kennedy in 1886, adding that "we shall be forced to reorganize as the Liverpool, St. Paul & Honolulu Island Railway Company." [56]

"You have all of Minnesota, north of the parallel of Minneapolis, into which to expand your system," Marvin Hughitt told Hill in 1886; "it should, I think, content your people." But Hill knew that his friend was merely trying to postpone the inevitable. When Washburn and his backers in Minneapolis moved to extend their Soo line northwestward between the Main and Branch lines of the Manitoba road,

Kennedy gave Hill the green light to adopt an aggressive policy.[57] As for Hill, his course had been clear for some time, and in his monthly letters to the executive committee at the height of operations in Montana he prepared them for more expansion in 1888:

> We are overrun daily with delegations and correspondence from the southwest covering southwestern Minnesota, Dakota and Nebraska for extension of our lines in that direction. . . . The localities are all prosperous and in a good country and sooner or later will secure their natural advantage of two to three hundred miles shorter distance to Lake Superior than to Chicago.

> Today there is a scarcity of tonnage [of Lake steamers]. . . . We will not get the benefit of our natural advantages until there is provided a line of steamers that will carry off this surplus business. We have now more than enough business from our own lines to sink a daily line of boats before they left the dock at Superior.[58]

So the Manitoba road was going into the steamship business. Grain would proceed eastward, on the company's own line of Lake steamers, from Superior all the way to Buffalo, from which point it would enjoy highly competitive rates to the seaboard; and the steamers would return laden with coal, which the Northwest was demanding in vaster quantities each year. But what did Hill know about Lake steamers? He had kept abreast of shipbuilding developments during the preceding decade, in which the reduction in the cost of steel had revolutionized the industry, and he knew that steel ships, although they would cost twice as much as wooden ones, would pay for themselves that much faster. Mark A. Hanna, his old friend, was building steel Lake steamers at Cleveland, and when Hanna got wind that Hill wanted a fleet he wrote him that that moment, when steel prices were depressed, was the time to buy. "I would not hurry you a moment, Jim, were it not very important to decide soon," he wrote. Hill wired him to lay the keels for four vessels at once. He sent his own man to oversee construction, but, as usual, took a direct hand in design and execution. "What do you know about Krupp's crucible steel shafts?" he wrote Hanna. "They are used on the ocean with good results." [59]

Kennedy proved his worth to the company once again. Hill, in his haste to launch his fleet, had done nothing about dock facilities at Buffalo, and he was greatly relieved to learn that Kennedy had: "I saw Mr. Sam Sloan, President of the Delaware, Lackawanna & Western Railroad Co., a short time ago . . . and he [said] that they would be very glad to give you all you need at Buffalo." The new ships were all to contain the word "Northern" in their names, as did the first, the *Northern Light*, launched in 1888. Hill met Hanna's requests to pay up delinquent bills, which the Manitoba road found more than a little inconvenient, with complaints about the poor quality of construction, but he confided to Nichols that he was greatly pleased with their speed and carrying capacity. Nichols, in turn, wrote proudly that New York applauded Hill's dramatic moves, and believed that the Manitoba road's strength in relation to the Chicago railroads had been greatly increased. "The feeling is that you hold the whip hand and can dictate your own terms," Nichols told Hill.[60]

Meanwhile, the Manitoba road, under Minot's direction, had been extended westward into what would soon become South Dakota, and southwestward in the direction of its ultimate goal, Sioux City, Iowa. These branches were spectacularly successful, bringing to the railroad an increased volume of business which promised to pay back their costs in short order. Hill was delighted, but he was at the same time troubled by the uncertain future which Minot faced with the Manitoba road. Minot, unhappy because he seemed to carry little weight in St. Paul—no one, he complained, would show up for his weekly staff meetings—told Hill frankly that no other work "would satisfy me [as much as] a share in the successful completion of the enterprise I have identified myself with, but there is plenty of other work for me to do." Bowing before Kennedy's near-hysteria, Minot resigned as vice president late in the summer of 1887, and the displeasure of the Boston people was quickly felt. Hill had anticipated such a crisis, however, and earlier that summer had gotten Kennedy's approval to set up the Lake Superior extension, which was to be built next summer, as a separate corporation, the Eastern Railway of Minnesota, with Minot as its president. The young man was delighted, stipulating only that there be "a definite understanding that the service is temporary . . . [and] will lead me back to a place next to you; that locally my position be autocratic"; and that he receive a salary of $20,000 a year. Hill agreed, and Henry D. Minot's short career with the Eastern was an outstanding success.[61]

As the spring of 1888 came on, Hill approached the most important junction of his career. The Manitoba road was now a major railroad, equipped to handle bulk freight from Buffalo, on the east, to Butte, Montana, on the west, at costs of operation which none but the leading Eastern trunklines could match. Each passing year seemed to bring the railroad more business than ever, yet everyone talked as though it was only temporary, that something cataclysmic was about to happen in the economic world, and that only the strong could hope to survive intact. The Manitoba road had seriously strained both its financial and its human relations. Such men as Samuel Thorne and D. Willis James made no effort to hide their belief that Hill was overextended, while Kennedy, his real pillar of strength, was passing out of the picture. It was a time for rest and consolidation of their position, they all said. Flushed with success, and exhausted by the hard work of the previous two years, Hill was eager to agree. "Our system is, I think, so far complete that we can make haste slowly for the next few years," he told his associates. But even as he spoke he was laying plans to break his promise.[62]

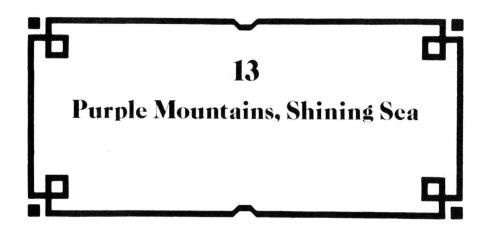

13

Purple Mountains, Shining Sea

What we want is the best possible line, shortest distance, lowest grades and least curvature that we can build. We do not care enough for Rocky Mountain scenery to spend a large sum of money developing it.

—James J. Hill, 1890

I

Riding westward from Fort Benton, Montana, on their first inspection trip in 1884, Hill and his friends were impressed by the grandeur of the major obstacle which stood between the Land of the Big Sky and the Pacific Northwest. By late afternoon, as they prepared to make camp for the night, the gently rolling hills of the Montana plateau to the east were still bathed in vivid sunlight, but to the west loomed the forbidding slopes of the Rocky Mountains, already deep purple in a premature twilight. It was hard to believe that the western slopes of these peaks were still in full sunlight and that across another wide plain, yet another range of mountains, the Cascades, repeated the process all over again before the land finally sloped down to the shining waters of Puget Sound and the great Pacific. Though deep in earnest conversation about their plans for Montana and, later, merry in song and story around the campfire, they still felt the presence of the ultimate challenge.

In the early months of 1889 James J. Hill committed the railroads under his leadership to extension to the Pacific. By then regional railroads like his were finally facing the decision of whether to become transcontinentals in their own right or to be absorbed by men of larger vision and greater daring. But Hill had been preparing for the decision for at least six years, and from the beginning of his career in railroading he had known that the Manitoba road would eventually have to acquire, or become part of, an untrammeled route to the Pacific Ocean. When the Northern Pacific, badly built and clumsily managed as it was, achieved transcontinental status in 1883 by tying up with Henry Villard's Oregon Railway & Navigation Company to Portland, Oregon, he had been filled with envy. "They are able to secure valuable concessions from the other Pacific lines," he explained to Stephen, "most of which I think comes to them in money. They receive bonuses on account of coast business and . . . the China and Japan trade." Still driven by the old ambition to help America achieve what he believed would be its ultimate destiny in the Far East, he could not bear to be left out. Soon he sent Major Rogers, who had completed his exploration work for the Canadian Pacific and was looking for new mountain passes to name for himself, on a "hunting trip" in the rugged territory west of Helena, and he complained bitterly when suspicious newspaper reporters found out what the colorful Major was really up to.[1]

Knowing that his associates already felt that he had more than he, or any other mortal, could handle, Hill explained his intentions when he sent Rogers's report to Kennedy late in 1886. "It is of great value to us to know just what is ahead of us, and I expect to keep Major R. at work until we know all the country between Sun River Valley and the Columbia or Puget Sound," he explained, adding that even if they did not take the initiative, the information would be valuable "in case another company was seeking to occupy that country." He was overjoyed when Kennedy accepted his trial balloon with enthusiasm. "I have no doubt but that sooner or later we will make use of it," Kennedy wrote, "for people all seem to be waking up to the idea that sooner or later we will become a transcontinental line." At the end of the year Hill forwarded a letter in which Rogers reported finding a pass, and as soon as spring came he had the intrepid Major follow up on his theories. "I write this hastily to let you know I still live," scribbled Rogers from Wolf Lodge Creek, in the wild country east of Fort Coeur d'Alene, Idaho. "Have found a feasible route as far west as the Coeur d'Alene mission . . . requiring a tunnel of about 4000 feet. . . . [The area] is fearfully cut up, and there is no trace or even a twig cut to show any human being has ever been through." [2] Even as he joined the Manitoba road to the Montana Central, thus appearing to

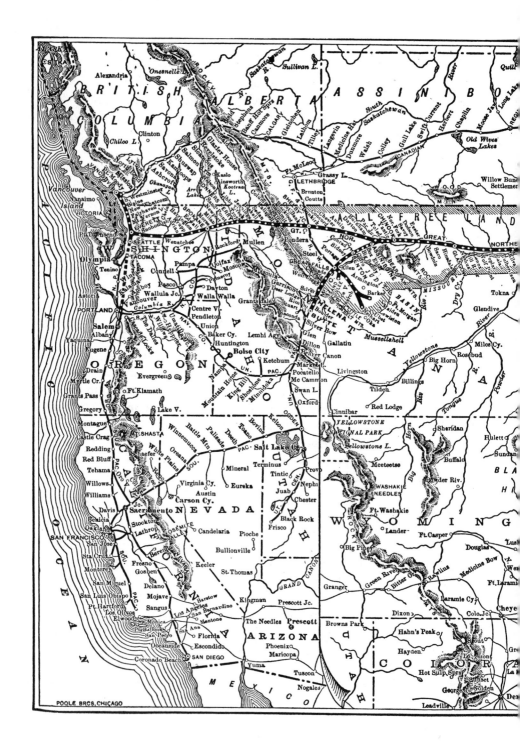

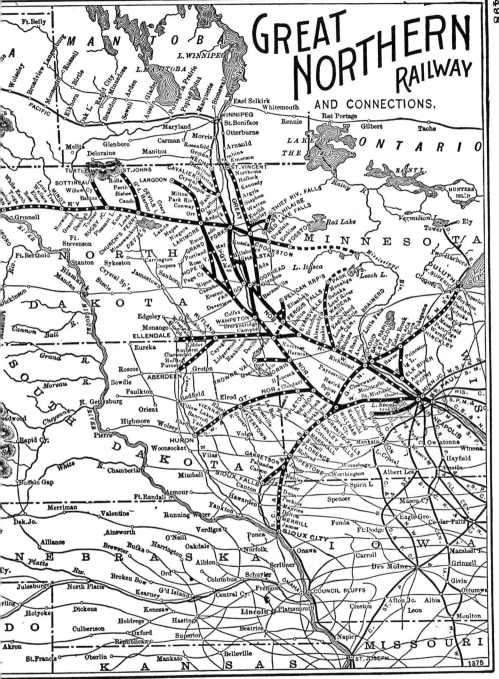

GREAT NORTHERN RAILWAY

AND CONNECTIONS.

1893 (*Official Railway Guide*, June 1893.)

cast the die in favor of a Pacific extension only a few miles to the north of the Northern Pacific, Hill was flirting with the idea of abandoning Great Falls and Helena in favor of a route straight west from Fort Assiniboine to Spokane Falls and Puget Sound, through some of the most desolate territory in the entire Northwest.

As the subsequent history of Midwestern railroads reveals, Hill was one of the few leaders of regional roads who realized by the end of the 1880s that the time for major decisions was at hand. The Chicago, Burlington & Quincy, under the competent leadership of Charles E. Perkins, had seen the need for some kind of firm connection to the Pacific Coast as early as 1883, but the Boston capitalists who had made the Burlington one of the strongest properties west of the Mississippi River shrank from major new undertakings. The Milwaukee Road, the Chicago & North Western, and the Rock Island all failed to evolve a master strategy which would have made them powerful transcontinental carriers. Meanwhile, the Union Pacific, despite the senseless financial handicaps placed upon it by a vindictive Congress after the Crédit Mobilier scandal, had achieved true transcontinental status by building the Oregon Short Line northwestward to a connection with the Oregon Railway & Navigation Company, in which it owned a large interest, thus bringing the road into Portland, then the only major port in the Pacific Northwest. Despite his shortcomings as an operating executive, Charles Francis Adams, Jr., was making something of this "apple tree without a limb," as the Union Pacific's chief builder, Sidney Dillon, had called it, although its huge debt to the government was coming due in a few years and the evil figure of Jay Gould lurked in the wings. Collis P. Huntington, the only real railroad man among the fabled "Big Four" (which had included Leland Stanford, Charles Crocker, and Mark Hopkins), was appealing to the venality of the California legislature and welding the Southern Pacific into a system whose strength would match Hill's Great Northern. Even the wobbly Atchison, Topeka & Santa Fe was emerging as a successful transcontinental, although its stubborn decision to build, rather than buy, an extension from Kansas City to Chicago was a fearful burden on its finances.

Most striking of all in the unfolding picture of the transcontinentals was the triumphant return of Henry Villard to leadership of the Northern Pacific. Forced to bow out during the panic of 1884, this promotional genius, who somehow still managed to inspire confidence among German investors in the Northern Pacific, was back in the saddle by 1889. He was determined to dominate the entire Northwestern railroad scene. Through his holding company, the Oregon Transcontinental, he narrowly controlled both the Northern Pacific and the Oregon Railway & Navigation Company, although he had to share the latter with the Union Pacific. During his absence the Northern Pacific, much to the Portlanders' disgust, had bored its Stampede Tunnel through the Cascades and had built its own line to tidewater at—of all places—Tacoma, Washington, and, under Villard had made half-hearted gestures toward bringing the raw new town of Seattle into its ken. The way Hill had made off with most of the mining traffic of Montana still rankled, and Villard continued what Hill considered the idiotic policy of building branches of the Northern Pacific into the province of Manitoba in cutthroat competition with both the Canadian Pacific and the Manitoba road. Very soon, Hill and nearly everybody else could plainly see, the question of whether the Northern Pacific or the Manitoba road would dominate the Northwestern transportation system would have to be settled.

There were even more fundamental, if less dramatic, reasons why the day of the vigorous regional railroad was coming to an end. As the nation became more highly industrialized and thus more regionally specialized, through traffic grew much faster than local business. By the end of the 1880s the railroads went nearly everywhere, some areas were over-supplied with rails, and the number of possible combinations of railroads that could form through routes had grown alarmingly. As rates declined along with nearly all other prices in the last quarter of the century, the need to increase traffic, and especially the more profitable through business, could not be ignored. Above all else, traffic managers had to be able to make contracts with big shippers which guaranteed rates between terminal points for the duration of the contract, and as long as a railroad man controlled only a segment of that route he could offer no such guarantee. What rate stability the railroads had been able to achieve, mainly through the practice of pooling, had been destroyed by the Interstate Commerce Act of 1887, which outlawed such collusive activities. Railroad experts could see no alternative to chaos except massive consolidation of the railroads, which, they freely predicted, would be the chief outcome of the new regulatory law. And even if Hill had not been perfectly aware of the woefully unstable financial structures of all but the strongest railroads, and the day of reckoning toward which they so clearly pointed, he had the gloomy predictions of men such as John S. Kennedy, Henry W. Cannon, Henry L. Higginson, and Jacob H. Schiff to remind him of it. Bad times, Hill knew, could be times of opportunity, but only for the strong.

Hill had begun to develop strength for his thrust to the Pacific by learning as much about the physical obstacles as he could. Then he turned to the matter of making common cause with Villard's enemies, who were legion, if poorly organized. "He is a very sanguine man, and full of his own importance," Hill said of Villard. He had also discovered that the Northern Pacific leader did not offer all the local promoters in the Pacific Northwest the kind of leadership they wanted. Men like Elijah Smith, who had built snippets of railroads around Puget Sound, were looking for a friskier dog. Smith had a substantial interest in Villard's holding company, and would be a valuable ally in case it came to a fight, so Hill carefully cultivated relations with him from the day they first met in 1886.[3]

Early in 1889, as he was wrestling with the question of how to go to the Pacific, Hill began to suspect that Villard was about to move against the Manitoba road. Cannon had written that the Union Pacific was inclined to give Villard his head in voting Oregon Transcontinental stock, and that was bad news indeed. A week later Cannon rushed to Nichols's office with the intelligence that Villard was indeed planning a takeover, with the help of Boston men who had their eyes on Kennedy's stock, which was thought to be lying around loose, and that of George Stephen and Donald Smith, who, gossip had it, had cast their lot irrevocably against Hill when he had refused to take the Soo roads off their hands. Nichols wired Hill and followed up with an anxious letter. "One thing is certain," he agonized, "Villard can carry the combination through or defeat it. I believe he has put [Charles] Fairchild up to attempt to secure control of Manitoba with or without your cooperation. He (Fairchild) says he will give 120 [dollars per share of Manitoba common stock]. . . . The most dangerous part is the unanimous action of the N.P. board in joining Adams [of the Union Pacific] . . . to bottle up the Manitoba at Helena and Butte." Hill dropped everything and wired Villard that he was coming to New York to see him.[4]

Arriving in New York, Hill went straight to Villard's townhouse on East 72 Street, where his adversary was sick abed. What Hill said to him is not on record, but he was well prepared to clear up a number of misapprehensions under which Villard seemed to be laboring. Kennedy's stock was not available, its owner having decided not to sell his substantial remaining holdings even to Hill, Stephen, and Smith, who had agreed to buy it up if it came to that. As for Sir George and Sir Donald, they were going to be Hill's staunchest supporters in the Pacific extension, had consented to rejoin the board of directors of the company, and were arranging to secure the bulk of the financing in England. The new line would run rings around the Northern Pacific as far as operating costs were concerned, and there was no question who would end up on top if it came to a fight. A low opinion of Hill's strength and determination seems never to have been one of Villard's follies, and he mounted no organized effort to gain control of the Manitoba road. Just to be sure, however, Hill and his associates, working through Cannon, bought 15,000 shares of Oregon Transcontinental, which, along with another 15,000 held by Smith and his friends, they were prepared to vote against Villard at the holding company's annual meeting. "Some of the large people are already deserting him," Cannon noted, laconically. Stephen was greatly relieved to learn that Hill had rejected Villard's overtures; he declared his complete confidence in Hill's loyalty to his own and Sir Donald's interests and passed along a letter from Schiff, "who is greatly relieved that the danger of the N.P. gobbling you up has passed away." [5]

Convinced by now that the interests of the Northwest demanded that domination of its railroads pass from Villard to himself, sooner or later and in one way or another, Hill was still not sure that an additional line to the Pacific could be justified. Writing to Sir George to thank him for his part in securing tighter control of Manitoba stock, he made a startling suggestion:

> You may think I am going pretty fast in Nor Pac matters but I am *very sure* that if we can get what we want there the results will be more than we considered in any other plan. . . . The entire property, controlled by a new company, would have an earning capacity of about $3,000,000 a month, and this with the advantages of removing all expensive rivalry and competition would alone save not less than 5%, which is $1,000,000 per annum. . . .[6]

And a month later he was full of enthusiasm for the idea:

> The more I think it over the more I am convinced that the thing for us to do is to "take the bull by the horns" and get control of the Northern Pacific, and by one stroke settle all questions at once. . . . It is pursuing a very aggressive course, almost regardless of permanent cost and business judgment . . . [and] doing both the Manitoba and the CPR great damage. . . . They cannot be held to any agreement. A starving man will usually get bread if it is to be had and a starving railway will not maintain rates.

Whenever I take up this question I want to go right at the work of getting control of that company. . . .[7]

But Stephen did not see how they could possibly snatch the Northern Pacific away from Villard, who was at the crest of his power. "I am 10 years your senior and not the man I was 10 years ago," Stephen admitted, "but would gladly put myself to more considerable inconvenience to capture the NP." But, he added, "I have no doubt of our ability to build a line on our own and think I can see my way to finance the extension to the coast on very economical terms."[8] Both men could see that a chance to build a superior line to the Pacific was a more alluring prospect than a bruising fight for a second-rate railroad, a fight which, after all, they might lose.

II

Terrified at the breakneck speed which the Hill express picked up as the year 1888 waned, two of his most important passengers jumped off at the first opportunity. Sam Thorne, conservative as ever, had no heart left for risk-taking after the exciting events of the previous year and a half, and he was content to retire to the less nerve-wracking occupation of managing his investments. D. Willis James, however, was convinced that Hill had lost all contact with reality, and he hinted at "madness." As serious-minded working directors of the corporations to which they lent their names, both were fed up with being kept in the dark by Hill. That busy man had no time, it seemed, to keep the New York directors up to date on costs of the Montana extension, the line to Lake Superior, and the growing fleet of Lake vessels which he was assembling, and his early, optimistic estimates bore little resemblance to actual costs. In February of 1889 James was furious to learn that not only had the company not used its recent bond issues to retire the million-dollar loan Hill had made to it, as had been solemnly resolved by the board of directors, but it had used up all its immediate collateral for loans even while needing yet more funds to meet firm commitments.

Henry Minot, at Hill's request, made a close study of the company's finances and he gave a soothing report to his chief, but nothing either man could say mollified the disgruntled New Yorkers. A month later Thorne walked into the Manitoba road's offices in New York and, finding no one around except a clerk and Minot, brusquely directed the young man to deliver a letter personally to Mr. Hill. Blandly observing that he presumed it was Thorne's resignation from the board, Minot cheerfully reported to Hill that "Mr. T. expressed himself as fully decided." James' "No" had resounded repeatedly at a recent board meeting as questions of further commitments were put, and he finally stalked out of his last meeting in the middle of the proceedings. But it was Kennedy's resignation Hill truly regretted. His old associate had sold 10,000 of his 25,000 shares of stock, and it was a great relief to get a letter from Naples, where Kennedy had wandered in search of relief from his insomnia, declaring, "My interest in the company is large, and I fully expect and believe it will continue more or less so as long as I live." His counsel was at Hill's disposal whenever he wanted it, he promised.[9]

It was Sir George Stephen, backed up by the benign presence of Sir Donald Smith, who stood staunchly behind Hill, from his first awareness that the railroad was to be extended to the Coast to the day when he succeeded in breaking down English investors' prejudice against Great Northern securities at the end of the century. As the busy summer of 1888 wore into fall, only one shadow lay across the bonds of sentiment and rich profits which bound Hill to his Canadian associates: the question of what they were to do with the Soo lines. Stephen, fishing at his lodge at Grand Metis, Quebec, that July, had assured Hill that he and Smith wanted to do whatever was best for the Manitoba road, in which "we each have a greater pecuniary interest than we have in the CPR." [10] Hill fenced with Stephen on the issue for the next several months, sensing, correctly, that it was not the time to bring it to a head.

Meanwhile, Sir George poured out his heart to Hill about the ingratitude of his fellow Canadians. They did not fully appreciate his nine years of backbreaking effort to make the Canadian Pacific a reality. The "Grits" of Manitoba—whose credo, like that of their American Populist counterparts, was composed of one part righteous indignation, one part routine demagogy, and one part abysmal ignorance— were attacking his stewardship mercilessly. The more he thought about the deteriorating Canadian situation, the more he relished the idea of completing the work the associates had begun south of the boundary in 1878. "We both have the same pride and confidence in the 'blessed old railway' we ever had," he confessed. As for his own people, he raged, "I am thoroughly disgusted and for the thousandth time bitterly repent that I ever had anything to do with them or their country. . . . I would like to shake the dust of Canada off my feet and turn my back on the country for ever." [11]

By spring of next year Hill, Stephen, and Smith had joined forces to buy up 12,000 shares of Manitoba common, virtually all of the floating supply to which any potential corporate raider might be attracted. Stephen was proudly reporting that he was advising friends to buy Manitoba, not Canadian Pacific; had persuaded one of the most efficient London brokers, Thomas Skinner, to become the company's agent; and, through his virtuoso New York lawyer, John W. Sterling, had assured such potential troublemakers as General Samuel Thomas and Calvin S. Brice, who knew a good thing when they saw it, that they would be properly taken care of when the time came. "The new scheme has taken complete possession of my mind," he wrote, adding wistfully that he wished there were some way to retain the word "Manitoba" in the new corporation name, which Hill was determined would be simply, "Great Northern Railway." Soon, Sir George added, they must tie up such loose ends as the Soo question. Meanwhile, Donald Smith found time to echo these sentiments in two letters. [12]

During the spring and summer of 1889 Stephen and Hill consulted frequently on how best to reorganize the Manitoba road for its great new venture. In July they spent several days closeted with Sterling, General Thomas, Brice, and others in New York, and Stephen was disquieted to note that Hill, whose rheumatism was troubling him again, was not in the best shape for heavy new burdens. Stephen had doubts, in fact, about the "wisdom of my undertaking more work after what I have gone through the last nine years." In St. Paul that September for the annual meeting of the Manitoba road, however, he and Hill resolved to carry the enterprise through on their own resources, if it should come to that. On his way back to Montreal Stephen heard much that reaffirmed his faith in their independent methods. At Sudbury, Ontario, he found his private car coupled onto the train that was pulling General Thomas's car. Thomas, a chief protagonist of such more-or-less blackmail projects as the Nickel Plate Railroad and the Duluth, South Shore & Atlantic (one of the Soo roads), was by no means in Stephen's confidence, but the General had acquired a major interest in the Chase National Bank and had to be reckoned with. Wandering into Sir George's car after dinner, Thomas delivered a two-hour monologue on the vast sums which they could make out of the Great Northern venture. "I thought it well to put you on your guard," Stephen wrote Hill; "the ways of Thomas and his friend, Brice, are not our ways and I see nothing in them to lead me to think we should give up our old and tried methods of working for the company rather than for our individual interests. . . ." [13]

Both Hill and Stephen realized that it would be difficult to convince European investors that the Great Northern was a virtuous and worthy suitor; the Europeans had suffered repeated disappointments at the hands of American transcontinental railroads. With skill and patience, however, it could be done, for, as Stephen never tired of pointing out, there was a great deal of money languishing at 3 per cent in England for want of more attractive investment opportunities. Judge Greenleaf Clark, one of Hill's oldest friends and most trusted advisers, joined with M. D. Grover, who was to make a brilliant reputation as the Great Northern's general counsel, in recommending that the new transcontinental be placed under the aegis of a combination holding and operating company, to be called the Great Northern Railway, to which the physical assets of the Manitoba road would be leased. They already owned the charter for such a company, for no better franchise could be hoped for than that of the Minneapolis & St. Cloud Railroad, under which Hill had built the line to Lake Superior. The St. Cloud charter had been issued by the territorial legislature in 1856—long before railroads were thought capable of doing any wrong—and it seemed to give Hill and his friends the power to do just about anything they wanted when it came to building new railroads or buying up competing lines. Legally, the birth of the new railroad amounted to no more than changing the name of the Minneapolis & St. Cloud to Great Northern.

Hill had intended from the beginning that the new company should be owned, for the most part, by the owners of the Manitoba road, and he worked out a sophisticated scheme to attain this end. Predictably, it aroused criticism for appearing to give somebody something for nothing. The Great Northern was authorized to issue $20 million (par value) of preferred and $20 million of common stock, but only the preferred was to be issued at the time of organization. Stockholders of the Manitoba road could subscribe for one $100 share of Great Northern preferred for each share of Manitoba common they owned, at only $50 cash. The remaining $ 10 million of the purchase price was made up by $22 million worth of stock the Manitoba road held in various subsidiary corporations to which it had advanced construction money, like the Eastern Railway of Minnesota. This stock was turned over to the Great Northern, subject to a "mortgage" represented by $8 million of collateral trust bonds, which the Great Northern would pay off with the cash proceeds of its preferred issue.

In modern jargon, the subsidiary stock was "spun off" by the Manitoba road to the Manitoba stockholders—who were its ultimate owners—and then immediately "spun back" to complete payment for the preferred stock. Such complicated maneuvers kicked up considerable dust, including a stockholder's lawsuit, but it settled quickly. Soon everyone understood that, by and large, the owners of the Manitoba road, on whose common stock the Great Northern guaranteed a 6 per cent dividend in perpetuity, were also the owners of the new railroad. The Manitoba road would build the extension, thus vesting title to the entire railroad from St. Paul to Seattle in the Manitoba, and its bonds, guaranteed by the Great Northern, would provide the money. Eventually, Hill and Stephen realized, they would want to simplify this corporate arrangement, but for now, while the credit of the Manitoba road was well established and that of the Great Northern was not, this was the way to do it.[14]

The Manitoba road's annual meeting was held in St. Paul on September 12, 1889, and four days later Hill boarded the Soo line train for Montreal, where he was joined by Sir George for the trip to New York. At a meeting of the full board of the Manitoba road on September 20 the plans for the Great Northern organization were spread on the minutes and adopted. Sir George and Sir Donald rejoined the board of the Manitoba road and accepted seats on the new Great Northern. Besides Hill and his associates, the directors of the new company included Samuel Hill, who was serving his father-in-law on the boards of several of the subsidiary companies; George Bliss and J. Kennedy Tod, representing the New York banking community; William P. Clough, vice president of the new company and Hill's right-hand man; and Edward Sawyer, treasurer. By 1891 the company was running smoothly, and Bliss and Sir George, the latter having taken up permanent residence in England, were replaced by Jacob Schiff, head of Kuhn, Loeb & Co., and Edward T. Nichols, Hill's chief financial representative in the New York office. Of all these men, none would be so helpful to Hill during the grueling construction period as Clough, a brilliant lawyer whom Hill had determined to pirate away from the Northern Pacific ever since Clough had revealed great skill when he had assembled that road's new right-of-way between St. Paul and Minneapolis.[15]

And now the real work could begin.

III

A more superstitious man than Hill might have been terrified at the
promptness with which his usual Christmas indisposition showed up
at the end of 1889. This time it was his rheumatism. It laid him low for
nearly four weeks, during which he raged at his inability to get on
with the great work. A trip to England which he had looked forward
to as his first Atlantic crossing had to be canceled. "My illness took
nearly four weeks of my time," he admitted to Stephen, "and the location of our lines, necessary legislation, &c have demonstrated that we
have too much of a load on one pair of shoulders. . . ." But neither
then nor later did either he or any of his associates give any hint that
anything had gone wrong with the leadership, much less that it might
happen again.[16]

Fortunately, he had been able to assemble several highly competent
subordinates just as the great adventure began. E. L. Mohler, his
plodding general manager, ran the railroad's day-to-day affairs from
the hot seat which Manvel had finally quit for an even more uncomfortable one as president of the ailing Santa Fe. Even before spring
signaled the beginning of construction in 1890, Hill had his chief engineer, E. H. Beckler, out in the mountains making preparations. The
two men knew each other well, for Beckler had had charge of the Montana Central work. He knew that Hill would demand every last gasp of
devotion to the Pacific extension. Slight of stature, well-educated, and
still in his thirties, Beckler had no illusions about the task that faced
him. He had learned well that, while Hill generally knew—or thought
he knew—the one best way to do everything, any man who interpreted his job simply as one of blindly carrying out his chief's
orders would not last very long. As Hill told one of Beckler's subordinates, they were free to alter plans on the spot, "so some fellow can't
come along in a few years and make a change in your work." [17]

But they had better be right.

The engineer who had received this sage advice was John F. Stevens, a wiry, athletic young man. This self-taught, tenacious New
Englander was to be the prime mover in establishing the route the GN
would follow across the two great mountain ranges that stood between
Pacific Junction and Puget Sound. If there was one thing which gave
Hill nightmares, it was the thought that he might, after putting everything he had into the greatest work of his life, build the railroad in the
wrong place. He wanted nothing less than the best possible line, he

The financier: Gaspard Farrer of Baring Bros. & Co., about 1937, forty years after Hill first met him.

The explorer: John F. Stevens, about 1900, a decade after his discovery of the Marias Pass. Burlington Northern.

The negotiator: William P. Clough in the late 1880's, when he went to work for Hill. Burlington Northern.

The politician: "Judge" Thomas E. Burke, pioneer builder of Seattle. University of Washington.

FOUR WHO HELPED BUILD THE GREAT NORTHERN RAILWAY——

said over and over, and this meant the straightest route, with the least possible grades and the lowest mileage over-all. Most fundamentally, it meant crossing the Continental Divide in as straight a westward line from Pacific Junction as could be surveyed. While deep in study of half a dozen possible routes west, Hill and Stephen had received a visit from D. C. Shepard, who shook his head at the route Major Rogers had recommended. "Shepherd's talk rather impressed me with the necessity of our not making a mistake in the location of the line to the coast," Sir George observed, with superb Scottish understatement. [18]

For all anyone knew, the best pass at the latitude which Hill wanted to occupy was the highly undesirable one which A. W. Tinkham, the young leader of one of the parties sent out by Congress to explore a route for a Pacific railroad in 1853–54, had dubbed *the* Marias Pass. Instructed to make one more foray before the winter of 1853 set in, Tinkham, moving from the western base of the Rocky Mountains eastward, had struggled up the appallingly steep valley of a tributary (the wrong one, it turned out) of the Flathead River. He and his men paused briefly to note that although it was late October, the previous winter's snow still lay, unmelted, at the summit of the pass, and they then hastened down the eastern slope and on to the welcome warmth of Fort Benton. The "mere brook," later named Cut Bank Creek, which Tinkham had followed down the eastern slope was indeed a tributary of the Marias River. This Marias Pass was 7600 feet above sea level, well above the line of perpetual snow, and a two-and-one-half-mile tunnel, cutting through the peak, would be required to cross at 5450 feet. Even if such a tunnel were constructed, no one could imagine a railroad descending the western slope under any circumstances.

Hill had been familiar with the findings of the Pacific Survey for many years, and in 1889 he had acquired a set of its thirteen volumes and maps. He frowned at its conclusion that the most northerly route "is not likely to come into competition with the passes farther south." But his heart leaped up at something which I. I. Stevens, Territorial Governor of Washington and head of the northern division of the Pacific Survey, had added:

> There are probably passages of the mountains connecting other branches of the Marias river with other tributaries of Flathead river, and giving, perhaps, opportunities for passing the divide with more ease than by the way explored; and should a line in this direction be thought desirable, it should be remembered that the field has been very partially explored. . . .[19]

Since the 1850s several parties had claimed to have crossed the Rockies via a low pass at the latitude in which Hill was interested, but none had noted its location. To the Indians, mountains were holy places, and fearing the displeasure of their gods more than the anger of white men, they were evasive when questioned about passes. And after the Northern Pacific selected its route to the south, further interest in the location of the "other" Marias pass waned. But Hill was determined that one more effort be made to find it. Unless it was found right away, however, all of his planning would be thrown into abeyance until the following spring. Reluctantly, for it was bitter cold in the mountains by the end of November, Beckler allowed the eager Stevens and a grumbling Flathead Indian named Coonsah to make one more expedition into the mountains before winter closed in.

Soon Stevens was plodding up the eastern slope of the Rocky Mountains, not far from what is today an entrance to Glacier National Park. Coonsah muttered gloomily as the cold, dark peaks closed around them, and finally he said that he would go no farther. But Stevens was determined to follow a provocative little stream to its source. The two men made camp, and Stevens, pausing only long enough to pull on his heaviest clothing and boots, pressed on alone into the wilderness. The little stream led him to its source, and Stevens could see that, a short distance farther on, another stream flowed, unmistakably, to the west. Trembling with excitement, he checked his barometer, which told him that he was barely 5000 feet above sea level. He had found the *real* Marias Pass. Not daring to pause long enough in the forty-below-zero cold to build a fire, he kept moving all that long night. It was December 11, 1889.[20]

"The more I think of the question the more I am impressed with the importance of the northern line via Flathead and Kootenai," Hill wrote Beckler two days after receiving the good news, and immediately he began to speculate on how they would cross the plain between Spokane and the base of the Cascades. "Some important questions have to be decided this winter," he continued, ordering Beckler to St. Paul without delay. "If I am not well enough to be at the office when you arrive, come right up to the house," directed Hill, who was the worst of patients by then. To Paris Gibson, who was devastated to learn that his beloved Great Falls would not be on the main line, he took the time to explain the hard facts: "It would be folly to make a detour as far south as Great Falls and turn around and go north, using two sides of a triangle when one of them could be saved. The nearer a railway line can be built in accordance with natural conditions the better, in the end." [21] But throughout the long winter he had to admit to himself, in an occasional bad moment, that they still did not know how they were going to cross the Cascades.

IV

At the end of February 1890 Hill made a fourteen-page report to Sir George, who was settled by then in a fine house at 25 St. James's Place, London:

> This work [finding the best route] has been very difficult, as we have had to cover over 1000 miles of route, mostly in the mountain region. The line via Dearborn to Missoula and Mullan [the southern route] has very heavy work with high and expensive trestles and over two miles of tunnels, with maximum grades of 117 feet per mile [2.3 per cent]. The northern route gives us our own line all the way to Spokane and the coast with lighter grades, less cost and shorter distances to all competing points . . . We

will have a line to the coast . . . two hundred miles shorter than the other lines, and I think our interest [charges] will be less per mile per annum than our competition, by one-half. . . .

So much for the good news. At last, however, it was time to grapple with the distasteful problem of the Soo line:

> I am, I assure you, desirous to carry out our understanding, but do not think you would advise a step that has on its face no justification and one that might, by our loading the Great Northern at the first, jeopardize its whole career. . . . I have had some inquiry . . . from Boston as to whether there was a deal on foot to saddle the Great Northern with the Soo, to which I replied that the owners of the Soo [are] too heavily interested in Great Northern . . . and further, that they did not do business that way. . . .[22]

He had decided to take a stand as a result of a letter from Donald Smith, who proposed that they meet at the "little Bank Cottage" in Montreal, where fourteen years before they had hatched their plan to take over the St. Paul & Pacific, and effect a fusion of the Soo and the Great Northern. Hill believed that as traffic grew the Soo might become, in time, a moderately profitable railroad, but he did not care to be saddled with it during its dependent years. The Soo line northwestward from the Twin Cities, which was in direct competition with the Great Northern, was not even earning its operating expenses, he told Stephen, and if he had his way about it he would take up the rails and re-lay them where they would do some good.

Later that winter he saw his way out of the difficulty. Now that Van Horne was running the Canadian Pacific, it was up to the Canadians to decide what kind of relations they would have with the Great Northern. On March 2 he sent Sir George a long cablegram, offering to take over the Soo if the Canadian Pacific would execute a "traffic contract of binding and perfectly equitable and effective character between Great Northern and Canadian Pacific." He could hardly lose. If Van Horne agreed at that stage to divide up all transcontinental traffic, for which the Great Northern would not even be in a position to bid for several years, it would be well worth the cost of the Soo. At the same time, it seemed a fair compromise to Stephen. But Hill knew Van Horne; such an agreement was the last thing Hill expected, and it was not forthcoming.[23]

It was a strategic victory for which Hill could be grateful, even if he had had to finesse his closest friends. At last they presented a solid front to the financial world. Offers to help in the financing of the Pacific extension now came in from all sides. Old John Murray Forbes, who that spring had been scribbling notes critical of Hill's business methods from his private car on the Burlington road, begged for a thirty-minute interview at Hill's hotel before he left New York. Failing that, he offered to ride in the train as far as Philadelphia to say what he had to say. Standing in the lobby of the Albemarle, Hill could smile as he weighed Forbes's letter in one hand and a similar one from Jacob Schiff in the other. It was the wary English, however, who won the business, for Sir George persuaded Baring Brothers & Company to lead a syndicate which was to take £6,000,000 worth of Manitoba road bonds, one of the largest financings ever achieved by an American railroad in Europe up to that time. Then, almost immediately, Baring's collapsed (as a result of unwise investments in Argentina). But Sir George counseled that he and Hill were not to worry. "The intrinsic merit of the security is sure to be appreciated more and more every day. . . . We must just put our hands into our pockets again next spring and find another million and hold them until the public wakens." Baring's struggled to its feet again, and £3,000,000 of the bonds were sold, enough to keep Hill in construction funds, but to complete the financing the Great Northern would have to look to its own resources.[24]

V

As work got under way that spring Hill's friends were surprised to learn that he was not to have the help of the one lieutenant whom, they thought, he had been grooming for a high post in the Great Northern organization. Hill's inability to tolerate for long any man who obviously had his eye on his job had seemed to have been overcome in the case of Henry D. Minot, but things were going altogether too slowly for that "round, rosy-cheeked boy," as Manvel described him. Once the line to Lake Superior was in operation Minot looked around for a new field to conquer, and he soon decided that the Pacific extension was it. "It would please me to assume, under your guidance, the task of the entire extension," he wrote Hill. "I believe that to segregate the whole undertaking from the Manitoba and to have one lieutenant in the field, with a single responsibility, at the head of the campaign, would develop the best results," reminding his chief that his services were now worth $25,000 elsewhere.[25] Hill's reply was quick and forthright:

> Now, in the first place I wish to say that it has been a principle of my life that no man should ever sacrifice his opportunities for advancement to an extent that might result in his failing to take the tide at its flood . . . and I would be the last person to find any fault with you for seeking your own advancement in every proper way.
>
> In regard to your taking charge of the work of building the entire western extension, while I have full confidence as to your efforts to do the best you can . . . Stephen and Bliss both felt that I must see the line to the coast, and after some further discussion I told them I would. . . .
>
> Your help in settling many matters of a general character would, if I could have it, save me much time and travel on the Pacific side, and . . . I would personally feel the value of your assistance [but] the questions that will arise are to be more complex and difficult than any we have heretofore been called on to settle, and will take all the knowledge [and] judgment we can muster to avoid mistakes, many of which no doubt will occur in any event.[26]

Minot gave Hill plenty of time to change his mind, but it was soon clear that the young man had little to offer the great adventure. With customary zeal he was soon immersed in new projects assigned him by the Boston interests who were trying desperately to make a go of the Santa Fe Railroad. He maintained his elegant bachelor establishment in St. Paul, but was on the road most of the time. On November 13, 1890, he left Washington, where he had been attending to the Santa Fe's affairs, to return to St. Paul. When his wooden Pullman car, the "Biscay," was coupled to the rear of the New York-to-Chicago limited at Harrisburg, Pennsylvania, late that night, Minot was asleep in his berth, at the very end of the car. Traffic in the East was already taxing the facilities of busy railroads like the Pennsylvania, and this train, one of its best, almost always ran in two or more sections, of which Minot's was the first. Early next morning most of the passengers, bound for Pittsburgh, were making their toilets in the washrooms at the front end of "Biscay" when the train stopped at Florence, Pennsylvania, to take on water. Out of the autumn mists roared the second section, and it did not stop until it had telescoped "Biscay" for a distance of twelve feet. Minot and one other passenger were killed instantly. Mary Hill was writing to her daughter, Clara, who was at school in New York, when her husband came up the front walk clutching telegrams confirming the tragic news.[27]

Hill's failure to make Minot his successor had not gone unnoticed, but railroad men could not agree on the reason. "Hill has never shown . . . very much ability in getting the most possible out of men," Charles E. Perkins observed to Henry Higginson; "that is, he has not built up able men because he has not given them a chance to develop. Whether this has been simply part of his policy, so as to give his boys a better chance, I do not know." Allen Manvel, who had frequently chafed at Hill's tendency to withhold authority, as president of the Santa Fe was working closely with Minot at the end. "I thought a great deal of that boy," he told reporters, "for he was only a boy, but with a will power and ability for work that I have rarely seen equaled, bright and witty but at business he was all business." Perkins, however, had found Minot sadly lacking in common sense. "I think Hill liked him and wanted him to grow into a useful man, but the experiment failed." Still, he added, "Some people say Hill is a damned hard man to get on with!" Not until the very end of his career would Hill give the nod to a successor, and in the interim James Norman and Louis Hill would be made to feel as subordinate as ever Henry Minot and the others had.[28]

Hill shared none of the laurels for the great work with Minot, but he had other good men to lean upon, as did the engineers who gained fame on the Great Northern construction. The working out of the Great Northern's position on the Pacific slope between the international boundary, Seattle, and Portland—a job which Hill had had in mind for Minot—was handled by William P. Clough, who thus relieved his chief of a crushing burden. These delicate negotiations, carried on with a number of proud, suspicious, ambitious, local men who were determined to leave their own mark on the Pacific Northwest, were probably better off in Clough's hands than in those of the blunt, single-minded Hill or the sometimes arrogant Minot. Beckler and Stevens were backed up by another brave young man, Charles F. B. Haskell, who endured great hardships in verifying the feasibility of passes with which more famous men are credited.[29] And from one end of the 900-mile project to the other swarmed thousands of ordinary laborers: Irishmen, Italians, Americans of every description. Deer hunters still stumble over the bones of the several score who perished from exposure during the winter of 1890–91. All of the builders might take their place alongside the huge bronze statue of John F. Stevens that stands at the summit of Marias Pass.

VI

"I do not think that during the whole time I have been with Mr. Hill I have had such a busy time as during the past two years," Will Stephens wrote C. H. Benedict, his former co-worker, in the fall of 1892; "it has been a desperate scramble to try and hold things together." In the twelve years that Stephens had stood at Hill's elbow the pace had seldom slackened, but he had never seen Hill drive himself as relentlessly as he had since the spring of 1890. It would be a severe strain for everyone connected with the Great Northern, and most of them, including Stephens, would be worn out and ready to move to more tranquil situations when it was over.[30]

It was almost as if Hill knew that he had barely three years to complete the Pacific extension and arrange for its permanent financing before the country would find itself in the grip of a major depression. The fast-growing new industries of the East hummed busily in 1890, employment was high, and wages were rising, but just below the surface there were signs of trouble. The fat years already had been succeeded by the lean on the Great Plains, where crops had failed two years in succession, cutting the Manitoba road's earnings at the moment when Hill needed all the cash he could scrape up. Farm prices sagged badly, as indeed they had been doing more or less consistently for two decades, and the sadly inadequate banking and currency system had become the target for increasingly radical political elements. Whether the United States would or could remain on the gold standard, which men like Hill considered vital to economic growth, was an ever more important question. It was not only necessary to build the best possible road to the Pacific, he realized; it must also be done without the waste of a single dollar or the loss of a single day.

At the end of 1889 Hill had once again found himself responsible for virtually every detail of running the railroad. For more than a year he had been convinced that the patient, hard-working, but unimaginative Manvel was actually incompetent. "It is quite as much work to look after his work as it would be to do it all," Hill remarked to Kennedy. He scoffed at the idea that Manvel could handle the top job on the Union Pacific, for which, it was rumored, he was under consideration, and cruelly hinted that he was considering putting A. L. Mohler, Manvel's subordinate, in Manvel's place. When the presidency of the Santa Fe was offered him, Manvel accepted, although it appeared to offer little more than the opportunity to work himself to death.[31]

Hill sought a good man to replace Manvel, but his own tyrannical reputation was a handicap. "You are in the prime of life," wrote the second vice president of the Erie, declining the job, "and however much you may feel disposed to do so, it would hardly be possible for you to permanently abandon a hearty interest in the daily . . . workings of your property." Meanwhile, Charles E. Perkins, who had been carefully grooming his own general manager for the top job on the Burlington, warned Hill not to try to lure the man to the Great Northern. There was nothing for it but to promote Mohler to the post and hope for the best.[32]

Meanwhile Hill gathered every phase of the Pacific extension under his direct supervision. He had seen what had happened to the Northern Pacific when Villard had "delegated" responsibility for construction to subordinates, and he meant to watch over every aspect of the engineering and construction of the line. It had always been his way, the secret of his success, and he saw no reason to change at that crucial juncture. A large staff of engineers, under Beckler, would set the specifications of the line, subject to his final approval. His old friend D. C. Shepard would be the prime contractor to whom dozens of local contractors would be responsible, but all questions affecting the permanent character of the line would be decided by the engineers, with Hill as the final ajudicator of disputes—of which, he knew full well, there would be many.

Hill had never tackled anything quite this big before. It was not just the length of the extension—some 900 miles—nor the ruggedness of the region through which it ran, but the appalling uncertainties which he faced even as he committed the Great Northern to multi-million-dollar expenditures. Even the relatively easy stretch from Havre, in western Montana, where the chief operations base was set up, to Two Medicine Creek, at the eastern base of the Rockies, posed major problems. At a place called Cut Bank a bridge of heroic proportions had to be thrown across a deep chasm. Then there was the question of the western slope of the Rockies, still barely explored, and after that the Cascades. Reluctantly, he agreed with Beckler that the chief engineer's decision to call Haskell and his exploring party out of the mountains until spring was right. As in the Red River Valley eleven years before, winter was to be his chief adversary.[33]

In 1890, two days before Minnesota's reluctant spring was due, Hill called Beckler to St. Paul to receive his orders for the season's work. He urged Stevens, who had spent the winter making some extra money by doing consulting work in the East, to get back into the mountains as quickly as possible. Soon Hill had Clough on his way to the Puget Sound area to complete negotiations for the line from the Canadian boundary to Seattle, to decide whether the line down the Sound into Seattle should run along the shore or inland, and to tie up a host of critical loose ends. "There is but one way to have it done," said Hill of railroad building, "[and] that is to make the work permanent and good in every respect so that it will not have to be done over again." But when he finally had Stevens's report on the pass through the Cascades, he realized that he would have to make some major compromises. The altitude of the pass was almost as low as that through which the Northern Pacific ran, but a considerably longer tunnel was required. There was no time for a tunnel, Hill sadly realized, so they would have to fall back on one of the most primitive expedients in railroading: a "switchback," which would crab its way back and forth up one side of the mountain and down the other, adding some twelve miles to the length of the road. As soon as there was time to breathe, Hill would replace the switchback with a tunnel, but the vaunted Stevens Pass was a problem spot for the Great Northern until the end of the 1920s, when a new seven-mile-long Cascade tunnel was completed.[34]

It was one thing, Hill soon discovered, to run a railroad line across a prairie, where the successive steps of surveying, grading, track-laying, surfacing, and ballasting could be planned to follow each other in logical order. From one end of the Pacific extension to the other, however, there were streams to be bridged, chasms to be spanned by elaborate trestles, embankments to be whittled out of mountainsides which always seemed to be made of either the hardest rock or the most unstable mud, tunnels to be bored, and flash floods, blizzards, and bitter cold weather to be contended with. They all threw his neat timetable into chaos. Throughout the summer of 1892 he fumed at the sight of grading and track-laying crews standing idly by while some major obstacle was conquered. Hill's flying trips to the scene of operations became more and more frequent—and not a little dangerous, as his business car had a tendency to slip off the rails—and he addressed himself to every detail. Sweeping across the flat country west of Havre, Montana, he fired volleys of telegrams scoring whoever it was who had located the water-supply reservoirs so stupidly. Mohler, back in St. Paul, was told to stop ordering replacement wheels for locomotives, since it should be plain to him that much larger engines were on the manufacturers' drawing boards. Hill tore up Beckler's plans for placement of sidetracks on the extension, noting that there should be fewer of them, and that they should be longer, to accommodate the longer trains that the bigger locomotives would haul. Along the way he found time to lay down his familiar law about speculation by Great Northern employees in the lands along the road and about political activity among the men (both were rigidly proscribed), and to see to it that the laws relating to the taking of sand and gravel from the Indian reservations through which the railroad passed were scrupulously observed.[35]

"Mr. Hill was a hard taskmaster," Stevens recalled in his memoirs. "He kept every one on the jump and not always by suave comments. . . . I learned early to answer [his questions] if I knew the correct answer, and if I did not I told him so. . . ." But there was only one answer which Hill wanted to hear in the summer of 1892, and that was that the Great Northern's eastern and western links would be joined, somewhere up there in the Cascades, before the winter set in. When Beckler broke the news to him that it was not to be, Hill was almost hysterical. His devoted men felt the lash:

> I can hardly tell you how much of a disappointment this is. . . . I see no reason why that work should not have been completed before now. . . . I dislike to find fault in this matter; but there has been so much delay on the part of your engineers that I am forced to the conclusion that your men were not well selected. . . . Mr. Haskell worked for this Company in Dakota, and his work was practically all thrown away. . . . I fear you . . . will jeopardize the Company's interests. . . . If you cannot get this line completed, let me know and I can then take whatever steps may be necessary. . . . I feel it is a duty, and one that I will not shirk. . . .

Yet a few days later he was doing everything he could to help the harried Beckler. He sent him one of the best Irish track-laying experts that that tough breed had ever produced, backed his chief engineer in disputes with contractors, and by fall was telling him to abandon minor economies wherever necessary in order to get the job done quickly.[36]

Meanwhile, he was playing a patient and skillful waiting game with the citizens of Spokane and Seattle. Seattle's waterfront on Puget Sound was badly congested, and Hill was appalled at the bitter struggle being waged between the railroads for the best terminal sites. "I am getting tired of trying to get into Seattle," he told one of Clough's lieutenants there, "and if we are unable to get what is necessary in time, we will be compelled to go on with our work elsewhere." He hit upon a memorable metaphor which rocked the men of Seattle: their city, he observed blandly, was only "the head of the rake" with which the Great Northern expected to grasp the trade of the Pacific Northwest, and that rake would have "prongs that will reach all the principal cities of the Northwest." As usual, he had been careful to enlist the support of the best man around. Thomas Burke, Seattle's most influential citizen, was on his side. This short, portly, talented, Irish-American lawyer vastly simplified the task of assembling terminal property, and he told Hill to keep his hands off during the delicate process. "He [Hill] is a direct, positive, straightforward businessman," Burke told his neighbors. "He knows what he wants and isn't afraid to ask for it, and, I may add, generally gets it." [37]

Meanwhile, in Spokane, where a right-of-way for the railroad through the heart of the city was hard to find, Hill resorted to some unseemly temporizing. The railroads which had already come to Spokane, he noted in a speech to the city fathers, were practicing the same kind of rate discrimination against their capital of the Inland Empire, and in favor of Seattle, that had characterized other areas of the country. The Great Northern would put an end to this, he promised, if it found it feasible to get into Spokane. He got the right-of-way, but in doing so he had to make a promise he knew he could not afford to keep. [38]

VII

Sir George Stephen was delighted to hear that early in 1891 Hill was finally coming to England. He had constantly reminded his friend that it was time to prove to European investors that such a remarkable person as James J. Hill actually existed, and that their money was in good hands. The trip across the Atlantic was no longer any obstacle, he assured Hill, for "by the new White Star boats leaving NY on Wednesdays you are sure to be in London the next Wednesday and the voyage in them, no matter what the weather, is comfortable as possible." But Hill did not suit his departure to the sailing dates of the big queens of the sea, as did Sir George and Sir Donald, but rather to his own hectic schedule. After several cancellations Nichols got Hill and Henry P. Upham, who was to be his traveling companion, two staterooms on the North German Lloyd steamer *Lahn*, which sailed from New York on January 21.[39]

"When the ship is plunging through the waves and the rain and wind, making the whole of our visible world gloomy, I am sure that you are all better at home," Hill wrote Mary on his last day at sea. He was delighted with the restfulness of a sea voyage, however, even on the North Atlantic in January, for he had slept fourteen hours out of every twenty-four. But he soon discovered, as all transatlantic travelers do, that the last stages of the voyage are invariably exhausting. Routed out of bed at 2:30 a.m. by the Germans, the passengers for Southampton were taken to shore on a lighter, and, at 5 a.m., having finally passed customs, they departed for London. Hill, who had slept not a wink that night, grumbled that the tranquil Upham slept soundly all the way to Waterloo Station, and that, later, after they were installed in their suite at Brown's Hotel, he sat before the fire studying his tourist's guidebook while Hill mapped out business appointments.[40]

Hill was impressed by London, "a much greater city than New York," but "heavy, and at this time of year, a dull place." He had little time to spare from business, however, for Sir George had arranged meetings with nearly everybody of consequence in the investing community. "We have been out to dinner five nights out of seven," he wrote Mary, and on one evening they had gone to see what Sir Arthur Sullivan had done to turn his old favorite, *Ivanhoe*, into an opera. (Like nearly everyone else, he damned it with faint praise: "serious and rather pretty music.") He spared one hour for the National Gallery, writing Clara that after seeing some of the finest pictures in the world there, he "was better satisfied with our own pictures, particularly those of the Barbizon school." "Tonight we dine at [Sir George and Lady] Stephen's," he reported a few days later, "to meet a lot of Nobs." Then he was off to Paris and Amsterdam, back for a quick trip to Edinburgh, and, by the end of February, with a reluctant Upham in tow, he had landed in New York.[41]

Sir George's help had been valuable, even indispensable, in the conception and birth of the Great Northern, but with the Barings' bankruptcy in 1890 Hill was thrown back on his own resources in the

United States for the completion of the Great Northern's financing. "Barings are rapidly finding their 'feet' again," Stephen reported at the end of the year, "though their former great prestige is a thing of the past, I fear, never to be restored at least in our day." That June the Queen had raised Sir George to the peerage, and the delighted colonial took the title of Lord Mount Stephen, after the peak in the Canadian Rockies which had been named for him. He bought Brocket Hall, once the country home of a former Prime Minister, Lord Palmerston, and settled down for the rest of his long life. Save for one more visit, he had shaken the dust of Canada from his feet forever. He stoutly resisted Hill's efforts to keep him on the Great Northern's board of directors after 1892, but his usefulness to Hill and the American railroad system was far from ended.[42]

As first Kennedy, then Thorne and James, and then Stephen ended their regular involvement in the Great Northern, Jacob Schiff, head of the powerful firm of Kuhn, Loeb & Company, became more prominent in Hill's affairs. Proud and dignified, handsomely bearded, radiating the cultivation of New York's upper-class German-Jewish financial world, Schiff's very person denied the fact that he had left school at the age of fourteen. The two men's lives had been strikingly similar, and Schiff found in Hill a worthy associate and a stimulating companion. Their business association was brief, extending only until 1897, when E. H. Harriman claimed Schiff's skills and loyalty, but their friendship endured. In the spring of 1891 Hill had taken Schiff and several other New Yorkers out along the railroad to the summit of the Rockies, and their reactions were gratifying. Schiff wrote warmly about the trip, recalling that Hill always seemed to be jotting down facts for future use but could seldom find a pencil though he searched from one end of the business car to the other; so he sent him one. Four days later Schiff applied his own pen to a contract to buy from Hill 7500 shares of Great Northern preferred stock, thus taking for his firm a $5 million interest in the railroad.[43]

Meanwhile, Hill continued to enlarge the base of financial support which he enjoyed in New York. Henry W. Cannon's Chase National Bank, which at that time was far from the largest in the nation's financial capital, was forging a front-rank place for itself, and its cashier remarked to Hill that the Great Northern's $2 million deposit was far and away the largest that the Chase held. J. Kennedy Tod, over whose banking firm the comforting wings of his uncle, John S. Kennedy, were still spread, and John N. Moore, of the up-and-coming invest-

ment banking house of Moore & Schley, were strong supporters. In April 1892, with the help of these experts, the question of what to do with the unsold one-half of the issue of sterling bonds, planned as the permanent financing of the GN, was finally settled. The Great Northern now issued its own bonds on Wall Street, taking the sterlings from the Manitoba road as collateral. Virtually all of the $11 million issue was subscribed by the stockholders of the Great Northern, and they were never to regret their decision.

Elated and greatly relieved, Hill left New York for St. Paul. Sitting in the library of the big new house on Summit Avenue the night he returned, he realized that he was all alone. Mary was still in Santa Barbara; she, with Mamie, and his granddaughter, Rachel, had gone there to escape the Minnesota winter. Clara, Charlotte, James Norman, and Louis were at school in the East, while Ruth, Gertrude, and seven-year-old Walter were tucked away in bed upstairs. In the stillness of the great house, his pen scratched across the paper. "While East I raised the last money to finish our lines to the Pacific Coast," he wrote his wife, "the greatest work I have ever done, or will have to do. I hope we are not to be separated so long again." [44]

VIII

There are fir trees in the mountains
   Higher than the Eiffel tower;
There are cedars in the hollows
   Growing bigger every hour;

But your axe is never ringing,
   Though the world demands our pine;
You are waiting for the prophet—
   You are waiting for a sign.

You are waiting for a prophet—
   James with hair *en aureole*—
James, who pushes through the mountains,
   For Fairhaven's final goal.[45]

Hill smiled broadly at this expression of impatience, written by a Puget Sound newspaperman who was fed up with his railroad-mad neighbors. The poet, however, had put his finger on one of the most attractive resources of the Pacific Northwest. The treeless plains of the Midwest did indeed "demand our pine," and millions of board feet

lumber made from its pine, spruce, and fir would soon be rumbling eastward over the new line. Hill himself was eloquent in explaining this important factor in his plans for the Great Northern. He wrote Mount Stephen:

> The timber between the Cascade Range and Puget Sound is the largest and of the best quality I have ever seen. The amount of merchantable lumber per acre is from six to ten times as great as the best Michigan or Wisconsin timber land. It is impossible to realize the immense growth of these trees without seeing them in their native forest.

> From the traffic in this lumber alone . . . will come our largest revenue. With our low grades and well constructed railway we can successfully transport this lumber to St. Paul, Chicago, and even to all points east as far as New York. . . .[46]

Hill had expected to be on hand beneath those towering trees when the last spike was driven on the Great Northern, on January 6, 1893, at a siding appropriately named Scenic, which is today a station at the west portal of the Cascade tunnel. But the event took place in the dead of winter, and two division superintendents were the highest ranking Great Northern officials who turned up for the occasion. The workmen, who were warming themselves in the cook shack, only reluctantly came outside to put on a show of celebration for the photographer. It was, after all, the fifth or sixth time a transcontinental route had been completed (depending on how you defined "route"); as an anticlimax it resembled the astronauts' fifth or sixth trip to the moon seventy-five years later. As for the man who had done the most to bring it about, he was, true to form, nursing his rheumatism in the master bedroom of his new mansion in St. Paul.[47]

It was another month before regularly scheduled trains could run over the new line, and the first through passenger train did not leave St. Paul for the coast until June 18, taking a leisurely four days for the trip. But the citizens of St. Paul were far from blasé about the accomplishment, and plans were laid for a monster celebration on June 8 and 9. This was, after all, St. Paul's first transcontinental road of its own, and the people of the city made the most of the event. Hill, who felt that the money might be better spent on a public library, and who frequently refused to allow news photographers to take his picture, winced at the gigantic pen-and-ink portrait of himself that stared from the front page of the *Pioneer Press* on the great day. The city was festive with elaborate decorations, the most notable being several osten-

tatious triumphal arches. Through them passed float after float proclaiming the pride which the fire department, the Historical Society, and many a prosperous local merchant felt in their fellow citizen's triumph. As for the honored one, he had remained busy down to the last hour before the grand banquet held to honor him at the Aberdeen Hotel. A few days earlier he had participated in the Second International Reciprocity Convention in St. Paul, delivering a long speech on the need to abolish tariff barriers with Canada and the rest of the world. Then fire broke out in Fargo, North Dakota, one of the most important points on the Great Northern's Red River Valley line, and the entire town burned to the ground. Hill took over, issuing orders for relief of the homeless, who depended heavily upon him and the railroad for help.[48]

The grand ballroom of the Aberdeen Hotel was crowded with many famous and important men on the night of June 9, 1893. From Chicago had come Marshall Field, George M. Pullman, and Marvin Hughitt, who all sat at Hill's table. Upham, Greenleaf Clark, H. R. Bigelow, and former Governor Merriam were there with their old friend, as were Minnesota's first Governor, the venerable Alexander Ramsey, and its then chief magistrate, Knute Nelson. Of Hill's original associates only Sir Donald Smith was there. When Hill introduced him, the people of St. Paul, recognizing that he had had almost as much to do with the growth of their city as had the honored guest, cheered the old gentleman lustily.

Congratulations poured in from Hill's friends, great and small, intimate and near-forgotten. President Cleveland sent a graceful letter of praise (Hill had contributed both money and hard work to his third and successful campaign). George Stephen reminded him that "the company never can find a man who will serve it with the devotion and ability which you have lavished upon it from the first day," and for perhaps the thousandth time told him that now it was time to take it easy. Some time earlier, the ailing C. A. Broadwater had sent him a stuffed mountain goat,—it eventually became the symbol of the Great Northern—and Bishop Whipple, busy with his Indian work, praised him as the first man to build a railroad to the Pacific "alone." All the way from Boston came a letter from George A. Blanchard, with whom Hill had worked on the levee thirty years before, reporting that William Wellington, Hill's benefactor in his early business days, was still living in Dubuque.[49]

But where were the great money men of New York—Kennedy, Cannon, Schiff, Tod, Moore, and the rest? They sent their congratulations, and their regrets, for they were at that moment attempting to save a financial ship that was almost on the rocks. The Panic of 1893 was raging, and the outcome was in doubt. There was little time for self-congratulation, Hill realized. The Great Northern was about to be buffeted by gales more violent than any that raged at the summit of Marias or Stevens Pass.[50]

PART THREE
HARVEST, 1895-1916

Eagerly, prayerfully, the "wretched refuse" of Europe's shores crowded after those who had opened the Northwest to them. Engebord Ryggen; Knute and Arne, the beardless youths who were dead Jacob's extension in time; and their sisters were among them.

Like James J. Hill, the Ryggens worked, they multiplied, and they prospered in a way that their countrymen back in Norway could never have imagined. They grew the hard spring wheat, like everyone else, but they plowed their profits back into their farm, just as they plowed the manure of their sturdy cows, horses, sheep, and pigs back into the soil. They learned the secrets of this new land, so cruel to the unfortunate and the foolish, and so bountiful to those who farmed smarter as well as harder, and had a little luck along the way.

Engebord's daughters married duplicates of her sons. Knute and Arne married duplicates of their sisters. But they married the soil, too. When the wildly profitable years arrived after 1897, they were ready. By 1916 Jacob Ryggen's sons were leading citizens of Polk County, Minnesota, and they owned large pieces of rich land where less than half a century before there had been no one to hear the piercing screams of a half-breed except the grim young man who was setting his dislocated shoulder.

Engebord bought a little house of her own, the last, greatest symbol of how far they had risen above the life they had led in the Old Country, and she played out her role of matriarch with style.

14
The Worst of Times

Some men have convictions and lack courage; some men have courage and lack convictions; and some men have both. The difference between civilization and barbarism may be measured by the degree of safety to life, property, and the pursuit of the various callings that men are engaged in.

—James J. Hill, 1894

I

Among the first to feel the impact of the Depression of the 1890s were the Eastern resort proprietors, for many of the guests whom they expected from Boston, New York, and Philadelphia never got away from their desks during the ghastly summer of 1893. Terror stalked State, Wall, and Chestnut Streets as stock prices collapsed, depositors demanded their money from hard-pressed banks, and fortunes old and new stood in imminent danger of being wiped out. It was a dangerous time for Hill. The Great Northern, sound as it was, needed credit as much as any other legitimate business enterprise did, but credit dried up when the jerry-built financial institutions felt the shocks of 1893. Once more Hill placed his faith in the New York connections he had nurtured for thirteen years, and that faith was justified. E. T. Nichols, Treasurer of the Great Northern, proved his worth to Hill that summer, and while pessimistic, he kept his brittle sense of humor. "I confess I fear that Stephen will be backward," he forecast, and he said that Kennedy, another man for whom he felt little warmth, was preoccupied with saving the Bank of the Manhattan Company. "Neither

Cannon nor I feel that we can rely on either Schiff or Tod," he wrote Hill, "Schiff keeps a stiff front, but Tod has been p-s-ing down his leg for the last month." [1]

No one with any talent for observation could claim to be surprised at what was happening. As the survivors picked their way over the rising piles of bodies of the weak, they realized that virtually every enterprise they had initiated during the preceding decade had been born under a fearsome question mark: would the political economy of this brash young nation hold together long enough for their project to gain its feet? In late 1890 John G. Moore had described the carnage created, notably for Henry Villard's supporters, by a stock exchange panic which was soon brought under control. Hill, telling Stephen about the measures the Great Northern had had to take then to keep its feet, was inclined to emphasize a want of character: "Our company is in the best financial shape and everything except the cowardly *panic* here looks well." But even Hill blanched when news of the Barings' failure came, and he offered to help by subscribing £50,000 of stock in the new firm which was to be erected on the ashes of the old. It was good training for the main event. [2]

Hill could not help smiling at the outrageous puns which the early stages of the 1893 panic inspired in his forgetful old friend, John Murray Forbes. Nearing the end of a long, full life during which he had seen half a dozen major panics, each more far-reaching in its effects than the last, Forbes was sanguine. He thanked Hill for reminding him to sell his Great Northern stock purchase rights before they expired, though he noted that they were "only a drop in the bucket now *since the stock took a drop too much,"* and complimented him for discouraging his idea of a syndicate to buy control of Union Pacific, "which would have been a *singed cat"* by then. [3]

But it was no laughing matter, as Hill noted in warning his son-in-law not to let sentiment influence his handling of the affairs of the Minneapolis Trust Company. Thomas Lowry, the Mill City's most flamboyant plunger, was in trouble, but that was no affair of theirs. "If his load crushes him it is his matter. We have nothing at stake," Hill asserted. Late in June Nichols warned him that loans made for a specific period of time at a fixed rate of interest, on which Hill personally and the Great Northern routinely depended, were impossible to secure, yet they must stay away from demand loans at all costs. Cannon, who was determined to make the Chase National Bank a bastion to which the financially prudent might repair, explained to Nichols what was happening. Everybody wanted currency, not bank drafts, for no one knew from one day to the next whether a bank would be able to honor its liabilities. Paper money (national bank notes, Treasury notes, and greenbacks) was at a premium of 2 per cent, and gold coin 4 per cent, over bank drafts. "Country banks," which kept their legal reserves on deposit in New York banks, were calling them back to meet the demands of their own depositors. Every evening the wagons of Wells, Fargo & Company, Adams Express, and United States Express clattered into Grand Central Station or onto the New Jersey ferries loaded with packages of currency which were fleeing the city.

Nichols, using his every wile to get a time loan, was jubilant when Richard A. McCurdy, president of the Mutual Life Insurance Company, agreed to advance $175,000 for four months at 6 per cent. The young treasurer juggled incoming bills skillfully—Cannon had begged him not to draw down their balance at the Chase any more than necessary—and transferred 3000 shares of Manitoba stock to Cannon, to use at his discretion to discourage the possibility of a bear raid on the company. Kennedy came to the rescue with $500,000 of Manitoba bonds to be used as collateral for loans once things eased up a bit.[4] By mid-August they could all pause to breathe, for somehow they had managed to keep the lid on things. It had not been just another financial brush fire. If they had failed, the history of the Northwestern railroads would have been vastly different.

What turned the panic of 1893 into the cruellest depression that the nation had seen up to that time was a combination of natural and man-made factors which, in retrospect, were the agents of major political and economic change. Agriculture had already suffered several years of distress, with major crop failures on the Great Plains. After the wheat crop had been lost two years in a row in the Dakotas, Hill and his fellow railroad leaders had taken steps to prevent a third disaster. In the spring of 1890 he reminded a group of influential North Dakotans that the Great Northern had paid for one-third of a shipment of 300,000 bushels of seed wheat consigned to their state, and had carried it free, along with many other shipments of feed, seed, and fuel. Now, Hill said, farmers must control their greedy impulses by planting *fewer* acres and taking better care of them, and that way they would be less likely to fail.

As commodity prices fell, Hill put pressure on the secretary of the Northwestern Elevator Company to lower storage charges so that farmers might recoup some of their losses. When the August frost, that grim specter of want, threatened the following year, he set up an early-warning system through station telegraphers along the road. As a result, the farmers, alerted to the danger, set out smudge pots, thus preventing any trace of frost-kill. Schiff raised a loan of $500,000 for Hill, who used it to help country grain elevators buy wheat and hold it for farmers' accounts until prices rose later in the season. By 1893 this source of credit had become routine, and Cannon's bank was participating enthusiastically. It did nothing to relieve the traditional drumfire of criticism which the railroads bore for the farmers' plight, but at least it kept everybody in business.[5]

The monetary system of the country, feeble as it was, would be the chief punching bag in the political battles which were threatening to breed a major third party and start the nation on the road to socialism—whatever one meant by that plastic term. Gold, which nearly everybody considered the best and, indeed, the only ultimate form of money, flowed out of the country at an increasing rate. No one could quite understand why, until the presidential campaigns of 1892 and 1896 made it clear that the demand for the free coinage of silver was rapidly eroding European confidence in American fiscal sanity. Hill and his friends well knew that "free silver" was at bottom a shameless attempt by silver-producing areas to exploit the sovereign power of coinage to enhance the market for what they had to sell; and when it began to appear in the early 1890s that the selfish arguments of silver men might be swallowed by an uninformed electorate, businessmen began to lose what confidence they had had.[6]

At the same time, the currency, inelastic as ever under the obsolete national banking system, continued to shrink just as the rapid expansion of industry and trade demanded that the money supply grow rapidly. In desperation, Hill brought to St. Paul $200,000 in gold to shore up the First National Bank of St. Paul, then watched helplessly as lesser banks went under. To the bank of Great Falls, Montana, he sent a package containing $45,000 in currency for the Lewisohn copper smelter's payroll.[7] Meanwhile, above the din of general dissatisfaction could be heard the mutterings of the emerging industrial working class, more and more of whom were crowding into the cities. Their wages, if they generally covered necessities, simply could not be stretched to produce the standard of living they felt they had a right to. More of them than ever before worked in plants producing capital goods—many of them for the hard-hit railroads—and when capitalists hysterically canceled orders for such goods, unemployment came suddenly and stayed long. Labor was also beginning to look to new leaders, and they, no less than the captains of industry, wondered nervously what would happen if the shaky machine coughed, stuttered, and ground to a stop.

II

The Depression of the 1890s had its profoundest effects on the railroads. For at least fifteen years this first and greatest of American big businesses had muddled along, unable, for a variety of reasons, to correct the irrational but very real faults that sapped its strength. Most important, because it was most pressing, was their shaky financial structure. "Over-capitalization," a rather empty term in the light of today's sophisticated financial history, but a powerful shibboleth then, was the cry from one end of the country to the other. The total value of bonds and stocks, *taken at par value*, grossly exceeded the actual sums which had gone into the railroads' physical plant and equipment. Some Western railroads, Great Northern among them, and such towers of financial strength as the New York Central, the Pennsylvania, the anthracite-carrying roads, the Burlington, and the Illinois Central, to mention the most obvious, were conservatively capitalized. But the Erie, the Baltimore & Ohio, the Northern Pacific, the Union Pacific, the Santa Fe, Gould's southwestern properties, and many lesser known roads, east and west, had nominal capitalizations which bore little resemblance to either their original or their replacement cost, and the public tarred all railroads with the same brush.

Many railroads had borrowed vast sums of money at steep discounts from par, on first mortgage bonds, and on several terraces of subordinate bonds; at the same time they had issued bales of common stock, with nothing but a residual claim on the property, for little or no consideration, despite the fact that it bore a "par" value. In the best of times most of these roads did well to earn enough to pay the high fixed interest charges on their bonds, and, like the farmers who were paying off 1880s mortgages with scarce dollars of higher 1890s purchasing power, they would be candidates for foreclosure when bad times came. Ample legal precedent had emerged during the 1880s to deal with insolvencies expeditiously and with an eye to maintaining and improving railroad service for the greater benefit of the American commonwealth. Hill knew that when the time came, the courts would use their new-found power freely.[8]

By 1893, however, a host of other obstacles to their future intelligent growth as a rational system had grown up, and these had to be removed without delay. The decline of voluntary coordination between a congeries of relatively small regional railroads meant that some form of involuntary coordination—no one knew just what kind—was inevitable. J. Pierpont Morgan, to name only one figure of increasing importance from outside the railroad industry, had emerged in the 1880s as a man who would knock together reluctant operating heads in order to resolve the most egregious evils of rugged individualism, but it was only a beginning. Meanwhile, everyone who used the railroads, shippers as well as hapless travelers like Henry Minot, would continue to suffer until transportation facilities were improved and expanded. Such a task, railroad men were beginning to suspect, would amount to a virtual rebuilding of the entire system.

It was their relations with government which gave railroad men their worst nightmares. Since the early 1870s state and local politicians had grown accustomed to pointing an accusing finger at the railroads, blaming them for nearly all the discontents of a still overwhelmingly agrarian society. Not all railroad men were wise enough to see that, notwithstanding the fact that the original discontent over high rates had long since ceased to be valid, the political usefulness of the anti-railroad stance was as powerful as ever. Indeed, it was indispensable for all politicians, high and low. Hill grieved at first, and then raged at the gulf which his old friend, Knute Nelson, deliberately opened between himself and his capitalist friend after his election to the governorship of Minnesota in 1892. Nelson had been politically embarrassed by a newspaperman who had reported the scandalous news that Nelson had lunched with Hill at the Minnesota Club, and during the campaign of 1892 Nelson had singled out the Great Northern as the villain that was guilty of the most outrageous disservices to the people of Minnesota. Time and again Hill tried to explain the situation to Nelson, until he finally began to suspect that the politician had known better all the time.

A few days before Nelson's inauguration Hill recommended that an upstate banker be made a member of the Railroad and Warehouse Commission. Nelson's rebuff drew this anguished reply:

> Your note by the hands of my messenger was duly received, and . . .
> after reading it, I destroyed it. . . . During your entire public career, I

have never asked you for any favor and I do not propose to begin or end your term as governor by asking for any favor. . . . I have a right to ask that interests which have been so much villified and misrepresented shall be placed in the hands of honest, intelligent, and fairminded men. . . .[9]

Even with state politicians, however, railroad men still had some standing. Two years later, when Nelson was running for the United States Senate, Sam Hill reported that the candidate wanted Hill's support, and had offered to go easy on the railroads in pending rate cases.[10] In the years that followed, Hill's opinion of Nelson would improve, as many a United States Senator gave way to much worse chicanery.

It was at the federal level, however, that the trend of regulation most directly brought about the grand railroad consolidations in which Hill was to play a key role. On top of the 1887 Act to Regulate Interstate Commerce, which had deprived the railroads of the right to pool traffic or revenues, Congress piled the Sherman Anti-Trust Act of 1890. Whether, to whom, and how this Act would be applied remained a question for over a decade in most branches of American big business, but not where the railroads were concerned. By 1893 the Supreme Court had begun to strike down all attempts by independent railroads to act collusively, even a pious agreement not to cut rates. As for the clause which forbade long-and-short-haul "discrimination," it was so fatuous that most railroad men believed it could not be enforced.[11]

Hill put little faith in independent railroad men's voluntary efforts to stop rebating, end long-and-short-haul discrimination, and maintain rate structures, whether in prosperity or depression. We have little hard statistical data on the actual extent of rebating on American railroads, but Hill's personal records clearly reveal that it was not ended by the Act of 1887. In 1888 his little Mason City & Fort Dodge Railroad had granted rebates which reduced its gross revenues by 3.4 per cent, completely eliminating the profit margin. His success in getting the copper ore traffic in Montana was based squarely on giving both Anaconda and the Lewisohn interests heavy "discounts"—i.e., rebates. When J. Pierpont Morgan sent telegrams inviting Western railroad men to a meeting at his Madison Avenue mansion, Hill went (he was already in New York), but he was contemptuous of the Western Traffic Association which grew out of it. "The Association is rapidly falling into the regular line of Chicago railway associations," he told Manvel less than a year later, "and at the next meeting our company will withdraw." [12] Five years after passage of the Act of 1887, the Great Northern, like its neighbors, was still granting heavy rebates on wheat.

Hill made his last effort to maintain rate structures by voluntary means at the time the Great Northern inaugurated through passenger service to Seattle in June 1893. As usual, there was a frustrating lack of coordination between the Great Northern and the Northern Pacific. The first-class Pullman sleeper fare on the run was very expensive, so the Northern Pacific carried second-class, or "tourist," sleepers, on which the fare was much lower, and dragged along a nearly empty first-class Pullman. Hill had no intention of investing in tourist sleepers at that time, nor did he intend to drag empty Pullmans back and forth across the Rockies and the Cascades. He suggested to the Northern Pacific that both companies cut first-class fares, and when the road refused he went ahead on his own. George Stephen complained bitterly that Hill was getting a reputation as a rate-cutter, but Hill had found out that the Northern Pacific had made a secret agreement with the Pullman Company not to cut first-class fares. Rate-cutter or not, he filled his own Pullmans with tourists, saved the cost of second-class equipment, and abandoned all hope of voluntary cooperation among railroad men. When lawyer Sterling asked him to help persuade crusty George Roberts of the Pennsylvania Railroad to support a bill in Congress to reinstate pooling, Hill did not respond. Both Roberts and Hill knew that the answer to the railroad's disciplinary problems lay elsewhere. [13]

The final hour struck in 1893 for the Victorian railroad corporation, its financiers, its managers, and its self-seeking antagonists. Allen Manvel was heartsick at what he discovered about the Santa Fe. "I am 'wading in' to my duties," he wrote Hill late in 1889; "the water is a *little cold*. I could write a small book of 'Revelations' now and it will be a large volume before I get thro'." Before long it was revealed that the profits the Santa Fe had reported in the preceding several years had been greatly overstated, and bankruptcy of the road was almost certain. Hill, who apparently was insensitive to his old friend's agonies, wrote Manvel condemning the suggestion then being bandied about that the government come to the aid of ailing transcontinentals with large loans:

> The government should not furnish capital to these companies, in addition to their enormous land subsidies, to enable them to conduct their business in competition with enterprises that have received no aid from

the public treasury. Our own line in the North, which protects the International Boundary line for a distance of 1600 miles, . . . was built without any government aid, even the right of way, through hundreds of miles of public lands, being paid for in cash.[14]

Manvel knew that Hill had every reason to be proud of his accomplishments, and he doubtless agreed with his individualistic philosophy. He responded with a brave little note suggesting that Hill join him on a vacation trip he was taking to California. A month later he was dead, and before the end of the year the Santa Fe had joined a growing party of major railroads at the bankruptcy bench. Hill knew of these failures even as they were about to happen, for his sources of information had never been better. That August he had cabled Stephen that the jig was up with Villard and that receivers would soon take possession of the Northern Pacific. Cannon soon predicted the same thing for the Union Pacific, and he noted that George Gould was struggling to keep his father's railroad legacy from slipping away. John G. Moore found it all very depressing, but at least the Great Northern was safe. "We have carried the load to the top of the hill," he reflected, "[and] the reward is certain." [15]

III

In the second year of the depression Hill explained to his general manager how the Great Northern was to survive. "The general outlook for business is not in the direction of an increase," he wrote, "and we must make our cloth cover our requirements, and the only safe way is to begin in time and make our reductions carefully and well. . . ." He had, in fact, taken the sternest possible measures, without regard to their unpopularity, from the very beginning of hard times. Scribbling a telegram with his stub of a pencil, somewhere out on the line in the late summer of 1893, he gave explicit orders to his chief lieutenant:

> Take whatever steps are necessary to reduce track, machinery, station, and other service to lowest point possible. Take off all extra gangs everywhere, except those relaying steel. Reduce wages section foremen to forty dollars [a month] east and forty-five west, and of section men to one dollar [a day] east and one dollar and quarter west. . . . There will be plenty of men to work at those rates. . . .[16]

There was to be no arguing over the reduction of expenses. If the general manager could not see his "way clearly to this end," he was to assemble all his facts and figures and then Hill would show him how it was to be done. He fixed his eagle eye on a sheaf of vouchers coming through for grading and filling of embankments, showing costs of 15¢ per cubic yard of material, and he was incensed. "I have worked hard for years to get these prices where they should be," he told his general manager, "and it is very disappointing to see all this work quietly ignored and contracts for work let at prices far beyond its value." It was the last time the contractor got more than 12¢ a cubic yard during the depression.[17]

The hot, dry summer of 1894 dramatized the need to be always prepared for the unexpected. Dense stands of rosin-fat pines along the Manitoba road's line to Lake Superior were like tinder by August every year, and Hill worried that sparks from a carelessly operated locomotive might set off a holocaust. Word went out each summer that engineers and firemen were to avoid such an occurrence, come what may. Whatever the source of the spark, however, the great Hinkley, Minnesota, fire of 1894 brought Hill's worst fears to pass. Thousands of acres of forest were destroyed, along with towns, sawmills, and human lives. Hill rejoiced at the news that the heroic crew of a little locomotive had got steam up in record time and had pulled a train, made up of every piece of rolling stock that Hinckley could supply and loaded with every human being in the neighborhood, across the burning trestles to safety. He threw himself into the massive job of relieving the victims, and was proud of the generous contributions that poured in from his old associates, Mount Stephen, Sir Donald, and Kennedy.[18]

In the fall of 1893 Hill confessed to Schiff that he was "a little short handed in the general office," and that he found it necessary to "stand at the helm nearly all the time." The fact is that he was no nearer a permanent day-to-day management than he had ever been. Manvel was the closest to a real general manager the railroad had ever had, but Mohler had discovered that, in effect, he had been demoted to general superintendent by Hill's close attention to operations. Hill had in mind the appointment of "an older and more experienced man" as operating vice president of the company, and intended to abolish the position of general manager. But such a man was not easily found, Hill's reputation being what it was.

W. A. Stephens, armed with an enthusiastic recommendation from Hill, heeded the call of the West in 1894, and he made good his escape from the crushing burden of work which his chief had piled on his shoulders for twelve years. Hill then tried to get along with an "assistant to the president," but when that gentleman began to display some of his chief's own autocratic methods, he did not last long. Hill appoined the genial Charles H. Warren, a longtime employee who had mastered such diverse branches of railroading as auditing and traffic management, to the position of general manager, and wore him out in barely two years. Two of the most important men in twentieth-century railroading, W. W. Finley, later president of the Southern Railway, and W. H. Newman, who was to head the New York Central in its most brilliant era, filled the position of first vice president briefly. But, as usual, there was little delegation of authority and no independence, and Hill continued to dominate the vastly enlarged railroad as completely as he had the newborn Manitoba road.[19]

Hill's business methods, or lack of them, severely strained relations with his associations. After the terrors of the summer of 1893 had passed, Nicholas told him frankly that he would have to mend his ways. "I am the company's financial representative here," he wrote from his office on Wall Street, "although not its chief financial officer, and our directors . . . do not hesitate to express irritation when I am unable to give them full details. It is mortifying to me. . . ." He noted wistfully that Stephen Baker, no older than he and once a fellow clerk in the old firm of John S. Kennedy & Company, had just been elected president of Bank of the Manhattan Company. Meanwhile, George Stephen, now wearing the ermine of a member of the House of Lords and bearing the hereditary title of first Baron Mount Stephen, kept up a steady fire of criticism. Hill failed to answer cables; he was reluctant to come to England ("friends need their blood up"); he was unable to get the annual report out on time; and, finally, his report was skimpy when it did come.[20] Hill, torn in a dozen different directions, lashed out at his old friend:

> I am extremely sorry that Your Lordship and Mr. Farrer should find so much disappointment in our Annual Report. . . . However, this begins a defense of our action and I do not intend to make any. . . . Our Report has been better received by the public this year than ever before. . . . If our friends abroad, after the various privileges and advantages they have received . . . are dissatisfied, I am very sorry. . . .[21]

Much sobered by this blast, His Lordship beat a hasty retreat and took refuge in unaccustomed flattery. Hill had not bragged enough, he protested: "It was entirely with your own way of *describing* what you had accomplished that I expressed my disappointment," he wrote.

The storm was over as quickly as it had begun, for the forces that united these busy men far exceeded the pressures that tended to divide them. Hill, resolving to pay more attention to public relations in the future, went to work on a long letter to Gaspard Farrer, the dignified, industrious young establishment gentleman at Baring Brothers who was becoming so useful to the Great Northern and such a good friend of Hill's. Soon the English allies had more intimate information about the affairs of the Great Northern and the other Northwestern railroads than anyone else in the City of London could have dreamed of getting.[22]

To everyone's delight and surprise, things did not turn out so badly for the Great Northern. A gigantic wheat crop was harvested in the same year the depression hit, and crops generally were abundant during these years. Rates were low, but the Great Northern could make money on a rate that would—and frequently did—land its competitors in the poorhouse. Basic improvements in efficiency paid off quickly, while the prices of everything the railroad bought, particularly labor, plummeted. The profits piled up, so much so that what to do with them became a problem. If he reported them, Hill realized, the familiar outcry for lower rates would be heard again, even though the "excess profits" were reflected not primarily in cash, but in permanent improvements to the railroad. Hill knew that all the profits the road could retain, and new money, too, would be barely enough, for he realized that prosperity would bring a burden of freight and passengers beyond anything the past had known. In the year ending June 30, 1896, Hill tucked away $1,350,000 of earnings beyond the amount reported in various accounts. It was an uncomfortable position to be in. "Our shareholders want to know how well we have done," he explained to Farrer, "while the State wants to limit our earnings to a reasonable return on our capital without [giving] any guarantee that we will have the traffic to make such return."[23]

Wall Street analysts did not have to look far for the reason for such profits. In just one year, from 1894 to 1895, the Great Northern had reduced its cost of carrying a ton of freight by 13 per cent. A typical Great Northern freight train was now carrying 300 tons of payload, and for the first time the railroad's total annual freight volume, measured in tons carried one mile, had exceeded one billion. Eastern businessmen pricked up their ears at such unheard-of results. "I am learning your lesson," George F. Baker, of New York's First National Bank, wrote admiringly, "that an increase of cost per train mile may

mean a material reduction in the cost per ton." The old-fashioned concept of the railroad as a light-duty facility was ending, and the heavy-
duty, high-volume, low-rate, low-cost railroad of the twentieth century was at hand. The trend was already marked in the East, but Hill
had played a major role in stimulating it in the West. Meanwhile, he
could not contain his pride in the fact that the Great Northern had survived while competitors all around it were succumbing to the depression. He wrote Mount Stephen:

> You will recall how often it has been said that when the Nor Pac, Union
> Pac and other competitors failed, our company would not be able to
> stand. . . . Now we have them all in bankruptcy . . . while we have gone
> along and met their competition. . . . I hope you will not consider this as
> self-praise, for . . . the quality is in the property. . . .[24]

The feat was not accomplished without personal cost. While Hill's
wage cuts were no deeper than those which terrified businessmen everywhere were making, the Great Northern's obvious prosperity made
it all the harder for the workers to accept them. They knew nothing
about operating ratios—much less about the handsome profits squirreled away in accounting holes—but they could see Hill straining
every muscle—their own muscle, in fact—to move the heavy volume
of traffic. In the spring of 1894 Hill had had to fight Eugene V. Debs,
whose new American Railway Union, having displaced the Knights of
Labor, was eager to show its members what it could do. There followed a costly strike on the Montana Central and, despite Marcus
Daly's reassurances, the Great Northern managment, from Hill down,
received most of the blame for the disruption in service and local hard
feelings.

Watching the strike spread to the west end of the railroad and eastward as far as the Dakotas, Hill offered to submit the dispute to arbitration by three outside railroad men. But the question of whether the
American Railway Union, or the resentful brotherhoods, or, indeed,
any union really represented the men haunted Debs, and after a conference in Hill's office he refused the offer. When the strike spread to
the Twin Cities area Hill defiantly sent through a freight train that had
been made up on the Lake Superior end of the railroad. Hearing that
mobs were threatening to shut down all operations, he lost his temper
and demanded that President Cleveland send in troops to help the
local authorities, who were being "prevented by turbulent mobs from
serving the civil and criminal process of the United States courts.
. . ." Fortunately, things did not go that far, although Cleveland was

to use troops later that year during the much more serious Pullman strike. Cooler heads proposed arbitration by a panel that would include non-railroad men from the Twin Cities, under the chairmanship of Charles A. Pillsbury. Matters were speedily settled, and James J. Hill, much relieved, congratulated a startled Eugene V. Debs on his "shrewd management" of the strike.

The union had achieved no great wage victory, but it had won the right to bargain for the men, and it approached the disastrous Pullman strike with confidence. It was quite a comedown for Hill, who had expressed the opinion during the epic strike of engineers on the Burlington system in 1888 that railroad men had to stand together solidly against union pressure.

Worst of all were the hate letters, some of which he was unable to hide from Mary:

> I pray the God of justice . . . may lay on you such a burden of adversity as will make you realize the pangs of hunger, the inability to provide the comforts and necessities of life to your loved ones. . . . It would be a fitting climax if you should be taken by your employees and *hung* by the neck till dead, from one of the triumphal arches so recently erected at the expense of the very people you are now defrauding of their hard earnings. . . . I send this to your wife in order that it may strike you in your home.[25]

IV

One blustery day in March 1890 Hill was startled to see his daughter Charlotte and her governess rush breathlessly into his office. At that moment he and fourteen-year-old Charlotte were presiding over his busy household in the absence of Mrs. Hill, who had gone to New York with Mamie to consult an eye specialist for the younger woman. He had just written Mary that "Charlotte has given me a great deal of satisfaction," and he was deep in plans for the first season's work on the Pacific extension when, suddenly his domestic world had fallen into chaos. Next day, after matters had been put right again, he had regained his good humor and could joke about what had happened, in a letter to Mary:

> March has gone out like a lion and in order to be in the mode we had at the house yesterday a full blown, all wool, three-ply, yard-wide circus. Three shows under one tent—with a matinee into the bargain.

V.* had been seeking spiritous consolation in the forward room in the cellar and as the boys say, got badly loaded, and under the influence manifested a strong disposition to stand guard over the house and took her place on the front steps bareheaded, from where she engaged the attention of at least our own household and a few strangers.

Charlotte and Miss Partridge came down to the office, and when I went up the show was all over, and V. was somewhat disfigured and weary looking, but kept or rather tried to keep out of sight. Mrs. Eaton was with the children in the Gallery, and aside from a subdued feeling of curious astonishment the children were about as usual.

It will not do to keep V., for the children are afraid of her and will never forget yesterday's show. Now, Mamma, do not allow this to worry you. . . . I will tell her today to take a couple of weeks vacation. . . .[26]

He liked to take Mary and the older girls with him on his travels, but the ladies had to expect to be left pretty much by themselves, especially in New York. They almost always stayed at the Albemarle, a comfortable family hotel on Madison Square from which Mary and Mamie could sally forth, as they did on a bright January afternoon in 1888 to hear a piano recital by a child prodigy, Josef Hoffmann. But one glorious July day in 1891, Hill took Mary on a tour of the elegant summer places of his powerful New York allies. From the James's "fine house" in Morristown, New Jersey (thriftily rented, as Mary noted), they drove to Bernardsville to visit Frederick P. Olcott and his family. "Imagine how you would enjoy riding along in a four-in-hand," Mary wrote her daughter, "where the cherry trees were many and loaded with ripe fruit." After almost forty summers in Minnesota, where peach trees could not survive, they were impressed by orchards laden with golden peaches. "We saw one in which there were 2500 trees," she explained, "and apples everywhere." From there they went to visit the Schiffs at Seabright, and then on to Hollywood, New Jersey, to pay their respects to the Heidelbachs. Outings like this, infrequent though they were, were valuable restoratives to a man whose efforts were being concentrated on bigger enterprises than ever before.[27]

Mary gave close attention to the family's moral and religious welfare, even if the increasingly frequent separations from their children made adjurations to spend Lent "seriously" sound rather weak. Art, of course, must not be neglected, but "Bernhardt's 'La Tosca' is said to

* Miss Veeley, the housekeeper, who had served the Hills for about ten years.

be very shocking [and] if you are to see her I trust it may be in some play of better morals," she counseled Clara. In the winter of 1891 Mary developed a wracking cough, as the "bronchitis" which would turn out to be tuberculosis asserted itself. The following winter Hill sent her and eleven-year-old Rachel to Santa Barbara, California, along with Mamie and little Mary. (Sam Hill, to avoid confusion, called them Mary the Second, Third and Fourth, the First being Mrs. Hill's mother, who was still living in St. Paul in her own little house.) Hill managed a brief visit with them, and when he went back to Europe in 1895, at Mount Stephen's insistence, he took Mary with him. Despite the rigors of a February crossing, they enjoyed their week's vacation aboard the *Majestic*.[28]

Ten years in the house on Canada Street had made it a warm, cheerful home in which the complicated ritual of Victorian life went on ceaselessly. In New York with her husband in 1888, Mary could imagine the scene in the kitchen, with twelve-year-old Charlotte lifting the covers off the pots on the huge kitchen range, disdainfully noting that it was "the same old thing," and being shooed out by the cook. With neither father nor mother present to frown them down, Rachel would whistle at table while "Geegee" (almost the only name little Gertrude had) delivered a lecture on the point that *Ruth* had not had to wear a bib when *she* was four years old, going on five. But already the new mansion was rising at 240 Summit Avenue, and the girls, lugging along their Kodak on inspection trips, were taking pictures of the massive sandstone and red brick pile, where architects, foremen, and laborers struggled to carry out the minutely detailed orders of their employer.[29]

Learning that his friend meant to build a mansion, Frank Thomson urged him to take the time to stop over in Philadelphia to inspect Alexander J. Cassatt's celebrated house. The Boston architectural firm of Peabody, Stearns & Furber were set to work sketching ideas and laying out plans, and they soon learned that they had a demanding client. The Philadelphia firm Hill retained to design the interiors found him surprisingly knowledgeable on matters of taste, and not at all shy about lecturing them. "What I desired was good, simple Louis XV style [but] your design seems to be a hybrid between half a dozen styles," he remarked, aware that at that height of the "picturesque eclectic" era a purist would have to fight for his beliefs. He crushed Tiffany's manager by returning sketches for windows with the blunt statement that they were "anything but what I want; I want very little

The mansion at 240 Summit Avenue, St. Paul, the Hill family home from 1891 until Mary Hill's death in 1921. Minnesota Historical Society.

stained or leaded glass, but want it good." The impressive gallery that was to open off the east wing of the house would need no such *fin de siècle* embellishments once it was filled with its owner's collection of paintings.[30]

As the house was to bear the stamp of Hill's individuality, it would also reflect his independence and self-sufficiency. In the basement there grew apace a striking collection of glassware: six hundred eight-gallon glass jars that made up a storage battery for what the engineer proudly promised would be the largest private electric lighting system in the United States. Hill found it and the newfangled engine which was to turn the generator constant headaches, but they were more than that for Hill's secretary, who had to contend with repeated pleas from embarrassed suppliers for their money. The notorious temper, never far below the surface, finally boiled over when Hill discovered that the architects had countermanded his instructions to the stonecutters for a second time. Not even a prestigious Boston architectural firm could get away with it twice. "Hereafter I will not allow you to come near the building," he thundered, demanding their bill in full. If he had to be his own contractor for a railroad to the Pacific to get it done right, he could do the same thing for a mere house, and what was more, he could do both at the same time.[31]

He was proud of the house, and eager to show it off to the curious who thronged about the site. The gentlefolk of St. Paul arrived with cards of admission from the owner, while the ordinary people trooped through almost at will. Finally James Brodie, the builder who had worked for Hill for years, pleaded with him. The picture gallery had no lock, he wrote, "and it is difficult to persuade people not to go in." But Hill's generosity, at least when it came to showing off his gallery, was soon a legend in St. Paul.[32]

In the spring of 1891 van after van arrived with elegant new furnishings which, their owner noted carefully in his inventory, in all had cost $132,532. In August he wrote Manvel that the old house "will be abandoned when you come to St. Paul again." The thrifty citizens of St. Paul were amazed at what he did next. Down came the sturdy, thirteen-year-old mansion, torn apart by the wreckers without ceremony. Soon there was nothing to mark the spot but a forlorn shed. Hill had not done it for profit, but out of the purest sentiment. The neighborhood was declining rapidly, he explained to Clara, and "I could not bear to drive by here, day after day, and see milk bottles in the windows." [33]

The thread of the Hill's domestic life continued almost without a break. Quiet dinners, receptions for Catholic dignitaries who were proud that a daughter of the Church was the mistress of such an establishment, and an occasional gala "at home" made up their social life. One fall Hill was proud to welcome the leaders of St. Paul, Catholic and Protestant alike, to a reception honoring the aging Right Reverend H. B. Whipple, Episcopalian bishop for the state and the chief benefactor of Minnesota's considerable Indian population. On New Year's Day of 1894 there was dancing at a party for the Yale Glee and Banjo clubs.[34]

V

No other major economic leader of the late nineteenth century had a family quite like Hill's. In size, cultural background, and family spirit it was unique. His letters abound with references to the nursery, the schoolroom, and the sickroom, giving them a domestic tone not to be found in the papers of any Vanderbilt, Rockefeller, Gould or Carnegie. His business associates, writing to thank him for his hospitality at North Oaks Farm or 240 Summit Avenue, declared their envy of Hill's blessings. He was indeed a fortunate man, most of all for the quiet dignity and warm affection that Mary brought to the large establishement. It was a Roman Catholic household, and strict observance of regimen was the rule. While Hill did not continue his early practice of accompanying the youngsters to church, his fireside was the scene of many long, earnest conversations over teacups or port glasses with Father Caillet and Bishop Ireland. After the two older boys went east to school, an atmosphere of feminine gentleness, one hardly broken by the little-boy misdemeanors of Walter, settled over the household. Clara, dignified and reserved, tutored the younger ones. Charlotte sawed away at her violin (she had some talent), and left-handed Rachel embroidered industriously. Gertrude—for a little while her father's favorite, it seems—gravely followed his dictation when she wrote to President Cleveland, informing him that his second inaugural and her ninth birthday were to occur on the same day. (She received an autographed picture for her pains.)

Hill gave the rearing of his sons both too much and too little attention. Acutely aware that his great work made the role of conventional father impossible, he tried to compensate by carefully planning that aspect of their upbringing which seemed most important: their education. He fondly hoped that one of the boys, at least, would follow him in the leadership of the great enterprise, of which, by 1893, he was the unchallenged master in the public mind. But by the time they were young men James Norman and Louis had come to expect that "papa" would make the important decisions, and their roles would be limited to carrying out the details. Hill made good decisions, on the whole, and showed more consideration for their temperaments and interests than many a Victorian father did. Inevitably, however, his sons, in the opinion of contemporary observers, were failing to develop that degree of independence and self-motivation which was the chief feature of their father's character, and which he most wanted them to emulate.

Louis had been scheduled to follow his brother from Exeter to Yale in 1890, but by the early spring of that year it was clear that the younger boy, despite the help of a tutor, would not be able to master the ancient languages which admission to the college demanded. He was enrolled, instead, in the three-year course in Yale's Sheffield Scientific School, which meant that if all went well both brothers would receive a Yale diploma in June 1893.

To tutor Louis, first for his entrance examinations and then as a first-year student at Yale, Hill engaged a poor but brilliant undergraduate, Irving Fisher, who later became a noted statistician and economist, and leased an apartment for them near the university. Fisher, not hesitating to remind Hill of the temptations to which Yale men were subject, worried that Louis's companions were a drain on his ambitions. When Louis was suspended and James Norman's grades deteriorated, Hill threatened to call off the trip to Europe they had looked forward to so eagerly. "Each [of you] should . . . work day and night to make examinations sure at close of term," he wired them. Fisher, for his part, concluded—reluctantly, for he needed the money badly—that as long as Louis had a tutor to shore him up he would never do more than the bare minimum required. The tutor was discharged, and a year later Louis's professor reported that the boy had developed "good spirit and deserves credit for the work he has done the past few weeks." [35]

Meanwhile, James Norman had been dropped from his class. Deeply despondent about his college career, he threatened to quit for good. He was in frequent pain from arthritis—then diagnosed as "rheumatism"—which may also have had something to do with his recurring eye troubles, and had little real interest in academic subjects, but both of his parents were determined to keep him at Yale. Frequent conferences with William Graham Sumner, the most popular teacher at Yale, and a timely intercession with Yale's president by John Sterling, the rich and powerful Old Blue who was Mount Stephen's lawyer, backed up by a surge of effort by James Norman, saved him for the Class of 1893. Graduation day was an anticlimax worthy of the *ennui* which was affected by the fashionable college man of that day. Too many things had come to fruition at once, it seems, for either father or mother to be present when the boys received their diplomas. Within hours the boys had turned their backs on the scene of their recent tortures and hurried off to join the festive citizens of St. Paul in celebrating their father's great triumph. [36]

From the walls of Hill's library smiled the portraits of his six daughters, who, one by one, as they finished their courses at the schools which the Diocese of St. Paul provided for the proper nurture of Roman Catholic girls, were sent off to finishing school in the East. In the fall of 1890 Clara had entered The Misses Ely's School, in then-fashionable Brooklyn, where she was followed by Charlotte and Ruth. They sent their parents scene after scene, filmed with the durable Kodak, of girls in costume from Arcadian to Shakespearean, and Hill laughed heartily when he came to Charlotte's candid shot of the fat little boy who lived next door. The three sisters, ostensibly bent on improving their knowledge of French and German, but enthralled at the prospect of a trip across the Atlantic with no supervisor but their German governness, when they did go were soon disillusioned by the Old World. As they, with sinking hearts, inspected the spartan accommodations in the convent in which they had expected to live, they quickly concluded that a *pension* was more to their taste.[37]

For twenty-five years, from 1868 to 1903, there was at least one school-age child in the Hill household. Walter was just starting to school when his father became the celebrated head of the nation's newest and most vigorous transcontinental railroad. "Papa," to Walter Hill, was a bustling, bearded man of booming voice and decisive manner, a man to whom other people paid obvious deference, and who generally disappeared from Walter's little world as quickly as he entered it. During the school year Walter sometimes was brought to New York by Mr. Bobbett, a clerk in the Great Northern office, so that he could accompany his father back to St. Paul for the Christmas holidays. It was great fun to sit in the dining car of the luxurious Pennsylvania Limited or Lake Shore Limited, ordering anything he wanted from the huge menu. And the handsome lad could hardly fail to notice how obsequious everybody was to a boy lucky enough to be in the company of James J. Hill. Walter showed a disposition to do as he pleased quite early. His father persuaded Horace D. Taft to enroll the boy at his school in Watertown, Connecticut, despite the headmaster's misgivings. "He does not seem to care for any of the regular things which the boys do," Taft wrote Hill. Walter had spurned the informal football games on the school green, preferring to hobnob with the older boys in the village.[38]

Meanwhile, in the already eventful summer of 1893, over at the Sam Hill's home in Minneapolis, Hill's first grandson was born. Sam, his father-in-law was pleased to reflect, had turned out to be a competent businessman. Marcus Daly, who was not given to unnecessary words, had grown fond of Sam during the young man's days as head of the Montana Central, and wrote that he was impressed by his "judgment, sagacity and business capacity." What Hill had to guard against, Daly warned, was a tendency of all of Hill's lieutenants to say, when the going got rough, that they were "just carrying out Jim Hill's orders." Sam himself let his father-in-law know that his role was not easy. "I sometimes think you do not know how difficult it is for me to speak or act lest such word or act should be thought coming from you or as an indication of your views," he complained.[39]

Soon after their graduation from Yale, Hill found places in the Great Northern for James Norman and Louis. The older boy took Minot's place on the Eastern Railway of Minnesota, suffering banishment to cold, dull Superior, Wisconsin, with good humor. He was a capable, conscientious worker with a talent for working with people. After he had discharged some troublesome duties for Hill in Seattle, his father was convinced that he had found the man who could eventually succeed him.[40] Louis also served his time at Superior, but Hill found it a great help and comfort to have him at his side, and he was soon accompanying his father on his increasingly frequent trips to Europe. In 1897 Gaspard Farrer braved the famous temper, warning Hill of the dangers of the crown prince's role:

> You both remember what a high opinion Lord M[ount] S[tephen] formed of Louis, of his thoughtfulness and sobriety of his judgment, and Lord M.S. does not often make a mistake in these matters. I cannot but think that it would be a great help to Louis if he had some definite work and responsibility and I am sure he would do it well; but he is such a modest, good fellow that he will never push himself forward and will need all the push and encouragement that you can give him to bring out his merits. . . .[41]

But Hill's sons found themselves with no more independence than any of his other lieutenants. While Mamie had received gifts totaling $200,000 at or shortly after her marriage, James Norman and Louis, still bachelors, received nothing beyond their living costs and a monthly allowance of $75 until 1898, when Hill transferred $100,000 of Great Northern preferred stock to each of them. The girls, living at home or at a school where money was doled out to them with Victorian frugality, required little. By 1900 Hill's personal ledger recorded only $31,000 paid out on account for Clara, including the cost of tuition and at least two trips to Europe. Successively smaller sums were recorded for the younger children. The girls received no regular allowance. If they needed to make a purchase, it was understood that Mr. Stephens would see that the bill was taken care of. In those days before the popularity of tax-free gifts, a young person might have great expectations and yet not be particularly aware of them.[42]

VI

Notwithstanding the brilliant success with which the Great Northern came through the depression of the 1890s, it was "the worst of times" for James J. Hill. It could hardly be otherwise for the men who shouldered the responsibility for guiding the clumsy young nation through such an uncertain era. To most men, of course, Hill's "worst of times" must still have looked good. The rewards, material and psychological, for his emergence as the most important economic leader in the Northwest were great, at least by the standards of an outside observer. Presiding over the gigantic ledgers, which contained the exquisitely detailed records his employer insisted upon, was a full-time bookkeeper, John J. Toomey, who had forsaken a thirteen-year career on the Grand Trunk Railway in Montreal to come to St. Paul in 1888. This pleasant, obliging, fiercely loyal, transplanted Irishman would be Hill's right-hand man in St. Paul and in New York to the end of Hill's life. Toomey recorded that from 1885 to 1890 his employer's net worth had grown from $7,700,000 to $9,600,000. Despite the depression it totaled $12,000,000 by 1895, and on January 1, 1901, it stood at $19,400,000.[43]

But Hill was overextended, psychologically, if not financially. He was engaged in an astonishing variety of major projects at a time when both he and the nation were at a major crossroads. The depression of the 1890s was a lull that preceded the climax of the era of settlement and basic development of the North American continent, a climax in which Hill was about to play a fundamental role. By 1897 both his age and the times dictated that the multifarious interests in which Hill had zestfully engaged would have to be put by in favor of the one "great adventure."

Besides building a railroad to the Pacific, acting as his own contractor on the new mansion, and overseeing every detail of the design and construction of the St. Paul Seminary (of which he was the chief patron), Hill waded rashly into the swirling waters of American politics in the elections of 1892 and 1896. He was as determined as ever to keep the Great Northern itself out of politics, issuing a stern warning to Mohler that any foreman who attempted to influence a man's vote was to be discharged, but as a private person he gave all the support he could muster behind the scenes, to Cleveland in 1892 and William McKinley in 1896.[44]

There was little if anything which he wanted from politicians, for himself or the Great Northern—except for the freedom to continue, without interference, at the work he and his fellow entrepreneurs had set for themselves following the Civil War, which many would soon judge to be the most outrageous demand of all. His relations with Cleveland were not close, for the President avoided identification with any railroad leader and Hill found the great, torpid man very dull company. The President took the initiative only once to write Hill informally. Half sick at "Gray Gables," his retreat on Buzzards Bay, Cape Cod, he scratched out a pathetic note asking Hill to do what he could to save from bankruptcy two favorite nephews, "who went west very young, have worked very hard, . . . have their little families about them and are taking care of their father and mother." Hill would help them, but in return he asked for reappointment of Mrs. Cavileer, his old friend, as postmistress of the decaying border town of Pembina and a federal judgeship for William Lochren, a sympathetic supporter of the railroads against the self-seeking state legislators.[45]

What Hill most wanted was repeal of the Sherman Silver Purchase Act and, in fact, an end to the insane silver issue that was ruining the country's international credit. He had for years, no less ardently, sought moderation, if not outright repeal, of the protective tariff. Cleveland's performance on these issues satisfied neither Hill nor anyone else, but the President's firm (and, some would say, unfair) action in the Pullman strike made up for a great deal. When Cleveland, deaf to Debs's offer to run mail trains if the hated Pullmans were cut off, called out the Army to end violence in Chicago and the threat of it elsewhere, Hill was delighted. He wrote the President:

> . . . nothing has occurred since the battle of Gettysburg that has borne as good fruit or that has done so much to restore order and confidence to the people that the nation will be preserved. . . . It seems as if Providence has lifted you up as others were lifted before.[46]

It was the silver issue which finally convinced Hill that the Democrats had to be retired from the presidency. He was not yet ready to agree with Philip D. Armour, who gloomily predicted that "you and I will never live long enough to see another Democratic party in power; this country ain't ready for free tariff," but long before Bryan captured the convention with his "Cross of Gold" speech in 1896, he knew that silver was not only a fraudulent issue, but a politically weak one as well. The gold loan which the government had authorized in a desperate attempt to maintain the Treasury reserve had been well subscribed despite the hard times, and Hill had noted an interesting phenomenon among working men, whose leaders were so insistent on cheap money. As he wrote Calvin S. Brice, a Democratic chieftain, "fully eighty per cent of the people in the northwest favor unconditional repeal [of the Sherman Silver Purchase Act]. Even the payment of a small proportion of monthly pay rolls in silver is not well received by wage-earners." He predicted that the Democratic party faced nothing but disaster at the polls unless it took a clear stand in support of the *de facto* gold standard on which the nation's dealings with the investing nations of the world was based.[47] For once his political divining rod was working.

Mark Hanna, the shrewd, affable, master politician, and Hill's friend of many years, had greatly expanded on his career as an iron ore and Great Lakes shipping magnate. In the campaign of 1896 he came into his own as kingmaker of the colorless William McKinley. The silver issue ("all he talks about is silver, and *that's* where we've got him," Hanna said of Bryan) was bringing even strong anti-tariff men like John S. Kennedy around to the Republican side. When Hanna went looking for someone to contribute both money and hard work for McKinley's election, Hill, with his reputation as a disgruntled Democratic leader in Minnesota and the Dakotas, was an obvious recruit. But Hill seems to have thrown himself into campaign work almost before he was asked, although, as he told Hanna, he had to be "very careful in anything I do." Through the late summer and autumn, Hill coordinated the flow of money and campaign speakers in his part of the country, where the outcome was greatly in doubt. The day after the election he awoke to discover that McKinley had carried not only Minnesota, but North Dakota as well. Almost overnight, Mount Stephen wrote him, they had heard in London about Hill's influence on the outcome in the Northwest. For his part, however, Hill had wise words for leaders of both parties. He wrote David B. Hill, Democratic leader in New York, that ". . . when the storm is over and men's common sense again controls their action you will find the old party with renewed strength, enjoying the confidence of those who wish the country well." And he told Mark Hanna that "The independent vote of the country, call it by whatever name you may seems to be increasing in numbers, and I think this vote will control National elections in the future more than in the past. . . ."

In a letter to Farrer he predicted the political climate of the United States for the next half-dozen years rather well:

. . . lately the people of the country are fixing their minds on social questions, . . . the result being a steady increase of the conservative feeling. . . . For ten years it has been "railroads, monopolies, trusts, &c," but

now it shows up as those who have nothing against those who have
something, and in this country those who have outnumber greatly those
who have not . . .[48]

His political cunning, however, seems to have left him almost as
abruptly as it had arrived. He had long been convinced that St. Paul
needed a strong Democratic newspaper. His old friend Norman Kittson, who felt the same way, had bought the *St. Paul Globe* in the
1880s, but had been reluctant either to put money behind it or to sell
out to Hill. Meanwhile, Hill's clerks had fretted for several years over
the affairs of the *Fargo Argus,* a provincial paper into which Hill had
poured money, time, and energy, to an avail. These experiences
should have been warning enough, but they were not. In 1893 Cannon
warned Nichols that Charles R. Flint, the New York merger-monger
whose name is at the roots of many a giant corporation's family tree,
"was going around the town trying to find [Hill] and induce him to
take an interest in the *New York Times.*" Both men begged Hill not to
do so, for there was no hope that the old management of the dowdy,
dull *Times* could make a go of it. Stubbornly, Hill put $25,000 into
Flint's scheme, and when, three years later, Nichols asked his approval to turn the stock over to the new party which was going to
reorganize the paper, he growled ungraciously, "I have no objection if
you donate the *Times* interest to Mr. Ochs." Yet on he blundered.
After turning down an offer of an interest in the *Minneapolis Tribune,*
which might at least have made him some money, he finally bought
up the old *Globe.*[49]

Hill might have made more money writing for periodicals than he
ever made as a publisher, for offers from such prestigious magazines
as *The Forum* poured in. He had no time for them, though he did take
the time to write a Chicago editor, giving his prescription for stopping
a wave of lawlessness on the railroads in which several express agents
had been murdered. Put a price on their heads, he advised, and the
murderers' dead bodies, with fifteen or twenty bullets in them, would
be on display on the courthouse steps by sundown. Activity, meanwhile, was piled on activity. He joined New York's Metropolitan Club
and was confirmed as a member of the exclusive Jekyl Island Club. His
list of new friends grew apace, while demands on his time continued
from old ones, like John Murray Forbes. On one occasion the old gentleman had insisted that the Hills come over from Exeter to lunch at
his home in Milton, even though they were in their traveling clothes
and had sent their baggage on ahead to St. Paul. Edward Tuck, charm-

ing, witty, and a marvelous raconteur, enticed the two of them all the way from London to his villa at Monte Carlo in 1895. Hill owed it to his wife, Tuck said, for having brought her across the Atlantic in February.[50]

Tough as he was, Hill was not made of steel. It had been sixteen years since George Stephen reminded him of that fact, and by 1894 Kennedy was genuinely alarmed at his friend's pace, which, it seemed, could no longer be intelligently controlled. In 1896 Hill came down with his usual Christmas illness, and this time he could not ignore it. He confessed to Mount Stephen that "After my return from NY on Christmas I found myself much run down and finally forced to remain *indoors away from work* for about two weeks. I was not down sick but afraid I might be, took the prudent course for a time and am now feeling very well in every way." [51]

More than one lady of their acquaintance gave voice to her amazement at the equanimity with which Mary Hill bore all the alarums and excursions which echoed through her dignified home. Had she asserted just a modicum of what today would be considered her rights, she could have made his burden unbearable. Even in the 1890s most women would have read a note of mild contempt into something Mrs. Samuel Thorne wrote Hill. "I have a purpose in writing this note directly to *headquarters*," complained the lady, who was quite put out by her failure to get the Hills up to Dutchess County for a weekend, "for that *poor, abused* wife never seems to know when or where you are going." [52]

The railroad had barely been completed to the Coast and its financial hatches secured when Mary Hill saw the next act begin to unfold. Sitting alone in the winter twilight, she read the note her inexhaustible husband had written her as their twenty-fifth anniversary approached:

> This year will mark the union of our lives for a quarter of a century, and while we began with youth and strength on our side, I am sure we have reason to be most thankful. . . . As the time rolls by I do not want to spend the weeks and days away from you. The years we have left, be they many or few, will I am sure be happier if we are left largely to our children and ourselves.[53]

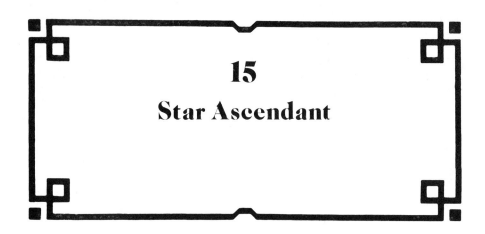

15

Star Ascendant

I see no reason why the Darwinian theory does not apply to railways. I do not think rates can ever be advanced in this country, and the very name of pool savors so much of trusts that it is unpopular. The only safe way I see for the railways is in more economical management, and with that their future should be good.

—James J. Hill, 1897, 1899

I

It was only another begging letter, of which James J. Hill received dozens each year, but as Edward T. Nichols slipped it into the envelope of mail to be forwarded to his chief in St. Paul, he smiled at the address. "James J. Hill, Wall Street, New York," was all it said, in a pathetic, painful pencil scrawl. But by the late 1890s it was all any envelope needed to find its way to Hill, who had come through the bitter depression with a greatly enhanced national reputation as one of the three or four leading railroad men of the day.[1] A transcontinental railroad built without land grants or other government assistance on the eve of the worst depression the raw new industrial society had ever seen was a conspicuous achievement. A railroad which thereupon proceeded to expand both its traffic volume and its profits was a miracle. Hill's dramatic success in every department of railroading caught the success-oriented society's fancy to a degree which made him a true celebrity.

By the summer of 1899 Hill's most insistent predictions were being borne out from one end of the land to the other. The old century was going out with a bang, after all, and the spindly railroads of America would soon collapse under their burden unless they were transformed into heavy-duty facilities as fast as human nature and scarce capital would permit. "Don't be even a little bit afraid of getting your engines too heavy or your cars of too big capacity," Hill advised William H. Newman, his former general manager, who was busy transforming the New York Central into one of the most efficient and most profitable enterprises in the world.[2]

No segment of the Great Northern got a respite from Hill's incessant improvement programs for very long. Motivated by a government policy which encouraged him to plow back much of his true profits into capital improvements that were charged to operating expense, and by rock-bottom prices for both labor and materials, Hill was soon able to report to Mount Stephen that no major wooden bridges and trestles remained in the system. Railroad men everywhere watched in admiration as the Great Northern's cost of carrying a ton of freight one mile approached the incredibly low figure of one-fourth of a cent. Soon there would be little more Hill could do to increase efficiency within his own railroad household, and few railroad men doubted that, one way or another, they would soon feel Hill's influence on a broader front.[3]

Hill laid down a stern line for his lieutenants to follow, and he set them a good example. He explained to a man in Superior, Wisconsin, that he had long since adopted a policy of never engaging in business deals along the line of the Great Northern, saying that "It has saved me a good deal of trouble." If a director or officer of a corporation can engage profitably in business deals *in competition with* his company, he lectured Chicago steel magnate H. H. Porter, he ought to be doing it *for* his company. He met the inevitable paradoxes of business organization head-on, though not always successfully. John F. Stevens remembered him as a man who was always pleased "to have an engineer leave the beaten path and find a better way," but Stevens was a brilliant individualist who was far better at his own particular job than his boss was; as for Hill, he had once told his old friend, Stanford Newel, that he did not care for men who were "too brilliant."[4]

He did care for men who were primarily trained to operate a railroad, which called for a good technical education. Remembering the many times he had envied the way Stevens could handle a difficult problem by the use of mathematics, he declared that "the best equipped men for railway [operation] are those who have taken a course at a good school of technology; the time spent at such a school would be gained two or three times over in the better start a young man would get." But Hill never solved the age-old problem of delegation of detail versus that responsible attention to every facet of operations that he expected his lieutenants to shoulder manfully. He nagged his general superintendent to discourage the flurry of telegrams which constantly poured into the main office from division superintendents seeking orders, because "it destroys their individuality." But where spending money was the issue, there was to be no such delegation. "It seems that almost everybody has got into the habit of leaving their requisitions to their clerks," he growled, and he wanted the practice stopped. While they were at it, his traffic executives might as well stop attending traffic managers' meetings in Chicago, which settled nothing anyway. His subordinates were astounded that a man who a few days before might have been sitting in J. P. Morgan's library discussing the acquisition of a major railroad could swoop down upon them with such an all-seeing eye for details. But it made for a high degree of pride in the road among men who appreciated having their abilities stretched to the limit, while those who did not could always go to work for a lesser railroad. He demanded absolute loyalty, and bitterly condemned a traffic man who accepted a better job with the Rock Island without giving him a chance to meet the offer. But he knew that loyalty was a two-way street, and when prosperity returned he announced a plan that would permit the Great Northern's employees to buy the company's stock at par ($100) at a time when it was heading for 200 on the stock exchange.[5]

He was besieged by requests to help clear away the wreckage left in the wake of the depression, and his natural enthusiasm, propelled by a good-sized ego, guaranteed that he would spend many hours at the task. When the inexperienced president of a fledgling railroad in the booming Southwest begged him to "take a little of your valuable time to tell me some of the duties of my office," he responded sympathetically, for it was a position he had been in two decades before. One of his general managers, transferring to the Cotton Belt railroad, asked him if he might take with him one experienced man from the car accounting department, and soon Hill's ideas of how to keep up with valuable rolling stock were taking root in East Texas. He sent his own statistical report to a vice president of the proud Milwaukee road who had asked for a look at the Great Northern's operating data. His rewards lay primarily in such things as a letter from Newman, whose prodigiously profitable Lake Shore subsidiary had managed to increase its average tonnage per train almost to that of the Great Northern. "How's this for one of your students," Newman crowed.[6]

This all took a great deal of time, but it also paid off handsomely in the profound respect it stimulated among the all-important Eastern railroad men. The powerful financiers who were reorganizing the Santa Fe consulted him about filling their top operating job, and soon Edward P. Ripley, who would become a railroad industry leader early in the new century, was hard at work bringing that road back to health. Hill declined to participate in the refinancing and rebuilding of the strategically important Alton road, perhaps reasoning that in Edward H. Harriman it had all the talent it could use. But when a group of Chicago financiers asked him to join them in refloating the venerable Baltimore & Ohio, Hill began one of the most fruitful consultations of his career. He set the tone of his participation high, rejecting a "quick stock turn" and demanding that the syndicate approach the deal as a long-term, constructive reorganization effort. Marshall Field and Philip D. Armour, who had got up the idea, were deeply impressed by Hill's description of its greater possibilities. "I guess I am more at home in the sausage business," Armour replied.[7]

Did it seem arrogant for this Westerner, who had been a coal merchant when the Baltimore & Ohio had been in operation for fifty years, to declare that he could increase the trunk line's net profits by several million dollars a year just by instituting shrewder operating methods? Did it seem insulting that Hill should lecture the receivers about the need to rebuild large sections of the road to get more favorable grades over which to haul its huge coal tonnages? And that they might as well do it right the first time, rather than rebuilding over and over as the Pennsylvania and the New York Central had done? Not to J. P. Morgan, who sent his man, Charles H. Coster, to tell Hill's man, Daniel S. Lamont, that he was delighted to hear that Hill was taking a hand. "Your connection with the B&O would remove a long standing irritating element in the railroad situation in this country," Morgan declared, with rare enthusiasm.

Hill was as good as his word. He traveled back and forth over the road, preparing an improvement program which totaled a staggering $20 million. He persuaded Frederick Douglass Underwood, another man destined for industry leadership, to leave the Soo road and become the Baltimore & Ohio's general manager. The road entered the twentieth century magnificently transformed from the rundown, rate-cutting, weak-sister trunk line it had been in the bad old days of the 1870s, 1880s, and 1890s, and in 1901 Hill helped place it in the Pennsylvania Railroad's "community of interests." His association with the Baltimore & Ohio did not ripen into the true coast-to-coast railroad which some had naïvely heralded, but among financiers it gave Hill a credit balance that would prove priceless as the pieces of the Northwestern railroad puzzle fell rapidly into place after 1898.[8]

II

"You don't answer telegrams worth a d—n, . . . so I try the mails, bad as they are," chided John Murray Forbes, Hill's Boston friend. The year was 1889, and the old gentleman still had a decade to live. Hill was always glad to get one of Forbes's breezy, confident letters, especially during the gloomy years of the depression, and he was saddened to see how his painful scrawl deteriorated. Still, Forbes insisted, writing was better than telegraphing, for, he said, George Gould, who had inherited the Western Union Company from his father, read all the telegrams before they were delivered. He chattered away about his new boat, the steam yacht *Wild Duck*. Knowing of Hill's growing interest in shipbuilding, he coaxed him to bring his family to the World's Columbian Exposition in Chicago while he was there with the yacht, for whose innovative Belville boilers Forbes's enthusiasm knew no bounds. "Tell me how to earn money enough to buy me a good saddle horse, to prolong the rather worthless days of your friend and admirer of your pluck and foresight," he joked.[9]

But it was not naval architecture or tips on the stock market that were really on the mind of old John Murray Forbes. The Chicago, Burlington & Quincy Railroad, that magnificent transportation machine which joined East and West in the very heart of the nation's breadbasket, was Forbes's greatest achievement in a long life of service. Not since he and his Boston associates had entered the picture almost half a century before had the Burlington's future seemed so uncertain. The problem it faced was a fundamental one for all of the so-called Granger roads: how it was to assure itself of a strong place in the rapidly changing railroad world of the 1890s? Whatever its relations with the Eastern trunk lines, one fact was obvious: it must secure a direct connection to the West Coast, and whether this meant building, or buying, or being bought by an existing railroad, Forbes and his associates knew that sooner or later the step would have to be taken. They had bought a large interest in the Manitoba road, the only concrete result of Charles E. Perkins's western trip to investigate possibilities ten years before. At that time Perkins had seen little to recommend purchase of the Oregon & Transcontinental Company, the holding company which controlled both the Northern Pacific and the Oregon Railway & Navigation Company. Although both the Northern Pacific and the Union Pacific (via the Oregon Short Line) used the Oregon Railway & Navigation as access to the rich Columbia River valley and Portland, it did not seem right for the Burlington. "The policy of the CB&Q up to this time has been not to speculate in railroads," Perkins had explained, "but to buy them after they have shown that they [are] valuable. . . . " By 1893 Forbes saw that it was time to do something, and it was to Hill, not Perkins, that he looked for the solution.[10]

Totally absorbed in extending the Great Northern to Puget Sound and consolidating his position, Hill had little time for the Burlington people and their problems in the 1890s. Running into one of them at the Harvard-Yale football game in 1890, he had ignored broad hints that the Great Northern could have a substantial stock interest in the Burlington's new line between Chicago and the Twin Cities if he wanted it. Two years later Perkins worried that the Union Pacific was about to fall apart. Charles Francis Adams, Jr., was out of the picture, Jay Gould had finally coughed himself to death in his lonely Fifth Avenue mansion, and the draconian debt repayment terms which the government had fastened upon the pioneer transcontinental were dragging it further down with each passing month. In a letter to Forbes recommending that they form a syndicate to buy control and "neutralize" the Union Pacific, Perkins wrote, optimistically, that "Hill will probably side with us in this." But when he visited St. Paul five days later, Hill told him that it would be best to wait, for rates were bound to come down when the last spike was driven in the Great Northern, and then they could get the Union Pacific at a bargain price.[11]

It was a dodging tactic, for Hill never wanted anything to do with the Union Pacific. He considered it primarily a road to serve the mining interest in the arid, rocky regions through which it ran. He did not believe that the Union Pacific, which was barely able to hold on to the Oregon Short Line and the Oregon Railway & Navigation, would remain a viable route to the Northwest, where his own interests lay. Thus, when Forbes and Perkins renewed the pressure the following year, Hill told Forbes, "I feel much less inclined to take any interest in it than when I saw you in Chicago. . . . The nation has had some pretty hard falls and I think it will take some time to recover." By 1895 Oregon Railway and Navigation was about to be foreclosed, and separated from the bankrupt transcontinental, presumably forever. Fearing the chaos this might produce in the Western railroad picture, Perkins begged Hill to take one-half of a syndicate which he, with the best Boston people, was forming to buy it. The Great Northern, which was totally dependent upon the Oregon Railway & Navigation for access to the thriving city of Portland, might well have jumped at the offer, but Hill was adamant. Five years later, when Hill and Perkins ran into each other on the Lake Shore Limited between Chicago and New York, Hill explained why he had spurned the offer: Jacob Schiff had by then undertaken the gigantic task of reorganizing the Union Pacific, and Hill would not make his friend's job any harder. Had he been a little less loyal, both Schiff's problems and Edward H. Harriman's position in railroad history might both have been considerably diminished.[12]

Hill and Perkins saw little of each other after 1895, until dramatic events brought them together again in 1900. Meanwhile, Hill and his old associates continued to cultivate each other with the mixture of sentiment and ambition which had worked so well for twenty years. Hill was deeply pleased to hear that his old friend Donald Smith, whose service to the British empire had been as great, many felt, as that of Stephen, was to follow Mount Stephen into the House of Lords. "He has not yet been able to make up his mind what title to call himself," Mount Stephen wrote; "what a strange creature he is, so Indian-like in his love of mystery and secretiveness." Hill was not surprised, therefore, to learn that his friend had finally settled on the unwieldy title of Lord Strathcona and Mount Royal. He promised to visit the new Baron and his lady in their massive new stone mansion in the loch country of Scotland, although Mount Stephen cattily remarked that the new laird never seemed to be able to alight there for more than three or four days at a time.[13]

For Mount Stephen, now well into his sixties, life had many changes in store. Shuttling between his country seat at Brocket Hall and the mansion at 25 St. James's Place, with frequent trips to confer with Gaspard Farrer and the Barings and an occasional look-in at the House of Lords, he savored his role as one of England's most financially sophisticated peers. He enjoyed showing off Hill on the latter's trips to

Europe, especially at functions such as the all-male dinner which he gave in February 1895 for twenty-two important people who came to see their friend's famous guest. Then, in 1896, Mount Stephen's wife of many years died. He had no children, and Hill worried what his friend would do now, especially after learning from some friends that they had decided to move in with him to take care of him. "I hope that we may be able to find some committee for him to serve on in the Lords," one of them wrote gloomily. But they all worried too soon, for barely a year later Mount Stephen announced his engagement to a thirty-five-year-old former lady-in-waiting to Mary of Teck (later consort to George V), and Hill noted that "since his wife's death he is more active than ever before." [14]

The old associates grouped more closely around Hill than ever as the nation began to pull out of the depression. In summer, Kennedy fled to Bar Harbor, Maine, far from the heat of New York and the gabble of the growing herd of tourists in Europe. During much of the rest of the year, accompanied by his wife and numerous female in-laws, he was at Aix-les-Bains and other dignified European watering spots. But he told Hill that he was his to command, and Hill knew that he meant it, for his Great Northern interests were larger than ever before. And Edward Tuck, whether he was staying at his villa in Monte Carlo or in his apartment on the Champs Elysées, made the Great Northern his chief hobby.

D. Willis James also renewed his loyalties, remarking that it was hard to believe that operating costs could be lowered to a quarter of a cent per ton per mile, "but after what you have done since I first knew you I shall never say anything you suggest is impossible." The allies whom Hill had made a decade before at the Chase National Bank and at Moore & Schley were more valuable than ever. Hill was worried about H. W. Cannon, for the financial genius was ailing, and he was saddened when news came that gentle, dignified John G. Moore, still in his fifties, had died. His relations with the Eastern railroads, always good, were made even better when George B. Roberts, president of the Pennsylvania Railroad, suddenly died and was succeeded by one of Hill's best friends, Frank Thomson. And despite the hard blows he had given over the years to Chicago, Hill's stock remained high among such leading citizens as Marshall Field, Philip D. Armour, H. H. Porter, and John W. Gates. [15]

Until the formidable figure of Edward H. Harriman burst upon the scene in the mid-1890s, however, nearly everyone had concluded, not always enthusiastically, that Hill's most important financial ally was to be Jacob H. Schiff. Schiff took his job as a director of the Great Northern seriously, and insisted that Nichols be kept better advised on the financial needs and resources of the company. No more one-man-bands seemed to be the price of Schiff's support, and Hill was glad to pay it. Apart from the great and growing strength of Schiff and his associates, and their unparalleled entrée to European purses, Hill was genuinely fond of Schiff and his family. He found their daughter, Frieda, and her husband, Felix Warburg, stimulating young friends, and he gave a stunning sable cape and a matched team of ponies to the newlyweds. Hill took Frieda's brother, Mortimer, or "Morti," as everyone called him, into the offices of the Great Northern in St. Paul, where he taught him railroading from the ground up, as he later did James Stillman's son, Chauncey.[16]

Schiff was anxious to do something to resettle the impoverished victims of Czarist anti-Judaism in America, and Hill, when he heard what his friends were contemplating, got entirely carried away. Various Jewish charities, Schiff told his friend, had been investigating the possibility of founding a colony of refugees in Minnesota, although previous attempts to do the same thing in Manitoba had ended unsuccessfully, even tragically. In a few days Hill overwhelmed Schiff with a complete plan to settle an initial colony of forty families on small farms to be carved out of cleared pinelands which Hill owned at Milaca, about seventy-five miles northwest of St. Paul.[17] Schiff was dumbfounded:

> The members of the Baron de Hirsch Committee feel deeply gratified. . . . At a time when so many of our own people are apathetic in the duties which they owe to our unfortunate persecuted co-religionists, it is most gratifying to get from one not belonging to our faith so much encouragement as we do from you.[18]

Before the New Yorkers knew what was happening, Hill announced that the forty houses were ready and that St. Paul's Jewish community had consented to look after the newcomers, albeit somewhat reluctantly. Now there arrived on the scene not the colonists, but a Dr. Rosenthal, who surveyed the ground with a critical eye, thanked Hill for his courtesies, and returned to New York with the urgent advice that the Russians were under no circumstances to be permitted to proceed to Minnesota.[19] Julius Goldman, chairman of the Baron de Hirsch fund, embarrassed beyond measure, explained frankly a few matters that even Schiff, urbane German Jew that he was, had not realized:

> The number of Jewish farmers in Russia [is] about 64,000 out of about five million Jews. Of those who immigrate from Russia to this country, . . . though many of them have the enthusiasm for agricultural pursuits, their enthusiasm is based upon ideas so different from the actual facts that their buoyant spirits are very apt to ooze out when the hard task that lies before them is actually encountered. The isolated life upon a farm, away from the cities, soon discourages the people. . . .[20]

Disappointed at the sudden collapse of his plan, Hill nevertheless assured Schiff that he was to feel no embarrassment. He was at no expense or inconvenience as a result of the miscarriage, he insisted, although his personal records show otherwise. As for the Russians, those who cared to try farming were soon raising chickens and vegetables on truck farms in New Jersey. The forty forlorn little houses were consumed in the great forest fire of 1894.[21]

Both men had thornier problems to solve. Disregarding his friend's warnings, Schiff had committed Kuhn, Loeb & Co. to reorganizing the Union Pacific. Not only was it going to take a very great deal of money, but there was no one in sight who could undertake the physical rehabilitation of the neglected old transcontinental. Hill firmly declined Schiff's offer to take a controlling interest. "I think it is doubtful if anyone can get either honor or profit out of it, "he said.[22]

III

The names of James J. Hill and Edward H. Harriman dominated Western railroading so completely in the decade following the depression of the 1890s that the evolutionary process which brought them to the fore has been all but forgotten. Not until a host of lesser men had worked unavailingly over the inert forms of the Union Pacific, the Northern Pacific, and the Santa Fe (to name only the more important bankrupt lines) did these two titans emerge. The Santa Fe receivership was not only a failure at first, but a scandalous feast for a pack of legal jackals as well, until the brilliant team of Victor Morawetz, a legal and financial expert who had been on J. P. Morgan's staff, and Edward P. Ripley routed the scavengers and rebuilt the Santa Fe into one of the West's great railroads. Meanwhile Schiff, who thought he had finally mastered the thorny Union Pacific situation, woke up one day to find that a droopy-moustached, bespectacled little broker named Harriman, who had seemed content with his work on the Illinois Central Railroad, was demanding a major role in the rebuilding of the road.

A new cast of characters would soon move on stage at the Northern Pacific, too. No railroad, it seems, ever enjoyed more trust, or was given the benefit of more doubts, and betrayed them more, than the Northern Pacific under Henry Villard. Under Villard is perhaps unfair, for the brilliant publicist and financial arranger was a poor builder and manager of railroads, and made little show of actually running the Northern Pacific from his headquarters in New York. Men like Hill and Perkins knew that Villard, at best, was closing his eyes to conflicts of interest between the railroad and its operating executives. Villard's strange power over investors, especially the Germans, who almost begged to be allowed to throw good money after bad, proved more of a handicap than an advantage, as the Northern Pacific paid dividends and even interest out of the proceeds of fresh issues of securities, while the crying need for physical improvements was ignored. Perkins had had so little faith in the road's management that when the company demanded a $15 per share assessment from stockholders at its first reorganization, he had forfeited all 4000 of his shares. As Hill pushed the Great Northern across the Cascades, Mount Stephen freely predicted that the Northern Pacific's weakness, and not any strength it might be said to have, was its main threat. As early as 1892 Schiff had warned Hill to be prepared to decide what role he would play in the inevitable reorganization of the road.[23]

With his own line to Puget Sound, which he knew could best the Northern Pacific in any rate war, Hill at first showed little interest in the road. Even the most favorable opinion of it—a report by an engineer hired by Dr. Georg Siemens, head of the Deutsche Bank and chief representative of the worried German bondholders—was scathing in its denunciation of the management. That highly confidential report, a copy of which the resourceful Schiff procured for Hill, noted that it was not the physical condition of the road which was so bad, but its burden of fixed interest charges, which it could not possibly carry so long as the management insisted on building sterile branch lines and cutting rates. Close to criminal was the Northern Pacific's insistence that it had to have a line to Chicago, which led it to buy the Wisconsin Central Railroad, the longest and most poorly built of the too-numerous Chicago lines. This step was unnecessary, and the price the Northern Pacific paid so excessive, that even a child could smell financial double-dealing. T. F. Oakes and J. M. Hannaford, operating and traffic vice presidents of the Northern Pacific, had fought the purchase tooth and nail, but not even Oakes's threats to resign could keep the New Yorkers from closing the deal. In the summer of 1893, the Northern Pacific collapsed into receivership.[24]

Both Hill and Schiff, reading the confidential report, had been amused at the German engineer's dismissal of the Great Northern as a factor to be reckoned with in the Northern Pacific situation:

> People who know Hill assert that it needs only an energetic decision to defeat him with his own weapons. . . . If the rate war could be carried to such a point that the best business of the Great Northern would be threatened, peace could be quickly gained. The very fact that the GN traverses some 1500 miles which has [*sic*] so far hardly any settlers, makes it especially vulnerable. . . . Mr. Hill runs the risk of a general rate war . . . but Hill is described as a man who is too wise to be stubborn. . . .[25]

Still, the danger that the Northern Pacific, freed, if only temporarily, from paying interest on its bonds, might slash rates to get business under depression conditions, had to be dealt with. This was all the more true since by the spring of 1894 men like Cannon had begun to fear that the receivership would be a protracted, indecisive affair. Control, if it could be called that, had reverted to the remnants of the old "Billings crowd": Brayton Ives, the brothers Johnston and Crawford Livingston of St. Paul, Charles Wright, and iron magnate Charlemagne Tower. A new personality, destined to serve largely as a front for a group of men whose interests were best served by a protracted receivership, was Edward D. Adams, who was elected chairman of the reorganization committee. Proud of his relationship with the famous Adams family of Boston, slight as it was, and equipped with a good, if not brilliant head for finance, Adams had played a role in several railroad refinancings in the past. His great handicaps were an ego all too large for its owner's accomplishments, a pathetically thin skin where criticism was concerned, and a cultivation bordering on the prissy, which from time to time led him to spurn an important business conference on the ground of a prior date to attend the opera. By fall it was obvious to the Germans that reorganization was not making any headway, and when Dr. Siemens, on a trip to London, confided his problems to his old friend Lord Mount Stephen, that gentleman told him that he thought there was only one sensible solution: "unification" of the Northern Pacific and the Great Northern under the aegis of James J. Hill.[26]

Mount Stephen was not the only person thinking along those lines, as Hill explained in a long letter:

> When I was in N.Y. some of the old "Billings" crowd as they call themselves . . . came to see me . . . wanting to know if I would take into consideration a plan of reorganization with a view of bringing the Nor. Pac. and our own property closer together. I told them I would consider it . . .

> If the Nor. Pac. could be handled as we handle our property, and all the wild and uncalled for rate cutting stopped, it could be made [a] great property. Its capacity to earn money is good, . . . but it has not been run as a railway for years, but as a device for creating bonds to be sold . . .[27]

Five days later he had the figures before him, and Hill gave Mount Stephen a picture of what a skillful railroad man, given a free hand, could do with the Northern Pacific:

> I think the Nor. Pac. could be made to earn net from traffic alone $8 million of which fully $2 million would come from saving in operating expenses and unnecessary train mileage. . . . The amount of work to be done would be very great, and the men who would be of use are very few. . . . The advantages to our company would mainly come from the freedom from competition and needless friction and expense in operation, all of which I think would be worth to us about $600,000 or $750,000 [a year]. We can get along without them and against them [but] at the same time the control of an empire such as lies between Lake Superior and the Pac. Ocean . . . would render the future secure. . . .[28]

He had talked himself into it. Perhaps because he and Mount Stephen were no longer young men, the burden they were about to shoulder intimidated them more than any such project had in the past. "After the work of reorganization is carried out the real drudgery will begin," Hill admitted to Farrer. But they never seriously considered shunning the task. Mount Stephen and Arthur Gwinner, English representative of the Deutsche Bank, who saw the man and the occasion meeting in Hill, urged him to come to England, and to bring Mary with him. Although they managed a short trip to Monte Carlo while there, business was never very far away. One morning the telegraph messenger pedaled up to the Tuck villa with a worried dispatch from Mount Stephen: the Northern Pacific receivers were about to sell off the company's express business. Don't let them do it, Hill wired; the business will be worth $5 million once it is merged with the Great Northern's express business. It was his first concrete step in the formation of the community of Northwestern railroads, a journey which would carry him further than he or anyone else dreamed.[29]

Back in the United States, Hill began the tiresome process of convincing Adams that the new turn of events was the best thing for the Northern Pacific's bondholders, who were the receiver's special responsibility, and, somehow, that it was all Adams's idea in the first place. "I may be wrong," Hill sarcastically wrote Mount Stephen, "but I think I could see in Mr. Adams' mind a somewhat remote desire towards a *unification* of the two corporations." Unfortunately, Adams was still capable of thinking for himself: when he unveiled a grandiose plan to merge (submerge, Mount Stephen and Farrer would scream), both the Northern Pacific and their proud Great Northern into a new proprietary company, Hill was appalled.[30]

He told Adams that that was definitely not what he and his London associates had agreed to do, but he trod lightly, for, as he told Mount Stephen in an agonized, fourteen-page letter, he had promised Dr. Siemens that if he and Adams were unable to agree, at least they would not disagree without further consultation. What the associates had agreed to do was to guarantee a reborn Northern Pacific's interest charges to the extent of $6 million a year (several million dollars more than anyone except Hill thought the Northern Pacific could earn in any year in the foreseeable future), in return for which the Great Northern would take possession of a majority of the Northern Pacific's capital stock. Clearly, they had left things too loosely arranged when he was in London in February, and it would be necessary to have the Germans firmly committed to the plan before they could jolt Adams off his side track.[31]

Under strict secrecy (the steamer ticket was bought in George Clark's name), Hill embarked on the next available boat. As he bobbed across the Atlantic in the North German Lloyd's *Trave* he scribbled out the terms of a definitive proposal to the Northern Pacific reorganization committee, calling for the $6 million guarantee. Landing in Queenstown on May 3, he went directly to Brocket Hall, where he and Mount Stephen discussed the situation. By now Hill's friend was enthusiastically in favor of "unification," as he called it, but only on terms which would preserve their "blessed old road." On May 10 they gathered at Mount Stephen's town house on St. James's Place, and there Hill, Mount Stephen, Edward Tuck, and Thomas Skinner (for the Deutsche Bank) signed the "London Agreement" to acquire the Northern Pacific on behalf of the Great Northern.[32]

The news leaked out almost immediately. Crawford Livingston, eager as ever to get on the bandwagon, begged for details. That very day, he confessed, he had sold his bonds and then turned around and bought them all back again. Schiff was delighted, and Charles A. Pillsbury, Hill's old Minneapolis friend, told him that "if you were not the foremost railroad man in the United States before, this would certainly make you so." A small broker in New York wrote that Hill's bargain reminded him of the businessman who, upon asking the female typist who had rendered her bill what she would take off for cash, was startled to hear her reply "Everything but my stockings." Perkins wondered what was afoot. "Hill is certainly up to something," he wrote Forbes, "and I suppose it must be to control the N Pac. . . . Such a combine would make him almost absolute over a pretty big country." [33] But it was not going to be that easy.

IV

St. Paul's dowdy, mansard-roofed Union Station, barely fifteen years old in the summer of 1895, was already operating at full capacity. Before long, it was predicted, there would be more than 200 trains arriving or departing every day. Four railroads competed vigorously for the lucrative passenger business between Chicago and St. Paul, and when their morning trains pulled in several hundred travelers poured into the station. The scene would have offended the senses of those born too late to savor the age of steam and horseflesh. Dozens of perspiring "drummers," their eyes red from a night's fitful sleep in an upper berth or long card games in the smoker, lugged their gladstones up the steps and headed for the baggage room, where they hoped to find their bulky sample cases awaiting them. Porters strained at clumsy baggage trucks piled high with the impedimenta of a society on the move, from ladies' elegant hatboxes to the cardboard suitcases of the Scandinavian immigrants. Outside under the corrugated iron roof men, women and children sought to pile into the carriages which swearing, sweating drivers struggled to bring up to the front entrance. The air was a rich mixture of soft coal smoke, horse droppings, and unwashed bodies.

Into their midst, one hot morning in early July, came a swarm of enterprising newspaper reporters, hot on the trail of St. Paul's most famous citizen. "Jim" Hill, who, it was rumored, had recently been in Europe raising money to buy the Northern Pacific, was returning that day from a hurried trip to New York, and someone, they had heard, was trying to throw a monkey wrench into his well-laid plans. "There he is," came the cry, and the reporters surged along the platform where the Burlington's Chicago train had just come to a stop. Barely giving the Pullman porter time to put down his footstep, Hill swung easily down the steps of the Pullman, his suit rumpled from two days on a train and his big, slightly squashed, western-style homburg clamped squarely on his head. He smiled broadly as the newspapermen bore down upon him, and soon the knot of men was moving in disorderly fashion through the waiting room and out onto the street. Stocky, grizzled Hill strode along, gesturing vigorously as he responded to their questions. Was it true that the Northern Pacific deal was off? "The deal will be successful; school is not dismissed, we're just having a recess," he retorted, and disappeared into the Great Northern building on the far side of Third Street.[34]

When Hill had landed in New York, seven days after signing the London agreement, he had paused only long enough to learn from Nichols that the Germans had unanimously ratified the document. On arriving back in St. Paul, however, he found that everything had begun to come apart. First he came down with another of his heavy colds. Mount Stephen, alarmed, cabled Mary to see that he stayed in bed until he was quite well. As soon as he was himself again, he had rushed back to New York for long, wearying conferences with the small army of people who, one way or another, had thrust themselves into the picture. He had known full well, that morning at the railroad station, that what he and his associates had agreed to do in London might prove to be impossible. But, confident that in the long run everyone would see that it was not only the best, but really the only workable solution for the railroads of the Northwest, he was now committed to throw all his energies into the struggle. Meanwhile, Schiff, reading about the railroad station interview in the New York papers, pleaded with him not to talk so much.[35]

J. P. Morgan, at least, was on his side. Charles H. Coster, Morgan's senior partner, and a specialist in railroad reorganizations, was deeply immersed in assembling the Southern Railway from the ruins of the old Richmond Terminal combine. Dividing his time between taking long, grueling trips over thousands of miles of bumpy railroad line, during which he examined every foot of the properties, and slaving at his desk at the corner of Wall Street and Broadway, Coster was, quite literally, working himself to death. Since Morgan & Company would head the syndicate to underwrite the securities of the reorganized Northern Pacific, which was their main business, it would be just as well to let Hill do the real work. Francis Lynde Stetson and Victor Morawetz, Morgan's senior legal counsel, shook their heads gravely at what Hill was about to do to the laws of the state of Minnesota, but Morgan told them, as he had once told Elbert Gary, that he paid them to tell him *how* to do something, not to tell him that he could not do it.[36]

It was true, of course, that in the 1870s and 1880s the state of Minnesota had amended its corporate charter laws to prevent a railroad from buying the securities or otherwise gaining control of any other railroad that it paralleled in the state. But several people, including W. P. Clough, Minnesota's prestigious Senator Cushman K. Davis, and the terribly expensive New York law firm of Simpson and Thacher, assured Hill that these amendments could not be applied *ex post facto* to a railroad that had been chartered in 1856.[37] Once again Hill would discover that the quality of legal advice is not always in direct proportion to its cost.

It was the greed and foolish pride of the Northern Pacific's reorganization committee, in fact, which frustrated Hill's program to put the London agreement into effect. He had barely arrived back in St. Paul in May when Nichols, his spy system a effective as ever, wired him that a meeting of the committee had revealed considerable opposition to the unification plan. But Adams would surely carry the question, Hill thought, with the associates, the Germans, and Morgan all behind him. Hill had reckoned without William Nelson Cromwell, whose law firm, archetype of the powerful Wall Street variety, served the committee on a fat retainer of $60,000 a year. Each time Hill thought he had persuaded Adams that his idea of a new proprietary company was impractical, Adams would have a conference with Cromwell, after which he would return more fired up for it than before. For his part, Cromwell made no effort to hide the fact that he was trying to break the London agreement, and from Hill's friends in North Dakota and Montana came word that he was sowing seeds of discontent among western interests. Hill finally agreed with Mount Stephen, who charged that Adams and the other receivers "had thought they were all in for a three or four year job with no end of opportunities of making money for themselves, and of course hated the London agreement as fatal to their schemes for sucking the life blood out of the NP."[38]

The legal guns of the state of Minnesota might never have been trained on the plan to unify the Great Northern and the Northern Pacific, but for Edward Adams's duplicity. During negotiations with

Adams and Morgan's people early in the summer, the chief obstacle seemed to be a demand for an increase in the guarantee to $6.2 million. D. Willis James thought it was too much, but Hill convinced him that they could handle it. On July 3 Adams asked Hill to meet him at Coster's office, and there, despite the devotion of the Morgan people to New-Jersey-model holding companies (which Hill felt would be pounced upon by Minnesota politicians), it was decided to proceed with the London agreement. Next day, sitting in his New York hotel room with the newspapers spread out around him, Hill took advantage of the Fourth of July lull to write Mount Stephen in detail of what had happened:

> With Mr. Coster, we went over the work of the lawyers and I stated that . . . Messrs Thacher & Simpson agreed that no serious obstacle interfered with carrying out the London agreement. Mr. Adams seemed very nervous and wanted me to reaffirm our London agreement and give assurance that we would carry it out. . . . I told him that we would continue in this to the end. . . . On my return to our office I found his public statement in print, that we had not the power without additional legislation, &c, which, if true, would do more to prevent the securing of any further legislation than anything which could be said or done. . . .[39]

In short, Adams had managed to put the state of Minnesota in the position of condoning a business deal which some of its major participants themselves considered to be illegal. Despite Stetson's warning that a court judgment in a private test case would carry no weight against the power of the attorney general of Minnesota, Hill rushed to institute such a case. In great secrecy, he persuaded Thomas Pearsall, the pliable broker who had feathered his nest with the help of the Manitoba road in the 1880s, and who was a stockholder in the Great Northern, to sue to permanently enjoin that company from making any guarantees to the Northern Pacific under the London agreement. As summer gave way to fall, Hill continued to put the bravest face he could on the situation. When Circuit Court Judge W. H. Sanborn, an old friend and outstanding jurist, ruled against Pearsall, he was delighted, and he enthusistically pressed Pearsall's New York lawyers (whom he himself had retained through a go-between) to appeal so that they might have the United States Supreme Court's reaffirmation. Meanwhile the various federal courts along the route of the Northern Pacific fell into bitter disagreement, and, reasoning, apparently, that if they could not split the patient's fee the next best thing was to split the patient, they appointed several competing receivers. Hill was

*HILL'S MAN AND MORGAN'S MAN IN THE TAKEOVER OF THE NORTH-
ERN PACIFIC RAILROAD:*

grateful to Thomas Burke, his old Seattle friend, for helping to break
up this unanticipated log jam.[40] Finally, in the hope that the political
leaders of Minnesota could yet be made to see where the real interests
of their constituents lay, he drafted an "open letter" to be issued over
the signatures of a number of Twin Cities businessmen. An end-to-
end merger of the Northern Pacific with a Chicago line, Hill argued,
while meeting the nominal requirements of doctrinaire "free competition," would in fact reestablish the tyranny which Chicago had exercised over the Twin Cities before the Great Northern had destroyed its
monopoloy of transportation facilities eastward:

OPPOSITE Daniel S. Lamont. Library of Congress.

ABOVE Charles H. Coster. Courtesy of Morgan Guaranty Trust Company.

If the NP is better off reorganized by a Chicago line, why not place the Great Northern control there also? We have all been in Chicago's grasp until we declared our independence after a long and bitter contest; and the business interests of Minnesota cannot now afford to go back to the conditions that have taken hard work to overcome, which would be the case should the Northern Pacific road be controlled by any Chicago—St. Paul line.[41]

But the days of reason were drawing to a close. As the Minnesota Supreme Court prepared to rule on the case which the state had brought against the unification, the hostile New York *Sun* predicted

"President Hill's defeat in his third attempt to get control of the Northern Pacific." The Northern Pacific, in fact, had improved its profits to the point where the $6 million guarantee no longer looked very generous. His hopes flagging, Hill left New York for St. Paul, but this time all he had to welcome him was the news that the state court had ruled against him. In the long run, however, as Schiff told him and as the Germans told Mount Stephen, it was not court decisions that counted. "We have felt—as Mr. Morgan did ever since August last—" Gwinner wrote from Berlin, "that as bankers we could not carry through a scheme against the unmistakable opposition of public opinion."

So J. P. Morgan would undertake an "independent" reorganization of the Northern Pacific. Would there be a place in it for Hill and the Great Northern, who were now so thoroughly tarred with the brush of monopoly? Exhausted by his labors, Hill almost did not care whether there was or not.[42]

V

It is ironic that Hill's expansive plans for unifying the railroads of the Northwest, which he expected to keep him busier than ever, seemed to have been dashed at a time when his other interests had declined. While few of his avocations ever lacked some practical aspect, his innovative mind had many fruits, and they did not always work out as he hoped. By 1890 he was ready to abandon as a failure his program for encouraging animal husbandry in Minnesota and the Dakotas. He had grown not a little bored with the stolid Anguses, Shorthorns, and Shropshires that absorbed the considerable money and increasingly scarce time he devoted to North Oaks Farm. As his children grew up, the somnolent atmosphere of the farm appealed to them less and less. Louis began to grumble at the long Sundays which his father expected him to spend with him at the farm, painstakingly going from stall to stall to check upon the care the animals were getting. Father and son never got back to Summit Avenue until nearly dark, and Louis often found in the silver bowl in the entrance hall the calling cards of his own friends, mute testimony to what his Sunday might have been.[43]

Hill had hoped that the farmers of the Northwest would see the futility of trying to live twelve months on seven months' work at wheat-growing, and that with his help and inspiration they would work hard at diversifying their farms, but it had not worked. After 1890 he usually left it to his secretary to decline the requests for free bulls which continued to trickle in, but one day in 1898 he scrawled across the face of a farmer's letter a reply which expressed his bitterness:

> Some years ago I made an effort to improve the livestock of the farmers in the several counties along our line and to that end gave them several hundred young bulls. The failure on the part of the farmers to even try to help themselves was very discouraging and for that reason I have for several years only raised such animals as I need for my own use.[44]

Even so, he was sometimes flattered by imitation, as when the receiver of the Oregon Railway & Navigation Company wrote to ask his advice on distributing purebred boars among the wheat farmers of the Inland Empire.[45]

Throughout the 1880s Hill had repeatedly resolved to improve his personal liquidity, but he was constantly pressed for cash during the depression of the 1890s. While his net worth rose consistently throughout these years, more and more of it reflected his deep personal commitment to railroad schemes, and the Great Northern, Northern Pacific, Baltimore & Ohio, and other railroad securities in which his cash was locked up could not be touched. He had to decline Robert Bacon's generous offer of a subscription to the stock of the Federal Steel Company, which J. P. Morgan & Company were organizing in defiance of Andrew Carnegie, and which would have paid off handsomely just a few years later, when the United States Steel Corporation was formed. Art dealers found the 1890s a lean time, although the energetic Durand-Ruel kept Hill's interest in collecting high, and he managed to sell him a Corot here and a Delacroix there. But he did not get very far with a realistic canvas by Honoré Daumier, "The Third Class Carriage," for Hill was not quite ready for the new school. Meanwhile, restless as ever, he had begun to try to grow orchids in Minnesota.[46]

His personal mail swelled with letters from people who hoped to get something from him. His usual response was a polite refusal, as he confined his philanthropy close to Minnesota and the still-poor Dakotas, but he generously rewarded free expressions of loyalty. Thus when the Pullman conductor of a Burlington train wrecked on its run from Chicago to St. Paul found Mrs. Hill, Clara, and Charlotte and saw them to safety, Hill surprised the man with a check for $500. He was flattered when the great or near-great looked him up in St. Paul, for he greatly enjoyed their conversation at dinner. (The intellectual climate of St. Paul was rather bleak just then.) Among them were Charles Trevelyan, nephew of Macaulay, the celebrated historian, and F. W. Taussig, the eminent Harvard economist—like Hill, a champion of free trade—who told Hill that "nothing gives the economist more food for reflection than the operations of the able captains of industry." Hill's reputation as a talker, in the lecture hall, the banquet chamber, or his business car, spread far and wide. A Chicago acquaintance remembered it vividly. "When we were last together at Duluth in 1893," he wrote at the end of the century, "it was three o'clock in the morning, the thermometer about 20° below zero, and you stood on the platform of your car and told me still more of your great plans for the future. I would have stayed there till daylight . . . and I told them in Chicago that Mr. Hill of St. Paul was the greatest railway president this country had ever produced. . . ." [47]

Hill was sometimes painfully blunt in his impatience with those who failed to pull their weight. In 1890 he told the Reverend Dr. Edward D. Neill, who was still pushing his idea for a reference library of high standards, that St. Paul was too preoccupied with plans for a public library to think about any other kind, and that the citizens did not even seem to be making much progress in that direction. The pastor of a Presbyterian congregation, which had erected an ugly, pretentious church and then had saddled it with a mortgage, got short shrift from a man who preferred to help "struggling communities who are unable without help to build even small churches." He was troubled by the inability of the Roman Catholics, the poorest of the sects, to provide an educated clergy for their rapidly growing numbers. Even as he lost patience with the chronically over-extended Bishop John Ireland, who had brought so many of his co-religionists to the Northwest, he resolved to build and endow the St. Paul Seminary. [48]

Through Hill's private office flowed all the details of the design and construction of that substantial educational institution. Cass Gilbert, St. Paul's celebrated architect, drew the plans, and Hill and his clerks supervised every phase of the construction and equipping of the buildings. By 1895 it was finished, and an impressive group of Catholic educators, headed by the apostolic delegate, Monsignor Satolli, came to St. Paul for the dedication. A series of dinners and receptions given them by the citizens of St. Paul was climaxed by a huge reception at 240 Summit Avenue, where the Hills threw open their doors to all who wished to meet the visitors. Before leaving the house for the Seminary on dedication day, Hill made some last-minute changes in his speech, sharpening his answer to local criticism of his benefactions to the Roman Catholic religion. Standing bareheaded in the bright September sunlight, chin thrust outward and index finger stabbing the air, he told them:

> Some of you may wonder why I, who am not a member of your church, should have undertaken the building and endowment of a Roman Catholic theological seminary. . . . Almost all other denominations have members who are able to help their church work in every material way, but the Catholic church, with its large number of working men and women, have little else than their faith in God and those devoted men who have been placed in charge of their spiritual welfare. . . .
>
> For nearly thirty years I have lived in a Roman Catholic household, and daily have had the earnest devotion, watchful care and Christian example of a Roman Catholic wife, of whom it may be said, "Blessed are the pure in heart, for they shall see God," and on whose behalf I desire to present the seminary and its endowment.[49]

Among the many messages of congratulation that poured in was one from an old friend and associate who was also one of the staunchest supporters of Protestant religious education in the United States. "That the Roman Catholic church is bound to have a most potent influence on the future of the United States is certain," wrote D. Willis James; "that an educated priesthood—educated in America, in touch with the life of America—will be a factor for good, I do not doubt."[50]

VI

As word went around the railroad world at the end of 1895 that Hill would not participate in the rehabilitation of the Northern Pacific, a general cry went up to keep him in the picture. Mount Stephen reported that even one of the attorneys for the reorganization committee, greatly troubled, had called on him in London to tell him that his associates were convinced that the Northern Pacific and the Great Northern should be unified under Hill. Schiff was relieved to hear that Hill had agreed to make another quick trip to England as soon as he had recovered from his regular winter cold, to see what new arrangements could be made. Charles D. Rose, of the London banking family, anxiously wrote that he had invested heavily in the Northern Pacific on the assurance that Hill would be its "guiding spirit." Most convincing of all was a letter from Daniel S. Lamont, now Cleveland's Secretary of War and a closer confidant of Hill's than ever. A very distinguished person had been to see him on other business, he wrote, and before leaving had commented that the Northern Pacific ought to be under Hill's control, and that he would be glad to do whatever he could to bring it about. The visitor had been Henry Villard.[51]

No one wanted Hill's help more than the man who had decided to lead the reorganization. J. Pierpont Morgan, who was nearing the peak of his career, let it be known that he expected to cooperate fully with Hill in both the financial reorganization and the rebuilding of the Northern Pacific, and that it would be brought under Hill's direction as quickly and as fully as could be done under the legal obstacles which had been raised. Years earlier Morgan had discovered the secret of success in the highly technical, time-consuming, and spirit-wearying world of financial reorganizations. It all lay in having dedicated, hard-working lieutenants who would pour all their skill and energies into the operation. (Although Morgan kept close control of the progress of a bewildering variety of reorganizations, his primary virtue was his prestige—he lent them the image of absolute legality and financial soundness so essential to their success.) But such lieutenants were always scarce, and Morgan wore them out at a prodigious rate. His banking firm, despite its worldwide reputation, was small, and only one man, Charles H. Coster, deserved the title of senior partner, in Hill's opinion. On a distinctly more junior plane were men like George Perkins, whom Morgan had stolen away from the New York Life Insurance Company, and Robert Bacon, both of whom would burn themselves out in his service. Morgan knew that he could not rely upon such a slender staff to rebuild the Northern Pacific, which was thousands of miles away in a country none of them knew much about. If Hill had not existed, Morgan would have had to invent him.

Mount Stephen had been at great pains to keep relations between Morgan and Hill cordial. When Morgan, a leading Episcopal layman, came to St. Paul in October 1895 for a church convention, he conferred repeatedly with Hill and spent several hours with him at dinner and, later, in the study at 240 Summit Avenue. Banker Cannon saw to it that Adams understood why the Morgan-Hill relations were important. As for Hill, be observed that "final settlement will come hard and call for firm and patient work of all our friends," but he would carry on. Early in 1896 Morgan invited him to New York for a first look at the reorganization plans his men had worked out.[52]

Naturally, Hill expected to control any situation for which he was going to be held responsible in the public eye. He discussed with Mount Stephen a plan involving a net investment of $10 million which would give them and their associates effective control of the old Northern Pacific, and thus a dominant role in the new company. He tried to convince Morgan that it was of crucial importance to reduce the per-mile capitalization of the Northern Pacific, and drafted a detailed reorganization plan which would have done so. A few days later he received a telegram from Morgan telling him that they had worked out a reorganization plan "conservative enough to meet your approval . . . and will gladly offer you any reasonable amount in a syndicate of forty millions." Morgan's counsel, Stetson, sent word via Lamont that it meant "you are to be in control of the property." Cannon advised him to be wary. "You will have to be as wise as a serpent and as harmless as a dove with these people," he warned. And he was right, for the key feature of Morgan's reorganizations—and this one was to be no exception—was a voting trust, which gave Morgan absolute control of a new company, without regard to what the investors or the directors might think of the outcome, for five years from its formation.[53]

Hill refused to discuss such a plan unless there was forthcoming some additional guarantee from Morgan that the "unification" of the Northern Pacific and Great Northern properties (which, he and Mount Stephen had agreed, was the only reason for their being in the affair) was a primary objective of the reorganization. Reluctantly, he strode up the gangplank of the Cunarder *Lucania* and followed Morgan's *Corsair II* across the Atlantic. On April 2, 1896, Mount Stephen's butler ushered the two men into the library of the mansion on St. James's Place, where their host and Arthur Gwinner awaited them. There they signed what Hill later called the "London memorandum," which covenanted that "GN and reorganized NP shall form a permanent alliance, defensive and in case of need offensive, with a view of avoiding competition and aggressive policy and of generally protecting the common interests of both companies." There would be no new construction into each other's territory; all competitive business, notably that of the Anaconda Company, the fast-growing copper producer, would be divided "upon equitable terms"; and both railroads would cooperate to keep the Oregon Railway & Navigation Company "independent and available on the same terms to all connecting railroads." All parties would vote for the same slate of directors for five years after termination of the voting trust. Hill and Mount Stephen, for themselves and their associates, agreed to buy at least $3 million, net, of the old company, to be exchanged for the securities of the new company when issued.

Mount Stephen was elated; he was convinced that "unification" had been virtually achieved. He saw Hill off on the boat train and a few days later reported to him on another meeting with Morgan, "who said you were the most satisfactory guardian of the property of other people he ever knew." As for Hill, he knew that, even under the best of circumstances, turning the Northern Pacific into a worthy sister of the Great Northern would be a big job. He could barely tolerate the idea of a voting trust, which he did not believe would be allowed "to retain property and mismanage it in this country."A month later the news arrived that Morgan, without any prior consultation, had appointed Edwin P. Winter, president of the North Western railroad's subsidiary "Omaha road," to head the new Northern Pacific.[54]

Hill was furious. He told his friends that Winter was not up to the job of operating the Northern Pacific; in fact, he had not run the much smaller "Omaha road" with anything but the most mediocre results. If Winter wanted Hill's help, he would have to come asking for it. "In the meantime," Hill growled, "I am anxious to do all I can for our own company." But he had already plunged into the mass of problems which would have to be solved if the Northern Pacific were to be effectively reorganized. Throughout Winter's short, rather bewildering career as president of the Northern Pacific, and through the even greater frustrations of the regime which Morgan installed thereafter, Hill went repeatedly through the familiar cycle of sweet reasonableness, righteous indignation, and kiss-and-make-up which are always the lot of men who occupy such anomalous situations. He lectured Morgan on the changes in operating policy which had to be made on the Northern Pacific, and was encouraged to find Morgan firmly behind him. Adams, who had become chairman of the board of the Northern Pacific and actually thought that *he* was running things, agreed to order a halt to all plans for constructing branch lines. Hill, acting as if the two railroads had been merged, ordered his traffic manager to turn over to the Northern Pacific at Spokane the Great Northern's Portland-bound freight, because the Northern Pacific would enjoy the longer haul. When the various state commissions demanded lower rates, he backed up the Northern Pacific's frightened officials, persuading them that it would be far better to lower them voluntarily than to be forced to by formal order.[55]

Meanwhile his relations with Coster, who was really running the

Northern Pacific, alternated between warm and cool. Morgan's man was far too sensible to do anything that would rupture his valuable relations with Hill, but at the same time he had strict orders to maintain the independent character of the reorganization at all costs. He agreed heartily with Hill's assertion that "unless the directors of the Northern Pacific have more and better knowledge than they can get sitting in the upper story of a New York office," they would not be worth much. He encouraged Hill to prepare lengthy reports on how the road could get its ton-mile costs down to the Great Northern's level, and Hill's advice is in two long letters to Adams on operating economies. Meanwhile, Hill worked closely with Winter and his successors to reduce costs, astounding everyone with the uncanny accuracy of his forecasts of the Northern Pacific's net profits. He opposed the declaring of a dividend on the common stock—successfully, for a while—in the hope that the stock might be retired and the excessive capitalization thereby reduced. By May of 1897 he was ready to bring matters to a head by demanding that his own men be put into the top positions on the road.[56]

"Now, when Mr. Morgan arrives in New York I mean to see him and again try to bring about the appointment of Mr. Lamont," he wrote his associates, "but if the policy of indefinite postponement is continued I am unwilling to accept any responsibility whatever." He wanted Lamont badly, for the two men worked together with total effectiveness. Cleveland's term had expired early that year, and although Lamont had received fat job offers from Standard Oil and the Mutual Insurance Company of New York, he told Hill that it was a railroad job he wanted. Hill also wanted F. D. Underwood as general manager. Instead, for president of the Northern Pacific he got Charles S. Mellen, whom few men liked, apparently for good reason, but who had been Morgan's trusted lieutenant at the helm of the rapidly expanding New Haven Railroad. And as for Underwood, that shrewd executive decided that no man could serve two masters. All, however, were agreed that they were able to dispense with the services of Adams, who, Hill said, "has made a mess of everything he has ever been associated with," and that gentleman woke up one day to find that the office of chairman had been abolished.[57]

Hill reluctantly agreed to continue his important, if vague, role in the Northern Pacific under the terms which Morgan, secure in the voting trust, laid down. He had no alternative. Early in 1897 he had tried to persuade his associates to join him in an effort to buy control of the road, although he had no reason to believe that Morgan would thereupon have felt a moral obligation to terminate the trust. It was a most uncharacteristic threat, and both Mount Stephen and Schiff recoiled in horror. Mount Stephen, in fact, worked harder than ever at keeping Morgan happy, and when Hill was in London again in the spring of 1897, he saw to it that the two of them, with Gwinner in tow, paid a call on Morgan at his house in Prince's Gate. At a dinner which Morgan's hostess gave for her famous guests, Hill told Morgan that sooner or later they must have unification or withdraw. "Myself and associates, including the German interests, own a large majority of the shares of the Northern Pacific Co.," he said, "purchased with the expectation that the London memorandum would be carried into effect. I think the time for this has come . . ." [58]

Charles S. Mellen was a hard man for Hill to take, even if Collis P. Huntington of the Southern Pacific and Frank Thomson of the Pennsylvania had sent congratulations on the appointment. He was a "yesman," in the opinion of those who were repelled by his blind obedience to Morgan in carrying out the latter's disastrous expansion plans for the New Haven Railroad after 1901. He was obsequious to his superiors and notoriously unpleasant to subordinates. To Underwood, who refused to serve under him, Mellen was a man who had risen "only by pulling other people down." He was, in short, an early model of one species of the hired professional manager, as he tried, on one or two occasions, to explain to Hill. "I fear you forget others are not all situated in their positions as you are," he remarked. "You control your company; you are in every sense its master; while I am but the 'hired man,' so to speak, of this one." Hill could not understand a man who would accept responsibility without the requisite authority. Mellen was either master in his own house or he was a fool. "Mellen has no business judgment more than a child," he growled. "He appears to have lost his head completely, and is unfit to occupy the position he does. . . ." [59]

By 1898 the reorganization was enormously successful, and Morgan was vastly pleased at this further dramatic proof of the efficacy of "Morganization." A full 4 per cent dividend was declared on the common stock, which rose higher and higher on the exchange, and Coster and Mellen settled in as managers of a thoroughly independent Northern Pacific. However, Mellen's policies in the Far Northwest threatened to destroy all that Morgan, Hill, and their associates had agreed they were working for. A pillar of the London memorandum, and one that Morgan was anxious to support now that the figure of Harriman threatened larger than ever on Wall Street, was the neutralization of the Oregon Railway & Navigation Co. Schiff, who was fast becoming Harriman's ally as their Union Pacific reorganization prospered, had agreed to keep this Portland gateway open to all, but it was clear that if Harriman decided to try for control Schiff would go along with him. Hill hoped that it would never be necessary to build a parallel line on the north bank of the Columbia River, and worked hard to keep the road in what he considered neutral hands. He persuaded W. L. Bull, the dignified former president of the New York Stock Exchange who headed the reorganized Oregon road, to appoint Hill's former general manager, A. L. Mohler, to run it. Soon Hill found himself feeding vital information about the Northern Pacific to Bull and Mohler, and encouraging them to take offensive steps against the Northern Pacific, whose Mr. Mellen was "flirting considerable with Harriman," Bull claimed. Mellen, meanwhile, had begun to make the same kind of aggressive noises in the Red River Valley and Manitoba that the old Northern Pacific had made.[60]

By mid-1898 Hill and Mount Stephen were both more frustrated than they could ever remember. Business throughout the nation was booming, and now, if ever, seemed the time to put "unification" into effect. Hill sat down in Morgan's office on visit after visit, determined to get his promise to end the voting trust, and each time came away with courtly protestations of faith in the ultimate fruits of their association, and nothing more. In Hill's opinion, it was greed, or ego, or just plain obtuseness that kept Morgan from carrying out what Hill understood to be the spirit, if not the letter, of the London memorandum. He demanded wider representation on the board, and did not get it. He recommended to Mount Stephen that they sell out, but Mount Stephen counseled patience. He sent voluminous letters to Coster, reciting the transgressions of the Mellen-Morgan regime, and received even more voluminous rebuttals which the harried Coster somehow found time to pen in the cold, formal tones of the highest echelons of Wall Street. Coster's bulldog determination was a full match for Hill's, up to a point. That point was reached on March 13, 1900. Ignoring a heavy cold until his doctor ordered him to bed, sickly, overworked Charles H. Coster quickly succumbed to pneumonia.

Morgan was now faced with running the Northern Pacific himself, and that was to make all the difference.[61]

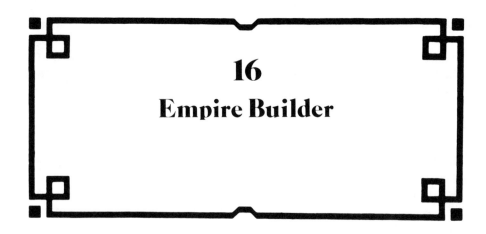

16
Empire Builder

The people are fixing their minds on social questions, the result being a steady increase of the conservative feeling. For ten years or more it has been "railroads, monopolies, trusts, &c," but now it shows up as those who have nothing against those who have something, and in this country those who have, outnumber greatly those who have not. The nation will have an era of prosperity fostered by the good, common sense of the people.

—James J. Hill, 1896

I

When James J. Hill tossed his $25,000 worth of *New York Times* stock into the pool which reorganized that venerable journal in 1896, he gave a big boost to the remarkable career of a man who shared his enthusiasm and optimism for the approaching twentieth century. Adolph S. Ochs, who was to turn the *Times* into the most influential newspaper in the Western Hemisphere, could hardly believe his good fortune at suddenly being propelled from Chattanooga, Tennessee, into the New York newspaper world. But talent, as Hill's own rise to national prominence proved, knew no province in that free world which Hill and his fellows had come to take for granted.

With such thoughts in mind, Ochs took his little daughter, Iphigene, downtown to the *Times* offices on Park Row after dinner one cold night in December of 1900. Through the windows of the grubby old offices, which the paper would soon quit for its new building on newly named Times Square, the little girl could see a group of revelers gathering in City Hall Park. The same thing was happening in cities and towns all over the world, her father explained. The people were saying goodbye to the old century and looking forward expectantly to the new. He wanted her to remember it because, he told her solemnly, "No person shall ever see two such celebrations." [1]

The wave of optimism which Ochs and Hill were riding as the brave new century came in is not quite unique in modern history. Henry Adams, in his *History of the United States*, wrote a classic description of a similar wave which followed the War of 1812. The atmosphere in the late 1890s was, in part, a reaction to thirty years of uneasy prosperity which had been punctuated and then terminated by panics and depressions and bitter, class-conscious political strife early in the decade. In 1896 William McKinley had been elected President of the United States, and the nation's businessmen looked forward to what promised to be the most congenial eight years since James Monroe's presidency. McKinley had ridden in on a resurgence of prosperity marked by the discovery of gold in the Klondike and more efficient techniques for extracting it; by the introduction of remarkable technologies which launched new industries in the chemical and electrical fields while invigorating the older iron, steel, and railroad industries; and by an upturn in the general level of prices which nearly everybody (except railroad men) received for their goods and services. On the political scene, it was as if the earth had opened up and swallowed the cheap-money, anti-business, populistic forces which had threatened a few years before to transform American politics into a three-way struggle. William Jennings Bryan, who had embraced free silver because, as he said, "Nebraska is for free silver," discovered that a remarkably broad segment of the electorate, including most of the country's workingmen and even a majority of the people in the West, wanted no tampering with the nation's basic institutions, which seemed, on the whole, to be the best guarantee of a rising standard of living.

By 1900 it was clear, even in the most remote backwaters of the nation, that the young giant, America, was ready to play a major role in the world. Cities large and small rang with construction hammers, which transformed them and created the urban society which is the chief trademark of the twentieth century. As myriad new opportunities to make money unfolded, businessmen scrambled for capital, and, in response, interest rates joined other prices in an upward spiral. With a wary eye on these developments and a profound faith in their ability to continue to reduce their costs of operation, business leaders plunged into an orgy of combinations which promised to place at the top of the American economic hierarchy a handful of men who had been heading for that role ever since the rough days of the 1870s and 1880s. As the new century dawned these men looked into the future, and thought they saw an era of good feeling in which the political leaders of the nation would join hands with its new economic potentates to produce a golden age.

No one reflected the optimism of the new century more clearly than James J. Hill. He had begun to wonder by 1899 whether there was any bottom to the new prosperity. "We have made estimates in the past," he exclaimed to Schiff, "and what seemed to be based more on hope than sound judgment has always been realized." He bombarded his Eastern associates with invitations to sally forth from their stuffy offices and somnolent clubs and take a trip on his special train to see what their money and brains had wrought. "I would not sell out for $200 a share," he told Gaspard Farrer early in 1900.[2]

In a major speech at the Immigration Convention which assembled in St. Paul at the depth of the 1890s' depression, Hill had noted the end of the era in which the railroads had been the chief colonizing agent. In the future a wider support for immigration must be forthcoming, he warned, and political leaders would have to take a more mature attitude toward the railroads if the carriers were to continue to bear up under the burdens which they had shouldered in the 1870s. By 1899 the flow of immigrants, in fact, was greater than ever before. "It looks as if we would receive 25,000 new settlers this year on the east end [of the Great Northern]," he told Farrer, while "there is a constant stream of people going to the west coast, from common laborers to miners to men with large capital who are going out to the timber districts and building large lumber mills." Thousands of miles away, Mount Stephen watched closely. "It makes me almost giddy when I think of the 'two streaks of rust' which we bought from the Dutchmen 21 years ago," he wrote. On May 23, 1899, twenty years after he had called to order the first meeting of the directors of the Manitoba road, Mount Stephen walked into a cable office in the City of London and scrawled out an unabashedly sentimental message: "Am thinking of this day twenty years ago and wondering what will be the position of the blessed thing twenty years hence." He would live to find out, even if his friend in St. Paul would not.[3]

Now began the process of bringing the Northern Pacific firmly under Hill's control. A few days after Coster's funeral, Lamont wrote that he had talked to Morgan about Northern Pacific matters and found him "disposed to relieve himself and his house of unnecessary burdens," while Robert Bacon, taking warning from Coster's fate, "tells me that he has no intention of assuming the direction of the property." But defrosting Morgan's glacial self-satisfaction in the Northern Pacific's brilliant reorganization was not easy, especially since Mellen seemed to be doing a satisfactory job of running it. "The Senior," as Morgan's men called him to distinguish him from his son "Jack" (J. P., Jr.), was rushing around Europe, buying up art treasures at a prodigious rate with the help of an expert who sneered at his employer behind his back. Off went Hill in pursuit. During the very pleasant month of May 1900 he managed to see more of England than in any of his previous visits, while conferring several times with Morgan. Mount Stephen and Farrer pressed Gwinner to get the Germans' assent to ending the voting trust and to turning a majority of the Northern Pacific's board over to Hill. In the meantime Hill dropped well-placed hints that Mellen was flirting with Harriman, which Morgan professed not to believe but which worried him all the same. With agonizing slowness Morgan worked out a plan calling for further substantial investment by Hill and his associates, which he revealed at a conference aboard his yacht that October. When the Morgans' daughter Louisa married Satterlee, Hill made her a timely present of some of the most beautiful bear, otter, and sable skins the Northwest had to offer. A month later he very quietly checked into the Netherlands Hotel in New York to await developments, and on the afternoon of November 12, 1900, Morgan, thinking that Hill was patiently standing by in St. Paul, wired him: "The voting trustees at their meeting two o'clock dissolved the voting trust. Many congratulations." [4]

II

Hill, with his immediate associates and the Germans, exercised working control of the Northern Pacific. At the beginning of 1901 they held a large minority of the common stock, and while their hold on the preferred, which also had voting rights, was much lighter, no one doubted their ability to elect their slate of directors and do with the company as they saw fit. Hill's direct investment in the Northern

Pacific, which was $1.5 million on January 1, 1901, would rise to nearly $10 million by 1906. He lost no time carrying out a *de facto* "unification" of the two properties. While formal amalgamation of the two railroads had been ruled out, apparently forever, by the laws of Minnesota, there seemed to be no brake at all on what could be done through personal ownership of stock. Hill told Bacon that the two companies would divide up the business of their common territory "equitably, giving to each its proper proportion." Above all, any future extensions of track would be non-competitive. Neither the Northern Pacific nor the Great Northern was expected to suffer from such brotherly sharing. In the wonderful new world of the twentieth century, there was business enough for all. The Northern Pacific was now in a position to share in the heavy lumber business that Hill and the Weyerhaeusers were developing, and which yielded a welcome eastbound return load to a railroad which for two decades had been dragging long strings of empty cars back to the Twin Cities. The Northern Pacific's need for fresh capital, Hill thought, would be a good place to park some of the Great Northern's surplus profits, which were more embarrassing than ever.[5]

Only one real problem remained as the first year of the new century began. Hill insisted that Charles S. Mellen was to be replaced just as quickly as Morgan could find a face-saving spot for him. In 1898 Hill had discovered, on the Missouri-Kansas-Texas Railroad in Texas, the first outsider to whom he seriously considered turning over a major share of the responsibility for the Hill roads. Darius Miller was a pleasant, broadfaced, balding man who had that talent for getting along with people and at the same time getting things done which, if Mellen had had it, would have made him a successful professional manager. Miller was soon hard at work as second vice president of the Great Northern, and, notwithstanding the fact that he was eleven years older than the first vice president, James Norman Hill, he had been given to understand that there was room for both men in the huge railroad empire which Hill had assembled. Mellen was quickly isolated and forbidden to make any important decisions for the Northern Pacific, and, after spending two unhappy years without Hill's confidence, returned to the East to take in hand the strange things that J. P. Morgan was doing to the railroads of New England.[6]

Meanwhile, the progress of the Great Northern was the wonder of the railroad world. By the spring of 1901 Louis Hill was hard at work supervising a major improvement program. Along almost the entire main line from Minot, North Dakota, to the eastern slope of the Rockies a swarm of workers were ripping up track, straightening curves, reducing grades, and then laying down heavier steel rail. "The changes have been so great that it is not the same railroad," Hill proudly told Schiff. It was not just that he preferred to build up the road rather than turn its immense profits back to the public in the form of lower rates. The next decade, in fact, would demonstrate that all of these improvements were barely enough in the face of the incredible growth of traffic. But the hard fact was that if he had allowed the various state commissions to mandate rate decreases beyond the substantial ones which he was periodically making anyway, there would have been real distress, since all railroads had to charge the same rates between common points. "As a matter of course, we will gradually be compelled to reduce our rates," he confided to Schiff, "[but] while with a six and one-half mill rate we would still have a surplus of a million and one-half to two million dollars, every other railway west of Chicago except the Alton would be unable to meet its interest charges." Meanwhile he heaved a great sigh of relief as the detested switchback in the Cascade mountains was replaced with one of the longest tunnels in North America. Yet it, too, he realized, would be obsolete someday.[7]

And always he hunted for new ideas. His neighbor on Summit Avenue, Frederick Weyerhaeuser, leader of the largest lumbering enterprise in the country, had finally been worn down by the rhetoric of night-owl Hill. He nodded before the fire in the "den" at 240 Summit Avenue as Hill droned on about the magnificent stands of timber on the Northern Pacific's vast granted lands in Washington state, and as the hands of the big clock passed midnight, he agreed to join with Hill in their exploitation. The deal, which included eastbound rates so low that they were unheard of, enormously invigorated the lumber industry and guaranteed the profitability of the Hill roads. Hill also investigated the possibility of generating great quantities of electric power at Great Falls, Montana, to drive the Great Northern's locomotives in that region. For a decade he followed a will-o'-the-wisp which attracted many another dreamer: the idea of a great coal, iron, and steel industry in Washington state, based on fuel from the Kootenai district, which straddled the international boundary in Idaho and Montana, and deposits of iron ore and limestone in the Puget Sound area. The railroads with which he complicated the Great Northern system's map, and his relations with the Canadian Pacific Railway in this vain enterprise, still puzzle those who believe that James J. Hill could not make big mistakes. But he did, just like anyone else.[8]

Railroad developments back East were also impressive, especially since the old-fashioned terminals which had been erected in the mushrooming cities in the last third of the nineteenth century were hopelessly outdated. The Baltimore & Ohio had plans for what Hill considered an overly expensive and inadequate new station in Washington, D.C. He persuaded Alexander Cassatt, who had replaced Frank Thomson as head of the Pennsylvania Railroad, to join the enterprise and make it a true union station scheme. The result was one of the most impressive portals any city ever had. In return Hill tried unsuccessfully to sell the Baltimore & Ohio and the Erie on Cassatt's grand plan for a New York terminal, to be served by a gigantic bridge over the Hudson River at 59th Street. And throughout these involvements he did his best to advance the efforts of the New York Central and the Pennsylvania to stabilize trunk-line railroad affairs through their communities of interest. In that exhilarating era, railroad men's heads were full of great plans for the future. They exulted over the discovery that, while government regulation of railroads had been proved a failure—for all time, they believed—their own plans for concerted action promised to make them, after three decades of chaos, masters in their own house. To cement the era of good feeling which was so well begun, ten men, including three of the most important railroad men in the nation, met in Edward H. Harriman's office in the Equitable Building a few days after the new century had begun. Signing the manifesto which announced to lesser railroad men the formation of the Railroad Advisory Committee were J. P. Morgan, Robert Bacon, George Gould, Jacob H. Schiff, E. H. Harriman, James Stillman, Stuyvesant Fish (of the Illinois Central), James Speyer, Aldace F. Walker (one of the original members of the Interstate Commerce Commission), and James J. Hill.[9]

III

No phase of Hill's long career seems more fortuitous, in view of the hundreds of millions of dollars it eventually brought the stockholders of the Great Northern, than his involvement in the iron ore deposits of the great Mesabi Range in northern Minnesota. Notwithstanding the glamorous new industries which burst upon the world scene at the end of the nineteenth century, it was the basic industries—railroads and steel—which were most fundamental to American economic growth in the first two decades of the twentieth. By the 1890s Andrew Carnegie and his followers were making better and cheaper steel than anyone else, except the redoubtable Germans, and selling it throughout the world. At about this time the open hearth process for making steel, superior in so many ways to the older Bessemer process, revolutionized the industry. And it created a dramatic increase in demand for all the materials which go into the making of steel. The older sources of ore were suddenly inadequate, and steelmakers quickly turned to the iron ranges which had been discovered a few years before in the wilds of northern Minnesota. In this land, previously shunned by all but the vicious black fly and the intrepid lumbermen who coveted its magnificent forests, the largest, and, save one, the westernmost, of these ranges was the fabled Mesabi. Until the end of World War II it was to supply the greater part of the Western Hemisphere's ores. By the middle of the twentieth century the prime ores, virtually pure ferric oxide, which, as they were in granular form, could be scooped up in a process which hardly deserved to be called mining, had been mined out. A few million tons are semi-permanently monumentalized in the skyscrapers of the new century, while many millions scuttle back and forth in the form of automobiles, ceaselessly recycled in a triumph of planned obsolesence. Some lie in rusting heaps at the bottom of the great oceans, unseen reminders of the folly of war. By far the greater part have been returned to the earth, lost to mankind in the thousands of refuse dumps that mark our tin-can civilization. But in the first half of the twentieth century the great Mesabi Range was the cornerstone of the American steel industry.

Hill's participation in the iron ore business was so little due to any well-planned, long-term program, one critic noted, as to "shatter all preconceptions of the genius necessary to achieve millionaireship." [10] Several factors accounted for his early reluctance to join in the boom in Mesabi iron lands. It would have been contrary to his long-standing policy of never becoming involved in business deals along the line of the railroad, which he intended to run through the area as soon as certain obstacles were removed. The Great Northern itself had no corporate power to hold iron ore lands or to engage in any other non-transportation business (though ways around these difficulties were found when the time came). More important was the fact that by the early 1890s two powerful groups of capitalists—the Rockefellers, father and son, and the Carnegie-Frick interests—were rapidly taking over the Minnesota iron lands and the railroads which had been built to bring the ores to Lake Superior. Most important, however, was the fact that until his railroad affairs reached a temporary lull in 1897, Hill was simply too busy with other things. Two developments thrust these objections aside: his victory in the fight to keep the Canadian Pacific Railway from acquiring a direct line from Winnipeg to the Lakes, and the persuasiveness of his sons, James and Louis, who had made good use of the years of apprenticeship they put in at Duluth in the service of the Eastern Railway of Minnesota.

Hill's great love affair with navigation on the Great Lakes had reached its climax in the unlikely month of January 1894, when his Northern Steamship Company and the Globe Iron Works proudly launched "the twin-screw, steel passenger steamship, *Northwest*," at Cleveland, Ohio. He was deeply proud that his development of lakes shipping had emancipated both the Great Northern and the Northern Pacific from the tyranny of the Chicago lines and the haughty trunk lines between Chicago and Buffalo, and that the passenger steamers, while they never made much money, were fitting advertisements for the water freight route. At the end of the 1880s, however, an impoverished little railroad which had been building westward from Duluth, making uncertainly for Winnipeg, had begun to show real vitality. Before he realize what was happening, the Canadian Pacific had seized control of the Duluth & Winnipeg (as the Canadians had renamed it), and were preparing to tie the Great Lakes directly into their great transcontinental railroad empire. Hill was furious, but the more he blustered the more Van Horne savored this opportunity to discomfit the man who, ten years before, had lectured him on railroading.[11]

Even Mount Stephen was inclined to twist the knife. It would teach Hill not to bet on the financial collapse of the Canadian Pacific, he said, when Van Horne came out of the depression still holding fast to the Duluth & Winnipeg. Then, having proved that his heart was still very much with his colonial countrymen, Mount Stephen relented, and went to work to persuade Van Horne to let the road go to Hill. The Canadian Pacific, in fact, had had a close call during the depression, and its obligations to the people of Canada left it no resources for adventures south of the border. Sir Donald Smith applied his pressure, and by spring of 1897 the Duluth & Winnepeg was Hill's. He quickly uncorked his long-made plans to rebuild the little road and extend it in a graceful arc across Minnesota, considerably north of the old Northern Pacific's main line, through the town of Fosston to a connection with the Great Northern at the Red River. John F. Stevens, stung at Hill's bet that he could not find a 0.8 per cent grade for this line, which was destined to carry some of the heaviest traffic in the world, located a line of 0.4 per cent, and by doing so won Hill's profound admiration. In one stroke the Great Northern's ability to haul great tonnages of food and feed grains due eastward and northeastward to the head of navigation on Lake Superior, and its power to bargain with the great railroads of the East, had been immeasurably strengthened. But that was not all.[12]

"The [Duluth & Winnepeg], of which we receive the stock, owns some very valuable iron properties in the neighborhood of the Biwabik and Mahoning mines," Hill wrote Cannon. "They were selected about as early and have always been considered among the most valuable properties in the Range." Indeed, the road's property which Van Horne had so reluctantly yielded boasted many acres of some of the richest ore lands on the Mesabi Range. Louis Hill was delighted. For several years, while living in a dreary hotel in Duluth, he had studied the iron ore situation, and had frequently preached to his father about it. Now he went to work buying up additional tracts on the Range which he had previously scouted.

But Louis knew that even more important quarry lay elsewhere. He had learned that two aging lumbermen, A. W. Wright and C. H. Davis, who had pioneered the logging off of the Mesabi's pineries, had some cut-over land they were anxious to sell so that they could retire. They had leased the lumbering rights to the Weyerhaeusers some years before, but could not convince those single-minded men to buy the land outright, even after the existence of the ore was known. They had not even been able to sell it on the open market for $3.00 an acre. But by 1897 the Rockefellers were moving ponderously in that direction. Meanwhile, Hill admitted to Louis that the rickety logging railroad which Wright and Davis had built south from the Mesabi to the Mississippi River would, when connected with the new Fosston line, produce huge tonnages of ores—if the right people controlled those ores. The "right people," Louis and James Norman were convinced, were the owners of the Great Northern, or the Hills, or both, and they soon convinced their father that the $4 million which the elderly lumbermen were now asking for their property was a bargain. It turned out to be one of the bargains of the century.[13]

The three Hills were of one mind as to what to do with the iron ore properties. Estimating that the ultimate yield in royalties might run as high as $900 million if shrewdly handled, they decided to hold the properties against the day when ore would be even more in demand than it was then, for the Mesabi was the last continental source in sight. Louis bought up another 17,000 acres in the next few years. They were dead right in their strategy. When the company which was formed to hold the properties ultimately signed a contract with the U. S. Steel Corporation in 1906 to mine the ore, it was on terms which no one would have dreamed of just six years before. They were pretty steep terms even for 1906, Hill admitted, but J. P. Morgan, fearing that its ore supply was the Steel Corporation's weakest link, had repeatedly urged him to come to terms. "I told them that was the price they could have it at, and it was a loss of their time and a waste of mine to ask for any other figure," Hill bragged to a congressional committee. And he was not negotiating just for himself and his family, for shortly after the Wright-Davis acquisition he sold all of these iron ore properties, for the $4 million he had paid for them, to a trust formed for the benefit of the stockholders of the Great Northern. [14]

Since Hill and his family were major stockholders in the Great Northern, their pro rata share of the Mesabi properties thus delivered was very large. Still, it was a remarkable decision, involving royalties that would eventually amount to at least $425 million, according to Hill's 1906 estimates. He had been under no pressure of any kind to transfer the properties, since the $4 million had come from his own funds. Indeed, the deal seemed so gratuitous that Hill was frequently called upon to explain it to suspicious legislators.

"You were in the position where, if you made money out of the transaction, that went to the stockholders, and if you lost money that came out of your own pocket?" one of them asked, incredulously.

Yes, Hill replied. Yet there was little risk involved, he added blandly.

But why had he done it, when it meant giving up millions of dollars which over the years might have gone directly into the pockets of his heirs?

By 1904 he had begun to reply, wearily, whenever the subject came up, that he had done it simply because he had *wanted* to. "I might, if I so desired, have quietly acquired it for myself," he told Farrer, "and no one would have had any reason to find fault."

Probably no other business decision ever gave him so much pure satisfaction. [15]

IV

"We have on land the cheapest transportation in the world, but just as soon as we take our commodities to the salt water the other nations make us drop our bundles and they carry them at our expense and make us pay them for doing our work." Hill paused until the wave of enthusiastic applause subsided. He was the principal speaker that evening in September 1898 at a reception for U. S. Senator Cushman K. Davis, the most prominent statesman Minnesota had produced up to that time. "It is sometimes said that men have hobbies," he continued; "maybe that is the trouble with me, but I am getting ready to ride mine."

His listeners had certainly had fair warning, for Hill's missionary faith in America's destiny in the Far East trade was well known. In a few weeks a conference was to convene at Paris to arrange a peace treaty with Spain, which the United States had so abruptly defeated on sea and on land. The young nation's future on the world scene had become the subject of much agonizing, both by men of good will and men of selfish motives, and the subject of Hill's speech was thus a popular one.[16]

Hill professed to see little opportunity for the United States to develop new markets for its feared industrial surpluses and its very real agricultural surplus in the Atlantic community. Europe was already buying more and more grain and meats from the Argentine. But "lying to the west of us is one-third of the population of the globe," he lectured. "That one-third is not an ignorant, barbarous people but a learned people. And he warmed to his subject:

> Go back and read the history of the world. The nation that has controlled the trade of the Orient has held the purse strings of the world. . . . Our country cannot stand still. She must go ahead or backwards. . . . Shall we take part in [the development of the Orient trade] or shall we . . . build a Chinese wall and go behind it?

But it was not just national pride which demanded that ships flying the American flag sail, half-empty, across the oceans. Would-be exporters of steel rails, cotton, and flour could not get shipping space from any nation's registry sufficient to meet the demand. What was needed was more ships in the Pacific trade, and an attractive through freight rate from points in the United States all the way to Japan, China, and eastern Russia. Russia? How about the fabulous new Trans-Siberian Railway? people asked. Forget it, Hill said. That railroad was so badly built and so incompetently run that it would cost the Russians $3.50 a hundredweight to ship flour from the Ukraine to Vladivostok. Under those conditions, the entire Asiatic market was the American businessman's, whenever he chose to take it. [17]

Hill's enthusiasm was infectious. D. Willis James told him that it was obvious that he knew more about the future of Pacific Ocean commerce than any other man in America. Henry L. Higginson renewed his correspondence with him, warning that the United States would have to move quickly to keep China from being "torn to pieces" by Russia, France, and Germany. If we saw to it that the door was left open "to all comers," he predicted, America could out-trade them all. Hill agreed, basing his faith not on a low wage scale, but on "the great mass of our manufacturing and commercial people, [who] are intelligent and ingenious, using mechanical force and human intelligence in place of human labor." [18]

With his usual thoroughness and respect for specialists, Hill had made a systematic study of Far Eastern trade opportunities. Before the first Great Northern passenger train had run through from St. Paul to Seattle, he had made a quick trip to Chicago to meet the representative of the General Steam Navigation Co. of Japan. Greatly impressed by this bright-eyed little man who spoke perfect English, Hill discussed with him the establishment of a trans-Pacific steamship line, and he then hired an expert to study the situation. By 1895 Hill was writing to Judge Burke in Seattle—with more enthusiasm than knowledge of sociology—about the great possibilities that lay in converting the Chinese from rice to wheat. In 1899 he hired a former consular officer to go to Russia and the Far East, and he received, in due course, a report which confirmed his convictions. [19]

But where would all the new ships come from? Would the United States build them? Would Hill? The answer in both cases was "yes," an answer well qualified by Hill's awareness that notwithstanding the great productivity of American workers, the big ships which he knew were necessary for such long voyages would require a subsidy or operating guarantee. Hill's idea was to take money out of that traditional pork barrel, the rivers-and-harbors projects, and put it in ship subsidies. This would do far more good, he noted sarcastically, than "to lath and plaster the bottoms of rivers called navigable, on which there has not been a steamboat floated in ten years." He wrote his old friend, Senator Mark A. Hanna, the strong man of the Republican party, about subsidies and received an enthusiastic reply. "You are dead right," wrote Hanna, "and if my life is spared I intend to devote my efforts in the Senate to our merchant marine." But the nation was not ready for such courageous use of the public purse, and Hanna's repeated efforts to push subsidy bills through Congress bore no fruit.[20]

Ever since Lenin elaborated upon the international implications of Marxist theory a surprisingly wide spectrum of political thinkers have been convinced that "imperialism" is a natural concomitant of capitalism. Whether Hill's agricultural and industrial friends were overproducing or not (many of them rather suspected that they were, in the early years of the new prosperity), it is a gross *non sequitur* to conclude that the United States had to have political control over those peoples upon whom we proposed to dump our surpluses. The Germans had disproved that myth in the two decades before World War I by selling more goods to the British colonies in Africa than the British themselves had. The theory owes more to the foggy thinking and foghorn oratory of men like Senator Albert J. Beveridge, a leader of the "imperialist" movement shortly after the turn of the century, than to important business leaders, for they saw no particular advantage, and many practical and ethical drawbacks, to the founding of an American "empire." When relations between the United States and Spain began to deteriorate in early 1898, Hill sent telegrams to the entire Minnesota delegation in Congress, warning that "all thinking people hope [that nothing will be done to] impair the agricultural and industrial interests of the nation." The fact was that a fragile new prosperity had finally emerged from the depression, and men like Hill wanted nothing done to upset it. Where the jingoism lay, if one wanted to look for it, was among such men as Beveridge and Knute Nelson, who always had their eyes on the political main chance.

Nelson responded to Hill's telegram: "War would not be wholly an unmixed evil. The farmers of the Northwest never prospered more than they did during the war of the rebellion."

Whatever happened, Hill shot back, they must not annex Cuba, "We have enough illiterate people who do not know how to use the privilege of self-government." [21]

As he had so many times before, Hill went ahead with his plans in the hope that slower men would catch up. In the spring of 1899 he grasped the opportunity to hire a first-class man to set up the trans-Pacific steamship service he had in mind. That summer he persuaded Scotland's leading authority on the design and construction of steamships to come to the Northwest with him to study the problem. "My idea is to build very large carriers," he told the Scot. As usual he was thinking big, and in the fall of 1900, supplying the collateral from his own strongbox, he borrowed $5 million from Kuhn, Loeb and the Chase National Bank. He spent it on the keels of two big ships.[22]

V

Hill had looked forward with relish to the completion of the Great Northern's line to Puget Sound, anticipating that it would significantly improve his bargaining position with the Canadian Pacific, of which Van Horne was by 1893 the undisputed master. The Canadians had not completed their line to western salt water until 1885, and another couple of years had passed before they were in shape to do an efficient transcontinental business, but by 1890 they were aggressively seeking traffic for their hungry railroad, going so far as to run steamers down the coast to Seattle, Portland, and, for a while even San Francisco to deliver highly profitable westbound freight snatched in the East and Midwest from under the noses of American railroads. The Central and the Union Pacific, Hill charged, were paying the Canadian Pacific a huge annual bribe to stay out of California's Golden Gate. If the Canadian Pacific tried similar blackmail on Hill, the Canadians realized, there would be trouble, for Hill had always demanded and usually got his share of competitive traffic.

The answer to the problem of international railroad relations in the Northwest—if there was an answer—would be a contract to divide traffic equitably. But what was equitable? "There is no difficulty in making a fair contract," Hill explained sardonically to Sir Donald Smith in the spring of 1890; "it is like a pledge to temperance, entirely depending on the intention of the parties from time to time." [23] He knew that Van Horne admired him as a man, just as he admired Van Horne. But when they were finished walking over heroic trestles or exclaiming over gigantic excavating or tunneling feats on visits to each other's roads, they went at the business of competition in a two fisted manner. In 1891 Van Horne had slammed the door on compromise when Mount Stephen tried to keep it open. He wrote Mount Stephen:

> I have passed the stage of distrust and feel sure now that Hill has neither good will nor good intentions towards yourself. . . . I was confidentially warned some months ago . . . that his apparently friendly disposition

towards the CPR came from his need of the assistance of yourself and Sir Donald in carrying out his Montana and Pacific Coast plans. . . .[24]

By 1893 the Canadian Pacific, through its ownership of the Soo line, was firmly established in the Great Northern's territory in the Dakotas and Minnesota, and Hill told Smith that he was being criticized by his American associates for not retaliating with Great Northern lines in Canada. He also warned Mount Stephen that "Mr. Van Horne can not continue to have his own way about everything, taking us whenever he wants to and putting us down when he is ready." He accused Van Horne of negotiating with them in bad faith, and Mount Stephen responded anxiously with the same sage advice he had offered in the hectic days of the 1880s: "It is impossible for either to *conquer* the other. . . . After useless waste of *credit, money & human energy,* a truce will be called and peace established. This is the end of all wars, and it must be the end of yours. . . ." Meanwhile, Van Horne dispatched smug broadsides to the Canadian Pacific's stockholders, bragging that "the CP is the only transcontinental line in North America." The interests south of the border which had tried to piece together transcontinental lines, he sniffed, were mainly dependent upon mining for their traffic. Such a dialogue might have led these two bearded giants into a head-on collision if the depression had not sent them both scurrying for shelter.[25]

Affairs between Hill and Van Horne remained in uneasy balance for the rest of the century, with small gains on both sides and nothing really resolved. Mount Stephen kept communications open between the two men, scoring a great victory for peace when he finally persuaded Van Horne to let Hill take the Duluth & Winnipeg Railroad. Hill tolerated the Canadian Pacific's draining off of transcontinental freight, there being little he could do about it. There was a general equilibrium, but it rested in a delicate balance, which the clumsy, insensitive and uninformed Mellen threatened to upset. Except for the lowest classes of freight, the Canadian Pacific could not compete for traffic originating or terminating at Seattle or Portland as long as it charged the same rates as the American lines, because the transportation time was much greater via Canada. If the Canadians lowered their rates they would merely precipitate a rate war, because Hill, like any sensible merchant, would not be undersold. What the Canadian Pacific had to have was a differential—a right, granted by the American lines in recognition of the Canadian's circuitous route, to charge a somewhat lower rate—and this Hill steadfastly refused to grant.

Meanwhile the Grits of Manitoba were playing directly into Hill's hands, to the detriment of their own countrymen. Threatening to establish a government-owned railroad in Manitoba to haul the farmers' produce at rates 40 per cent below the Canadian Pacific's charges, they had also forced through the provincial parliment a law forbidding the Canadian road the right to buy the unprofitable Manitoba branches of the Northern Pacific. Thus, the possibility that the Northern Pacific might sell these branches to the Canadian government for incorporation in its subsidized railroad was a terrible sword which Hill held over Van Horne.

If Hill had any doubt that he had to have real control of the Northern Pacific and had to banish Mellen from the Northwest, it was removed by Mellen's efforts to manipulate the questions of the differential and the Manitoba branches independently of Hill. At one stage he promised the Canadian Pacific a differential, whereupon Hill almost had apoplexy by telegram. One day Mellen was threatening to expand the Northern Pacific in Manitoba, and the next he let it be known that the government of Manitoba could buy the Northern Pacific's Canadian lines. These moves greatly upset Thomas G. Shaughnessy, the canny, diplomatic, Canadian Pacific executive who had succeeded Van Horne in the presidency and with whom Hill was anxious to cultivate better relations. It was not that Hill was above manipulating these points—or additional ones, such as supporting the Canadian Pacific's competitors in the coal country of southeastern British Columbia. But he could not do it with Mellen in the picture, and this was one more good argument for unification. Like many stories of grand railroad strategy, this one settled into a stalemate made bearable by the fact that everybody involved had more business than he could adequately handle. Meanwhile, in 1900, Van Horne, having proved that the frigid wastes of North America were no match for his brand of railroading, had gone off to Cuba to help rebuild and extend the railroads of that ravaged paradise. (He did not neglect to tap Hill for a substantial subscription to his stock issue.)

From these episodes Hill learned to support more determinedly than ever the idea of trade reciprocity between the two nations, which he had always favored. He saw that the policies of the United States and Canada were out of balance and that this could lead to serious trouble between American and Canadian railroads sooner or later. "They are determined to keep out all American competition," he complained to S. B. Elkins of the Senate Committee on Interstate Commerce, and "while the American lines are subject to all the whims and prejudices of the demagogues, the Canadian lines are supported by subsidies." [26]

VI

"The key to the Pacific Railroad situation is the control of the Oregon Short Line. Anyone owning the majority of its stock can do more to keep the peace west of the Missouri River than all other influences put together." Thus did Charles E. Perkins, nearing the end of his long railroad career in 1897, unburden himself in a memorandum to his letterbook. The Short Line, as well as the Oregon Railway & Navigation Co., were very much on his mind. They were on other men's minds, too.

Mesmerized by such sterile abstractions as "competition," and an unshakeable belief in the innate tendency of businessmen to destroy it, the critics of Hill's domination of the Northern Pacific have consistently ignored its importance in resolving the relations of the Great Northern and Northern Pacific with their astonishingly reinvigorated neighbor to the south, the Union Pacific. Hill's rivalry with Edward H. Harriman reached its peak after the Northern Pacific had been settled (securely, everyone thought) in Hill's corner, and hardly ended until the premature death in 1909 of the "little man," as Schiff fondly called Harriman. A precursor of this epic struggle was the effort made by Hill, Harriman, and their supporters—Morgan, Bacon, Schiff, and Stillman—to untangle the railroad affairs of the Far Northwest between 1895 and 1900.

The geography of the Pacific Northwest is almost too much for the reader who tries to understand the origins of the Hill-Harriman tensions in the last years of the old century. Their rivalry originally had to do mainly with control of the Oregon Railway & Navigation Co., but why was that railroad so important to all three of the contending railroads, the Northern Pacific, the Great Northern, and the Union Pacific? The Oregon road had been the Northern Pacific's link between Spokane and the Pacific—at Portland, Oregon—in the early 1880s, to be sure, but the Northern Pacific, like the Great Northern, had built its own direct line to Puget Sound soon thereafter. The Union Pacific, of course, operated a transcontinental service between the Midwest and the Far Northwest via the Oregon Short Line, which wriggled up from

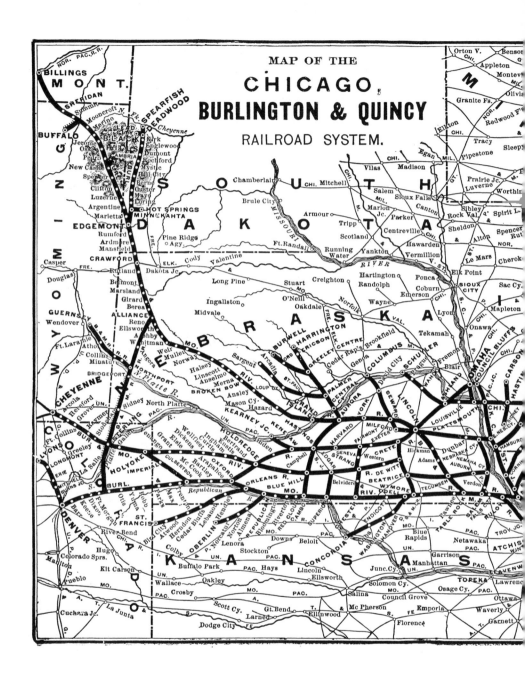

MAP OF THE

CHICAGO,
BURLINGTON & QUINCY

RAILROAD SYSTEM.

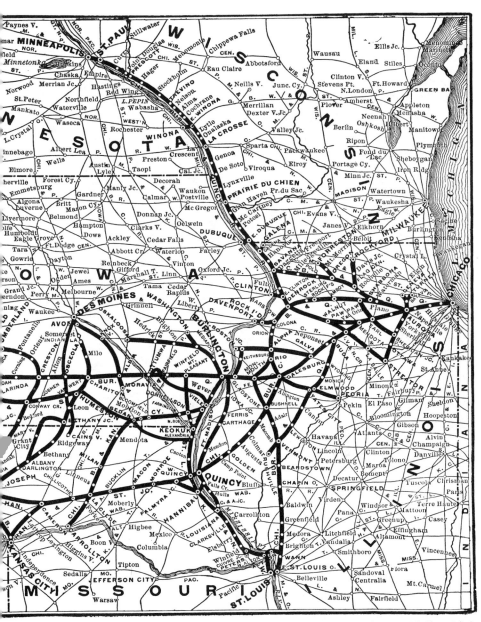

1901   *(Commercial and Financial Chronicle.)*

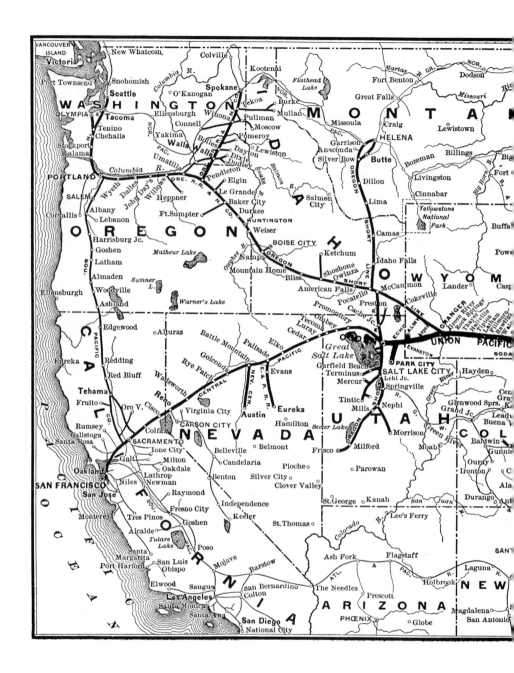

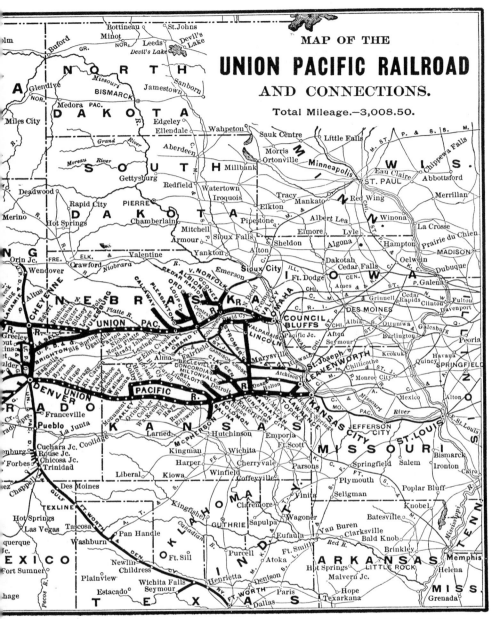

MAP OF THE

UNION PACIFIC RAILROAD

AND CONNECTIONS.

Total Mileage.—3,008.50.

1901 (*Commercial and Financial Chronicle.*)

a point on the Union Pacific mainline at Granger, Wyoming, to a point on the Oregon Railway & Navigation Co., by which it ran into Portland. But did not the Union Pacific's real destiny lie in a straight westward line across the high Sierras to San Francisco?

The answer to this riddle lies in three factors: first, the naïve arrangements which the youthful nation had made in the early 1860s to get the first transcontinental railroad built from Council Bluffs, Iowa, to San Francisco; second, the formidable barrier of the Cascade Range in Washington State; and, third, the fabulous valley of the lower Columbia River. When the government gave the contract to build the western segment of the transcontinental (between San Francisco and a point just west of Salt Lake City) to the Central Pacific Railroad, under Collis P. Huntington and his associates, it created one of the most irrational features of the transcontinental railroad system. For the men who built the Central Pacific immediately turned their attention to the building of the Southern Pacific, which eventually controlled practically everything that moved in the State of California, and built its own transcontinental line all the way from Southern California to New Orleans. At the same time they tightened their bulldog grip on the Central Pacific, refusing to allow it to fulfill its destiny as the Union Pacific's westward extension. Huntington demanded a high through rate from Council Bluffs to San Francisco via the Union Pacific and Central Pacific, while offering lower rates via the Southern Pacific a "sunset route" from New Orleans. In the 1880s the Union Pacific had fought its way out of this trap by building the Oregon Short Line (thereby virtually assuring its own eventual bankruptcy, since it could not well spare the money). When, as part of Harriman's plans to rebuild the system, it secured working control of the Oregon Railway & Navigation Co., the Union Pacific became, for all intents and purposes, a Northwestern transcontinental in direct competition with the Northern Pacific and the Great Northern.

But was not Portland a rather unsatisfactory seaport, situated as it was on the Willamette River, nearly a hundred miles up the Columbia River from the ocean at Astoria, and bound to give way to Seattle and Tacoma on Puget Sound? This might well have happened if the enterprising Portlanders had not stubbornly improved their estuary to the sea, and if the Cascades, despite the Stampede and Cascade Tunnels bored by the Northern Pacific and the Great Northern, had not remained a formidable, costly barrier and—if one wanted to go to Portland—an unnecessary one. For that was the significance of the third factor: the Columbia River. At a point some hundred miles due south of Spokane, the Oregon Railway & Navigation Company's line struck the Snake River, tributary of the Columbia, and, following its south bank and then the south bank of the Columbia, provided a water-level route to Portland through some of the most rugged territory in the Northwest. At the turn of the century, therefore, the Oregon Railway & Navigation Co. was one of the most strategically important railroads in the United States.

The Northern Pacific and the Great Northern had to have access to the Oregon Railway & Navigation Co. if they were to serve Portland efficiently, and the Union Pacific had to have access to the Northern Pacific's line north from Portland if it was to serve the rapidly growing ports of Tacoma and Seattle. Hill had reluctantly entered into a contract with the pre-Harriman Union Pacific to build a joint line from Portland to Seattle, the Northern Pacific, under Villard, being then unwilling to share its line. But when the depression came and the Northern Pacific and the Great Northern were united, the project was permanently abandoned. Meanwhile there was general agreement among railroad men that the Oregon Railway & Navigation Co. had to be "neutralized," and it appeared by 1895 that, with Jacob Schiff's earnest cooperation, that had been accomplished. But that was before Harriman demanded and won a major role in the rebuilding of the Union Pacific. By the time prosperity returned it was obvious that he was going to control the Oregon Short Line, and with Schiff's rather reluctant help, the Oregon Railway & Navigation Co. as well. The future balance between the Union Pacific, the Northern Pacific, and the Great Northern in the Far Northwest was now anybody's guess.

Hill, for his part, was determined to have access to Portland without crossing the Cascades, even if he had to build his own line on the *north* bank of the Columbia. It was a familiar situation: he had to decide whether to use, as a vital connection, an aging, poorly engineered railroad, at a high annual rental charge, or whether to exploit what he and the industry had learned about railroad building in the intervening years and build a much better connection of his own. Eventually he would do just that, but in 1898 he was not ready and he continued to preach that there were too many railroads in Washington State already. He hoped that he and Harriman could divide up the territory in the triangle formed by Spokane, Portland, and Seattle This would be easy to accomplish for local freight—i.e. freight originating or terminating on points within the triangle—but through freight involved the extremely sensitive question of how much of the transcontinental traffic that might otherwise be carried between Spokane and the Twin Cities by the Northern Pacific or the Great Northern ought, in fact, to be carried via the Oregon Short Line and the Union Pacific. Or, to look at it from Harriman's point of view, how much—if any, really—of the freight between Portland and the East, which the Union Pacific could handle quite efficiently over its own lines, should be turned over to Hill?

The two men knew well that there was no unique answer to these questions, and that only an arbitrary compromise, which might well come apart almost before it went into effect, was possible. The tempo and the temperature of the communications between Hill and Harriman and of their meetings at the Auditorium Hotel in Chicago, Schiff's and Morgan's offices in New York, and Harriman's baronial estate at Arden, New York, increased steadily as the old century approached its end. Both men held themselves under great personal control, for the entire railroad world was watching closely. In a formal meeting on the relatively neutral ground of the Northern Pacific's New York offices in October 1898, with a stenographer present, the problem was thoroughly aired. Said Harriman:

> I do not want to divide territory. That did not seem to be in contemplation when any of the agreements [to acquire stock of the OR&N by UP] were made. I read them carefully . . . and came to the conclusion that it was . . . practicable that the Union Pacific might be the owner. Nothing was said about any territorial division.

Coster remarked weakly that he felt very apprehensive. Hill said very little at all.[27]

They had come to another stalemate. For the moment, all parties were evenly matched, and there was little to do but study maps, insinuate surveying parties into the territory (while protesting loudly if the other side followed suit), and make plans to fight when the time came. With his usual frankness, and the hope that even Harriman could be scared by threats to build into Portland via the north bank of the Columbia, Hill told him:

> It may appear to you that the GN is assuming a great deal when it has not a mile of railroad at this time in the territory occupied by the OR&N and the UP has a large majority of the shares of the OR&N. But I think that with five million dollars I could build a much better line [than the OR&N] from [Spokane] into Portland . . . for an annual charge of less than we would pay the OR&N. . . .[28]

Hill received the most valuable advice on what he and his powerful New York associates were getting into from Lamont, whose usefulness to Hill reached its peak at the turn of the century:

> I am satisfied that Mr. Harriman is disposed to delay and will not of himself promote any early agreement. He is very close to Mr. Stillman these days and the latter rates him very high as a business man and a great railroad leader on broad and comprehensive lines—says we have had no such man in the east in a long time; that he is very rich, can command any amount of money, is independent of any man or any banking house and is very ambitious. . . .
>
> He takes great pride in his Union Pacific achievement; says he has established a great property between Chicago and Portland and San Francisco. . . .[29]

It was no longer merely a nineteenth-century-style struggle between two stubborn railroad men. The entire financial structure of the nation was involved.

VII

The six months following his assumption of full control of the Northern Pacific were among the most exciting and eventful of Hill's life. Returning to St. Paul in mid-May 1901, after several hectic weeks in New York, he watched the miracle of the Minnesota spring unfold outside the windows of his study on Summit Avenue. Never had the smart equipages which clopped proudly past the mansion seemed to gleam so handsomely. Even the pedestrians strolling up the beautiful, broad, tree-lined avenue walked with a quicker, more expectant step. At least it seemed that way to Hill as he sat down to explain to his closest friends the sensational events with which he had had so much to do. As he wrote he savored the final victory of his plans for the Northwest, which he had been maturing, it now seemed to him, since the day he stepped off the steamboat at St. Paul nearly half a century before.

Hill had never believed that the railroads of the United States would end up under one monolithic corporate control, like the telegraph and telephone systems, although he appreciated that this would remove many of the irritations that he and his fellows had had to contend with for so many wearying years. Penning a letter to Alexander Cassatt, now the leader of the "standard railway of the world," as the Pennsylvania Railroad proudly called itself, he assured his friend,

> I do not believe it is possible to make a strong combination covering the country between the Atlantic and the Pacific. The ownership of much the largest portion of the traffic from the west breaks at the Great Lakes or Chicago, and . . . the GN, NP, and Burlington have no desire to be a disturbing element east of Chicago.[30]

But Hill had become convinced years before that the Great Northern and the Northern Pacific had to control their own destinies as far east as Chicago if they were to deal firmly with the proud, Eastern trunk lines. That was what the excitement of the past six months, which had seen the Burlington Railroad brought firmly under his control, had been all about. As he explained to Mount Stephen:

> The trunk lines east to Buffalo demanded from us that we should hand over to them the ratemaking power. . . . So far we have been able to prevent this, for the reason that our lines originate so large a grain and flour traffic that we have been able to hold open both the Lackawanna and the Lehigh [Valley]. However, even these lines were during the past year passing into the control of the trunk lines.

> The time had arrived when we should make our own territorial combination. . . . Under one general control we have placed ourselves in a position of strength as to traffic, terminal cities, terminal facilities, and territorial control, which is now the strongest in the west and will daily grow stronger.[31]

The time had indeed arrived for the railroads of the Midwest to come in out of the cold or see their historical importance wither. The Alton, the Rock Island, the North Western, and the Milwaukee would stubbornly ignore this hard fact, and as a result the role they would play in the twentieth century would never match that which they had played in the earlier phases of the railroad era. The Burlington saw what they had to do, and, not without much agonizing, finally fell into the most welcome of the many arms that were outstretched to catch them. Albert E. Touzalin, the hard-driving Burlington executive who had detached himself from the parent corporation to build the Chicago, Burlington & Northern (the Burlington line from Chicago to the Twin Cities), did not live to see the consequences of his work. But as early as 1887 he had told Hill that the CB&N, the Burlington, and the Manitoba road would sooner or later make common cause, and he was all for their doing it sooner rather than later. Perkins, bemused by the idea of end-to-end, East-West mergers, flirted primly with Frank Thomson in the early 1890s and the rumor persisted that the Pennsylvania Railroad would help the Burlington build its own line from its terminus at Denver to the Pacific. Charles S. Mellen, even as Hill was preparing to take his scalp, deluded himself into thinking that the Northern Pacific was in a position to talk a deal with the fine old Midwestern road. The Burlington was the most eligible belle in the West, and she did not want for suitors.[32]

There were, of course, other railroads one might buy if all one wanted was a link between the Twin Cities and Chicago. There is no evidence that Hill ever considered the Rock Island or the Wisconsin Central. Both were relatively indirect routes, and the former entertained a high opinion of itself that is laughable in the light of subsequent events. The latter, less attractive physically, was slipping into the collection of second-rate railroads which the Canadian Pacific controlled under the general rubric of the "Soo." A. B. Stickney's spunky little Chicago Great Western, also an indirect line, was going its own way in a constructive manner which Hill would not have thought of disturbing. The Vanderbilts had controlled the North Western since the days of William H. in the 1880s, although they did not seem to know what to do with it. That left the Milwaukee and the Burlington, both with superb routes along the Mississippi River. J. P. Morgan, desiring to give Hill his Chicago line and at the same time remove the confused management of the Milwaukee from the Western railroad picture, urged Hill to go after it. Morgan had not overlooked the fact that William Rockefeller, a large investor in the Milwaukee, also loomed as his most troublesome competitor for leadership in Wall Street. Hill talked halfheartedly to the Milwaukee's officers and was relieved to learn that Rockefeller and Philip D. Armour, the other major stockholder, had an inflated idea of the line's worth. As Hill told Mount Stephen, the Burlington was a far better partner for the "northern lines," even if the price turned out to be higher.[33]

What made the Burlington so much more attractive to Hill? He wanted a line to Chicago, but that was not *all* he wanted. Mergers have their offensive as well as their defensive sides. Someone else wanted the Burlington very badly—in fact, was already negotiating heavily for it—and just as Harriman wanted to keep it out of Hill's hands, Hill had to have it. The deciding factor was the line which the Burlington had built in the 1880s and 1890s from its very heart in Nebraska northwestward to a connection with the Northern Pacific at

Billings, Montana. This line was to the Burlington what the Oregon Short Line was to the Union Pacific, as it enabled the Burlington to do a through business with the Northwest in cooperation with the Hill lines and in total independence of the Union Pacific. Symmetrical to it, and showing great promise as the Southwest boomed, was the line to Texas and the Gulf of Mexico which could be acquired when the time was ripe. The opportunity to carry the billions of board feet of Cascades lumber for which the treeless plains yearned, and to haul back the meats and cotton of those plains, entirely on his own lines, was overwhelmingly seductive to Hill. And the need to keep this traffic for the Union Pacific was just as pressing to Harriman.[34]

"I believe Schiff and Harriman have some big combination in mind, and perhaps in hand, and there can be no doubt about the value of the CB&Q to any scheme for combining roads west of Chicago. . . . The CB&Q cannot control any such combination without taking risks which I do not suppose our present stockholders want to take. . . ." This was the way Perkins explained to Thomas Jefferson Coolidge, Boston financier, that the Burlington's role as an independent railroad was coming to an end, and that the Bostonians would play no part in its next role. "If it [the sale of the Burlington] comes about, it means New York management," Perkins wrote sadly. He was sure that the heavy buying of Burlington stock in the spring of 1900 was being done by Kuhn, Loeb & Co. for Harriman's account, and he wondered how two such brilliant financiers as Harriman and Schiff could be so naïve as to think they could get control in the open market. The Burlington was one of the most widely held widows-and-orphans securities in the Western world. No one could buy control of it in the market, even if they were willing to bid the $100-par-value stock above 140 or 150. Perkins made up his mind that he would recommend sale of his loyal followers' stock when and if someone made a cash offer of $200 for all of it. As for the rumor that the Burlington would build its own line to the West Coast, of course they could do it, and it would be a far better line than the Union Pacific's just as Hill's line on the north bank of the Columbia would be a far better line than the Oregon Railway & Navigation Company's, if he ever built it. But Perkins knew that a Pacific extension would never be built under the independent banner of the Burlington.[35]

Harriman, deeply involved elsewhere at that critical juncture, was never able to screw up his courage to come anywhere near the $200 figure which Perkins stubbornly insisted upon. Perkins knew that eventually either Harriman or Hill would control the road, and he hoped it would be Hill. While he showed Hill the same Yankee poker face that he showed Harriman, he stiff-armed the latter (so Hill claimed) with the remark that with 49 per cent of the Burlington stock Harriman would not elect a single director, but with 51 per cent of it he could have the entire board. By February Hill had told Perkins, figuratively, to "do nothing until you hear from me." At the end of that month Perkins invited George B. Harris, to whom he had just given the nod to be his successor as president, to his home in Burlington, Iowa, for a conference. "Our conclusion," he told a Boston associate, "was that if Hill means also Morgan and the Northern Pacific, as he says it does, that would be the stronger and safer place for us to land." His reasons, which he spelled out in his careful, precise manner, were overwhelming.[36]

Hill had taken an agonizingly long time to put in his oar, but on February 11, 1901, Perkins, who had just had another indecisive meeting with Harriman, agreed to stay over in Chicago to discuss the possibility that the Northern Pacific and the Great Northern might take the Burlington. Hill was just as stunned by the $200-a-share price as Harriman had been. If Perkins had been willing to recommend to the Burlington stockholders that they take a 3.5 per cent bond in return for their shares, it would have been easy to swallow the price, for this would only have amounted to a guarantee of 7 per cent on the par value of the stock. The Burlington stockholders had come to expect such a return, anyway. But Perkins held out for an alternative offer of $200 *in cash*. If a stockholder took a bond for his Burlington stock it would be on his own responsibility, not Perkins's, who could go to his grave saying that he had got them a cash price come what may. The widows and orphans were in very good hands. As for Hill, he needed some moral support at this point. Out went a telegram to J. P. Morgan:

> Had long interview with President of CB&O. Think I can arrange to purchase control and possibly entire capital. . . . Am thoroughly satisfied Q more valuable than St. Paul [the old-fashioned term for the Milwaukee road] and at less cost. I can take no further action for both companies [NP and GN] until you advise me your desire to act together as understood in New York. . . .[37]

Morgan, according to legend, told Andrew Carnegie shortly after formation of the United States Steel Corporation that if Carnegie had asked much more for his steel properties than he did, he would have gotten it. Whether the story is true or not, it is clear that to Morgan, where the long-term stability of a basic industry like railroads or steel was concerned, price was secondary. His response to Hill's telegram reflects this philosophy:

> I am distinctly in favor of the business to which you allude on fair terms. You can say to the president if you so desire that I am working with you and shall do everything in my power to carry out any contract that can be made, but come what may I wish you to understand distinctly that until I tell you to the contrary, which is not likely, I am acting with you in good faith to carry out what was agreed to in New York in October last. . . .[38]

There followed a period of heavy activity in Burlington stock on the exchange. Perkins thought Hill was buying; Hill, that Perkins's people were getting in on the ground floor, although that was out of character. Later they realized that Harriman, now out of the running, was laying the groundwork for a demand that he be represented on the Burlington board. By March 2 Hill could bear the tension no longer. Morgan is going to Europe at the end of March, he warned Perkins, who agreed to meet Hill in Chicago again. The $200 price still stood. "[Hill] seems to be much in earnest," Perkins wrote his Boston associates; "he professed to think the price too high, but he wants to talk and said he would write me from New York after he had seen Morgan." By mid-month Hill was back, more eager than ever, and Perkins suggested that they meet secretly at the Victoria, a quiet, sedate Boston hotel, toward the end of the month. Hill took Perkins so literally that he had Nichols lie to his private secretary, J. J. Toomey, that he had "gone yachting." [39]

Beginning about March 25, when Perkins and Hill met privately at the Victoria, and continuing until April 9 in consultation with George F. Baker and four of Perkins's associates, the conditions of sale were thrashed out. The few months' delay had been costly, for against the background of a skyrocketing stock market, Perkins insisted that only a 4 per cent bond could conscientiously be recommended to the stockholders, and that the $200 cash alternative still stood. Hill winced at the price, but the time for decision was at hand and, with the full support of the strongest banking house in the western hemisphere, he made it quickly. Perkins was as good as his word, and at his call some 97 per cent of the stock came in from the obedient, trusting stockholders. Boston, in its last act in their behalf, had done them proud. But what looked like a high price, Hill reassured the worried Mount Stephen, would look cheap in a few years. That was not the main point, his friend replied: "It is a big farm for you to work. If anyone but you undertook the job I should be afraid of the final outcome." [40]

Perkins, meanwhile, assured his associates that the man was up to the job. "Hill is in many ways a wonderful man, not only a prophet and a dreamer. . . . He is a great man—there is no mistake about it." As for the object of their concern, he was back in St. Paul. It was the 26th of April. Now, he thought, he could turn his back on the East for a good long while as he looked to the new duties he had shouldered in the West. Euphoria leaked from his pen as he wrote Mount Stephen that he would not see him in London that year:

> We have been making railway history pretty fast for some time, in our own part of the country. . . . I think it safe to estimate our net income at $25,000,000 by the end of 1906. . . . It is true we pay a good price for the CB&Q. This could not be avoided. . . .

Halfway through the letter he burst forth with a breathtaking forecast of what the Northern Pacific and the Great Northern (which would hold the stock of the Burlington jointly) could expect in dividends from their new investment when he got through refinancing the company:

> Now, these figures look very large and are as easy to place on paper as much smaller ones, but I cannot see where they can be materially reduced.

> The United States have grown in population since 1790 at the rate of about doubling every 30 years. Since the close of the Civil War, the increase has been over 41,000,000. If we maintain anything like the above rates, and I see no reason why we shall not do so, we would have a population of 150,000,000 by 1930. . . .

> However, let the increase in population be ever so slow, the fact remains that the country served by the Gt. Nor., the Nor. Pac., and the Q can take better care of more people than any other section of the country. For that reason I expect our growth will not be diminished. [41]

Genial, tight-fisted, skullcapped old Collis Potter Huntington had died a few months before. With the help of Stillman, Schiff, and the Speyers, Harriman had scooped up a controlling interest in the Southern Pacific and was proceeding to unify it with the Union Pacific. Rumors flew that he also had his eye on the Santa Fe. Meanwhile, George Gould, preoccupied with chorus girls, was neglecting his Southwestern empire. Once there had been many great leaders of Western railroads. Now there were only two.

ALLIES AND ANTAGONISTS IN THE STRUGGLE FOR CONTROL OF THE BURLINGTON AND THE NORTHERN PACIFIC:

RIGHT J. Pierpont Morgan. Courtesy of Morgan Guaranty Trust Company.

BELOW Edward H. Harriman at his desk in the Equitable Building. Courtesy of E. Roland Harriman.

OPPOSITE TOP Robert Bacon. Courtesy of Morgan Guaranty Trust Company.

OPPOSITE BOTTOM Jacob H. Schiff. Library of Congress.

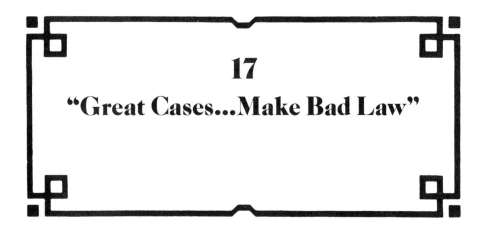

17
"Great Cases...Make Bad Law"

It really seems hard, when we look back at what we have done in opening the country and carrying at the lowest rates, that we should be compelled to fight political adventurers who have never done anything but pose and draw a salary.

—James J. Hill, 1902

I

After it was all over, nobody could remember who started the rumor that a very important meeting was going on somewhere in New York's Waldorf-Astoria Hotel that night of May 8, 1901. Few of the recently rich who patronized the ornate pile would have been welcome among the fabled Four Hundred who had once congregated in Mrs. William B. Astor's ballroom, now vanished from the site. Still, they expected a pretentious elegance, and that had been quite shattered by a horde of businessmen, most of them brokers from Wall Street, who chattered noisily in the strictly masculine precincts of the bar, then surged through the billiard room, and finally crowded into the café, where they gathered in groups around such prominent speculators as John W. "Bet-a-Million" Gates.

Was it true, they demanded to know, that the common stock of the Northern Pacific Railway had been cornered? It if had been bought up and squirreled away, where would the many brokers who had sold it short during the past week buy the shares they were obligated to deliver? Was it true that Gates himself had sold 60,000 shares short and, during the closing hours of trading that afternoon, had found himself unable to buy except at ruinous prices? "Do I look like it?" Gates replied, smiling knowingly at his companion and private attorney, Max Pam. Off went the herd of worried brokers, their rumpled street clothes contrasting harshly with the elegant dinner suits of the startled guests against whom they brushed. "The air was thick with rumors, with tobacco smoke, and with the fumes of various fluids which the brokers, bankers and financiers were consuming in order to steady their nerves," wrote one reporter. They needed steadying, for many of them faced ruin.[1]

No securities exchange anywhere in the world had ever been the victim of such a panic as that which had begun to sweep the New York Stock Exchange that afternoon. For weeks Wall Street and Main Street alike had been jittery. No one had ever seen the like of the vast outpouring of new securities of the last two or three years, and the rise in market speculation which had accompanied it. Stocks and bonds had been steadily rising for over three years, floating upward on a series of earnings reports, each better than the last. Newcomers to the financial jungle eagerly plunged their arms into a golden stream, which, they began to tell each other, had no bottom. Older men knew, however, that all that was needed to dry up the stream was some factor, not especially important in itself, which would set off a rush to turn the paper profits of the preceding several months into real cash. Stocks would then be thrown onto the market for whatever they would bring, toppling the entire structure, as it had been toppled repeatedly in the rugged days of the 1880s and 1890s.

That factor was provided shortly after one o'clock on May 8, 1901. The Stock Exchange, its magnificent new building then under construction, was struggling to carry on trading in temporary quarters in the Produce Exchange. The pandemonium was all the greater, therefore, when word raced across the floor that Northern Pacific's stock had been cornered. For weeks dozens of brokers had been selling Northern Pacific stock they did not have, at prices ranging up to 143½ on May 7, in full confidence that such prices could not be sustained and that they would be able to buy stock to deliver in a few days at much lower prices and a tidy profit. Now they tried frantically to "cover." At the closing bell the price of Northern Pacific stood at 180, with little offered. When the Exchange opened the next morning the carnage was all that had been expected. Traders dumped blue-chip stocks for whatever they would bring, only to find that in the meantime Northern Pacific had soared above 700. At that point the quotation clerks gave up, but at least three shares traded, unrecorded, for $1000 each. Several affluent investors in Northern Pacific from upstate New York, who had hired a special train the night before to rush their shares to the city, made a killing.

The Northern Pacific corner of May 9, 1901, bid fair to wipe out a good part of the Wall Street tribe until it was recognized all around that the circumstances were unique and called for extraordinary measures to be made by those few financial leaders to whom it regularly fell, in times of crisis, to patch things up and get them going again. Within a week the thundering locomotive of economic growth was proceeding at top speed, almost as though nothing had happened. But the corner profoundly affected the future of two men, Edward H. Harriman and James J. Hill, whose plans for reorganizing America's Western railroads had been its main cause. The notoriety which the panic brought in its train meant that in the future they would be familiar figures to the most unlettered citizen in the sleepiest backwoods town in the nation. But more important, it guaranteed that everything they did thereafter to compromise their differences and recast the structure of the railroads of the Northwest would be done in the full glare of publicity, at a time when the concentration of economic power was becoming the hottest political issue in the nation.

II

Hill always claimed that he had told Harriman he was buying the Burlington Railroad. "So as to remove any ground for the charge that we were working secretly to acquire the CB&Q, I said to Harriman in January [1901] that if he at any time heard that we were conferring with the Q Board of Directors looking to the joint acquisition of that property, I wanted to be the first one to tell him that we intended to take the matter up seriously," he told Kennedy when the excitement had died down. In March, therefore, when the deal with Perkins was all but final, Hill was surprised to learn that Harriman did not want Hill to have exclusive access to the Burlington, which would place the Great Northern and the Northern Pacific on the same basis as the Union Pacific in tapping the rapidly growing markets of the Northwest. Word went to Schiff that he was to get hold of Hill and keep the Harriman foot in the Burlington door, regardless of what he had to do to achieve it.[2]

According to Schiff, however, Hill denied flatly, as late as "the second half of March," that he was buying the Burlington, though Schiff did not say how, and, again according to Schiff, very shortly thereafter, "it became evident that . . . negotiations were being carried on between him and the Burlington. . . ." Learning that Hill, who had been visiting Mamie in Washington, was en route to Boston to close the deal with Perkins, Schiff sent his son Mortimer to intercept Hill at the Pennsylvania Railroad's Desbrosses Street ferry slip. "Morti," as instructed, persuaded Hill to go with him to George F. Baker's house to hear what Harriman had to say. There, Schiff first reproached Hill for not telling him what was going on and then made an impassioned appeal that he allow the Union Pacific a one-third interest. "To this Mr. Hill replied with platitudes," Schiff told Morgan later, "and soon went on his way to Boston." [3]

Dreading the titanic struggle which he knew Harriman and Hill were capable of, Schiff hurried to the offices of J. P. Morgan and Co. to consult with Robert Bacon. "It is a grave mistake for the two Northern roads to control the Burlington system," he told Bacon, who coldly replied that it was already too late to do anything about it. At this point, Schiff said, he actually began to share Harriman's fear that Hill was out to wreck the Union Pacific, which had always found the Burlington "a factor for worriment and anxiety while independent." Morgan himself could well understand that both Harriman and Schiff had known Hill long enough to fear his wrath, if it were roused, but he must have frowned at Schiff's later reference to "the methods . . . which Mr. Hill employed to bring down the Northern Pacific in its earlier career." And when Schiff tactlessly referred to "the profits which apparently had first been made [in Burlington stock during negotiations] by the friends of Mr. Hill," the battle lines began to be drawn, for in the Burlington deal Hill had no closer friend than J. P. Morgan. [4]

Back in New York with the Burlington tucked (safely as he thought) in his pocket, Hill was handed a personal letter which seemed to convey Schiff's reluctant resignation to Hill's exclusive control of the Burlington. Hill was paying too much for it, Schiff warned, and he could not resist insinuating once more that Hill had been used by "others" who wanted only to make a quick killing. But, "your judgment as to this is, to me, final," his old friend wrote, and "as to the Union Pacific, it must take care of itself, as it will be able to do. . . ." [5]

Stabbing energetically at his inkwell, Hill dashed off a three-page reply in which he tried to smooth things over. "I have missed your counsel in the CB&Q matter," he declared, "but I felt with the knowledge I had of the situation that any discussion of the subject between us would only lead to mutual embarrassment. However, I took occasion to say to Mr. Harriman a day or two after my arrival that if he should ask me if there was any truth in the rumor that the Gt. Nor. and Nor. Pac. were working for control of the 'Q,' I could not say the rumor had no foundation. I wanted Mr. Harriman's first information to come from me." As for the Union Pacific's insistence on being included in the deal, it was not only illegal, but not even in Harriman's best interest, as he proceeded to explain:

> My astonishment is very great at the position of the Un. Pac. today. It could not legally take a single step towards its control of the CB&Q west of the Mo. River. [The Burlington] can build a much shorter line [than the UP] to San Francisco, with lower grades and with 3½ per cent money. They have a connection over the Nor. Pac. with the Puget Sound country, and do not desire to extend in that direction. . . .

> We do not need any more through coast lines. Therefore, I was strongly of the opinion that a control of the CB&Q by the Gt. Northern & Nor. Pac. would remove any object for extending to the Pacific, and insure the greatest harmony. However, I find myself mistaken. . . .

> I like peace, and am not ashamed or afraid to work for it. . . . On the other hand, I do not think the time has come when we must acknowledge that we have no rights which our neighbors claim for themselves, or such as we are willing to accord to them. . . .[6]

Hill knew that Harriman would undo the Burlington trade if he could, and that Schiff, however reluctantly, would follow him into battle. He also knew that Morgan was about to leave for a long trip to divest Europe of its art treasures, and it would be well to keep in close touch with Bacon and Perkins, Morgan's able lieutenants. Meanwhile, Hill had more constructive work to do. He had repeatedly urged Edward Tuck to take a trip over the vastly improved Great Northern, and Tuck and his nephew, Amos French, were at that moment due to land at the Cunard line pier. What these influential expatriates would see in the West they would convey to a host of Frenchmen and Germans who were finally beginning to look across the Atlantic for investment opportunities. It was also a good opportunity to show off his eldest son, in whose hands the sixty-three-year-old Hill hoped he would soon be placing the day-to-day operation of the many thousands of miles of Hill roads. All arrangements had been made, and Hill saw no reason to stay in New York. He, Tuck, and French visited briefly with Mary in St. Paul, and on Monday, April 15, at 1:30 p.m., she saw them off for the West.

III

"We see by the papers that papa is hurrying back from the coast," Mary wrote in her diary on April 19; "it is indeed a quick trip to Seattle since Monday. . . ." The newspapers seemed to know a great deal more than Mrs. Hill did about her husband's movements. He had been called to New York on urgent business, they claimed, and, arriving in Seattle in the small hours of the morning of April 18, had ordered the tracks cleared all the way to St. Paul and departed for the East on the same morning, at 10:30 a.m. The run was expected to set a new record between St. Paul and Seattle, the papers reported breathlessly, although one noted that for that matter the trip out had also set a record—60½ hours.[7]

Hill's quick trip has been blown up by enthusiastic writers into a mad dash all the way from Seattle to New York, presumably with all traffic shunted aside right into Grand Central Station, and with Hill standing at the engineer's elbow, urging him to get yet more speed out of a careening locomotive. It was no such thing. Hill had known before he left St. Paul that an unusually large amount of trading was taking place in Northern Pacific stock, even for a security which was "on the street," as he contemptuously referred to a security which was not, for the most part, locked up in investors' strong boxes. His guests had been anxious to make the trip as quickly as possible, and Hill had nothing in particular to do in Seattle except turn around and come back. Once back in St. Paul, he was glad to be with Mary again, to talk with her before the fire in his study of the years of leisure they would soon be enjoying together, and to write his optimistic letter to Mount Stephen on the future of the Northwest.

But just as he was folding the letter, on the Friday afternoon nearly a week after his return from Seattle, a clerk brought him disturbing news. Sales of Northern Pacific stock on the exchange that day had reached the incredible volume of 106,500 shares and the price had advanced three points. Obviously, Harriman had made his decision to grab the Northern Pacific, and, as Hill explained to Mary that evening at dinner, if he were successful, he got everything, for he would then control two of the four routes to the Northwest and would have an equal voice in the third, the Burlington. The Great Northern would stand alone, and in that case "we would not have held it a day longer than we could have sold it." The following night, Saturday, April 27, he climbed aboard the Burlington's overnight express to Chicago. On Monday morning, at the opening bell of the Stock Exchange, he would be at his post. If only the sore throat which he felt coming on did not turn into one of his famous bad colds! [8]

Hill strode in the front door of 27 Pine Street, the headquarters of the Great Northern and of Kuhn, Loeb & Co., on that blustery Monday morning, feeling well rested from his Sunday on the train. Outside the door he was surprised to find Schiff waiting for him. Taking Hill by the arm, the banker guided him into his private office. Hill wrote Mount Stephen what happened next:

> He told me they had bought sixty millions of Northern Pacific, which, with what myself and friends owned, would give an absolute control, and we would put the whole thing in together with the Union and Southern Pacific, and that I should make my own terms and take general direction of the combined properties. Harriman came in often and repeatedly said, "You are the boss. We are all working for you. Give me your orders." [9]

It was quite out of the question, Hill responded, and on he went to his own office. Something did not ring true about all this. Surely Harriman was not really as worried as he seemed about the Union Pacific's ability to hold its own in the competition for business in the Northwest. The Union Pacific and the strong men behind it had resources far exceeding his own. In fact, that road was all but coining money—no one was more surprised at that than James J. Hill—and the Southern Pacific acquisition made Harriman master of everything south of the Washington-Oregon boundary. He came to believe that Harriman, like Schiff, was more the driven than the driving force in a much broader financial intrigue, as he explained to John S. Kennedy, that veteran of the rugged early days of New York banking:

> In my own judgment they did not expect us to give them an interest [in the Burlington] but were using this as a reason for attacking Morgan in the Nor. Pac. during his absence. . . . They offered me all manner of things by way of control of Un. & So. Pac., as well as Nor. Pac., &c. I simply said that it was not necessary to bribe me to do the fair and respect-

able thing toward as close a neighbor as the Un. Pac., and on the other hand I could not be bribed to do wrong in any way. . . .

I am sure the main motive was truly expressed by Stillman and others who said they would show the world that Morgan was not the only banker in America, &c, that all other banking houses were nothing more than his clerks, and talked of cutting his wings, &c. . . .

I at once told Messrs. Bacon and Perkins, and at once they wired Mr. Morgan. You know the result. . . .[10]

And Mount Stephen must have been dumbfounded at what Hill told him:

They offered me their Nor. Pac. proxy for ten years if myself and friends would cooperate with them and throw Morgan overboard, and they actually had the gall to suppose that I would consider such a proposal. When they found I refused to abandon Morgan and join them in their plan of piracy, they made a struggle to gain the actual majority of all the stock. . . .[11]

If Harriman was not at the very bottom of the business, who was? Stillman would have welcomed a signal victory over Morgan. His National City Bank was growing apace in that golden era of commercial banking, and would soon be contending with the Chase National for first place. But Stillman's resources would not have supported a frontal attack against the enormous reserves, domestic and foreign, of J. P. Morgan & Co. The answer, Hill was convinced, lay in the Rockefeller millions: rich profits from the Standard Oil Company of New Jersey, only a portion of which could be profitably plowed back in that fabulously successful enterprise. These funds were flowing into the New York commercial banking world via both the Chase and the National City Banks, where they provided the greatly increased capital base which the growing American business community demanded. It was a classic case of the migration of capital across industrial lines, which is fundamental to the development of a vigorous economy. William Rockefeller, John D.'s younger brother, was in charge of these developments. Hill suspected that it was William's large interest in the Milwaukee Railroad, the line that would be frozen out of the Northwestern transcontinental business if the Northern Pacific and the Great Northern made good their exclusive control of the Burlington, coupled with his ambitions in Wall Street, which fueled the parallel ambitions of Harriman in the West. The enemy that Hill faced was more powerful than anyone had supposed.

IV

The American millionaire, John S. Kennedy, might have been observed walking agitatedly through the lobby of the Regina Grand
Hotel in Aix-les-Bains one day early in May. He had just come from a
talk with J. P. Morgan, who was also visiting the picturesque old
French watering place at the foot of the Alps. Someone is trying to get
control of the Northern Pacific, Morgan had told him. Kennedy knew
what that meant to the Hill roads, in which much of his life's work
was centered, and he pledged vigorous cooperation in fighting off the
raiders. Similar pledges of help came from Lord Mount Stephen, Lord
Strathcona and Mount Royal, and Gaspard Farrer, and from Edward
Tuck, who had just unpacked his bags at his apartment on the
Champs Elysées.[12]

Luck turned out to be on Hill's side, as it had been so many times
before. Though his own men made glaring tactical errors in the
struggle, his enemies made a fatal strategic blunder. Hill had found
little awareness of the danger among the men at J. P. Morgan & Co.,
and no plan of action. Looking over the stock transfer books, which
Nichols was carefully keeping up to date, he noted that Harriman
seemed to be settling for a majority of the combined preferred and
common stocks, both of which had voting rights. If he stayed with
that strategy they would have little to worry about, but Hill knew that
Harriman would soon realize what a mistake he was making.

Absolute control of the Northern Pacific lay with a majority of the
common shares, which possessed the right to retire the preferred
shares on January 1, 1902; and, further, the present board had the
power to delay the annual meeting, scheduled for October 1901, at
which Harriman hoped to elect his own slate of directors, until well
past the New Year. Eighty million dollars worth of common stock, at
par value, was outstanding, of which the Hill-Morgan forces had recently controlled $30 to $35 million. But the recent dramatic rise in the
market price of Northern Pacific had greatly altered the situation.
"About the closest estimate I could make [of our Northern Pacific
holdings on May 2 and 3] was about between $20 and $21 million,"
Hill recalled. When he discovered that some of the stock Harriman
was buying had come from the treasury of the Northern Pacific itself
and from a Morgan trust fund, he was furious, and he came down
hard on the entire crew. Off went an urgent cable to Aix-les-Bains,
and back came Morgan's approval to buy whatever common was nec-

essary, at any price, to assure control. By this time it was the afternoon of Saturday, May 4, and the market was closed. The buy order for $15 to $16 million worth of common stock would lie over until Monday. It almost turned out to be too late. It was not too late to cause the worst stock market panic anyone had ever seen.[13]

The huge buy order quickly soaked up all of the Northern Pacific common that was still "on the street," and then some, as it turned out. If Harriman had had his way, little would have been available that Monday morning. As he later explained:

> On the morning of Saturday, May 4th, I was at home, ill. We had some-what over $42,000,000 of the preferred shares of the Northern Pacific, or a clear majority of that issue, and somewhat over $37,000,000 of the common shares, which lacked being a majority of the common by about 40,000 shares. But we had a majority of the entire capital stock . . . and I had been competently advised, and was convinced, that this holding was sufficient to enable us to control the Company. Nevertheless, the fact that the Northern Pacific could, on the 1st of January following, retire the preferred shares . . . bothered me somewhat. . . .
>
> I made up my mind that we should have a majority of the common shares, and on that morning I called up Heinsheimer (one of the partners in the firm of Kuhn, Loeb & Co.) and gave him an order to buy, at the market, 40,000 shares of Northern Pacific common. . . .
>
> On Monday, the 6th of May, . . . having had no confirmation from Kuhn, Loeb & Co., . . . I called Heinsheimer up and asked him why. . . . He told me that before giving out the order he had to reach Schiff, who was at the synagogue. Schiff instructed him not to execute the order and said that he (Schiff) would be responsible. . . . Meanwhile . . . prices of Northern Pacific shares had gone so high that I realized the impossibility of buying . . . 40,000 shares of stock. So I determined . . . to fight the question out with what material I had in hand.[14]

Northern Pacific common soared 17½ points that day, on a volume of 350,000 shares ($35 million worth), which would have been a respectable total daily volume of all stocks a year or two earlier. St. Paul's leading newspaper sent its New York representative for a "heart to heart talk with James J. Hill," who declared that the country was economically healthy, but decried the speculation in Wall Street. "I can't explain the rise in NP," he said, placing prudence ahead of veracity. Next day the *Pioneer Press* concluded that the "Harriman syndicate" had defeated the "Great Northern magnate," and that Hill had lost control of the Northern Pacific. The same conclusion swept through European financial capitals, but Hill's friends knew better.

"We are letting enemy think they have control," he cabled Mount Stephen; "we have the present board and will elect the next one if our friends stand firm. Kennedy and Morgan at Aix and working together." Hill's files bulge with cables and telegrams reflecting the confusions and the irritations which the hectic days of early May had brought. As they sought to reckon where they stood, they counted some stock twice, while other shares they had controlled all the time turned up only after it was all over. Hill "ran scared," as he had done all his life, and by the time it was clear that there was no more stock available, he had just enough of the common to assure absolute control of the Northern Pacific. In Aix-les-Bains, seated at dinner in the staid restaurant of the Regina Grand Hotel, John S. Kennedy smiled broadly at the victory cablegram which the page brought to his table.[15]

Clearing away the debris and reestablishing the stability of the huge and vitally important railroad properties which had hung in the balance for days was a long-drawn-out task. First, however, Wall Street itself had to be rescued. The Hill-Morgan men sat down with the enemy in a series of meetings which lasted all day May 9, while a few blocks away panic reigned. After others had concluded preliminary negotiations, first in Harriman's offices in the Equitable Building and then at Kuhn, Loeb's offices, Hill agreed to attend a late afternoon meeting at J. P. Morgan & Co. Flanked by his lieutenants, Daniel S. Lamont and George F. Baker, and acknowledging the good offices of Harrison McK. Twombly, a Vanderbilt son-in-law, Hill listened to what a lonely Jacob Schiff proposed. Would they agree to deliver, at $150 a share, enough common (heaven knows they had plenty) to the pathetic, unsuspecting brokers who had sold it short, and thus get them off the hook? If they would, Schiff would bring Harriman to the conference table, where he was sure they could compromise their differences over the Burlington. Hill agreed. And so the Northern Pacific panic ended almost as quickly as it had begun.

Word that Hill was still in control spread quickly through the financial district. Besieged by reporters as he stepped out of Morgan's office, he spoke to them willingly: "I state without any reservation that the control of the Northern Pacific is in the same hands in which it has rested for the past five years, and where it will remain for five years to come. The truth is, that I have been engaged in no fight—although there are some people who have been throwing stones into my yard." A proud Montreal newspaper headlined the story, "The Canadian Has Won!"[16]

V

In agreeing to a truce, the Hill-Morgan and the Harriman-Schiff-Rockefeller forces recognized that they had been about to bring the temple down on their own heads. The naked power—if such uncontrolled forces deserve to be called power—which their struggle had revealed unleashed bitter criticism of these titans of industry. Realizing that Hill and Morgan had a perfect right to demand delivery of every last share of nonexistent Northern Pacific common they had bought, and that by so doing they would drive dozens of financial firms, large and small, to the wall, Harriman had no choice but to agree to allow Morgan to name the next board of directors of the Northern Pacific at its next annual meeting. It was this concession which persuaded his opponents to let go of enough stock to slake Wall Street's thirst. But getting Harriman to follow through on his agreement was another matter, and Hill and his friends suffered many an anxious moment before that goal was reached.[17]

At first, Hill was barely cordial with Harriman, especially after George Perkins reported that Harriman controlled somewhat less Northern Pacific stock than he had claimed at the May 9 conferences. Hill was back in New York on May 19, much refreshed by a short cruise on his new yacht *Wacouta,* to New London, Connecticut, where he had inspected the "big ships" being built there. But he declined an invitation to spend the weekend at "Arden," Harriman's grand estate in the Ramapo Mountains of New York's Rockland County. Robert Bacon told him a few days later that Harriman was demanding "common methods of management and accounting" for the Hill roads and his own, which had an ominous ring. At the end of May, Tuck wrote from Paris that Mortimer Schiff was in London bragging that his father and Harriman had absolute control of the Northern Pacific. "I cannot understand Mr. Schiff's being a party to [such] acts of brigandage," he grieved. On that same day, however, the contending parties put their hands to an agreement which would bind up their wounds.[18]

Sitting around a big table in a private dining room of New York's exclusive Metropolitan Club, they signed an agreement to cooperate fully in the operation of all of the transcontinental railroads. The instrument called for "the establishment and maintenance of uniform methods of management and accounting of the transcontinental lines," including, if they chose to join (they could hardly refuse), the North Western, the Milwaukee, the Santa Fe, and the Missouri Pacific, and provided "also for the settlement of any grievances or differences which may now exist or hereafter arise between said companies or any two or more of them in their relations to and with each other." The parties were to appoint four representatives "to formulate a plan by which the purposes may be lawfully accomplished." (Hill may have smiled sardonically at this clause, but he kept his own counsel and hoped for the best.) Disagreements were to be arbitrated by William K. Vanderbilt, of the New York Central, or in case Vanderbilt should be unable to serve, Alexander J. Cassatt, of the Pennsylvania.[19]

Still cautious, Hill repeatedly urged his friends to hold on to their shares until all danger had passed. He ordered Nichols to buy every share of Northern Pacific common that came along at a price below 200. By June 7, he wrote Mount Stephen, he personally owned $13 million of Northern Pacific common. (His personal net worth at that time was slightly less than $20 million, but his financial liquidity had been drastically curtailed.) "Nothing more can be done until Morgan arrives," he said. Morgan was full of praise for their allies in Europe when the two met in New York in July. Hill was proud of them too, having told Morgan during the darkest days of May, "Myself and friends will stand without hitching." Still, it had been a very close call. When the score was finally totaled up late that summer, Harriman and company were found to have $37 million of Northern Pacific common and Hill's group $42 million, a little more than a majority. Only $1 million of the $80 million issue was held outside these two groups.[20]

On September 6 Hill cabled his European friends, "Very confidential. Harriman has turned over their proxy to Morgan for October election. That settles it." It was fully the equivalent of a great general handing over his sword in defeat. Harriman made a few more minor irritations and last-minute objections, but a month later George Perkins wired Hill, "In case you have not heard from Mr. Schiff, this is to put you to bed with the good news that he [Harriman] has withdrawn from his position and . . . everything looks as lovely as a May morning." There had been some pretty bleak May mornings that year, however, and there were more to come. For on September 6, the same day Hill sent his cable, William McKinley, at a reception following a speech at Buffalo's Pan-American Exposition, offered his hand to a man who thereupon fired a revolver into the President's stomach. In a little more than a week McKinley was dead, and he had been succeeded by the youngest man ever to hold the office up to that time. As soon as the new occupant had moved into the White House, Hill asked for an audience and received an invitation to lunch. It was time, Hill knew, to explain to Theodore Roosevelt what the new railroad arrangements meant for the West they both loved so much.[21]

VI

Twice before in his hardworking life, Hill had seen his energies taxed almost to their limit: during the summer of 1878, when he pushed the old St. Paul & Pacific Railroad to completion and laid the foundations of the Manitoba road; and in 1889–93, when the Great Northern was financed and completed to Puget Sound on the eve of a great depression. Now, as the spring of 1902 ripened into summer, he was well into the most demanding period of his life, a period which had begun with the fight for control of the Northern Pacific and would not end until the final defeat of Harriman in 1905 and the virtual dissolution of the Northern Securities Company. In these years Hill met four great challenges, any one of which would have been sufficient to absorb the skills of an ordinary man. First, he had to carry out the integration of the Burlington into the Great Northern–Northern Pacific system, a very critical step because, as he was fond of observing, they had paid a handsome price for it and would have to work hard to make the investment good. Second, he had to work out a practical plan for teaming up with Harriman in the operation of the railroads of the Northwest, a task that was not made easier by the fact that Hill had been sedulously avoiding such an association for five years. Third, he had to find for the Northern Pacific and the Great Northern, and the valuable Burlington which they controlled, a corporate haven in which they would be safe from future raids. And, finally, he had to defend his efforts to perfect his Northwestern "community of interests" in one of the most celebrated lawsuits in American legal history.

He waded into the Burlington with all the gusto of a child with a new toy. His first move was to persuade plain-spoken John F. Stevens, then making a good living as a consulting engineer, to take an inspection trip over the road. He was determined to have Stevens as general manager, and one day when the two men's private cars were coupled to the same train, he pressed him to take the job. But Stevens, who knew that the very able men who had been running the Burlington would resent having an outsider placed over them, turned him down flat. Hill, furious, demanded that his car be detached from Stevens's without delay. But he quickly came to see that Stevens, once again, was right. He learned to work smoothly with George B. Harris, who had succeeded Perkins as president of the Burlington, and Daniel Willard, a rapidly rising railroad star. But he constantly kept them just slightly off balance, repeatedly preaching his cost-cutting doctrine. He said that the Burlington was not run very economically so many times that Perkins, who was justly proud of his life's work, pointed out that the dense network of branch lines which the Burlington had to operate in the Midwest made for higher costs than the Great Northern and the Northern Pacific with their slender ribbons of steel stretching mile after mile across the Northern plains had to pay. The fact is that Hill was privately delighted to find that his acquisition was even more valuable than he had imagined. "I am more pleased with the CB&Q purchase every day," he wrote Kennedy; "it is really the strongest property of the three. . . ." [22]

Making peace with Harriman was one thing; keeping that peace, Hill realized, could be quite another unless he used all the power and determination at his command. This meant that he and Morgan must proceed with the huge job of retiring the Northern Pacific's preferred stock. Otherwise, they would be back where they had been on May 9. Before the job was finished, there would be another cliffhanging lawsuit in which an injunction against retirement would be lifted only at the very last moment, on December 31, 1901. The suit required days of testimony on the details of the complicated events leading up to the retirement, and Hill wearied of it. He could not know then that the days on the witness stand in St. Paul's chateau-like Federal Court House would save them all a great deal of time in a much more important lawsuit. [23]

"Here, we will put Mr. Harriman on this board, and Mr. Schiff, too, to show them we are not afraid of them," Morgan proposed to Hill one day that summer. Taking advantage of the particularly jovial mood Hill was in, Morgan received his approval of a step the banker knew was absolutely necessary. Harriman and his lieutenants, Stillman and Schiff, were given seats on the Northern Pacific and, later that year, the Burlington and the new Northern Securities Company as well. Hill and Morgan, with their absolute control of the Northern Pacific, ran no risk in making such concessions, and it might persuade Harriman to put his great block of Northern Pacific stock into a giant holding company, which, they were convinced, was where both Northern railroads should be safely and permanently lodged. [24]

In the years that followed Hill always insisted that the Northern

Securities Company, as the holding company was named, was not intended to stifle competition, nor, indeed, to carry out any operating purpose whatever. Its sole purpose, he maintained, was to provide a safe place for the railroad securities which he and a few elderly associates of considerable wealth had accumulated, and which represented their lives' work, which they did not want to see quickly torn down. He had decided to form a holding company several years before the struggle with Harriman, he revealed, and would have done so even if the events of 1901 had never taken place. The first point will continue to be debated inconclusively as long as such words as "competition" lack precise meaning. The second is probably not quite true, inasmuch as Morgan, at least, assiduously encouraged Harriman's participation. But the third point is beyond question. In February of 1899 Hill had had his lawyers draw up a detailed blueprint of a holding company to be called "Northern Securities Co., Ltd." (A secondary purpose of a holding company, he noted at the time, would be to receive the surplus earnings of the operating companies, which the State of Minnesota would not countenance their distributing as dividends.)[25]

Harriman, on the other hand, considered the securities company a device for locking him into a situation which gave him considerably less freedom of action than he longed for. "The conversion [of a majority of Northern Pacific common stock to securities company stock] . . . was a foregone conclusion unless we were prepared to commence litigation, which would be protracted and which would probably be detrimental to the value of all railroad securities in view of the panic of May 9, 1901." [26] From England, meanwhile, there emanated a coldness toward Hill's request that his friends buy and convert some of the Northern Pacific stock which Hill, Morgan, and others were carrying with great difficulty. "Your proposition is not one of business," sniffed Farrer. Hill then sent off an earnest, almost pleading cable to Mount Stephen:

> The whole plan is based upon our friends in London putting into holding company five millions of pool stock. Without this I cannot go on. I am ready to put in seven and half millions NP common, Kennedy four, Morgan and Baker about ten, . . . and others in proportions. It would be very unfortunate if the stock is scattered. It could never again be brought together. The profit made by our London friends in NP is almost equal the sum required. And the benefits are much greater. I hope the plan will not go down for want of the support to the extent asked. . . .[27]

By the time Northern Securities shares were ready for exchange for Northern Pacific and Great Northern stock (at $115 and $180, respectively), Hill had managed to persuade Mount Stephen and Farrer that they and their friends would have no more reason to regret sticking with him in this instance than they had in the past. Northern Securities stock was already selling at twelve dollars above par, even before organized trading started. He recommended the stock widely, taking care that Minnesota businessmen with whom he had dealt for years were given a chance to subscribe. In early August the largest investors in Great Northern signed an agreement to turn in their stock for that of the new company. Leading the list was Hill, with 80,049 shares of Great Northern. Kennedy had 75,000 shares; Strathcona, 54,000; and Mount Stephen, nearly 50,000 in various trusts. About 370,000 shares, or nearly 30 per cent of all Great Northern stock, was represented, and the psychological effect was to bring the smaller shareholders into the holding company on the run. Eventually about three-fourths of Great Northern stock, and nearly all of Northern Pacific, was gathered into the fold.[28]

The new corporation, one of the largest in the world, with its capitalization at $400 million, filed for incorporation in the very cooperative State of New Jersey on November 12, 1901. Next day the stockholders elected a board of directors: Hill, Sam Thorne, D. Willis James, George F. Baker, Robert Bacon, George W. Perkins, Nichols, Lamont, Clough, George C. Clark, Kennedy, and Nicholas Terhune (cashier of the Great Northern), all for the Hill-Morgan interests; and Harriman, Schiff, and Stillman. Harriman, with 23 per cent of the stock, had 20 per cent of the directors. Hill was thereupon elected president, while Harriman went unrepresented on the list of officers. Charles E. Perkins had followed the proceedings with amazement and admiration, and he wrote in his letterbook: "Hill, being in snug shape, . . . could afford to fight, if necessary but, wanting substance and not shadow, was willing to make a fair and logical settlement. . . . But five years from now, more or less, look out!"[29]

Hill was glad to see the approach of what he hoped was the end of his exhausting labors. "It is the hardest job I have ever undertaken," he wrote Mary from New York a month before the incorporation, "but I must go through with it all no matter what occurs or where it leads, as the result is of the greatest importance to us all . . . and will leave my labors practically at an end. . . ." Mary had heard it all before, but she came on to New York to be with him, noting in her diary on November 13, "A busy day for Papa. . . . He gave me the first twenty dollar gold piece he received [as a director's fee] after the first meeting of the new organization." As for resting on his oars, there was one who could tell him how little rest there was for the famous. "Merry Christmas, Colossus!" read an end-of-year note from Andrew Carnegie, who wanted him to come to dinner. "We shall have the two most famous Scots together. J. S. Kennedy, the third Scot, is also coming." [30]

VII

Neither Hill nor Morgan had an illusion that the Northern Securities Company would go unchallenged in the trust-conscious world of 1901. In forming the company they had followed their usual policy of selecting the ideal solution from a number of possibilities, putting the best face possible on it, and hoping that they could carry it through. They were well aware that relations between government and propertied interests were taking on a strong political hue, and statute law was rapidly replacing the common law of equity, making their past experience a poor guide to what they might be allowed to do in the future. Their lawyers, however, with nothing but the past to guide them, counseled that the company clashed with neither the Sherman Anti-Trust Act of 1890 nor any of the judicial decisions which were painfully building up some substance to that vague statute. In the 1895 case of *U. S. v. E. C. Knight Co.*, the Supreme Court had established the principle that restrictive agreements which related only to manufacturing were not in violation of the Act of 1890, regardless of what restrictions on the actual marketing of the manufactured goods were subsequently entered into. Surely, then, a corporation formed merely to hold the securities of two railroads, and claiming no role in their operation, had nothing to fear. [31]

The Trans-Missouri and Joint Traffic Association decisions of 1897 and 1898, which struck down agreements to maintain rates, were the only applications of the Act of 1890 to railroads at that time. The great railroad consolidations which had transformed the structure of the industry in the 1890s had not yet been challenged. Public distaste for the Northern Securities Company, latent at first, was a weed which would thrive mightily, however, with a little encouragement. The country was sick of bickering over the tariff, high-blown rhetoric about America's responsibilities in Cuba and the Philippines, "free silver," and conventional party politics. But the question of what to do about the vast power that a few wealthy men had acquired, entirely outside the political system, which controlled the lives of the people seemed to grow more urgent every day. No one knew this better than Governor Samuel R. Van Sant of Minnesota, who faced an uphill fight the following year in his bid for a second term.[32]

Hill felt he had little to fear from Van Sant. The State of Minnesota had blocked his plan to have the Great Northern acquire the Northern Pacific five years before, but the securities company was an entirely different matter. He laughed at Governor Van Sant's unsuccessful attempt to whip-up enthusiasm among the governors of the Northwestern tier of states for the suit which he brought against the company. James Norman, viewing the situation in St. Paul, felt that all his father had to do to frustrate Van Sant was to stay in New York and out of sight, because it was Hill, not the Governor, who made news and kept the politician before the public. But Hill, annoyed by a steady stream of newspaper inaccuracies, many of which he believed were inspired by the Soo and the Milwaukee Railroads, released to the press a carefully worded statement explaining the entire affair. "Jacob Schiff has been very near convulsions," Clough told Hill, reporting on New York reaction to the statement, but the national response seemed favorable.

Early in January Hill went to Fargo, North Dakota, to deliver an address at the state's grain and cattle growers' convention. Arriving on a clear and remarkably mild afternoon, he insisted that he and the welcoming committee walk to the Opera House. "Remember that whatever helps you, helps the railroad . . .," he trumpeted at the multitude who had come to hear him; "we will always prosper together or be poor together," and the waves of thunderous applause rolled over him like a warm blanket. The cheers were for Jim Hill, not the Northern Securities Company, but still, Van Sant would have had a lonely fight if it had not been for the phenomenon of Theodore Roosevelt.[33]

Another time, another place, TR and Hill might have been the best of friends. Scion of an old Dutch family which was firmly planted among New York's *haute bourgeoisie,* Roosevelt had congratulated himself that he was well down in rank in his class at Harvard College, as befitted a gentleman, and had rejoiced that he had remained a virgin until his wedding night. Not one to enter business, despite the flagging fortunes of his family, he esteemed public service in and out of uniform above all other callings. But, like Hill, he had an inquiring mind and a thirst for knowledge of the world around him which he never lost. Both men faced the future with the deep optimism that marked the Progressive era, and both yearned for the great outdoors, even as they sat chained to their desks. Both eagerly sought the company of the fresh new thinkers which the brave new century enjoyed, and both were outgoing in their personalities. It is not too difficult to imagine their roles reversed, though TR held the edge when it came to firing the imaginations of the masses. His grinning countenance was instantly recognizable at a time when the "gravy section" was bringing lavish rotogravure illustrations to newspaper readers everywhere. As for his unresonant voice, his luck still held, for radio and talking pictures were twenty years in the future. It was inevitable that such a man should be pressed to the bosom of the reformers who gave the name to the Progressive era and who were, for the most part not dull businessmen but, like TR, gentlemen and scholars. But Roosevelt's most enthusiastic supporters were uncomfortable in their awareness that he was also a politician of consummate skill, well equipped to practice the art of survival once Fate had put him in the seat of power.

Four Vice Presidents before Theodore Roosevelt had been elevated to the presidency by a President's death, and not one of them had subsequently received his party's nomination for a term in his own right. But for a proud man like Roosevelt, who adored leading other men, it would be a cruel fate to serve nearly a full term as President and then not even have the chance to submit his stewardship to the judgment of the electorate. He was determined to get the nomination even if it meant destroying political boss Mark Hanna. Roosevelt began to lay his plans the day he moved, with his large, noisy, and highly photogenic family, into the White House, and he was equal to all of the political expediency that was required of him. No one had ever claimed to hate compromise more, or practiced it with greater skill, than TR did.

He knew that his major appeal would have to be directed to the voters of the West, who thought Republican but often voted Democratic. Those Westerners who had helped to build the Republican party in Civil War days, and had maintained it against Rum, Romanism, and Rebellion ever since, would find a special attractiveness in a fresh voice which spoke for the commonwealth above the trust, the independent businessman above the plutocrat, the law above naked economic power. Not to become the prisoner of a principle, however, as William Jennings Bryan had done—*that* was the trick. Later, he would abandon plans to cut the tariff, which a large segment of labor opposed as bitterly as did the Eastern capitalists, and concentrated instead upon a strong railroad regulation law, which hardly anybody opposed except railroad men. He tried to look the other way when reformers pointed a finger at the arrogant beef trust, which could make common cause with livestock farmers, or at J. P. Morgan's mammoth United States Steel combine, which only bothered a few reluctant independent steel men. And then he looked at the Northern Securities Company, and he saw that it was good—that is, bad.

Hill himself had said, and not very privately, that the organizers of the Northern Securities Company would control the three railroads whether the holding company stood or fell. To sacrifice it in the name of trust-busting, therefore, could do no harm, and sooner or later, TR reasoned, the proud men who had created it would realize that the future of the Republican party depended upon their sacrifice. In order to implement these tactics, TR needed the support of Mark Hanna, who spoke both for capitalism and for hardheaded, pragmatic politics. One day in February 1902 he invited Hanna and Postmaster General Henry W. Paine to breakfast at the White House, and all during the meal he talked animatedly on a variety of inconsequential matters. But as his guests were taking their leave, he turned to his old friend and asked, "Mr. Hanna, what do you think about the Northern Securities Company?"

Hanna replied that it was the best thing possible for the future of the whole Northwest country.

Next day Hanna went to New York, and a few days later he boarded a train at Jersey City for the return to Washington. Already seated in the parlor car was John W. Griggs, who had been McKinley's Attorney General and now had a private law practice in Washington. When Hanna asked Griggs why he was going to Washington, Griggs realized that Hanna did not know what had happened.

"The government has brought a suit against the Northern Securities Co.," he said.

Hanna was flabbergasted.

Late that evening George W. Perkins, Morgan's right-hand man, called on Hanna at his suite in the Arlington Hotel. Perkins, who had rushed to Washington to try to get the President to relent, reproved Hanna for not having given him advance warning when they ran into each other in New York a few days before. When Hanna replied that he had known nothing about the President's intentions, Perkins, incredulous, exclaimed, "But I have just come from the White House and the President told me that before any decision was reached, you had been consulted."

TR's breakfast "conference" with Hanna was as far as he ever went in consulting with any of his advisers on the question of taking over the Northern Securities prosecution from the bumbling Minnesotans, with one exception: his Attorney General, Philander C. Knox. Knox had long been convinced that the federal government would sooner or later have to establish its right to strike down huge combinations of economic power when it felt such use of the sovereign power was in the public interest, and he had watched Van Sant's flounderings closely. So had his President, and soon the two of them were closeted in conferences from which even the prestigious Elihu Root ("the only one [of my Cabinet] who will fight with me"), to his great chagrin, was excluded. Afterwards, Roosevelt always gave Knox full credit for the decision to prosecute, while Knox would insist that his President was "the inspiring and unwavering cause of it all." [34]

VIII

"I have ordered taken down the fences of a very great and very arrogant corporation," Roosevelt told Western author Hamlin Garland that spring. And he wrote to Oswald Garrison Villard: "The rich Wall Street man, the so-called trust magnate, who attempts to do what the law forbids; the labor leader who attempts to do what the law forbids; and the white man who attempts to act outside the law against a colored man—must all three be made to understand that the law applies to them as well as to their fellows." But the law, as everyone knew, was whatever the United States Supreme Court said it was. The President himself knew that a legislative function lurks beneath the judicial act. "It seems to me that the head of the Supreme Court should be not merely a learned lawyer but a constructive statesman," Roosevelt pointedly remarked, as he prepared to elevate the very learned Oliver Wendell Holmes, Jr., to the highest court.

Looking back on the forces arrayed against the securities company, it seems remarkable that Hill insisted so doggedly that the fight be carried to the very finish. Morgan and his associates never shared Hill's determination to maintain the legality of the Northern Securities Company, and Hill had to argue heatedly to get them to continue the struggle. More than anything else, Morgan wanted to keep his great steel merger, his consolidation of New England railroads, and his shipping combine out of the jaws of anti-trust. But the Northern Securities Company, in the minds of most Americans, if not in actuality, was the culmination of Hill's life work, and he would not leave it hanging.[35] He managed every aspect of the three-year battle with his usual command of detail. He insisted that the case be tried in Minnesota, and that such local men as his old friend George B. Young and the able lawyers of the Great Northern and the Northern Pacific head the defense. "It is well understood that the judges do not regard a case with favor, which has to be tried by imported talent," he explained to Morgan's partner Charles Steele. He contributed to the defense a voluminous presentation of the complex corporate structure of several Eastern railroads which, he emphasized, involved dozens of consolidations of parallel railroads, and he was bitterly disappointed when the court took no note of the argument. He was greatly relieved when both sides agreed to read into the record the testimony in the case, just concluded, which had arisen out of the efforts of local men to block the Northern Pacific stock retirement. And he fretted at the rather uncooperative attitudes which Schiff and Harriman adopted on the witness stand.[36]

The struggle was taking a great deal out of him, Mary realized, when he came home in March of 1903 for a few weeks' rest. Never content in New York hotels, he had recently leased a big, comfortable apartment in a new building, the Bolkenhayn, on Fifth Avenue near 58 Street. James Norman, who had his own bachelor "digs" at the University Club, kept him company on many an otherwise lonely evening, the two of them sitting in their shirt-sleeves at the massive walnut dining table, playing double solitaire or whistling tunes in the old-fashioned harmonic style. Ruth, who had married a New York lawyer, Anson Beard, took him out for long walks, and somehow he found time to write "Dear Tolly" (his name for Clara) about it.[37] But there was no escaping the fact that living half in New York and half in St. Paul was dispiriting, as he had explained to Mary early in his ordeal:

> I am hard at work every day. To the office in the morning, work all day long, and return at night. My fingernails are broken and worn, mainly due to incorrigible sleeve buttons and unmanageable shirt studs. Nearly all of my clean linen has been worn. I do not know the address of a single laundry in this whole city. Many of my articles of wearing apparel are in a

state of decay that is actually alarming. Winter is rapidly approaching, I am growing old and helpless, and what am I to do!! [38]

The unanimous decision of the Circuit Court on April 9, 1903, was all the more disappointing because Hill's old friend, Walter H. Sanborn, chief judge of the court, was one of the four judges. It was a very narrow interpretation of the Act of 1890, taking its cue from the decisions which the Supreme Court had rendered in the traffic association cases. Whether the defendants had restrained commerce was immaterial, the court declared; the combine gave them the power to do so, and that was enough. There was no room for the concept of good and bad trusts, or even for the "rule of reason," which the Supreme Court would adopt eight years later to replace the view that *every* agreement in restraint of trade was unlawful. Brutally rejected as irrelevant was all evidence that the securities company may have had a constructive purpose:

> It may be that the motives which inspired the combination are unselfish . . . [and] would prove to be of inestimable value to the communities which these roads serve and to the country at large. We shall neither affirm nor deny either of these propositions because they present issues which we are not called upon to determine, and some of them are issues which no court is empowered to decide, involving questions of public policy which Congress must decide. [39]

When one reflected that it had been freely stated on the floor of Congress, during debate on the Sherman Act of 1890, that the courts would decide what the Act really meant, it was obvious that the constitutional separation of powers had created a dangerous vacuum.

Hill could not believe that the Supreme Court would allow the decision to stand. In his opinion, at least so he said, Washington was horrified, the Cabinet was pleading with the President to abandon his role of "trust breaker" before the nation was plunged into depression, and a special session of Congress would be called to amend the Act of 1890. He was glad to find that friends in Europe were, as Tuck said, "generally unterrified," but in June he made a trip to England to make sure of his ground. When his friends urged him to make a holiday of it, he went sightseeing in London with Stanford Newel, minister to The Hague, who wrote Clara that her father was "on occasion, the best loafer I know, what the French call 'flaneur.' " [40]

Brief encouragement came that summer when Judge William Lochren, who had heard the parallel suit of the State of Minnesota, ruled that the securities company had broken no law. Hill redoubled his efforts to make a strong appeal to the Supreme Court. On the advice of John W. Sterling he persuaded John G. Johnson, who was cast in the classic mold of the Philadelphia lawyer, to head the battery of attorneys. "He was the successful warrior in the Knight sugar case," Sterling noted, "and would consider the opportunity as the greatest of the closing years of his eventful life." [41] Johnson wrote one of the greatest briefs of his career, but it betrays a less-in-anger-than-in-sadness tone which suggests that he knew perfectly well that it was a political and not a judicial process in which he was participating:

> To a certain extent, the NP and GN are competitive, but about 75% of the business of each is non-competitive, because it originates or is consigned to a point or points on the line of one, not reached by the other. About 22%, nominally competitive, can be transported by other systems. . . . No concert of action between NP and GN . . . would be possible, because such action would give the transportation to competing lines. . . .

> We have been taught to believe that it was the greatest injustice towards the common people of old Rome when the laws they were commanded to obey, under Caligula, were written in small characters, and hung upon high pillars, thus more effectually to ensnare the people. How much advantage may we justly claim over the old Roman, if our criminal laws are so obscurely written that one cannot tell when he is violating them? . . .

> If this court is embarrassed as to the true meaning of the Act, it will not legislate. . . . It was the duty of Congress to put its intent in unequivocal language, and if its intent was to itself unknown . . . there can be no conviction. [42]

In March 1904, in a split decision, 5 to 4, the Supreme Court ruled that Congress had known exactly what it intended, which was to destroy the great power that men might arrogate to themselves in such a combination as the Northern Securities Company. On this point Justice John Marshall Harlan, who wrote the majority opinion, expressed himself as emphatically as the English language permitted:

> It need not be shown that the combination, in fact, results or will result, in a total suppression of trade or in a complete monopoly, but it is only essential to show that by its necessary operation it tends to restrain . . . commerce or tends to create a monopoly . . . and to deprive the public of . . . free competition. . . .

> Whether the free operation of the normal laws of competition is a wise and wholesome rule is an economic question which this court need not

consider. . . . If Congress has not, by the [Act of 1890] described this and like cases, it would, we apprehend, be impossible to find words that would describe them. . . . The court . . . may mould its decree so as to accomplish practical results—such results as law and justice demand. . . .[43]

To Hill, the major surprise in the decision was that Justice David J. Brewer had helped make the majority. It did not square with a career in which the Justice had usually resolved such knotty cases on the side of those who wished to carry on constructive work. "Possibly, the dazzling influence of the 'newly established court at Washington,' with all its tinsel and red-stockinged and gilded flunkies, has got the better of [him]," Hill growled to Charles E. Perkins, in a reference to the imperial atmosphere of the White House. There was some comfort in Holmes's dissent, the first of many for which TR's appointee would become famous. Harlan's turgid opinion decided the case, but it was Holmes's beautifully written dissent, embodying a little gem of a lecture on the historical meaning of "restraint of trade," which was in demand and quickly disappeared from the Supreme Court's stockroom: [44]

Great cases like hard cases make bad law. For great cases are called great, not by reason of their real importance in shaping the law of the future, but because of some accident of immediate overwhelming interest which appeals to the feelings and distorts the judgment. These immediate interests exercise a kind of hydraulic pressure which makes what previously was clear seem doubtful, and before which even well settled principles of law will bend. . . .

Much trouble is made by substituting other phrases assumed to be equivalent, which then are reasoned from as if they were in the act. . . . The act says nothing about competition. . . .

There is a natural feeling that somehow or other the statute meant to strike at combinations great enough to cause just anxiety on the part of those who love their country more than money. . . . This notion, it may be said, somehow breathes from the pores of the act, although it seems to be contradicted in every way by the words in detail. . . .

I am happy to know that only a minority of my brethren adopt an interpretation of the law which in my opinion would make eternal the *bellum omnium contra omnes*. . . . If that were its intent I should regard calling such a law a regulation of commerce as a mere pretence. . . .[45]

The Northern Securities Case was not even a great case, as it turned out. The Hepburn Act of 1906 and the Mann-Elkins Act of 1910, which gave government the power to set rates, replaced "competition" as the primary economic force ruling the railroads. And the "rule of reason," enunciated in the Standard Oil and American Tobacco cases in 1911, reversed the earlier notion that *every* restraining agreement was unlawful. The Hill roads were soldily merged in 1970, and now all that remains of the Northern Securities Case are two principles: the general principle that the antitrust law is whatever the Court said it was the last time it ruled, and the principle, so fundamental to the American system, that great concentrations of power are bad in and of themselves. In the Northern Securities Case, the American fear of great concentrations of power triumphed over evidence that great power had been greatly used. A mutilated eagle is a sorry sight, but at least he cannot soar above the pedestrian beings who clipped his wings.

IX

The Hill-Harriman rivalry was discreetly muted during the Northern Securities litigation, but it continued unabated beneath the surface. Harriman, determined to make the most of his minority position in the securities company, pressured Nichols to set up the offices of the new company in the Equitable Building at 120 Broadway, where Harriman had his offices and the Union Pacific had its New York headquarters. Nichols resisted, and with the help of the waspish, intensely loyal Clough, torpedoed the idea. Meanwhile, Harriman continued his surveys on the north bank of the Columbia River and took steps which, Hill felt, were designed to block any railroad that Hill might build there. When evidence came to hand that Harriman was trying to inaugurate business practices that Hill had proscribed for himself and his lieutenants for over two decades, Hill was outraged. Louis Hill, routinely checking the Northern Pacific purchasing agent's plans to buy new rolling stock, discovered that that gentleman, no doubt dazzled by Harriman's direct interest in his plans, had agreed to give the order, at $1200 a car, to "Diamond Jim" Brady's Pressed Steel Car Co. The Great Northern had been getting all of this type of car it wanted for $900 each, and Louis intervened just in time to save the Northern Pacific $400,000. When Hill learned that Harriman had a substantial interest in Brady's company, the bonds of trust were damaged beyond repair.[46]

If Harriman had had his way, the Court's order to the securities company to get rid of its railroad stock would have put them all right back where they had been on May 9, 1901. To Hill's atonishment, Harriman first agreed to, and then brought suit to enjoin, Hill's plan of redistribution. Hill had always assumed that if it came to that, the assets of the company would be redistributed *pro rata,* rather than in kind, which simply meant that investors would not get back shares in the specific company whose shares they had sold to the securities company, but shares of both the Great Northern and the Northern Pacific in proportion to the company's holdings of such securities. This meant little to the average investor, but to Harriman, who had turned in only Northern Pacific stock, it meant that he would get back a much smaller amount of Northern Pacific and a substantial block of Great Northern stock. He claimed that this would mean a financial loss to him, inasmuch as the price of Northern Pacific relative to Great Northern had improved since the spring of 1901. To Hill, and, as it turned out, to the United States Supreme Court, this was beside the point, for all of the investors had come in on the same basis, and they had to go out the same way.[47]

To Hill, it was the Rockefeller influence all over again. By this time the Milwaukee road was involved in a disastrously costly plan to build its own line to the West Coast, and if it could get control of the Northern Pacific, its future would be vastly improved. How else could one explain the bitter, pointless lawsuit which Harriman instituted, unless once again he was not the driver but the driven? This time, despite Harriman's assiduous efforts in England to court Mount Stephen's favor, Hill's old friend sided with Hill, and fiercely. "Harriman told me two years ago when I first met him that it was a great mistake the Nor Pacific fight was not then fought to a finish and that he foresaw it would have to be fought out again. This is the man you have to deal with. . . . It is quite clear that the time has not yet come for you and Harriman to run in the same team."[48]

And Hill did deal with him, all the weary way to the Supreme Court. Finally, early in 1905, it was all over. During the next three years the Harriman interests gradually sold their stock in the Hill roads. Harriman, deeply involved in making his acquisition of the Southern Pacific stick in the face of bitter government opposition, spread himself thinner and thinner. He endured a searching investigation of his massive railroad reorganizations by the Interstate Commerce Commission and, just as he had expected, the clean bill of health he received did not prevent the politicians from nailing his hide to the wall. Still, he continued to capture the fancy of that schizoid beast, the general public, and when word leaked out that he was very sick a general feeling of malaise crept over Wall Street. In the late summer of 1909, after a disappointing visit to European specialists, he came back just in time to die in his own bed at "Arden." Hill, whose respect for Harriman, justly or unjustly, had been finally snuffed out by the last court battle, sent not a word of condolence.[49]

Schiff was still his friend, although their business association was at an end. And Hill could hardly turn his back on the President, especially when Roosevelt repeatedly made it clear, through third parties, that he harbored no ill will and, in fact, counted himself an enthusiastic admirer of Hill. Bidding farewell to an English journalist toward the end of his term in office, Roosevelt was delighted to hear that his visitor had just come from an interview with Hill. "Oh! I know Jim Hill well," Roosevelt burst out; "he opposed me in politics; but I like him! I like him very much! And he can tell you a great deal worth learning!" It was Mr. Justice Holmes who got TR's cold shoulder, but the jurist let it be known that he did not "care a damn" whether he ever went to the White House again. Teddy Roosevelt, Holmes said, was "very likeable, a big figure, a rather ordinary intellect, with extraordinary gifts, a shrewd and I think pretty unscrupulous politician. He played all his cards—if not more." [50]

One thing was certain. Now that the securities company was dead, or practically so, Hill would have to continue to look after these three great railroads himself, while he renewed the search for younger hands in which to entrust them. The next several years promised to be the most critical in the history of American railroads, and they would be Roosevelt years. The President had got the nomination in 1904 and, with his incredible luck, had found himself pitted against colorless Judge Alton B. Parker. Next March, Theodore Roosevelt was inaugurated President in his own right, the youngest ever up to that time, and he has remained one of the most colorful and popular Presidents in American history. A quarter of a century later two of the nation's leading poets undertook to write a book introducing children to famous Americans, among whom were included Jesse James but not a single captain of industry. When they came to Theodore Roosevelt, Rosemary and Stephen Vincent Benét captured his popular image with perfect accuracy:

> T.R. is spanking a Senator,
>   T.R. is chasing a bear;
> T.R.is busting an awful trust,
>   And dragging it from its lair.
>
> They're calling T.R. a lot of things,
>   The men in the private car—
> But the day-coach likes exciting folks,
>   And the day-coach likes T.R.[51]

Of such gossamer stuff are historical reputations made.

18

A Public Man

Your reminiscences would be a monumental book and a valuable contribution to the real *history of the United States, as distinguished from the mere stories of wars and politics.*

—Walter Hines Page to Hill, 1908

I

History does not record whether James J. Hill ever saw the Sunday, October 9, 1910, issue of *The New York Times*, nor, if he did, how he reacted to the Knox Hat advertisement in the rotogravure section. Twenty years earlier a cigar manufacturer had timidly asked, and had been sternly refused, permission to put Hill's likeness on a cigar band. But times had changed. The photograph which New York's Pach Brothers had made of Hill, pencil in hand, promised to become almost as familiar to Americans as one of Theodore Roosevelt. Hill could hardly complain, then, when an enterprising pencil manufacturer pasted a photograph of his own product over the pencil in the portrait, reproduced it on a blotter, and mailed thousands of them to stationery stores across the nation. The Knox advertisement was the ultimate testimonial to his popularity. It was the age of the "comer," the young man who was told over and over again, from the pulpit and the college lecture platform, by the pompous business-college brochure and the popular press, that to get ahead he had to emulate those greatly successful men of the previous generation. One way was to dress up to the part, and in the years before World War I men's fashions improved dramatically, culminating in the Arrow Collar Man of the 1920s. The Knox advertisement reproduced a crayon drawing in which a godlike young man, hat in hand, approaches his "prospect" at his desk. Unmistakably, the "prospect," his attention riveted on the Knox label in the young man's hat, is intended to be James J. Hill.

In the decade following the battles with Harriman and the culmination of the Northern Securities Case, Hill became one of the best known men in the United States. Partly by default (Rockefeller and Morgan had no use for publicity, and Carneigie occupied rather too lofty a plane for the average man), but even more so because of his tireless writing and speaking on subjects which were directly related to the daily work of the people, Hill became the symbol of the doer of hard, constructive work whom the age of progress admired. He was rich—although much less rich, many would have been surprised to learn, than the titans of manufacturing—and by 1910 he was the unquestioned dean of American railroad men. Except for Hill, none remained from the heroic age of enterprise which had brought cheap dependable transportation to virtually every hamlet in the nation.

He was busier than ever. He continued to work out of three offices, as he had for twenty years. By the end of the old century, William C. Toomey presided over a staff of seven clerks, taking care of Hill's personal business in the office rented from the Great Northern in St. Paul, while upstairs Hill carried on as president of the railroad in an only slightly less bleak office. In New York, the faithful Nichols had evaded Harriman's efforts to lure the securities company into the Equitable Building and had secured spacious new quarters for that company and the Great Northern at 32 Nassau Street. The return of the bull market after the wreckage of the Northern Pacific corner had been cleared away brought a dramatic rise in all of the railroad securities in which Hill had sunk so much money. His personal net worth on January 1, 1901, had been $19 million, but just a year later Mr. Toomey entered $32 million on the summary sheet of the ledger. But net worth was not the same thing as liquidity. Early in 1902 John J. Mitchell, president of the Illinois Trust and Savings Bank, offered him a chance to subscribe for the much sought after stock of his institution, but Hill admitted sadly, "I am too much in debt to buy anything [but] I am glad to say that I am in sight of the shore." The ensuing decade was very good to him, however, as it was to most shrewd men of property, and by 1910 John J. Toomey, who had replaced his brother as Hill's chief clerk, recorded the figure of $53 million in the big ledger.[1]

Hill was the most domestic of the great business leaders of his era. His children remained modestly out of the limelight—no Italian counts as husbands for his six daughters! But in St. Paul their comings and goings were watched with the mixture of pride and envy which the Hills had long since grown accustomed to. Until they married, the girls lived at home, in the great sandstone mansion which never boasted any more pretentious name than "240 Summit Avenue." It was a large, efficient establishment, the multitude of brick chimneys testifying to the numerous bedrooms, most of which had a fireplace and, as the owner had dictated after a decade of Spartan living on Canada Street, a bathroom. The place ran smoothly under Mary's watchful eye, and with the hard work of a small army of Scandinavian, Irish, and German domestics. With some pressure from young Walter, who had begun to drive an automobile at sixteen, Hill bought a "machine" sometime before 1907. Soon the horses which occupied the spacious stables, carefully built of Milwaukee white brick salvaged from the old house, were joined by a Pierce Arrow, a Studebaker, and a touring car, handmade by Charrow, Giradet & Voight. Before long the Hills were going out to North Oaks after lunch on summer Sundays, staying for tea, and returning to 240 Summit for dinner. The new routine which the automobile made possible impressed Mary, who also noted that the machine did not panic at the sound of Fourth of July firecrackers.[2]

Old friends had begun to join the great majority. All of the Hills were saddened to learn of the violent end of stoop-shouldered old Mr. Chemidlin, who had presided over Louis and James Norman's schoolroom at Ninth and Canada almost twenty-five years before. Trudging up St. Paul's crowded Seventh Street in the dusk of a July day on which the temperature had reached 100 degrees, he stepped or was jostled from the sidewalk directly into the path of a clanging, smoke-belching fire engine and the galloping horses which pulled it. With this kindly man's help, Mary reflected, she had reared all nine of her children in the Catholic faith, and with Walter's confirmation in 1899 her responsibilities in that regard were ended. Soon she would have to face the fact that, just as in her own case, religion usually passes through the female line, but she would never entirely accept the fact that Louis's children would be Episcopalian. In such matters her husband held himself discreetly aloof.[3]

Leaving the details of the Northern Pacific settlement with Wall Street's embarrassed speculators to be ironed out by subordinates, Hill shepherded Mary and Gertrude up the gangplank of the new yacht, *Wacouta,* at the end of May 1901. After a short cruise up Long Island Sound, they disembarked at New Haven, climbed aboard a trolley, and rode into the city for a visit with the faculty at Yale. Arriving back in New York in a dense fog, the three were glad to transfer to a train, which took them to Tuxedo Park. They were much impressed with George F. Baker's gracious mansion in that beautiful enclave of millionaires. Two days later they were back in New York, where Mary was relieved to find that the new clothes which her husband had ordered from his harried tailor in St. Paul had arrived. "Now we are ready for the wedding," she noted in her diary. On June 6, 1901, in an informal ceremony at the New York home of the bride's brother, Louis married Maud Van Cortlandt Taylor. The Kennedys, the J. P. Morgans, the Stephen Bakers and a number of Maud's girlfriends, including Gertrude, Ruth, and Charlotte Hill, and a few other close friends were the only guests. Maude was a beautiful, sunny girl; she had grown up on Staten Island and had lived for some years in St. Paul, and she was pleased that her new husband intended to build a handsome Georgian house at 260 Summit Avenue, next door to 240.

Later that year, in an elegant formal wedding held at 240 Summit on one of Minnesota's beautiful October days, Charlotte married George T. Slade, an ambitious young railroad man who faced a brilliant future with the Erie Railroad. The host of guests fitted gracefully into the great art gallery; the organ, thoroughly repaired for the occasion, worked perfectly; and the 175 cooked crabs which the bride's father brought from Seattle disappeared quickly. Ten plainclothesmen, personally hired by Charlotte, kept an eye on things. The photographer managed to get the entire family, save for Walter, whose father had sternly forbidden him to leave his school in the East, on the rear terrace of the mansion for a wedding picture. It had been thirteen years since Mamie had married Sam Hill—exciting, eventful years in which James J. Hill had grown old while his burdens had grown heavier. Now, with Louis and George Slade, there were two young railroad men in the family, and the future took on more of an air of certainty than Hill could ever remember.[4]

By the end of 1906, of all the children who had enlivened the Hill household over a period of thirty-five years, only Clara and Rachel remained at home. Ruth, who had married lawyer Anson Beard in 1902, was an elegant New York matron by then. Slender, graceful Gertrude had been graduated from Miss Spence's school in the hectic

month of May 1901, and her father had found the time to be present and applaud as the beaming principal handed her her diploma. When she married young Michael Gavin in 1906 it was the first ceremony in the family which was permitted to be performed in the sanctuary of the Catholic church. The groom, a native of Memphis, Tennessee, and a junior partner in the investment banking firm of Moore & Schley, was himself a Catholic, and Gertrude marked the occasion by choosing the late Father Caillet's own parish church, St. Mary's.

Meanwhile, Walter was off on his own, learning railroading and then farming, so the big mansion bustled only occasionally, when the children and a growing list of grandchildren arrived for visits. Quiet, dignified Rachel concentrated on the extensive gardens at 240 Summit Avenue, and on numerous charities. Clara shared her interest in charity work, but spent more and more of her time as companion to her father. She accompanied him on several of the short, hurried voyages to Europe which Mary Hill avoided, especially now that grandchildren were beginning to arrive at frequent intervals. Clara and Rachel lived simply, while the married girls used the trust funds which their father settled on them to live in the greater luxury which the East expected of them.[5]

II

Mary and her husband watched sadly as the marriage of Mamie, their first-born, and Samuel Hill died in all but name. Sam was in love with the Pacific Northwest and spent more and more of his time there, but Mamie had formed an attachment for the kaleidoscopic social life of Washington, D.C., and determined to live there permanently. Mary Mendenhall, Hill's first grandchild, darkly pretty like her mother and her aunts, fared poorly in the strained domestic atmosphere. Hill had

The entire Hill family, except for Walter, on the terrace of 240 Summit Avenue following Charlotte and George T. Slade's wedding reception, October 1901. Left to right: Louis W. and Maud Hill, married the previous June; Clara; James Norman Branson Hill, 8, son of Sam and Mary Frances Hill Hill; George Slade's father; Charlotte; George T. Slade; James Norman Hill; Mrs. James J. Hill; Gertrude; Rachel; Ruth; Mary Mendenhall Hill, 12, standing in front of her father, Samuel Hill; her mother, Mary Frances Hill Hill; and James J. Hill, who was about to leave for New York to organize the Northern Securities Company. Photograph by Zimmerman, St. Paul.

observed her intense, anxious approach to her schoolwork. Her brother, James N. B., who spent much time with his father in Washington State and his grandparents in St. Paul, fared better, but by 1910 Mary Mendenhall had begun to suffer the severe and recurring depressions from which she would be released only by death. By the end of the decade Hill had nine more grandchildren: Louis and Maud's three boys, Louis, Jr., James Jerome II, and Cortlandt, and their daughter, Maud; George and Charlotte's son, George Norman, and their daughter, Georgiana; Ruth and Anson's son, Anson, Jr., and their daughter, Mary; and Walter's daughter, Dorothy, but Hill would always have a special feeling for this first grandchild, who had written him so joyously of her first sight of spring in the Pacific Northwest.[6]

"I hope you will always remember how anxious I am to have you do well," Hill had wired his youngest son in September 1901. Walter was just about to leave for Lakeville, Connecticut, where his father, with some difficulty, had got him admitted to the Hotchkiss School. Hill himself was in Seattle and deeply involved in working out his future relations with Harriman in the Northwest, but Walter was very much on his mind. This was the boy's last chance to make a success of his education, and his prospects were not good. Walter had had all the schooling he wanted or could profit from, and by the following spring the headmaster managed to convince the boy's disappointed father of that fact. The handsome lad, who charmed nearly everyone he met, saw little future in the role of dutiful son when he had two older brothers who were already playing it. He had meanwhile developed a real interest in farming and livestock raising, and once he convinced his father that he cherished no ambition beyond that of country squire, Hill supported him enthusiastically. In 1908 Walter married a St. Paul girl, Dorothy Barrows, and his father bought them Samuel Stickney's fine house on Summit Avenue for a wedding present. At Northcote Farm, one of the huge spreads which Hill had owned for years in the Red River Valley, he set Walter up to grow wheat and raise shorthorn cattle. Presently a handsome residence—every detail of its construction watched over by Hill—rose on the prairie for the new squire.[7]

In the summer of 1899, when Mary Brooks visited her famous brother and his family in St. Paul, Hill saw his sister for the last time. Two years later her husband gave up his forty-year battle to support his big family, and in 1905 Emma A. Brooks, their spinster daughter, wrote that Mary Brooks herself was dying of cancer. The family was destitute, and to make matters worse, brother Alec was not doing well either. The help which Hill gave was not lavish, nor even particularly generous, but it was regular and just sufficient to keep the Canadian Hills from the poorhouse.[8]

"Louis, Maud and the children left for Manchester [New Hampshire] Thursday afternoon," Mary Hill wrote Clara on June 2, 1906. "They had a great time getting off, as you may imagine. Three servants, besides three nurses, four babies and the little dogs! the whole arrangement being very much on Louis' mind. He and George go fishing later, with Papa." When June arrived each year and the eager report came from the River St. John that the salmon were running, Mary was glad that her husband refused to let anything prevent his taking "that one vacation" which seemed to be about all his busy schedule would permit. Mount Stephen continued to urge Hill to enjoy more leisure; like Stanford Newel, who had once gotten Hill to pause long enough to see London, he realized that his friend had a talent for loafing, if he would only indulge it. "If you were another kind of man, say like Russell Sage, I would not be so urgent," he wrote at the height of the Northern Securities lawsuit.

Hill had bought the exclusive rights to fish the River St. John, a tributary of the St. Lawrence, in 1899, and with each passing year the June trip to "kill" as many salmon as possible became more and more complicated. By 1901 a comfortable log lodge stood on the site, in readiness, along with several dozen of the local population, to accommodate Hill and his close friends, generally including Sam Thorne, Dan Lamont, Robert Bacon, and Earl Grey (Governor General of Canada) and the Earl's wife and daughter, all avid fishermen. In 1901 the camp entertained its most distinguished visitor, Grover Cleveland, who created a sensation when he slipped, fell, and became wedged in one of the canoes. Whether it really came to that or not, the story of how the guides had to lift the canoe out of the water, turn it upside down, and shake the former President of the United States free lives on among Hill's descendants, who still fish the river. It was only at salmon-fishing time that Hill made much use of his yacht, which he had bought in 1900 for $150,000, and which cost him over $60,000 a year to operate.[9]

The rumor that the Hills were preparing to abandon St. Paul and move permanently to New York became more frequent as the girls settled there, and as business kept Hill in the East for weeks at a time. But he always denied the rumors flatly, and there is no evidence that there was any other place he would rather have been than St. Paul, other than the salmon river and his beloved North Oaks Farm. But in 1906 he gave up the apartment in the Bolkenhayn and ordered $3500 worth of undistinguished furniture from a firm in Chicago for a new house which he had bought in New York. The handsome limestone mansion, at 8 East 65 Street, was spacious; it was forty-three feet wide and five stories tall. At $422,500, the house, which had been built only a short time earlier, was a good investment, for the block just off Fifth Avenue in the sixties and seventies was fast becoming the most fashionable in the city. He also took the lot next door, No. 12, where he built a house for Gertrude and Michael Gavin (having done the same for Ruth and Anson Beard on East 68 Street) and the lot behind, on 64 Street, to protect his light. The new establishment was prevented from becoming just one more burden by Hill's great luck in hiring Ernst Kurth and wife to run the place, which they did with efficiency. They even bought fresh flowers every morning before dawn at the wholesale flower market. Almost as an afterthought, Hill sent J. J. Toomey and his daughter on a junket to Paris to close the apartment which Hill had optimistically leased the year before the exposition of 1900. His old friend Tuck, who had lived for years in the building next door, watched sadly as most of the furniture was auctioned off and Hill's promise of leisurely trips to Europe faded, along with the plan to take the *Wacouta* across the Atlantic.[10]

III

The final resolution of the difficulties with Harriman over the securities company left Hill busier and lonelier than ever. By the late spring of 1905 he was testifying at length before the Senate Committee on Interstate Commerce, which was wrestling with the red-hot question of railroad rate regulation. He accepted only a fraction of the invitations to speak which came from dozens of groups between New York and the Pacific Northwest. But he found himself rushing more and more often to catch the train to one of the major market towns in the Red River Valley, the Dakotas, and Montana, for he was reluctant to miss an opportunity to convey to the farmers of these areas the passionate ideas on agriculture which he held. He was lonely because Mary's health had broken down badly early in 1905 and she was spending the winter of 1905–6 in an elegant Southern mansion which Hill had rented, lavishly furnished and equipped with servants and horses, in Aiken, South Carolina. In the cold dark days of January 1906, he sat in his study at 240 Summit and wrote her as cheerfully as he could:

> I arrived home from Chicago on Wednesday morning and left the same evening for Grand Forks where I made two speeches and came home that night. I was a little tired but feel well rested now, and will hurry up my work so that I can go south and see my—my—my family, who are at present living on Whiskey Road near Aiken, S. C.

> The house is very quiet these days and nights too. I come home, eat, read, and sleep. Walter is the only one at home. . . .

> I hope that with "Charley" and your own horses you are enjoying, as far as a lone woman can, the outdoor life. You have horses enough to furnish saddles for all the girls. Tell Clara that I hope she has taken up horseback riding again and that she will be able to accompany me on long and arduous trips across country. . . .

> I am "achin' " to be there and to be on hand to see that you and Clara do not get too giddy. . . .[11]

Worn out from the strain of waiting for the Supreme Court's decision in the Northern Securities Case, Hill had decided in February 1904 that the time had come for the Hills to get some use out of their apartment in the lodge at the Jekyl Island Club, which he had been a member of for years. Splendidly isolated on one of the coastal islands of Georgia, the Club was a tropical paradise, while St. Paul still lay under a season's accumulation of snow. Everyone at this "millionaire's club," as D. C. Shepard, who spent his winters in Thomasville, Georgia, called it, brought their finest horses, both to ride and to pull their carriages from tea party to tea party. Even the servants whom these rich people brought along could almost think of it as a vacation, for the hordes of servants recruited from the local black folk did all the work, of which there was a great deal. It was an arduous, twenty-five-hour trip from New York to Brunswick, Georgia, where one got the Club ferry to the island, and the plumbing was no better than it should have been in that typhoid-conscious age, but to the Hills it made an ideal vacation spot. But back in St. Paul in the winter of 1904–5, while her husband worried over the Harriman litigation, Mary took cold and lingered for weeks on the verge of pneumonia. The following spring, with Harriman fended off, Hill insisted that they go to Jekyl Island where, a day or two after the trip down, Mary collapsed.

With Mary at Aiken, South Carolina. Winter 1906.

It was the old tuberculosis, now vigorously reasserting itself, and the complication of a weak heart, which almost carried her off during the next few days. Down from New York, on a train that was five hours late, came Hill's personal physician and salmon fishing companion, Dr. Stewart, who took one look and advised that Dr. Herman Biggs, general medical officer of New York City and a leading specialist in the prevention and treatment of tuberculosis, be summoned immediately. But Mary was so much better a day later that they decided to spare Biggs the trip. Stewart recommended however, that as soon as the hot weather made its appearance at Jekyl Island, Mary should be transferred to a cool, dry lodge in the Adirondacks, and in no case was she to spend the following winter in St. Paul. Later that summer she was to go to the renowned sanitarium at Saranac Lake, New York, for observation. By the late spring of 1906, after a winter in Aiken, she was well enough to telegraph her husband that she and the girls had secured perfectly good accommodations on the Palm Limited for the trip from Aiken to St. Paul, and there was no need to send the private car.[12]

As it has always been with northern peoples, though winter brought care and worry, summer usually seemed to bring things right again. Soon the Hills were looking forward to an old-fashioned Fourth of July at North Oaks. Gaspard Farrer was paying them the visit he had promised for so long, and, to rescue him from the non-stop conversation which her husband expected, Mary challenged Farrer to a game of pool, and beat him, after which he taught her a new game of solitaire. While Farrer and Mrs. Hill played games, Hill turned to D. C. Shepard, who had dropped by to be brought up to date on railroad affairs. He was describing the recent trip to the River St. John, and the 500 salmon that the party had killed, when Norman and Georgiana rushed in to report that their Aunt Gertrude had caught a five-pound bass in the pond and they had landed forty-three sunfish and crappies. "Everything is comparative, you know," Mary observed.[13]

IV

Few members of Congress then knew much about the complicated issue of railroad rate regulation, and not many pretended that they did. But nearly all of the members of the House of Representatives knew which side their bread was buttered on when the time came to vote on the Esch-Townsend bill in January 1905. This radical measure, which would have given the nearly moribund Interstate Commerce Commission virtually dictatorial powers over railroad rates, had no chance of becoming law. The fact that the Congressmen knew it, yet insisted on voting for the bill, 326 to 17, in the confidence that the Senate would bring things back to an even keel, brought some of the harshest criticism of the House since Woodrow Wilson's 1885 treatise on congressional government. Meanwhile, the Senate went dutifully to work and, as the raw, unpleasant Washington winter gave way to the short, glorious spring and then the steamy days of May, doggedly assembled 1700 pages of evidence for and against strict regulation. One of the railroad "stars" whom they looked forward to putting on their witness stand was James J. Hill.[14]

Hill had known, even before Leon Czolgosz made Theodore Roosevelt President, that the vaguely *laissez faire* arrangement which had marked relations between shippers and the railroads in the nineteenth century was doomed. In a long letter to Jacob Schiff, in which he sought to mend their badly strained relations following the Northern Pacific corner, he had summed up the mood of the country eloquently:

> I feel very strongly that we are approaching the time when new political lines will be forced upon the country. . . . There is a widespread and general feeling of dissatisfaction which will, I think, increase as we go on

and will by, say, 1903 be in full blast. The pulpit and the press are doing their full share to draw intelligent people into the fold of agitation. College professors who, as a rule, are not well qualified to speak, are active, all inciting the public mind. I have never seen a time when I felt as strongly the absolute need of great caution and wise counsel in order to preserve the great railway properties of the country. . . .[15]

It was a brilliant prediction of the Progressive era of reform as applied to the business world, but neither the need for nor the danger of strict rate regulation was what worried Hill most. Since the 1880s he had agonized over the average politician's insistence upon regarding the net profits of railroads as a tax levied upon the many for the benefit of the few stockholders. For over two decades he had used his ingenuity to find ways to keep surplus funds in his railroad companies. Great as those funds were, they never were sufficient to provide the capital for increased carrying capacity and for improved efficiency. The latter goal, in fact, was becoming paramount, as wages and materials costs rose far more rapidly than railroad rates. The nation's transportation "plant" was simply inadequate, in the most fundamental sense, and as early as 1902 Hill was telling everyone who would listen just how critical the situation had become:

The railway situation east of Chicago is rapidly coming to a point where the facilities are taxed to their full capacity. There has been a freight blockade on all the lines. The business has grown so rapidly that the terminal facilities of five years ago are no longer equal to the service. In the past eleven years the ton-miles have grown from 76 billions to 165 billions, or 120%, while the additional mileage has only increased 18%. . . . The average daily movement of cars has been reduced from 30 miles to less than 20 miles . . . which goes to show the inability of the railways to handle the cars. . . . The increase in passenger traffic has been very great, and the speed of passenger trains has been materially increased. . . . The business of the country has outgrown the transportation in all the great centers. . . .[16]

The main difficulty which the railways have to overcome is the greater movement of cars, and this calls for a large increase in terminals . . . Many think the only solution will be a decentralization of terminals . . . but this would be very strongly resisted by all the large commercial centers. . . .[17]

It is difficult to bore an inch hole with a half-inch auger. . . .[18]

Hill's views on the quantity and quality of transportation facilities were, if anything, conservative, for extreme congestion all but shut down many lines for weeks in the winter of 1906–7. The result was bitter recriminations from shippers, a government investigation, and a covert sigh of relief from railroad men when the recession of 1907–8 brought some respite. One way or another, however, the American railroad network was transformed in the two decades before World War I, in a herculean labor which an ungrateful public took little note of and has long since forgotten. Almost no section of line that carried a heavy volume of traffic failed to be more or less rebuilt: curves straightened, grades reduced, rails ripped up and relaid with heavier ones, and wooden bridges and trestles replaced with steel. But the record-breaking sums which railroad men had to spend for new facilities were never enough, especially when it came to relieving the situation at the terminals. And as far as improving the attitude which Americans adopted toward the railroads, the money might as well never have been spent. But it did make it possible, somehow, to keep the great tonnages of freight and the hordes of passengers moving.[19]

Only Hill and a few other railroad leaders saw the chief paradox of railroad public relations in the Progressive era. Whereas by 1900 the ability of the carriers to deny "rebates" to their best or most powerful customers had been immeasurably improved by the great consolidations and the communities of interest of the 1890s, Americans were demanding even higher standards of impartiality. The rhetoric of the period turns almost entirely on "fairness" of treatment of weak shippers by powerful railroads, but it is clear, looking back, that what many shippers—large and small, agricultural, mercantile, or industrial—wanted was more unfairness. They wanted to propel the mechanism of ratemaking into the public arena where, hardly anyone doubted, they would be able to manipulate the process and keep rates frozen, and this at a time when virtually all other prices had been going up from 5 to 10 per cent a year since 1898. In the short run, such tactics would spell even greater profits for shippers. In the long run they would lead to a crippled transportation system, higher costs, and great inconvenience for everybody who used the railroads.

Hill expected Congress to pass a more stringent law, one making the seeking as well as the giving of rebates criminal. He welcomed it, although all of his experience told him that no law was a satisfactory substitute for a railroad's inherent power to maintain its rate schedule on its own. At the same time, he expressed nothing but contempt for legalized pooling, although this old idea continued to be brought up. He went to Washington to confer with West Virginia's earnest, bumbling Senator Stephen B. Elkins, chairman of the Committee on Interstate Commerce, who was trying to draft what in 1903 became the anti-rebating law that bears his name. Hill was deeply troubled to learn the dangerous game which the powerful leaders of the Pennsylvania Railroad were playing. In order to get a law which would protect them from the demands of powerful shippers for rebates (as if anyone could be made to believe that the Pennsylvania needed protecting!) they were willing to draft the law themselves; and they hinted that they might not mind if the ICC were given the power to set maximum rates, on application by dissatisfied shippers, *so long as such orders were subject to full review by the courts.* It was a desperate gamble, Hill realized, to keep the real rate-making power in the hands of railroad men, with recourse to the courts in which the carriers would at least have the protection of the common law of equity as they understood it; and out of the hands of a dictatorial, bureaucratic commission beholden to no one and to nothing except expediency. Hill's fears were shared by western railroad men and by Samuel Spencer, president of the Southern Railway and an intense, hard-bitten enemy of government regulation, who was the unofficial head of the railroads' joint effort to fight it. They were right to be afraid, for the gamble failed.[20]

"If Roosevelt is bound to have more law about rates," Charles E. Perkins wrote Hill in 1905, "the sooner we put the fire out the better. With Cummins and La Follette and Van Sant and Bryan . . . , to say nothing of the Boss Lunatic himself, doing all they can to fan the flame, it will be hard to extinguish—and we may get something really bad." Spencer felt the same way, and he pressed Hill for his views on what action the railroads could reasonably take. Hill contributed to the war chest that Spencer collected to wage a hard-hitting publicity campaign during the critical year of 1905, but his experience gave him little reason to believe it would work. As it turned out, it backfired badly when the unemployed hack newspapermen whom Spencer hired as publicists resorted to devious tactics which influential critics of the railroads, such as Professor William Z. Ripley of Harvard, condemned. All their strength, Hill warned, should be put behind an effort to preserve judicial review, for the rate-making power was about to be shared with the ICC whether railroad men liked it or not:

> If the power to make rates and establish rules is given to any Interstate Commission without the right to appeal to the Federal courts and secure a stay of proceedings until the question is determined by the Court, the end of it will be most harmful to all the railway interests in the nation.[21]

V

Ever since his appearance before the Minnesota state legislature back in 1885, Hill had believed that lawmakers were educable on the subject of railroad regulation. Longer than almost anyone else among the big business leaders of his day, he struggled to reason with them and with the general public. The alternative, he realized, was the end of the spirit of enterprise which had given the United States the finest and cheapest transportation system in the world in the space of barely four decades. He was beginning to realize even before the turn of the century that some legislators could not be reached with the facts, as when Senator Knute Nelson insisted upon giving the Canadian Pacific credit for bringing down rates in the Northwest in spite of data which Hill furnished to the contrary. He suspected that the political process was rapidly deteriorating, as the average legislator, his eyes on the main chance, gave more and more of his time to local "woodchuck bills" and less and less to complex national problems. As colleges and universities grew in influence, and religion became increasingly secularized, new candidates for his scorn took up the railroad problem. Much of the agitation for authoritarian railroad regulation, he told Spencer, "does not come from those who use the railways but rather from a lot of doctrinaires, . . . college tack-head philosophers and preachers. . . ." [22]

Hill appeared before the Senate Committee on Interstate Commerce at Washington, which was wrestling with the problem of a strict regulatory law, on May 3, 1905. Throughout the long day he was questioned by the three lawmakers who were the most knowledgeable on the subject: Elkins, the chairman; Shelby M. Cullom of Illinois, whose work on regulatory legislation went back to his chairmanship of the committee which had produced the Interstate Commerce Act of 1887; and Joseph B. Foraker of Ohio. These men, all Republicans, were true conservatives, in that they believed that a strong regulatory commission involved the very real risk of destroying whatever it was that had produced the American railroad miracle in the past, and which they knew would be needed even more in the future. Their line of questioning would have benefitted greatly if, like modern congressional committees, they had had the services of an expert counsel. Even so, they could piece together from Hill's response as clear a picture of the dangers involved in commission rate-making as they were ever going to get from anyone:

There is only one safe basis upon which low rates can be made, and that is a low cost of producing the transportation. It is not and never can be a safe basis for the business of the country to be built upon [the idea that] the party that furnishes the transportation must furnish it at a loss. . . .

It is [believed] throughout the country that a rate once made is always a rate that is compulsory; that if a railway voluntarily makes a rate from one point to another . . . it follows that that rate . . . is a fair and compensatory rate. . . . It would be a very difficult thing to convince a judge or a jury that the railway could not make that rate under all conditions.

The conditions under which rates are made vary almost daily. . . . The railway is up against the proposition that if you ever make a rate that rate must stand for all time against you. And that alone goes further to hold up rates than anything else.

There is but one true basis for determining the reasonableness of a rate . . . and that is the value of the service. . . . Rates vary with conditions. They vary from day to day, almost. I was much struck by some of the questions [addressed to the previous witness] as to the difficulty in fixing what is a reasonable rate, by law. You are dealing with the questions that exist today. Can you apply the conditions that exist today to tomorrow or next week or next month? It is absolutely impossible. . . .[23]

A system in which the railroads would be deprived of the ability to discriminate in any situation, Hill declared, would be a great backward step. He explained that the great lumber trade of the Pacific Northwest was based on constructive discrimination:

If there were no discrimination the people would come down here in great throngs and ask you to authorize discriminations. We have to discriminate against ourselves. We discriminated against the lumber on the eastern end of our own road. . . . The road was finished [to Puget Sound] in 1893. In 1897 we were carrying about four trains a week eastward over the Cascade Mountains. We are now carrying four trains a day, and the lumbermen in the East have not suffered. We had to discriminate against them, because if you can not carry to market what the country produces . . . you will have nothing else to carry.

The only amendment to the Interstate Commerce Act Hill wanted was one which would exempt freight destined for export from the rules of the Commission, and he explained at length how and why that business would die, in fact was even then dying, without such relief. He pleaded eloquently for fair treatment of the railroads, for a recognition that their great power, on the whole, had been used well, and for a law which would leave railroad men with the power to

discharge the responsibilities that the country would continue to expect them to shoulder:

> We have not contaminated the air. We have not deprived [the government
> and the people] of any highway or byway they had before the railroad
> was built. We have not destroyed the water. We have given them better
> and cheaper facilities for communication than they had before. . . . Is
> there any reason why we should get a different measure of justice from
> any other class of property owners? It comes home to us. We feel that we
> are sort of outlaws. . . .

> Allow the railroad company, under the closest scrutiny of an intelligent
> Commission, to make the rate, and if they transgress in making the rate
> too high, take them to court. . . . But leave the ratemaking power with
> them. . . .[24]

In the next few months Hill prepared elaborate statistics to prove to
the Senators that, contrary to much irresponsible testimony which
they had heard, railroad rates on the Great Northern had been reduced
dramatically in the twenty-five years since the Manitoba road had
been formed. He cut rates further, and gave short shrift to less efficient competitors who resented his action, declaring that in the existing political climate the Great Northern could not do otherwise, whatever the impact on the profits of railroads like the Milwaukee. As the
legislative battle narrowed down to the question of judicial review
early in 1906, Spencer urged him to join top railroad officials from
other sections of the country at a secret meeting to plan last-ditch
strategy. It was to be held in a private dining room at the St. Regis
Hotel in New York, Spencer told him, adding, "It is suggested that no
inquiries be made at the desk, but that you go direct to the room.
. . ." W. P. Clough, however, told them they were wasting their time,
and he was right. In March Congress passed the Hepburn Act, giving
the ICC the right, upon complaint of shippers, to fix maximum rates
finally and absolutely, with no right of judicial review.[25]

To a railroad man who was also a free trader, the Hepburn Act was a
double insult, for Roosevelt was thought to have traded away tariff
reduction in return for the cooperation of conservative Senators on the
rate bill. But Hill seemed to place his faith in the ability of the ICC to
interpret the law intelligently, and did not agree with Charles E. Perkins's assertion that it was unconstitutional, although he admitted that
it would have been adjudged so five or ten years before. Nor did Hill
believe that a spiteful reaction, such as Henry L. Higginson recommended, would help. The main thing was to see to it that Hepburn

marked the high-water mark in regulation, and Hill agreed to continue his support of Spencer's lobbying organization. But Spencer was not to lead the fight against further legislation. Late in 1906 he and three friends, asleep in Spencer's private railroad car coupled to the end of a train which had stopped momentarily just south of Lynchburg, Virginia, were instantly killed when a following train plowed into theirs. Railroad men entered the most critical period in their history badly divided and without effective leadership.[26]

Hill had been predicting a severe business crisis for over a year when a brief but sharp panic gave the country clear warning, in October 1907, that its obsolete monetary and banking system had to be thoroughly remodeled. The following spring, with signs of business recovery beginning to appear, Hill told Senator Moses E. Clapp of Minnesota that he expected William Jennings Bryan to be nominated for a third try for the presidency, and that he would poll his largest vote ever. Meanwhile he wrote Robert Bacon, who was resting from his years of overwork at J. P. Morgan & Co. as Assistant Secretary of State, that he hoped the national attitude toward the railroads would take a constructive turn. Most important, the recession convinced Hill that the railroads could no longer do without a substantial general increase in rates.[27]

In the spring of 1908 railroad leaders agreed upon a step which had never even been considered before in the long, turbulent history of railroads: a general increase in freight rates. The carriers had come out of the depression of the 1890s with a seriously depressed average rate level, and while prices of labor and materials had risen steeply—from 30 to 50 per cent—between 1897 and 1907, railroad rates had climbed only about 7 per cent. How was this possible, inasmuch as the railroads had made good profits in these years? The answer, Hill knew, was, first, intensive utilization of the existing system, which was now feeling the strain; and, second, a truly spectacular increase in productivity per man-hour and per train-mile as a result of the rebuilding and re-equipping of the lines, a process which was far from complete and which, in fact, needed to be speeded up. To Hill, the rate constriction was a national problem which transcended mere politics. "I left Washington yesterday," he wrote Darius Miller of the Burlington on April 8, 1908, "having spent two days there. There is no question but the Interstate Commerce Commission and the administration would be willing to see rates generally advanced." The irrepressible George W.

At Billings, Montana, October 16, 1909, with Louis W. Hill, Sr. (right), and Howard Elliott, president of the Northern Pacific.

Perkins, minimizing the dangers of such a move, went to Washington to cultivate his old friend Roosevelt, and he felt he had the President's acquiescence. Both men had been misled. Writing from the summer White House at Oyster Bay, Long Island, late that summer, Roosevelt told Perkins that a general raise "is simply an invitation to an attack" during an election year, and he wrote his Attorney General, Charles J. Bonaparte, to begin an investigation under the antitrust law if the railroad men tried to ram their proposed general increase through.

It was all downhill thereafter. We shall never know whether the Hepburn Act, which empowered the ICC to lower rates that had turned out to be unreasonable, would have worked, for that progressive law was soon replaced by truly repressive legislation. The struggle of 1905–6 had demonstrated the political popularity of the railroad question to Albert B. Cummins, an Iowa Governor who wanted to be a Senator, and Robert M. La Follette, a Wisconsin Senator who wanted to be President, as well as a large number of other politicians, most of them from the West, who would soon challenge the conservative leadership of the Republican party and revel in the name Insurgent. When the bumbling railroad men, having for the most part dutifully supported William Howard Taft to succeed the "Boss Lunatic," renewed their efforts for a 10 per cent general rate increase early in 1910 they soon discovered that they had traded the pragmatism of TR for the anarchy of Taft. The new President had not seemed to be able to do anything right. Now he tried to out-Insurgent the Insurgents by getting an injunction against the increase on the ground of possible violation of the Anti-Trust Act. He had his Attorney General, George W. Wickersham, who was an even worse politician than Taft, draw up a new regulatory law for the guidance of Congress, and the Insurgents, incensed at this example of presidential "dictation," rammed through the Mann-Elkins Act. As the next seven months would prove, the new legislation made it impossible, as a practical matter, for railroad men to increase rates or even for the ICC to grant a raise out of sheer pity. For the railroads, it marked the end of the age of enterprise that had produced men like James J. Hill.[28]

VI

There they stood, their gaunt shapes towering over the squat sheds of the shipbuilders: the hulls of the two "big ships" with which Hill hoped to prove that the United States could build an Oriental trade. After the River St. John, the shipyard at New London, Connecticut, was the most likely place for the *Wacouta* to head on the pitifully few occasions when her commodore took her out. "We walked under them, over them, and around them," Mary wrote in her diary after the first of several inspection trips, and she might have recalled strolls on the bluff overlooking the lake at Milwaukee, nearly forty years before, when her fiancé had told her of his plans for the Orient.[29]

Hill knew that if the United States were to compete effectively with the subsidies and low wages of the English and Japanese who dominated the trans-Pacific carrying trade, his ships would have to be very big and very fast. They certainly were big—nearly three times the size of a standard Pacific freighter and able to carry 21,000 tons of cargo—and they were rated at fifteen knots. They would carry a few first and second class passengers, and the lower decks had many feet of space in which the narrow bunks, all that the Chinese immigrants would need or expect, could be installed. But their main excuse for being was to carry the great tonnages of cotton, wheat, and other commodities

Hill hoped to ship westward on the growing fleet of railroad cars that the eastward flow of lumber required. But how about the Panama Canal, and the Trans-Siberian Railroad? he was asked. He attached little importance to either. The Russian railroad was so badly built and incompetently run that it would never, in his opinion, deflect the flow of Oriental goods westward across Europe. As for Roosevelt's "big ditch," Hill was as proud of it as the next moderately chauvinistic American, but he had a hard time concealing his conviction that, economically speaking, it was a boondoggle. And if the railroads had been able to sustain their remarkable record of cutting costs of transportation in the early years of the twentieth century, the railroad "land bridge" between Europe and the Orient, which Hill dreamed of and which promised to become a reality in the last third of the century, would have proved him right in his own lifetime.[30]

The first of the big ships, the *Minnesota*, was launched on April 16, 1902, and her sister, the *Dakota*, about a year later. To the first launching, by special train provided by their host, came some 300 invited guests who cheered as Clara swung the bottle of champagne against the bow. Afterward, at a luncheon held in the cavernous loft of the shipbuilder, Thomas Burke, Hill's old friend and a leading citizen of Seattle, praised the great ships, which would soon make his city their home port, and the farsighted man who had brought them into being. The garrulous "Judge" Burke was briefer than usual that day because Nichols had got hold of a copy of his prepared remarks and cut it drastically in order not to delay return of the train to New York.[31]

The cherished dream began to fall apart almost immediately. It was a time of rapid change in the art of steam propulsion, on land and on sea. And just as the turbine made the mammoth power plant of New York City's new subway system obsolete even before the first giant piston slid in its cylinder, so it quickly turned the big ships into "Hill's white elephants." They were too slow, and they never navigated very well, especially under their temperamental American crews, who had a tendency to settle disputes with their fists. First Louis and then Walter were sent to see what the trouble was. Walter even made the tedious trip out to Hong Kong and back, and if he had ever had any maritime ambitions he was permanently cured of them. Both ships went into service in 1905, and before the year was out their speed was being regularly bested by others. The *Minnesota*, literally staggering from the multiple blows of faulty boilers, the La Follette Seaman's Act, and the insanities of American railroad rate regulation, was sold in 1915 to a company which used her to carry munitions to the beleaguered Allies.[32] The *Dakota* found a more dramatic end in 1907: she ran aground, a total loss, on the coast of Japan.

Even the White Queen might have found it hard to believe that the Interstate Commerce Commission would insist on applying to export rates its requirement that all railroad rates be published well in advance of their effective date. In order to get the business from an interior point in the United States via rail to Seattle and via one of the big ships to the Orient, the Great Northern had to be able to make a "through" rate, of which the land component would be considerably less than a shipper would pay if his freight were going no further than Seattle. And it had to be able to quote its rate on the spot, without advance notice, or else foreign carriers would undercut them on the water component, and take the business. The first requirement technically violated the strict law against discrimination, both as between shippers and as between the long and the short haul; the latter technically violated the advance notice rule. As far as the ICC was concerned, there was nothing technical about the violations, and Congress stubbornly refused to amend the law to make an exception for the export trade. Exports, which had grown since Hill, in cooperation with Japanese and English ships, had first begun to promote them, withered on the vine. By 1909 Hill had turned his back on his old dream, not without considerable bitterness, for he realized how few Americans really cared. "America is not a commercial nation," he said, "and until she has to make greater efforts to support her population than has been necessary in the past, I do not see how she will become important among the leading exporting nations of the world." [33]

VII

Railroad politics and the launching of the big ships were making a public man of Hill by 1905, but the process was greatly accelerated thereafter by his energetic support of better relations with Canada and the reciprocal trade agreement which had been under consideration for so many years. By 1902, with the last great land rush under way in the United States, Hill had predicted correctly that the tide of immigration between the two countries would be reversed as more Americans sought cheap farms in Manitoba. Behind his last great railroad building ventures in the Pacific Northwest, in fact, lay a desire to open central Oregon to this tide.[34] By 1905 he was convinced that trade relations between Canada and the United States had to be placed upon a special basis. As he told the president of the Illinois Manufacturers Association,

We are deliberately creating a trade rival where our second best customer should be found. . . . The farmers of Canada want to trade with us. They will do so if we allow them. . . . If we throw them back upon their own resources, they are not helpless. . . . Canada is capable of becoming our most formidable competitor; and that it will, unless our eyes are opened by intelligent self interest.[35]

In November of 1906 he made a speech on Canadian reciprocity before the Merchants Club of Chicago which drew widespread attention. "One blast from your bugle is worth a thousand from us students and literary men," James Ford Rhodes, the historian, wrote him. Two years later, as Roosevelt's administration neared its end, Hill told the prestigious New York Chamber of Commerce at its annual banquet that the United States would benefit from abolition of duties "on the natural products of both countries." A month thereafter he shared his views with President Nicholas Murray Butler of Columbia University and Sir James P. Whitney, premier of Ontario, before the Rochester Chamber of Commerce. The Canadians welcomed him enthusiastically as the reciprocity movement slowly gained momentum. In 1906, before the salmon-fishing began, he was feted in Ottawa by the Canadian Club at a reception and luncheon and that evening dined at Government House with the Governor General. It all made celebrity-loving Sam Hill, who went along, "very happy." Three years later, at his reunion with Donald Smith (Lord Strathcona and Mount Royal) in Winnipeg, Hill was more optimistic than ever.[36]

But, like constructive railroad regulation, tariff reciprocity is one of those measures which only a small segment of the electorate actively want, yet which carry politically dangerous overtones. American farmers, who saw Canada becoming a competitor in the world market and standing ready to flood the United States with its growing agricultural surplus, believed that they would lose more than they would gain. Hill argued earnestly that transportation economics ruled out the danger, but the argument was too sophisticated to neutralize the obvious demagogic potential of the anti-reciprocity stand. And Canadian capitalists and workers, for their part, feared to be deluged by American manufactured goods. The battle would not be easy, Mount Stephen told Hill, in a letter in which he enclosed a suspicious editorial from the London *Times*. Hill had the most politically adept man in his great organization, the shrewd and personable J. H. Carroll, nominally of the Burlington's law department in St. Louis, do some virtuoso lobbying in Washington. His chief target was Champ Clark of Missouri, leader of the Democrats in the House of Representatives and a presidential hopeful for 1912. "You captured soul, body and breeches of the minority leader," Carroll crowed after he had managed to get Hill and Clark together. But the indifference of Washington's leaders soon became clear. "The party that you dined with is not doing anything—not opposing and not pushing," Carroll wrote a week later.[37]

By February 1911 the battle lines were drawn, and, as Hill had feared, major opposition to the reciprocity measure in Congress had appeared in the Northwest. At a banquet in Minneapolis he seized the opportunity to plead his case: "I came to Minnesota to help build it up fifty-five years ago," he declared, "and if I did not think reciprocity with Canada would help Minnesota, I would not be here tonight." He carefully cultivated his long acquaintance with William Howard Taft, who had followed Roosevelt in the White House, from the day he jokingly wired the new President not to take his snowbound inauguration day as an evil omen for his administration. At Taft's request he went to the White House on several occasions to explain a knotty point in the arguments for and against reciprocity. He reasoned patiently with Knute Nelson, who wrote him complimentary, even affectionate replies and prepared to vote as common sense told him to. He persuaded a very brave economics professor from the University of North Dakota, James E. Boyle, to go to Washington and testify in favor of reciprocity. When the bill finally passed and was sent to the White House, Hill sent Taft an exultant telegram and received a grateful letter in return. In the end, however, it was all just one more bitter disappointment, for the Canadians, whose chauvinism was never less than a match for that of their southern cousins, decided that they could do very well without reciprocity and refused to ratify the treaty. Hill could only shrug and repeat what he had said so many times before, "Trade will go her own way, even though she must walk in leg irons."[38]

VIII

No foreign enemy that might invade our shores, Hill was fond of saying, posed as much potential danger to the United States as the inability of the nation to feed itself. No one who regularly watched the golden harvests of the Northwest from the platform of a Great Northern business car could count it a present danger, to be sure, but Hill was convinced that such a day was coming unless the nation mended its ways. Concern for the food supply, which has become fashionable in America in the last third of the twentieth century, was also a popular topic for a few years at the turn of the century. The natural population growth of the bustling nation, to which was added in the 1890s a spectacular flood of immigrants who tended for the most part to settle in the urban, industrial areas, led many to fear that the age of agricultural surpluses was drawing to a close. Serious observers of the process by which the North American continent had been occupied realized that the rise in food production owed nothing to better methods of farming or husbanding of the land resources. On the contrary, grain yields per acre had fallen as the Great Plains had become the center of production. These ruminations were the foundation of Hill's deep interest in the twin issues of soil conservation and scientific farming, interests which he had cherished since he was a young man and which, in the last decade of his life, led him squarely into the national spotlight.

Conservation and scientific farming were fields in which the knowledgeable amateur, like Hill, plunged as bravely as the most thoroughly trained scientist, for both fields were in their infancy. His work at North Oaks Farm, and the results he obtained at his huge bonanza farms in the Red River Valley, all of which he delighted in telling about at every opportunity, would have given him some stature as an authority even if he had not been the head of the greatest transportation agency serving the richest agricultural lands on the globe. By the time he was preparing to lay down the reins of day-to-day operation of the Hill roads, his old adversary, Theodore Roosevelt, with less than a year left as President, decided that he wanted Hill's advice and influence in a cause which had grown close to his own heart: the conservation of national resources. When Roosevelt called all of the nation's governors to the White House on May 13, 1908, for a Conference on the Conservation of Natural Resources, he also invited a few influential men from other walks of life to participate. To Hill he wrote, "In view of your experience in dealing with problems of transportation and the general confidence reposed in your judgment concerning the commercial development of the country, I should be pleased to have you participate in the Conference. . . ." When all had assembled, the President led them out to the front portico of the White House for the official photograph. The governors dutifully lined up on the steps behind the row of chairs which had been reserved for the celebrities: the President, flanked by Andrew Carnegie, John Mitchell of the United Mineworkers, the Chief Justice, and James J. Hill, who glared sideways with his good eye as the cameraman disappeared behind his black cloth.[39]

Inevitably, the Conference gave birth to a commission. This one was to have forty-eight members, of whom more than half were either politicians or government employees. Hill, invited to sit on the subcommittee on lands, accepted, but he told Gifford Pinchot, the elegantly educated forester who had been appointed chairman of the executive committee, that running the railroads would leave him no time in which to participate actively in committee work. What Hill wanted to see was neither conferences, nor committees, nor even educational programs, because to him there was no time to lose. He wanted action. As he told a man in Melrose, Minnesota, "It will not do to wait until the children grow up, go to the agricultural college and come back to the farm, fifteen or eighteen years hence. . . ."[40]

But what *was* conservation? Three-quarters of a century later, between the proponents of scientific forest management on the one hand and advocates of "forever wild" woodlands on the other, there was no unanimity on what conservation implies, and there was none in 1911, when Hill wrote Henry Wallace his views. To this influential Iowan, editor of *Wallace's Farmer*, father of a future Secretary of Agriculture, and grandfather of another who also became Vice President of the United States, he explained:

> Conservation should mean the saving of our resources for future use by providing for an economic, scientific and self-perpetuating present use of them. The locking up of resources indefinitely, the exclusion of the people from those natural sources of wealth to which they have a right to access, is not Conservation. It is now too often held to be so. . . . "They make a desert and call it Conservation," might be said of certain administrators. . . . I have always regarded the proper utilization of the soil as the first and most necessary item of Conservation.[41]

Like hungry ants before whom a picnic is spread, the politicians swarmed upon this fruit of others' labors and devoured it. With misgivings, Hill watched the first Conservation Congress convene at St. Paul. He welcomed the delegates with a blast against the proliferation of government at all levels, warning that it was just another example of the nation's chief malady, which was "not the high cost of living, but the cost of high living," then settled back to see whether anything good would come out of the meetings. His disappointment was not long in coming, and it was quickly dissolved in disgust and anger. From San Francisco and his triumphs as prosecutor in that wicked city's spectacular graft cases came Francis J. Heney to this springboard to fame. As a battery of straw-hatted telegraphic reporters, sitting at the foot of the rostrum, clicked away furiously at their keys, the delegates listened, open-mouthed. Disposing of the topic of conservation in a few sentences, Heney launched into a wild attack on James J. Hill and his "misuse" of sixty million acres of lands which Heney somehow thought had been granted to the Great Northern.

Heney's vicious attack had been prompted by Hill's denunciation of big government. This servant of the people had taken up the cudgels with all the fervor of the Progressive reformer who saw government as the last, best hope for the solution of men's problems. "He marshalled facts and figures, ridicule and irony, in an attack on the arguments of James J. Hill," gushed the *Pioneer Press*, "and divided with Gifford Pinchot the honors of the afternoon." Anything, the delegates may have thought, was an improvement over Pinchot's soppy beginning, for that gentleman, overcome with emotion as his life's dream of a great conservation movement became real, had blubbered, "I wish my mother were here." [42]

Hill, furious, composed a hot rejoinder to Heney's libels. "There is not a rag of truth to cover its nakedness," he thundered in the reply, which the *Pioneer Press* printed next day. "If Mr. Heney did not know the facts, [which have been] public property now for nearly fifty years, what shall the public call a man who brings to important occasions such incredible ignorance? If he did know them, what still shorter and more unpleasant name does he deserve?" To J. H. Carroll, the Burlington's man in Washington, he reported that "the conservation congress broke up in a row; the attempt to run the entire thing for the benefit of personal politicians sent the delegates of the Western States away from the convention. . . ." When Wallace wrote him the following spring for a contribution to the fund to print the proceedings of the congress, he let the newspaper man feel the full impact of his indignation. He was for conservation as strongly as ever, he said, but he would waste no more time on such sterile activities as conferences and committees, congresses and conventions. [43]

IX

The problems of agriculture, Hill had begun to realize, were as much sociological as scientific. In company with many other men and women of good will whose faith in the power of education to lift an entire people had been unbounded, he was flabbergasted to see that the young men—and a few of the women—of the farming areas were indeed using the greatly expanded college and university system to lift themselves right out of farming and into urban occupations. Noting that agriculture, railroading, mining, construction, and practically every other line of work in the Northwest were suffering from a lack of manual labor, he commented that "the children of the farmer are mostly ambitious to get an education with the idea that it will enable them to live without actual work." Having lived his entire life in an era in which farming methods had hardly been improved, but, on the contrary, had deteriorated, he could see only eventual famine in the growing movement from farm to city. Not realizing that the farm boy who took an engineering degree might eventually do more to raise farm output by his work in the chemical fertilizer and insecticide industries, which did not yet exist, or in the designing of better farm machinery, than the addition of two men to the farm population would do, he wrung his hands over the situation. Like many others who cling to the idea of virtue in the soil, he could not divorce the economic from the moralistic. To Sir Horace Plunkett, a knowledgeable Irishman whose country had been wrestling with the problem for a century, he wrote, "There is no other question which bears so directly on the comfort, well-being and prosperity of so many people as the improvement of rural life, and the keeping of the population on the soil and away from the large cities." [44]

To those who did choose to remain on the farm, Hill's advice was very simple: they had to farm better, and they had to do so right away. He first claimed national attention in 1906 with a speech at the Minnesota State Fair that was later widely read in *World's Work* magazine as "What We Must Do To Be Fed." From then almost to the end of his life he followed the county and state fair trail, spreading his gospel. Each fall, many of the farmers of Minnesota, the Dakotas, and Montana who brought their exhibits, their wives, and their excited children into town for the fair, went back home with the memory of a stocky, grizzled man in a slightly squashed western-style homburg, swinging down from the platform of a special train and, sometimes

Speaking to a group of farmers at Wenatchee, Washington. October 1905.

followed by a dignified woman, climbing into the best automobile that the community could muster for a boisterous ride to the fairgrounds. There, to a forest of derbies and artificial flowers, his fist pounding the palm of his hand, "Jim" Hill expounded his program: rotate your crops; diversify into livestock; fertilize your lands with the manure the livestock will produce; select better seed; and learn how to prepare the ground and cultivate your land in the most scientific manner.[45]

Hill believed that the rewards of better farming lay not only in the future, but also in the present. He did not preach sacrifice by the present generation for their young people, knowing the economic and psychological limitations on such a philosophy. As for pushing back the frontiers of knowledge, he decried the tendency of college agricultural experiment stations to make this their first order of business. The work these schools were doing did not seem to be focussed on the practical problems whose solution would bring immediate rewards and thus stimulate broader interest in scientific farming. He wanted to bring home to the average farmer, in a dramatic way he could not ignore, the large rewards of relatively slight improvements in farming methods. A model farm of not more than thirty or forty acres in every rural congressional district would be the most effective tool, he believed. And when the experiment stations failed to change their ways, he did not hesitate to condemn them in his speeches and strike out on his own. In 1912 the Great Northern, at Hill's direction, inaugurated several hundred demonstration plots on farms along the railroad and established its Agricultural Extension Department to oversee them.

Meanwhile the universities, which had their own breed of zealot, plunged ahead in the exciting new fields of soil and plant chemistry. Hill might never have lived to learn how much men like him needed this kind of basic research if it had not been for Cyril G. Hopkins of the University of Illinois Experiment Station. Hopkins, a "real fighter" in the words of one who has studied his work, was deeply disturbed that an influential, newsworthy man like Hill was retailing the ideas of certain highly placed charlatans that crop rotation actually enriched the soil, or Hill's own notion that manure was the best fertilizer available. At dinner with James R. Forgan, president of the First National Bank of Chicago, Hopkins was excited to learn that the banker was a good friend of Hill's, and asked him to bring them together. "He is very desirous of meeting you and having an hour or two's talk with you," Forgan wrote Hill next day. "To put it plainly, he thinks that in some matters you have been misinformed in connection with the rotation of crops." Hopkins knew that Hill was about to publish a book which would get widespread attention, so he was willing to meet him in Chicago, or to ride east on the train with him (he had to go east anyway), if necessary, to have a talk with him. It was the beginning of a relationship which gradually converted Hill to Hopkins's ideas. Hill ordered carloads of representative Northwestern soils shipped to St. Paul for intensive study. Soon the greenhouses at 240 Summit Avenue where he had once dabbled briefly with orchids had been transformed into an agronomical laboratory.[46]

Looking backward from the era of the Great Depression, when much of the Northern plains lay prostrated by a decade of overproduction followed by one of drought and the dust storms of the 1930s, historians have questioned the social worth of Hill's agricultural development work. The extreme view is that railroad men, in a selfish quest for profits, built railroads which lured men and women into areas that were not fit for farming and where, once the rainfall cycle turned against them, they were ruined. Professional controversialists like to have it both ways. During Hill's lifetime he had been accused of try-

Addressing some farmers from the observation platform of business car A-1 at Litchfield, Minnesota. Spring 1914. From a photograph by Harry Williams, 14, a contestant in Hill's corn-plot project.

ing to destroy the wheat-growing economy of the Northwest with his ideas about livestock diversification. None of this bothered Hill much, since the most energetic of the activist organizations, the Farmers' Alliance, supported his activities enthusiastically.[47]

Hill always knew that farming beyond the Red River Valley, especially in the semi-arid tablelands of Montana, would be a gamble calling for a degree of foresight which the American farmers had seldom displayed. He warned that it would probably be necessary to allow much of the land to lie fallow every third year to preserve the scarce moisture, a technique which eventually became universal. Irrigation, he felt, was the only way in which much of the land could be farmed, and he urged that this technique be thoroughly studied. With care, he believed, the deep, rich soils of northern Montana could be put to intelligent use. Sooner or later, he knew, the steady stream of immigration which was passing up Montana for lands in Washington and Oregon would turn to the dry plains. He was eager for them to settle Montana, and when they did, he could only pray that they would do so intelligently.[48]

X

Hill went to his office in the Great Northern building at his usual time
on September 16, 1908. He had agreed to place himself that afternoon
in the hands of a group of old-time employees of the railroad who
were making plans in which he figured importantly. Obviously, it was
some kind of celebration in honor of his seventieth birthday. But they
were up to something unusual, as anyone who observed the whispers
of the office staff could see. At three o'clock he strolled across the street
to Union Station, and in a few minutes the men unveiled their surprise. Freshly painted and polished for the occasion, its diamond stack
belching smoke and hauling a single coach from the days of the old St.
Paul & Pacific, the William Crooks chugged into the station. Its tender
was piled high with firewood and the ornate No. 1, symbol of its place
on the locomotive roster of the Great Northern, was proudly displayed. Seventy men, all of whom had been hard at work on the St.
Paul & Pacific on the day that it had become the Manitoba road
twenty-nine years before, welcomed their guest of honor aboard, and
the old engine headed out the Lake Minnetonka branch. After a banquet followed by many speeches and reminiscences at the old Lafayette Hotel, Hill told reporters that it was one of the happiest evenings of his life.[49]

Hill's incisive prose style, so thoroughly exercised over a lifetime of
letter writing and now well mellowed by his years, seemed to demand
a wider audience. There was so much Hill wanted to say. When a perfect stranger wrote to ask him for his "philosophy of life," he dashed
off a reply in the optimistic vein of the age:

> I have always lived the life of a man endeavoring to be usefully busy. The
> working hours are those in which there is necessary work to be done,
> whatever time that may require. Spare hours are well spent upon the
> study of history, literature and art. Whatever any able mind or great ge-
> nius has given for the instruction or enjoyment of the world is worth
> while. In books and pictures, as in practical things, only the best are
> worth anyone's time and attention. . . .
>
> The boy or girl who is taught to be obedient and affectionate and consid-
> erate of others, and who receives, after leaving the home, such education
> as the best schools and universities have to offer, has all the preparation
> for life that it is possible to give. . . .
>
> There are no new recipes for success in life. Get knowledge and under-
> standing. Determine to make the most possible of yourself by doing such

useful work as comes your way. Some opportunity will come at some time to every man. Then it depends upon him, what he makes of it, and what it will make of him.[50]

He soon had his chance to reach a larger audience, for there were others who realized that he had become a public man. As the long Minnesota winter came to its end early in 1909, once again he found himself all alone in the great house, writing to Clara, who was at Jekyl Island with Mary. "I am trying to persuade myself that my solitariness is my way of keeping Lent," he joked; "I have spent my evenings reading and writing—the latter for a book, which I may show you sometime."

Among the perceptive men of the publishing world who had watched with interest Hill's growing fame was Walter Hines Page, former editor of the influential magazines *Forum* and *Atlantic,* and by 1908 a partner in Doubleday, Page & Co. He urged Hill to adapt his speeches to book form, "grouped around certain large subjects," and let Doubleday publish them. A few weeks later Hines had matured the idea even further. The highly successful magazine he had founded some years before, *World's Work,* was the ideal place for the chapters of the book to appear first. Among its subscribers he would reach an audience that might never go out and buy his book. With the help of Joseph G. Pyle, former editor of the defunct St. Paul *Globe,* Hill went energetically to work, and the first article appeared in the fall of 1909. "I think that no other subject in any other magazine has attracted so much attention and so much discussion in every part of the world," Hines exulted the following spring. By that time the book, *Highways of Progress,* was coming off the press.[51]

He had toiled over the introduction until he finally distilled into it the optimism that had sustained him over a period of more than fifty years. The book was a challenge to Americans everywhere, and in all callings, to address themselves to a rational solution of those problems which barred the way to indefinite material and spiritual progress:

> Nations, like men, are travellers. Each one of them moves, through history, toward what we call progress and a new life or toward decay and death. As it is the first concern of every man to know that he is achieving something, advancing in material wealth, industrial power, intellectual strength and moral purpose, so it is vital to a nation to know that its years are milestones along the way of progress.
>
> About this conviction centre much of our public thought, most of our public discussion, nearly all of our public action. . . . Down to within a

century [the] study of ways and means dealt almost wholly with abstractions. It sought to establish certain general principles and universal laws. . . . But the application of a system of unchanging laws to those variable quantities, man and society, proved unworkable. . . .

This has been followed by a period of almost pure empiricism in our economic thought and conduct. Each incident, each danger and each need has been isolated, enlarged and studied alone, with little regard to the organic relation between the different interests in the life of man. . . . The result is conflict, confusion, failure and waste of material and mental forces. . . . There is great need of a broader understanding of the relation of one interest to another in the social life of man; of their interdependence as well as their separate values; of the community as an economic whole. . . .

This volume does not attempt to cover the immense field; but simply . . . to erect here and there, along the road the nation travels, certain signboards where the ways diverge and mark them, "Highways of Progress." The effort may not be successful, but it is at least sincere. . . .

Facts, and powerful analysis of those facts—the technique which had seldom failed him in a lifetime of dealing with problems that had often seemed larger than any possible solution—are the basis of the book. The sixteen chapters embrace nearly all of the major subjects that he had wrestled with throughout his life: agriculture, relations with Canada, foreign and domestic commerce, the operation and financing of railroads, conservation, and, most elusive of all, the relationship of the state to economic activity. *Highways of Progress* was a notable success for such a serious book, and it was prominently and favorably reviewed in the *New York Times Book Review:*

Mr. Hill long ago made manifest in his public addresses, in his occasional writings, and especially in his practical activities, that he possesses in high degree the quality of imagination . . . without which no man can be great. . . . He was one of the first of our great railroad makers to plan his work—to see the vision of vast miles of country as they might be, and then go to work patiently to make the vision real. . . .

It was this address [1906, reproduced as Chapter 1] that turned President Roosevelt's attention to the subject of conservation as a whole. What he says on this subject deserves the widest possible study and discussion.

[On the railroad question] he manifests a fairness, a sense of justice, an ability to see the question in its due proportions and its vital relations upon both sides. . . . The book cannot fail to have an effect at once stimulating and sobering upon general thought.[52]

Honors for a life well lived were coming in too fast for a man who had so much left to do. He had gone to Seattle in June, 1909 to speak at the opening of the Alaska-Yukon-Pacific Exposition, and was to join Judge Burke afterward but lost him in the crowd of well-wishers that surrounded him. "What has become of the leisure that you were going to have?" chided Burke, who found that Hill had gone back East the same evening. Three weeks later the leading Seattle citizens revealed that they were about to unveil a bronze bust of him on a pedestal on the state university campus, and they expected him to be present. But by that time Hill was on the opposite edge of the continent, immersed in entirely different matters. He did consent to go to New Haven in June 1910 to receive the honorary doctor of laws degree from Yale, and found it even more of an ordeal than he had expected. Jane Addams, who was on the platform with him, looked cool as her doctoral hood was placed on her shoulders, but Hill was miserable in his academic regalia. "I am sending you my new gown," he joked to Mary, "which may serve you as an automobile garment, although the hat and hood may not be so useful." [53]

His special relationship to the Scandinavians of the Northwest was soon a part of the national folklore. "Yem Hill" almost became one word in the lexicon of Minnesotans living north and west of the Twin Cities, and at least one new American addressed a letter to him just that way.[54] Someone sent him a Swedish dialect poem, composed by an Irishman, which precisely captured the admiration of the Swedes and the Norwegians for their famous fellow Minnesotan, and their own determination to emulate his courage and stubbornness:

> Ve got little faller har,
>   Name ban Yem;
> Das whole ralroad over dar
>   Blong to him. . . .
>
> Fallers laugh ven he come har,
>   Das man Yem;
> But he ain't ban fraid for scare,
>   Not for hem.
> Call das ralroad strak o' rust
>   An say Yem vill go clean bust;
> But he keep still and he yust
>   Vork for Yem.
>
> Val, Ay tal you Ay don laugh,
>   Ay explode

Van his inyine kal my calf
    On das road. . . .
An he wrote me letter, too,
    An say: "Ole, Ay lak you,
An how much you tenk ban due
    On das calf?" . . .

Val, Ay got my gude hard mun
    From das Yem,
An Ay lat das ralroad run
    Yust for hem;
An Ay tenk das Nortvest har
    Yump ahead gude many yar
Yust by not ban fraid for scare,
    Me and Yem.[55]

19
"The Way For Me To Quit Is To Quit"

Most men who have really lived have had, in some shape, their great adventure. This railway is mine.

—James J. Hill, 1912

I

D. C. Shepard, who had built thousands of miles of railroads in the Upper Midwest, was growing quite feeble by 1910, but he still managed to get to his beloved Georgia in the winter. Basking in the warm sun of late February, he scribbled a letter to his famous friend in St. Paul. He apologized for the pencil—"It is so *easy*," he explained—as he told Hill of the impressive news about the Great Northern, the Northern Pacific, the Burlington, and their many affiliates that filled the pages of the newspapers. "My first Minnesota love of 1857 is surely making a great record," he wrote, recalling through the mists of half a century the shovels of earth he had helped to turn on the first thousand feet of Minnesota's first railroad. "I am proud of it and of *you* who have done so much to accomplish it."

The first decade of the new century had brought Hill and the railroads he controlled something less than total dominance of the Pacific Northwest. But in one way or another he, his friends, and his erstwhile adversaries had achieved a mature, stabilized relationship between three vast Western railroad interests: the Hill roads, the Harriman properties, and the sprawling Canadian Pacific system. The stability of the transportation system was the most important factor in the rational development of one of the fastest growing areas of North America. Beginning with acquisition of the Burlington in 1901, Hill had shown his willingness to challenge Harriman's Union Pacific-Southern Pacific empire at the strategic line of the Columbia River. In the decade that followed he had gone on to force a compromise that gave the Hill roads as good an entrance to the Southern Pacific's jealously guarded empire south of the river as Harriman had grasped, during the confused years of the late 1890s, for his roads north of it. The cost had been great, and not only in money, for during this hectic decade Mary Hill and most of her husband's many friends came to realize that he never intended to lay his burdens down.[1]

By the middle of the decade Hill saw that the most optimistic of the predictions he had made to Mount Stephen, Farrer, and other supporters during the gloomy days of the 1890s depression had been conservative. "Our whole enterprise [is] growing faster than our present plans cover," he cabled Farrer in May 1906, and he urged his friend to spare some time during his approaching trip to America for long, private conversations about the future at Hill's salmon-fishing lodge in Quebec. Traffic density—total tonnage divided by the total mileage of the system—on the Great Northern had eclipsed that of older and once stronger Midwestern roads like the Chicago North Western and the Milwaukee. Both of those roads, in fact, had finally begun to realize that a railroad without its own line to the Pacific faced an uncertain future. The Milwaukee, which, during the crucial decade of the 1880s had had the best chance of all Midwestern railroads to become a transcontinental, had wallowed in indecision for twenty years. Finally, in 1901, after the era of low-cost railroad building had passed forever, the Milwaukee decided to extend its line from the railhead in South Dakota to Puget Sound.[2]

Hill was of two minds about the Milwaukee's move. In private he sometimes deplored the extension, declaring to Robert Bacon that "it is hardly probable that [the extension] would enable that company to secure . . . one-third of the total business." To George B. Harris he rationalized, on the other hand, that completion of another transcontinental railroad to Seattle might make Puget Sound a more important port than San Francisco. "If I were the head of the North Western or the [Milwaukee]," he admitted, "I would never be satisfied with a connection over some other line . . . [and] I have no idea that the existing lines can carry the business to and from the West Coast in the next ten or fifteen years. . . ." To Mount Stephen, he was all calm confidence: "These two lines [the Chicago North Western and the

Milwaukee] were all right for a time, until the transcontenental lines began to dominate the situation . . . And they will remain [at the mercy of their competitors] until they build a line to the coast, which I hope they will do . . . and in the end do us much more good than harm." [3]

The birth of this third Northern transcontinental, where two decades before a single line had found the going difficult, forced Hill to tighten his grasp on the traffic to and from the booming Pacific Northwest. Eastern Washington State had become a leading wheat-growing area, and Hill noted that because this grain tended to flow to Gulf Coast ports for export, and the Burlington was in danger of losing as much as one-half of its grain traffic. In 1905 he instructed his son James N. to make a thorough study of transportation routes from Denver to the Texas Gulf Coast areas, which led to the acquisition of the Colorado and Southern lines to Galveston in 1908. Meanwhile Hill accepted the fact that the best fuel in the age of steam was the coal which lay in such incredible quantities beneath the fertile fields of southern Illinois. It was the end of Hamilton Browne's dream of a coal empire in Iowa and, in Hill's lifetime, of Hill's own hopes for the coal of Montana and southern Canada, when the Burlington acquired its own line southward through the coal towns of southern Illinois to Paducah, Kentucky. Before long Hill was astonishing his friends with the information that the Burlington now had a higher traffic density on its north-south axis than on its east-west lines. To the casual observer, James J. Hill was still firmly identified with the Great Northern, but he and a growing number of his associates knew that the brightest jewel in their collection was the Burlington. Meanwhile, the Far Western end of the system, at Portland, had become the weakest part of the whole, and, once the moral imperative for collaboration with Harriman had been removed in 1904–5, Hill intended to do something about the situation. [4]

II

"The joint line north of the Columbia is growing in importance and length," Hill wrote Gaspard Farrer in the fall of 1906. "It will run from Spokane to Portland and thence to Puget Sound and later the mouth of the Columbia River, in all about 600 miles . . . and will cost . . . from $40 million to $45 million. . . ." Farrer and his fellow bankers all but fainted at the price tag which Hill placed on this child of his old age,

Showing the Pacific Northwest to two powerful New Yorkers: Charles Steele (left), of J. P. Morgan & Co., and George F. Baker, Sr., chairman of the First National Bank of New York, at Portland, Oregon, May 5, 1910.

and they eventually withdrew from a major role in its financing. It certainly was a lot more money than the $5 million which, Hill had bragged to Harriman in 1899, was all he needed to build a "north bank" line that would be far superior to the Union Pacific's aging Oregon Railway & Navigation Company. But inflation had caught up with Hill, as it had caught up with the Milwaukee Railroad. And he was about to relearn the principle of railroading which he had preached in the 1880s: that a railroad's success was in direct proportion to the closeness with which its affairs are looked after.[5]

The first task was to remove Harriman's forces from the north bank of the Columbia, where they had been pretending for several years to build a railroad. Hill went into action on two fronts. Into the valley he sent 300 teams in the spring of 1906 to begin the earthmoving work, which was to turn out to be far heavier than anyone had anticipated. And in Washington, D.C., he put C. W. Bunn, the able general counsel of the Northern Pacific, and W. P. Clough, who was still looking after the Great Northern's affairs in the East, to work on getting Congress to pass a law declaring that the Harriman venture had forfeited its clearance to build through federal lands. Clough found that "our friend, Hansbrough" (Minnesota Senator Henry Clay Hansbrough, Chairman of the Committee on Public Lands) required a great deal of persuading before Hill finally had clearance to actually build a railroad where the Union Pacific had only dawdled.[6] The work was pushed rapidly by the Northern Pacific and the Great Northern, which were to own the new Spokane, Portland & Seattle Railroad jointly. Despite the mention of Seattle in the name, Hill had no intention of building another line from Portland to Seattle, choosing instead to double track the old Northern Pacific line. Extended to Astoria, where the Columbia empties into the Pacific, the Spokane, Portland & Seattle was to connect with a line of fast coastal steamships which Hill believed would take as much business from the Union Pacific's heartland as the Union Pacific was taking from what he considered his own province, north of Portland.[7]

But the Spokane, Portland & Seattle was a long time living up to his expectations for it. A year later Howard Elliott, the hard-driving Easterner who had done so much to relieve Hill's mind about the proper operation of the Northern Pacific, reported that most of his line's traffic still seemed to be going across the Cascade Range. Since the Spokane road was intended to take the Northern Pacific and the Great Northern to tidewater at Portland without their having to cross the mountains, this was a severe disappointment to Hill, who had constantly preached that "what that line wants, with its capacity to haul traffic at low cost, is a heavy traffic; the rates are of less consequence than the volume of business."[8]

But what hurt even more was the excessive cost of the new line—at least $10 million over the original estimate—and the realization that he had lost control of the undertaking, something that he had never done before where so much was at stake. As he confessed to George F. Baker,

> There has been a great deal of money spent which can never be recovered.
> . . . If I had at all supposed that the construction was being carried on as

subsequent reports had shown, I would have tried to have cured it at the time, but I had no idea. . . . On the whole it is the most unsatisfactory thing that has ever occurred in my experience.[9]

The truth was that he was having a difficult time financing the last section of the line, and when Farrer turned down his request for a loan of $5 million on his own signature until satisfactory long-term arrangements could be made, he was mortified. Meanwhile, the strong, able men whom he had placed in charge of the Northern Pacific objected to the accounting statement which Hill rendered them for their share of the joint venture. For months the lawyers of the two companies argued back and forth while Hill fumed at the delay. George F. Baker, who played an important role in forming Northern Pacific policy, finally dressed him down for the increasingly accusatory tone of his letters. "There is not a member of the [Northern Pacific executive] Committee who would for a moment submit to the GN being 'outrageously wronged to the extent of millions of dollars,' " Baker retorted. Then, realizing how deeply Hill's pride had been wounded by the Spokane affair, he added, "It disturbs me that you should have so much worry over this matter." [10]

Charles Steele, also stung by the efforts of Great Northern officials to make the Northern Pacific appear remiss in the project, was equally frank in telling Hill where his problem lay. "One of the great difficulties about a man who has attained such a position as you have is the practical impossibility of getting accurate information, for all the people who are around you are naturally anxious to tell you something which would be agreeable rather than the exact facts [which are] not quite so pleasant," he preached. But Steele was not altogether right, for Hill knew one man who would tell him the truth come what may, and he had managed to get him back to carry through one more project.

John F. Stevens had compiled a remarkable record since he left the Great Northern in 1903. After two years as chief engineer with the Rock Island, he had gone to the Canal Zone to save Theodore Roosevelt's favorite project. It was Hill, in fact, who urged the President to turn to Stevens, and his faith was not misplaced. For it was Stevens who whipped the Panama Canal project into shape, supplied Dr. William C. Gorgas with the resources he needed to eliminate yellow fever, and calmly made a hard decision from which lesser men had shrunk: to drop the plans for a sea-level canal. Stevens recommended a canal with a series of locks, which would be less impressive and slower of transit, but which could be dug in the lifetimes of those involved.

From Panama he had returned East to supervise the electrification of the New Haven Railroad's lines north of New York. Hill rushed Stevens out to Puget Sound, where he first ascertained that the problem of the Spokane, Portland & Seattle was its thoroughly incompetent president—he fired him—and then turned his attention to the real work Hill had sent him out to do.[11]

By the end of the first decade of the new century central Oregon was the last untapped center of great agricultural promise in the region. The Southern Pacific, which ran along the rich western slope of the Cascade Range through Eugene, was content in its monopoly of rail service between San Francisco and Portland. At the base of the eastern slope of the Cascades, however, was the canyon of the Deschutes River, a possible but most unlikely route up which someone might someday decide to build a railroad from a point on the Columbia at about The Dalles. Harriman's men had done a little work on the route, but after the Panic of 1907 activity had ceased. Hill decided in 1909 that the Canyon was the key with which he could unlock the potential traffic of central Oregon and, perhaps in combination with George Gould, provide an independent inland route to San Francisco that would smash the Southern Pacific's monopoly. This was what Stevens went to the Northwest in 1909 for, putting up at one fleabag hotel after another, talking big deals with ranchers whose lands were strategically located, and settling those deals with a checkbook that seemed inexhaustible.[12]

There is a breed of historian for whom the saga of the West cannot possibly be too hairy-chested, and to them the story of this last confrontation between Hill and Harriman before Harriman's premature death quickly became the "Deschutes Canyon War." There was no violence, although for a time it was threatened as each group frantically sought to turn more of the narrow, twisted ravine into a railroad route than did the other. The natural outcome was joint occupation of the line, which Hill worked out the following year with "Judge" Robert S. Lovett, who had succeeded to the dead Harriman's leadership of the Union Pacific-Southern Pacific railroads, and his able lieutenant, Julius Kruttschnitt. Stevens remained in the Northwest for a short while to integrate the new line northward into the Spokane line, but the fun was over, the challenge exhausted, and the age of compromise in full sway, so by 1911 he left for new adventures. As for Hill, he made one more strenuous effort—this one less successful and more costly than all the rest—to confirm his dominance of the Pacific Northwest.[13]

Driving the last spike on the Oregon Trunk Railway. Burlington Northern.

III

At least Hill had known where he stood with Harriman. Both men played the game according to the same set of rules, as far as the law was concerned. But the Canadian Pacific, which was as much of an upsetting factor during the decade of prosperity as it had ever been in the hungry days of the 1890s, hid behind the wall of the international boundary, from which it raided the territory to the south. Free to make whatever rates it liked, the Canadian Pacific horned in on the rich transcontinental traffic between terminals in the United States. Its agents boldly solicited freight in Seattle, Tacoma, Portland, and even San Francisco, carried it north in its ships, placed it on the rails at Vancouver and—most insulting of all—frequently transferred it to its American subsidiary, the Soo line, which dipped down from Saskatchewan to the Twin Cities, the very heart of Hill's empire. In 1909 the Soo bought control of the Wisconsin Central route to Chicago, which the Northern Pacific had gotten rid of years before as part of its reorganization therapy. It was not much of a line to Chicago, but in combination with the other Soo lines and the Canadian system it made the Canadian Pacific a fearsome competitor for through traffic between the East and the Pacific Northwest. These developments were all the more galling when Hill reflected that both Mount Stephen and Strathcona had once begged him to take the Soo off their hands!

William C. Van Horne had managed to maintain good relations with Hill despite the growing tensions of competition. This was owing, in good measure, to Van Horne's remarkable forbearance, his understanding of Hill's motivations and tactics, and his determination not to let business poison their personal relations. In the early 1880s, when Hill's general manager, Manvel, had worried that tensions between Van Horne and Hill which had developed during the early years of the Canadian Pacific's construction might affect relations between the Canadian Pacific and the Manitoba road, Van Horne had reassured him: "When I damn you or him for your numerous sins, as, unhappily, you give me frequent occasion to do, I beg to assure you that you are damned in a strictly official sense."

It was, rather, the Canadian Pacific's pressing need to share in United States transcontinental traffic that led Van Horne to press his competitive edge so fiercely. (And he did have the edge, for there was little traffic for the Great Northern to take away from the Canadians.) By the end of the 1890s, however, Van Horne was losing patience. He was tired of Hill's tactics, which consisted of interminable talk around the edges of a subject, during which he hoped that his adversary, out of impatience or sheer exhaustion, would cave in and give him what he wanted. After one such session in Montreal in 1894, Hill would have missed his train to St. Paul if his host had not rushed him to the railroad station. Van Horne wrote Mount Stephen cynically about Hill's farewell speech:

> Taking me by the arm, he said, "Van, it is a very nice thing that although we may disagree about business matters, our personal relations are so pleasant. We would do anything for each other." (The skunk.) [14]

Four years later, having finally induced Van Horne, with the help of great pressure from Mount Stephen, to relinquish the Duluth & Winnipeg Railroad, Hill appeared to be surveying new lines in Manitoba and the Kootenay district of British Columbia, the Canadian Pacific's softest points. Much upset, Van Horne went to St. Paul "and had two long interviews with him, which resulted in nothing but hunger and fatigue." Hill, for his part, claimed that the Northern Pacific was the guilty party, and that the Manitoba activity was "a wild move on the part of 'that lunatic Mellen.' " This, Van Horne thought, was an insult to his intelligence, for he was certain, in that year of 1898, that Hill was calling the tune on the Northern Pacific. "We are now quite at a loss to know how to deal with Mr. Hill," he wrote Mount Stephen. "His statements and promises are absolutely worthless. . . . We have lost the only arm that he was afraid of [the Duluth & Winnipeg] and we must somehow replace it with an equally effective one. . . ." Three weeks later Van Horne wrote Mount Stephen in great embarrassment that he had learned that Hill was not in control of the Northern Pacific after all. But the damage had been done, and for the rest of his life Hill's attitude toward the Canadian Pacific would be one of controlled aggression. It would cost the Hill lines many millions of dollars in hopeless investments, and load upon the Canadian system, already fully occupied with parrying the blows of a hostile Liberal government at home, an additional burden.[15]

Hill's retaliations took two forms. Into Manitoba the Great Northern and, with Hill's full support, the Northern Pacific, built lines to tap the east-west traffic of the Canadian Pacific. Eventually the Great Northern even had its own line from the boundary to Winnipeg. But it was to southeastern British Columbia that Hill carried the struggle with the least profit to all concerned. At the turn of the century he sent James N. to get control of a railroad that was inching eastward from Vancouver to the Kootenay district. The economic value of the coal and other mineral deposits in the region were already being questioned, but Hill proceeded to build railroads in the area while at the same time he sought to assure them of traffic by buying control of the coal mines at Crows Nest Pass and nonferrous metals workings at Granby. The Canadian Pacific, of course, retaliated with its own lines in the area, and what ensued was an east-west arrangement not unlike that which Hill had had to settle for in the Deschutes Canyon. The difference was that Hill's railroad ventures into these isolated parts of Canada amounted to very little. At the height of the Canadians' own railroad mania in 1906, when they were already engaged in building two new transcontinentals for which they had little need, Hill bandied it about that he intended to build his own transcontinental between Vancouver and Winnipeg. "We expect . . . that the Grand Trunk or Canadian Pacific, or both, will be glad to carry all the business we can give them from the west to eastern Canada," he wrote a man in Montreal; "of course, we always have the line to Lake Superior in reserve. . . ." A great railroad building career was threatening to end not with a bang, but a bluster.[16]

IV

As the Progressive era unfolded, the challenge was rapidly being drained from railroading for men like Hill. After trying unsuccessfully to head off laws which gave the Interstate Commerce Commission the power to fix specific maximum rates for the railroads, he had watched a group of lawmakers ram through regulatory legislation which threatened to be truly repressive. The Mann-Elkins Act of 1910 not only gave the ICC the power to suspend a rate increase pending investigation, but it also placed upon the railroads the burden of proof of the reasonableness of the higher rate. Since the commissioners themselves had admitted on the record some years before that no objective proof of reasonableness of rates existed, it did indeed appear that the real purpose of the Act was to fasten a ceiling on railroad rates and keep it there, come what may.

That is exactly what happened. Between 1910 and 1917 railroad men tried time after time to get moderate general increases in rates, with virtually no success. Meanwhile the inflation rolled on, and while each dollar the railroads took in was worth less and less, traffic grew relentlessly, demanding fresh capital which was increasingly hard to get. Labor pressed its demands for big increases in wages—the men, too, had been hurt by the inflation—and few doubted that they would get them. The tragic, ludicrous impasse was finally resolved by the demands of World War I, but to Hill it marked the end of an era in which a man of enterprise, willing to shoulder great risks and expecting to wield great discretionary power, could contribute to American transportation. He had seen the end coming as early as the Northern Securities decision. "By the time you're forty," he advised Louis, "be out of the railroad business." [17]

Hill's favorite photograph with "Lou." On the station platform at Billings, Montana, October 16, 1909.

But meanwhile there was a railroad to run, a "very big farm," indeed, as Mount Stephen had called the Great Northern-Northern Pacific-Burlington system. New problems arose, and all of the old ones remained. The jerry-built American monetary system brought more grief in the fall of 1907, but Hill was ready. George F. Baker had warned him in August that "Wall St. is in condition to swallow whole almost anything bearish," and Hill put well-oiled emergency machinery into action to assure Northwestern farmers and middlemen that there would be sufficient funds to keep the grain and other crops moving to market. George C. Clark sent a frantic wire asking Hill to help guarantee J. P. Morgan's plan to save the New York banks, but Hill replied that he was too deeply committed to similar efforts at home. He expected a long recession. Lacking any other source of relief from the burdens of prosperity, railroad men might almost have welcomed such an event, but by the end of 1908 the country was booming again. There was nothing to do but take the larger view. Hill went to work on what he hoped would provide a solid financial foundation for the Great Northern until well past the middle of the century: a new $600 million mortgage, to replace all existing financing, which would reflect the $325 million that had been poured into the railroad since 1879 and provide $270 million for further enlargement and improvement.[18]

As it had been thirty years before, the weather continued to be Hill's cruelest adversary, especially since there were now more people living on the vast lands through which the Hill roads ran than ever before. As each winter brought fresh tales of hardship, he placed the railroads on an emergency basis, hauling coal and hay hundreds of miles at special low rates to keep the settlers from freezing and their animals from starving. "We are having more difficulty from snow than I have ever known," Hill wired Nichols in the brutal January of 1907. He lived in dread that the next telegram might bring news of some disaster in the Cascades, through which the Great Northern hauled thousands of passengers every day. The worst time was late winter, when a warming trend sometimes loosened countless tons of snow and rock and sent an avalanche hurtling down upon the puny railroad below. Miles of snow sheds and fences had been installed, but not everywhere they were needed. Late in February of 1910 a slide came down at the east portal of the Cascade tunnel, demolishing the boarding house and killing the cook. Inspection revealed that an even worse slide at the west portal seemed likely, and that any train blockaded by snow that took refuge just inside the tunnel would probably be buried; smoke from the locomotives would have been intolerable, in any case. But just beyond the west portal was a little station called Wellington, which Hill considered a "safe harbor."

On the night of March 1, 1910, two trains took refuge on the siding while snowplows up ahead struggled to clear the tracks, which sometimes took days. Asleep in the Pullmans were nearly a hundred people, while in the mail cars in front seven clerks prepared to bed down for the night. Rending the cold silence of the night, the worst avalanche in the history of the Great Northern roared down the mountainside, sweeping the three steam locomotives, four huge electric helper locomotives, and every one of the Pullmans and mail cars into oblivion. Days later the toll stood at 87 people, either known dead or buried forever in the rubble. Hill's shoulders drooped as he surveyed the scene some weeks later. The vast new system of snowsheds which he ordered would never wipe out the memory of the ghastly tragedy.[19]

V

"My active work will, I hope, soon be lightened," Hill wrote a friend at the beginning of 1906. "While I do not feel that I am an old man, I would certainly enjoy a little more leisure and opportunity to occasionally look into what other people are thinking about or doing." He thought that "another year or two" would see his building plans in the Northwest completed; until then, he had no intention of relaxing his hold on the thousands of miles of railroad for which he was responsible.[20]

He faced three handicaps in providing for his succession. First, there was his natural reluctance to turn over authority to others or even to train them for the inevitable time when he would be unable to act, a reluctance which Charles E. Perkins had commented on twenty years before. Then there was the problem of getting good men at a time when first-class managers were in great demand by the busy, expanding railroads, a problem which was not helped by Hill's obvious intention to pass the top position along to one of his sons. And then there was his reluctance to face the fact of the declining health of his oldest son, which would ultimately have ruled out his assuming responsibility for the system even if the young man had been enthusiastic about such expectations.

"Jimmy" and "Lou," Hill's older sons, had behind them twelve years of conscientious work with the Hill lines by the time the strife with Harriman was resolved in 1905. Hill's pride in James N. grew rapidly in the early years. "The Eastern [the subsidiary line from the Twin Cities to Duluth] is being operated entirely by a young man of 27 years with only three and a half years [experience] since he was graduated from Yale College," he told J. P. Morgan in 1897. Two years later he made James N. a vice president of the Great Northern and sent him west, confidently informing the division superintendent on the troublesome Montana Central that "he will want to put Montana Division in better shape at once." When Hill went to London in pursuit of Morgan in the spring of 1900, he left the young man in charge and was pleased to receive detailed reports on his skillful handling of half a dozen complex negotiations in the region of Puget Sound and British Columbia. By the beginning of 1902 James N. had reported favorably to his father on the proposed Seattle tunnel, which assured the Great Northern its dominant position in that city. Always popular with Mount Stephen, Farrer, and the other powerful Englishmen whose support remained so vital, James N. was eminently successful in reassuring them that his father had full control of the situation during the uncertain months following the Northern Securities decision. By the time James N. was back in the United States, his father was convinced that he would soon qualify for real, formal responsibility if he could conquer the "rheumatism" that made him miserable for weeks at a time and, now and then, laid him low.[21]

But the ailment, which may actually have been arthritis, and which Hill traced back to a childhood case of measles, never was conquered. As the new century began James N. was in Hot Springs, Arkansas, in search of a cure. Slowly, Hill's deep sympathy for his bright, articulate, personable young son began to be edged with impatience. As in his own case, Hill interpreted each remission as a permanent cure, and in 1903, after several weeks at Jekyl Island, even James N. caught the spirit:

> I have thought over your talk about my doing nothing and have concluded to offer to do what you may want me to. I feel better than I did. Well enough to work & help to such an extent as I may be able if you wish my help. . . .[22]

But the rheumatism came back, worse than before, and there were other problems. It is not likely, moreover, that young Hill would have thrived in St. Paul as nominal head of the Hill lines under the close, daily supervision of his father. He developed early a taste for the cosmopolitan atmosphere of New York, and enjoyed his bachelor life at the University Club. By 1905 it had been decided that he would live in New York, with no day-to-day responsibilities, as a director of the Northern Pacific, and help his father keep an eye on that independent-minded railroad. He also dabbled in other enterprises, as when his father supplied $300,000 for him to invest in a disappointing cement-making process. But his big opportunity came when the Texas Company, which was destined to grow into one of the largest petroleum companies in the world, was organized. John W. Gates had urged his old friend, James J. Hill, to take part of a large block of common stock that was being offered in 1910, and invited him to join a party that would include such astute money men as John J. Mitchell, A. B. Hepburn, and Hepburn's brilliant lieutenant, Albert Wiggin, to tour the new company's properties by special train. Although the world stood on the threshold of the automobile age, Hill had no time for such ventures. But his son invested heavily in the oil company, and he ended up a very rich man in his own right.[23]

At the end of 1904 Hill wrote Mount Stephen, "Louis is running the

Gt. Northern, and while he is not quite so quick as Jim, he is very sound and careful, and is doing the best railroad operation I have ever seen." [24] Devoted to his father and eager for his approval, this second son would be the successor to James J. Hill in the leadership of the Great Northern. He had learned his father's ways, and when guidance was lacking did not attempt to second-guess him, as when he was sent on a very vague mission to see what was holding up the maiden voyage of the *S. S. Dakota* in 1905:

> I do not wish to shirk any duty you may put on me, or work you may wish me to do, but having never been instructed of any duties or authority in connection with the movement of the boats, I have hesitated to assume any. . . .[25]

"Hope you will hold everybody fully up to his work, with a firm and steady hand, and I will be right behind you," Hill told Louis in 1907 when he took the newly created post of chairman of the board of the Great Northern and his son assumed the presidency. But there could be only one source of authority in any enterprise of which James J. Hill was a part, and he did not hesitate to make decisions for his son which Louis might just as well have made for himself. A year later Louis, who soon bought a superb homesite overlooking the Pacific Ocean at what became Pebble Beach, dutifully asked his father's permission to take Maud and their large family out for a part of the winter. In 1910, when Louis had been president for three years, Hill saw nothing bizarre in telegraphing his son after several weeks' absence that he had had enough vacation and should get back to work.[26]

The time for a man like Louis, however, was at hand for the Great Northern. The father-and-son team made a striking picture at a wide variety of public events throughout the Northwest in Hill's last decade. The old man, smiling broadly or gesturing energetically, took the foreground while Louis, dignified and rather old-world-looking in his pince nez and dark red beard, stood near by. Louis's handsome sons—Louis, Jr., James J. II ("Romie"), and Cortlandt—made photogenic companions for their grandfather. At Glacier Park in 1913, during his seventy-fifth birthday celebration, Hill stood in an open touring car to address the crowd, while curly-haired "Corty," aged seven, struggled to stay awake on the seat beside him. Louis, too, was a good public speaker, and devoted himself to the long-neglected public relations of the railroad. He emphasized agricultural development, creating a "western grain and fruit exhibit" that toured the country extolling the land from Minnesota westward. Louis was a talented painter, and he saw the wild beauty of the Rocky Mountains where the Great Northern crossed them. He made Glacier National Park into one of America's most popular playgrounds and his own monument. Slowly the competent, ambitious men who made up the day-to-day management of the Hill railroads came to look to Louis Hill for their orders. "If I had Lou to make over," his father told an old friend, "I wouldn't change a thing." [27]

When he started the long process of retiring from active management, Hill redoubled his efforts to get strong men into the key positions of the three railroads under his direction. For the Burlington, one of the most demanding posts in the country, he pinned his hopes on Daniel Willard, whom he took from the Erie. But Hill could not hope to keep a man like Willard, who eventually became the unofficial spokesman for all American railroads, in a subordinate position, and he soon lost him to the Baltimore & Ohio. Darius Miller, sent to the Burlington from the Great Northern, was on a clear track to the number two position in the Hill roads until an attack of acute appendicitis and the ministrations of an incompetent doctor at Glacier National Park Lodge in August of 1914 brought his promising career to a tragic end. First-class management was turning out to be the scarcest of all resources.

In 1903 Hill persuaded his daughter Charlotte's husband, able, hardworking George T. Slade, who was making a successful career on the Erie Railroad, to take an operating position on the Great Northern in St. Paul. When Slade intimated a few years later that he did not think that there was much opportunity for both a son and a son-in-law of James J. Hill on the same railroad, Hill moved him to the Northern Pacific. Hill had replaced Mellen, putting in the presidency Howard Elliott, and under Elliott Slade quickly earned a place in line for the post. When Elliott went east in 1913 to rescue the ailing New Haven Railroad, Hill let it be known that he preferred Slade for the presidency of the Northern Pacific, and was taken aback when Slade declined. It belongs to Jule M. Hannaford, his son-in-law said. Hannaford had worked faithfully to keep the old Northern Pacific in business in its darkest days. Meanwhile, Hill had formally recognized the priceless services of a man who had labored for the Great Northern in New York since it was the bankrupt old St. Paul & Pacific, by making E. T. Nichols a director and first vice president of the company. [28]

It was on the Great Northern that Hill faced the biggest problem in finding and keeping expert management. When he turned the presidency over to Louis, he had hired a man from the Grand Trunk to become vice president and general manager, but he had lasted barely six months. When John F. Stevens's work in Oregon was finished Hill apparently tried, as he had tried when he bought the Burlington in 1901, to get this independent spirit to stay on, but Stevens wanted no part of such an arrangement. (Hill, even angrier than after the first refusal, a few months later refused to recommend Stevens for an important post in Brazil.) When Louis moved up to the chairmanship in 1912, Carl R. Gray, a first-class railroad man who later rose to the presidency of the Union Pacific, assumed the number two job on the Great Northern. But he and Louis could not work together, and Hill asked Gray for an undated resignation, which he intended to use when he was ready. Meanwhile, Hill told Louis, Gray's assistant, Ralph Budd, a brilliant young engineer with exceptional credentials including a period of service on the Panama Railroad, could assume Gray's duties without the title. Hill had indeed found a "safe harbor" in Budd, and near the end of his life he let it be known that he wanted Budd to become chief operating officer and, along with Louis, to continue his work of thirty-eight years.[29]

VI

When James J. Hill made his first trip east from St. Paul to New York in the late 1860s, "Commodore" Cornelius Vanderbilt was a newcomer to the railroad business and the New York Central was still a primitive agency of transportation. The Pennsylvania Railroad, twisting and climbing through the rugged mountains east of Pittsburgh, was hardly any better. Back and forth over these railroads, which soon became two of the most successful and vital enterprises in the world, Hill made perhaps 400 to 500 round trips between 1868 and 1916. He watched them being almost continuously rebuilt, learning from their mistakes as well as their triumphs, and, with his book or his letter-writing portfolio or his sheaf of operating and financial reports at his side, he kept busy on his trips. These little respites from the constant demands upon his time provided a chance to reflect, to plan, and to decide upon increasingly important matters. In our air age the lack of similar escapes is keenly felt by men and women of all responsible callings.

In the 1870s and 1880s the Hills—"Papa," "Mama," and an increasing stream of sons and daughters who shuttled between home in St. Paul and their schools in the East—had preferred riding the Pennsylvania Railroad, which pioneered the fast, luxurious, all-Pullman "limited train." By 1893 the "Pennsylvania Limited" required less than twenty-one hours for the run between the "Fort Wayne" Depot in Chicago (named for the Pennsylvania's west-of-Pittsburgh subsidiary, the Pittsburgh, Fort Wayne & Chicago Railroad) and the Jersey City terminal on the Hudson River opposite Gotham's rapidly rising skyline. Both the Milwaukee and, after 1886, the Burlington trains from St. Paul arrived at the Fort Wayne road's depot in Chicago, and the ferry trip across the Hudson was not only a treat, but, inasmuch as Hill could take it direct to the financial district, a great convenience in the days before New York solved its rapid transit problems.

Competition between the two great Eastern trunk lines for the lucrative passenger business grew dramatically in the 1880s. Not to serve the public ("The public be damned," a weary William H. Vanderbilt had retorted to a fatuous, pushy newspaper reporter in 1883), but to compete with its arch-rival, the New York Central copied and improved upon the Pennsylvania's limited trains. By the end of the century nothing could match the swift, smooth run of the Lake Shore Limited over the Central's "water level route" through the Mohawk River valley of upstate New York; nor the sparkling, starched elegance of its dining car service; nor the ministrations of the cheerful sleeping car porters, who stood at the pinnacle of their profession; nor the convenience of arriving at Grand Central Depot in the fast-growing midtown section of Manhattan. And then, in 1901, the Central introduced the Twentieth Century Limited, which for fifty years set the standard for first-class land travel throughout the world. The Pennsylvania's Broadway Limited (named not for the New York thoroughfare, but for the mighty Pennsylvania's superb four-track "broadway of steel" between the East and West) could never quite match the Central's apotheosis of the Brave New Century. Ordinary people rode the train, but the rich and important, and their mimics, "took the Century."

James J. Hill was a member of that most exclusive of clubs, the powerful men who held passes on the Century, but now and then he took the Broadway and, very infrequently, the Baltimore & Ohio or even the Erie if his interest warranted and time permitted. Almost never did "car A-1," Hill's private business car, in which he click-clacked all over the country northwest of Chicago, ever go east of the Windy City.

A drawing room on the regular train was good enough for Hill and his family. Not until the last decade of his life was he persuaded to engage a traveling secretary. By 1905 he had found an ideal right-hand man in efficient, diplomatic, and taciturn Martin R. Brown, who went nearly everywhere with Hill.

As he approached his seventy-fifth year, Hill was beginning to face the hard truth that he soon would be unable to endure such constant travel. Nobody, least of all Mary, believed his resolutions about retiring any more, but when Crawford Livingston importuned him to take an interest in a coal deal late in 1912, Hill replied, "I am aiming to get out of active work and . . . as Greeley said, 'The way to resume is to resume,' and the way for me to quit is to quit." [30] That summer, in fact, he had broken the longest and strongest tie of his life: he had resigned as chairman of the board of the Great Northern. Louis took his place. For days Hill had sat at his desk, drafting a letter of farewell to his co-workers. Finally he had it just as he wanted it:

> Not lightly may the relation between a man and the work in which he has had a vital part be set aside. My personal interest in the Great Northern remains as keen as ever. . . . While I shall be no longer the responsible head of the Great Northern I will contribute henceforth such counsel and advice as may seem best from one no longer holding the throttle valve or controlling the brake.
>
> Most men who have really lived have had, in some shape, their great adventure. This railway is mine. I feel that a labor and a service so called into being, touching at so many points the lives of so many millions with its ability to serve the country, and its firmly established credit and reputation, will be the best evidence of its permanent value and that it no longer depends upon the life or labor of any single individual.

The letter, which was separately printed, ran to twenty-three pages. It was a history of the Great Northern since Hill's earliest involvement with it. It was also a frank *apologia* for his long stewardship. As far as he was concerned, the two came down to the same thing. [31]

When released to the press, the letter attracted widespread attention. *The New York Times* of Sunday, June 30, 1912, featured it in an article that detailed Hill's rise to first place among the nation's railroad leaders. Two days later there came an urgent letter from publisher George H. Putnam, begging him to write "a volume of your reminiscences" for Putnam to publish. From Europe came a letter from Edward Tuck, who confided that "parts of your address are, as Ambassador Jusserand said to me the other evening, 'touching and almost

At Vancouver, Washington, about 1910.

pathetic.' " [32] Truly pathetic was a letter from Senator Paris Gibson. Despite its tone of self-pity, the final salute from this complicated man who had kept the faith for so many years in bleak Montana was to be treasured, all the same:

I must lay down my burden, a poor man and with nothing accomplished worth remembering. I hope you will live many years longer . . . to shape the development of the Northwest whose upbuilding, so far, is mainly due to you. [33]

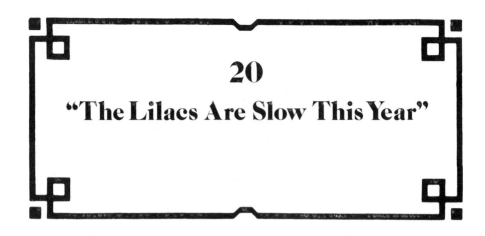

20

"The Lilacs Are Slow This Year"

. . . a figure carved in massive proportions out of man's necessity to act heroically upon his hostile environment.

—New York Times, 1916

"If he'd of lived, he'd of been a great man. A man like James J. Hill. He'd of helped build up the country."

—F. Scott Fitzgerald, *The Great Gatsby*

I

Barely three months after his "retirement," Hill began a new career. "I have bought a bank and will want $250,000 this week," he wired Nichols in October 1912. He had, in fact, bought two banks, the First National and the Second National of St. Paul. To the stockholders of the First National, which seemed destined to become the most important financial institution in the Northwest, he offered a cash dividend of 25 per cent and $310 a share for their holdings. He soon had virtually all of the stock, and his investment in the newly organized First National Bank of St. Paul reached $3.8 million.

The following January, Hill was summoned to Washington to appear before Representative Arsène Pujo's committee, which was investigating what Pujo called the "money trust." Samuel Untermeyer, the hired counsel who was actually running the committee, tried to force Hill into simple "yes" or "no" answers to a line of questioning that was intended to prove that Hill was leading a move to consolidate the banks of the Northwest into one powerful trust. But Hill ignored Untermeyer's high-handed manner and launched into his own explanation of his bank acquisitions. "The stock had drifted into the estates of dead men," he said, thinking of his old friend, Henry P. Upham, nearly four years dead, "and there was no active interest in the ownership of the stock. I bought . . . every share of both banks and distributed what I desired to, to men who would take an active part in it—younger men."

Pressing Hill for the answer he wanted, Untermeyer asked whether he thought cumulative voting—a method of giving greater weight to minority stock interests—would be a good thing to require by law. Hill gave him a piece of his philosophy about what could be accomplished by laws, and what had to be left to leadership. "In trying to do good you are liable to do harm; . . . it depends upon the individual man. All acts are personal things, and the mind and conscience of that individual man is what is going to govern his actions." Between the nineteenth-century individualist and the twentieth-century authoritarian—between a James J. Hill and a Samuel Untermeyer—yawned a chasm which is still widening.[1]

What *did* Hill want with a bank? He and his associates knew perfectly well what economic historians seem determined to forget: that the weakest link in the American economic system in 1912 was, as it had been practically from the beginning, the agricultural credit system. To Hill, neither the short-term credit machinery, by which farmers tried to finance their highly seasonal operations until crops could be sold off, nor long-term farm mortgage credit were adequate. Throughout most of Hill's life farmers had financed their land purchases through local private bankers who marshalled surplus funds from the East, but that breed had been made virtually extinct by the depression of the 1890s, and no replacement had appeared. The National banking system, based on emergency Civil War legislation, worked less and less well as a short-term credit mechanism. If, as the Democrats and a growing number of Republican "Insurgents" liked to say, the tariff was "the mother of trusts," Eastern Republicans and conservative Democrats—who would have liked to resurrect the Bank of the United States, Nicholas Biddle and all—might have retorted that the National banking system was the "father of panics."

Had he lived another decade, and had World War I not intervened, Hill might have accomplished significant innovations in agricultural credit institutions. With Chicago banker John J. Mitchell and the Santa

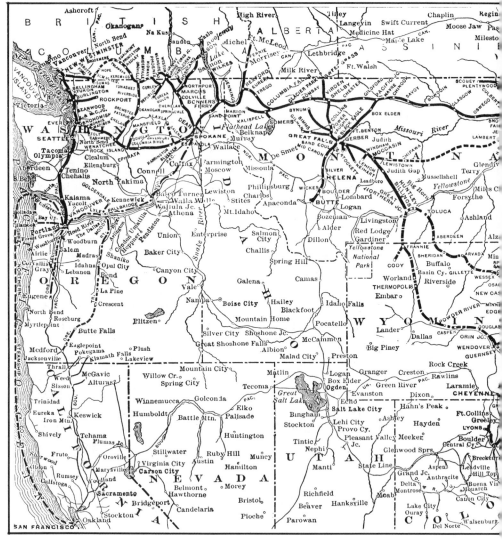

The Great Northern Railway and the Chicago, Burlington & Quincy Railway, 1916.

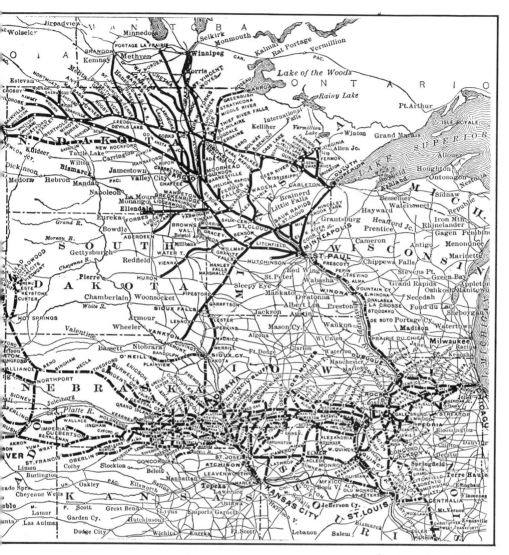

Great Northern Railway.

Fe's virtuoso president, Edward P. Ripley, he discussed the formation of a "central farm mortgage bank," and on the staff of the First National he placed H. R. Smith, professor of agricultural husbandry at the University of Minnesota, to promote an innovative program of livestock financing. "I have still about five and a half years' work laid out before me," Hill told a New York reporter a few weeks after his appearance before the Pujo committee; "[then] I'll be 80 years old, and I guess then I can find something else to do." But social institutions change slowly and Hill's declining energies were claimed by the vast majority of bankers who preferred to savor the status quo. Soon he was receiving a steady stream of invitations to speak at meetings of bankers' associations, of which, it seemed, there were dozens. In June 1913 he consented to go to Ottawa to address the annual convention of the New York State Bankers Association. But he had two ulterior motives. The following year would be the one-hundredth anniversary of the "peace of Christmas eve," the Treaty of Ghent, which had ended the War of 1812 and brought a century of peace between the two great English-speaking nations. Gesturing enthusiastically before a sea of well-fed, well-starched shirtfronts in the ballroom of the elegant new Chateau Laurier (which the ailing Grand Trunk Railway had built, as if to prove its own senescence), he spoke on "some victories of peace." And next day he enjoyed a long inspection tour of the Canadian experimental farm on the edge of the capital city, and a jovial chat on the lawn with some of Canada's most distinguished supporters of better agriculture. The old yearning to diversify Northwestern farming came back with a rush, and soon his representative was off to England again to buy new herds of blooded Anguses, Ayrshires, and Shorthorns.[2]

In his last years, however, Hill had to resist a growing cynicism about the many programs to improve farming in the United States that he saw around him. What had appeared to be a generous if misguided effort to kill the farmer with kindness seemed to him to stem increasingly from the most selfish of motives. On the one hand, the attainable objectives were being overstated:

> . . . what the farmer can be taught to do with his own hands on his own land is about all that can be done for him. The question of social uplift and others of that nature will amount to very little for the farmer if his

At the Canadian Government's experimental farm in Ottawa. With him are J. J. Booth, a Canadian lumberman (left), and Sir James Grant, a leading physician of the Dominion. July 1913.

work does not bring him a return in money value. The first step is to enable him to get more value out of the ground for the labor he puts upon it.

On the other, too many people were feathering their own nests in a manner that was sure sooner or later to reflect discredit on all such programs:

> Many new propositions are mere schemes to use the alleged interest of the farmer to create new places and salaries. Such is a federal system of rural credits that contradicts the experience of all the older countries and the facts of human nature. Such are those projects for road improvement that aim at big appropriations. . . . In trying to promote agriculture, care is necessary that it may not suffer from the current mistaken tendency to organize everything to death.[3]

II

Every spring Captain Weed came down to New London, Connecticut, to put the steam yacht *Wacouta* in shape for what he kept hoping would be an active summer of cruising for the large Hill family and their many friends. His employer was spending $60,000 a year to keep the ship in commission, nearly half what she had cost him to buy, even though the Captain made do with considerably fewer hands than the thirty-two-man crew for which she was designed. The summer began each year with a great flourish of activity, for Hill never allowed anything to stand in the way of his annual trip to the salmon river in Quebec, and he expected to use the *Wacouta* between Montreal and the mouth of the St. John. By the middle of June Hill's chief clerk, John J. Toomey, was in Canada confirming that all preparations had been made at the big, seven-bedroom lodge which Hill had built on the bank of the river. His employer, with such friends as Dan Lamont, Sam Thorne, William H. Dunwoody (the Minneapolis flour milling magnate), Robert Bacon, Charles Steele, and Dr. George D. Stewart in tow, usually took the overnight train from Grand Central to Montreal, where Weed stood by with orders to sail immediately upon their arrival. At Montreal they might be met by Louis, who made a quick trip by the Soo line from St. Paul to join in "killing" the Atlantic salmon, which, unlike less noble fish, is never merely "caught." [4]

Each in his own canoe, the members of the party set forth early every fair morning, with two French-Canadian canoeists, one in the stern, paddling, and the other up front, re-baiting the hook. At lunch-

Shoving off for a day of salmon fishing at the St. John River, Quebec, June 1913. From a photograph.

time the fishermen reassembled at the lodge, where the ceremony of counting, measuring, and weighing the kill was performed. The region had a short, late summer, Mary Hill noted in her diary one year, and the wild strawberries did not ripen until August. The crisp nights, like the frequent rainy days, were ideal for singing, story-telling and much serious talk about the future of the great enterprises which, despite a swiftly changing society, these men still hoped to remain the stewards of. But it was not a strictly masculine or grown-up excursion. At least two years in a row, Hill had as his guests in the last days of his stay Lord Grey, Governor General of Canada, and his wife and daughter, Lady Sibyl, formidable sportswomen who could show the men a thing or two about killing salmon. The season of 1912 turned out to be a family affair, with Mary carefully noting in her diary the kill scores of her grandsons.

But for the rest of the summer the *Wacouta* could lie rusting at the dock in New London for all Hill seemed to care. Except for a rather rough, foggy sail with Mary at the end of the 1912 fishing trip, down the St. Lawrence, the Maine coast, and in Long Island Sound, Hill almost never used the handsome yacht after the fishing. In 1911 Hill had coaxed Mary and such of her daughters and grandchildren as she could get to accompany her to take a cruise on the Great Lakes, as they had done in 1901, when the *Wacouta* was new, but at the last minute he decided that he could not join them. "Were you but here the day would be very happy; we have much to rejoice us," his wife wired on August 19. It was their forty-fourth wedding anniversary. Meanwhile, Jekyl Island stood by each winter. When he resigned the chairmanship in 1912, Hill resolved to spend more time at that paradise, but after he had balanced teacups for two weeks amid the jasmine and bougain-villea he escaped back North a month or more ahead of the reluctant spring, leaving the ladies behind.[5]

The moment it began to look as though he would have the leisure to look at them, Hill resumed buying pictures. The painters of the Bar-bizon school, of which he had one of the finest collections in the world, were often in his mind. "The banks of the River below Quebec are a constant Daubigny landscape," he wrote Mary in 1911. Durand-Ruel, Knoedler & Company, and even gregarious little August Jacacci, his old St. Paul art adviser, who was getting along very well as an art-ists' agent and art publisher in New York, brought him canvases. Corots, Rousseaus, Troyons, Decamps, and Millets, Hill bought gladly. A fine Constable required little soul-searching, and a Renoir only slightly more. But when a Dutch dealer armed with an enthusi-astic letter from that accomplished amateur painter, William C. Van Horne, and Durand-Ruel pressed him to buy works of Honoré Dau-mier, he found himself not quite ready, even though he was intrigued by the Frenchman's realistic picture of the interior of a third-class railway carriage. Hill had barely begun to think about what would happen to all these pictures when he was gone. To the Minneapolis Institute of Arts he gave his big, expensive de Neuville, "The Storming of Tel-el-Kebir," and was glad that the director had had the good sense to hang it where visitors had room to get well back and have a good look at it. Meanwhile there were letters from young artists seeking patrons, but that had never been Hill's role. When a young man, comfortably employed and with a wife and family, begged him to stake him to two years of painting, in return for which he would gladly give Hill all his work in that period, Hill had his secretary reply that he was not interested. He believed that real genius can and should make it on its own, and he was not mistaken in this case, for the young artist was Rockwell Kent.[6]

Hill's many interests cost a great deal of money, even though he had little time to devote to them. The fine house at 8 East 65 Street in New York was always ready for Mr. and Mrs. Hill, their daughters Clara and Rachel, or, on short notice, such guests as a Prussian prince, whose stay was the high point of major domo Kurth's service with Hill. In September 1912, a typical month, Toomey disbursed $1600 for Northcote Farm, where Walter was struggling to become a successful farm manager; $1000 for the *Wacouta*, even though it had been laid up for the season; $500 for servants' wages at the New York house; and $243 to the caretakers at the salmon river. None of this, of course, paid for the expenses of the mansion at 240 Summit. In 1905 Hill had reluctantly decided to liquidate his venture into newspaper publishing, the St. Paul *Globe*, after an accumulated loss of half a million dollars, but he kept Joseph G. Pyle, whom he had coaxed from Seattle to edit the paper, on his staff as personal editor at $500 a month. Seven or more clerks continued to labor under Toomey, keeping the elaborate records of Hill's various enterprises. His most expensive hobby continued to be North Oaks Farm, where the monthly payroll alone had come to exceed $1500. It was not only money that these interests absorbed, however, for he threw himself into the minutest details of their operations. Near the end of his life he built a big new mansion to replace the old farmhouse at North Oaks. After luncheon one hot day in July 1914 he insisted that he and Mary go out to the farm. Once there, she found herself immediately abandoned, and sat down at her writing table to compose a letter to Clara. "He is off somewhere in his shirt sleeves," she wrote.[7]

Their greatest good fortune, they and their friends agreed, was their family. By 1912 only James N., Rachel, and Clara remained unmarried, and both girls were being seriously courted. Egil Boeckmann, a big, handsome Norwegian, had come from the Old Country as a boy with his father, a doctor who had endeared himself to both the rich and the poor of St. Paul. Everybody knew Egil's performance on the University of Minnesota football team in those days of skimpy leather helmets and the flying tackle, and they noted proudly that these activities had not kept him from becoming a highly successful doctor himself. He and Rachel were engaged by 1912, and it looked as though Erasmus C. Lindley, general counsel of the Northern Pacific, might finally persuade Clara to marry him. It remained for James N. to sound the jarring note.

For some time, "Jim" had been courting a New York woman who would have been an eligible bride in every way, his parents thought, if she had not been a divorcée. Mary Hill, ultra-conservative Irish-American Roman Catholic that she was, even felt there was something not quite right about a widow marrying again, especially if she had been Mrs. Grover Cleveland; but a divorcée was quite out of the question. Hill was only slightly less opposed to the match. But James N. was aboard the *S. S. Kronprinzessin Cecilie*, on his way to England and his fiancée, before anyone knew it. Gaspard Farrer stood up for him when he married Margaret Fahnestock, and the very proper Lord and Lady Mount Stephen received the honeymooning couple at Brockett Hall, but Mrs. James Norman Hill never set foot in her mother-in-law's drawing room.[8]

Well before his retirement from the Great Northern, Hill had begun to simplify his complicated finances. He would not make a will just yet: it was probably an old wives' tale that men who made wills were bound to die soon, but still he had not yet made up his mind what to do with his money. There were things, however, that were better done during his lifetime. One was to get rid of the Great Falls, Montana, Townsite Company, a perennial disappointment, which he sold, on behalf of the stockholders, in 1908. Another was to dispose of the 24,000 acres of land which he had held for so many years in the Red River Valley. By 1909 prime farming land was bringing record prices, and Hill was able to sell even his unbroken land at $22 to $30 an acre. As usual, he was anxious to get bona fide farmers instead of speculators as buyers. The terms of payment were generous; they allowed six years for payment, and "a little diversion from this would be allowed with good reliable parties." In 1911 he decided to buy control of the Northern Securities Company, which had survived as a shell containing not much besides the Crows Nest Pass Coal Company, and for which he alone was morally responsible. By 1915 he held 54 per cent of the stock.[9]

III

Even if he had no intimations of his own mortality, Hill was acutely aware of how quickly his old friends were falling away. The first to go was Dan Lamont, stricken by a heart attack in July 1905, only a few weeks after returning from the salmon river. Hill's grief was all the greater because this stimulating companion and sturdy lieutenant at the Northern Pacific had been still in his fifties. The following year Hill found himself writing to the bereaved Mrs. Marshall Field, "He was my friend for more than 30 years," and he hastily departed for Chicago, where he served as pallbearer. When D. Willis James, summering at Bretton Woods, New Hampshire, succumbed to a heart attack in 1907, the old associates felt the loss deeply. "I cannot tell you how lonely I feel when he and other friends like him are called away to join the great majority," Kennedy wrote Hill. And Mount Stephen, recalling the Manitoba road's perilous early years, cabled from England, "It is the first break in the old front line." [10]

When Hill visited Charles E. Perkins at his home in Burlington, Iowa, in the spring of 1907, he was saddened by his old friend's gloomy outlook. Perkins was taking very hard the "Progressives'" savage repudiation of the work of his generation in building up the country. When it came time to leave he insisted on seeing Hill to the front gate of "The Apple Trees," the Victorian mansion in which he had labored so many years to make the Burlington the servant of the Midwest. Taking Perkins by the arm, Hill looked him sternly in the eye and said, "Mr. Perkins, you and I will go to heaven or to hell— *together,*" and rejoiced at his friend's hearty laugh. One day that summer, Perkins wired Hill at St. Paul that he was coming through in his private car, the *Blackhawk,* and hoped for a few hours' visit, but Hill had left for New York the night before. They never saw each other again, for Perkins died November 8. Another who did not last out the year was Stanford Newel, who had been Hill's best man at his marriage forty years before. Returning from The Hague that spring, broken in health and fortune, Newel had been cheered by an unsolicited loan of $5000, one which both men knew was not going to be repaid.[11]

As the year 1909 sped by, Hill paid his last respects to Thomas Lowry, who for years had amazed and exasperated Hill with his wheeling and dealing in Minneapolis; and Henry P. Upham, who only yesterday, it seemed, had rather bashfully joined Hill, William P. Merriam, and Emerson Lewis in presenting Conrad Gotzian with a wide-muzzled old gun that might improve his luck at bird hunting. It had been twenty-six years since they hired the stuffed buffalo and the photographer for the tableau they had laughed over so much since. Nobody, it seemed, had time for that kind of fun any more. And that October, sober, dignified, elderly John S. Kennedy fell victim to whooping cough. Try as he might, Hill could find no way to get to New York in time for the funeral. One thing he could do was to learn from Kennedy, and a few weeks later he asked for a copy of the banker's will. Next year word came that Colonel Chauncey W. Griggs, Hill's partner in the wood and coal business forty years before, had died in Seattle. And then, in the early spring of 1913, as Hill was preparing to send a rare musk ox skin to J. P. Morgan, who liked such things, he was shocked to learn that his most powerful associate had died in Rome. He sent the skin to "Jack," instead, with his condolences.[12]

Donald Smith, Lord Strathcona and Mount Royal, grieved briefly for his wife, who had died, leaving him alone in huge, drafty Knebworth Castle, and then, as the year of 1914 began, died himself at the age of ninety-three. Only two of the original associates, Hill and George Stephen, Lord Mount Stephen, remained. "The Boss," as Mount Stephen's subordinates and, now and then, even Hill called him, was having a little trouble with his "locomotion," Farrer wrote, but was still eager for news about the Hill railroads. He no longer wrote letters if he could avoid it—his handwriting had been bad enough in his youth—but he passed the word through Farrer that he hoped the Hills would make their long-promised trip to England soon, for they had much to remember and be proud of. Hill agreed, declaring that no men would ever again have the chance to do what they had done:

> The old days and their associations will always be nearer our hearts than any other period of our lives. They can never come back to us, or to any others, for the reason that there are no such opportunities to open up new countries of imperial size as we had.[13]

In the spring of 1914 Hill helped to lay to rest two of his oldest friends in the Twin Cities: William H. Dunwoody, who had milled some of the flour that young Hill had stored in his warehouse on the river over forty-five years before; and Frederick Weyerhaeuser, his next-door neighbor for over twenty years, whose faith in Hill's ability to lower railroad rates was the cornerstone of the lumber industry of the Pacific Northwest. Hill, realizing that he would soon be eighty himself, began to talk seriously about a trip to Europe with Mary, but she would not go until Mary Boeckmann, first child of Rachel and Egil, who had married the year before, was born, and by then the season was too far advanced.[14] At the end of June the assassination of the Austrian archduke at faraway Sarajevo ended any hope that they would ever stroll on the banks of the Ganges, recalling the time when he wanted to put steamboats on it; or even sit on the Tucks' verandah in Nice and watch the informal new generation at play. Mary regretted that time had seemed to run out so abruptly, but then, as she told Clara at the end of her own life, it had been running out for a long time:

> If I succeeded in getting "Ras" [Clara's husband, Erasmus C. Lindley] to stop to think whether it was worthwhile to sacrifice every other thing to work, I did something. How well I can remember the different efforts I tried with Papa, all to no purpose as far as I know!

> How many things we were going to do in the future, that might have been done in the past. The present is all that is ours. . . .[15]

IV

The American educational system was dramatically transformed during the last two decades of Hill's life—by rapid population growth; a nationwide feeling of euphoria brought on by unparalleled prosperity, especially on the farm; and by complete surrender to the belief that social mobility was directly proportional to the amount of education to which the young are subjected. Slowly at first, then very rapidly, Hill began to doubt the social worth of many of the changes that were taking place, as the colleges grew to enormous size and became almost entirely secularized; as private colleges struggled to attract students in the face of competition from proliferating free state schools; as the elementary schools embraced a rigid system of graded classes; as rural school districts consolidated into pathetically inadequate "high" schools; and as the quality of the education diminished alarmingly despite soaring expenditures of public funds. In these years Hill wrote and spoke passionately on education, and he warned of the educational problems which Americans would be wrestling with at the end of the century.

By 1909 Hill had decided that the best way he could contribute to the American college movement was to give modest sums of money to private, church-related schools. He was convinced that these institutions, small in size, possessing a true community spirit, and kept alive by the efforts of dedicated—if not always brilliant—men and women, provided the best kind of education. Not himself a communicant of any organized religion, he yet believed that these schools, cleaving as they did to a historical body of religious doctrine, provided a civilizing and inspirational atmosphere which, sooner or later, would be recognized as the chief lack of the large state universities. He stopped giving to churches, for he wanted "to get a number of our Northwestern denominational colleges on their feet so that they can go on in a permanent way. . . ." When the new edition of the *Encyclopaedia Britannica* included in its biographical sketch of him the statement that he had given $1.5 million to the building fund for St. Paul's new Roman Catholic Cathedral, he wrote the editor an indignant denial.[16]

Nothing seemed more irrational to Hill than for the state legislatures to vote huge sums of money for more and bigger free colleges and universities when there were private institutions struggling to fill their classrooms. To the president of the Twin Cities' excellent Macalester College, one of his beneficiaries, Hill wrote in 1911 describing a plan which sixty years later, in new dress, was being advanced as the "voucher plan" for assistance to private schools and colleges:

> A simple plan which would be both just and free from all political interference would be a commission to examine all applicants for admission to the state university, granting a scholarship to such as passed, good at any denominational college whose curriculum was sufficiently high. . . . This would relieve the state university from over-crowding, and would allow parents and students to continue their work in the religious atmosphere of their choice, &c.[17]

By the time Hill was halfway through his speech to the Yale Club of Minneapolis, given one cold night in January 1914, the uncomfortable members had begun to wonder if inviting him had been a good idea after all. "He put the present day school system on a spit and roasted it brown," said one newspaper next day.[18] His remarks were not popular, for the assembled Old Blues, whether they were hard-headed businessmen, clergymen, or school officials, were proud of the big new public schools that were making little red schoolhouses things of the past. Indignant letters flowed in, and Hill took pains to explain why he opposed uncontrolled consolidation of schools and the graded class system, two of the central pillars of the new education:

> Rural school consolidation has become something of a fad. Where there are several small country schools . . . it may often be an advantage to have one good building and a smaller number of more competent teachers. . . . But where the idea is merely to ape the city high school the change may be for the worse. . . .

> The adoption of the graded system, applying a common mold, compelling children to develop along fixed lines instead of according to their individual aptitudes, holding back the bright and forced to promote the stupid, is one of the curses of modern education.

> I have felt for a long time the injustice of the present method to the scholars. . . . They do not teach them to write a plain hand, to spell correctly or give them a thorough drill in arithmetic and constantly impress upon their minds the necessity and importance of doing their work with the greatest accuracy. We find . . . that the graduates from the public schools are totally unfit. . . .[19]

Like most people in 1914, Hill assumed that the majority of young men and women would end their formal schooling at about the eighth grade. Whether they did or not, however, it was clear that if the public schools were going to do such a poor job of teaching those who went on to high school, a wise society would provide every reasonable facility for the highly motivated ones to instruct themselves. St. Paul had finally decided to build an adequate public library on the old farmers' market property near the Mississippi River, at the south end of Rice Park. Hill agreed to give the city the "reference library" which he and old Rev. Dr. Edward Neill, long since dead, had discussed twenty years before. It would become the east wing of the public library, the whole forming a handsome building in the elegant, restrained Venetian palazzo style which had begun to grace such thoroughfares as New York's Fifth Avenue. Hill gave no lump sum endowment, but chose, as usual, to supervise the project himself, directing Toomey to pay Butler Brothers, the contractors, monthly as their invoices came in.[20]

Meanwhile, a senior partner at J. P. Morgan & Company, Thomas W. Lamont, decided that Hill would make an exception to his desire to have no buildings or professorships named after him, if what was involved was a "James J. Hill Professorship of Railroad Transportation," to be established in the Graduate School of Business Administration of Harvard University. He was right, for Hill was greatly pleased when Lamont announced the project as a *fait accompli,* with $125,000 in pledges. He soon discovered, however, that the ultimate goal Lamont had in mind was $250,000, and he contributed another $125,000 himself. He recommended that the occupant of the chair be no mere theorist, but someone who knew how railroads were operated, and above all, who recognized good performance and what was required to get it from railroad people, high-ranking and low. Dean Edwin F. Gay of the Harvard Business School recommended William J. Cunningham, a Canadian by birth, who had had twenty-three years of railroad experience, and Hill approved, with the understanding that the new professor would spend several months on the Hill roads learning how Western railroads were run. Cunningham accepted, and much of what he taught and wrote at Harvard in the later decades showed the effects of Hill's tutelage.[21]

As these substantial sums passed back and forth, one good work involving only a few dollars at a time gave Hill as much satisfaction as anything else. For years Morgan L. Hutchins had run the Society for the Relief of the Poor in St. Paul. Up and down the byways of the rapidly growing city he went, his old horse clopping on the cobblestones as it pulled Hutchins's small covered van. Painstakingly he investigated tale after tale of woe, indignantly eliminating the deadbeats and bringing the deserving cases to Hill's attention. Twenty-five dollars here, fifty dollars there—rarely more—was sufficient to buy food and pay the rent for destitute but proud old people until other arrangements could be made, as well as for the growing number of women whose husbands had deserted them and their small children. No money was wasted, no pride destroyed. The critical factor in charitable work, Hutchins and Hill both knew, was not the amount of money available, but the skill and tact with which it was applied. Hill could only shake his head in admiration when Hutchins declined the gift of a handsome young horse from North Oaks Farm; Hutchins felt that it was far too elegant and high-spirited for his work.[22]

By 1912 politics had little remaining interest for Hill; he only wanted to help defeat Theodore Roosevelt in his bid for the presidency. He feared that the long trend of bad political talent driving out the good would not be reversed in his time, and the apparent collapse of the two-party system between 1910 and 1912 seemed to bear him out. Taft was "a platter of mush, a jellyfish," he told Pyle, who was gathering material for a biography of Hill; while Woodrow Wilson was "a fighter, but obstinate as a mule." What infuriated Hill most was the demagogues' talent for taking the people's money and then giving it back to them in a wide variety of social projects. At the National Foreign Trade Convention in Washington in 1914 he pointed to Great Britain as an example of how such domestic policies could handicap a great commercial nation in world markets and thus destroy its prosperity in the long run. The speech drew angry comments from David Lloyd George, Britain's radical chancellor of the exchequer, and the admiration of long-suffering conservatives.[23]

Offers to build a monument to him kept coming in. The architect of the Reference Library (Electus D. Litchfield, the talented young descendant of the "old rat" who had given the associates so much trouble in the last stages of their takeover of the St. Paul and Pacific) asked what he had in mind for a cornerstone. "No cornerstone," Hill scribbled on the margin of Litchfield's letter. "Wait until I am dead," he told the American Historical Association, which wanted to publish a biographical sketch. Nor would he write his reminiscences, although he told publisher F. N. Doubleday that "I may leave such a story as you request among my papers when I 'shuffle off.' " [24] And he did, a seven-page draft which left no doubt as to how he wanted to be remembered:

> From one point of view the relation of James J. Hill to the development of American material prosperity is unique. There is no other instance recorded of the exclusive conception by the mind of one man of the construction of one of the world's great railway systems. He believed that it was commercially practicable and scientifically feasible . . . to construct a line of railroad from an eastern terminus upon the Great Lakes to a western terminus at some point on the North Pacific Coast. He possessed the practical qualities which, within the working years of a single lifetime, crystallized that conception into accomplished fact. . . .[25]

Even though the turgid prose was probably Pyle's, it seemed rather immodest. Looking back sixty years, he may have felt that the idea of the Great Northern had, indeed, occurred to him in those summer days of 1856 when he had made good use of the time "from 6 o'clock every evening to walk around and enjoy myself." And no doubt he was greatly pleased when the Governor of Minnesota declared him "first citizen" of Minnesota in 1915.

Meanwhile, he went right on making the big decisions for the Hill roads, just as though he had never retired. Louis sought his counsel on many matters, notably on the purchase of large shipments of steel rails. Hill supervised the planning of a huge new building in which the Great Northern and the Northern Pacific, well separated by a thick partition down the center, were to have their St. Paul headquarters. And when the Great Northern found itself short of cash in the recession summer of 1913, he lent it $2.5 million from his personal funds. Nothing really seemed to have changed. His eye was as critically observant as ever. Riding through the yards in Chicago, he thought he saw far too many Great Northern freight cars loafing down there, and sent word to his men to get them back home. Louis, faced with a battery of Wall Street lawyers who were interposing one technicality after another in the new blanket mortgage, got his father into a room with George F. Baker. The pettifoggers were quickly straightened out. Tough problems concerning the Burlington's entrance into Kansas City had to be solved, and nobody else seemed able to do it. Meanwhile the new steamships *Great Northern* and *Northern Pacific*, with which he had hoped to compete for business between Puget Sound and San Francisco, developed one mechanical problem after another. They seemed about to prove once again that he should have stuck exclusively to railroads.[26]

It was harder than ever for Hill to keep up his spirits, that spring of 1914. Not long after Woodrow Wilson had moved into the White House the nation had slid into a recession that looked far more serious than the panic of 1907. In the spring of 1913 the railroads had applied for a second time for a token general increase in rates, and the Interstate Commerce Commission had been fretting over the case for more than a year. Traffic had declined sharply, and railroads that, unlike Hill's, did not know how to cut expenses just as sharply were in deep trouble. Throwing off these cares, Hill met Gaspard Farrer at St. Paul's Union Station in late May of 1914 and brought him up to Summit Avenue for an informal dinner with Mary. Next day he bundled Farrer and Ralph Budd, who was the railroad's *de facto* president, into his car A-1, and off they went for a trip over the Great Northern to Puget Sound. The Cascades give no hint of their winter terrors as they crossed them on a glorious spring day. Hill reminisced about the hard decision he had had to make in settling for a switchback until the tunnel could be completed. In another few years, he told Budd, a new and much longer Cascade tunnel would have to be built. It was his last trip over the line.

A month later Hill was at the salmon river, gloomy at the absence of nearly every one of his old friends. Sam Thorne was recovering from a heart attack that had almost carried him off. George Clark had made some kind of excuse. Dr. Stewart was attending an international medical congress in Europe. Even Louis, who had accompanied Maud to the Mayo Clinic, was missing. There were no newspapers to read, of course. A telegram from Nichols provided a good excuse to get back to New York and find out whether Archduke Ferdinand's assassination meant anything to the shaky peace of Europe. The bickering between Austria and Serbia was soon relegated to the inside pages of the papers, but Nichols went daily to consult with Jacob Schiff, whose European agents were close to the chancelleries of Vienna, Berlin, and St. Petersburg. By late July they were all deeply worried.[27]

V

Like many another American parent in the early days of August 1914, Hill's first concern was to get the members of his family who had been touring in Europe safely back to the United States. Europe had welcomed a record number of American visitors in June—tourists of all ranks, from impecunious language teachers, who went on walking tours with little more than bread and cheese in their knapsacks, to the wealthy, who were relaxing at Baden-Baden, Aix-les-Bains, and elsewhere. Among the latter were Gertrude and Michael Gavin and Clara. All commercial cable circuits were jammed, but J. H. Carroll, busier than ever with the railroads' business in Washington now that the storm had broken, persuaded his old friend Joseph Tumulty, the President's secretary, to use the State Department's circuit, and the Hills were soon relieved to learn that everybody was safe at Brown's Hotel in London.[28]

Historians of the great American financial panics usually ignore the panic that followed the news that Germany had invaded Belgium. Stocks did not merely slump. They collapsed, especially those to which British and French investors were heavily committed. And Wall Street's leaders prudently shut the Stock Exchange for the rest of the year. After the First Battle of the Marne, at the end of August, the long years of stalemated trench warfare began. Hill's pen flew as he asked his friends abroad what they thought lay ahead and told them of his own ideas. To Farrer, he gave his flat opinion that, in spite of neutrality, which he ardently supported, at least for the moment, the United States, and even the Midwest, despite its large German-American population, was on the side of the Allies. To those who wanted the United States to arm against the most pessimistic contingencies, Hill wrote that he had long considered the existence of large standing armies to be almost a guarantee of war, and he believed that the events in Europe had proved his theory. On the other hand, he had only contempt for weekend militia soldiers and reluctantly recommended some form of universal military training for one year to produce a large force of professionally trained reservists. The most important thing, he felt, was to keep the size of the active, professional army to a minimum.[29]

But there was more to do than talk and write letters. Ignoring his retired status, he issued orders to tighten the railroad belt even further. He rejoiced that the Hill roads had long ago made generous provision for terminal facilities, which he freely predicted would be a bottleneck in the near future. To a New York broker who asked him if this would not be a good time for the railroads to demand from Congress the rate increases they needed, and relief from the depredations of state commissions, he wrote a stern warning that it was no time for radical policies. "This is not the cause of the railroads, merely; it is that of the whole people," he counseled.[30]

In St. Paul Clara Hill quickly took a leading role in the campaign to raise food and clothing for the Belgians, whose courageous opposition to the Germans had made a shambles of the invaders' plan to subdue France in a few short weeks. She had an efficient lieutenant in her father, and both of them were proud of the warm letters of gratitude from Albert, King of the Belgians, whom they had first met when he was a young tourist in the Northwest over twenty years before. Hill was soon shuttling back and forth between St. Paul and Washington at the urgent call of Secretary of the Treasury William Gibbs McAdoo. The Secretary and his father-in-law, the President, who was still disabled by grief over the recent death of his wife, had finally awakened to the fact that the irrational policies of the preceding twenty years had left the United States with no merchant marine of its own to carry its goods. The first fruits of their hectic conferences were war-risk insurance for ships willing to register under the American flag, and emergency federal credits to finance marketing of the grain crop under circumstances that no one had ever foreseen.[31]

The long, boring winter of 1914–15 was followed by the renewed horrors of war on the western front. The terrible truth was beginning to hit home: it was to be a war of attrition, a war in the style of the American Civil War, one which would not end until one side or the other had been beaten into submission. Hill grieved with Gaspard Farrer as the calamitous death toll among young officers carried away many of the men who would have been Britain's future leaders. Men like Hill, however, knew that it was the problem of supply that would soon have the Allies in a desperate position. While England controlled the sea lanes and effectively shut Germany and her co-belligerents off from the farms and factories of the New World, the Allies were simply running out of money. Cash-and-carry neutrality, American policy since the beginning of the war, had been strained but not reversed by the sinking of the *Lusitania*. The short-term balances of English and French banks in the United States had soon been exhausted, and their people's holdings of bonds and stocks in American business were rapidly being liquidated. Soon the Americans would have to show whether they really cared who won the war.

Meanwhile, the annual trip to the River St. John to kill salmon was approaching, and Hill rejoiced that it was almost going to be like old times. Sam Thorne wanted very much to go, and his doctor, upon learning that Dr. Stewart and Thorne's son, William, would be in the party, gave his permission. Things got off to a bad start when a member of the *Wacouta*'s crew came down with smallpox early in June at the dock in New London, and to make matters worse, the salmon had arrived at the river unusually early that year. But after a short quarantine and a thorough disinfection, Captain Weed sailed in good time, and by early July the party had killed several hundred fish in one of the best seasons they had ever seen. On the afternoon of July 3, Thorne excitedly displayed a twenty-eight-pounder. Early next morning he awoke with pains in his chest, and a few hours later was dead. The party quickly broke camp, and the *Wacouta* sailed within hours.[32]

Hill's family and friends were not prepared for the profound effect Thorne's death had on him. When Toomey came into his office with a telegraphic offer to charter the yacht—they received several such offers each year—Hill waved him aside. "The *Wacouta* is being permanently laid up," he murmured. Some weeks later Brown risked a scowl to tell him that an offer to buy the ship had been received, and was surprised to hear his employer say that, yes, he would consider an offer. More depressing events followed. Returning to New York from the isolated salmon river, Hill was shocked to learn that on July 3 an unbalanced teacher of German at Cornell University had forced his way past the guard at J. P. Morgan's Long Island mansion and pumped two pistol bullets into the banker before being overpowered. Morgan was all right, but it had been a close call. And a few weeks later word came from Montreal that Sir William C. Van Horne, who had accepted a knighthood on the assurance that it would not compromise his American citizenship, had died—not so much from a lifetime of hard work, overeating, cigar smoking, brandy drinking, and all-night poker playing as from a restless spirit that preferred death to idleness.[33]

For months Hill had been resisting the signs that his own health was far from perfect. There was no one thing critically wrong with him; his heart and lungs were as strong as ever, and the rheumatism which had often laid him low as a younger man seldom gave him trouble. But there were problems which he had been trying to ignore for years. His teeth were a family joke, and not a good one. By 1910 they were threatening to undermine his health, and the entire family was worried about him. Anson Beard had written him a stern lecture which sent him off to the dentist for the little that could be done. By 1911 Hill was annoyed by a moderate enlargement of the prostate, "something every man must face, sooner or later, if he lives long enough," a doctor has said. In 1915, upon his doctor's advice that he get more exercise, he bought a saddle horse, which he rode now and then. The biggest nuisance—he was determined to consider it nothing more than that—was beneath his dignity to mention, humiliating, and damnably uncomfortable. The condition would have responded well to simple, if painful, surgery, but doctors were handicapped, then as now, by their patients' dependence upon quacks and palliatives. In 1899 Hill had carefully filed away an announcement from a New York doctor who had advertised, "Hemorrhoids radically cured by a new method, and without operation or pain." Dr. Stewart tried to convince him that there was but one remedy. George B. Harris and J. H. Carroll tried applied psychology on him in 1911, the former writing a shrewd letter telling of the latter's successful operation for a similar problem, and how it had made a new man of him.[34] By late summer of 1915 the condition was growing acute, but at that moment Hill was preparing to play the last and greatest role of his life.

VI

Gaspard Farrer had admitted ruefully that their letters were likely to end up in the censor's wastebasket or at the bottom of the sea, but still they wrote. Farrer, who knew that Lord Reading had left for America in search of financial help for the staggering Allies, was delighted to get Hill's letter of September 5, 1915:

> Sterling exchange today sold in New York at $4.51. Surely this cannot go on much farther or much longer. . . . The shipment of gold . . . will not stop the fall in exchange. . . . This country does not need any more gold. I am convinced that a credit of $500 million could be arranged here, to be followed by more later, if necessary. . . . Leading bankers are beginning to realize that while we have large amounts of grain, provisions and cotton to sell, our customers must be able to pay us for what we deliver. . . .
>
> If England cannot buy what we have to sell . . . who else will buy it?

As the leaders of the United States came to realize these hard facts, twentieth-century America, with all its international obligations, was born. James J. Hill was one of the midwives. On September 7 Lord Revelstoke, senior partner in Farrer's firm of Baring Brothers & Company, dispatched a cable whose impulses flashed beneath the ship that was carrying Hill's letter to England. Revelstoke was "anxious some friends arriving New York this week should have advantage of meeting you." On the same day a telegram arrived from J. P. Morgan, who was taking the lead in arranging an Anglo-French loan, as it was to be called. Could Hill be in New York by Friday afternoon of the tenth? Monday the thirteenth was the best he could manage, Hill replied. He sent his regrets to the disappointed officials of the county fairs at Long Prairie, Barnesville, and Bagley, Minnesota, where he had promised to speak. And, pawing through a mound of papers in his office late Saturday afternoon just before train time, he came upon his invitation to his birthday banquet, which the Great Northern Veterans' Association had made an annual affair. Hurriedly he dictated an apologetic note of explanation, adding, "I must resign the pleasure of looking into your familiar faces and clasping again your friendly hands." [35]

In the days of its greatness, newspaper reporters and photographers met the Twentieth Century Limited as conscientiously as they met the *S. S. Mauretania* or the *Olympic*. On Monday morning, September 13, there promised to be an important arrival at Grand Central Terminal, for James J. Hill was coming to town to confer with the Englishmen and Frenchmen who were seeking, and the big bankers who were considering, a huge loan. It was hot. New York City was sweltering under "the most prolonged spell of severe hot weather in September recorded by the local weather bureau," the *Times* reported four days later, noting that seven people had died from the heat the day before. The Century rolled in, its huge, new, green Pullmans stained with the September dust of five states, and then, down the red carpet, came the reporters' quarry, the short, burly man with a grizzled white beard that would never look well barbered, a big, slightly squashed, western-style homburg clamped on his head, and a face crinkling into a smile. The reporters also saw how small and tired he looked after his long, hot journey. But his wave of greeting was, if anything, more confident than ever.

Hill went directly to the Biltmore Hotel, where the six Anglo-French commissioners had their headquarters, and the conferences began behind doors that were closely guarded by private detectives. On Hill's side of the table, among others, were Willard Straight, the State Department's specialist in international finance, James B. Forgan of the First National Bank of Chicago, Frank A. Vanderlip of the National City Bank, Benjamin Strong of the newly organized Federal Reserve Bank of New York, and, of course, Morgan. Like his father, Morgan knew what to do when business negotiations threatened to bog down in New York's hot, muggy weather, and he took the group for a cruise on his yacht, *Corsair*. All week long they negotiated, and on one evening Hill eased the proceedings with an elegant dinner at 8 East 65 Street, flawlessly served under the cold eye of Ernst Kurth.[36]

Hill's role was a major one. For although the loan was to be a private affair—bonds were to be bought by a group of underwriters and then sold to the public—it was, obviously, a departure from strict neutrality. The Germans declared sarcastically that the Americans were submitting to a "hold-up" by an "insolvent" nation. It was crucial, therefore, that the loan have *national* support, especially in the Midwest, where pro-German sentiment was thought to be a fatal obstacle, even though most of the loan would be subscribed in the East. Hill told them how it could be done.

In the first place, he explained, it had to be made perfectly clear that no part of the loan would be used for munitions purchases. In fact, he had a telegram from Louis stating baldly that "word should go out from New York all over the country that this is a grain, livestock, cotton and wool proposition." There must be no sales commission to the bankers beyond their underwriting fee. Amounts subscribed in places outside New York must not be immediately drained off by New York banks, but retained on deposit locally until the proceeds were needed

Back at his desk in the Great Northern Building, St. Paul, in late September 1915, after the Anglo-French loan negotiations in New York. Photograph by Lee Bros., St. Paul.

to pay invoices for goods delivered. If they would make these conditions explicit, said Hill, there would be no problem. And later on, when it appeared that explicit clauses on these points were not going into the prospectus, he hastened to remind Morgan that a promise was a promise.[37]

By Friday he was exhausted, his spirits drained. Relaxing at the Great Northern office at 32 Nassau Street, he was greatly pleased to receive a visit from John F. Stevens. As Stevens later recalled,

He drifted into reminiscences about the old days. As I left his office he came with me to the elevator, something that he never did before, put his hand on my shoulder and said, "John, is there anything in the world that

I can do for you? If there ever is, you know where to find me." I left him with the sad foreboding that I would never see him again.[38]

When Hill got back to St. Paul he ignored threats from depositors and gave orders that the First National Bank of St. Paul was to subscribe heavily to the loan. Then he began to get frantic telegrams from Morgan, J. Ogden Armour, and Thomas W. Lamont, begging him to go to Chicago, where, Lamont said, "Mitchell . . . and all the other big banks want to [subscribe] but are afraid to come out into the open." [39] But he had done all he could. His doctor told him not to set foot on another train until he had had a good, long rest. Meanwhile he could savor some of the reaction his labors were getting from the angry German-Americans of Minnesota. Wrote a doctor in Melrose,

> I heard you are interested in a good fertilizing agent. No doubt you must have heard that bone meal is a good fertilizer. How many thousand pounds of human bone meal will your billion dollar loan produce if the by-product were properly taken care of . . . ?

He filed it along with Lord Reading's letter of gratitude.[40]

VII

"In the Northwest we have had a wonderful year for grain," Hill wrote Farrer, as the precious foodstuffs began to flow eastward. "On the lines of the Great Northern Railroad from the Twin Cities to the Rocky Mountains it is a grain field. All through Montana, where we used to hope the bench lands would be used for grazing, we have a continuous grain field." The success of the loan negotiations and the bountifulness of the harvest cheered him up remarkably. As a beautiful October unfolded, he even thought of going to Lafayette College, in Pennsylvania, to receive the honorary degree for which he had been nominated, and which could not be conferred *in absentia*. The school was planning a parade of notables: "Judge" Elbert Gary of United States Steel, Ambassador Jusserand of France, Cyrus Hall McCormick, Elihu Root—even the pacifist editor and son of Hill's old adversary, Oswald Garrison Villard. But the doctor was horrified at the thought. Still, by October 15, doctor or not, he went off to the Fergus Falls, Minnesota, fair and to other county fairs to fulfill his long-standing speaking engagements. In November he took Clara and Mary to New York, where they spent long hours in the art galleries. Back in St. Paul for Christmas, he was laid up again. "While I am not confined to the house, I am under the doctor's care and he advises that I remain quiet and forego any traveling," he explained to the secretary of the National Foreign Trade Council; to Henry M. Rice's daughter, who wanted him to unveil the statue of the late Senator in Statuary Hall in the capitol at Washington; to E. T. Stotesbury, who was active in the preparedness drive in Philadelphia; and to many others. To the president of Dartmouth College, which offered an honorary degree to be conferred the following June, he replied, "D.V. [*Deo volente*] I expect to be with you on June 18th." [41]

He was determined, however, that he and Mary should not spend the winter in St. Paul. Toward the end of January the two of them, with Clara, took the train to New York and then to Philadelphia, where he called on Samuel Rea, his ailing old friend who had headed the Pennsylvania Railroad. By February 1 the Hills were at Jekyl Island. He busied himself with plans for a cottage of their own, having decided that their apartment at the "Sans Souci", one of the first condominiums in the nation, was not adequate, but by February 24 he had fled back to New York. "Go ahead with building and send me the bill," he wrote the contractor from his desk at the Great Northern offices on Nassau Street. The office boy routinely pressed the letter in Hill's New York letterbook, as office boys had been doing for thirty-six years, and none would ever do again. That afternoon he saw Mike and Gertrude off for Jekyl, and two days later he left for St. Paul and the lonely mansion on Summit Avenue. [42]

He wrote to Clara on March 10, 1916, reporting that a shipment of medical supplies had been dispatched to a Belgian hospital, and asking whether she really liked the painting by Constable which they had seen at Knoedler's in November. He admitted that things were pretty "quiet" with him. He dined alone on many evenings, not wanting to accept all of the invitations which Rachel and Egil pressed on him. Rachel was very well, he thought, considering that she had presented Egil with two daughters in three years. The second, baby Gertrude, was his thirteenth grandchild. He played solitaire at a table near the window in his den. When that palled there were the big, beautifully cut jigsaw puzzles that he had grown fond of, and most of the latest non-fiction books, which he read sitting in a great wing chair near the fire. Louis and his large family, although they lived just next door, were in California for much of each winter. Charlotte dropped by now and then, and left her daughter Georgiana to visit with her grandfa-

The last trip to Jekyl Island, Georgia. February 1916.

ther. "Gian," still in pigtails, cooperated zestfully in Hill's ritual: a squeal as his rough beard scratched her cheek during their first kiss of greeting; giggles as he chanted the name he had made up for her, "Georgiana Phoebiana Concertina Brown"; and finally loud protestations when he accused her of coming to see not him, but the gardener, an ancient Irishman who never bathed.[43]

Over the years he had made few cronies. An exception was George A. McPherson, a local merchant of modest ability who represented, largely as a result of Hill's influence, a number of manufacturers of railroad and building materials. One evening their talk drifted to the subject of wills. Hill told his friend that he had decided to make a will in which he would leave only half as much to Walter, who had no head for money, as to the others, and nothing at all to James N. Hill. McPherson, though he knew how Hill hated to be disagreed with, nevertheless pointed out that such a will could cause family troubles for many years. The will was drawn up, shoved into a desk unsigned, and forgotten, as it turned out, forever. There was no hurry, Hill reasoned. Under the laws of Minnesota one-third of his estate, carried on Toomey's big master ledger at $63 million, would go to Mary. She would administer the rest of it, and her ideas and his were identical.[44]

Mary, Clara, and the Gavins returned to New York in March, and Hill joined them there. The elegant house on 65 Street was a cheerful place during the wild March days. They looked at more pictures at Knoedler's, where he bought another Millet and, finally, Daumier's "Third Class Carriage." He tried sitting for a new photographer, Pierce, and the results, although coldly formal, pleased him enough that he ordered several dozen copies. But spring was coming to the Northwest, and that was the time to be at home. By April 13 they were all back in St. Paul.[45]

Almost every day he went to his office, which by then was in the new Great Northern Building. He looked forward to Toomey's warm greeting, and the bashful "good morning's" of the young clerks, among whom there always seemed to be a new one. He issued instructions for furnishing the big new "bungalow" at North Oaks; wrote a letter to a budding valedictorian who wanted his recipe for success ("Honest application to the work you have to do"); agreed with Irving Fisher, by then a professor at Yale, that liquor was a curse; and laughed at George W. Perkins's suggestion that he support Theodore Roosevelt for the Republican nomination that summer.[46]

Returning home in late afternoon, he liked to poke around the grounds for a few minutes before going in. "The lilacs are slow this year," he observed to the gardener as he inspected the big bushes that framed the windows of the mansion. The longed-for symbol of spring's arrival was indeed slow that year; Mary noted in her diary on Sunday, May 7, 1916, that although it had turned very warm the lilacs were barely in leaf. The following Friday, May 12, Hill went to North Oaks to make sure that repairs to the porch were being done properly. Next day he stayed in his room, coming down only for dinner. The following Wednesday the weather degenerated into winter again. There was frost that morning, but Hill decided to go to the office. He returned after a few hours, feeling very bad and running a slight fever.

His last portrait. New York, March 1916.

On Friday morning, May 19, Louis and fourteen-year-old Louis Jr., both of them celebrating their birthdays that day, came through the hedge from next door to receive Hill's greetings. After they had gone he tried to get comfortable enough to read a new book in which he was deeply absorbed, *The Heritage of Tyre* by W. B. Meloney, which chronicled the steps by which America had destroyed its once-great merchant marine and offered an energetic program to redeem her place. By May 23 he was in great pain. When word got out that Hill was sick in bed, Mary sent a reassuring telegram to Roland F. Knoedler, and Toomey sent messages to George F. Baker and J. H. Carroll in Washington. Hill continued to conduct business from his sickbed, with Brown bringing all the mail and noting the replies to be made. Toomey came in every day to receive his orders, which one day included detailed instructions to be relayed to Walter at Northcote Farm. In the confusion Toomey suddenly realized that he had nearly forgotten to wire Captain Weed not to set sail on the *Wacouta;* Hill had stubbornly kept her in commission.

Dr. Herman Biggs hurried in from New York to help his old friend and benefactor. By May 27 the doctors were shaking their heads. What had been an ordinary hemorrhoid, sadly neglected and abused, had suddenly flared into a serious infection. Other lesions followed. Gangrene had set in and was proceeding down the patient's left thigh, probably out of control. In the first operation they ever performed outside their clinic at Rochester, Minnesota, Doctors William J. and Charles H. Mayo, assisted by Biggs and Hill's personal physician, James S. Gilfillan, lanced and drained the infection. But Hill was seventy-seven, and there was little hope that he could recover. Finally a coma brought relief from his deep, unyielding pain.

"At 9:50 A.M. today, Papa very peacefully breathed his last. All here but Ruth, who comes this evening," Mary wrote in her dairy on May 29. Still on the initial edge of grief, she had shut herself in her own room and carefully written the entry in the leather-bound book. She was sitting in her big wing chair when Clara came to tell her that the Slade children had arrived from George and Charlotte's place in Fenlea. She asked for Georgiana and, saying nothing, held her hand for a few minutes as the little girl sat on the footstool, wondering at the subdued atmosphere that pervaded the house. Clara suggested that she and her brother might join Louis and Maud's four children, from next door, in picking lilies of the valley in the broad yard of the mansion. By the time someone remembered to fetch them they had gathered several huge bunches. Only Clara was left with her mother, who softly began to tell her daughter of her early days as friend, then fiancée, and finally wife of James J. Hill.

Across the hall of their suite, her husband of not quite fifty years was laid out in his big corner bedroom, surrounded by vases of great bunches of lilies of the valley. It was a superb May day, the kind that finally announces the longed-for Northwestern spring. Almost reaching to the window-sill was a lilac bush in full bloom. Somewhere at the foot of the bluff a steamboat, one of a few left on the Mississippi, sounded its whistle. In the distance two smudges of smoke marked the St. Paul Union Station, where the Great Northern and Northern Pacific's transcontinental limiteds prepared to start their dash for Puget Sound. The Northwest was open.

At the hour of the funeral, 2 p.m. on May 31, every train on the Hill railroads, wherever it was, stopped for five minutes. The passengers of a Northern Pacific train high in the Rockies, at lunch in the diner, laid down their knives and forks in embarrassed silence when the conductor told them the reason for their unscheduled stop. Later that afternoon a small group of invited mourners braved a wild rainstorm to say their last goodbyes to James J. Hill in the little private cemetery at North Oaks Farm, which would not, in the end, be his and Mary's last resting place.[47]

From the porch of her own little house, from the fields where he was finishing the spring plowing, Engebord and Knute Ryggen might have seen the train pause amid the freshly turned furrows that ran right up to the tracks that Hill and his associates had laid through the valley nearly forty years before. They knew who "Yem" Hill was, well enough, and he, who had never met them, had yet met them a thousand times. Here, in the valley of the Red River of the North, their lives had all come together to form a common story. Receiving nothing from the past save the gift of life, they had put their hands to the work they encountered. Finding no place laid for them at Nature's table, they made places for themselves and countless more whose names they never knew. The abundance they created embarrassed the next generation, but their grandchildren would learn what they had always known: that abundance has always been the exception, and not the rule, in the human story. It is the creation of the Hills and the Ryggens, who will yet be the true heroes of the twentieth century. When we need them again they will be found walking in our midst.

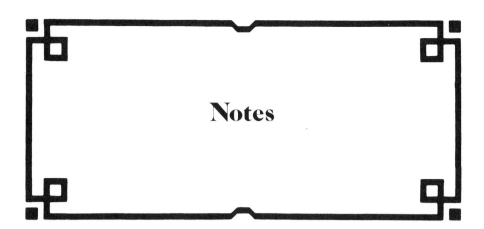

Notes

CHAPTER ONE

1. Written on the back of an old photograph in the possession of Mrs. Charles Rungeling, Fenwick, Ont., and quoted in "Famous School to be Commemorated," press release and MS biography of William Wetherald, Department of Travel and Publicity, Province of Ontario, Canada, June 21, 1962, 2.
2. Wetherald to his sister, Jan. 12, 1862, letterbook in possession of Mrs. Charles Rungeling, quoted in Province of Ontario, "Famous School," 2.
3. Wetherald's reminiscences of his early life are in Arthur G. Dorland, *A History of the Society of Friends (Quakers) in Canada* (Toronto, 1927), 187–89.
4. Frank Day, *Here and There in Eramosa* (Rockwood, Ont., 1952), 7, 26–34, 96; Province of Ontario, "Famous School," 3–4.
5. Ibid. 5; "J. J. Hill's Life Story; Powerful Railroad Magnate Relates His Early History," Philadelphia *Record*, Feb. 1, 1902, Scrapbook No. 1, p. 197, JJHP.
6. Province of Ontario, "Famous School," 11, 12.
7. Hill to Wetherald, June 23, 1881.
8. Ledger, "Subscriptions, Donations, etc., J. J. Hill, Nov. 23, 1880–Apr. 9, 1908," Stack XVII, Shelf 5, JJHP; Wetherald to Hill, Aug. 23, 1881.
9. MS genealogy in Accession 16 (Eleanor E. Pearce Papers), JJHP; reminiscences of Alexander S. D. Hill, 1916, and letter from Mrs. James N. Dunbar, Brookline, Mass., Oct. 9, 1916, to Joseph G. Pyle, in Pyle, Notes for a Biography of James J. Hill, James J. Hill Reference Library, St. Paul, Minn. (1917); Clara Hill Lindley, *James J. and Mary T. Hill, An Unfinished Chronicle by their Daughter* (New York, privately printed, 1948), 1–12. Neither a Colonel John Riggs nor an Admiral Warren Riggs, another military forebear claimed by A. S. D. Hill, appears in British records; Public Records Office, Jan. 31, 1974, and Ministry of Defense, Jan. 10, 1974, to Albro Martin.
10. Joseph G. Pyle, *The Life of James J. Hill* (2 vols., New York, 1916–17), I, 3.
11. Graham Hill to Alexander Riggs Hill, Oct. 19, 1842, Accession 16 (Eleanor E. Pearce Papers), JJHP. Details of the boyhood of James J. and Alexander S. D. Hill are from the reminiscences of A. S. D. Hill, in Pyle's Notes, and Lindley, *James J. and Mary T. Hill*, 12–13.
12. Reminiscences of A. S. D. Hill, in Pyle, Notes. Mrs. G. S. Reny discovered that, in a picture of Hill and his two older sons hunting birds in a field, Chelminski painted

Hill with his left hand on the trigger of his gun and the right hand supporting the base of the barrel, a characteristic pose of one who is prepared to lift the weapon to his left shoulder and sight with the left eye.

13. Lindley, *James J. and Mary T. Hill,* 12–14, 17–18.
14. A. S. D. Hill, Reminiscences, in Pyle, Notes; Lindley, *James J. and Mary T. Hill,* 16–17.
15. Reminiscences of A. S. D. Hill, in Pyle, Notes; Lindley, *James J. and Mary T. Hill,* 16–18.
16. Marcus L. Hansen, *The Mingling of the Canadian and American Peoples,* (New Haven, 1940).
17. *Ibid.* 115.
18. J. Bartlett Brebner, *Canada* (Ann Arbor, 1960), Ch. 18.
19. Hansen, *Mingling of the Canadian and American Peoples,* 135.
20. *Ibid.* 128–32.
21. C. W. Dana, *The Great West; or, The Garden of the World* (Boston, 1856), 14.
22. Thurlow Weed, in *New York Semi-weekly Tribune,* June 20, 1854, quoted in William J. Petersen, *Steamboating on the Upper Mississippi* (Iowa City, 1937; reprinted 1968), 343.
23. Reminiscences of A. S. D. Hill, in Pyle, Notes; Lindley, *James J. and Mary T. Hill,* 18–19; James J. Hill to Arch. H. Stuart, Mar. 27, 1889.

CHAPTER TWO

1. For a brief sketch of St. Paul's founding see William Watts Folwell, *A History of Minnesota* (4 vols., St. Paul, 1926), I, 222–30.
2. Original letter in possession of the Northwest Area Foundation, photocopy in JJHP, GC.
3. See Hill's corrections of MS accompanying Cy Warman to Hill, Dec. 7, 1901, JJHP, GC; Alexander Hill claimed that James J. arrived in St. Paul on July 15, 1856, but both Joseph G. Pyle and Clara Hill Lindley apparently had it from Mr. Hill himself that the date was July 21, 1856; Joseph G. Pyle, Notes for a Biography of James J. Hill; Pyle, *The Life of James J. Hill* (2 vols., Garden City, N.Y., 1917), I, 24; Clara Hill Lindley, *James J. and Mary T. Hill, An Unfinished Chronicle by their Daughter* (New York, privately printed, 1948), 20–21.
4. C. W. Dana, *The Great West; or, The Garden of the World* (Boston, 1856), 244.
5. Mary Ellen Ellet, *Summer Rambles in the West* (New York, 1853), 80–81; Harriet Bishop, *Floral Home; or, First Years in Minnesota* (New York, 1857), 125.
6. JJHP, Accession 16, contains a clipping which is a letter to the editor of an unidentified newspaper from one A. P. Hechtman of Osseo, Minnesota, asserting that the neighbor was one Joe Cardinal, who lived until 1918. For the influence of William Farrish and friends, see Lindley, *James J. and Mary T. Hill,* 20.
7. T. M. Newson, *Pen Pictures of St. Paul* (St. Paul, 1886), 564–65.
8. Newson, *Pen Pictures,* 568–69; St. Paul *Pioneer Press,* interview with Dr. Charles E. Smith, Mar. 5, 1922.
9. Newson, *Pen Pictures,* 540, 570, 654; James J. Reardon, *The Catholic Church in the Diocese of Saint Paul* (St. Paul, 1952), cited in James P. Shannon, *Catholic Colonization on the Western Frontier* (New Haven, 1957), 34, 43.
10. William J. Petersen, *Steamboating on the Upper Mississippi* (Iowa City, 1968), is the best summary; see 57, 77, 80, 105.
11. Mildred L. Hartsough, *From Canoe to Steel Barge on the Upper Mississippi* (Minneapolis-St. Paul, 1934), 160–65.

12. The St. Anthony *Express Weekly* printed data on steamboat arrivals at St. Paul for the years 1844–56 on Nov. 22, 1856; Hartsough, *Canoe to Steel Barge*, 164–71; Petersen, *Steamboating*, 229–34; Louis C. Hunter, *Steamboats on the Western Rivers* (Cambridge, Mass., 1949), 334–35, 488, 630–35. See also Robert C. Toole, "Steamboat Pioneer, The Early History of William F. Davidson," *Minnesota History*, XXXVI (Sept. 1959), 250–58.

13. Dubuque Daily *Express & Herald,* May 8, 1857, quoted in Petersen, *Steamboating,* 348.

14. Hill to J. A. Wheelock, May 20, 1893; Folwell, *Minnesota,* II *passim;* Col. George D. Rogers, "History of Flour Manufacture in Minnesota," *Collections of the Minnesota Historical Society,* X, Pt. 1 (1905), 34–55; N. S. B. Gras, *A History of Agriculture* (New York, 1925), 292–93.

15. Hill to J. A. Wheelock, May 20, 1893; Waybill, JJHP, GC, Nov. 6, 1864.

16. D. S. B. Johnson to Hill, Jan. 18, 1907; St. Paul *Daily Press,* Aug. 30, 1864; Mar. 28, 1863; Dec. 12, 1863.

17. Minnesota Historical Society, No. 1102, Minnehaha Engine Co. No. 2 of the City of St. Paul, Papers, 1857–1859 (1 vol.).

18. Montage photograph, JJHP, "Museum Pieces"; Folwell, *Minnesota,* II, 28–30; C. C. Andrews (ed.), *History of St. Paul, Minnesota* (Syracuse, 1890), 76; Lindley, *James J. and Mary T. Hill,* 72–74; Ulysses S. Grant, *Memoirs* (2 vols. in 1, New York, 1894), 132; St. Paul *Daily Press,* May 14, 1861.

19. Lindley, *James J. and Mary T. Hill,* 71–72; interview with Miss Leslie Hill, granddaughter of A. S. D. Hill.

20. St. Paul *Pioneer & Democrat,* Sept. 10, 1861; St. Paul *Daily Press,* Apr. 2, May 2, June 29, 1862.

21. Hartsough, *From Canoe to Steel Barge,* 168–70.

22. Petersen, *Steamboating,* 390; St. Paul *Daily Press,* Jan. 1, 1865; Lindley, *James J. and Mary T. Hill,* 81.

23. Wellington to Hill, Jan. 4, 1865.

24. Wellington to Hill, Jan. 22, 1866.

25. Wellington to Hill, Feb. 2, 1865.

26. Wellington to Hill, Mar. 28, 1865.

27. St. Paul *Pioneer & Democrat,* Mar. 5, 1865; St. Paul *Daily Press,* Mar. 7, 1865.

28. Lease, JJHP, GC.

29. St. Paul *Pioneer & Democrat,* Mar. 16, 1866.

30. Articles of Agreement, Apr. 1, 1866, JJHP, GC.

31. Hill to Wellington, Apr. 2, 1866.

32. St. Paul *Pioneer & Democrat,* May 17, 1866.

33. Memorandum of Agreement, Jan. 15, 1867, JJHP, GC.

34. Hill to Wellington, Jan. 12, 1867.

35. Articles of Agreement, Sept. 16, 1867, JJHP, GC; St. Paul *Daily Press,* Dec. 10, 1867.

36. Hill to L. L. Davis, Mankato, Minn., Apr. 30, 1866; to Albert Cushman, Boston, Nov. 23, 1866; to H. P. Wilkins, Milwaukee, Aug. 9, Nov. 21, 1866.

37. Hill to W. H. Dike Co., Faribault, Apr. 25, 1866; to Richard & Bond, Chicago, May 1, 1866; to E. J. Baldwin, Faribault, July 19, 1867; to H. W. Carr, Chicago, June 27, 1866; to H. C. Wentworth, Chicago, Jan. 15, 1867; St. Paul *Daily Press,* Jan. 3, 1868.

38. Hill to Mr. Sproat, New York, June 29, 1866; to John Haycock, Shakopee, Minn., June 29, 1866; to A. T. Wild, New York, June 29, 1866.

39. Hill to H. W. Carr, Chicago, July 9, 1867; to W. G. Swan, July 26, 1867; to J. J. Merrill, Milwaukee, Aug. 9, 1867. Wellington to Hill, July 21, 1867.

CHAPTER THREE

1. This account of James J. and Mary T. Hill's courtship and marriage, and Mrs. Hill's family background, is taken for the most part from Clara Hill Lindley, *James J. and Mary T. Hill, An Unfinished Chronicle by their Daughter* (New York, privately printed, 1948). Patti toured Minnesota with Ole Bull; *Minnesota History*, Winter 1965, 321. Clara, who married late, spent much time in conversation with her father and, especially after his death, with her mother. She recorded their reminiscences over a period of years. Deed to Timothy Mehegan's burial plot in JJHP, GC, 1889. Marriage license in JJHP, GC; Hill to Swan, Sept. 2, 1867.

2. The story of the development of the Red River country has received the attention of historians for over 100 years. See esp. John Harnsberger and Robert P. Wilkins, "Transportation on the Northern Plains: I, The Genesis of Commerce," *North Dakota Quarterly* (Winter 1961), 20–27.

3. St. Paul *Pioneer & Democrat*, July 2, 1856; Daily *Minnesotian*, July 1, 1856; Alvin C. Gluek, Jr., *Minnesota and the Manifest Destiny of the Canadian Northwest; A Study in Canadian-American Relations* (Toronto, 1965), 137–38, 140–50, 168.

4. St. Anthony *Express*, Nov. 22, 1856; St. Paul *Daily Press*, July 2, 1870; JJH, Diary, 1869, privately owned; St. Paul *Daily Pioneer*, July 17, 1870.

5. Hill to F. E. Kew, London, Aug. 31, 1868.

6. Hill to Kew, May 18, 1868.

7. Hill to Kew, May 18, 26, 1868; to H. E. Sargent, General Superintendent, Michigan Central Railroad, Chicago, May 25, June 5, 1868.

8. Hill to Messrs. Henry Callender & Co., Boston, Aug. 29, 1868.

9. Hill to P. D. Armour, Milwaukee, June 17, 1868.

10. The circumstances leading to the Riel rebellion and Donald Smith's role in settling it, as well as Smith's meeting with Hill, are in Beckles Willson, *The Life of Lord Strathcona and Mount Royal* (2 vols., Boston and New York, 1915), esp. I, 368. Smith's description of the meeting is in the transcript of *Farley v. Kittson et al.*, Vol. II, Part 1, 1132. The standard history of the rebellion is G. F. G. Stanley, *The Birth of Western Canada* (New York, 1936). Hill's telegrams, Feb. 11, 28, letters Apr. 22, 29, 1870, to Joseph Howe, Public Archives of Canada, Rb.6, Cl, Vol. 12. Hill's account of setting his companion's arm was printed in the *Quarterly Journal of the University of North Dakota*, Inauguration No. (1911), 112–19.

11. The main works on the rise of navigation on the Red River are summarized in John Harnsberger and Robert P. Wilkins, "Transportation on the Northern Plains; II, Steamboating North of Fargo," *North Dakota Quarterly* (Spring 1961), 57–64.

12. Articles of Co-partnership between Hill, Griggs, and William B. Newcomb, Aug. 20, 1869, JJHP, GC; attached to the agreement of Jan. 1, 1872, formalizing the Red River enterprise, are agreements of Aug. 2, 1870, Feb. 20, 1871; Marion Herriot, "Steamboat Transportation on the Red River," *Minnesota History*, XXI (Sept. 1940), 245–71; St. Paul *Daily Pioneer*, Nov. 19, 1870; St. Paul *Daily Press*, Apr. 29, 1871.

13. Mr. Royall and party were Canadians; Diary, 1871, JJHP.

14. Gluek, *Minnesota and the Manifest Destiny of Canada*, 113; Diary, 1873, JJHP.

15. Herriot, "Steamboat Transportation," 254, 270; Harnsberger and Wilkins, "Transportation," 64–65; Hill, Diary, 1873, JJHP; T. M. Newson, *Pen Pictures of St. Paul* (St. Paul, 1886), 431.

16. Diary, 1869, privately owned.

17. St. Paul *Daily Press*, Apr. 30, 1869.

18. Receipt signed by D. M. Robbins, for payment for Sioux half-breed scrip; Jackman to Hill, Mar. 23, 1874; Taylor to Hill, July 26, 1877; recapitulation of expenses, Aug. 1, 1877, JJHP, GC.

19. Indenture, mortgage deed, warranty deed, JJHP, GC, May 25, 1871; canceled note, Sept. 13, 1872; St. Paul *Pioneer & Democrat*, May 27, 1869; St. Paul *Daily Press*, June 6, 1871; Diary, 1873; Lindley, *James J. and Mary T. Hill*, 84–86; Diary, 1873.
20. Diaries, privately owned; George E. Warner and Charles M. Foote (eds.), *History of Ramsey County and the City of St. Paul* (Minneapolis, 1881), 537–38; Newson, *Pen Pictures of St. Paul*, 672.
21. Diaries, 1869, 1873; Lindley, *James J. and Mary T. Hill*, 85, 97.

CHAPTER FOUR

1. Robert T. Haslam and Robert P. Russell, *Fuels and Their Combustion* (New York, 1936), 2; Howard N. Eavenson, *First Century and a Quarter of the American Coal Industry* (Baltimore, 1942), 418–19.
2. Partnership agreement, Aug. 25, 1869, JJHP, GC; St. Anthony Falls *Democrat*, July 20, 1871; St. Paul *Daily Press*, Feb. 3, 1870, Nov. 3, 1872.
3. Diary, Jan. 14–19, 1876; E. A. Sewall, Superintendent, First Division, St. Paul & Pacific Railroad, to Hill, Oct. 19, 1876.
4. James Macfarlane, *Coal-Regions of America; Their Topography, Geology, and Development* (New York, 1873); Richard C. Taylor, *Statistics of Coal* (Philadelphia, rev. ed., 1855); J. P. Lesley, *Manual of Coal and Its Topography* (Philadelphia, 1856). In contrast, Mildred L. Hartsough, *Twin Cities as a Metropolitan Market* (Minneapolis, 1925), completely ignores the role of coal in the development of the Twin Cities as the economic center of the Northwest.
5. Hill to Robert Law, July 19, 1867.
6. Hill to Law, Sept. 10, 1867; to O. E. Britt, July 21, 1868.
7. Hill to Wellington, June 20, 1867.
8. St. Paul *Daily Press*, May 25, 1867.
9. St. Paul *Daily Press*, Dec. 20, 1870; Articles of Co-partnership, Aug. 20, 25, 1869; Articles of Co-partnership, Jan. 1, 1872.
10. Memorandum of Agreement, May 10, 1872; memorandum in files, May 6, 1873, JJHP, GC; Becker to "Dear Colonel," March 4, 1874.
11. Diary, 1873, JJHP, GC; Memorandum of Agreement with C. W. Griggs, May 1, 1875; Articles of Agreement between JJH, Acker, Armstrong, and Saunders, May 1, 1875; Hill to C. M. Underhill, Buffalo, May 3, 1875.
12. *Farley v. Kittson et al.*, Transcript, II, Part 2, Deposition of Edward N. Saunders, 1487–88.
13. Diary, 1874.
14. Hill to Underhill, May 3, 1875; to R. C. Elmore & Co., June 9, 1875; to Underhill, June 26, 1875.
15. St. Paul *Daily Press*, July 12, 1873; Underhill to Hill and Acker, Apr. 19, 1876; Hill to Underhill, Dec. 6, 1875.
16. Diary, 1873; St. Paul *Pioneer & Democrat*, June 20, 1875; St. Paul *Daily Dispatch*, July 10, 1875.
17. "E.M.P." to Hill & Acker, Nov. 29, 1875; Hill to Armstrong, Dec. 26, 1876.
18. Theodore Macy, Duluth, to Hill, Dec. 7, 1874.
19. Hanna to Hill, Aug. 24, Sept. 16, 1875; E. N. Saunders, Cleveland (on Hanna & Co. letterhead), to Hill, Nov. 9; Jones to Hill, Oct. 19, Nov. 29, 1875.
20. Jones to Hill, Sept. 11, 1875; Hill to F. B. Clarke, June 7, 1877; to George Repplier, New York, Dec. 29, 1876; to Charles Mackall, Baltimore, June 29, 1877; Acker to Messrs. Jones & Parkhurst, Sheldon, Minn., Jan. 15, 1877.
21. Hill to C. M. Underhill, Sept. 7, 1875.

22. Hill to C. M. Underhill, Sept. 20, 1875.
23. C. M. Underhill to Hill, Sept. 20, 1875.
24. Hill to Underhill, Nov. 19, 1875, Mar. 16, Apr. 13, 1876; Underhill to Hill, Dec. 2, 1875; Hill to Griggs, May 30, 1876.
25. Hill to J. P. Illsley, Mar. 17; Illsley to Hill, Mar. 25; Hill to Britt, Sept. 20; Britt to Hill, Sept. 22, 1876.
26. A. G. Yates, Rochester, N.Y., to Hill, Oct. 21; Lambie & Bates, Cleveland, to Hill, Oct. 24, 1876; Articles of Incorporation, May 1, JJHP, GC; St. Paul *Daily Dispatch,* May 25, 1877.
27. Clara Hill Lindley, *James J. and Mary T. Hill* (New York, privately printed, 1948), 83.
28. Lindley, *James J. and Mary T. Hill,* 84; Hill, Saunders & Acker, Profit & Loss Statement, May 31, 1878, JJHP, LB.
29. JJHP, GC; J. H. Pearl to Hill, Dec. 19, 1875.
30. Diary, 1873; Lindley, *James J. and Mary T. Hill,* 85.
31. Diary, 1873, 1874.
32. Diary, 1873.
33. Hill to Hon. L. A. Evans, St. Cloud, Minn., Aug. 21, 1876; to W. M. McNair, Feb. 3, Apr. 19, 1877; to Judge William Lochren, Feb. 2, 1877.
34. Diary, 1873; St. Paul *Daily Pioneer,* Jan. 13, May 24, 1874; JJHP, LB, 1876 *passim;* Hill to Members (circular letter), Aug. 21, 1876; A. Morton, Farmers' & Mechanics' Bank, to Hill, Dec. 10, 1875.
35. A. S. D. Hill to Hill, July 1, 1874.
36. Hill's papers relating to the Iowa coal properties, covering a period of almost thirty years, are voluminous and for the most part are filed separately under "Iowa Coal Properties," JJHP. Browne wrote Hill hundreds of letters, many of which Hill was neither able nor inclined to answer. See esp. Browne to Hill, Apr. 2, 1877; Hill to Browne, Feb. 4, 1873, May 9; Hill to W. D. Washburn, Minneapolis, May 31, 1877, all in JJHP, GC and LB. E. R. Landis and Orville J. Van Eck, *Coal Resources of Iowa* (Technical Paper No. 4, Iowa Geological Survey, Iowa City, 1965), summarizes the disappointing story of coal mining in Iowa. "Webster County became a coal producer early in the history of Iowa, but its coal-mining industry has been defunct or nearly so for many years," they note, but they reassure the reader that the state contains vast reserves of perfectly good coal whenever we shall want it, 54. See also *passim.*

CHAPTER FIVE

1. Holcombe to Hill, Aug. 24, 1877.
2. Hill to Holcombe, Aug. 28, 1877.
3. *Farley v. Kittson et al.,* Transcript of Testimony, II, 1, Testimony of Henry P. Upham.
4. The early history of the Northern Pacific and the St. Paul & Pacific Railroads is summarized in John L. Harnsberger, "Transportation on the Northern Plains," *North Dakota Quarterly,* XXIX (1961), Nos. 3, 4.
5. The best study of the early years of the NP is John L. Harnsberger, "Jay Cooke and Minnesota: The Formative Years of the Northern Pacific, 1868–1873" (unpubl. Ph.D. dissertation, Univ. of Minnesota, 1956). See also Henrietta M. Larson, *Jay Cooke, Private Banker* (Cambridge, Mass., 1936).
6. "Norman Wolfred Kittson," *Dictionary of American Biography;* C. W. Rife, "Norman W. Kittson, a Fur-Trader at Pembina," *Minnesota History,* VI (Sept. 1925), 225–52; Beckles Willson, *The Life of Lord Strathcona and Mount Royal* (2 vols., Boston and New York, 1915), I *passim.* For the Canadian nationalists' views, see William Mc-

Dougall to John Macdonald, Oct. 31, 1869, in Joseph Pope (ed.), *Correspondence of Sir John Macdonald* (Toronto, 1921), 101–2. Donald Creighton, *John A. Macdonald, The Old Chieftain* (Boston, 1956) *passim.*

7. Hill had forgotten the 1869 meeting over the years, but when he went to Winnipeg in 1909 for the celebration of the centennial of the original Selkirk settlements, where he visited with Smith, he recalled it; Winnipeg *Telegram*, Aug. 27, 1909. Diary, 1873, 1874; *Farley v. Kittson et al.*, Transcript of Testimony, II, 1, Testimony of Sir Donald Smith, 1147.

8. St. Paul *Daily Pioneer*, Feb. 1, 1874. Hill's friends Chauncey W. Griggs and P. H. Kelly were among the incorporators; Diary, 1874.

9. Reprinted in *Farley v. Kittson et al.*, Defendant's Exhibit 120, 254–89.

10. John S. Kennedy to Hon. T. B. Clements, Feb. 3, 1875, *Farley v. Kittson et al.*, Transcript, II, 2, Defendant's Exhibit 120, 1296–300.

11. J. Botsford, Treasurer, First Division of St. Paul & Pacific Railroad, Chicago, to "My dear Henry," Sept. 5, 1876, JJHP, GC.

12. Hill to C. Klein, London, May 12, 1877.

13. *Farley v. Kittson et al.*, Transcript, I, 2, Testimony of James J. Hill *passim.*

14. JJHP, Private vouchers, Sept. 19, 1876; *Farley v. Kittson et al.*, Transcript, I, 2, Testimony of James J. Hill, 592.

15. *Farley v. Kittson et al.*, Transcript, I, 2, Testimony of James J. Hill, 593–95. Hill's recollections of the events beginning with his meeting with Smith in Ottawa in the spring of 1876 are summarized in Hill to George Bryce, Winnipeg, May 5, 1915.

16. A copy of Hill's calculations is attached to Kittson to George Stephen, Sept. 17, 1877, Montreal, JJHP, GC.

17. Kittson to Stephen, Sept. 17, 1877, attachment, JJHP, GC.

18. He was energetic in reducing obstacles to immigration at the border; see Hill to Thomas Spencer, May 30, 1877.

19. Heather Gilbert, *Awakening Continent; The Life of Lord Mount Stephen Vol. I, 1829–91* (Aberdeen, 1966), 6, 27, 30–31.

20. *Farley v. Kittson et al.*, Transcript, I, 2, Testimony of James J. Hill, 596–8, 602–3. The cablegram is confirmed in Kittson and Hill to Carp, May 26, 1877.

21. Kittson and Hill to Carp, May 26, 1877.

22. JJHP, GC, May 15–31, 1877. The decoded message is on a separate scrap of paper.

23. Hill to Smith, June 11, 1877; Hiram M. Drache, *Day of the Bonanza* (Fargo, 1964).

24. Hill to Kittson, July 31, 1877; to Smith, Aug. 7, 1877.

25. Hill to Smith, Aug. 23, 1877.

26. Hill to Stephen, Chicago, Aug. 29, 1877; *Farley v. Kittson et al.*, Transcript, I, 2, Testimony of James J. Hill, 611; Testimony of Donald Smith, 1180; Testimony of George Stephen, 1233–34; James P. Shannon, *Catholic Colonization on the Western Frontier* (New Haven, 1957).

27. Kittson to Stephen, Sept. 17, 1877, copy in JJHP, GC.

28. J. S. Kennedy & Co. to Farley, Sept. 29, Oct. 2, 1877, in *Farley v. Kittson et al.*, Plaintiff's Evidence, 463–65.

29. J. S. Kennedy & Co. to Farley, June 19, 1877, *Farley v. Kittson et al.*, Plaintiff's Testimony, 434.

30. Recollections of Rachel Hill Boeckmann as recorded by Mrs. G. S. Reny. Clara Hill Lindley recalled the years on Dayton's Bluff in *James J. and Mary T. Hill*, 124–26.

31. Hill to Jno. Dick, Philadelphia, Feb. 23, 1877; to E. P. Bassford Co., St. Paul, May 2, 30, 1877.

32. St. Paul *Daily Dispatch*, Oct. 11, 1877.

33. Lindley, *James J. and Mary T. Hill*, 132–4; Hill to Messrs Herts Bros., New York, Jan. 26, 1878.

34. Hill to Alexander Hill, Mar. 10, 1878.
35. Hill to Mary Elizabeth Hill Brooks, Mar. 10, 1878.
36. *Farley v. Kittson et al.*, Transcript, II, 1, Testimony of George Stephen, 1237, and I, 2; Testimony of James J. Hill, 615.
37. Albro Martin, "Crisis of Rugged Individualism: The West Shore–South Pennsylvania Railroad Affair, 1880–1885," *Pennsylvania Magazine of History and Biography,* XCIII (Apr. 1969), 218–43.
38. *Farley v. Kittson et al.*, Transcript, I, 2, Testimony of James J. Hill, 615.

CHAPTER SIX

1. St. Paul *Pioneer Press,* Oct. 26; Smith to Kittson, Oct. 31, Nov. 1; Browne to Hill, Nov. 9; Holcombe to Hill, Oct. 28,1877.
2. *Farley v. Kittson et al.*, Transcript, I, 3, Testimony of George Stephen, 1237–38; Testimony of James J. Hill, I, 2, 617–18; Hill's memorandum book of expenses, Sept. 11, 1877, to Aug. 1878, JJHP, GC.
3. Smith to Kittson, Jan. 8, 1878, JJHP, GC.
4. Hill to Stephen, Jan. 16, 1878, italics added. Stephen testified a decade later, in *Farley v. Kittson et al.*, that no thought had been given to a loan from the Bank of Montreal before the formal purchase contract was signed on March 13, 1878; Transcript, 1244. But he had had Hill and Kittson execute a note to the bank five weeks earlier; Stephen to Hill, telegram, Feb. 7, 1878.
5. Stephen and Smith to Kennedy, Jan. 29, 1878, letterpress copy, JJHP, GC; Hill to Kennedy, Feb. 2, 1878.
6. Stephen and Smith to Kennedy Jan. 29; letterpress copy, JJHP, GC; Hill to Kennedy, Feb. 2; telegram, Stephen to Hill, Jan. 15; Hill to Kennedy, Jan. 18, to Kennedy, telegram, Feb. 6; to Stephen, Feb. 6, Stephen to Hill, telegram, Feb. 7; Hill to Stephen, Feb. 8; Stephen to Hill, Feb. 12, 1878.
7. Articles of Agreement between James J. Hill, John Armstrong, and Edward N. Saunders, June 1; JJHP, GC; Hill to Smith, June 7; to Stephen, Oct. 28, 30, Dec. 31, to James Roberts, St. Paul, Aug. 7, 1878.
8. Hill to Kennedy, to Stephen, Mar. 8, 1878; copy of contract in JJHP, GC.
9. *Farley v. Kittson et al.*, Transcript, II, 1, Testimony of Donald Smith, 1142, 1149; of George Stephen, 1243.
10. The draft of the preliminary agreement, signed and sealed, is in JJHP, GC. The final version was Defendants' Exhibit No. 118 in *Farley v. Kittson et al.*, reprinted in Joseph G. Pyle, *The Life of James J. Hill* (2 vols., New York, 1916–17), II, Appendix 5-B.
11. *Farley v. Kittson et al.*, Transcript, I, 3, Testimony of James J. Hill, 637–38; Hill to Stephen, Feb. 13; to Kennedy, Feb. 12, 1878.
12. Hill to Stephen, June 20; Stephen to Hill, July 9; Hill to Nelson, Oct. 7; to Farley, May 2; Taylor to Hill, Mar. 12, 1878.
13. Hill to A. E. Rice, Willmar, Minn., Apr. 18; to Kennedy, May 7; to Stephen, May 10, June 22, to Horace Thompson, July 16, to Stephen, July 22, Stephen to Hill, Aug. 21, 1878; *Farley v. Kittson et al.*, Transcript, I, 3, Testimony of James J. Hill, 627–29.
14. Stephen to Hill, Aug. 21, 1878.
15. Hill to Stephen, July 12, 1878.
16. Draft proposal to complete extension line from end of track at Snake River to St. Vincent and from Melrose to Alexandria, JJHP, GC, Apr. 1878; Hill, Jefferson City, Mo., to Kennedy, Apr. 19, 21, 1878; John F. Dillon, Des Moines, telegram to J. P. Farley, May 20, 1878, JJHP, GC; Hill to Stephen, June 1, 1878.

17. "John Stewart Kennedy," *Dictionary of American Biography*. There is no biography.
18. For Kennedy's reticence on this point see *Farley v. Kittson et al.*, Transcript, II, 3, Testimony of J. S. Kennedy, 1609–10.
19. Hill to Stephen, June 5, 1878.
20. Farley to Kennedy, June 13, 1878; *Farley v. Kittson et al.*, Transcript, II, 1, Defendants' Exhibit 94.
21. Kennedy to Farley, June 18, *Farley v. Kittson et al.*, Transcript, II, 1, Defendants' Exhibit 49; Stephen to Hill, July 10; Hill to Stephen, Oct. 12, 1878.
22. Hill to Kennedy, July 20, 22, 1878; to Stephen, Sept. 8, 1878.
23. Hill to Stephen, Jan. 10, 1879.
24. Hill to Robbins, Aug. 12, Sept. 16, 1878.
25. Clara Hill Lindley, *James J. and Mary T. Hill* (New York, 1948), 134–35.
26. Hill to Stephen, Feb. 23; to Robbins, Aug. 12; to Stephen, Aug. 18; to L. E. Torinus, Stillwater, Sept. 2; to Stephen, Oct. 18, 1878.
27. Hill to Stephen, July 23, Sept. 13, Oct. 19, 1878.
28. Hill to Stephen, April 5, 1878.
29. Hill to Smith, June 5; to Kennedy, June 17; to Stephen, June 23; to Kennedy, July 29, Aug. 21; to Stephen, Oct. 31, 1878.
30. Hill to Kennedy, Apr. 10, 1878.
31. Hill to Kennedy, Apr. 11, 1878.
32. Hill to W. J. S. Truitt, May 24, 1878.
33. Hill to Joe Upper, Aug. 29, 1878.
34. Hill to Stephen, Sept. 8, 1878.
35. Hill to Stephen, May 17, 1878.
36. Hill to W. F. Luxton, Jan. 14, 1878.
37. Donald Creighton, *John A. Macdonald: The Old Chieftain* (Boston, 1956), 237–40, quoting House of Commons Debates, 1878, II, 2564; Beckles Willson, *The Life of Lord Strathcona and Mount Royal* (2 vols., Boston and New York, 1915), II, 78.
38. Hill to Smith, Sept. 9, undated (about Sept. 10); to Upper, Sept. 10, 14; to Smith, Sept. 29; to Upper and Willis, Nov. 13; to William Harty, Sept. 12, 1878.
39. Hill to Kittson, Oct. 6, 1878.
40. Stephen to Hill, July 10, 1878.
41. Stephen to Hill, Oct. 1, 3, 24, 1878.
42. E. C. Holcombe to Hill, Sept. 21, 1878.
43. Hill to Stephen, Dec. 26, 1878.
44. Stephen to Hill, Oct. 8, 1878.
45. Hill to Stephen, Oct. 28, 1878.

CHAPTER SEVEN

1. Clara Hill Lindley (ed.), *Some Letters of Monsignor Louis E. Caillet and August N. Chemidlin, 1868–1899* (St. Paul, 1922), 29–33.
2. JJHP, Private vouchers, Aug. 1878, Jan. 1879; Hill to Mrs. A. H. Defoe, telegram, Jan. 29; JJHP, Diary, 1879; Clara Hill Lindley, *James J. and Mary T. Hill, An Unfinished Chronicle by Their Daughter* (New York, privately printed, 1948), 135.
3. Hill to W. F. Luxton, Dec. 6; to Stephen, Nov. 4, Dec. 4, 24, 1878.
4. Stephen to Hill, Oct. 1, 1878.
5. Hill to Kennedy, Oct. 7, 11; to Stephen, telegrams, Oct. 28, 30, letter, Oct. 30, 1878.
6. Hill to Stephen, Dec. 21; to Farley, Dec. 24, 1878.
7. St. Paul *Daily Globe*, Dec. 3, 1878; "Great Northern Railway Original Track-Laying Record," map furnished by the Burlington Northern Railroad.

8. John L. Harnsberger, "Jay Cooke and Minnesota: The Formative Years of the Northern Pacific, 1868–1873" (unpubl. Ph.D. dissertation, Univ. of Minnesota, 1956), 189, 191, 192–93.

9. Holcombe to Hill, Sept. 12, 1877; Hill to Stephen, Sept. 6; to Kennedy, Apr. 11, 1878.

10. Hill to Stephen, June 5; to Merrill, June 29; to Stephen, July 10, 1878. James W. Taylor had tried to get Jay Cooke to build a line north to Pembina as early as 1869. See Harnsberger, "Jay Cooke and Minnesota," 188. Hill to Mitchell, Oct. 30, 1878.

11. Hill to Donald Smith, July 12; to Stephen, July 12, 18; Stephen to Hill, July 10, 1878.

12. Hill to Stephen, Sept. 8, 1878 (one of two eight-page letters Hill wrote to Stephen on that date).

13. Hill to Stephen, Sept. 14, 24; Stephen to Stark, Sept. 27, Oct. 4, 12, 28, 1878, NP Archives, Minnesota Historical Society.

14. Stark to Mitchell, Oct. 2; to Wright, Oct. 30, 1878, NP Archives.

15. William Harty to Wright, Oct. 12; Wright to Stark, telegram, n.d., Oct.; Wilkie to Stark, Oct. 15; Wright to Macdonald, Oct. 11, 1878; NP Archives.

16. Sargent to Wright, Oct. 5, 16, 1878, NP Archives.

17. Stephen to Stark, Nov. 5; Resolution of Board of Directors of Northern Pacific Railroad, Nov. 8; Washburn to Billings, Nov. 16, 1878; NP Archives.

18. Hill to Kennedy, June 19, _Farley v. Hill_, Transcript, I, 2, 600; Stephen to Hill, July 10, Aug. 26; Stephen to Horace Thompson, Oct. 23; JJHP, GC; Hill to Stephen, Oct. 16, 19, 1878.

19. Billings to Stephen, Nov. 28; to Litchfield, Nov. 23, 1878; NP Archives.

20. Litchfield to Stephen, Nov. 27, 1878, copy in NP Archives. Italics added.

21. Stephen to Billings, Nov. 26, 1878, NP Archives.

22. Billings to Stephen, Dec. 7; Barnes to Billings, Dec. 9, 1878, NP Archives; Hill to Stephen, Jan. 6 (two letters); Stephen to Hill, telegram, Jan. 15, 1879; _Farley v. Hill_, Transcript, I, 3, 943.

23. Stephen to Hill, Jan. 17, 18, 1879.

24. Hill to Stephen, Jan. 22; Diary, Jan. 23, 1879.

25. Hotel bill, Feb. 7, 1879, JJHP, private vouchers.

26. Hill to Young, telegram, Mar. 30; Hill to Stephen, Mar. 21; Stephen to Hill, Mar. 26; Hill to Kennedy, Apr. 14, 1879.

27. Kennedy to Stephen, Apr. 16, copy in JJHP, GC; Hill to Hughitt, Apr. 23, 1879; Minutes of the Board of Directors of the St. Paul, Minneapolis and Manitoba Railway Co., 1–8, GN Archives, Minnesota Historical Society.

28. Minute Book, St. P. M. & M. Ry. Co., GN Archives.

29. Barnes, Amsterdam, to Kennedy, Apr. 3, copy in JJHP, GC; Kennedy to Stephen, Nov. 21, 1879, copy in JJHP, GC; Minute Book, St. P. M. & M. Ry. Co., GN Archives.

30. Hill to Stephen, Nov. 1, 1879; Minute Book, St. P. M. & M. Ry. Co.; Stock Transfer Book No. 1; GN Archives.

31. "Memorandum of cash transactions including analysis of George Stephen and Associates' account with J. S. Kennedy & Co., N.Y.," JJHP, GC, May 1880.

32. In November 1885 the second mortgage bonds, according to the _Commercial and Financial Chronicle_, sold for as high as 116 and the common stock, 108.

33. _Farley v. Kittson et al._, Transcript, Testimony of Donald Smith, II, 1, 1142, 1149, 1192; II, 3, Testimony of J. S. Kennedy _passim;_ Stephen to Sir Arthur Bigge, Oct. 16, 1908, quoted in Heather Gilbert, "The Unaccountable Fifth," _Minnesota History_ (Spring 1971), 176, emphasis in original.

34. Hill to Stephen, Jan. 22, 1879.

35. *Farley v. Kittson et al.,* Transcript, I, 3, Testimony of James J. Hill, 693–94; Farley to Kennedy, n.d., probably May 20, 1879, from J. S. Kennedy's deposition in *Sahlgaard v. J. S. Kennedy et al.,* Dec. 10, 1881, read into record of *Farley v. Kittson et al.,* Transcript, II, 3, 1751–52.

36. Farley to Kennedy, May 29, 1879, in *Farley v. Kittson et al.,* Defendants' Exhibit No. 141.

37. Hill to Mrs. John A. Armstrong, May 9; Memorandum of Agreement, May 1, 1879, JJHP, GC.

38. St. P., M. & M. Ry. Co., Timetable No. 1, Nov. 9, 1879, JJHP, GC.

CHAPTER EIGHT

1. Certificate of Citizenship, Oct. 18, 1880, JJHP, GC.
2. Proclamation, JJHP, GC, 1879; Stephen to Hill, Mar. 24, 1879; Hill to Barnes, Feb. 21, 1879, original in JJHP, GC; to Kennedy, Apr. 7, 1879.
3. St. Paul *Daily Globe,* May 2, 1881; Hill to Stephen, July 11, 1879.
4. Hill to Stephen, July 11, Sept. 6, 1879, latter in Manitoba LB-1; diaries, 1880–84 *passim.*
5. Hill to Angus, Oct. 14, 1879; Angus to Hill, Nov. 3, 1879; St. Paul *Daily Globe,* Nov. 27, 1879; Hill to Angus, Jan. 21; and to Charles R. Tuttle, Mar. 18, 1881.
6. St. Paul *Daily Globe,* Feb. 4; Hill to T. A. Finney, Jan. 29, 1881; to C. C. Wheeler, Nov. 23, 1880.
7. Hill to Kennedy, Sept. 15, 1882.
8. JJHP, GC, and Personal and Manitoba Letterbooks, 1880–81 *passim.*
9. Hill to Manvel, Dec. 16, 1880, Jan. 17, 1881, Manitoba LB-4; to Angus, Dec. 17; to Manvel, Dec. 28, 1880.
10. Hill to Manvel, Mar. 15, 1881; Notice signed by George Stephen, President, St. P. M. & M. Ry. Co., Nov. 28, 1881, JJHP, GC; Angus to Hill, Dec. 2; Stephen to Hill, Nov. 30, 1881.
11. Hill to Stephen, Apr. 12, 1879.
12. *Poor's Manual of Railroads for 1886,* 749; Hill to Angus, Mar. 20, 1882, Manitoba LB-5.
13. Hill to Angus, Dec. 17, 1880; St. Paul *Daily Globe,* Sept. 29, 1879; Hill was quoted in the *Globe* (Nov. 24, 1880) to the effect that the Manitoba road had hauled over 4000 cords to its stations for public sale in October.
14. Manitoba LB-2.
15. Ives to Hill, Feb. 6, 1881; Washburn to Hill, Sept. 17, 1882.
16. Hill to Andrews, Feb. 19, 1883; to Kennedy, Mar. 5, 6, 1881; Sept. 4, 1879, Manitoba LB-1.
17. Hill to Kennedy, Mar. 5, 1881; to Angus, Mar. 27; to Stephen, Apr. 6, 1882; Ives to Hill, Feb. 6, 1881.
18. Hill to J. S. Kennedy & Co., Apr. 28; to Angus, May 8, 1882; Manitoba LB-6.
19. Hill to Angus, Mar. 27, 1882; Stansbury & Munn, patent attorneys, to R. B. Galusha, Mar. 30; U.S. Patent No. 227,434, May 11, 1880, JJHP, GC; Hill to Thompson, Oct. 7; to Jackson & Woodin Mfg. Co., Dec. 26, 1878.
20. Hill to Kennedy, Sept. 16, 1879, Manitoba LB-1.
21. Hill to Kennedy, April 14, Sept. 4, 1879 (Manitoba LB-1); to J. S. Kennedy & Co., May 1, 1882, Manitoba LB-6; Ives to Hill, Aug. 21; Joliet Steel Co. to William Munroe, Bank of Montreal, Aug. 23, 1879, JJHP, GC.
22. St. Paul *Daily Globe,* Dec. 5, 1880; St. Paul *Pioneer Press,* June 26; Stephen to Hill, June 26, 1882.

23. Jordan to Hill, April 13, 1881; Hill to A. E. Rice, Mar. 31, 1883; St. Paul *Daily Globe,* Jan. 13, Minneapolis *Tribune,* Jan. 9, St. Paul *Daily Globe,* Apr. 7, 1880.

24. This is a synthesis of Hill's remarks on that day and at a second meeting the next day. To what extent the newspaper reporter actually took his remarks down verbatim is not known; St. Paul *Daily Globe,* Aug. 23, 24, 1880.

25. St. Paul *Daily Globe,* June 16, 1881, quoting Fargo *Argus.*

26. JJHP, Jan. 1879 to May 1880 *passim,* esp. Hill to Stephen, Jan. 11, 1879; Stephen to Hill, Jan. 18, Feb. 20; to Joseph Pope, Feb. 22, 1879, copy in JJHP, GC; to Hill, Feb. 25, and Apr. 18, 1879; Hill to Stephen, Apr. 22, 1879, May 31, 1880 (Manitoba LB-3).

27. Diary, 1879; Hill to Stephen, March 8, 26, 1879.

28. St. Paul *Daily Globe,* Apr. 21, Dec. 2, 1881; Hill to Kennedy, Feb. 4, 1882, Manitoba LB-4.

29. Hill to Kennedy, Nov. 12, 1884, Manitoba LB-7. The Milwaukee road toyed with the idea, but could not bring itself to become a tenant in someone else's depot; it built its own. The bridge is 2100 feet long, 28 feet wide (to accommodate two tracks), and consists of 23 arches. It was the only structure on the railroad upon which he permitted his name to be placed. Its completion was the occasion of a gala celebration at which the citizens of Minneapolis presented Hill with an exceptionally ornate example of the silversmith's craft, a large tray on which a view of the new bridge was ringed with representations, in deep relief, of his career including a highly literal portrayal of him setting the half-breed's dislocated shoulder during his 1870 trip down the Red River Valley. Minneapolis *Tribune,* Nov. 23, 1883, Sept. 11, 1884.

30. Great Northern Track Laying Record.

31. Hill to Kennedy, Mar. 8, Dec. 5, 1879; St. Paul *Pioneer Press,* Jan. 20, 1880; St. Paul *Daily Globe,* Dec. 21, 1881.

32. Hill to Stephen, July 25, Aug. 5, 1879, both Manitoba LB-1; Kennedy to Stephen, Apr. 16, 1879, copy in JJHP, GC.

33. Hill to Stephen, Jan. 11, July 6, 9, 1879, Manitoba LB-1; Kennedy to Hill, Feb. 21, 1881; Hill to Kennedy, Mar. 5, 1881; to Stephen, Apr. 6, 1882.

34. Hill to Angus, Dec. 17; to Kennedy, Oct. 22, 1880, Manitoba LB-4.

35. Hill to Angus, Mar. 27; to Stephen, June 2, 1882, Manitoba LB-6; to David Young, Jan. 2, 1883.

36. Hill to Selah Chamberlain, Mar. 21, to Stephen, July 26, Aug. 5, 1879, Manitoba LB-1; to Merrill, Mar. 13, Aug. 15, 1882, Manitoba LB-5.

37. Kennedy to Hill, Nov. 15; Hill to Stephen, Nov. 19; Stephen to Hill, Nov. 14, 1883. With Hill's firm support, the railroads in the Twin Cities area had forestalled a takeover of the strategically important St. Paul & Duluth by the Milwaukee Road. It became a joint property of the Manitoba and other railroads in the area; Minneapolis *Tribune,* July 8, 9, 1879.

38. Hill to Stephen, Jan. 11, 1879; to Shepherd, Jan. 8; to Stephen, June 26, 1882.

39. James Bryce, *The American Commonwealth* (2 vols., London and New York, 1889), 506–16.

40. Hill to Stephen, June 3, 1879; *Poor's Manual of Railroads for 1884,* 749.

41. Kennedy to Hill, Dec. 21; Account Rendered by J. S. Kennedy & Co. to James J. Hill, Oct. 12, 1881, JJHP, GC; Hill to Kennedy, Aug. 3, 1882; Stephen to Hill, Dec. 19, 1881.

42. Minutes of the Board of Directors' Meetings, Mar. 19, Apr. 12, 1883; Annual Report, 1882–83, p. 17, St. P. M. & M. Ry. Co.; *Railroad Gazette,* XV (Apr. 20, 1883), 256; Hill to Kennedy, Apr. 3; to Thomas W. Pearsall, July 26, 1883.

43. Donnelly to Hill, Nov. 19; Hill to Stephen, Oct. 21, 1879; George B. Wright to Hill, Mar. 2, 1881; Hill to Belmont, Nov. 19, 1883; to Kennedy, Apr. 22, 1884, Manitoba LB-7; to J. M. Spicer, Mar. 30, 1886, Manitoba LB-8.

44. Holcombe to Hill, Sept. 10, 25, Oct. 21, 1879; Hill to Holcombe, June 26, 1881; to
   C. H. Pettitt, July 23, 1884; Minneapolis *Tribune*, Mar. 12, 20, 1880, June 24, 1881;
   Hill to George B. Christian, June 10, 1881; contract with Andrew Tod in Mille Lacs
   Lumber Co., May 27, 1882, JJHP, GC. The correspondence with Stephen and Kennedy concerning Lord Elphinstone's "machine" dragged on through the decade.
45. Most of the voluminous papers relating to the Iowa coal properties are filed separately in JJHP. But see Hill to Browne, Mar. 12; to W. C. Van Horne, June 23; to
   Angus, Dec. 17, 1880; to Browne, Mar. 10; to John Turnbull (Stephen's secretary),
   Apr. 12, 1883; to E. W. Gaylor, Oct. 15, 1884; all in JJHP, LB; to Kennedy, May 30,
   1884, Manitoba LB-7.
46. Adam Stein to Hill, Jan. 12, 1882.
47. P. B. Douglas, Ottawa, to Hill, Mar. 1, 1882.
48. Holcombe to Hill, Oct. 12, 1884; D. A. Monfort, Second National Bank, to Hill, July
   7, 1885; Hill to Superintendent of House of Correction, Detroit, Aug. 25, 1877; to
   "Friend McLean," Bismarck, D.T., Oct. 14, 1880; George W. Smith to Hill, Apr. 25,
   1883.
49. Hill to T. A. Finney, Jan. 29, 1881; credit memo, Private Vouchers, Jan. 1887; to Kennedy, Nov. 25, 1884; to J. S. Kennedy & Co., July 18, 1883; to H. A. Foster, July 31,
   1884; to C. A. Broadwater, Feb. 5, 1886.
50. Manvel Letterbooks *passim*; Hill to Angus, Feb. 12, 1882, Manitoba LB-5; Wakeman
   to Hill, Apr. 26; Hill to Wakeman, Apr. 27; Manvel to Hill, July 16, 1882.
51. Hill to Stephen, Apr. 6, 1882.
52. Angus to Hill, June 19, 1882.

CHAPTER NINE

1. Pierre Berton, *The National Dream* and *The Last Spike* (Toronto, 1970, 1971), a two-
   volume history of the C. P. R. down to 1885, published in the United States in a
   single volume as *The Impossible Railway* (New York, 1972), is a highly readable account based on published works and some additional manuscript material. Still
   valuable, however, is Harold A. Innis, *A History of the Canadian Pacific Railway*
   (Toronto, 1923), esp. 102–3. The "practical" route for a transcontinental Canadian
   railroad was described in 1860 by Edward W. Watkin, English businessman and
   member of the International Financial Society: ". . . commence at Halifax, strike
   . . . to Sarnia; extend that system to Chicago; use, under a treaty of neutralization,
   the U.S. lines from Chicago to St. Paul; build a line from St. Paul to Fort Garry by
   English and American capital, and then extend this line to the Yellowhead Pass,
   there to meet a railway through British Columbia starting from the Pacific." Quoted
   in J. Bartlett Brebner, *Canada, A Modern History* (Ann Arbor, 1960), 283–84. See also
   W. Kaye Lamb, *History of the Canadian Pacific Railway* (New York, forthcoming,
   1976).
2. Quoted in Brebner, *Canada,* 399.
3. Stephen to Macdonald, Nov. 13, 1880, Public Archives of Canada (PAC).
4. Berton, *Impossible Railway,* 215–36; Stephen to Sir William Van Horne, n.d., enclosed in Van Horne to Beckles Willson, Nov. 14, 1914, PAC; receipt from C. P. Ry.
   Co., Feb. 17, 1881, JJHP, GC.
5. Hill to Moberly, June 4, 1881.
6. Hill to Angus, Oct. 14, 1881.
7. Angus to Hill, Dec. 2, 1881.
8. Berton, *Impossible Railway,* 296–98; Hill to Angus, Jan. 3, 1882.
9. B. W. [Mrs. Thomas L.] Rosser to Hill, Feb. 2; Hill to Angus, Feb. 12; Manitoba

LB-5; Stephen to Hill, March 4; Van Horne to Hill, Mar. 18, 1882, Great Northern Archives, Minnesota Historical Society (MHS-GN), uncatalogued file.

10. Hill to Angus, Oct. 14, 1881. Macoun recorded his beliefs in his encyclopedic and widely read *Manitoba and the Great Northwest* (Guelph, Ontario, 1882).

11. Hill to Stephen, Oct. 17, 1881.

12. Hill to Angus, Dec. 17, 1880; to Rogers, Mar. 18, Sept. 25, to Van Horne, Dec. 16, 1881; to Stephen, Sept. 18, Manitoba LB-6; to Van Horne, Oct. 31, 1882, Manitoba LB-6.

13. Hill to Angus, July 8, 1880.

14. Hill to Angus, Oct. 19, 1880.

15. Angus to C. Drinkwater, Secretary, C.P.R., July 20, copy in JJHP, GC; to Hill, Dec. 31, 1881.

16. Hill to Kennedy, Feb. 1; to Stephen, June 30, 1882.

17. Van Horne to Beckles Willson, Sept. 10, 1914, PAC.

18. Hill to Stephen, Oct. 17, to Van Horne, Oct. 17, 1881.

19. Stephen to Hill, Mar. 4, 1882; Hill to Stephen, Apr. 6; to Van Horne, May 16, July 7, 1882, both Manitoba LB-6.

20. Hill to Stephen, June 30; to R. B. Langdon, June 10; to Stephen, June 16; Manitoba LB-6; Stephen to Hill, June 26; Hill to Stephen, June 26, July 9, latter Manitoba LB-6; to Van Horne, July 1, Manitoba LB-6; to Stephen, Nov. 11; Angus to Hill, June 19, 1882.

21. Hill to Kennedy, Oct. 5, 1882.

22. Hill to Kennedy, Jan. 10; to Angus, Jan. 10, 1883.

23. Angus to Hill, Jan. 15; Hill to Angus, Jan. 18, 1883; Kennedy to Hill, April 30; Hill to Angus, May 3; to Kennedy, May 4, 1883.

24. Reminiscences of Rachel Hill Boeckmann; private vouchers, Aug. 1884; Hill to Angus, Feb. 19, 1882; Oehmer to Hill, Oct. 1, 1884; Hill to M. Knoedler, Apr. 25, 1883; private vouchers, 1886; Hill to Angus, Feb. 19; to Stephen, Sept. 18, 1882, Manitoba LB-6.

25. Private vouchers, Aug. 1886, Jan. 1885, Jan. 1886; Mehl to Hill, Dec. 23, 1882.

26. Private vouchers, Jan. 1885; Hill to Thorne, telegram, Nov. 24, 1884; private vouchers, 1880, 1883, 1884, 1885; N. Matson & Co., Chicago, to Hill, Dec. 22, 1881.

27. Private vouchers 1881, 1887, 1882, 1886.

28. Private vouchers, Aug. 1884; Hill to W. G. Swan, Aug. 9, 1882; St. Paul *Daily Globe,* July 27, 1882; Hill to J. A. Chandler, Nov. 28, 1885; private vouchers, household payroll, June 1883.

29. Hill to Mehl, Dec. 19, 1882; Mehl to Hill, Dec. 25, 1883; Hill to Mehl, Jan. 20, 1883.

30. Hill to Browne, May 14, 1880; private vouchers, 1880; to Messrs. Brewster & Co.; to Charles S. Caffrey Co., Dec. 21, 1881; Diary, Jan. 12, 1879; private vouchers, 1878, 1879, Aug. 1884, Jan. 1887.

31. Hill to Angus, Dec. 17, 1880; Minneapolis *Tribune,* Jan. 31, 1881; private vouchers, Apr. 1881; JJHP, GC, Jan.–Mar. 1881 *passim;* private vouchers, Dec. 1883; Hill to Mrs. Hill, letter, privately owned.

32. Hill to George Seibert, Aug. 3; Hill LB, spring *passim;* Mehl to Hill, Dec. 23; Hill to Messrs. C. Cavaroe & Son, July 29, 1882; S. S. Simrall to Hill, Dec. 31, 1885; Minneapolis *Tribune,* Mar. 4, 8, Apr. 23, 1882; May 13, July 27, 1883.

33. Hill to Carnegie, Feb. 10, 1882.

34. Private vouchers, Jan. 1885, Jan. 1886; W. A. Stephens to Hill, telegram, Jan. 30, 1884.

35. Hill to Angus, Apr. 24 and 28, Manitoba LB-6; to Stephen, June 16, 1882, Manitoba LB-6.

36. Hill to Stephen, June 16, 1882, Manitoba LB-6.
37. Hill to Van Horne, May 10, June 7, 20, 22, 1882, Manitoba LB-6.
38. Hill to Angus, June 22; Manitoba LB-6; to Stephen, June 30; Van Horne to Hill, May 20, June 26, July 3, 4, 1882, MHS-GN (uncatalogued).
39. James to Hill, July 24; Hill to James, July 25, 1883.
40. Hill to Kennedy, May 15, 1883, Manitoba LB-7.
41. Stephen to Hill, June 7; Hill to Stephen, July 12, Manitoba LB-7; D. Willis James to Hill, Aug. 1, 1883.
42. James to Hill, July 25; Hill to James, Aug. 21, 1883.
43. Stephen to Hill, Nov. 14, 1883.
44. Hill to J. M. Stirling, Mar. 1, 1884; to Stephen, Apr. 21; Stephen to Hill, Apr. 18; Hill to Stephen, Jan. 18, Apr. 21, 1885.
45. Stephen to Hill, "Xmas Day," 1884; Hill to Van Horne, Apr. 24, 1886; to Tod, July 26, 1883.
46. James A. Ward, *That Man Haupt; A Biography of Herman Haupt* (Baton Rouge, 1973); Minneapolis *Daily Tribune,* Aug. 30; St. Paul *Pioneer Press,* Sept. 4, 1883.

CHAPTER TEN

1. Farrish to Hill, Nov. 22, 1887; Aug. 28, Sept. 28, Oct. 16, 1883; June 21, 1884. Hill to Farrish, Aug. 24, 1883, Manitoba LB-7; and Aug. 1, 1884.
2. A. V. McCleneghan to Hill, Sept. 4, 1883; William Wetherald to Hill, Aug. 23, 1881; Samuel Wetherald to Hill, Sept. 8, 24, Dec. 7, 1881.
3. Hill to B. P. Hinman, Jan. 31, 1882; to Nelson, Jan. 7, Sept. 5, 1887; to Stephen, Aug. 8, 1884; to Kennedy, Aug. 13, 1885; to Henry C. E. Stuart, Apr. 16, 1889; to Kennedy, Apr. 12, 1888.
4. Hill's agricultural philosophies and his efforts to promote livestock-raising in the Northwest are dealt with in Chapter Eleven.
5. The Minneapolis and St. Paul newspapers, taking the millers' and the farmers' sides, respectively, hurled thunderbolts at each other during the early years of the decade before both settled on the railroads as the most deserving victim; see Minneapolis *Tribune,* Nov. 3, 4, 1881; St. Paul *Daily Globe,* Feb. 18. 1882.
6. Hill to Forbes, July 3; Kennedy to Hill, Aug. 10, 1888.
7. Hill to E. T. Nichols, telegram, Aug. 29; to C. A. Broadwater, Oct. 6; to James Cudhie, Nov. 6; to 50 station agents, Nov. 16, 1888; to George H. Walsh, Mar. 30; to John M. Forbes, April 17, 1889.
8. Kennedy to Hill, Oct. 11, 1884.
9. J. Kennedy Tod to Hill, Mar. 18; Kennedy to Hill, Nov. 1, Dec. 20; Stephen to Hill, Mar. 4, 1882; Stephen to Hill, Mar. 22, 1884.
10. Kennedy to Hill, Mar. 23, May 7; J. Kennedy Tod to Hill, May 1; Kennedy to Hill, May 28, 1883.
11. Pearsall to Hill, July 17; Hill to Tod, July 17; Hill to Tod (quoting Stephen's telegram), July 24; Hill to Pearsall, July 26; J. S. Kennedy & Co. to Hill, July 28, 1883.
12. Hill to Kennedy, Jan. 10, 1885; to E. T. Nichols Jr., July 24; Kennedy to Hill, June 25, 1884; Nichols to Hill, Jan. 5; Kennedy to Hill, Jan. 13; Hill to Kennedy, Jan. 18, 1885; Nichols to Hill, Nov. 21, 1887.
13. Kennedy to Hill, Oct. 30, 1883, July 1, 1885; Stephen to Hill, Sept. 21, 1882, Mar. 22; Hill to Stephen, March 27, 1884.
14. Kennedy to Hill, Feb. 10, 1886, July 22, 1887; D. Willis James to Hill, Mar. 3, 1888.
15. Kennedy to Hill, June 3, 1884.

16. Manvel to Hill, telegram, June 1; Kennedy to Hill, June 6, 1884; D. Willis James to Hill, Jan. 23; T. W. Pearsall and Kennedy to Hill, telegram, Jan. 27; Kennedy to Hill, Jan. 27, 1886.

17. Ransom Phillips to Hill, Oct. 15; H. A. Foster to Hill, June 6; Kennedy to Hill, May 29, 1884; S. G. Comstock to Hill, Aug. 21, 1885.

18. Hill to W. J. Mooney, Sept. 23, 1885, Manitoba LB-8; to J. S. Kennedy, Jan. 4, 1884; to T. F. Oakes, Mar. 20, 1885, Manitoba LB-8.

19. Hill to W. L. Scott, May 2, 1888; T. A. Scoble to Hill, July 19, 1884.

20. Hill to R. V. Martinsen, Oct. 12, 1886.

21. Hill to Stephen, May 27, 1886.

22. Hill to Stephen, May 11, 1886.

23. Stephen to Hill, May 23, 31, 1886.

24. Samuel Thorne, a Manitoba director resident in New York, used his excellent contacts to confirm Hill's suspicions about the source of the Soo's financial vigor; Thorne to Hill, July 30, 1886. See also Hill to Stephen, May 18, 1887.

25. Stephen's biographer accepts the traditional interpretation that Hill had somehow obligated himself to buy the Soo, but it was clearly wishful thinking on Stephen's part; Heather Gilbert, *Awakening Continent, The Life of Lord Mount Stephen*, Vol. I (2 vols., Aberdeen, 1965), 250–51; Minneapolis *Tribune*, Oct. 16, 1886; Stephen to Hill, Sept. 7, 1889.

26. Hill to Forbes, May 20, 1889.

27. Manvel, Paris, to Hill, Apr. 12, 1886.

28. Hill to Thomson, Apr. 6, 1886.

29. Nichols to Hill, Mar. 1, 1889.

30. Whipple to Hill, June 27; C. P. Jones to Hill, Nov. 10, 1885; L. L. Baxter to Hill, Sept. 10, 1884; V. Hjortsberg to Hill, Jan. 3, 1880.

31. Hill to W. H. Fisher, Dec. 30, 1886; to Adams, June 6, 1889; to Whipple, Aug. 2, 1889, Nov. 26, 1887, May 23, 1889.

32. E. T. Jahr to Hill, Sept. 3, 1879; Hill to Marvin Hughitt, Sept. 29; to Hamilton Browne, Oct. 8, 1883; G. E. Cary to William Secombe, May 26, 1884.

33. Hill to Messrs. Rand, Avery & Co., Jan. 15, 1883.

34. Kennedy to Hill, Feb. 13, 1885; "Speech of Mr. James J. Hill, Delivered before the Railroad Committee of the House of Representatives, St. Paul, Minnesota, Jan. 28, 1885" (pamphlet, JJHP, GC, 1885); for a discussion of the general lack of understanding of the railroad problems of the Victorian era, which has persisted into the present, see Albro Martin, "The Troubled Subject of Railroad Regulation in the Gilded Age—A Reappraisal," *Journal of American History*, LXI (Sept. 1974), 339–71.

35. "Speech of Mr. James J. Hill . . . Jan. 28, 1885"; Kennedy to Hill, Feb. 13, 1885.

36. E. S. Warner to Hill, June 10; Hill to Kennedy, July 8, 1886; tabulation of railroad rates, 1881–86, LB, June 6, 1887.

37. E. Mattson to Hill, Feb. 13, 1887; to Sterling, Apr. 16, 1889.

38. Nimmo to Hill, June 30, 1885; Manvel, London, to Hill, Mar. 31, 1886; Hill to H. C. Waite, Feb. 2, to Charles T. Hinde, Feb. 12, 1887.

39. Hill to Manvel, telegram, Nov. 15, 1888. Paul W. MacAvoy, *The Economic Effects of Regulation: The Trunk-Line Railroad Cartels and the Interstate Commerce Commission Before 1900* (Cambridge, Mass., 1965), 110–53, is the most scholarly statement of the theory that the railroads benefited from the Act of 1887 in these respects; for the opposing view, see Martin, "Troubled Subject of Railroad Regulation."

40. Hill to D. R. Noyes, Sept. 5, 1888.

41. A. E. Touzalin to Hill, Mar. 7, 1887; Hill to Editor, *Bradstreet's Magazine*, telegram, Nov. 8, 1888.

42. Cannon to Hill, Nov. 22, 1888.

43. Higginson to Hill, Feb. 3, 1889.
44. Hill to John J. McCook, Aug. 2, 1889.
45. Strait to Hill, Oct. 10, 1888.
46. D. M. Sabin to E. T. Nichols, Jr., July 28, 1889; Harrison to Hill, Mar. 12; Hill to C. A. Broadwater, Mar. 13, 1888.
47. Hill to Thomas Greenway, telegram, Nov. 9; Greenway to Hill, telegram, Nov. 9, 1888.
48. Hill and P. H. Kelley to "The President of the United States," LB (n.d.); Hill to William C. Whitney, May 19, 1885; Knute Nelson to Hill, July 15; to William F. Vilas, July 15; Vilas to Hill, July 20; Hill to Strait, Mar. 29; to Nelson, July 19, 1886.
49. Rose to Hill, Mar. 17; Hill to Rose, Apr. 9, 1884 (italics added).

CHAPTER ELEVEN

1. See W. G. Constable, *Art Collecting in the United States of America* (London, 1964) *passim*; Avery to Hill, Sept. 9, 1885.
2. Durand-Ruel to Hill, May 28, 1888.
3. Durand-Ruel to Hill, July 5, 1889; Hill to Goupil & Co., Mar. 30, 1882; William Secombe to Hill, Mar. 15, 1883.
4. Kennedy to Hill, Oct. 30, 1883; Jacacci to Hill, Jan. 27, 1885; Kennedy and Thorne both sent Hill catalogues of the Mary J. Morgan estate sale in 1886; private vouchers, Aug. 1884, May 1886; "The Collection of James J. Hill, A Loan Exhibition Celebrating the Minnesota Statehood Centennial, April 15–June 1, 1958," Catalogue of the Minnesota Institute of Arts; Higginson to Hill, Feb. 3, 1889.
5. Record book, "Pictures," JJHP.
6. C. R. Cummings to Hill, Oct. 5, 1881; C. L. Hutchinson to Hill, Nov. 22, 1887; James Allison to Hill, June 14; C. Ralph Evans to Hill, July 10, 1888; W. A. Stephens to Judge M. B. Koon, July 3, 1889.
7. Hill paid $2450 for the Jefferson and $5141 for the Madison and Adams together, Record book, "Pictures," JJHP; Hill to Walter, Apr. 7; to E. L. Wakeman, Apr. 7, 1883; Walter to Hill, Sept. 20, 1883, Apr. 12, 1884; Massachusetts Historical Society Records, 1886–87, Vol. III, 2nd ser., 179–87, 219, quoted in Katherine McCook Knox, *The Sharples, Their Portraits of George Washington and His Contemporaries* (New Haven, 1930; reprinted 1974), 63–64; Adams to Hill, Oct. 14, 1888.
8. Hill to D. S. Lamont, Jan. 7; Thomson to Hill, telegram, Jan. 10, 1889; Hill's opinion of the President's personality was formed at an earlier reception; Hill to W. E. Smith, Oct. 14, 1887.
9. Mary T. Hill to Miss Veeley, telegram, Jan. 14; D. S. Lamont to Hill, telegrams, Jan. 11, 19, 1889.
10. William Watts Folwell, *A History of Minnesota* (4 vols., St. Paul, 1926), III, 186–87.
11. A typical viewpoint is Horace Samuel Merrill, "Ignatius Donnelly, James J. Hill, and Cleveland Administration Patronage," *Mississippi Valley Historical Review*, XXXIX (June 1952–Mar. 1953), 505–18, but see Martin Ridge, *Ignatius Donnelly* (Chicago, 1962), 218–20; Hill to Nelson, Apr. 22, 1884; Kennedy to Hill, Oct. 31, 1884; July 24; Hill to Kennedy, June 11, 1886.
12. Hill to J. L. MacDonald, Oct. 29, 1887; Kennedy to Hill, May 8, 1884; Hill to Smith M. Weed, Nov. 8, 1886.
13. Hill to Kelly, May 19, 1885.
14. H. W. Cannon to Hill, May 4; H. B. Strait to Hill, Jan. 7; Hill to Kelly, May 19; H. C. Doughty to Hill, July 1, 1885.
15. Dinner invitation, Feb. 3, 1886, JJHP, GC; E. T. Nichols to C. H. Benedict, July 28,

W. L. Scott to Hill, Sept. 17, 1888; George F. Parker, *Recollections of Grover Cleveland* (New York, 1909), 326–27.

16. Allen Weinstein, "Was there a 'Crime of 1873'?: The Case of the Demonetized Dollar," *Journal of American History*, LIV (Sept. 1967), 307–26; Knox to Hill, July 11, 1887.

17. St. Paul *Pioneer Press*, May 4, 1886.

18. Gilbert A. Pierce, May 6; H. W. Cannon, May 7; Charles B. Lamborn, May 20, 1886, to Hill.

19. Hill to W. J. Murphy, Feb. 17, 1886; to Nimmo, June 22; William G. LeDuc to Hill, Dec. 28, 1885, enclosing P. B. Young, U.S. Consulate General, St. Petersburg, to LeDuc (n.d.).

20. Hill to C. H. Burwell, May 2; Minneapolis *Daily Tribune*, Aug. 7, 1883; Hill to Mrs. H. A. Freeman, Apr. 3, 1889; Mary T. Hill to W. A. Stephens, Jan. 1, 14, 1885, JJHP, GC; Hill to Farwell & Co., Oct. 6, 1883.

21. Hill to Thorne, Mar. 4; to *Gardener's Monthly*, May 19, 1884; private vouchers, JJHP, Nov. 1883; W. Secombe to W. A. Dolby, Nov. 12, 1883; Hill to Gibson, Oct. 2, 1885, June 7, 1887.

22. Hill to George Laidlaw, Apr. 28, 1883; to Hon. Andrew Nelson, Jan. 4, 1884.

23. Hill to John D. Wing, Mar. 30; W. Secombe to Hill, enclosing Hume to Hill, cablegram, May 19, 1883; Hill to J. Kennedy Tod & Co. and to Hume, Feb. 16, 1884; to Dr. E. F. Thayer, Aug. 3, 1883; to W. M. Clark, Feb. 10, 1885; to Hon. Joseph Henry Pope, Oct. 13, 1883; to John Porter, Jan. 8, 1884.

24. Hill to Thorne, Mar. 4; to J. F. Harkness, Mar. 26; to Messrs Lamb Bros., May 4, 1884.

25. Hill to Kennedy, Jan. 10; private vouchers, Jan. 1885; to J. W. Pusher, Feb. 17, 1887; to Ole A. Hangerud, Oct. 30; to M. McMahon, Oct. 30, 1885.

26. Hill to Fleming, Apr. 14, 1888; Armour to Hill, Dec. 1; Field to Hill, Dec. 31; Thomson to Hill, Dec. 21, 1885.

27. H. C. Hewes to Hill, Nov. 15, 1885.

28. Mary T. Hill to Stephens, July 7, 1885; note in Mary T. Hill's handwriting, June 25, 1885 GC.

29. Hill to Tod, Apr. 23, 1883; to John D. Wing, July 21; Wing to Hill, July 1, 1884; Hill to George Clark, Nov. 17, 1883; T. Edwards to Hill, Aug. 17, Sept. 10, 1886.

30. A. S. D. Hill to Hill, May 22, 1883, July 22, 1887, Oct. 8, 1888, Jan. 2, 1889.

31. Donations Ledger, JJHP; Hill to Payne, Apr. 8; Payne to Hill, telegram, Apr. 7, 1886; Johns to Hill, Mar. 17, 1884, Mar. 21, 1885; Herman Biron to Hill, Nov. 23; Harlan W. Page to Hill, Dec. 9, 1887.

32. J. Holman and J. R. Bennett, Jr., telegram, to Hill, Apr. 14; Hill to Hon. C. F. MacDonald, Apr. 19; MacDonald to Hill, Apr. 20; St. Paul *Pioneer Press*, April 15, 16, 1886.

33. Mrs. W. S. Fowlin to Hill, Oct. 18, 1884.

34. Frank (last name illegible) to Hill, Jan. 9, 1888.

35. Hill to Booth, Aug. 17, 1887; Kennedy to Hill, Sept. 14, 1885; Hill to Thorne, Oct. 20, 1887; to Lord Latham, Aug. 23, 1884; to "Estevan" (Stephen), cablegram (copy on scrap paper, n.d.), 1889; to Thomson, Jan. 3, 1888; to Weed, July 24; Kennedy to Hill, July 21, 1886.

36. Hill to Jas. Brodie, Dec. 1, 1886.

37. The dissolution document is in JJHP, GC, Oct. 18, 1883; Hill to Cavileer, Mar. 22, 1886; Stephen to Hill, June 7, July 12, 14, 1883, Mar. 22, 1884; Kennedy to Hill, July 9, 1884.

38. Hill to Kennedy, Oct. 5; to Stephen, Oct. 5 (enclosed with letter to Kennedy); Kennedy to Hill, Oct. 9; Stephen to Hill, telegram, Oct. 9; Hill to Thorne, Oct. 26, 1886.

39. Field to Hill, Aug. 3, 1881; Hill to Kennedy, Nov. 4, 1882; to Field, May 5, 1884, Manitoba LB-7.

40. Kennedy to Hill, Nov. 8; Kennedy to Hill, April 30, May 28, 1884; Thorne to Hill, Jan. 15, 1883; Hill to Kennedy, May 6, 1884; Kennedy to Hill, Sept. 27, 1886; Hill to Kennedy, May 6, 1884.
41. Ch. Hallock to Hill, Aug. 7; to James Brodie, Aug. 24, 1884.
42. Hill to James, Feb. 6, 1885.
43. James to Hill, Feb. 9, 1885.
44. Thorne to Hill, Feb. 14, 1885, LWHP; James to Hill, Apr. 12, 1886.
45. Clark to Hill, Dec. 18, 1883; Hill to Mary T. Hill, telegram, Nov. 30, 1885; private vouchers, Jan. 1886; Rockefeller to T. W. Pearsall, Apr. 17; JJHP, GC; Henry W. DeForest to Hill, Feb. 23; Clark, Dodge & Co. to Hill, Feb. 28, 1888; Stephen to Hill, Mar. 4, 1882; Manvel to Hill, July 8, 1885; Hill to Thorne, Oct. 20, 1887.
46. Stephen to Hill, Mar. 4, 1882; Manvel to Hill, July 8, 1885; Hill to Thorne, Oct. 20, 1887; Cannon to Hill, Jan. 10, 1888; Sterling to Hill, Mar. 20, 1884, Apr. 1, 1886; Farrer to Hill, July 20, 1888; Thomson to Hill, Aug. 13, 1885.
47. Hill to Kennedy, July 20, 1885.
48. Hill to Kennedy, Nov. 21; Perkins to Forbes, Oct. 20, 1883, Charles E. Perkins Papers, Newberry Library, Chicago; T. J. Potter to Hill, Apr. 11, 1884; Forbes to Hill, Jan. 1885.
49. The correspondence between Touzalin and Hill is extensive, but see esp. Touzalin to Hill, July 29, 1885. Lee, Higginson & Co. to Hill, Aug. 17; subscription call from CB&N, Sept. 15, 1885; E. T. Nichols, Jr., to Hill, Feb. 17, 1886; Hill to Kennedy, Apr. 21, 1885.
50. Stephen to Hill, telegram, Jan. 24, 1885; Kennedy to Hill, Apr. 24; Hill to Kennedy, June 8, July 20, 1885.
51. Kennedy to Hill, July 22, 23; Forbes to Hill, Apr.; Touzalin to Kennedy, July 30, copy in JJHP, GC; Kennedy to Hill, Aug. 14, 1885. The correspondence between Hill and Minot in the summer of 1885 on the subject of what Minot was to get out of the deal is extensive and reveals much about Minot's personality.
52. Nichols to Hill, Aug. 22; Minot to Hill, July 31, Aug. 5; Kennedy to Hill, Sept. 14, 1885.
53. Minot to Hill, Nov. 24, 27, 1885; Hill to Henry L. Higginson, Nov. 18, 1887. Minot's letterbooks, which reveal his many activities, are in JJHP.
54. Minot to Kennedy, Jan. 22, Feb. 17, 1886; to Hill, Apr. 15, 1886, Nov. 5, 1885; Kennedy to Hill, Oct. 4, 1886 (in which Kennedy enclosed Minot's letter to him of Oct. 1), Minot LB-1.
55. Minot to Hill, Nov. 5, 1885; Hill to H. A. Foster, Jan. 21, 1884; to Stephen, Jan. 24, 1885; to Kennedy, Feb. 17; Kennedy to Hill, Feb. 26, 1886.
56. Tod to Hill, Feb. 1; Kennedy to Hill, Oct. 2, 1886.
57. Kennedy to Hill, Apr. 5, May 21, 1886; Feb. 11, 1887.
58. Forbes to Hill, Oct. 12, 1886.

CHAPTER TWELVE

1. Hill to Thomson, Jan. 3, 1888.
2. See Maginnis to Hill, Sept. 16. 1884.
3. Gibson to Hill, June 17; Hill to Gibson, Aug. 10, 1881.
4. Gibson to Hill, Aug. 22, Sept. 2, 1881.
5. Gibson to Hill, Aug. 6, 1885; JJHP, private vouchers, Aug. 1886; Gibson to Hill, Sept. 18, 1883.
6. Hill to Gibson, Sept. 25, 1883.
7. Hill to Gibson, May 5, 1884.

8. Hill to Broadwater, Mar. 20; to E. T. Nichols, Jr., Mar. 20, 1888; Hill to George Stephen, Sept. 10, 1889; to Gibson, Feb. 12, 1883. Local newspapers watched the visitors like hawks; see Helena Weekly *Independent*, Apr. 17, June 19, 1884; Helena *Weekly Herald*, May 14, 1885.

9. Broadwater to Hill, June 15; Hill to Broadwater, June 19, July 23; J. T. Dodge to Hill, June 21, 1884.

10. Hill to Clark, July 30; to Thorne, July 30; to J. W. Sterling, Sept. 1, 1884; to Byron M. Smith, Sept. 28, 1883; to Broadwater, June 19, 1884.

11. Report by Newberry is in JJHP, GC, Oct; Dennis Ryan to Hill, Oct. 14; Hill to Broadwater, Sept. 17; to Gibson, Oct. 17, 1884. Broadwater to Hill, Sept. 21, 1884.

12. Broadwater to Hill, Nov. 25, 1884, Jan. 12, 1885; Hill to Broadwater, Jan. 16, 1885; Hill to Kennedy, Apr. 21, May 1; T. E. Collins and C. E. Conrad to Hill, Nov. 16; Broadwater to Hill, Nov. 27, 1885.

13. The correspondence on right-of-way and related matters is extensive; see esp. Maginnis to Hill, Apr. 3; H. B. Strait to Hill, June 19, 1884; Maginnis to Hill, June 7, 22, 1885; Hill to Strait, July 20; Strait to Hill, Dec. 11; Kennedy to Hill, Oct. 2; Hill to Hon. Benjamin Harrison, July 8, 1886.

14. Hill to W. E. Smith, Oct. 15, 1886.

15. Thorne to Hill, Dec. 24, 1885, Feb. 18, 1886; Maginnis to Hill, Feb. 23, 1886.

16. Manvel to Hill, Mar. 16; Kennedy to Hill, Mar. 19, 1886.

17. Hill to Broadwater, Mar. 19; R. B. Harrison to Hill, Mar. 23; Thorne to Hill, Mar. 27, 1886.

18. Kennedy to Hill, Mar. 20, 1886.

19. Hill to Kennedy, Apr. 3, 1886.

20. Hill to Kennedy, Apr. 10, 1886.

21. Kennedy to Hill, Apr. 8; Stephen to Hill, May 16; Hill to Kennedy, Mar. 27, 1886. The subscribers' names may be learned from the numerous subscription calls which fill Hill's private letterbooks during this period.

22. Hill to Stephen, Aug. 31; to D. Willis James, Aug. 31; to Kennedy, May 31, Oct. 9; to Frank Thomson, Oct. 25, 1886.

23. Shepard to Hill, Feb. 24, 1887.

24. Hill to Thorne, Oct. 26, 1886; Thorne to Hill, Feb. 10; Hill to James, Jan. 10, 1887.

25. Hill to Kennedy, telegram, Oct. 22, 1886.

26. Hill to James, Oct. 15, 1886.

27. Kennedy to Hill, Oct. 15; telegram, early Oct.; Nov. 16, 1886; telegram, Aug. 31, Sept. 1; Nichols to Hill, Nov. 21, 1887.

28. Hill to Kennedy, Jan. 10; to S. J. R. McMillan, telegram, Jan. 27; to Charles W. Johnson, Feb. 7; to J. D. P. Atkins, Aug. 6; to Kennedy, Sept. 7, 1887.

29. David Chauncey Shepard, *Memoirs and Atlas* (St. Paul, 1898); Hill to Kennedy, Sept. 25; Manitoba LB-9; Minot to Hill, Nov. 4, 1886, Minot LB; Hill to Executive Committee, Apr. 25, 1887.

30. Hill to Executive Committee, May 7; to Kennedy, May 7, July 22; to Donald Grant, Aug. 10; to Kennedy, Sept. 7; to Paris Gibson, telegram, Sept. 26; and to Kennedy, Nov. 18, 1887.

31. Hill to Perkins, July 22; to Higginson, July 23, 1887; to W. P. Clough, Dec. 3, 1888.

32. Hill to Daly, Oct. 12, 1886; Hill to Forbes, Jan. 26, 1888; Forbes to Hill, Apr. 18; Nichols to Hill, Apr. 1; Nichols to Hill, June 13; Parsons to Hill, Oct. 21; Hill to Nichols, Oct. 24, 31; Nichols to Hill, July 29, 1889.

33. Kennedy to Hill, May 12, July 22, Oct. 29; Hill to Kennedy, July 22; Kennedy to Hill, Nov. 19, 1887.

34. Hill to Thomson, Jan. 24, 1887.

35. W. J. Macaulay to Hill, Feb. 17, 1886; Charles R. Flint to Hill, Oct. 13, 22, 1885.

36. Hill to Dr. John T. Metcalfe, Dec. 4; to Kennedy, Dec. 3; to Mary T. Hill, telegram, Dec. 8, 1887.

37. Hill to Kennedy, Jan. 12, Mar. 13, 1888; W. H. Fuller to Hill, Mar. 27, 1887; Hill to Nichols, May 18; to Belmont, May 21; to D. S. Lamont, Aug. 26, 1888; to Frank Thomson, telegram, Jan. 2; to E. H. Beckler, telegram, Dec. 27, 1889.

38. Hill to Matthew Wilson, Apr. 16, 1889; George Palmes to Hill, Oct. 21, 1885; Weed to Hill, Aug. 4, 1888.

39. Hill to Sterling, Mar. 1, 1884; A. Chemidlin to Hill, Aug. 28, 1884; Fairbanks to Hill, telegram and letter, Aug. 7; Hill to Fairbanks, Aug. 13, 1884; Manvel to Hill, telegram, Aug. 5, 1885; J. Kennedy Tod to Hill, Sept. 2, 1885; Diary of Mary T. Hill, 1885, copy in JJHP.

40. W. S. Scott to Hill, Aug. 30; Hill to Fairbanks, Dec. 3, 1887.

41. Fairbanks to Hill, Nov. 1, 1887; Cole, Bramhall & Morris to Hill, July 2, 1888.

42. Hill to John L. Cadwalader, July 5, 1888; to Charles Benedict, telegram, Jan. 25, 1889; Mary T. Hill to James Norman Hill, telegram (n.d.) 1888; Mary T. Hill to James N. Hill, telegram, Mar. 9, 1889; James N. Hill to "Dear Papa," Sept. 25, 1889.

43. James N. Hill to Hill, Oct. 19, 1888; W. A. Stephens to Hill, June 20; James N. Hill to Hill, Jan. 27; to W. A. Stephens, Sept. 19; Louis W. Hill to Hill, June 18; G. A. Wentworth to Hill, Sept. 12, 1889; Hill to Wentworth, Oct. 10, 1888; Rick Mahony, Director of Alumni Affairs, Phillips Exeter Academy, to author, Mar. 31, 1975.

44. Samuel Hill to C. H. Benedict, Sept. 21, on letterhead of his law firm; JJHP, private vouchers, May–Aug.; Hill to E. T. Nichols, Oct. 8; Benedict to Samuel Hill, Oct. 15, 1888; "Mary" to Hill, cablegram from Paris, Jan. 21; Samuel Hill to Hill, confirming telegram, July 3; Samuel Hill to Hill, July 8, 1889.

45. C. H. Johnston to Hill, May 16; interview with Cortlandt T. Hill, Apr. 1974; Oakes to Hill, July 30; C. E. Otis to Hill, Oct. 7, 1885; Peabody & Stearns to Hill, July 2; Hill to E. S. Goodrich, Apr. 29, 1887; P. P. Furber to Hill, Mar. 28, 1888; W. P. Stymus to Hill, Jan. 23, 1889.

46. E. T. Nichols to Hill, Jan. 7; Forbes to Hill, Jan. 7; E. F. Cragin to Hill, Oct. 12, 1889; Rev. Edward Neill to Hill, July 27, 1887; Griggs to Hill, July 8, 1889.

47. Hill to Stephen, Oct. 20, 1880, Manitoba LB-4.

48. 14. Fed. Rep. 114, 117, 1882.

49. Kennedy to Hill, Mar. 16, 18; Young to Hill, Mar. 25, 1886.

50. 120 U.S. 303, 312–18; Kennedy to Hill, Feb. 8; Hill to S. M. Pinney, Feb. 12; Hill to Kittson, Aug. 18, 1887; William Watts Folwell, Notes for a History of Minnesota, 1906, in MHS, esp. interviews with William P. Murray, James M. Gilman, and Farley's nephew, W. H. Fisher.

51. Hill to Kennedy, Apr. 12; Stephen to Hill, Jan. 18; Hill to Kennedy, Jan. 12; Hill to Stephen, April 12; Hill to Kennedy, July 12, 1888; Folwell, Notes, interview with Daniel Murphy.

52. A handwritten note in JJHP, GC, Jan. 1–15, 1889 (n.d.), signed by one M. Denny, tells Hill that "Farley will not consent as I am informed unless he is paid a considerable sum." Hill to Stephen, April 12; Stephen and Smith to Hill, telegrams, May 11, 1888; 39 Fed. Rep. 513; Comstock to Hill, Sept. 14, 1889; Clark to Hill, Sept. 18, 1889; 150 U.S. 572, 574–77. R. B. Galusha to Hill, Feb. 1, 1894, enclosing copy of Kittson to Galusha, Mar. 15, 1888, confirms that Kittson did not intend to bribe Farley.

53. Hill to Kennedy, Mar. 6; Washburn to Hill, April 2, 1881; Hill to Charles S. Fairchild, July 1; Charles A. Pillsbury to Hill, Oct. 26, 1889; Hill to S. J. R. McMillan, June 23, 1884; F. H. Weeks to Hill, Feb. 13, 1885; Hill to William F. Phelps, Mar. 8, 1887.

54. Hill to E. W. Cummings, Nov. 29, 1886.

55. Kennedy to Hill, Aug. 26; Hill to Kennedy, Sept. 23, 1885; Hill to Rhawn, Aug. 30,

1886, Manitoba LB-9, all maintain that the St. Paul & Duluth Railroad was no longer a satisfactory link to the Great Lakes. That Hill was already planning an even more radical step, an east-west direct link between Crookston and the Lakes in direct competition with the Northern Pacific, is revealed in Hill to F. L. Brown, Apr. 20, 1887. George C. Stone to Hill, Oct. 7, 1885; Marshall Field to Hill, May 4; H. H. Porter to Hill, May 4; Hill to W. E. Smith, July 18, 1887; to Porter, Mar. 4, 1889.

56. Hill to William Minot, Jr., Mar. 2, 1889; Henry D. Minot to Hill, May 22, 1888; Hill to Minot, Aug. 25, 1888; Minot to Kennedy, Feb. 12, 1886.

57. Hill to Hughitt, Jan. 25; Hughitt to Hill, Jan. 21, July 29; Kennedy to Hill, June 11, 1886.

58. Hill to Executive Committee, April 25, May 18, 1887.

59. Hanna to Hill, May 23; Hill to Hanna, May 26, Aug. 15, 1887.

60. Kennedy to Hill, Sept. 8, 1887; Hill to T. Jefferson Coolidge, Aug. 8, 1888; John Gordon to Hill, May 28, 1889; Hill to Nichols, June 30, 1888; Nichols to Hill, Mar. 1, 1889.

61. Minot to Hill, Mar. 11, Aug. 12, 1887, Feb. 13, 1888; William Minot, Jr., to Hill, Nov. 3; Henry L. Higginson to Hill, Nov. 4; Hill to Kennedy, July 22; Minot to Hill, Aug. 21, 1887; Minot to Hill, Feb. 13, 1888, in Executive Committee Letterbook, JJHP.

62. Hill to Kennedy, Mar. 13; to James, Mar. 9, 1888.

CHAPTER THIRTEEN

1. Hill to Stephen, Jan. 18, 1885; to Kennedy, Mar. 27; Rogers to Hill, May 9, 1886.

2. Hill to Kennedy, Oct. 9; Kennedy to Hill, Oct. 14; Hill to Kennedy, Dec. 28, 1886; Rogers to Hill, May 22, 1887.

3. Hill to Kennedy, Nov. 26, 1886; to Elijah Smith, Jan. 24, 1887; to Stephen, June 9; Smith to Hill, Feb. 7, Mar. 12, 1889.

4. Cannon to Hill, Feb. 13; Nichols to Hill, Feb. 25, 1889.

5. Villard to Hill, telegram, Mar. 3; Villard to Hill, note, Mar. 1889; Minot to Hill, Mar. 15; Cannon to Hill, May 14; Stephen to Hill, cable, Mar. 14; Nichols to Hill, telegram, June 3; Stephen to Hill, May 21, 1889.

6. Hill to Stephen, May 10, 1889.

7. Hill to Stephen, June 9, 1889.

8. Stephen to Hill, June 19, 1889.

9. Thorne to Hill, Oct. 1, 1888; James to Minot, Feb. 15; Minot to Hill, Feb. 18, Mar. 15, 1889; Charles Fairchild to Hill, Aug. 24; Hill to Messrs. Lee, Higginson & Co., Sept. 7; Fairchild to Hill, Sept. 12, 1888; Kennedy to Hill, Jan. 16, 1889.

10. Stephen to Hill, July 16, 1888.

11. Stephen to Hill, Aug. 4 (First part of quotation), and July 16 (second part); Stephen to Hill, Aug. 18, 1888.

12. Hill to Stephen, May 10; Stephen to Hill, May 21 (there are two letters from Stephen of this date), 31; Smith to Hill, Jan. 15, Sept. 5, 1889.

13. Stephen to Hill, telegram, Aug. 7; Stephen to Hill, Sept. 6, 1889.

14. Circular of the St. Paul, Minneapolis & Manitoba Railway Co., Oct. 2, 1889, JJHP, GC; official details are in Minutes of the Board of Directors. The pattern of initial suspicion followed by general acceptance is reflected in *Railroad Gazette*, Oct. 11, 1889, Vol. XXI, 664 *et seq.*

15. Hill to William Minot and other directors, telegram, Sept. 16; to Nichols, Sept. 16, 1889.

16. Hill to Stephen, Feb. 23, 1890.

17. John F. Stevens, *An Engineer's Recollections* (New York, 1935), originally a series of articles in *Engineering News-Record*, 33.

18. One attraction of the more southerly route was the Union Pacific's promise to provide a link to the coast; see Hill to C. F. Adams, Jr., Sept. 9, 12; to Stephen, Sept. 14, 1889. Stephen to Hill, Sept. 6 (quotation); Hill to Beckler, Oct. 9, 1889.

19. U.S. War Dept., *Reports of Explorations and Surveys to Ascertain the Most Practicable and Economical Route for a Railroad from the Mississippi River to the Pacific Ocean* (13 volumes and maps, Washington, 1853–54), I, pp. 97–98 of Part II, paginated separately.

20. John M. Budd wrote me on July 18, 1975, after reading a draft of this chapter, that Stevens declared to Ralph Budd many years later that he had never even heard of the reports of the Pacific Survey when he went looking for the Marias Pass. The younger Budd, and others, believe that the gap in the silhouette of the Rocky Mountains at that point declares the existence of a pass. But, like gold in the mountains, it had to be found. Stevens's grim determination led him past a point now called False Summit, which may have kept earlier explorers from going farther west. Stevens recalled these events in a letter of May 31, 1928, to Gen. William C. Brown, quoted in its entirety in George F. Brimlow (ed.), "Marias Pass Explorer John F. Stevens," *Montana Magazine of History*, III (Summer 1953), 39–44, which John M. Budd called to my attention. See also Stevens, *Engineer's Recollections*, 21–26; Beckler to Hill, Dec. 24, 1889, July 3, 1890, GN Archives, Minnesota Historical Society (hereafter cited GN-MHS); E. H. Beckler, "Location of the Pacific Extension of the Great Northern," *Railway Gazette*, XXV (Oct. 11, 1889), 744–45; Ralph Budd, "Railway Routes Across the Rocky Mountains," *Transactions of the Newcomen Society*, XVIII (1938), 219. Tinkham's pass is shown as Cut Bank Pass on modern topographical maps. The little stream that Stevens followed into the pass was later named Summit Creek. The westward-flowing stream, named Bear Creek, led to the Middle Branch of the Flathead River, down which the railroad makes its way gently to the plain. That there are many tributaries of the Marias River has been known since the day in 1806 when Meriwether Lewis named it "in honor of Miss Maria Wood, . . . that lovely fair one"; see Milo M. Quaife (ed.), *The Journals of Captain Meriwether Lewis and Sergeant John Ordway, Kept on the Expedition of Western Exploration, 1803–1806* (Madison, 1916), 228n1. An exhaustive study of the history of the "real" Marias Pass, in the 75 years before John F. Stevens explored it, has been made by Warren L. Hanna, who graciously allowed me to read a portion of the MS of "Many-Splendored Glacierland, The Story of Glacier National Park," tentatively scheduled for publication in 1976 by Superior Publishing Co., Seattle, Washington.

21. Hill to Beckler, Dec. 27; to Gibson, Dec. 31, 1889, Mar. 27, 1890.

22. Hill to Stephen, Feb. 23, 1890.

23. Hill to George Stephen, Feb. 23; Donald Smith to Hill, Feb. 19; Hill to Stephen, cable, Mar. 2; Stephen to Numoilet (his agent in Montreal), cable, Mar. 3; to Hill, Mar. 14, 1890.

24. Forbes to Hill, Apr. 18, Dec. 7; Schiff to Hill, Dec. 7, 1889; Stephen to Hill, May 12; Nichols to Hill, May 22; Hill to Thomas Skinner, cable, June 9, 1890; Stephen to Hill, July 29, 1891.

25. Minot to Hill, Jan. 26, 1890.

26. Hill to Minot, Jan. 28, 1890.

27. Minot to Hill, Jan. 30, Apr. 16; resignation, JJHP, GC, July 6, 1890; *New York Times* and St. Paul *Pioneer Press*, Nov. 15; Mary T. Hill to Clara Hill, Nov. 14, 1890, letter, privately owned.

28. Perkins to Higginson, Nov. 18, 1901, Charles E. Perkins Papers, Newberry Library, Chicago; *New York Times*, Nov. 15, 1890; Perkins to William Forbes, Oct. 14, 1890.

29. Daniel C. Haskell (ed.), "On Reconnaissance for the Great Northern—Letters of C. F. B. Haskell," reprint, *Bulletin of the New York Public Library* (New York, 1948).

30. Stephens to Benedict, Oct. 7, 1892.

31. Hill to Manvel, May 18; Manvel to Hill, Mar. 27; Hill to Kennedy, Apr. 4; to D. Willis James, Apr. 5, 1888.
32. E. B. Thomas to Hill, Jan. 11, 1890; Perkins to Hill, Dec. 23, 1889.
33. Hill to Beckler, Jan. 21, 1890.
34. Hill to Beckler, 2 telegrams, Mar. 19; to Samuel Thomas, telegram, Apr. 8; to Beckler, letter, June 18; to Mohler, June 20; Beckler to Hill, June 22, 1890.
35. Hill to N. D. Miller, telegram, Aug. 5, 3 telegrams, Aug. 6; to Mohler, letter, Mar. 25, 1890; to Beckler, Dec. 27, 1889, June 18, Aug. 29, 1890; to Hon. W. F. Sanders, July 18, 1890.
36. Stevens, *Engineer's Recollections;* Hill to Beckler, July 2, 6, Aug. 7, Oct. 15, 16, 1892, GN Archives.
37. Hill to P. P. Shelby, June 21, 1892, GN Archives; *Seattle Post-Intelligencer,* Mar. 8, 1890, quoted in Frederick James Grant (ed.), *History of Seattle, Washington* (New York, 1891), 278; Burke to D. H. Gilman, quoted in Robert C. Nesbit, *"He Built Seattle": A Biography of Thomas Burke* (Seattle, 1961), 213.
38. Glenn Chesney Quiett, *They Built the West, An Epic of Rails and Cities* (New York, 1934).
39. Stephen to Hill, Dec. 30, 1890.
40. Hill to Mary T. Hill, Jan. 28, 29, 1891, letters, privately owned.
41. Hill to Clara Hill, Feb. 6; to Mary T. Hill, Feb. 3, 7, 1891, letters, privately owned.
42. Stephen to Hill, Dec. 28, 1890; Hill to Stephen, cable, June 9, 1891; to Stephen, July 1; Stephen to Hill, July 27, 1892.
43. Nichols to Hill, Apr. 22; Schiff to Hill, May 4, 8, 1891.
44. W. H. Porter to Hill, Dec. 19, 1891; Hill to Mary T. Hill, Apr. 4, 1892, letter, privately owned.
45. Clipping from unidentified newspaper, enclosed in C. X. Larrabee to Hill, Mar. 21, 1893.
46. Hill to Stephen, Dec. 9, 1890.
47. Hill to Frank Thomson, Jan. 9; to Hon. J. T. Ronald, Jan. 9, 1893, GN-MHS.
48. D. R. McGinnis to Hill, May 26, 1893; W. A. Stephens to Frank A. Flower, Dec. 15, 1889; St. Paul *Pioneer Press,* June 7, 8, and 9, 1893; C. F. Peterson to S. S. Breed, June 7; E. T. Nichols to Hill, June 8; Hill to S. G. Comstock, June 8, 1893.
49. Grover Cleveland to Hill, May 29, 1893, in Allan Nevins (ed.), *Letters of Grover Cleveland, 1850–1908* (New York, 1933), 325; Stephen to Hill, May 23, 1893; Broadwater to Hill, July 12, 1890; Whipple to Hill, Nov. 28, 1892; Blanchard to Hill, June 14, 1893.
50. Armour to Hill, June 8; Schiff to Hill, Mar. 26; St. Paul *Pioneer Press,* June 10, 1893.

CHAPTER FOURTEEN

1. Nichols to Hill, Aug. 7, 1893.
2. Moore to Hill, Nov. 12; Hill to Stephen, Dec. 8; Stephen to Hill, Dec. 28, 30, 1890.
3. Forbes to Hill, May 16, 1893.
4. Hill to Samuel Hill, telegram, May 19; Nichols to Hill, June 21; to Hill, 2 telegrams, June 21, 22; to Hill, June 20, 23, 27, July 26; Cannon to Hill, telegram, Aug. 4; Kennedy to Hill, Aug. 15, 1893.
5. Hill to Messrs. Ferdinand Bussinger, etc., Apr. 2; to C. A. Magnuson, July 24, 1890; to Schiff, Aug. 30, 1891; William H. Dunwoody to Hill, telegrams, Apr. 29, May 1, 1893.
6. Hill to Nichols, June 9, 1891; to Stephen, July 1, 1892; to President Cleveland, June 15, 1893; Schiff to Hill, June 16, 1893.

7. W. A. Stephens to Hill, Aug. 22; Nichols to Hill, Aug. 22; Hill to Nichols, Aug. 3; Lewisohn Bros. to and from Hill, June 14, 1893.

8. Albro Martin, "Railroads and the Equity Receivership: An Essay on Institutional Change," *Journal of Economic History,* XXXIV (Sept. 1974), 685–709, explains the legal climate on the eve of the 1890's depression.

9. Hill to Nelson, Dec. 18, 31, 1892.

10. Sam Hill to Hill, Mar. 21, 1894.

11. Hill to Senator C. K. Davis, Jan. 9, 1893, GN Archives; to Schiff, Apr. 20, 1893. The origins and effects of federal regulation, never understood by the Progressive historians, have subsequently been badly obfuscated by writers whose chief aim seems to be to rationalize the failure of Marxian socialism to emerge in the United States. See Gabriel Kolko, *Railroads and Regulation* (Princeton, 1965), whose discourse on railroad men's motivations bears little resemblance to the anguished thoughts which Charles E. Perkins dictated into his private letterbook, Jan. 7, 1895, Perkins Papers. An effort to clear away the confusion is Albro Martin, "The Troubled Subject of Railroad Regulation in the 'Gilded Age'—A Reappraisal," *Journal of American History,* XLI (Sept. 1974), 339–71.

12. W. A. Stephens to C. C. Burdick, Jan. 22, 1890; W. S. Gurnee to Hill, Feb. 4, 1892; Morgan to Hill, telegram, repeated in John N. Abbott to Hill, telegram, Dec. 9, 1890, GN Archives; Hill to Manvel, Oct. 14; to Roswell Miller, Oct. 2, 1891, GN-MHS.

13. Hill to Edward Tuck, June 15; to Sir Donald Smith, June 15; Stephen to Hill, July 20; to Hill, cablegram, Aug. 26, 1893; Sterling to Hill, Dec. 15, 1894.

14. Manvel to Hill, Sept. 14, 1889; Hill to Manvel, Jan. 9, 1893.

15. Manvel to Hill, Jan. 22; J. D. Springer to Hill, Feb. 24; Hill to Stephen, cable, Aug.; Cannon to Hill, Oct. 20; Moore to Hill, Dec. 24, Sept. 3, 1893.

16. Hill to C. H. Warren, Apr. 20, 1895; to Mohler, telegram, quoted in letter, Aug. 7, 1893, GN Archives.

17. Hill to Schiff, Aug. 7, 1893; to C. H. Warren, Apr. 20, Aug. 17, 1895.

18. Hill to Mohler, Mar. 25; to Minot, Apr. 8, 1890; St. Paul *Pioneer Press,* Sept. 3, 5; Nichols to Hill, Sept. 6; F. E. Ward to Hill, Sept. 2; to Nichols, Sept. 3; to W. Munro, Sept. 5, 7; to Hill, Sept. 6; Hill to Smith, Sept. 5; Kennedy to Hill, Sept. 8, 1894.

19. Hill to Schiff, Oct. 19, 1893; Hill "to whom it may concern," Sept. 21; F. E. Ward to Stephens, Aug. 22, 1894; Hill to C. H. Warren, July 20, to Lord Mount Stephen, Aug. 21; to Finley, May; to E. B. Thomas, Sept. 15, 1896.

20. Nichols to Hill, Oct. 17, Dec. 15; Hill to Stephen, cable, Dec. 18; Stephen to Hill, cable, Dec. 20; Stephen to Hill, cable, Nov. 3, 1893; Gaspard Farrer to Hill, Nov. 29; Stephen to Hill, Nov. 30, 1895.

21. Hill to Stephen, Dec. 17, 1895.

22. Mount Stephen to Hill, Jan. 1; Hill to Farrer, Feb. 3, 1896.

23. Hill to Stephen, Aug. 2, 1895; to Schiff, May 25, 1892; to Tuck, Feb. 5, to Farrer, Oct. 16, 1896.

24. Hill to Tuck, Feb. 5; Baker to Hill, May 27, 1896; Hill to Mount Stephen, Oct. 20, 1894.

25. Nichols to Hill, Apr. 16; to Hill, telegram, Apr. 19; Daly to Hill, May 4; 1894. Most of the records of the American Railway Union Strike of 1894 are in the Great Northern records, Minnesota Historical Society; see esp. Hill to Grover Cleveland, Apr. 28; to C. A. Pillsbury, *et al.,* Committee, Apr. 30, 1894. The hate letter, A. Freeman to Hill, Aug. 7, 1893, is in JJHP, as are the following, which reveal Hill's earlier labor union policy: Hill to T. Jefferson Coolidge, Apr. 3; to D. Willis James, Apr. 5, 1888. Ray Ginger, *The Bending Cross, A Biography of Eugene Victor Debs* (New Brunswick, N.J., 1949), 100–106, is more favorable to Debs and generally overstates the American Railway Union's claims to represent the Great Northern employees.

26. Hill to Mary T. Hill, Apr. 1, 1890, letter, privately owned.
27. Mary T. Hill to Clara, Jan. 18, 1888; Jan. 12, 1889; July 3, 1891; letters, privately owned.
28. Mary T. Hill to Clara, Feb. 12, 1891, letter, privately owned; Mary T. Hill to W. A. Stephens, Mar. 14; Hill to W. A. Stephens, Apr. 27, 1892; Nichols to Hill, telegram, Feb. 16, 1894; Sam Hill to Hill, Mar. 21, 1894.
29. Mary T. Hill to Clara, Jan. 16, 1888, letter, privately owned.
30. Thomson to Hill, telegrams, Dec. 4, 5, 1889; Hill to Furness & Evans, Jan. 14, to A. G. Wilbar, Jr., of Tiffany's, May 23, 1890.
31. W. W. Griscom to Hill, Aug. 5, 1891; to Peabody, et al., Aug. 7, 1889; Whitehead & Suydam, lawyers, to Hill, Oct. 26, 1893.
32. James Brodie to W. A. Stephens, May 7, 1891.
33. Inventory, JJHP, GC, Mar. 5; Hill to Manvel, Aug. 7, 1891, GN-MHS; E. Feldhauser to Hill, Aug. 18, 1893; conversation with Mrs. G. S. Reny.
34. Invitations in JJHP, GC, Oct. 14, Jan. 1, 1894.
35. Gertrude Hill to President Cleveland, Mar. 4, 1893; G. A. Wentworth to Hill, Nov. 8, 1889; Fisher to Hill, Apr. 13, 1890, Jan. 14, 1891; Hill to James N. Hill, May 25; W. G. Mixter to Hill, June 17, 1891; Henry W. Farnum to Hill, Jan. 26, 1892. The boys got to make the trip, after all; see Hill to Frank Thomson, telegram, Aug. 19, 1891.
36. Mary T. Hill to Hill, telegrams, June 28, Aug. 11; Sterling to Hill, telegram, Aug. 19; Mary T. Hill to W. A. Stephens, telegram, Oct. 7, 1892; James N. Hill to Hill, telegram, June 28, 1893.
37. Bill from the Misses Ely's School, Oct. 31, 1890, JJHP, GC; Hill to D. S. Lamont, Feb. 12, 1897; Clara to Mary T. Hill, Nov. 1895, letter, privately owned; conversation with Mrs. G. S. Reny.
38. Hill to Jacob Schiff, Sept. 17, 1895; Taft to Hill, Oct. 5, Dec. 8; Hill to Taft, Dec. 18, 1897.
39. Samuel Hill to Hill, Aug. 23, 1893, Nov. 12, 1895; Daly to Hill, May 30, 1894.
40. Hill to Mount Stephen, Oct. 20, 1894.
41. Farrer to Hill, Nov. 26, 1897.
42. JJHP, Ledger No. 5.
43. See correspondence between W. A. Stephens and Toomey, Mar. 22 to May 1, 1888, JJHP, GC.
44. Hill to Mohler, May 19, 1890.
45. Cleveland to Hill, July 10, 1893; William L. Wilson to Hill, Apr. 4; Hill to Cleveland, July 19, 1894.
46. Hill to Cleveland, July 18, 1894.
47. Armour to Hill, Jan. 11, 1894; Hill to Mount Stephen, Feb. 10, 1896; to Brice, Oct. 9, 1893.
48. Kennedy to Hill, Sept. 3; Mount Stephen to Hill, Nov. 20; Hill to David B. Hill, Sept. 16; Hill to Farrer, Oct. 1, 1896. Campaign letters of Hill to Mark Hanna are in a separate letterbook in JJHP.
49. Sterling to Hill, Feb. 24; Kittson to Sterling, Mar. 22, 1887, in JJHP, GC; Cannon to Nichols, Feb. 28, 1893; Nichols to Hill, Apr. 29, July 28; Hill to Nichols, telegram, Aug. 7, 1896; W. J. Murphy to Hill, May 15, 1894; Hill to Cleveland, Apr. 20, 1895.
50. Isaac L. Rice to Hill, July 31, 1895; Hill to H. H. Kohlsaat, Aug. 28, 1895; Mary T. Hill to Clara, Jan. 29, 1889, letter, privately owned; Forbes to Hill, June 9, 1891; Mount Stephen to Hill, Feb. 7, 1895.
51. Kennedy to Hill, June 2, 1894; Hill to Mount Stephen, Feb. 10, 1896.
52. Mrs. Samuel Thorne to Hill, June 29, 1890.
53. Hill to Mary T. Hill, Apr. 6, 1892, letter, privately owned.

CHAPTER FIFTEEN

1. Mrs. A. Clark to Hill, May 3, 1897.
2. Hill to Newman, Aug. 14, 1899.
3. Hill to Mount Stephen, Aug. 2, 1897.
4. Hill to A. A. Freeman, Mar. 20, 1890, GN Archives; to Porter, Mar. 1, 1892; Stevens, *Engineer's Recollections,* 37; Newel to Hill, Jan. 6, 1898.
5. Hill to G. A. Wentworth, Sept. 29, 1888; to F. E. Ward, Nov. 7, 1898, June 27, 1900; Hill to F. B. Clarke, Aug. 30, 1898; Edward Tuck to Hill, Jan. 11, 1900; Hill to H. E. Byram, Nov. 5, 1902.
6. Russell Harding to Hill, Dec. 13, 1898; Hill to A. J. Earling, Nov. 4, 1897; Newman to Hill, Aug. 12, 1899. When the Interstate Commerce Commission set up a uniform system of railroad accounts, it followed the Great Northern system closely.
7. Hill to Ripley, Apr. 6, 1895; to H. W. Cannon, Nov. 7, 1898; to Armour, Aug. 26, 1896; to E. R. Bacon, Sept. 20, 1898; Armour to Hill, telegram, Sept. 7, 1898.
8. Lamont to Hill, telegram, Sept. 16; Hill to W. H. Newman, Sept. 21; Hill to Mount Stephen, Oct. 9, 1898; to J. W. Gates, Dec. 11, 1899; to Schiff, Sept. 7, 1899, June 20, 1900; to Robert Bacon, May 22, 1901.
9. Forbes to Hill, Dec. 3, 1889, May 26, Aug. 1893.
10. Ray Morris, "The Trans-Continental Situation and the Far West," courtesy of Richard C. Overton. Morris, a close associate of Perkins, wrote this memoir of Perkins's policies in 1909.
11. Perkins to Forbes, Dec. 3, 1890; Dec. 12, 17, 1892; Perkins Papers.
12. Perkins to Hill, Aug. 8; Forbes to Hill, Aug. 20; Hill to Forbes, Aug. 22, 1893; Perkins, memorandum to self in LB, June 1901, Perkins Papers.
13. Hill to "Leanchoil" (Sir Donald Smith), cable, June 24, 1897; Mount Stephen to Hill, Aug. 23, 1897, Aug. 17, 1896.
14. Mount Stephen to Hill, Feb. 7, 1895; Hill to Farrer, Apr. 13; H. D. Northcote to Hill, May 2, 1896; Mount Stephen to Hill, Aug. 23, 1897; Hill to Schiff, June 8, 1896; Farrer to Hill, Oct. 16, 1897.
15. Mount Stephen to Hill, Mar. 16; Kennedy to Hill, telegram, July 25, 1895, July 27, 1898; D. Willis James to Hill, Aug. 6; Cannon to Hill, Dec. 17, 1898; Grant B. Schley to Hill, Feb. 3, 1900; Cannon to Hill, June 23, 1899; Thomson to Hill, telegram, Jan. 31, 1897; Hill to Thomson, Feb. 4; Thomson to Hill, Feb. 5, 1897; Field to Hill, Nov. 27, 1900.
16. Schiff to Hill, June 28, Oct. 9, 13, 1893; Hill to Schiff, telegram, Oct. 16, letter, Oct. 19, 1893; Hill to Schiff, Aug. 20, 1891; Mr. and Mrs. F. Warburg to Hill, Aug. 4, 1896; Schiff to Hill, Oct. 6, 1895; Hill to Schiff, Oct. 12, 1895, May 21, 1896; Schiff to Hill, May 22, 1896. See also Cyrus Adler, *Jacob H. Schiff: His Life and Letters* (2 vols., Garden City, N.Y., 1928), I, 82–87. (Neither Mount Stephen nor Nichols liked or trusted Schiff; see Mount Stephen to Hill, cable, Oct. 20, Mount Stephen to Hill, Nov. 30, 1894, Mar. 26, 1895; Nichols to Hill, Oct. 24, 1894.) James Stillman to Hill, Sept. 21, 1900.
17. Hill to Schiff, Aug. 6, 1891, GN-MHS; to Schiff, Aug. 20, 1891.
18. Schiff to Hill, Dec. 14, 1891.
19. Hill to Schiff, Jan. 16, May 25; Schiff to Hill, May 26, 1892.
20. Goldman to Schiff, enclosed in Schiff to Hill, June 3, 1892.
21. F. E. Ward to Hill, Sept. 3, 1894.
22. Cannon to Hill, May 1896; Nichols to Hill, telegram, Oct. 25, 1897; Schiff to Hill, Aug. 13, 1892; Hill to Schiff, Aug. 20, 1891.

23. Perkins, memorandum to his LB, June 1901, Perkins Papers; Mount Stephen to Hill, Oct. 30, 1891; Schiff to Hill, Dec. 29, 1892.
24. Report of Georg Siemens, Nov. 1893, JJHP, GC, to which is appended a report by T. Barth, engineer, enclosed in Schiff to Hill, Feb. 16, 1894; see also Hill to Schiff, Aug. 7, 1893.
25. Report of Georg Siemens, Nov. 1893, JJHP, GC.
26. Cannon to Hill, May 9; Mount Stephen to Hill, cable, Oct. 18, 1894.
27. Hill to Stephen, Oct. 20, 1894.
28. Hill to Mount Stephen, Oct. 25, 1894.
29. Mount Stephen to Hill, cable, Nov. 6, 1894; to Farrer, Jan. 4; Mount Stephen to Siemens, Feb. 9, 1895.
30. Hill to Mount Stephen, March 19, 1895.
31. Hill to Stephen, April 6; Mount Stephen to Hill, cable, April 8; Farrer to Hill, April 10; Hill to Mount Stephen, April 17, 1895.
32. Hill, two telegrams, and George Clark, telegram, to F. E. Ward, Apr. 26; Hill to St. Paul office, cable, May 10, 1895. The London agreement is in JJHP, GC (NP Reorganization Box 1).
33. Mount Stephen to Hill, May 15; Livingston to Hill, May 12; Schiff to Hill, telegram, May 20; Pillsbury to Hill, May 21; James McNaught to Hill, Aug. 2; Perkins to Forbes, May 15, 1895, Perkins Papers.
34. St. Paul *Pioneer Press*, July 9, 1895.
35. Mount Stephen to Mary T. Hill, cable, May 27; Nichols to Hill, telegram, quoting Schiff, July 9, 1895.
36. Hill to J. P. Morgan & Co., July 4; Nichols to Hill, telegram, July 17; JJHP, GC, 1895 *passim.*
37. Clough to Hill, June 12; Nichols to Hill, telegram, quoting telegram from Schiff, July 11; Hill to Schiff, Aug. 10; to Mount Stephen, July 10, 14; Nichols to Hill, telegram, quoting telegram from Schiff, July 15, 1895.
38. Nichols to Hill, telegram, May 22; James McNaught to Hill, Aug. 5; Hill to Farrer, Aug. 12, to Thomas Burke, Oct. 2; Marcus Daly to Hill, telegram, Aug. 6; Nichols to Hill, Aug. 16; Hill to Farrer, Sept. 12; Mount Stephen to Hill, Sept. 10, 1895.
39. Hill to Mount Stephen, June 24, July 4; Schiff to Hill, July 14; Hill to Mount Stephen, July 14, Aug. 2, 21; Schiff to Hill, telegram, Aug. 13, 1895.
40. Henry J. Horn to Jacob Halstead, Sept. 16, 1895 (forwarded by Halstead with his bill); Hill to Nichols, telegram, for transmittal to Schiff, Sept. 21; Hill to John W. Sterling, Oct. 11; to Charles C. Beaman, Oct. 7; to Schiff, Oct. 11, 1895.
41. Undated draft, JJHP (NP Reorganization Box 1).
42. Nichols to Hill, Aug. 22; Adams to Hill, Nov. 8; Schiff to Hill, Nov. 18; Gwinner to Mount Stephen, Dec. 11, 1895, enclosed in Mount Stephen to Hill, Jan. 7, 1896; Hill to Adams, Nov. 26; to Mount Stephen, Sept. 21, Dec. 17, 1895.
43. Interview with Cortlandt T. Hill, Apr. 1974.
44. Pencil note on Herman Gratz to Hill, Dec. 27, 1898.
45. E. McNeill to Hill, Oct. 29, 1895; JJHP, GC, 1892–93 *passim.*
46. F. E. Ward to E. T. Nichols, Feb. 1, 1895; Hill to Bacon, Oct. 14, 1898; Sam P. Avery, Jr., to Hill, Aug. 19, 1893; G. Durand-Ruel to Hill, Mar. 29, 1893, Mar. 20, 1895; Hill to Durand-Ruel, Dec. 20, 1893; W. C. Toomey to Messrs Lager & Hurrell, June 6, 1902.
47. George F. Brown to W. C. Toomey, June 12; Trevelyan to Hill, Mar. 28, 1899; Taussig to Hill, Dec. 26, 1900; Chester D. Wright to Hill, Jan. 7, 1901.
48. Neill to Hill, March 1; Hill to Neill, March 25, 1890; W. C. Toomey to Rev. Winthrop Allison, June 16, 1898; Rev. Mr. Ireland to Hill, Jan. 25, 1897; St. Paul *Dispatch*, Sept. 3, 1890.

49. Hyett & Smith Mfg. Co. to Hill, June 16, 1892, and many similar letters in JJHP, GC, 1892–95; St. Paul *Pioneer Press,* Sept. 5, 13; draft in JJHP, GC, Sept. 4, 1895.
50. James to Hill, Sept. 10, 1895.
51. Mount Stephen to Hill, Jan. 11; Schiff to Hill, Mar. 16, 1896; Rose to Hill, Dec. 1 [n.d., apparently 1895]; Lamont to Hill, Dec. 3; Villard to Hill, Dec. 18, 1895.
52. Mount Stephen to Hill, July 19; Hill to Adams, Oct. 11; Cannon to Hill, telegram, Nov. 29, 1895; Morgan to Hill, telegram, Jan. 21, 1896.
53. Hill to Mount Stephen, Feb. 15; Morgan to Hill, telegram, Feb. 25; Lamont to Hill, Feb. 26; Cannon to Hill, Feb. 26, 1896.
54. Mount Stephen to Hill, Feb. 27, Mar. 2 (via Nichols), 4, 17 (cable), 18; Nichols to F. E. Ward, Mar. 11; Hill to Schiff, Mar. 11; Agreement, Apr. 2, in JJHP, NP Reorganization Box 1; Hill to Mount Stephen, Aug. 25; Mount Stephen to Hill, May 19, 1896; Hill to Adams, May 23, 1897; J. P. Morgan & Co. to Hill, telegram, June 24, 1896.
55. Hill to Mount Stephen, July 3; Adams to Hill, May 9; Hill to Mount Stephen, Aug. 25; to Adams, Aug. 26; to Mount Stephen, Aug. 21, 1896; to Adams, July 27, 1897; to J. P. Morgan & Co., Sept. 27, 1898.
56. Hill to Coster, June 4, 1898; to Adams, May 23, 25; to Morgan, July 3; Morgan to Hill, Sept. 23; Hill to Morgan (quoted in Hill to Mount Stephen), telegram, Sept. 23; Hill to Morgan, Sept. 24, 1897; Hill to Mount Stephen, Aug. 21, 1896.
57. Hill to Mount Stephen, May 23; to Gaspard Farrer, Nov. 22, 1897; Lamont to Hill, Nov. 15, 1896; Hill to Lamont, July 17, 1898; Morgan to Hill, telegram, Sept. 27, 1897.
58. Mount Stephen to Hill, cable, Jan. 26; Schiff to Hill, Jan. 29, 1897; Mount Stephen to Hill, Apr. 1897; Hill to Morgan, June 21, 1897.
59. Thomson to Hill, Aug. 18; Huntington to Hill, Oct. 11; Crawford Livingston to Hill (quoting Underwood), Aug. 12; Coster to Hill, Aug. 6, 1897; Mellen to Hill, Sept. 3, 17, 1898; Hill to Lamont, July 17, 1898.
60. Schiff to Hill, Feb. 9, 1897; Hill to Mohler, Nov. 3, 1897; Bull to Hill, Oct. 29, 1898, Aug. 15, 1899; Hill to Nichols, telegram to be relayed to Schiff, Nov. 2, 1898; Hill to Coster, telegram, Feb. 1, 1900.
61. Mount Stephen to Hill, Nov. 9; Hill to Mount Stephen, July 2, Sept. 30; to Mohler, Nov. 5; to J. P. Morgan & Co., Sept. 27, Nov. 8; J. P. Morgan & Co. to Hill, Oct. 8, 1898. *New York Times,* Mar. 14, 1900.

CHAPTER SIXTEEN

1. Meyer Berger, *The Story of the New York Times, 1851–1951* (New York, 1951), 134–35.
2. Hill to Schiff, Feb. 2, 1899; to Kennedy, July 17, 30, 1898; to Farrer, Feb. 5, 1900.
3. St. Paul *Pioneer Press,* Dec. 9, 1895; Oliver Dalrymple to Hill, July 26; Hill to Henry D. Hurley, July 26, 1899; Hill to Farrer, Mar. 31, 1900; Mount Stephen to Hill, letter, Feb. 26, cable, May 23, 1899. At the end of 1895 the Great Northern and its predecessor companies had sold more than two million acres of its land grant to settlers in the 37 years since incorporation of the Minnesota & Pacific Railroad; but in the next 21 years down to Hill's death, another one million acres were sold. In 1895 the record number of acres sold in a single year since formation of the Manitoba road was 259,000 in 1880, but in 1902, 403,815 acres were sold. I thank Mr. Howard Dickman for allowing me to use this data from his forthcoming doctoral dissertation on James J. Hill's contributions to agricultural development in the Northwest.
4. Hill to Farrer, Mar. 31; Nichols to Hill, cable, May 18; Gwinner to Hill, May 18; Farrer to Hill, May 19; Morgan to Hill, June 1; Hill to Mount Stephen, cable, June 15;

Lamont to Hill, telegram, Oct. 24; Louisa Pierpont Satterlee to Hill, Dec. 14; Bacon to Hill, Nov. 2; Hill to Mount Stephen, Nov. 5; Morgan to Hill, telegram, Nov. 12; Mount Stephen to Hill, Dec. 7, 1900.

5. JJHP, Ledger 6; Hill to Bacon, June 18; to Nichols, Jan. 19; to Farrer, March 31; to Lamont, March 31, 1900. The outward identity of the Northern Pacific was so well preserved until the Burlington Northern merger of 1970 that for seventy years many of the rank-and-file employees of the Great Northern and the Northern Pacific had no inkling of the liaison.

6. Hill to Miller, Oct. 24, 1898; to Lamont, Mar. 31, 1900; Mellen to Hill, Dec. 16, 1900; Hill to Bacon, Feb. 9, June 12, July 19, Sept. 12, 1901.

7. Hill to Schiff, Feb. 2, 1899; to Strathcona, Aug. 19, 1898; to Schiff, Feb. 1, 2; to Farrer, Mar. 31; to Nichols, Jan. 19.

8. Ralph W. Hidy, Frank E. Hill, and Allan Nevins, *Timber and Men; the Weyerhaeuser Story* (New York, 1963), 207, 212–13; Hill to Mount Stephen, Aug. 2, 1897; to Marcus Daly, Sept. 26; Prospectus for Kootenay Railway & Navigation Co., JJHP, GC, Aug. 10; Hill to J. W. Gates, Aug. 12, 1898; to Farrer, Mar. 31, 1900; to Elias Rogers, Dec. 13, 1900.

9. Hill to Schiff, Jan. 22, 27; Samuel Rea to Hill, Dec. 20, 1900; copy of memorandum in JJHP, GC, Jan. 19, 1901.

10. Dwight E. Woodbridge, *History of St. Louis County* (2 vols., Chicago, 1910), II, 414, quoted in Joseph Wilmer Thompson, "An Economic History of the Mesabi Division of the Great Northern Railway Company to 1915," (unpublished Ph.D. dissertation, University of Illinois, 1956), 200, of which Ch. VI is an excellent summary of Hill's involvement of the Great Northern in the iron ore business.

11. Hill to Nichols, Sept. 26, 1892; Walter Vaughan, *The Life and Work of Sir William Van Horne* (New York, 1920), 225–26; 252–55; Van Horne to Mount Stephen, Apr. 19, copy in JJHP, GC, Apr. 19–30; Schiff to Hill, May 22; JJHP, NP Reorganization Box 1; Mount Stephen to Hill, May 29; Hill to Mount Stephen, July 2, 1896.

12. Mount Stephen to Hill, cable, Dec. 2, 1897; Hill to Van Horne, Mar. 11; John W. Sterling to Mount Stephen, Mar. 19 (enclosed with Mount Stephen to Hill, Apr. 1897); Stevens, *Engineer's Recollections*, 34.

13. Hill to Cannon, May 23, 1897; to Kennedy, July 30, 1898. "My son was very anxious that I should come up and look the ground over," Hill told the Congressional Committee that investigated the U.S. Steel merger in 1912; "he attached a great deal of importance to the transportation of the ore." U.S. Congress, *Hearings before the Committee on Investigation of the United States Steel Corporation*, 62d Cong., 2d sess., Washington, D.C., 1912, 3155, quoted in Thompson, "Mesabi Division of the Great Northern," 207.

14. Hill to Farrer, Jan. 23, 1906, letter, privately owned; to Lamont, May 24; James N. Hill to Hill, July 1, 1901; Hill to C. E. Perkins, Oct. 31; to Farrer, Feb. 20; to Tuck, May 18, 1902; Thompson, "Mesabi Division of the Great Northern," 213; *U. S. Steel Hearings*, 3242, quoted in Thompson, 216; Hill to Mount Stephen, Dec. 9, 1904, letter privately owned.

15. *U.S. Steel Hearings*, 3172, quoted in Thompson, "Mesabi Division of the Great Northern," 211; Hill to Farrer, Oct. 20, 1906, Dec. 13, 1904, letters, privately owned.

16. Speech printed in St. Paul *Pioneer Press*, Sept. 11, 1898.

17. See also Hill to Mount Stephen, Oct. 9, 1898.

18. James to Hill, Sept. 20, 1898; Higginson to Hill, Sept. 4; Hill to Higginson, Sept. 30, 1899.

19. Hill to Nichols, June 15, 1893; to Burke, Sept. 17, 1895; to Schiff, June 7, 1896; correspondence with J. G. Pangborn, JJHP, GC, 1899 *passim*.

20. St. Paul *Pioneer Press*, Sept. 11; Hill to Hanna, July 27, 1898; Hanna to Hill, July 29, 1898, May 13, 1899.

21. A sophisticated and well-written study of opposition to the annexation of the Phillipines after the Spanish-American War, which is the chief test of whether one was pro- or anti-"imperialist," is Robert L. Beisner, *Twelve Against Empire: The Anti-Imperialists, 1898–1900* (New York, 1968). Beisner demonstrates that political control of potential customer nations was not essential to commercial relations, and that such influential businessmen as Andrew Carnegie knew this. For the opposite view, see Walter LaFeber, *The New Empire* (New York, 1963).

22. Hill to A. B. Wolvin, Apr. 15; J. H. Biles to Hill, Aug. 12; Hill to Biles, Sept. 4, 1899; Nichols to Hill, Oct. 25, 1900.

23. Hill to Smith, March 11, 1890.

24. Van Horne to Stephen [n.d.], 1891, quoted in John Murray Gibbon, *Steel of Empire* (London, 1935), 338.

25. Hill to Smith, June 15; to Mount Stephen, August; Stephen to Hill, July 5; Van Horne, letter to CPR stockholders, Oct. 28, 1893, copy in JJHP, GC.

26. Hill to Lamont, Mar. 12; to Mount Stephen, Oct. 9; "Memo in Connection with a Possible Settlement with the CPR," handwritten by C. S. Mellen, JJHP, GC, July 16, 1898; Shaughnessy to Hill, Jan. 9, 1901; Hill to Gaspard Farrer, Nov. 22, 1897; Shaughnessy to Hill, Feb. 6, 1901, June 16, 1899; Hill to Shaughnessy, June 24, 1899; Van Horne to Hill, Mar. 30, 1900; Hill to Senator S. B. Elkins, Apr. 9; to Lamont, July 17, 1898.

27. Adler, *Jacob H. Schiff*, 88–91; Hill to E. D. Adams, Mar. 28; to Lamont, July 17; Mellen to Hill, Feb. 18; Harriman to Hill, telegrams, July 6, 7; Hill to Harriman, telegram, July 9; Harriman to Schiff (who sent it to Hill), telegram, Sept. 29; Schiff to Hill, Sept. 30; Minutes of Meeting of Oct. 3, JJHP, GC, 1898.

28. Hill to Harriman, Sept. 12, 1899. Robert Bacon was about to conclude that the north bank road would have to be built sooner or later; E. T. Nichols to Hill, Dec. 18, 1900.

29. Lamont to Hill, July 31, 1900.

30. Hill to Cassatt, May 16, 1901.

31. Hill to Mount Stephen, May 25, 1901.

32. Hill to Mount Stephen, May 25, 1901; Touzalin to Hill, Apr. 15, 1887; Perkins to John Murray Forbes, Aug. 27, 1892, Perkins Papers; J. W. Kendrick, second vice-president of Northern Pacific, to Mellen, Feb. 14, 1899, JJHP, GC; J. S. Kennedy to Hill, Nov. 20, 1900.

33. Luxton to Hill, Jan. 5; Mount Stephen to Hill, Jan. 18, 1901.

34. By far the best account of the strategic position of the Burlington and of its wooing by Harriman and Hill is Richard C. Overton, *Burlington Route: A History of the Burlington Lines* (New York, 1965), Ch. 14, one of the best of the modern business histories.

35. Perkins to Coolidge, May 31; to C. J. Paine, May 19; to Paine, June 30, 1900 (not sent), Perkins Papers.

36. Hill to Mount Stephen, Apr. 26; Perkins to F. W. Hunnewell, Feb. 25, 1901, Perkins Papers; see also Overton, *Burlington Route*, 256–58.

37. Overton, *Burlington Route*, 255; Hill to Morgan, telegram, Feb. 13, 1901.

38. Morgan to Hill, telegram, Feb. 14, 1901; he was referring to the alliance entered into at the time it was agreed to terminate the Northern Pacific voting trust.

39. Hill to Morgan, Feb. 18; to Perkins, Feb. 18; Perkins to Hill, Feb. 19; Perkins to J. Malcolm Forbes, Feb. 22; to F. W. Hunnewell, Feb. 25, Perkins Papers; Hill to Perkins, Mar. 2; Perkins to Hunnewell, Mar. 9, Perkins Papers; to Hill, Mar. 19; Nichols to Toomey, Mar. 25, 1901.

40. Overton, *Burlington Route*, 258–60; Hill to Mount Stephen, cable, Apr. 11, 1901; Mount Stephen to Hill, cable, Apr. 12, 1901.
41. Perkins to Henry L. Higginson, Nov. 18, 1901, Perkins Papers; Hill to Mount Stephen, Apr. 26, 1901.

CHAPTER SEVENTEEN

1. *New York Times* (hereafter cited as *NYT*), May 9, 1901.
2. Hill to Kennedy, May 16, 1901. Both Harriman and Schiff denied that they knew Hill was seriously negotiating for the Burlington until March; see George Kennan, *E. H. Harriman, A Biography* (2 vols., Boston and New York, 1922), I, 294–96, quoting Pyle's biography of Hill, in which Pyle for some reason changed the word, "Harriman," to "a representative of the Union Pacific interests" in Hill's letter to Kennedy; see Pyle, *Hill*, II, 138, and Schiff to J. P. Morgan, May 16, 1901, in Cyrus Adler, *Jacob H. Schiff, His Life and Letters* (2 vols., New York, 1928), II, 102–3, in which Schiff asserts that Hill denied any interest in the Burlington to his and Harriman's face. For Harriman's reasons for opposing Hill's control of the Burlington, about which there is little controversy, see *U.S. vs. Northern Securities Co.*, Record, I, 44–45, 135, Testimony of James J. Hill; Adler, *Schiff*, I, 98–100, 104–6; and Kennan, *Harriman*, I, 294–95.
3. Schiff to Morgan, May 16, 1901, in Adler, *Schiff*, 102–7.
4. *Ibid.*
5. Schiff to Hill, Apr. 8, 1901; this letter is also in Adler, *Schiff*, I, 100.
6. Hill to Schiff, Apr. 9, 1901, loose letterpress copy in JJHP, GC, bearing the obviously incorrect date of April 9, 1900. Compare this letter with Hill's assertion to Kennedy, May 16, 1901, that he informed Harriman of the negotiations in January, which this letter to Schiff does not quite contradict.
7. Diary of Mary T. Hill; St. Paul *Pioneer Press*, Apr. 19, 1901.
8. Hill to Mount Stephen, Apr. 26; St. Paul *Pioneer Press*, Apr. 27, 1901; *U.S. vs. Northern Securities Co.*, Record, I, 84; Diary of Mary T. Hill. For the myth, see, for example, Stewart H. Holbrook, *The Age of the Moguls* (New York, 1954), 196.
9. Hill to Mount Stephen, July 22, 1904.
10. Hill to Kennedy, May 16, 1901.
11. Hill to Mount Stephen, July 22, 1904.
12. *U.S. vs. Northern Securities Co.*, Record, I, 187, Testimony of John S. Kennedy. For the cooperation of Hill's European friends, see esp. Hill to Mount Stephen, cable, May 7; Lefevre & Co. to Hill, cable, May 8; Hill to Strathcona, Aug. 13; Strathcona to Hill, Sept. 25; Hill to Lefevre, May 8; Mount Stephen to Hill, cable, May 9; Charles Ellis to Hill, cable, May 9; Farrer to Hill, Sept. 16, 1901; Mount Stephen to Hill, May 27, 1902.
13. *U.S. vs. Northern Securities Co.*, III, 688–89, and I, 63, 46–47; Testimony of James J. Hill.
14. Harriman to G. W. Batson, quoted in Kennan, *Harriman*, I, 305–6. Harriman maintained for several years after the event that he had not given any serious consideration to the status of the preferred stock; see *U.S. vs. Northern Securities Co.*, Record, II, 615, Testimony of E. H. Harriman. Charles E. Perkins was convinced that much of Harriman's subsequent truculence reflected his great mortification at having overlooked the point; Memorandum, Nov. 10, 1901, CEPP. Hill had also been inconvenienced by Schiff's careful observance of the Jewish Sabbath; see Nichols to Hill, Oct. 15, 1892.

15. St. Paul *Pioneer Press*, May 7, 8; Hill to Mount Stephen, cable, May 8; Kennedy to Hill, May 9, 1901.
16. Schiff recalled that Hill was at the conference in Harriman's office, but the *New York Times* placed him only at the Morgan conference; *U.S. vs. Northern Securities Co.*, Record, I, 263–64, Testimony of Jacob H. Schiff; *NYT*, May 10, 1901. Charles Steele said that Harriman authorized Schiff to capitulate at the first meeting, held in Harriman's office; *U.S. vs. Northern Securities Co.*, Record, I, 287, Testimony of Charles Steele. Hill quotation, *NYT*, May 10; clipping from unidentified Montreal newspaper in Mrs. H. M. Simpson to Hill, May 10, 1901.
17. Mount Stephen was deeply worried over the effects of the struggle; Mount Stephen to Hill, cable, May 17; Hill to Mount Stephen, May 18; Mount Stephen to Hill, May 21, 1901. Many small investors lost shares of perfectly good stocks which they had bought on margin just before the panic; see, e.g., Cornelia A. Lyon to Hill, May 30, 1901.
18. *U.S. vs. Northern Securities Co.*, Record, I, 241, Testimony of George W. Perkins; Hill to Harriman, May 19; Bacon to Hill, telegram, May 23; Tuck to Hill, May 31, 1901. See also Mount Stephen to Hill, cable, May 22, 1901.
19. JJHP, GC, May 31, 1901.
20. Tuck to Hill, May 31; Hill to Bacon, and to Nichols, telegrams, May 21; Hill to Mount Stephen, June 7; JJHP, Ledger No. 5; Hill to Kennedy, July 18; *U.S. vs. Northern Securities Co.*, Record, I, 46–47, 57, 62 (quotation about "hitching"), Testimony of James J. Hill. The outcome of the struggle to acquire Northern Pacific common stock is summarized in *U.S. vs. Northern Securities Co.*, A43–44, 91, Reply of Defendants.
21. Hill to Bacon, Sept. 2; to Lefevre, cable, Sept. 6; Bacon to Hill, telegrams, Oct. 10, 11; Perkins to Hill (n.d.); George B. Cortelyou, secretary to President Roosevelt, Oct. 29, 1901.
22. John F. Stevens, *An Engineer's Recollections* (New York, 1935), 36; Perkins to Hill, Jan. 10, 1903. An idea of Hill's close supervision of the Burlington can be had from Hill to Harris, June 13, July 18, Sept. 21, Dec. 23, 24, 1901, Jan. 6 and 14, 1902; and Hill to D. S. Lamont, Jan. 8, 1902. Hill to Kennedy, Sept. 7, 1901.
23. Resolution of Board of Directors of Northern Pacific Railway Co., Nov. 13, 1901, JJHP, GC; Hill to Lefevre & Co., cable, Nov. 13; George W. Perkins to Hill, telegram, Dec. 31, 1901; *Oral Decision of Charles F. Amidon, Judge of the U.S. Circuit Court, District of Minnesota, Fourth Division, in Case of Peter Power and Camille Weidenfeld v. Northern Pacific Railway Company*, JJHP, GC.
24. *U.S. vs. Northern Securities Co.*, Record, I, 135, Testimony of Hill; Hill to Clough, Nov. 6, 1901.
25. Hill to Great Northern stockholders, form letter, Nov. 30, 1901, JJHP, GC; *U.S. vs. Northern Securities Co.*, Record, A44–45, Reply of Defendants, and I, 92–93, Testimony of James J. Hill; Memorandum on proposed holding company, Feb. 8, 1899, JJHP, GC; Hill to Schiff, Sept. 9, 1899. Morgan testified that the purpose of the holding company was "not to keep it [the stock of the Northern Pacific and Great Northern] in one place, but to keep it so that the policy of the company upon which its future depended could be continued. We didn't want convulsions going on . . . ," *U.S. vs. Northern Securities Co.*, Record, I, 345, Testimony of J. P. Morgan.
26. *Northern Securities Co. vs. Harriman*, 1903, Affidavit of E. H. Harriman.
27. Farrer to Hill, Aug. 14; Hill to Mount Stephen, Aug. 13, 1901.
28. Hill to Mount Stephen, cable, Nov. 18; Nichols to Toomey, Sept. 21, 1901, acknowledging Hill's instructions to see that Archibald Guthrie, a contractor who had built many miles of Great Northern line, was allotted 1000 shares; Agreement to deposit

Great Northern shares, with list of shareholders attached, Aug. 7, 1901, JJHP, GC; Balthasar H. Meyer, *A History of the Northern Securities Case* (Madison, Wis. 1906), 240. This valuable monograph by Meyers is the standard history of the case, but a modern study is badly needed.

29. *U.S. vs. Northern Securities Co.*, Record, A19, Certificate of Incorporation; *Commercial and Financial Chronicle*, LXXIII [Nov. 16, 1901], 1062. Schiff told his friends that the Union Pacific would wield considerable influence over the Northern Pacific and the Great Northern as a result of its share in the Northern Securities Co.; Schiff to Ernest Cassel, Adler, *Schiff*, I, 110. Perkins, Memorandum for his letterbook, Nov. 10, 1901, CEPP.

30. Hill to Mary T. Hill, Oct. 26, 1901, letter, privately owned; Diary of Mary T. Hill, Nov. 13, 1901; Carnegie to Hill, Dec. 1901.

31. The traffic association cases are 166 U.S. 290 (1897) and 171 U.S. 205 (1898).

32. Unsolicited letters to the Attorney General of the U.S. seldom distinguished between the power of the Northern Securities Co. and that of Hill as an individual, demanding that both be crushed; see, e.g., H. M. Crittenton to U.S. Attorney General, Apr. 30, 1902, National Archives. An investigator for the Attorney General reported widespread belief in Wall Street that the Company was merely the first step in the consolidation of all the nation's railroads into one giant corporation; W. A. Day to P. C. Knox, Feb. 28, 1902, National Archives.

33. Hill to Harriman, telegram, Dec. 24, 1901; David G. Browne to Paris Gibson, Jan. 1, 1902, enclosed in Gibson to Hill, Jan. 6; Hill to Lamont, telegram, Jan. 4; to Lamont, Jan. 7, 8, 1902; James N. Hill to Hill, [n.d.], 1902; *Commercial and Financial Chronicle*, LXXIII (Dec. 28, 1901), 1357 (statement on formation of the Northern Securities Co.); Clough to Hill, Dec. 24, 1901; St. Paul *Pioneer Press*, Jan. 11, 1902. For Van Sant's efforts, see Meyer, *Northern Securities Case*, Ch. 4.

34. Hanna related these conversations to Charles E. Perkins a few weeks before Hanna died (early in 1904); Perkins's Memorandum to his letterbook, July 11, 1904, courtesy Richard C. Overton. Roosevelt gave various reasons during the course of the lawsuit for attacking the securities company; see Elting E. Morrison, *The Letters of Theodore Roosevelt* (8 vols., New York, 1951–54), III, esp. TR to Joseph Gurney Cannon, Sept. 12, 1904; to Edwin Packard, Nov. 26, 1903, on the power of the press to mold an image of the President; to Paul Dana, Nov. 18, 1901, on "the revolt that would be caused if I did nothing in the matter"; to Herschel V. Jones, Feb. 16, 1901, denying pressure from the State of Minnesota; to Carl Schurz, Dec. 24, 1903, asserting that "the men of very great wealth . . . totally failed to understand the temper of the country and its needs, as well as their own needs"; to William Howard Taft, Mar. 19, 1903, claiming that once he, Roosevelt, had explained his position on trusts to them, Senators Hanna and Nelson Aldrich were "far more satisfactory to work with than . . . the radical 'reformers' "; to Elon R. Brown, May 12, 1902, rationalizing his position on the beef trust; and to Anna Roosevelt Cowles, Aug. 26, 1903, claiming that the suit would discourage excessive financial speculation and thus reestablish economic stability.

     Roosevelt's desire to give full credit to Knox is clear in *Theodore Roosevelt, An Autobiography* (New York, 1924), 426–29. Roosevelt's description of Root is in H. F. Pringle, *Theodore Roosevelt, A Biography* (New York, 1931), 255. W. H. Harbaugh's excellent study, *Power and Responsibility: The Life and Times of Theodore Roosevelt* (New York, 1961), adds nothing on the subject of the Northern Securities prosecution. The definitive study of Knox's role is Anita T. Eitler, "Philander Chase Knox, First Attorney-General of Theodore Roosevelt, 1901–1904," unpublished Ph.D. dissertation, Catholic University of America, 1959, 63–87.

35. Roosevelt to Garland, May 5, 1902; to Villard, July 25, 1903; to Benjamin Ide Whee-

ler, Dec. 12, 1901, in Morison (ed.), *Letters of Theodore Roosevelt,* III. Hill to Farrer, Apr. 27, 1903, letter, privately owned.

36. Hill to Clough, Feb. 20; to Steele, Mar. 31; to Clough, telegram, Apr.; to various railroad presidents, Oct. 1902; *U.S. vs. Northern Securities Co.,* Record, I, 8, 258, Testimony of Schiff, and III, 899, Testimony of Harriman.

37. Mary T. Hill to Clara Hill, March 1; Hill to "Dear Tolly," Oct. 12, 1903, letter, privately owned.

38. Hill to Mary T. Hill, Oct. 30, 1901, letter, privately owned.

39. Opinion on Final Hearing, 120 Federal Reporter 721.

40. Hill to Farrer, Apr. 27, and Newel to Clara Hill, June 15, 1903, letters, privately owned; Tuck to Hill, cable, Apr. 10, 1903.

41. Nichols to Hill, Aug. 5; Clough to Hill, Aug. 6; Sterling to Hill, May 22; Hill to Johnson, telegram, Aug. 11, 1903.

42. Brief for the Northern Securities Co., *Northern Securities Co. et al., Apellants, vs. U.S.,* 5, 21; the remark about Caligula is a quotation from *U.S. vs. Comerford,* 25 Federal Reporter 902.

43. 193 U.S. 197, Opinion of Mr. Justice Harlan, Mar. 14, 1904.

44. Hill to Perkins, Mar. 21, 1904; James H. McKenney, clerk, U.S. Supreme Court, to Joseph Nimmo, Jr., Aug. 10, 1904, National Archives.

45. Dissenting opinion of Mr. Justice Holmes, Justices White and Peckham and Chief Justice Fuller concurring. Brewer, in a separate opinion, had refused to accept Harlan's doctrine that every agreement in restraint of trade was unlawful. Latin: "the war of all against all."

46. Hill to Farrer, July 22, 1904.

47. Since many of the shares of the securities company had been purchased from the company for cash, or traded repeatedly on the stock exchange, it was obviously impossible to make a redistribution in kind to all stockholders. When the company was formed, Hill's old friend, Judge Greenleaf Clark, living in retirement in California, had written him that if he ever had to redistribute, *pro rata* would be the only possible way; Clark to Hill, Dec. 5, 1901. See Northern Securities Co., Circular, March 22, 1904, JJHP, GC, for the redistribution plan.

48. Hill to Farrer, cable, Oct. 5; to James N. Hill, c/o Barings, cable, Oct. 6; to Mount Stephen, Dec. 12; Nichols to Hill, Aug. 5; Farrer to Hill, Aug. 25, 1904. Hill to Farrer, Dec. 13, 1904, letter, privately owned; Mount Stephen to Hill, Dec. 30, Aug. 10, 1904.

49. Hill's bitterness toward Harriman is stated without reserve in Hill to Farrer, Jan. 9, 1905, letter, privately owned.

50. Schiff to Hill, Mar. 7, Apr. 17; Hill to Schiff, Mar. 10, 1905. For the President's overtures, see Don. M. Dickinson to Hill, Mar. 24, 1902; Senator A. G. Foster to Hill, May 16; Hill to Lamont, May 25, 1903; Kennedy to Hill, Jan. 1, 1904; Hill to Mary T. Hill, Jan. 19, 1905, letter, privately owned; Goldwin Smith to Hill, Dec. 9, 1908 (quotation); Holmes to Sir Frederick Pollock, Feb. 9, 1921, in Mark De Wolfe Howe (ed.), *The Holmes-Pollock Letters. The Correspondence of Mr. Justice Holmes and Sir Frederick Pollock, 1874–1932* (Cambridge, Mass., 1941).

51. Reprinted by permission of Farrar, Strauss & Giroux, from *A Book of Americans* (New York, 1933), 111.

CHAPTER EIGHTEEN

1. W. C. Toomey to A. J. Blethen, Dec. 12, 1899; Hill to Mitchell, Feb. 24, 1902; Personal Ledgers Nos. 5, 6, and 7. When the securities company redistributed its

railroad stock, Hill's Northern Pacific and Great Northern shares were worth about $37 million, $1 million less than if redistribution had been made in kind, as Harriman had demanded; Nichols to Hill, Oct. 15, 1904.

2. Diary of Mary T. Hill, Nov. 29, 1901; J. J. Toomey to George N. Pierce, telegram, Dec. 17; J. H. Probst to J. J. Toomey, June 15, 1907; J. M. Studebaker to Hill, Apr. 2, 1908; Mary T. Hill to Clara Hill, July 8, 1906, letter, privately owned.

3. Mary T. Hill to Clara Hill, May 7, 10, 1899, letters, privately owned; Diary of Mary T. Hill, July 16, 1901.

4. Diary of Mary T. Hill, May 30–June 4; *NYT,* June 6; W. C. Toomey to Hill, June 1; Hill to Mount Stephen, May 25; Diary of Mary T. Hill, July 17; JJHP, GC, Oct.; St. Paul *Pioneer Press,* Oct. 10; Diary of Mary T. Hill, Sept. 23, 1901.

5. Diary of Mary T. Hill, May 28, 1901; St. Paul *Pioneer Press,* Nov. 22, 1906; Hill to Nichols, July 28, 1902.

6. Hill to Mary T. Hill, Feb. 11, 1906, private collection; Mary Hill Hill ("Mamie") to Mary T. Hill, Nov. 20, 1906; Mary T. Hill to Hill, telegram, Mar. 8; Hill to Samuel Hill, Apr. 19, 1910; Mary Mendenhall Hill to Hill, May 31, 1910.

7. Hill to Walter Hill, telegram, Sept. 13, 1901; Edward G. Coy to Hill, June 27, 1902; Hill to Clara Hill, Aug. 17, 1905, and to Mary T. Hill, Mar. 21, 1909, letters, privately owned; J. J. Toomey to Hill, May 1, 1909; Walter J. Hill to Hill, Nov. 8, 1910.

8. Diary of Mary T. Hill, Aug. 1899, June 21, 1901; Emma Brooks to Hill, May 27, Aug. 28, 1905; A. S. D. Hill to Hill, July 4, 1906.

9. Mary T. Hill to Clara Hill, May 26, June 2, 1906, letters, privately owned; Mount Stephen to Hill, Apr. 4, 1903; Hill to Frank Thomson, June 22, 1898; Cleveland to Hill, July 12, 1901; Nichols to Hill, May 14, 1900.

10. William C. Pope to Hill, Dec. 6, 1901; Hill to Mary T. Hill, Nov. 3, 1905, letters, privately owned; Nichols to Hill, June 5, 1906; J. J. Toomey to Messrs. S. Karpen & Bros., Jan. 5, 1907; Michael Gavin to Hill, Aug. 14, 1908; Edward A. LeRoy to Hill, Sept. 27, 1906; Ernst Kurth to J. J. Toomey, April 9, 1907; Hill to Mary T. Hill, March 6, 1907, private collection; JJHP, GC, Feb. 1909.

11. Hill to Mary T. Hill, Jan. 14 and 16, 1906, letters, privately owned.

12. D. S. Lamont to Hill, Feb. 1904; Hill to Louis W. Hill, telegram, Mar. 7; Martin R. Brown (Hill's private secretary) to Louis W. Hill, telegram, Mar. 8; Hill to George C. Clark, Mar. 10; Herman Biggs to Hill, Aug. 5, Sept. 21; George T. Slade to Hill, Aug. 16; Hill to Messrs. John Laird & Son, Oct. 14, 1905; Mary T. Hill to Hill, telegram, Mar. 29, 1906.

13. Mary T. Hill to Clara Hill, July 8, 1906, letter, privately owned.

14. There is no definitive study of the extended political maneuverings that finally produced the Hepburn Act of 1906 and gave the ICC the power to set maximum rates without review by the federal courts; but see John M. Blum's essay, "Theodore Roosevelt and the Hepburn Act: Toward an Orderly System of Control," in Elting E. Morison (ed.), *The Letters of Theodore Roosevelt* (8 vols., Cambridge, Mass., 1951–54), VI, 1558–71, and Albro Martin, *Enterprise Denied: Origins of the Decline of American Railroads, 1897–1917* (New York, 1971), 112–14.

15. Hill to Schiff, June 13, 1901.

16. Hill to Farrer, Feb. 20, 1902.

17. Hill to unknown correspondent, [n.d.], 1909; there is a draft of this letter in Hill's own hand in JJHP, GC, 1909.

18. Note in Hill's hand on Howard Elliott to Hill, Jan. 5, 1906.

19. Martin, *Enterprise Denied passim,* esp. Chs. I–IV.

20. Hill to Spencer, May 15, Nov. 5; to George B. Harris, Feb. 14; Spencer to Hill, Apr. 26, 1902; Hill to Charles E. Perkins, July 31, 1906. Gabriel Kolko, who sought to demonstrate that the railroads actively sought the regulation enacted from 1887 to

1920, emphasized that the Pennsylvania Railroad supported maximum rate regulation, but omitted to mention their insistence on judicial review; Kolko, *Railroads and Regulation* (Princeton, 1965), 118. Martin, *Enterprise Denied*, 113–14, corrects this deficiency, but it is only from such private sources as this correspondence between Hill and other concerned individuals in the period 1902–6 that the devastating consequences of the Pennsylvania's clumsy strategy can be fully grasped.

21. Perkins to Hill, Jan. 10; Spencer to Hill, Feb. 14; Hill to Spencer, Feb. 20, 1905.
22. Hill to Senator S. B. Elkins, Mar. 3, 1898; to Tuck, Feb. 17, 1900; to Spencer, Dec. 14, 1905.
23. *Regulation of Railway Rates; Hearings before the Committee on Interstate Commerce, Senate of the United States, December 16, 1904 to May 23, 1905, on Bills to Amend the Interstate Commerce Act.* Senate Document 243, 59th Cong., 1st sess. [5 vols.], Testimony of James J. Hill, 701–2.
24. Ibid. 717, 721.
25. Hill to Elkins, Sept. 12; to D. Miller, Aug. 24, 1905; Spencer to Hill, Jan. 6; Clough to Hill, Apr. 9, 1906.
26. Perkins to Hill, July 21; Hill to Perkins, July 31; Higginson to Hill, Oct. 3, 1906, Mar. 26, 1907; Spencer to Hill, May 28; Lewis W. Hill to Hill, telegram, Nov. 30, 1906.
27. Hill to D. C. Shepard, Mar. 7, 1907; to Clapp, Mar. 4, 1908; to Bacon, Mar. 23, 1907; D. Miller to Hill, Apr. 6, 1908.
28. The disappointments of 1908 are treated in Robert H. Wiebe, *Business and Reform* (Cambridge, Mass., 1962), 85. Martin, *Enterprise Denied*, is a detailed study of the railroads' needs for a general rate increase and the reasons why they did not get one until 1918. The source of Hill's comment about the future of railroading as a career is Louis Hill's son, Cortlandt T. Hill.
29. Diary of Mary T. Hill, May 30, 1901.
30. Hill to Charles Steele, Jan. 16, 1903; Count Matsukata to Hill, June 27; Hill to Matsukata, Aug. 17, 1903; Hill to Mark Hanna, May 12, 1902.
31. Charles R. Hanscom, "Description of the Design and Building of the 21,000-Ton Steamships Minnesota and Dakota," Paper read at 11th general meeting of Society of Naval Architects and Marine Engineers, New York, Nov. 19, 20, 1903; printed copy in JJHP, GC; the copy of Burke's speech is in JJHP, GC, Apr. 16, 1903.
32. H. W. McCurdy, *Marine History of the Pacific Northwest*, [no place, no date], 109–10, 251; J. J. Toomey to Mary T. Hill, Apr. 19, 1905.
33. D. Miller to Hill, 2 letters Mar. 21; Hill to Louis W. Hill, Mar. 21, 1904; Miller to Hill, Dec. 15; Hill to Miller, Dec. 25, 1905; Hill to Francis B. Thurber, Sept. 20, 1906; to Hon. Moreton Frewen, March 30, 1909.
34. Hill to George W. Perkins, Feb. 22, 1902; to William Howard Taft, Mar. 26, 1910.
35. Hill to U. G. Orendorff, Dec. 21, 1905.
36. Rhodes to Hill, Dec. 8, 1906; Hill to A. B. Hepburn, Nov. 16; Charles F. Garfield to Hill, Nov. 17, 1908; Hill to Mary T. Hill, June 9, 1906, letter, privately owned; to R. H. Smith, telegram, Aug. 23, 1909.
37. Carroll to Hill, Feb. 8, 13, 1909.
38. St. Paul *Pioneer Press*, Feb. 10, 1911; Hill to Taft, telegram, Mar. 4, letter, July 27, 1909; Taft to Hill, Feb. 6; Hill to Taft, Feb. 8, Oct. 19; to Nelson, Feb. 13; Nelson to Hill, Feb. 18, 25; Hill to Charles D. Hilles, secretary to President Taft, May 5; Hill to Taft, telegram, July 24; Taft to Hill, July 25, 1911; quotation in James J. Hill, *Highways of Progress* (New York, 1910), 92.
39. Roosevelt to Hill, Mar. 4; Hill to Roosevelt, Mar. 20, 1908.
40. Roosevelt to Hill, June 8; Hill to Roosevelt, June 11, 1908; to Pinchot, Feb. 15; to Rev. Mr. Leon S. Koch, Mar. 3, 1909.
41. Hill to Wallace, Aug. 28, 1911.

42. St. Paul *Pioneer Press,* Sept. 9, 1910.
43. St. Paul *Pioneer Press,* Sept. 10; Hill to J. H. Carroll, Sept. 9, 1910; Wallace to Hill, Mar. 16, 18; Hill to Wallace, Mar. 16, 1911.
44. Hill to J. D. Turner, May 20, 1907; to W. H. Stafford, Aug. 19, 1911; to C. F. Manderson, Aug. 1, 1909; to Sir Horace Plunkett, Mar. 22, 1909.
45. *World's Work,* XIX (Nov. 1909). In the fall of 1909, for example, Hill kept eleven such speaking engagements.
46. Forgan to Hill, Dec. 7; Hill to Forgan, Dec. 11, 1909. This summary of Hill's agricultural development activities is based in large part on the work of Howard L. Dickman, who has generously allowed me to read an early draft of his Ph.D. dissertation, to be submitted to the University of Michigan.
47. The extreme example of the effort to make the railroads the scapegoat is Richard Connor, *Iron Wheels and Broken Men* (New York, 1973). A more subtle one is James Michener, *Centennial* (New York, 1974). See J. C. Hanley, president and general business agent of the Farmers Alliance, to W. C. Toomey, Mar. 7, 1904, JJHP, GC.
48. Hill to Senator Thomas H. Carter, Mar. 14, 1908; to George F. Baker, June 14, 1910.
49. St. Paul *Pioneer Press,* Sept. 17, 1908.
50. Hill to A. H. Horwood, July 23, 1907.
51. Hill to Clara Hill, Mar. 8, 1909, Page to Hill, Aug. 13, Oct. 29, 1908, Mar. 29, 1910.
52. *New York Times Book Review,* July 9, 1910.
53. Burke to Hill, June 2; Hill to Burke, June 9; A. J. Blethen, etc., to Hill, June 23; Hill to same, July 25, 1909; Anson Phelps Stokes, Jr., to Hill, May 9, 1910; Hill to Mary T. Hill, June 24, 1910, letter, privately owned.
54. George Lingard to "Yem Hill," Sept. 27, 1903.
55. "Me and Yem," by J. W. Foley, copy in JJHP, GC, 1912.

CHAPTER NINETEEN

1. Shepard to Hill, Feb. 22, 1910.
2. Hill to Farrer, cable, May 28; to D. C. Shepard, Mar. 7; M. R. Brown to E. S. Meade (economics instructor at University of Pennsylvania), Mar. 17, 1906.
3. Hill to Harris, May 19, 1905; to Mount Stephen, June 15, 1904.
4. Hill to J. N. Hill, telegram, Oct. 17, 1905; to Charles Steele, Nov. 7, 1909; Richard C. Overton, *Burlington Route; A History of the Burlington Lines* (New York, 1965), 271–79.
5. Hill to Farrer, Oct. 20; to Barings, cable, Sept. 29, 1906.
6. Hill to Clough, Apr. 2; Clough to Hill, Apr. 9, 1906.
7. Hill to Charles Steele, Oct. 26, 1910.
8. Elliott to Hill, Oct. 21, 1909; Hill to Charles Steele, Oct. 26, 1910.
9. Hill to Baker, June 14, 1910; see also Clough to Hill, Sept. 17, 1910.
10. Baker to Hill, Sept. 27, 1910. The Great Northern and Northern Pacific finally had to reduce their agreement on a settlement formula to writing; JJHP, GC, Oct. 14, 1910.
11. Steele to Hill, Sept. 28, 1910. Stevens's role in the building of the Panama Canal was quickly forgotten, but this historical wrong seems destined to be righted; see David G. McCullough, "A Man, A Plan, A Canal, Panama!" *American Heritage,* XXII (June 1971).
12. Hill's strategy is fully explained in two letters to Charles Steele, May 26 and June 8, 1911.
13. Stevens told his version of the Deschutes Canyon affair in Chapter XII, "The Railway Invasion of Central Oregon," in *An Engineer's Recollections* (New York, 1935). For the informal relationship between Hill and Stevens during the secret phase of

the "invasion," see e.g. Stevens to Hill, May 4, July 4; Hill to E. T. Nichols, telegram, July 30, to Nichols, Oct. 14; to Stevens, Aug. 14, 23, 1909. For the settlement, see Hill to Stevens, Feb. 7; to R. S. Lovett, Mar. 14; to J. Kruttschnitt, Mar. 16, 1910.

14. Van Horne to Stephen, June 20, 1894, Van Horne-to-Stephen Letterbook, typewritten transcript in Public Archives of Canada, original in archives of Canadian Pacific Railway.

15. Van Horne to Mount Stephen, Oct. 7, 29, 1898, Public Archives of Canada.

16. Hill to Andrew Strang, Apr. 3; to Robert Reford (quotation), June 9, 1906. The *Annual Report of the Great Northern Railway for 1916* gave the total investment in Canadian railroad properties as nearly $37 million. For a quarter of a century after Hill's death the Great Northern struggled to disentangle itself from these investments.

17. The evolution of the Mann-Elkins Act and its consequences are treated in Albro Martin, *Enterprise Denied: Origins of the Decline of American Railroads, 1897–1917* (New York, 1971). Louis told his youngest son what James J. Hill had said about getting out of the railroad business; conversation with Cortlandt T. Hill, Apr. 1974.

18. Baker to Hill, Aug. 16; Clark to Hill, telegram, Nov. 5; Hill to Baker, Nov. 7, 1907; to George B. Harris, Jan. 17, 1908; text of mortgage announcement in JJHP, GC, May 1, 1911.

19. Thomas O'Hanlon to J. J. Toomey, Jan. 30; B. Campbell to O'Hanlon, Feb. 4; Hill to Nichols, telegram, Jan. 10, 1907; Hill to Samuel Hill, Mar. 26, 1910; St. Paul *Pioneer Press*, Mar. 2–8, 1910.

20. Hill to Alex K. McClure, Jan. 7; to W. W. Finley, Jan. 7, 1906.

21. Hill to Morgan, June 29, 1897; to F. E. Ward, telegram, Aug. 28, 1899; J. N. Hill to "My dear Father," May 17, 1900; to Hill, Jan. 27, 1902; Mount Stephen to Hill, Apr. 4, 1903; Farrer to Hill, Nov. 7, 1904.

22. James N. Hill, Mar. 14, 1903.

23. Hill to James N. Hill, Apr. 25, 1908; J. W. Gates to Hill, May 10, Oct. 21; Hill to Gates, telegram, May 16; Gates to Hill, May 17, 1910.

24. Hill to Mount Stephen, Dec. 9, 1904, letter, privately owned.

25. Louis W. Hill to Hill, May 4, 1905.

26. Hill to Louis W. Hill, July 14, 1907; W. C. Toomey to C. H. Huttig, Jan. 26, 1903, conveying Hill's decision that Louis was too busy to become a director of the Third National Bank of St. Louis; L. W. Hill to Hill, telegram, Feb. 22, 1908; Hill to L. W. Hill, telegram, Mar. 23, 1910.

27. Interview with Cortlandt T. Hill, Apr. 1974.

28. Hill to Willard, Dec. 22, 1909; Slade to Hill, Mar. 4, 1903; Louis W. Hill to Nichols, telegram, Oct. 8, 1908. For the sickness and death of Miller, see messages from L. W. Hill, at Glacier National Park, to Hill, Aug. 21–23, 1914; on the Northern Pacific succession, Hill to George F. Baker, telegram, July 24; Charles Steele to Hill, July 25, 1913.

29. Hill to Louis W. Hill, Oct. 6, 1910; to Farrer, Aug. 30, 1911; to L. W. Hill, telegram, Feb. 1913; L. W. Hill to Hill, Mar. 23, 1913; Hill to L. W. Hill, Feb. 11, 1914.

30. Hill to Livingston, Nov. 16, 1912.

31. Letter of resignation, July 1, 1912, separately issued in pamphlet form as "The Great Northern and the Northwest." Hill remained a director of the Great Northern until his death.

32. Putnam to Hill, July 2, 1912; Tuck to Hill, July 30, 1912.

33. Gibson to Hill, July 9, 1912.

CHAPTER TWENTY

1. Hill to Nichols, Oct. 7; to E. H. Bailey, Oct. 16; to Nichols, telegram, Dec. 27, 1912; Untermeyer to Hill, telegram, Jan 16; Testimony before "Money Trust Investigation," Vol. 26, Jan. 24, 1913, stenographic transcript in JJHP, GC.

2. Hill to Elmer Larson, Feb. 9; Andrew R. Sheriff to Hill, Feb. 25, 1912; B. F. Harris to Hill, Mar. 25, 1915; quotation about working past 80, Bagley-Clearwater (Minnesota) *Gazette,* Feb. 21, 1913; convention program, Friday, June 13, 1913, in JJHP, GC; Thomas Shaw to Hill, Aug. 12, 1913.

3. Hill to Kenyon L. Butterfield, Apr. 27, 1915; to W. P. Kirkwood, May 17, 1916; to Charles W. Holman, May 10, 1916.

4. Special File "Wacouta," JJHP; preparations for a typical trip to the salmon river may be found in JJHP, GC, June 1911.

5. Diary of Mary T. Hill, 1912; Mary T. Hill to Clara Hill, July 13, 1912, letter, privately owned; Mary T. Hill to Hill, telegram, Aug. 19, 1911; JJHP, GC, Feb. 1915 *passim.*

6. Hill's Private Voucher Record, 1912–16, provides a key to the numbered vouchers, to which are frequently attached the description and "pedigree" of the paintings involved; Jacacci to Hill, Jan. 30, 1913; P. C. Eilers, Jr., to Hill, Dec. 4, 1912; G. Durand-Ruel to Hill, Feb. 3, 1913; Joseph Breck to Hill, Sept. 30, 1915; Kent to Hill, Dec. 3; M. R. Brown to Kent, Dec. 7, 1912.

7. Payroll in JJHP, GC, Sept., 1912; the final accounting on the *Globe* property is in JJHP, GC, June 30, 1905; Mary T. Hill to Clara Hill, July 15, 1914, letter, privately owned.

8. E. T. Nichols to Hill, telegram, July 10; Mary T. Hill to Clara Hill, Oct. 30, letter, privately owned; Farrer to Hill, cable, Aug. 23; Mount Stephen to Farrer, Aug. 26, included with Farrer to Hill, Aug. 27, 1912; August Jacacci tactlessly dilated on the new Mrs. Hill's hopeless position in society in a letter to Hill, Jan. 4, 1913.

9. The Great Falls sale documents, JJHP, GC, June–July, 1908; J. J. Toomey to Messrs. McDonald & Murphy, Oct. 19, 1909; Hill to Farrer, Aug. 4, 1911; E. T. Nichols to Hill, July 23, 1915.

10. Lamont obituary, *New York Times,* July 24, 1905; Hill to Mrs. Marshall Field, Mar. 16, 1906; James obituary, *New York Times,* Sept. 12, 1907; Kennedy to Hill, Sept. 13; Mount Stephen to Hill, cable, Sept. 13, 1907.

11. Leita Amory Perkins to Hill, Nov. 14, 1907 (quotation); Edith F. Perkins to Hill, Jan. 8, 1909; Edith F. Perkins to Hill, Dec. 15; Perkins to Howard Elliott, telegram, July 22; Hill to Mrs. Charles E. Perkins, telegram, Nov. 9; Newel to Hill, Mar. 3, 1907.

12. Lowry died Feb. 4; Upham, May 1; Kennedy, Oct. 31, 1909. See Charlotte Hill Slade to Hill, telegram, May 1; Stephen Baker to Hill, Oct. 31; Hill to William Stewart Tod, telegram, Nov. 1, 1909; Griggs's firm's notice of his death, JJHP, GC, Oct. 29, 1910; Hill to J. P. Morgan, Jr., telegram, Apr. 1, 1913 (Morgan died Mar. 31).

13. Hill to Strathcona, Nov. 13, 1913; to Farrer, Feb. 11, 1914; Farrer to Hill, Mar. 31, 1911; Hill to Farrer, Jan. 13, 1912, referring to Farrer to Hill, Dec. 30, 1911, not in JJHP, GC.

14. P. L. Howe to Hill, telegram, Feb. 8; J. P. Weyerhaeuser to Hill, Apr. 4; Hill to Farrer, Feb. 11, 1914.

15. Mary T. Hill to Clara Hill, Apr. 19, 1921, letter, privately owned. Clara married Erasmus ("Ras") C. Lindley in 1918.

16. Hill to Rev. Mr. Leon S. Koch, Mar. 3, 1909; to F. H. Hooper, Jan. 15, 1916.

17. Hill to T. M. Hodgman, Dec. 5, 1911. For Hill's opposition to the centralizing of higher education in large public institutions, see Hill to E. P. Craighead, president, University of Montana, Dec. 28, 1912.

18. Clipping, unidentified newspaper, JJHP, GC, Jan. 5, 1914.

19. Hill to Carl Berg, Feb. 5, to John A. Seeger, Jan. 7 (on consolidation and the graded system); see also Hill to Charles McCarthy, Chief, Legislative Reference Library, Madison, Wis., Jan. 12, 1914.

20. Voucher Record No. 9, JJHP.

21. Lamont to Hill, May 11, with copy of announcement circular signed by Robert Bacon, George F. Baker, Howard Elliott, Arthur Curtiss James (son of D. Willis), Thomas W. Lamont, Robert T. Lincoln, and J. P. Morgan, Jr.; Lamont to Hill, Jan. 14; Hill to Lamont, June 18; Lamont to Hill, Oct. 11, 1914; Private Voucher No. 56014, Oct. 16, 1915; Gay to Hill, Oct. 20, 1915.

22. Hutchins to Hill, Oct. 5, 1909, June 28, 1910.

23. Hill to Nichols and to Senator J. H. Bankhead, telegrams, Apr. 23, 1912; Joseph G. Pyle, Notes for a Biography of James J. Hill, James J. Hill Reference Library, St. Paul, Minn. (1917); the speech was published in pamphlet form as "The Future of Foreign Trade"; Bullen, *Daily Telegraph,* to Hill, telegram, June 22, 1914.

24. Litchfield to Hill, Aug. 2, 1914; note in margin of American Historical Assn. to Hill, Dec. 30, 1915; Hill to Doubleday, Aug. 5, 1912.

25. Undated MS, about Mar. 16, 1914, typewritten, pressed in one of Hill's last personal letterbooks, beginning at page 537.

26. L. W. Hill to Hill, telegram, Oct. 10; sketch, in Hill's hand, attached to "Real Estate Officer" to Louis W. Hill, May 6, showing the parcels of land to be acquired and probable cost of each, JJHP, GC; E. T. Nichols to Hill, July 14; W. C. Watrous to M. R. Brown, telegrams, July 31, Aug. 2, 1913; L. W. Hill to Hill, telegram, Nov. 25, 1914; Hill to Hale Holden, Apr. 1; L. W. Hill, San Francisco, to Hill, telegram, March 30, 1915.

27. Hill to A. L. Ordean, May 23; to Farrer, June 6; Thorne to Hill, May 14; Nichols to Hill, telegram and letter, July 30, 1914.

28. Gavin to Hill, cable from Brussels, in J. J. Toomey to Hill, telegram, July 31; Carroll to Hill, 2 telegrams, Aug. 6, 1914.

29. For Hill's views of the war and its consequences, see esp. Hill to Farrer, Nov. 11, 1914, Sept. 16, 1915, Mar. 14, 1916; on preparedness to Dr. John E. Hausman, May 5, 1915, Mrs. Sara Forbes Hughes, Jan. 1, Lt. Gen. S. B. M. Young, May 10, 1916.

30. Hill to Louis W. Hill, Aug. 13; to Farrer, Nov. 11; to Walter S. Case, Aug. 25, 1914.

31. See JJHP, GC, Nov. 1914 *passim,* esp. Farrer to Hill, Nov. 18; Minister of the Interior of Belgium to Hill, Nov. 24; Hill to J. A. Farrell, telegram, Aug. 3; to McAdoo, Aug. 3; McAdoo to Hill, telegrams, Aug. 6, 7, 10, 1914.

32. M. R. Brown to Nichols, telegram, June 7, 11; Hill to Farrer, July 14; Brown to Edwin Thorne, July 22, 1915.

33. Hill to Nichols, telegram, July 23; Brown to John Damers & Co., Sept. 10; *New York Times,* July 5, 1915. Van Horne died Sept. 11, 1915.

34. Beard to Hill, Apr. 17, 1910; J. A. Grant to Hill, Mar. 14, 1911; Leslie M. Scott to Hill, July 20, 1914; Hill to H. H. Gross, May 12, 1915; to Judge O. M. Spencer, telegram, May 25, 1915; doctor's announcement, JJHP, GC, 1899; Stewart to Hill, Nov. 30, 1911; Harris to Hill, May 25; Carroll to Hill, May 25, 1911.

35. Revelstoke to Hill, cable, Sept. 7; Morgan to Hill, telegram, Sept. 7; Hill to Morgan, telegram, Sept. 9; Hill "To the Great Northern Veterans' Association," Sept. 11, 1915.

36. A news photograph of Hill's arrival in New York in JJHP, Photographs; *New York Times,* Sept. 13–20, 1915, headlining Hill's arrival and his optimistic reports on the progress of the negotiations.

37. Louis W. Hill to Hill, telegram, Sept. 13; Hill to L. W. Hill, telegram, Sept. 15; to J. P. Morgan, Sept. 21; to J. P. Morgan, telegram, Sept. 29; Morgan to Hill, long night message giving details of loan, Sept. 29; Hill to N. Terhune, telegram, for per-

sonal delivery to Morgan, Sept. 30; Terhune to Hill and Morgan to Hill, telegrams, Oct. 1, 1915; for the German attitude, see Heinrich Charles, Secretary, Chamber of German-American Commerce, Inc., to Hill, Sept. 15, Hill's reply, same date, and Charles's rejoinder, Sept. 16, 1915.

38. John F. Stevens, *An Engineer's Recollections* (New York, 1935), 37.

39. Morgan to Hill, Sept. 26; Hill to Armour, telegrams, Sept. 27, 28; Hill to Morgan, and Lamont to Hill, telegrams, Sept. 29, 1915.

40. A. Kuhlman,, M.D., to Hill, Oct. 3, 1915; Reading to Hill, Oct. 15, 1915.

41. Hill to Farrer, Sept. 2; to John H. McCracken, telegram, Oct. 14; J. J. Toomey to Hill, telegram to Fergus Falls, Oct. 15; E. H. Bailey to Hill, Nov. 29; Hill to Robert H. Patchin and Mrs. Matilda Rice Auerbach, Dec. 29; to E. T. Stotesbury, Dec. 30; to Ernest Fox Nichols, Dec. 29, 1915.

42. Hill to Rea, Jan. 1; to Mrs. Samuel Hill, Jan. 25; to Mary T. Hill, telegram, Feb. 24, 1916.

43. Hill to Clara Hill, Mar. 10, 1916, and Mary T. Hill to Clara Hill, Nov. 24, 1912, and Nov. 25, 1915, about jigsaw puzzles, letters, privately owned; conversations with Mrs. G. S. Reny.

44. McPherson's influence upon Hill's attitude toward a will, conversation with Cortlandt T. Hill, April 1974.

45. The package of pictures from Pierce was put aside among the other papers in Hill's office and, apparently, forgotten; they are in the photograph section, JJHP. Hill to Mary T. Hill, telegram, Mar. 15; to H. H. Gross, telegram, Mar. 29, ,1916.

46. Hill to Ambrose Loidolt, May 9; to Fisher, May 10, 1916; Perkins to Hill, May 1916.

47. The chronology of Hill's last weeks is based on the Diary of Mary T. Hill. Additional details are in JJHP, GC, May 1916 *passim,* and in St. Paul *Pioneer Press* and *New York Times,* May 27–30, 1916. Twenty years later, when the little cemetery was threatened by waters of Pleasant Lake, the graves of James J. and Mary T. Hill were moved to Resurrection Cemetery in St. Paul.

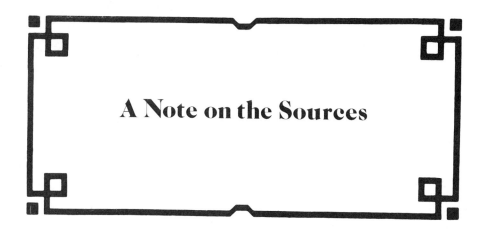

A Note on the Sources

From his debut as an independent businessman in 1866 to his death almost exactly half a century later, James J. Hill carefully preserved all of the documentary evidence of his career, which by 1893 had made him the chief figure in the Northwest and, by 1910, the leader of the American railroad industry. By nature a gregarious, articulate man, and by conviction an evangelist for the intelligent growth of the Northwest, Hill fortunately lived before the telephone had quite begun to wipe out the written record of human affairs. His letters are voluminous and, until the mid-1880s, were written entirely in his own highly legible hand. Until the end of his life, moreover, he continued to pen confidential business letters to his chief associates. The special value of such letters in understanding the complex problems which Hill faced, and the paths he followed in solving them, needs no elaboration.

The letters received by Hill are the only substantial collection of papers of at least two men whose historical importance has been obscured by their failure to preserve their own papers. Most notable are several hundred letters from George Stephen, Lord Mount Stephen, dating from 1877, when Hill first met him, until the second decade of the twentieth century. Only slightly less important are several hundred letters from John S. Kennedy, a seminal figure in the history of American banking and the New York business community, whose career, as it coincided with that of Hill, may now be documented in great detail. There are, however, disappointingly few letters from Donald Smith, Lord Strathcona and Mount Royal, whose own papers were destroyed by fire.

Hill, of course, had many other business leaders as correspondents, of whom I should mention John Murray Forbes, Jacob Schiff, Henry L. Higginson, D. Willis James, George F. Baker, James Stillman, Edward Tuck, and Gaspard Farrer (of the English firm of Baring Brothers and Company). Hill apparently found J. P. Morgan as disinclined to write letters as did everyone else.

Among early Western figures, the career of Paris Gibson, of Montana, may be followed closely in the Hill Papers, and historians may learn much more therein about C. A. Broadwater, a neglected figure in Montana history. "Judge" Thomas Burke of Washington is represented by several letters, as are most of the Governors, Senators, and Congressmen from the Northwest. Hill's activities in national politics, his growing disenchantment with the Cleveland Democrats, his usefulness to Mark A. Hanna in carrying the Northwest in the watershed election of 1896, and his final disgust with the Western wing of the Republican party are well documented.

The James J. Hill Papers are a unique collection, being the complete body of papers of a major business leader of late-nineteenth and early twentieth-century America, professionally cataloged and deposited in one place, and open to scholars without restriction as to their contents. Located in a special room in the James J. Hill Reference Library, St. Paul, Minnesota, they include two main bodies of documents: (1) The letterbooks, comprising Hill's personal letterbooks; many volumes filled by the employees in his personal office; the letterbooks of the president of the St. Paul, Minneapolis & Manitoba Railroad, containing letters written by Hill or his assistants; the letterbook of Henry D. Minot in his brief service under Hill; and certain other items which somehow found their way permanently into one or the other of the two offices which Hill always maintained; and (2) The General Correspondence, which is a chronological file of all incoming correspondence from 1856 to 1916 except for certain subjects which have been allocated separate files. The items from 1838 to 1866, of course, are not numerous, but young Hill's odyssey from Rockwood to St. Paul in 1856 is fully documented in a priceless letter which was not available to earlier writers.

In addition, there are the complete records of a number of enterprises into which Hill plunged, such as North Oaks Farm, the farms in the Red River Valley, the Northern Pacific reorganization, and the Iowa coal properties; and those which he took over from Kennedy's nephew, Andrew Tod, such as the Mille Lacs Lumber Co. and the Red River Roller Mills. Most of these records have figured only slightly in this biography, but for special studies they will prove of great value. There are also many special files on Hill's avocations, real estate holdings, and other miscellaneous subjects. Particularly striking is the complete collection of personal vouchers, which detail every expenditure made by Hill from the early 1870s to the end of his life. They provide a rich insight into the life style of a well-to-do Victorian Midwestern family, and will also yield the kind of information about the collecting of paintings of the Barbizon school which art historians long for. The personal ledgers bare all of the financial details of Hill's life that were put on paper.

Several of Mr. Hill's descendants generously lent me materials which are not part of the Hill Papers, including personal letters that passed between James J., Mary T., and Clara Hill; a number of original letters from Hill to Gaspard Farrer, of which no copies were made; and a large collection of old snapshots which, if Hill did not get into them himself, nevertheless richly portray his domestic world. There is also a typewritten transcript of Mary T. Hill's diaries in the Papers.

With the establishment of the Hill Papers and the deposit of the Great Northern and Northern Pacific archives in the Minnesota Historical Society, St. Paul became the major center for research in the transportation history of the Northwest. The Burlington Northern Company transferred these enormous bodies of Northern Pacific and Great Northern records, along with a generous grant for cataloging, to the Society, thereby benefitting both posterity and their stockholders, who will no longer have to pay for their storage. The message for other holders of corporate records of historical value is loud and clear: Go thou and do likewise. The Northern Pacific records contain answers to many questions about the complex negotiations which saw the Manitoba road emerge as a strong, independent railroad despite the prior presence of the Northern Pacific, while the Great Northern records constitute, to a considerable degree, an extension of the Hill Papers.

The Newberry Library in Chicago, possessing one of the largest collections of railroad materials in the country, has the papers of Charles E. Perkins of the Chicago, Burlington & Quincy Railroad. While all of Perkins's letters to and from Hill are available in the Hill Papers, the Newberry's materials provided an insight into what Perkins and his friends thought privately of Hill, his enterprises, and the future of Western railroads in general. Other scholars will find Perkins's shrewd and fully informed observations on American railroading of equal value.

The Public Archives of Canada, in Ottawa, have made a good start on a collection relating to the Canadian Pacific Railway. Their typescripts of confidential letters between William C. Van Horne and Lord Mount Stephen, which contain many frank comments about relations with Hill, added an important dimension to this biography.

Less rewarding were the documents in public repositories in Washington, D.C. The records of the office of the Attorney General, in the National Archives, provide some insight into the way the government went about building its case against the Northern Securities Company, but nothing on the critical role of President Theodore Roosevelt in initiating the prosecution. The Papers of Theodore Roosevelt in the Manuscript Division of the Library of Congress were thoroughly gleaned on the question of Roosevelt's role by Elting E. Morison in Vol. III of his edition of *The Letters of Theodore Roosevelt* (8 vols., New York, 1951–54). When read along with a vital item from Charles E. Perkins's letterbook, generously lent me by Richard C. Overton, Roosevelt's casual utterances on the Northern Securities Case should remove any remaining doubt that the prosecution was a cornerstone of his fight to win the Presidency in his own right.

As to the "inner history" of the origins of the Northern Securities affair, we shall probably have to be content with the story as told by Hill to his oldest and closest associates in confidential letters which he wrote from the time of the Northern Pacific "corner" in May 1901 to Edward H. Harriman's final defeat in the Supreme Court in 1905. Both W. Averell and Roland Harriman confirm that all of their father's papers were destroyed in the epic fire which consumed the old Equitable Building at 120 Broadway, New York City, in 1912. George Kennan, *E. H. Harriman, A Biography* (2 vols., New York and Boston, 1922), leaned heavily upon Joseph G. Pyle, *The Life of James J. Hill* (2 vols., New York, 1916–17) in composing his narrative of these events, but he apparently did have direct from Harriman the story of Harriman's indisposition on that fateful Saturday morning when Schiff decided to ignore his order to buy Northern Pacific stock. The papers of Jacob Schiff in the American Jewish Archives in Cincinnati, Ohio, contain no business materials, but Cyrus Adler, *Jacob H. Schiff, His Life and Letters* (2 vols., New York, 1928), includes important items on the Northern Pacific affair.

Previously published material on Hill is much less voluminous than that on others who more closely fitted the "robber baron" stereotype, and is either a paraphrase of Pyle's biography or fiction. Gustavus Myers's *History of the Great American Fortunes* (3 vols., New York, 1910) is one long sneer. Myers hopelessly lost his way in trying to follow Hill's career and ended up confusing the St. Paul & Pacific Railroad with the Iowa Central, and Hill with Russell Sage. With Pyle's help, Matthew Josephson, *The Robber Barons* (New York, 1934), cleared up the confusion, but retained the sneer. Pyle's two volumes were a valuable research tool for nearly sixty years, although the author was handicapped by his closeness in time and space to his subject, the relative inaccessibility of much of Hill's files, and the haste with which the biography was published after Hill's unexpected death.

Jacob, Engebord, and Knute Ryggen and Ole Rynning were real people whom I have taken as the symbol of the transatlantic Scandinavian migration. There is a biographical sketch of Knute in *History of Polk County* (Crookston, Minn., 1916), while T. C. Blegen's magisterial *Norwegian Immigration to America* (2 vols., Northfield, Minn., 1931–40), tells Rynning's story.

Neither the economics of publishing nor the character of this book justify a lengthy discourse on the hundreds of published materials I have consulted in writing this biography. Where a work has contributed directly to an interpretation that has not yet achieved universal acceptance, I have cited it in the notes. Let them constitute my bibliography of published sources. I would remind the larger number whom I have not cited that we all stand squarely on the shoulders of those who have gone before. I shall be greatly pleased if others use this book as confidently as I have used yours.

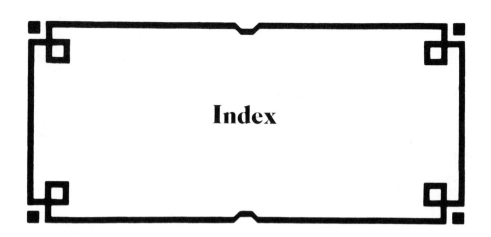

Index

Acker, George S., 97, 98, 99, 101, 106, 107
Ackerly, A. A., 219
Adams, Charles Francis, Jr., 292, 305, 370, 372, 435
Adams, Edward D., 441, 443, 446-47, 454, 457
Agriculture: Hill's views on, 309-10, 532, 552-55; agricultural credit, 583, 587-88
Alexander, W. S., 209
Alton Railroad, see Chicago & Alton Railroad
American Railway Union, 415-16
Andrews, C. C., 215
Angus, R. B., 137, 154, 175, 192; vice president of Manitoba Railroad, 210, 214, 217; and Canadian Pacific, 240, 241, 246, 265, 266
Anthracite Association, 99, 105-6
Armour, Philip D., 71, 212, 285, 313, 426, 433, 437, 487
Armstrong, John A., 96, 97, 98, 101, 104-5, 197
Atchison, Topeka & Santa Fe Railroad, 370, 386, 407, 410-11, 491; bankruptcy and reorganization, 410, 439

Bacon, Robert, 451, 463, 464, 466, 477, 497, 498, 505, 510, 542, 562, 588; photo, 493

Baker, George F., 414, 490, 504, 510, 527, 566, 600, 613; photo, 564
Baltimore & Ohio Railroad, 104, 135, 345-46, 407; Hill and, 433-34, 453, 466, 579
Bank of Montreal, 132, 137, 151-54 passim, 175, 178, 192, 211, 288
Banking: Hill's views on, 583, 587-88
Baring & Company, 414, 436; failure, 385, 404; as Baring Brothers & Company, 605
Barnes, John S.: and St. Paul & Pacific, 128, 129, 130, 134, 139, 147, 157, 160, 184, 188, 189; and Manitoba Railroad, 190, 191, 197, 229
Beard, Anson (son-in-law), 516, 527, 532
Becker, George L., 45, 84, 97, 117, 182
Beckler, E. H., 379, 382, 383, 390, 391
Belmont, August, Jr., 231, 351
Benedict, Charles H., 234, 318, 329, 388
Bigelow, H. R.: and Manitoba Railroad, 190, 195, 224, 397
Billings, Frederick C., 181, 184, 188, 224
Blakeley, Capt. Russell, 79
Blanchard, George, 47, 49n, 50, 397
Boeckmann, Egil (son-in-law), 595, 609
Borup & Champlin, 38-39, 45-47, 48-49

Brewer, Judge David, 358-59; Justice, 519
Brice, Calvin S., 306, 323, 376, 427
Broadwater, Charles A., 335-39, 340, 397; photo, 336
Brodie, James, 351, 420
Brown, Martin H., 580, 603
Browne, Hamilton, 113, 147, 152, 232, 233, 260, 337, 563
Brunson, Lewis & White, 35-36
Bryan, William Jennings, 461, 538, 542
Budd, Ralph, 578, 600
Bull, W. L., 459
Bunn, C. W., 565
Burke, Thomas, 392, 448, 545, 559; photo, 381
Burlington Railroad, *see* Chicago, Burlington & Quincy Railroad

Caillet, Father, 60, 61, 63, 84, 175, 257, 354, 421, 529
Cambria Iron Works, 161, 166-67
Canada: railroad competition with U.S., 19, 238-40, 289-90; government and geography in *1856*, 20-21; as Dominion, British America Act (1867), 72; Riel rebellions, 72-75, 125, 269; Hill's relations with *re* railroad from St. Paul to Winnipeg, 124-25, 169-71, 185, 239, 287 (*see also* Duluth & Winnipeg Railroad); reciprocal trade agreements, 289-90, 546-48
  political parties: Conservative, 124, 169, 238, 240; Liberal, 164, 169, 185, 240; "Grits" allied with Liberals, 224, 238, 240, 248, 287
Canadian Pacific Railroad, 19, 125, 153, 164, 167, 182, 237-53, 264-70, 287, 465-66, 468, 474-75, 568-70, 572-73; and St. Paul & Pacific, 115; Emerson-Winnipeg line, 118 (map); construction, 177-78, 221, 241-48, 250, 252, 266, 270, 281; and Manitoba Railroad, 214, 239-40, 247, 248, 252-53, 281, 287, 338; financing, 248, 252-53, 268-69, 280-81, 468; acquisition

of Soo Line, 247, 289, 475, 569; map, 244-45; Hill and, 240-42, 568-70
Cannon, Henry W., 296, 297, 299, 308-9, 323, 329, 372, 373, 394, 397, 404-6, 428, 437, 441, 454, 469
Carnegie, Andrew, 103, 109, 166, 263, 451, 467-68, 489-90, 550
Carp, Johan, 128, 130, 138, 139, 143, 148, 151, 153
Carroll, J. H., 547-48, 604, 613
Cassatt, Alexander, 313, 466, 485-86, 506
Central Pacific Railroad, 474, 482; map, 480
Chase National Bank, 296, 309, 323, 394, 405-6, 437, 501
Chemidlin, August N., 175, 256, 258, 352, 526
Chicago & Alton Railroad, 433, 486
Chicago, Burlington & Northern Railroad, 324, 486
Chicago, Burlington & Quincy, 285, 323, 407, 579; construction, 324, 370; Hill and, before purchase, 324, 434-35, 486, 491; engineers strike (1888), 416; map, 478-79; purchase by Hill, 487-91, 496-99, 507, 562
Chicago & Great Western Railroad, 487
Chicago, Milwaukee & St. Paul Railroad, 54, 231, 241, 270, 286, 486; Hill and, 51, 100, 106, 110, 136, 153, 182-83, 210, 226-27, 285; construction, 110, 185, 231, 370, 521; St. Paul terminal, 628*n*29
Chicago & North Western Railway, 100, 103-4, 139, 156, 182-83, 190, 211, 233, 270, 285, 361, 370, 486, 562-63
Chicago, Rock Island & Pacific Railroad, 211, 213, 233, 319, 486, 487
City Bank of St. Paul, 84
Clark, Champ, 548
Clark, George C., 510, 601
Clark, Greenleaf, 85; Judge, 304, 377, 397, 651*n*47
Cleveland, President Grover, 299; Hill's friendship with, 305-9, 338, 346, 352, 397, 415, 421, 425-27, 457

Climax Coal Company, 113, 147, 152, 197, 232-33, 234
Clough, William P., 387, 390, 446, 510, 520, 541, 565; photo, 381
Coal, 88-90, 92, 93-95, 214; transportation of, 38, 47, 89-90, 91, 100, 103, 216, 233, competition, 93-106 *passim*, 476; rates, 93, 102-4, 106, 293; as locomotive fuel, 90, 94-95, 219; Hill businesses, 93-107 *passim*, 109, 113, 147, 152-53, 199, 232-33, 234, 341, 593; in Montana, 337-38, 241, in Canada, 476
Colleges and universities: Hill's views on and gifts to, 595-98
Cooke, Jay, 81, 117, 119, 130, 183, 186
Coster, Charles H., 433, 445-46, 447, 454, 458-59, 463, 485; photo, 449
Cotton Belt Railroad, 432
Cromwell, William N., 446
Crooks, William, 45-46, 122
Crows Nest Pass Coal Company, 593
Cullom, Shelby M., 539
Cummins, Albert B., 538, 543

Daly, Marcus, 348, 415, 423
Davidson, Commodore, 35, 39, 40; and Northwest Packet Company, 46-47, 48, 96
Davis, Sen. Cushman K., 471
Debs, Eugene V., 415-16, 426
De Graff & Company, 127, 134-35, 156
Delano, Francis R., 45, 50, 127
Depression of *1893*, 405-7, 562; effect on railroad industry, 398, 403-16
Dillon, Judge John F., 159, 162, 164, 171, 178-79, 189-90
Dillon, Sidney, 370
Donnelly, Ignatius, 81, 111, 231, 295, 306-8
Duluth Railroad, 100-1, 105, 106
Duluth & Winnipeg Railroad, 468-69, 475, 570
Dunwoody, William H., 588, 294-95
Durand-Ruel, George, 302-3, 590

Eastern Railway of Minnesota, 364, 377, 424, 468
Edmunds, George, 358

Elkins, Sen. Stephen B., 476, 538, 539
Elliott, Howard, 565, 577; photo, 543
Elphinstone, Lord, 232
Erie Railroad, 238, 579; receivership, 104
Evarts, William N., 358

Fairbanks, J. W., 352-53
Fairchild, Charles, 372
Fargo Argus, 428
Fargo & Southern Railroad, 241, 286
Farley, J. P., 121, 122, 134, 138, 139, 140, 148, 154, 156; receiver of St. Paul & Pacific, 158, 162-66, 171, 179, 180, 193, 194-95, 197, 208; suit (*Farley v. St. Paul, Minneapolis & Manitoba Railway, et al.*), 356-60
Farrer, Gaspard, 414, 424, 427, 436, 443, 462, 463, 509-10, 562, 566, 594, 600, 604-5; photo, 380
Farrish, William, 29, 40, 44, 275
Field, Marshall, 313, 317, 319, 325, 356, 397, 433, 437, 593
Finley, W. W., 413
First National Bank of St. Paul, 45, 84, 185, 406; Hill purchase of, 582-83, 608
Fleming, Sandford, 242, 243
Flour: milling and shipping in Minnesota, 36, 37-38, 49, 51, 53-55, 184, 214, 278, 287, 360-61; *see also* Wheat
Foraker, Joseph B., 539
Forbes, John Murray, 22, 278, 289, 323-25, 331, 347, 385, 404, 428, 434-36; photo, 326
Fort Garry, 65, 67-68, 73; Hill's trip to, 73-76, 86, 125, 233, 316
Fur Trade, 22, 23, 36-37, 64-65, 69-70

Galusha, R. B., 133, 147, 148, 154, 179, 180, 188, 189, 190-91, 195
Gates, John W., 437, 494, 575
Gavin, Michael (son-in-law), 528, 532, 601, 611
General Steam Navigation Company, 472
Gibson, Paris, 333-35, 347, 383, 581; photo, 336

Globe Iron Works, 468

Gotzian, Conrad, 33, 111, 141, 257, 594; photo, 196

Gould, George, 407, 411, 434, 466, 491, 567

Gould, Jay, 370

Grand Trunk Railway, 288, 425

Gray, Carl R., 578

Great Falls Townsite Company, 298, 334, 349, 592

Great Falls Water Power & Light Company, 298, 334, 341, 465

Great Lakes steamship companies, 363-64, 427, 468

Great Northern Elevator Company, 361

Great Northern Pacific Steamship Company, 600

Great Northern Railway: outgrowth of St. Paul, Minneapolis & Manitoba, 279, 396; maps, 368-69, 584-85; choice of name, 376; proposed organization, 377; officers, 378, 395; construction, 379, 381, 387-92, 477, 483-84, Marias Pass (Pacific Survey), 381-83, 639*n*20, completion, 396-98; competition with Soo Line, 384, 475, 569; finances, 389, 393-95, stock, 377-78, 385, 394, 404, 407, 470, 1893 financial crisis, 398, rates, 410, 414; Seattle terminal, 392; mountain goat as symbol, 397; unification with Northern Pacific, 455-59, 464-65, 477, 486, 520-21; extension into Oregon, 482-83; building of Spokane, Portland & Seattle Railroad, 563-67; 1910 wreck, 573; *see also* Northern Pacific

Great Northern Steamship Line, 473-74, 544-46

Griggs, Capt. Alexander, 78, 80, 83, 265, 356

Griggs, Col. Chauncey W., 78, 80, 83, 99, 104-5, 107, 594; *see also* Hill, Griggs & Company

Griggs, John W., 514

Griggs & Johnson, 106

Grover, M. D., 377

Gwinner, Arthur, 442, 455, 458, 463

Hand, Dr. Daniel W., 86, 110, 176

Hanna, Mark, 99, 102, 105, 363-64, 427, 472-73, 513-15

Hannaford, Jule M., 411, 577

Hansbrough, Sen. Henry C., 565

Harlan, Justice John Marshall, 518

Harriman, Edward H., 394, 436, 466, 477, 522; and Alton Railroad, 433, 486; and Northern Pacific, 439-41, 459, 463, 477, 482, buying into, 484-85, 496-99, 502-7, 508-9, 520-23, 567; and Union Pacific, 459, 488, 491, 500-1, 564-65; and Burlington, 487-88, 496-99; acquisition of Southern Pacific, 491, 500, 521, 562; and Northern Securities Company, 509-10, suit to prevent distribution of stock, 520-22; Interstate Commerce Commission investigation, 521-22; photo, 492

Harris, George B., 489, 508, 562, 604

Harrison, President Benjamin, 298, 359

Haskell, Charles F., 387, 390

Hastings & Dakota Railroad, 226

Haupt, Herman, 270

Hauser, Samuel T., 339, 340

Heney, Francis J., 551

Higginson, Henry L., 297, 299, 303, 330, 347, 372, 387, 541

Highways of Progress (Hill), 557-59

Hill, Alexander (brother Alec), 14, 15, 19, 44, 86, 112-13, 142-43, 175, 315, 531

Hill, Ann Dunbar (mother), 15, 18-19, 45, 86, 111, 112-13; photo, 24

Hill, Charlotte (daughter), 140, 255, 416-17, 418, 421, 423, 424, 451; marriage to George Slade, 527, 609-10, 613

Hill, Clara (daughter), 111, 140, 174-75, 177, 255, 257, 418, 421, 423, 424, 451, 527, 529, 591; marriage to Erasmus C. Lindley, 595, 601, 602, 608-9, 611, 613

Hill, Gertrude (daughter), 255, 256, 418, 421, 527; marriage to Michael Gavin, 529, 532, 601, 611

Hill, James (father, 1811-52), 11, 13-15, 17, 113

Hill, James (grandfather, 1780-1845), 13, 14

Hill, James J.: *1838-79*, 3-198; blindness in one eye, 16, 108; photos, 25, 62, 123, 197, 235, 534, 553, 555, 564, 568, 571, 581, 586, 607, 610, 612; journey to St. Paul, 26-31; volunteer fireman and militiaman, 41-44; marriage, 57, 60-64 (*see also* family life); net wealth, 109, 425, 451, 525, 617; *1877*, 114-45; *1878*, 146-73; *1879*, 174-98; U.S. citizenship, 207; *1879-95*, 207-398; European trips, 392-93, 418, 424, 429, 437, 442, 443-44, 455-56, 463; and Depression of *1893*, 398, 403-16 *passim*; in 1890s, 425-29; *1895-1916*, 403-615; after Northern Securities case, *1904-10*, 524-60; celebration of 70th birthday, 556-57; *Highways of Progress* (book), 557-59; later years, 561-611; preparations for "retirement," 574-78, "first citizen" of Minnesota, 599; and Anglo-French loan, 605-8; honorary degrees, 608-9; will, 611; final illness, death and funeral, 613-15

early life and youth, *1838-56*: education, 7-12; family background, 12-17; early employment, 18-25

family life: 73, 84-87, 107-13, 140-43, 174-76, 234, 253-65, 310, 314-17, 350-55, 395, 416-24, 429, 437, 450-53, 526-32; children, 73, 84, 85, 86, 107, 111, 130, 141, 143, 173, 175, 177, 255-58, 262, 264, 351-54, 395, 416-24, 526-32, 591-92, 613-14 (*see also names*); photos, *1886*, 262, *1901*, 528; grandchildren, 355, 423, 529, 530, 595, 608-10, 613-14

homes: in St. Paul, 64, 85-86, 140-42, 175, 254-55, 262, 310-11, 355, 418-20, 453, 526, 591; photos, 254, 419; North Oaks Farm, 263, 282, 310-11, 321, 421, 451, 591, 611; in New York City, 532, 591; Canadian lodge, 588

non-railroad businesses: shipping, river, 49-57, 76, 78, 80-84, 91, 95, 96-98, 105, 109; wood-fuel, 91-92; coal, 93-107 *passim*, 109, 113, 147, 152-53, 197, 232-34, 341, 593; lumber, 232, 259, 318; electric and waterpower, 341, 465; grain storage, 361, 405-6; shipping, steamship, 363-64, 427, 468, 472-74, 544-46, 600; iron, 468; mining, 469-70; banks, First and Second of St. Paul, 582-83

personal interests: art collector, 110, 257, 259, 263, 301-5, 351, 420, 451, 463, 590-91, 611; politics, 111-12, 207, 305-9, 425-28, 598-99, 611; fishing and hunting, 143, 160, 314-15, 322-23, 351, 352, 531, 562, 588-90 (photo), 605; farming and cattle, 263, 282, 309-14, 450-51, 587, 591; philanthropy, 304, 315-16, 356, 452-53, 591, 595-98; newspaper publishing, 428, 461, 591

railroads, *see under names of individual railroads*

Hill, Mrs. James J. (Mary); as Mary Mehegan, 59-61; engagement and marriage, 57, 60-64; photo, 63; *see also* family and private life *under* Hill, James J.

Hill, James Norman (son), 85, 86, 140, 175, 258-59, 263, 353-54, 421, 422, 516, 526, 530, 575, 591; education, 175, 259, 352, 353-54, 422; president of Eastern Railway, 424, 468, 574; with Great Northern, 424, 464, 512, 563, vice president, 574-75; marriage, 592

Hill, James N. B. (grandson) 530

Hill, "Katie" (daughter, died in infancy), 130

Hill, Louis W. (son), 85, 110, 140, 263, 351, 353-54, 520, 526, 545, 580, 613; education, 175, 259, 352, 421-22; with Eastern Railway, 364, 377, 468; with Great Northern, 424, 464, 469, 575-76, board chairman, 576-77, 600; marriage, 527; photos, 543, 572

Hill, Mary Elizabeth (sister, Mrs. James Brooks), 19, 142-43, 315, 530-31

Hill, Mary Frances (daughter "Mamie"), 84, 85, 175, 259, 314, 416, 417, 418; marriage to Samuel Hill, 354-55, 424, 527, 529-30

Hill, Mary Mendenhall (granddaughter) 529-30

Hill, Mary Riggs (grandmother), 13, 14, 26, 27

Hill, Rachel (daughter), 140, 255, 350-51, 418, 421, 527, 529, 591; marriage to Egil Boeckmann, 595, 609, children, 609

Hill, Ruth (daughter), 177, 255, 256, 423; marriage to Anson Beard, 516, 527, 532

Hill, Samuel (son-in-law), 354-55, 404, 527, 529-30; president of Montana Central, 423-24

Hill, Walter J. (son), 255, 256, 416, 423, 545; education, 526, 529, 531; marriage, 530; large-scale farming, 530

Hill, Acker & Saunders, 98-99, 100-101, 105, 106, 109

Hill & Company, J. J., 49-57

Hill, Griggs & Company, 80, 82-84, 91, 93, 95, 96-98, 105

Hinman, A. B., 97, 98

Holcombe, Capt. E. V., 38, 78, 114-15, 147, 172, 182, 233

Holmes, Justice Oliver Wendell, 522

Hudson's Bay Company, 37, 45, 65-66, 68, 72, 74, 78, 81, 82, 83, 123, 124

Hughitt, Marvin, 156, 361, 362, 397

Huntington, Collis P., 300, 302, 370, 458, 482, 491

Immigration to Minnesota, 3-4, 36, 115-16, 201, 214-15, 276-77, 401, 462

Interstate Commerce Commission: investigation of Harriman, 521-22; rate hearings, 532, 535, 539-40, 542, 600; rebate hearings, 539; export rates hearings, 546

Ireland, John, 60, 63; Bishop, 421, 452

Iron: production and shipment of, 89, 109, 177, 218, 266, 468; rails, 161, 165-66, 167, 177, 219, 362; in Mesabi Range, 466-70 *passim*

Ives, H. C., 211, 212, 215, 234

Jacacci, August, 140, 303, 590

James, D. Willis, 266, 267, 268, 319, 320, 321-22, 344-45, 365, 374, 437, 447, 453, 510, 593; photo, 321

Johnson, John G., 518

Jones, A. C., 101-4 *passim*

Kelly, P. H., 39, 86, 108, 195, 281, 307

Kennedy, John S., 160-61, 279-80, 403, 502, 510, 594; and St. Paul & Pacific case, 121, 127-28, 134, 147-57 *passim*, 159-64, 178, 180-81, 186, 191, 192-94; as financial adviser to Manitoba Railroad, 193, 194, 208, 211-12, 224, 230, 239, 264, 274, 280, as vice president, 283-84, 317, 318-19, 328-30, 339, 349, 363, 365, 375, 397; and Canadian Pacific, 239, 240, 252, 265; photo, 136

Kennedy, John S., & Company, 139, 147-57 *passim*, 160, 187, 191, 192-94, 229, 234

Kittson, Norman W., 33, 45, 66, 69, 78, 79, 359, 428; partner on steamboat line, 78, 80-84, 90, 114, 122-24; and control of St. Paul & Pacific, 124, 130-33, 135, 138, 145, 146-61 *passim*, 170-71; and Manitoba Railroad, 190-91, 192, 194, 208, 229-30, 318, 357-59; photo, 126

Knoedler, M., & Company, 303, 590

Knox, John Jay, 308-9, 329

Knox, Philander C., 515

Kuhn, Loeb & Company, investment bankers, 284, 345, 394, 488, 500, 503-4

La Follette, Sen. Robert M., 538, 543, 545

Lake Superior & Mississippi Railroad, 100

Lamont, Daniel S., 298, 308-9, 433, 454, 455, 457, 463, 485, 504, 510, 588, 593; photo, 448

Law, Robert, 93-94, 95, 98

Lindley, Erasmus (son-in-law), 595

Litchfield brothers, 45, 54; Egbert S., 45, 54, 69, 79; William B., 45, 84;

E. B., 117, 120; E. Darwin, and First Division of St. Paul & Pacific, 120-21, 122, 128, 157-58, 160, 180, 187-89
Livestock, Hill and improvements in, 310-14
Livingston, Crawford, 441
Lochren, Judge William, 517-18
Lovett, Robert S., 567
Lowry, Thomas, 404, 594
Lumber, 90, 92, 232, 259, 295-96, 469; transportation of, 396, 464-65, 488

Macalester College, 356, 597
Macdonald, John A., 72, 74, 124, 169, 185, 194, 224; and Canadian Pacific, 238, 240, 287
Mackenzie, Alexander, 164, 169, 185, 238
Macoun, John, 243
Maginnis, Martin, 334, 339
McCurdy, Richard A., 405
McIntyre, Duncan, 241, 248
McKinley, President William, 425, 427, 461, 506
McPherson, George A., 610-11
Malmros, Oscar, 74, 81
Manitoba, Province of, 66, 72-75, 78
Manitoba Railroad, *see* St. Paul, Minneapolis & Manitoba Railroad
Manitoba & Southwestern Colonization Railroad, 224, 248, 266-67
Manvel, Allen: and Manitoba Railroad, superintendent, 211, 212-13, 217, 234-36, vice president and general manager, 290, 295, 328, 338-89 *passim*, 412, 569; president of Santa Fe, 379, 387, 410-11; photo, 291
Mason City & Fort Dodge Railroad, 329, 409
Mattock, Rev. John, 33
Mehl, Eugene, 257, 259, 261
Mellen, Charles S., 457-58, 459, 462, 464, 475, 570, 577
Merriam, Governor William R., 397; photo, 397
Merrill, S. S., 153, 182-83, 226
Metcalfe, Dr. John T., 323

Michigan Central Railroad, 70-71
Mille Lacs Lumber Company, 232, 259, 318
Miller, Darius, 464, 542, 577
Milwaukee & Mississippi Railroad: Hill as agent of, 49
Milwaukee Railroad, *see* Chicago, Milwaukee & St. Paul Railroad
Mining: in Montana, 333, 341, 348, 455; in Minnesota (Mesabi Range), 466-70; Washington State, 465
Minneapolis & Pacific Railroad, proposed, 287
Minneapolis & St. Cloud Railroad: charter, 331
Minneapolis & St. Louis Railroad, 216, 233
Minneapolis, St. Paul & Sault Ste. Marie Railroad (Soo Line), 287-89, 372, 375, 376; sale to Canadian Pacific, 247, 289, 384, 475, 487, 569; construction, 362-63
Minnesota House of Representatives: Railroad Committee, 128, 293-94
Minnesota & Pacific Railroad, 39, 227; reorganization as St. Paul & Pacific Railroad, 39, 46
Minnesota Railroad Commission, 294-96
Minnesota Supreme Court: Northern Pacific case, 449-50
Minot, Henry D., 325-30, 345, 362, 364, 374-75, 385-87, North Dakota city, 346-47; photo, 327
Mississippi River steamboat transportation, 31, 33-35, 38, 46-47, 50, 54, 56
Missouri, Kansas & Texas Railroad, 464
Mitchell, Alexander, 183, 185
Mitchell, John J., 583, 608
Moberly, Walter, 241
Moffett, F. L., 318
Mohler, A. L., 379, 391, 412, 425
Montana Central Railroad, 298, 336, 338, 340, 360, 367, 379; construction, 339, 341, 344, 346-48; map, 344; finances, 341, 344-46, 348;

Montana Central Railroad (*cont.*)
acquisition by Manitoba Railroad, 348; 1894 strike, 415-16
Montana Territory: Hill's extension in, 298-99, 333-49 *passim; see also* Montana Central Railroad
Moore, John G., 308, 323, 394-95, 398, 404, 411, 437
Moorhead, William, 117, 122, 181
Morawetz, Victor, 439, 446
Morgan, J. Pierpont, 160, 295, 408, 409-10, 466, 594, 603-8; and Northern Pacific, 433, 434-59 *passim*, 463, 490, 502-7, 509; photo, 492; and Burlington, 497, 498
Mount Stephen, Lord, *see*, Stephen, George

Natural resources, conservation of, 548-51: Hill at Washington Conference, 549-50, at Congress in St. Paul, 550-51
Neill, Rev. Edward, 356, 452, 597
Nelson, Knute, 112, 260, 276, 299, 307, 397, 408-9, 539, 548
Newcomb, William B., 96
Newel, Stanford, 63, 85, 129, 517, 531, 593
Newman, William H., 431, 432
New York Central Railroad, 55, 104, 407, 413, 466, 506, 578-79
New York, New Haven & Hartford Railroad, 457, 458
New York Times, 428, 460
Nichols, Edward T, Jr.: and Manitoba Railroad, 291-92, 346, 348, 364, 372; and Great Northern, treasurer, 403, 428, 446, 506, 510, 521, 545, 573, vice president, 577, 601; photo, 291
Nimmo, Joseph E., Jr., 295
Northern Pacific "Corner," 494-96, 499-500, 502-6, 521
Northern Pacific Railroad: construction and extensions, 81, 83, 119, 180-81, 223, 224, 239, 334-35, 370, 440-41, St. Vincent Extension, 117, 118 (map), 119, completion, 270-71, 367; and Hill before takeover, 102, 106, 126, 164, 180,

182-86, 188, 194, 216, 223-24, 298, 333-34, 441-44; purchase and sale of St. Paul & Pacific, 117, 119, 134-35, 181-86, 194; bankruptcy and receivership, 119, 181, 225, 411, 441; competition with St. Paul & Pacific, 181-86, 194; competition with Manitoba road (protocol), 223-26, 231, 239, 286-87, 298, 333, 337-38; and Montana route, 333, 337-38, 339, 340-41, 348; attempted takeover of Manitoba Railroad, 367, 370-71, 372-74; and Union Pacific, 371, 372, 435, 474, 477; finances, 414-15, rates, 410
acquisition by Hill (London agreement), 443-50, Minnesota state challenge, 466-50; reorganization plan, 431-44, 446-57, approval (London memorandum), 455-59; finances, stocks, 432, 440, 441, 451; directors, 455, 459, 463; officers, 456, 457-58
under Hill reorganization: unification with Great Northern, 455-59, 464-65, 477, 486, 520-21; construction, 464-65 477, 482-83, 520, building of Spokane, Portland & Seattle Railroad, 563-67; extension into Canada, 570-71; finances, 464, stock, 1901 "corner" of market, 494-96, 499-500, 502-6, 521; *see also* Northern Securities Company
Northern Securities Company: incorporation, 508-9, 510; stock, 509-10, disposal of, 521, 592-93; board of directors, 510; Circuit Court case, 512, 517-18; Roosevelt and, 513-15, 519; Supreme Court case, 514, 517-19, 521
Northern Steamship Company, 468
Northwest Packet Company, 47-48, 50-53, 57, 95
Northwestern Elevator Company, 405-6
Northwestern Fuel Company, 107, 109, 130, 152-53, 197
North Western Railroad, *see* Chicago & North Western Railroad

Oakes, Thomas F., 286, 337, 339, 355, 441
Ochs, Adolph S., 428, 460-61
Omaha Railroad, 456
Oregon Railway & Navigation Company, 270, 367, 370, 371, 435-36, 459, 477, 482-84, 486, 564; foreclosure and receivership, 436, 451, 455
Oregon Short Line, 370, 435, 477-84 *passim*, 488; map, 480
Oregon & Transcontinental Company, 371-73, 435

Parsons, Charles O., 348
Pearsall, Thomas, 282, 447
Pembina, Minn.: Fenian attack on, 81-82, 174
Pennsylvania Railroad, 135, 238, 434, 437, 466, 486, 487, 538, 579-80
Perkins, Charles E., president of Burlington Railroad, 324, 348, 370, 387, 389, 435-36, 477, 486-91 *passim*, 496, 498, 519, 538, 541, 574, 593; photo, 327
Perkins, George W., 454, 505, 510, 514
Philadelphia & Erie Railroad, 181
Pillsbury, Charles A., 416, 444
Pillsbury, John S., 155, 208
Pinchot, Gilbert, 550, 551
Porter, H. H., 431, 437
Proctor, John, 233
Pujo, Arsène, 582
Pujo Committee, 582, 587
Pyle, Joseph G., 591

Railroad legislation: federal, 275, 278, 292-93, 295, 371, 409, 519-20, 535, 539-42, 544 (see also U.S. legislation); Minnesota, 293, 295, 408-9, 539
Railroads: industry, early opportunities in, 23-24; growth in 1880s, 272-75, 277-78, 284-85; regional, decline of, 371-72; Midwestern, East-West mergers, 486-87; effect of antitrust cases on, 511-12, 514, 520, 522; in Progressive era, 536-38; Eastern, development of passenger service, 578-79
Railway Advisory Committee, 466
Ramsey, Gov. Alexander, 270, 397
Rate regulation, federal, 292-97, 409-10, 511-12, 519-20, 535-36, 539-42, 544; 600, 602; exports, 546
Rebate system, 409-10, 537-38
Red Mountain Coal Mining Company, 341
Red River country: maps, 67, 77; development of trade in, 64-72; railroads in, 76, 77 (maps), 79; steamboat transportation, development of, 76, 77 (maps), 82-84, 90, 114-15, 170
Red River & Manitoba Railroad, 161-63
Red River Transportation Company, 76, 78, 82-84, 109, 114-15, 116, 149, 152, 170
Red River Valley Railroad, 121, 135
Rhodes, William, 107
Rice, J. B., 219
Riel rebellions: *1869-70*, 72-75, 125; *1885*, 269
Ripley, Edward P., 433, 439, 587
Ripley, William Z., 538
Rockefeller, William, 323, 487, 501
Rock Island Railroad, *see* Chicago, Rock Island & Pacific Railroad
Rockwood, Canada (Hill's birthplace), 7-12, 44-45, 86, 113, 315
Rogers, A. B., 243, 246, 367
Roosevelt, Theodore, 507, 513, 522-25, 543, 549-50, 611; and Northern Securities case, 513-15, 519
Rose, Charles, 453
Rose, Sir John, 129, 143, 145, 239-40, 246, 300
Rosser, Thomas L., 241-42
Ryggen family, 3-4, 201, 401

Sage, Russell, 226
St. Paul, Minn.: in *1856*, 28-29, 31-33; photos, 30, 52; as transportation hub, 66-68; Public Library, 452, 597, 599; Union Station, 55, 221-22, 318, 444, 556, 614

St. Paul, Minn. (*cont.*)
  newspapers: *Daily Pioneer*, 49, 50;
    Daily Press, 55; *Pioneer Press*,
    146, 299, 317, 396, 503, 551; *Daily*
    Globe, 154-55, 180-81, 210; *Globe*,
    428, 591
St. Paul Coal Company, 106
St. Paul & Duluth Railroad, 361-62,
  628*n*37
St. Paul, Minneapolis & Manitoba
  Railroad: under Hill, 190-98,
  207-23, 227-35; organization,
  190-91; state acceptance and land
  grants, 208; organizational structure, 209-13, 317-23; freight and
  passenger traffic, 213-16; rolling
  stock, 217-19; and Canadian
  Pacific, 214, 239-40, 247, 248,
  252-53, 281, 287, 338; employees
  strike, 219-20; expansion and
  improvements, 220-23, 230-31,
  287-88, 300, 328, 360-72; construction, 223-24, 229, 252, 266,
  286, 362; competition with
  Northern Pacific, 223-26, 231,
  239, 286-87, 298, 333, 337-38;
  finances, 228-32, 252-53, 374-75,
  stock, 280-82, 284, 300, 320, 322,
  324-28, 331, 354, 375, 376, 388;
  reorganization as Great Northern, 279, 396; rates controversy,
  293-97; Montana Central Railroad, 298-99, 333-49 *passim*; St.
  Paul passenger depot, 222-23;
  Stone Arch Bridge, 223, 628*n*29;
  office building, 318; map,
  344-45; Great Lakes steamship
  company, 363-64; Farley suit,
  356-60
St. Paul & Pacific Railroad, 36, 39, 46,
  79; Hill and, 49, 50, 53, 54, 91, 95,
  109, 115-16 (*see also* financial
  difficulties); construction, 68, 74,
  118 (map), 148, 161-71, 178, Extension Line, plans, 117, 118
  (map), 119, 121, 122, 130-31,
  133-34, 135, 151; construction of,
  159, 161-71, 173, 178; in *1873*, 118
  (map); Red River Valley Railroad, 121, 135; linkup with
  Canadian Pacific, 118 (map), 164,
  167, 177-78, 180-81; competition

with Northern Pacific, 181-86,
  194
financial difficulties, 97, 100, 115,
  119, 229; receivership, 116, 120,
  325; control by Northern Pacific,
  117, 119, 121-22, 134-35, 181; default in payment of bonds,
  119-20, settlement with Dutch
  purchasers, 120, 121, 127-35 *pas-*
  sim, 143-45, 146-61 *passim*,
  178-80, 186-89, 191-93; First Division Company, 120, 187, 188,
  189, bond issue, 120, 189, default and receivership, 120-21;
  negotiations by Hill and Smith
  for takeover, 122-40 *passim*,
  143-45, 146-61 *passim*, 186-90;
  foreclosure, 189-90; acquisition
  by Manitoba Railroad, 190 (*see*
  also St. Paul, Minneapolis &
  Manitoba Railroad); celebration
  of 29th anniversary of acquisition by Manitoba Railroad and
  Hill's 70th birthday (1908), 556-
  57
St. Paul & Sioux City Railroad, 100
St. Paul Railroad, *see* Chicago, Milwaukee & St. Paul Railroad
St. Paul Seminary, 425; construction
  of, 452-53
Sanborn, Judge W. H., 447, 517
Santa Fe Railroad, *see* Atchison, Topeka & Santa Fe Railroad
Sargent, Homer E., 182, 183
Saunders, Edward N., 98, 99, 101,
  104-5, 106, 107, 153, 197, 233
Sawyer, Edward, 190-91, 198
Schiff, Jacob H., 372, 398, 466, 491,
  601; and Manitoba Railroad, 284,
  345, 373, 385; and Great North-
  ern, 394, 404, 406, 412, coloniza-
  tion plan, 438-39; and Union
  Pacific, 439, 440-41, 444, 459, 477,
  496-98, 500; and Northern
  Pacific, 440-41, 444, 445, 450, 453,
  462, 496-98, 500, 503-7, 522; and
  Burlington, 488; and Northern
  Securities Company, 510, 522;
  photo, 493
Schultz, John C., 224, 248
Secombe, William, 211, 212, 234, 259,
  318

Second National Bank of St. Paul, 582
Shepard, David C., 227, 344, 347, 381, 389, 533, 561
Sheridan, Gen. Philip, 323, 356
Sherman Anti-Trust Act (1890), 296, 511, 544; and Northern Securities case, 517, 518-19
Shipping, transpacific exports: development of, 471-74, 544-46
Sibley, Gen. H. H., 33, 84, 154
Siemens, Dr. George, 440-41, 443, 445
Sioux City & St. Paul Railroad, 100
Skinner, Thomas, 376
Slade, George T. (son-in-law), 527; with Erie and Great Northern Railroads, 577
Smith, Donald A., 594; and Hudson's Bay Company, 73, 74-75, 124-25; and St. Paul & Pacific, 125-33 *passim*, 144, 146-58 *passim*, 180; and Canadian Pacific, 164, 177, 185, 240, 241, 249, 251, 318; director of Manitoba Railroad, 190-91, 192, 208, 280, 289, 317, 318, 319, 359, 372, 373, 375, 397; Lord Strathcona and Mount Royal, 249*n*, 436, 510, 547; photo, 127
Smith, J. Gregory, 119
Smith, Elijah, 372
Soo Railroad, *see* Minneapolis, St. Paul & Sault Ste. Marie Railroad
Southern Pacific Railroad, 300, 482, 500, 521, 562, 567
Spencer, Samuel, 538, 541-42
Spokane, Portland & Seattle Railroad, 563-67
Standard Oil Company, 96, 297, 501, 520
Stark, Gen. George, 181, 184, 185, 186
Steel, 363, 451, 467; rails, 103, 166, 218, 224, 274, 286, 300, 307, 347
Steele, Charles, 566, 588
Stephen, George, 132, 317, 403, 510; and St. Paul & Pacific, 133, 135-38, 140, 144, 146-61 *passim*, 164, 169, 171, 173, 178, 179-80, 183-84, 186-90 *passim*; president of Canadian Pacific, 164, 208, 210, 237, 243, 246, 249, 265, 266-70, 287, 318, 375-76; chairman of Manitoba Railroad, 190, 192, 194, 208, 213, 229, 233, 249, 280,

288, 289, 317-19, 329, 340, 359, 367, 372-76, 393-94, 397, 413-14, 462; Lord Mount Stephen, 394, 436-37; and Northern Pacific takeover, 440-43, 446, 453, 455-56, 458; photo, 137
Stephens, W. A., 234, 264, 318, 388
Sterling, John W., 295, 323, 376, 410, 518
Stetson, Francis L., 446, 447, 455
Stevens, I. I., 382
Stevens, John F., 379, 381, 382-83, 390-91, 431, 507-8, 566-67, 578, 607-8; photo, 380
Stewart, Dr. George D., 588, 601, 603, 604
Stickney, A. B., 242, 309, 487
Stillman, James, 466, 477, 485, 491, 501; and Northern Securities Company, 510
Strait, Rep. H. B., 297-98, 299
Strathcona and Mount Royal, Lord, *see* Smith, Donald A.
Strikes, 135, 219-20, 415-16, 426
Swan, W. G., 94, 110

Taft, President William Howard, 544, 548
Taylor, James W., 81, 150, 181
Terhune, Nicholas, 510
Thomas, Gen. Samuel, 376-77
Thomas, Horace, 45, 84, 185-86, 195, 217
Thomson, Frank, 290-91, 306, 313, 323, 350, 418, 437, 458, 466, 487
Thorne, Samuel, 308, 510, 531, 589, 601, 603; and Manitoba Railroad, 317, 319-20, 329, 335-36, 365, 374-75; photo, 321
Tinkham, A. W., 381-82, 639*n*20
Tod, Andrew, 232, 318
Tod, J. Kennedy: and Manitoba Railroad, 229, 232, 270, 283, 314, 330, 395, 397, 404
Toomey, John J., 425, 490, 525, 532, 588, 603, 611, 613
Touzalin, A. E., 296, 324, 486
Treat, Judge Samuel, 357
Tuck, Edward, 308, 323, 429, 437, 443, 499, 505, 517, 532, 580, 595
Tupper, Charles, 169, 188, 194

Underhill, C. M., 98-99, 105, 106
Underwood, Frederick D., 433-34, 457, 458
Union Pacific Railroad, 292, 334, 448; financing, 238, 407; and Manitoba Railroad, 298; Oregon Short Line, construction of, 370, 435, 477-84 *passim*, map, 480; construction of, 370, 483-84; and Northern Pacific, 371, 372 435, 474, 477; bankruptcy and reorganization, 411, 439, 459; Schiff and, 459, 477; Harriman and, 459, 488, 491, 500-501, 564-65; map, 480-81
U.S. House of Representatives: Money Trust Investigation and Hill, 582-83, 587
U.S. legislation: Interstate Commerce Act (1887), 292-93, 295, 371, 409-10, 539; Sherman Anti-Trust Act (1890), 296, 511, 517, 518-19, 544; Hepburn Act (1906), 519-20, 541-44; Mann-Elkins Act (1910), 519-20, 544; Esch-Townsend bill (1905), 535; *see also* Railroad regulation; Rate regulation; Rebate system
U.S. Senate: Committee on Interstate Commerce, 289-90, 476-77, 539; Committee on Indian Affairs, 346
U.S. Steel Corporation, 451, 470, 489-90, 514
U.S. Supreme Court: Farley case, 356-60; Northern Securities Company case, 514, 517-19
Untermeyer, Samuel, 582-83
Upham, Henry P., 45, 84-85, 111, 115, 195, 256-57, 355, 393, 397, 583, 594; photo, 196
Upper, Joseph, 169, 177, 185

Vanderbilt, William H., 104, 112, 145, 302, 309, 487
Vanderbilt, William K., 506
Van Horne, William C., 241-42, 246, 251, 604; general manager of Canadian Pacific, 248-53, 264-70, 384, 468, 474-75, 569-70; photo, 251
Van Sant, Samuel R., 512, 515, 538

Villard, Henry: and Northern Pacific, 225-26, 270-71, 283, 334-35, 348, 367, 370-71, 404, 411, 440, 454, 483; *see also* Oregon Railway & Navigation Company

Wabash Railroad, 357
Wakeman, E. B.; general superintendent of Manitoba Railroad, 208, 209, 213, 219, 234
Wallace, Henry, 550, 551
Walter, Maj. James, 304-5
Warren, Charles H., 413
Washburn, W. D., 184, 186, 215, 287-88, 306, 361, 362
Weed, Smith M., 317, 352
Wellington, William A., 47-48, 50-53, 57, 85, 95, 397
West, mid-19th century; opportunities in, 23-24
Western Railroad of Minnesota, 126
Western Traffic Association, 409-10
West Wisconsin Railroad, 100
Wetherald family, 261, 275
Wetherald, Rev. William, 1, 7-12, 44; photo, 13
Weyerhaeuser, Frederick, 464, 465, 469, 595
Wheat: cultivation and transportation of, 214, 227, 276-79, 285, 287-88, 405-6, 414; *see also* Flour
Wheeler, C. C., 211
Wilkins, H. B., 53
Willard, Daniel, 577
Willis, H. B., 170, 177
Wilson, President Woodrow, 600
Winslow, Gen. Edward, 144, 145
Winter, Edwin P., 456, 457
Wisconsin Central Railroad, 441, 487, 569
Wood, 165, 340, 396; fuel business, 28, 91-92, 97, 214; railroad ties, 91, 164-65; *see also* Timber
World War I, 601-3; Anglo-French loan, 604-8
Wright, Charles B., 181-84 *passim*, 441

Young, George B.: and St. Paul & Pacific, 133, 188, 190; and Manitoba Railroad, 178, 190, 357-58